The Comprehensive Dictionary
of English & Hebrew First Names

THE COMPREHENSIVE

Dictionary of
English & Hebrew
First Names

Alfred J. Kolatch

JONATHAN DAVID PUBLISHERS, INC.
MIDDLE VILLAGE, NEW YORK 11379

THE COMPREHENSIVE DICTIONARY
OF ENGLISH & HEBREW FIRST NAMES

Copyright © 2005
by Alfred J. Kolatch

Jonathan David Publishers, Inc.
68-22 Eliot Avenue
Middle Village, New York 11379

www.jdbooks.com

2 4 6 8 10 9 7 5 3 1

Library of Congress Cataloging-in-Publication Data

Kolatch, Alfred J.
    The comprehensive dictionary of English and Hebrew first names / Alfred J. Kolatch.
        p. cm.
    Includes index.
    ISBN 0-8246-0455-5
        1. Names, Personal—English—Dictionaries—English. 2. Names, Personal—Jewish—
Dictionaries—English. I. Title.
    CS2377.K59 2005
    929.4'4'089924—dc22

                                                                        2004047758

Book design and composition by John Reinhardt Book Design

Printed in the United States of America

Dedicated with love to the memory of
Anna and Samuel Rubin

CONTENTS

PREFACE

M Y INTEREST IN NOMENCLATURE grew out of a practical need to assign Hebrew names to the students of my congregational school in Columbia, South Carolina. Many of the youngsters had never been given a Hebrew name, and the parents of children who had received one often were unable to recall them.

In selecting names, I decided to follow a system that has been used for centuries in Jewish communities worldwide: selecting a Hebrew name based on its similarity in meaning to the person's secular name. That method was used to determine the entries in my first book, *These Are the Names* (1948), as well as in *The Name Dictionary: Modern English and Hebrew Names* (1967), *The Complete Dictionary of English and Hebrew First Names* (1984), and *The New Name Dictionary* (1989), all of which expanded upon the initial effort. This volume is a greatly enlarged edition of the earlier works.

The process of gathering the names that appear in this volume began in 1942, when I conducted the first of three surveys aimed at discovering which Hebrew names were popular and what correlation in meaning, if any, existed between a child's English and Hebrew names. Questionnaires were mailed to the heads of forty-nine Hebrew schools in thirteen states, and follow-ups were sent in 1943 and 1945. From the 15,000 names submitted, it was evident that in most cases the meanings of a child's Hebrew and English names had no relationship.

In 1966, at my request, Hagai Lev, a member of the Institute of Contemporary Jewry at Jerusalem's Hebrew University, combed through Israel's Registry of Births, which is under the supervision of the Ministry of the Interior, as well as lists of elementary and high-school students. Of approximately 100,000 Hebrew names, he selected several thousand of the most popular, many of which appear in these pages.

In 1983, Elinor Slater, of French Hill, Jerusalem, conducted extensive research on Hebrew names that had come into being during the previous two decades. Her findings have also been incorporated into this volume. Two years later, in 1985, and once again in 2002, I scanned the pages of telephone books from various parts of Israel in search of new first names. Those efforts yielded a rich harvest of unusual names.

Also used extensively in the preparation of this work was a publication issued by the Academy of the Hebrew Language in Israel that proposes names for newborn children, as well as a list of masculine and feminine names found in Abraham Even-Shoshan's *Ha-Milon He-Chadash*, likely the most useful Hebrew dictionary ever published.

The names that appear in *The Comprehensive Dictionary of English & Hebrew First Names* include both the new and the old, the popular and the unusual. It is hoped that those searching for a name for a newborn will find many appealing choices.

ALFRED J. KOLATCH

INTRODUCTION

THROUGHOUT MOST OF HISTORY, Jews have carried both secular and Hebrew names. The Talmud (*Gittin* 11b) states that "the majority of Jews in the Diaspora have Gentile names," an observation that can be applied to every period from the Babylonian Exile (586 B.C.E.) onward. Daniel, of lion's den fame, had the Aramaic (Babylonian) name Beltshatzar (Daniel 4:16) in addition to his Hebrew name. His friends Shadrach, Meshach, and Abed-nego were known also by their Hebrew names—Chananya, Mishael, and Azarya.

In the fourth century, with Alexander the Great's conquest of Palestine, Jews became exposed to Greek (Hellenistic) culture, and they soon began taking Greek names. The practice spread, and some of the greatest of the early talmudic masters, as well as some of the most revered leaders of the Jewish people in the early centuries B.C.E., carried names such as Antigonus, Avtalyon, Jason, Onias, and Alexander. A Greek name was selected based on a similarity in meaning to the person's Hebrew name. Thus, an individual with the Hebrew name Netanel or Yonatan would choose a Greek name meaning "gift of God," such as Dositheus or Theodotian. In the same manner, Tobiah (Tuviya) also became known as Agathou, Uri became known as Phoebus, and Tzadok became known as Justus.

The practice of pairing secular and Hebrew names based on meaning grew increasingly popular among Jews worldwide. The Italian names Diofatto and Tranquillo were paired with the Hebrew Asael and Manoach, respectively. The great thirteenth-century French leader Rabbi Yechiel of Paris also bore the name Vivant. Frenchmen with the

Hebrew name Matityahu also were known as Dieudonne, those with the name Chaim as Vive, those called Ovadya as Serfdieu, and those with the name Gamliel as Dieulecresse.

Jews living in the Arab world used Arabic names along with their Hebrew names. Thus, Abraham also was called Ibrahim, David was also known as Daoud, Eliezer as Mansur, and Matzliach as Maimun.

The Jews of a congregation in India, known as Bene Israel, modified their Hebrew names to give them a Hindi sound. Thus, Benjamin became Benmanjee, Abraham became Abrajee, David became Dawoodjee, and Jacob became Akkoobjee.

The practice of giving a child a Hebrew (or Yiddish) name in addition to a secular name continues today. More often than not, however, the only similarity between the two is in sound, and that is most often confined to the first letter or syllable.

THE BIBLE AS A SOURCE OF NAMES

The Bible is the moral guide of the Jewish people and the centerpiece of its religious life. Given its status, it is not surprising that the Bible has long been a favored source of names for children.

Biblical names are most often used in their original form—Abraham, Isaac, Sarah, Leah, for example—but they are also sometimes modified. Abraham has yielded such forms as Avrum, Bram, and Brasha; Isaac has become Ike, Isa, and Zak; Jacob has been transformed into Jack, Kivi, and Kobe; Sarah has become Sadie, Sirele, Sorele, and Tzirel; Miriam has yielded Mimi and Mirele; and the name Binyamin (Benjamin) has led to such variants as Minyamin, Minyomi, and Yummy.

For the most part, the meanings of biblical names are easy to analyze because their roots are readily traced, usually to the Hebrew. In fact, the significance of many biblical names are explained in the Bible itself:

- The Hebrew root of the name Cain is *kanoh*, meaning "to buy, to acquire." Genesis 4:1 explains the association: "And she [Eve] conceived and bore Cain, and said, 'I have *acquired* a man with the help of the Lord.'"
- Adam and Eve's son was named Seth. In Genesis 4:25, Eve says, "For God has given me another seed [child] instead of Abel, for

Cain slew him." The name of this child, Seth (Shet in Hebrew), means "to give, put, appoint."

• Abraham and Sarah named their son Isaac, the Hebrew root of which is *tzachok*, meaning "laughter." At the time of Isaac's birth, Abraham was one hundred years old and Sarah was ninety. When told that she was to bear a child, Sarah exclaimed, "Everyone who hears about it will *laugh*!" (Genesis 21:6).

• Jacob and Leah were so excited over the birth of their first son that they called him Reuben, meaning "Behold, a son!" (Genesis 29:32).

Old Testament names are generally divided into six categories:

1. *Names describing a physical characteristic:* Laban means "white"; Korach means "bald"; Charim means "flat-nosed."

2. *Names inspired by particular experiences in the life of the mother or newborn:* Eve was so called "because she was the mother of all *living* beings" (Genesis 3:20); the name Eve in Hebrew is Chava, meaning "life." Moses was so named by Pharaoh's daughter because she "*drew* him out of the water" (Exodus 2:10).

3. *Names of animals.* Devora means "bee"; Jonah means "dove"; Hulda means "weasel"; Tzipora means "bird"; Yael means "goat." Animal names might have been chosen because the parents had a particular fondness for an animal, or a particular animal was prevalent in the locale of the child's birth, or even perhaps because the newborn in some way resembled an aspect of the animal.

4. *Names of plants or flowers:* Tamar, the name of the wife of Judah's eldest son, means "date" or "date palm." A descendant of Caleb was named Tappuach, meaning "apple." A grandson of Jacob was called Elon, meaning "oak tree." Joseph's second son was given the name Ephraim, meaning "fruitfulness."

5. *God-centered names:* Yonatan (Jonathan) means "gift of God"; Yoel (Joel), "God is willing"; Iddo, "God's friend"; Daniel, "God is my judge"; Jehoiakim, "God will establish"; Isaiah, "salvation of the Lord."

6. *Names that express hope for the future or a desire for improved circumstances:* When Joseph was born to Rachel, she said, "May the Lord add to me another son" (Genesis 30:24). Joseph (Yosef in Hebrew) means "to add, increase."

Biblical Names in Contemporary Times

Biblical names have been used by Jews and Christians throughout history. United States Social Security Administration (USSSA) statistics show that from 1880 to 1925 the New Testament names John and Mary were the most popular male and female baby names, respectively. In 1926 the nonbiblical name Robert replaced John and the nonbiblical name Linda replaced Mary, a trend that continued until 1953. The biblical names James and Thomas were repeatedly among the top ten New Testament male names for newborns.

The most popular Old Testament name given to boys between 1880 and 1919 was Joseph. Sara and Anna (a form of Hannah) were among the most popular female names.

In a study of 10,000 personal names appearing in the birth columns of *The New York Times* between 1943 and 1946, of the ten most popular masculine names six were biblical or of biblical derivation, two (Michael and David) from the Old Testament and four (Stephen, Peter, Steven, Mark) from the New Testament. Among the female names, four of the ten most popular were of biblical derivation: Ann and three of its variant forms—Jane, Joan, and Nancy.

The 1948 New York City birth records reveal that among the ten most popular masculine names that year were John, James, Michael, Joseph, Thomas, Stephen, and David, three from the Old Testament and four from the New Testament. The ten most popular feminine names included two names of biblical origin: Mary and Nancy.

Studies of the 1980 birth rolls of the State of Pennsylvania and the 1981 birth records of the cities of New York and Detroit reveal a striking similarity in the selection of biblical names. The 1980 Pennsylvania listings include seven biblical names (Michael, Jason, Matthew, David, John, James, Joseph) among the ten most popular male names, and two biblical names—Jessica (a feminine form of Jesse) and

Sarah—among the ten most popular feminine names. The next four names on the feminine list (Rebecca, Stephanie, Elizabeth, Lisa) are also of biblical origin or derivation.

Beginning in 1960 and continuing into the twenty-first century, David and Michael alternate as the most popular male Old Testament names. Joshua and Daniel began to find favor around 1975. Among the most popular female Old Testament names during that same period were Deborah, Sarah, and Elizabeth, an Anglicized form of Elisheva.

In the decade before the new millennium, biblical names continued to achieve popularity. USSSA records for the 1990s include Sarah, Elizabeth, Rachel, and Hannah among the most popular names for girls. Michael is listed as the most popular boy's name of that decade, with Joshua, Jacob, Daniel, and David also in fashion. That trend continued into the twenty-first century.

NAMES IN ISRAEL

As elsewhere, the names favored by Israelis have changed with the generations. For many years prior to the establishment of the Jewish state, the biblical names Amnon, Yonatan, Naomi, and Noa were fashionable. In the 1950s, the feminine name Anat gained preference along with such names as Hila, Hadas, Orit, and Tal. Popular masculine names in those years were Alon, Ehud, Eyal, Gil, Guy, Nir, Oren, Oz, and Ron.

As increasing numbers of Jews immigrated to Israel from the Diaspora—particularly the former Soviet Union—more and more non-Hebrew names, spelled with Hebrew characters, were introduced. Nonetheless, biblical names continued to be popular. A 2002 survey includes Daniel, Itai, David, Iddo, and Amit (a form of Amitai) among the most popular biblical names for boys. The most popular female biblical names were Yael and Tamar.

CHRISTIAN NAMES

In the early centuries of the Common Era, Christians freely used Old Testament Hebrew names, but in time those names were abandoned by many New Testament figures as a form of protest against Judaism.

Thus, the man once known as Simon bar Jonah came to be called Peter, and Saul of Tarsus came to be known as Paul.

During the early centuries of the Common Era, Christians often chose names associated with mythology and idolatry, even though they abhorred both. The names Phoebe, Olympius, and Jovianus were common, which outraged the seventh-century Bishop of Seville. In his *Etymologia*, he urged Christians to return to the use of biblical names, but to no avail.

THE REFORMATION

Not until the sixteenth century, when attempts at reforming the Roman Catholic Church resulted in the establishment of Protestant churches, did biblical names—particularly from the Old Testament—again find favor. In seventeenth-century Puritan England, where the Reformation turned into a crusade against all Church dogma and ceremonials, New Testament names were even more strongly renounced in favor of Old Testament names.

As late as the eighteenth and nineteenth centuries, Puritan extremists went so far as to choose the most obscure and odd-sounding appellations they could find. Sometimes phrases were borrowed from Scripture and used in their entirety as names. Ernest Weekley, in his book *Jack and Jill*, notes that at the beginning of the twentieth century members of a single family carried the names Asenath Zaphnath Paaneah, Kezia Jemima Keren Happuch, and Maher Shalal Hashbaz. However, average Puritans were satisfied with Old Testament names as well as those derived from abstract virtues, such as Perseverance, Faith, Hope, Humility, Charity, and Repentance. A pair of twin girls born to the English Wycliffe family in 1710 were named Favour and Fortune.

OPPOSITION TO NEW TESTAMENT NAMES

The Quakers (Society of Friends), like the Puritans, preferred Old Testament over New Testament nomenclature. This was no doubt a reflection of their extreme distaste for the elaborate ceremonies of the Church of England, with which they broke in 1648.

The life of John Bunyan (1628–1688), author of *Pilgrim's Progress*, epitomizes the conflict between the Quakers and Puritans and their adversaries. In his early years, Bunyan was an antagonist of the Quakers, which explains his choice of Mary, John, Thomas, and Elizabeth— all but the last from the New Testament—as names for his children. By the time of Bunyan's second marriage, his philosophy had changed. No longer an adversary of the Quakers, he had become intensely opposed to the established Church and its bishops. His children by his second wife were named Joseph and Sara, after Old Testament figures.

NAMES FROM PLACES

Many first names, like surnames, were originally the names of places. The Bible contains numerous examples: in the Book of Genesis, Efrat is the place where Rachel died and was buried; Efrata is the name of Caleb's wife in the Book of Chronicles. Ofra, the name of a city in the Book of Joshua, is also a masculine first name that appears in the Book of Chronicles.

In more recent times, the actress Myrna Loy was named after the whistle-stop Myrna, which her father found intriguing. Portland Hoffa, the radio comedienne and wife of Fred Allen, was named after Portland, Oregon. Actress Tallulah Bankhead was named after Tallulah Falls, Georgia.

NAMES WITH POSITIVE ATTRIBUTES

Names representing strength, courage, and other positive attributes have been used since biblical times. The male names Ari and Aryeh (lion), Ariel (lion of God), Gidon (warrior, hero), and Gavriel (strength of God) fall into this category.

The female names Abira, Amitza, Azriela, Aziza, Gibora, and Uza all represent strength; Gidona and Tigra mean "warrior"; and Ariela, Kefira, and Levia refer to leonine characteristics.

CALENDAR AND HOLIDAY NAMES

Some names used by Jews are derived from the calendar and holidays. In fact, the Hebrew term for holiday, *yom tov*, is sometimes taken as a personal name. In the Middle Ages, it was common to call boys who were circumcised on Purim by the name Mordechai, in honor of the hero of the holiday. Those born on Tisha B'Av were often named Menachem, meaning "comforter," because the ninth (*tisha*) day of the month Av is a fast day commemorating the destruction of the Temple in Jerusalem, and in the Prophetic portion (Isaiah 40) read in the synagogue on the Sabbath following that fast day the Prophet *comforts* Israel. Among the Jews of Eastern Europe, a son born on Chanukah was usually named after that holiday.

Particularly among Sephardic Jews, children born on Yom Kippur were often called Rachamim ("mercy"), and those born on Passover were sometimes called Pesach. Shabbat and Shabbetai were popular Sephardic names for boys born on the Sabbath. One rabbi, the father of twelve sons, is reported to have named each son after a different Hebrew month.

Names associated with holidays, as well as names of the days of the week and the months of the year, are used by the general population: Natalie, Noel, Tuesday, April, May, June, and so on.

Numeral Names

Although numeral names do not appear frequently in the Bible, in the Book of Genesis (35:27) we find the name Arba, meaning "four," and in I Kings (4:3) we find the name Shisha, meaning "six."

The Romans seemed particularly fond of numeral names, among the more common of which were Quintus (5), Octavius (8), and Septimus (7). Among Tripolitan Jews of North Africa, the feminine name Hmessa and the masculine name Mammus, both meaning "five," have been used.

Numeral names are used less commonly today, although a Michigan family with the surname Stickaway named their three boys One, Two, Three, and their three girls First, Second, Third. And a young rabbi, having difficulty finding a satisfactory Hebrew name for his first daughter, decided to use the name Rishona, meaning "first."

Interestingly, the Puritans, and especially the Quakers, refrained from using the months of the year as names, substituting numbers instead. Since the names of most months were of pagan origin, it was considered best to avoid them. Official records and tombstone engravings of the seventeenth century therefore show months referred to by number rather than name—January as 1, February as 2, and so on.

Occupational Names

Although the names of occupations are more frequently taken as surnames, many have come to be used as first names. George ("farmer"), Mason ("worker in stone"), Safran ("scribe"), Benaya ("builder"), and Sarag ("tailor, weaver of cloth") are all masculine occupational names. Farrah ("iron worker, blacksmith"), Bona ("builder"), Eda ("poet, songwriter"), Zemira ("singer"), and Mishmeret ("guardian") are examples of feminine occupational names.

Celebrity Names

Children are sometimes named after charismatic historical or contemporary figures. Alexander the Great entered Palestine in 333 B.C.E., and according to legend all Jewish boys born that year were named Alexander in his honor. Although there are no records indicating the degree of popularity the name achieved among the masses in the years immediately following Alexander's visit, we do know that one Jewish king (Alexander Janneus) and one queen (Salome Alexandra) adopted it. Somewhat later, in talmudic times, we find the name being used by the scholar Rabbi Alexandri (*Yoma* 53b).

Over the years many Jewish boys have been named Theodor Herzl, after the founder of modern Zionism, and more recently the names of two of Israel's most popular prime ministers, (David) Ben-Gurion and Golda (Meir), have been used. Inspired by the Israel-Egypt Peace Treaty, signed in Washington, D.C., in March 1979, Mr. and Mrs. Hotam El Kabassi named their triplets, born on April 5, 1979, Carter, Begin, and Sadat, thereby honoring the three principals at the signing: U.S. President Jimmy Carter, Israeli Prime Minister Menachem Begin, and Egyptian President Anwar Sadat.

Following the death on February 24, 2003, of Israeli astronaut Ilan Ramon, who perished tragically when the space shuttle *Columbia* disintegrated, many Israeli newborns were named Ilan.

The above notwithstanding, the custom of naming children after celebrities has not been as popular among Jews as among other groups. In the Bible itself one finds that the names of early heroes are not shared by characters that appear later in the biblical narrative. Thus, only the original Abraham, Sarah, Isaac, Rebecca, Jacob, Rachel, Leah, Joseph, Moses, Aaron, Miriam, Isaiah, and Jeremiah carry those names. Why these names are not used more than once has not been adequately explained.

It is also not clear why not a single scholar in the Talmud is named after Abraham, Israel, or David, who are among the most revered biblical personalities. It is true that the names of some of Jacob's sons are used, but Dan, Gad, and Asher are not among them. Of the Prophets, the names Isaiah, Hosea, Joel, Amos, Obadiah, Micah, Habakkuk, Zephaniah, and Malachi do not appear in the Talmud at all.

It is indeed difficult to explain why many Rabbis of the Talmud are named Ishmael, but only one is named Moses. Rabbi Jose (*Genesis Rabbah* 71:3) finds some justification for use of the name Ishmael in the explanation that the biblical character who bore that name exemplifies a person whose "name was beautiful but whose actions were ugly." The commentary *Tosafot* on *Berachot* 7b justifies the use of the name by observing that Ishmael, Abraham's son by his concubine Hagar, was a sinner who later repented.

Name-Changing

Since early Bible times, it has been customary for an individual's name to be modified when a change in status was achieved or was imminent. Among the more prominent examples are Abraham (from Abram), Sarah (from Sarai), Israel (from Jacob), Joshua (from Hosea), Jerubaal (from Gideon), Zedekiah (from Mattaniah), and Jehoiakim (from Eliakim).

Alhough name-changing is no longer common, the ancient Jewish custom of altering a person's name in time of serious illness still persists in some circles. It is hoped that the alteration will cause the angel of death to doubt the identity of the person he is about to visit. If the patient is a young male, the name Alter or Zaken ("old one" in Yiddish and Hebrew, respectively) or Chaim ("life" in Hebrew) is sometimes added to or substituted for the original name. If the patient is female, the feminine equivalent—Alterke, Zekena, or Chaya—is used.

Masculine/Feminine Interchanges

The Bible contains many examples of names used by both males and females. In II Kings 8:26 Athaliah is the daughter of Ahab and Jezebel, while in I Chronicles 8:26 Athaliah is used as a masculine name. The name Efah, grandson of Abraham and Keturah in Genesis 25:4, is used as a feminine name for the concubine of Caleb in I Chronicles 2:46. The names Shlomit, Tzivya, Bilga, Chuba, Noga, Chupa, Gover, Buna, Bina, Aviya, Ofra, Rina, Chavila, and Simcha also appear as both masculine and feminine names. Among the popular unisex Hebrew names currently in use are Adi, Adiel, Amal, Anat, Ariel, Carmel, Giora, Hadar, Inbal, Mazal, Orli, Ron, Tal, Yarden, and Zohar.

Numerous women's first names in use today are adaptations of masculine forms. In many instances, the feminine name is so long established and accepted that we no longer realize that it has its origin in a masculine name. In this group we find Alexandra and Alexandria from Alexander; Charlotte and Charlene from Charles; Davi, Davida, and Davita from David; Erica from Eric; Frederica from Frederic; Georgia, Georgine, and Georgette from George; Harriet and Harri from Harry; Henrietta, Henri, and Henria from Henry; Herma and Hermine from Herman; Josepha and Josephine from Joseph; Louisa and Louise from Louis; Roberta from Robert; Stephanie from Stephan; and Willa and Willene from Will or William.

Unconventional Spellings and Variant Forms

Out of a desire to give their children distinctive first names, parents sometimes alter the spelling of a popular name to give it a new "look." Most commonly, the change is accomplished by substituting a "y" for an "i" or by adding an "e." Thus, Fannie becomes Fannye, Mollie becomes Mollye, Sadie becomes Sadye, and Edith becomes Edyth or Edythe. Shirley might become Shirlee, Shirlie, or Sherle; and Toby, Tony, and Ricky might become Tobi, Toni, and Ricki, respectively.

Spellings are sometimes altered by dropping a consonant. Thus, Sarah becomes Sara, and Hannah becomes Hanna. Esther might be changed to Ester by dropping the "h," or it might be more radically modified to create variant forms such as Esta or Estee.

Among the feminine names with one or more variant spellings or variant forms are Rosalind (Roslin, Rosaline, Rosalyn, Roselyn, Roslyn, Roslyne, Rosylin); Deborah (Debra, Dobra); Caroline (Karolyn, Carolyn); Alice (Alyce, Alyse); Gail (Gale, Gayle); Elaine (Elane, Elayne); Eileen (Ilene, Iline); Ethel (Ethyl, Ethyle); Madeleine (Madeline, Madelon, Madelyn, Madelyne, Madlyn); Marilyn (Marilin, Marylin); and Vivian (Vivien, Vyvyan).

Among the masculine names with one or more variant spellings or variant forms are Alan (Allan, Alyn, Allyn, Allen); Frederick (Fredric, Fredrick); Irvin (Irwin, Erwin, Irving, Irvine); Isidor (Isodore, Isador, Isadore); Lawrence (Laurance, Laurence, Lawrance, Lorence); and Morris (Maury, Morey, Morry).

Pet Forms

Pet forms, also called *diminutives* or *nicknames*, make up a large portion of our contemporary first names, and the percentage continues to grow with an increased desire for self-expression.

In some cases, an individual's nickname becomes so widely used and accepted that it virtually replaces the person's given name. James Earl Carter, thirty-ninth president of the United States, preferred the nickname Jimmy, and that was what he affixed to official documents. William Jefferson Clinton, forty-second president of the United States, liked to be called Bill, even though he was named after his birth father, William Jefferson Blythe II.

Apocopation—cutting off or shortening the last sound or sounds of a word—is characteristic of many pet forms, including Jake (for Jacob), Tom (for Thomas), Bob (for Robert), Cal (for Calvin), and Pete (for Peter).

Names to Be Avoided

Jewish religious law does not specify criteria to be used in selecting a name for a child, but tradition suggests the wisdom of avoiding specific names. In the Midrash (*Genesis Rabbah* 49:1), for example, the Sages suggest that one not use the names of wicked people such as Pharaoh,

Sisera, and Sennacherib. This admonition seems to have been heeded over the centuries.

Rabbi Chayim Azulai, the eighteenth-century author of an encyclopedia containing the biographies of 1,300 scholars and writers, suggested that Jews avoid using all names that appear in the Bible before Abraham, the first Jew. Thus, he considered it improper to name a child after Adam or Noah or Shem or Ever. Azulai also condemned the selection of the name Yafet (Japheth), which belonged to the father of third-century Palestinian scholar Benjamin ben Yafet (*Berachot* 33a).

Elazar Fleckeles, a noted contemporary of Azulai, disagreed, asserting that it was quite proper to use pre-Abrahamitic names. Fleckeles calls attention to the talmudic scholars Benjamin ben Yafet and Akavya ben Mehalalel (both Yafet and Mehalalel are pre-Abrahamitic biblical names).

The cautions of Rabbi Azulai have been largely ignored, evidenced by the fact that for the past two centuries many illustrious persons have carried pre-Abrahamitic names.

Naming Children After Relatives

Ashkenazic Jews—those of Middle and East European ancestry—subscribe to the ancient Jewish belief that a man's name is his soul, the essence of his being. When given a relative's name, the child also receives that person's soul. If the relative is alive, the soul would then have to be shared by two, which might result in the shortening of the older person's life. Following this reasoning, Ashkenazic Jews discourage naming newborns after living relatives, although they generally do name them after deceased relatives.

In the twelfth century, the noted mystic Judah ben Samuel of Regenburg (popularly known as Rabbi Yehudah He-Chasid, "Judah the Pious One") introduced the prohibition against a man's marrying a woman with the same name as his mother. Rabbi Yehudah feared that this might lead to the embarrassing situation of the mother erroneously answering when the wife was actually being addressed. This concern aside, Ashkenazic Jews in particular consider such marriages ill-advised. The reasoning is as follows: if a man were to marry a woman with the same first name as that of his mother, and his mother were to die, the man would not be able to honor his deceased mother by naming a future daughter after her, based on the fact that his wife, still living, carries that name.

Generally speaking, Yehudah He-Chasid disapproved of naming any child after a living relative; but he also disapproved of naming a child after a deceased relative, out of fear that the soul of the deceased might be disturbed. In his will, the rabbi instructed that none of his descendants be called by his name or the name of his father, Samuel.

Sephardic Jews—those whose ancestry can be traced to pre-Inquisition Spain and Portugal—do not share the Ashkenazic belief that a person's life will be shortened if a newborn is given that person's name. Sephardim therefore do not hesitate to name their offspring after living grandparents, and occasionally, though infrequently, even after themselves.

A longstanding tradition justifies the Sephardic practice. As far back as the fourth century B.C.E., at the height of the Greek influence in Palestine, Jews took the names of living relatives. In the family of the High Priests, the names Onias and Simon were used alternately, between 332 and 165 B.C.E. In the early talmudic period, beginning with the first century B.C.E., Hillel the Great's family repeated the names Gamaliel and Judah for several generations, with occasional use of the names Simon and Hillel.

The practice continued throughout the Middle Ages, and many examples can be found. Typically, the eldest son in a family was named after the paternal (or sometimes maternal) grandfather. The grandson of the eminent eleventh- and twelfth-century philosopher and poet Yehuda Halevi was also named Yehuda during the poet's lifetime. The grandfather of twelfth-century scholar Moses Maimonides was Yosef, son of Isaac, son of Yosef, son of Ovadyah, son of Shlomo, son of Ovadyah. Similarly, the maternal grandfather of the thirteenth-century Italian talmudist Rabbi Isaiah ben Elijah de Trani was also Isaiah.

In most Sephardic communities today, the general practice is to name the first son in a family after the paternal grandfather, living or dead. The sole exception is found among Jews of Spanish and Portuguese extraction whose ancestors settled in Holland; they do not name children after living relatives.

Sephardim sometimes name their first male child Bechor, meaning "firstborn," or by the diminutive form Buki. The first female child in the family is frequently named Bechora or Becharetta. But most often the first male in a family is named after a paternal grandfather, alive or deceased, and the first female child after the paternal grandmother, alive or deceased.

Naming Children After Non-Relatives

The Talmud cites instances where, for a variety of reasons, children were named after living or dead persons not within their own family. In one case (*Shabbat* 134a), the second-century scholar Nathan of Babylonia (Natan Ha-Bavli), a contemporary of Judah the Prince, advised a mother who had lost two sons as a result of the circumcision procedure not to circumcise her third son. She followed the scholar's advice, her son survived, and in gratitude she named the boy Nathan, meaning "He [God] gave [life]." In another instance (*Bava Metzia* 84b), Rabbi Eliezer ben Hyrcanus, a first-century C.E. scholar and disciple of Yochanan ben Zakkai, was considered so helpful by several women whose questions he answered that they later named their children Yochanan.

Aside from Chasidim who have occasionally named children after a deceased *rebbe*, and Jews who have named offspring after personal historical favorites, the idea of naming children after celebrated persons never took root in Jewish tradition. The reason is quite likely linked to the belief that a man's name is his person, his soul. Jews who may have wanted to name a child after a celebrity have chosen not do so out of fear that the soul of the person would be acquired along with the name. This would place a grave responsibility on the child, who would have to measure up to the life of the soul now occupying his or her body.

Naming a Boy

Although there is an old tradition of naming boys and girls in the synagogue on the first Sabbath after birth, today it is established custom to name a boy at his *brit* (circumcision), held on the eighth day after birth. However, neither the Bible nor the Talmud alludes to this. In the few instances where the circumcision rite is mentioned (Genesis 17:24 for Abraham; Genesis 17:25 for Ishmael; Genesis 21:4 for Isaac; and Exodus 4:25, where Tzipora, wife of Moses, circumcises her son), no reference is made to naming a child. The accepted biblical practice seems to have been to name children at the time of birth, not later. This was true of the naming of Jacob's sons (Genesis 29, 30); the naming of Gershom by Tzipora (Exodus 2:22); and the naming of Samson (Judges 13:4). Interestingly, it appears that in practically all cases of naming recorded in the Bible it is the mother who took that responsibility.

Only in the New Testament do we find reference to naming a child at his circumcision. In Luke 1:59, a son born to Zacharias and Elizabeth is named John at the time of circumcision, and in Luke 2:21 Jesus is given his name at the time of circumcision.

At least two references in talmudic literature describe what transpires at a circumcision ceremony. The Midrash (*Ruth Rabbah* 6:6) gives a detailed description of the proceedings at the *brit* of Elisha ben Avuya. All segments of the population of Jerusalem—rich and poor—were invited. A banquet was prepared and much merrymaking ensued after the circumcision ceremony. The celebration lasted for hours, with many participants singing, dancing, and playing games, while the more learned gathered in a separate room to discuss Torah. But no mention was made of naming the child.

The Midrash (*Kohelet Rabbah* 3:4) describes a similar joyous celebration taking place about one hundred years later, in the northern Palestinian city of Sepphoris. Again no mention of a baby naming is made.

Scholars concur that the formal naming of a child at the *brit* began some time in the middle of the twelfth century, but what prompted the institution of the practice is not known. Nonetheless, the *brit* being the first major religious event in the life of a male child, it is quite understandable that the naming should take place then. By the sixteenth century, baby namings at circumcisions were commonplace.

Nowadays, many Ashkenazim hold the circumcision ceremony in the home, preferably in the morning hours, although some prefer to hold it in the synagogue. Sephardim generally hold it in the synagogue in the late afternoon, when more people are free to attend.

Shalom Zachar Ceremony

The celebration known as *shalom zachar* ("welcome to the male child") or *ben zachar* is of kabbalistic origin. During this ceremony, relatives and friends gather to socialize in the home of the newborn's parents. Among the foods served are cooked legumes (beans, peas, etc.), which are believed to be an effective charm against spirits and demons that could potentially harm the boy.

Among Sephardic Jews, the *shalom zachar* is held on the night before the circumcision. The practice is based on the belief that the presence of a group of people will deter Satan, who is eager to prevent Jews from observing the rite of circumcision. The Ashkenazic community, which rejects this belief, observes the *shalom zachar* celebration on the Friday night following the child's birth.

Naming Ceremony for a Boy

Before commencing the actual circumcision, the *mohel*, who is serving as the father's surrogate, recites the following blessing in Hebrew: "Blessed art Thou, O Lord our God, King of the universe, Who has hallowed us by Thy commandments and commanded us to circumcise [our sons]."

The father then says: "Blessed art Thou, O Lord our God, King of the universe, Who has hallowed us by Thy commandments and commanded us to enter this child into the Covenant of Abraham our father."

Upon completing the surgical procedure, the *mohel* holds up a cup of wine and pronounces the appropriate blessing. He then continues with a prayer for the welfare of the child and his parents, which includes the words, "And may he henceforth be known in Israel as '(*baby's name*) son of (*father's name*).'" This prayer, which includes verses from Proverbs 23:25, Ezekiel 16:6, Psalms 105:8-10 and 118:1, and Genesis 21:4, concludes with the words, "This little child named (*baby's name*) may he grow to be great. Even as he now enters the Covenant [of Abraham], so may he enter the world of Torah study, a life of marital bliss, and a life in which he will perform good deeds."

The *sandek* (godfather), who holds the baby during the circumcision, then drinks some of the wine and dabs a few drops on the lips of the infant.

Naming a Girl

Ashkenazim and most Sephardim name newborn girls in the synagogue on the first Sabbath after birth, where a *minyan* (religious quorum) is assembled. On that occasion the father is honored with an *aliyah* (called to the Torah), following which the formal naming takes place. Since the Torah is also read at Monday, Thursday, and Rosh Chodesh (New Moon) morning services, the naming may take place on those occasions as well.

Moroccan Jews, as well as those from Turkey and other countries once part of the Ottoman Empire, name girls in a home ceremony called *zeved* (or *zebed*) *ha-bat* ("gift of the daughter"). The ceremony is held as soon as the mother has recovered from childbirth. If the girl is the family's firstborn, she is generally named Bechora or Becharetta, or by the diminutive form Buzika.

Traditionally, the name of the newborn and the name of the father is mentioned as part of the baby-naming ceremony for both boys and girls. Today, it is common for the name of the mother to be mentioned as well.

Naming Ceremony for a Girl

The naming ceremony for a girl is simpler than that for a boy. Among Ashkenazim and most Sephardim, on the Sabbath following the baby's birth the father visits the synagogue and receives an *aliyah*. After his portion of the Torah is read and the father recites the final Torah blessing, the sexton or rabbi recites a special prayer for the welfare of the mother, asking for her return to good health following childbirth. This prayer is known as *Mi-Shebeirach*, meaning "May He who blessed." A second *Mi-Shebeirach* is then recited, and as part of this prayer the baby is named.

The general wording of the prayer is, "May He who blessed our forefathers Abraham, Isaac, and Jacob bless (*father's name*) and the daughter just born to him, and she shall henceforth be known in Israel by the name '(*baby's name*) daughter of (*father's name*).'" Guard and protect her father and mother. May they live to rear her to be a God-fearing person, and may they raise her to achieve marital bliss and a life of meritorious deeds."

In some Reform congregations today, the child is named on the first Sabbath during which mother and child are well enough to visit the synagogue together. A similar custom seems to have been followed in some communities in medieval Germany.

NAMING AN ADOPTED CHILD

The Talmud (*Sanhedrin* 19b) says, "Whoever raised an orphan may be considered his parent." This statement led later authorities to conclude that if one adopts an unnamed child, the name of the adoptive father may be referred to as if he were the natural father. Thus, for example, if the adoptive father's Hebrew name is Moshe, a girl may be called "(*baby's name*) bat Moshe," and a boy may be called "(*baby's name*) ben Moshe." If the child was named before being given up for adoption, the name of the natural father is to be retained.

The Talmud arrives at the same conclusion based on the biblical account of King Saul and his daughters, Michal and Merav. Merav had several children who were raised by her younger sister, Michal; and the Bible refers to these children as Michal's children. By extension, it was concluded that it is proper for an adopted child to be called by the name of his or her adoptive parents. It must be said, however, that in Jewish law natural parents never relinquish their rights or status, and a child is obligated to mourn for them upon their death. The child is also obligated to say *Kaddish* for adoptive parents, who have raised and cared for him.

NAMES FOR CONVERTS

There is a longstanding tradition, although no legal requirement, that a male convert take the name Abraham and a female convert take the name Ruth or Sarah as a first name. The male convert is most frequently referred to as "Avraham ben Avraham Avinu" (Abraham, son of Abraham our father), and the female convert as "Rut bat Avraham Avinu" (Ruth, daughter of Abraham our father) or "Sara bat Avraham Avinu" (Sarah, daughter of Abraham our father). The use of "ben Avraham" and "bat Avraham" is generally insisted upon for purposes of identifying an individual as a proselyte (*Shulchan Aruch*, Even Ha'ezer 129:20).

Two reasons are offered for using the name Avraham. First, the Bible (Genesis 17:5) speaks of Abraham as "the father of a multitude of nations." Since proselytes come from diverse backgrounds, it is appropriate that they be called sons of Abraham.

The Midrash (*Genesis Rabbah* 39:8-11) offers a second explanation: In Isaiah 41:8 the Children of Israel are called God's friends, as it is written, "The seed of Abraham My [God's] friend." And in Deuteronomy 10: 18 proselytes are called God's friends, as it is written, "God is the friend of the proselyte." From these references the conclusion is drawn that Abraham has a special relationship to proselytes. In Jewish tradition, Abraham has become known as "the father of proselytes." When a proselyte converts to Judaism, the family of Abraham becomes his family. The Talmud (*Yevamot* 22a) calls converts to Judaism "newborn babes."

Offering the convert the name of Abraham is explained by the Midrash (*Deuteronomy Rabbah* 8:2) to be an expression of deep love: "God loves proselytes dearly. And we, too, should show our love for them because they left their father's house, and their people...and have joined us."

It is, of course, a matter of record that not all proselytes have taken the name Abraham. The scholar Onkelos was a proselyte. Flavius Clemens, nephew of the Roman Vespasian, was a proselyte. The Talmud (*Berachot* 28a) also refers to a proselyte named Judah the Ammonite.

Female converts take the name of Sarah because she was the First Lady of Israel, the wife of Abraham; and they take the name of the biblical Ruth because she epitomizes loyalty to Judaism. Ruth is famous for swearing her eternal allegiance to her mother-in-law, Naomi, which was expressed in these immortal words (Ruth 1:16):

> *Whither thou goest, I will go,*
> *Where thou lodgest, I will lodge.*
> *Thy people shall be my people,*
> *And thy God my God.*

Using the Matronymic in a Prayer for Health

Modern Orthodox feminists have been promoting the idea that when called to the Torah for an *aliyah*, a person should be identified as the child of the mother as well as that of the father. Traditionally, however, in Jewish life a man or woman is identified by the father's name: "(*person's name*) ben/bat (*father's name*)." This patronymic form is used in the Jewish marriage contract (*ketubah*) and divorce document (*get*). An exception has always been made, however, when reciting the prayer for recovery from illness. On that occasion, the mother's name—the matronymic—is substituted for the patronymic.

The custom of using the matronymic form in this instance developed quite early and was already in vogue in talmudic times. The fourth-century scholar Abayei said: "My mother told me that all incantations [prayers for recovery] that are repeated several times must contain the name of the mother ..." (*Shabbat* 66b).

The *Zohar*, commenting on the Bible portion *Lech Lecha*, makes a similar point when it says that all appeals to supernatural beings, whether in prayers or on charms, must be made in the name of the mother. To find biblical justification for the practice, the Sages pointed to the verse, "I am the servant, the son of Thy handmaid, Thou hast loosened my bonds [saved me]" (Psalms 116:16). From this verse the inference is drawn that in an emergency, when one prays to be saved, the matronymic form is preferred over the patronymic.

Using the Matronymic to Avoid Confusion

There are times when the matronymic form is used simply to identify a person and avoid misunderstanding. Thus, we find the talmudic scholar Mari, a proselyte, identified as Mari ben Rachel (mother's name), thereby making his status immediately known.

It is considered important that the individual's standing as a Jew be readily apparent, because in large part it determines his or her legal rights and helps mitigate confusion. Thus, for example, since a proselyte may not marry a *Kohen*, a member of the Priestly family (*Shulchan Aruch*, Even Ha'ezer 6:8), someone named Mari ben Rachel would not find himself placed in the position of being introduced to the daughter of a *Kohen* with an eye toward marriage.

The noted eighteenth-century Polish scholar Ezekiel Landau made the point that when one writes a document of divorce for a proselyte, the matronymic rather than the patronymic should be used. The fact that many proselytes are named "(*person's name*) ben Avraham" could conceivably lead to confusion at a later date, since many born Jews are so named. By using the matronymic, a misunderstanding may be avoided. In fact, some scholars favor using the matronymic form in the divorce document in cases where the mother in the family is better known than the father.

Naming an Illegitimate Child

If a child is born out of wedlock to a Jewish mother and the father's identity is unknown, the child should be named at the appropriate time and place (at the *brit* for a boy; in the synagogue for a girl), and he or she should be identified as the child of the mother—for example, "(*baby's name*) ben Rachel" or "(*baby's name*) bat Rachel." According to Moses Isserles, in his Notes on the *Shulchan Aruch*, Orach Chayim 139:3, when such a child (known in Hebrew as a *shetuki*) is given an *aliyah*, he should be called to the Torah by the name of his maternal grandfather in order to avoid the embarrassment that might result if the mother's name is used.

A NOTE ON STYLE

The task of transliterating Hebrew, Yiddish, and Aramaic names into English is not as simple as it might seem, owing to the fact that there are two styles of pronunciation: Ashkenazic and Sephardic. In this dictionary, transliterated names are rendered in the Sephardic dialect, although frequently used Askenazic pronunciations of some names are also included as variant forms.

KEY TO TRANSLITERATION

- When transliterating from Hebrew into English, scholars make a distinction between the gutteral-sounding *chaf* (כ) and the gutteral-sounding *chet* (ח), the *kh* being used for the former and the *ch* for the latter. In this volume, for simplicity's sake, both the *chaf* and the *chet* are represented by the letters *ch*. For some names, alternate spellings using the *kh* are indicated.

- The vowel sound in the English word *pique* and the Hebrew word *bimah* is represented by the letter *i*.

- The vowel sound in the English word *pin* and the Hebrew word *minchah* is also represented by the letter *i*.

- The diphthong sound in the English word *find* and the Hebrew word *chai* is represented by the letters *ai*.

- The diphthong sound in the English word *eight* and the Hebrew word *eish* is represented by the letters *ei*.

- The vowel sound in the English word *far* and the Hebrew word *chag* is represented by the letter *a*.

- The vowel sound in the English word *met* and the Hebrew word *get* is represented by the letter *e*.

- The vowel sound in the English word *do* and the Hebrew word *zu* is represented by the letter *u*.

LANGUAGES REFERRED TO

Aside from the familiar languages (Hebrew, Greek, Latin, French, Dutch, etc.) referred to in the text of this dictionary, the following lesser-known languages are sometimes mentioned as the source of a name:

- *Anglo-Saxon*, the Germanic language used by the three Teutonic tribal groups living in England before the Norman Conquest (1066): The Angles, the Saxons, and the Jutes. Used synonymously with Old English.

- *British*, the language used by the ancient Britons beginning about 400 A.D. It includes many of the Celtic languages.

- *Celtic*, a family of languages used in the British Isles dating back to 1000 B.C. It includes Eise, Scottish, Gaelic, Irish Manx, Breton, Cornish, and Welsh.

- *Danish*, the Germanic language spoken in Denmark.

- *Gaelic*, a subbranch of the Celtic family of languages.

- *Irish Gaelic*, the Celtic language of Ireland.

- *High German*, consisting of dialects spoken in southern Germany.

- *Low German*, consisting of dialects spoken in northern Germany.

- *Middle Latin*, used in Europe from about 700 to 1500. Also called Medieval Latin.

- *Old English*, the Germanic language (or dialect) of the Anglo-Saxons spoken in England from the fifth to the eleventh century. Used synonymously with Anglo-Saxon.

- *Old Low German*, the language used in the northern part of Germany and in the Netherlands from the eighth to the twelfth century.

- *Old Norse*, the language used in Denmark, Iceland, and Norway between the eighth and the fourteenth centuries.

- *Scotch Gaelic*, the Celtic language of Scotland.

- *Scottish*, the dialect of the English language used in Scotland.

- *Slavic*, a subbranch of the Indo-European family of languages. It includes Polish, Czech, Slovak, Serbo-Croation, Slovenian, Bulgarian, Russian, and Ukrainian.

- *Slavonic*, used synonymously with the word Slavic.

- *Syriac*, the ancient Aramaic language of Syria, used from the third to the thirteenth centuries.

- *Yiddish*, a dialect of High German into which Hebrew, Russian, Polish, and words from other East European languages have been incorporated.

How to Use This Dictionary

The entries in this book are presented alphabetically in two sections: masculine and feminine. Immediately following the entry, where applicable, the Hebrew spelling is provided in Hebrew script.

Each entry specifies the language or languages from which the name derives as well as its literal meaning. Both masculine and feminine Hebrew equivalents are then offered.

The Index of Names by Meaning will be extremely helpful to those seeking a name with a specific meaning or significance.

MASCULINE
NAMES

⁓ A ⁓

Aaron (אַהֲרֹן) The Anglicized form of Aharon. *See* Aharon.

Abba (אַבָּא) From the Aramaic, meaning "father." The exact Hebrew equivalent is Abba. FEMININE HEBREW EQUIVALENTS: Avi, Aviya.

Abbahu (אַבָּחוּ) From the Aramaic, meaning "God is my father." The exact Hebrew equivalent is Abahu. FEMININE HEBREW EQUIVALENTS: Avi, Avicha'yil, Avi'em.

Abbayei (אַבָּיֵי) From the Aramaic, meaning "little father." The exact Hebrew equivalent is Aba'yei. FEMININE HEBREW EQUIVALENTS: Avi'ela, Aviga'yil, Avishag.

Abbe, Abbey From the Old French and Latin, meaning "head of a monastery, abbot." *See* Abbot.

Abbie A variant spelling of Abbey. *See* Abbey. Also, a pet form of Abba. *See* Abba.

Abbot, Abbott Greek and Latin forms of the Aramaic name Abba. *See* Abba.

Abe A pet form of Abraham. *See* Abraham.

Abel (הֶבֶל) From the Assyrian, meaning "meadow," or from the Hebrew, meaning "breath." The exact Hebrew equivalent is Hevel. FEMININE HEBREW EQUIVALENTS: Carmela, Gana, Nirel. In Genesis 4:2, the younger son of Adam and Eve.

29

Abelard From the Anglo-Saxon, meaning "noble, nobly resolute." HE-BREW EQUIVALENTS: Achiram, Aminadav, Ish-hod, Yehonadav, Yisra'el. FEMININE HEBREW EQUIVALENTS: Nedira, Ne'edara, Sara.

Aberlin A Yiddish form of Abraham. *See* Abraham.

Abi A pet form of Abraham. *See* Abraham. Also, a variant spelling of Avi. *See* Avi.

Abida A variant spelling of Avida. *See* Avida.

Abie A short form of Abraham. *See* Abraham.

Abiezer A variant spelling of Aviezer. *See* Aviezer.

Abihu A variant spelling of Avihu. *See* Avihu.

Abimelech A variant spelling of Avimelech. *See* Avimelech.

Abimi A variant spelling of Avimi. *See* Avimi.

Abin A variant spelling of Avin. *See* Avin.

Abina A variant spelling of Avina. *See* Avina.

Abinadab A variant spelling of Avinadav. *See* Avinadav.

Abinoam A variant spelling of Avinoam. *See* Avinoam.

Abir (אָבִּיר) From the Hebrew, meaning "hero, strong." The exact Hebrew equivalent is Abir. The exact feminine equivalent is Abira.

Abiram A variant spelling of Aviram. *See* Aviram.

Abiri (אֲבִּירִי) A unisex name. From the Hebrew, meaning "my hero; my gallant one." The exact Hebrew equivalent is Abiri.

Able A variant spelling of Abel. *See* Abel.

Abner A variant spelling of Avner. *See* Avner.

Abraham The Anglicized spelling of Avraham. *See* Avraham.

Abram A variant spelling of Avram. *See* Avram.

Abrasha A variant form of Avraham. *See* Avraham.

Absalom A variant form of Avshalom. *See* Avshalom.

Achav (אַחְאָב) From the Hebrew, meaning "uncle." The exact Hebrew equivalent is Achav. Ahab is the Anglicized form. In I Kings 16:29, the seventh king of Israel, after the monarchy split.

Achban (אַחְבָּן) From the Hebrew, meaning "brother of intelligence." The exact Hebrew equivalent is Achban. FEMININE HEBREW EQUIVALENTS: Da'at, Dei'a. In I Chronicles 2:29, a leader of the tribe of Judah.

Acher (אַחֵר) From the Hebrew, meaning "the other one, another." The exact Hebrew equivalent is Acher. In I Chronicles 7:12, a leader of the tribe of Benjamin.

Achi (אֲחִי) From the Hebrew, meaning "my brother." The exact Hebrew equivalent is Achi. In I Chronicles 5:15, a leader of the tribe of Gad.

Achiezer (אֲחִיעֶזֶר) From the Hebrew, meaning "my brother is my support." The exact Hebrew equivalent is Achi'ezer. FEMININE HEBREW EQUIVALENTS: Mashena, Sa'ada. In Numbers 1:12, a leader of the tribe of Dan.

Achihud (אֲחִיהוּד) From the Hebrew, meaning "my brother is majestic." The exact Hebrew equivalent is Achihud. FEMININE HEBREW EQUIVALENTS: Adira, Ge'ona, Nediva. In Numbers 34:27, a leader of the tribe of Asher.

Achinadav (אֲחִינָדָב) From the Hebrew, meaning "my brother is noble." The exact Hebrew equivalent is Achinadav. FEMININE HEBREW EQUIVALENTS: Adira, Nediva. In I Kings 4:14, one of King Solomon's officials.

Achinoam (אֲחִינֹעַם) A unisex name. *See* Achinoam (*feminine section*).

Adad A variant form of Hadad. *See* Hadad.

Adael (עֲדָאֵל) From the Hebrew, meaning "God is witness" or "adorned by God." The exact Hebrew equivalent is Ada'el. FEMININE HEBREW EQUIVALENTS: Ada, Ada'ya, Adi.

Adair From the Celtic, meaning "food near the oak tree." HEBREW EQUIVALENTS: Ela, Oren, Rechov. FEMININE HEBREW EQUIVALENTS: Alona, Ela, Selila.

Adam (אָדָם) From the Hebrew, meaning "earth." Also, of Phoenician and Babylonian origin, meaning "man, mankind." The exact Hebrew equivalent is Adam. The exact feminine equivalent is Adama. In Genesis 3:17, the first man on earth.

Adar (אֲדָר) From the Babylonian *daru*, meaning "darkened," or from the Hebrew, meaning "noble, exalted." The exact Hebrew equivalent is Adar. The exact feminine equivalent is Adara.

Adda (אַדָּא) From the Aramaic, meaning "this one." The exact Hebrew equivalent is Adda.

Addison From the Old English, meaning "son of Adam." *See* Adam.

Adelbert A variant form of the Old High German, meaning "noble" and "bright," hence "illustrious person." HEBREW EQUIVALENTS: Avihud, Avner, Nadav. FEMININE HEBREW EQUIVALENTS: Behira, Me'ira, Nediva.

Aden A variant spelling of Adin. *See* Adin.

Adi, **Addi**, **Addie** (עֲדִי) A unisex name. From the Hebrew, meaning "my adornment" or "my witness." The exact Hebrew equivalent is Adi.

Adiel (עֲדִיאֵל) From the Hebrew, meaning "adorned by God" or "God is my witness." The exact Hebrew equivalent is Adi'el. The exact feminine equivalent is Adi'ela.

Adif (עָדִיף) From the Hebrew, meaning "excellent." The exact Hebrew equivalent is Adif. The exact feminine equivalent is Adifa.

Adin (עָדִין) From the Hebrew, meaning "beautiful, pleasant, gentle." The exact Hebrew equivalent is Adin. The exact feminine equivalent is Adina. In Ezra 2:15, a contemporary of Zerubabel.

Adina, **Adinah** (עֲדִינָה) A unisex name. From the Hebrew, meaning "delicate." The exact Hebrew equivalent is Adina. In I Chronicles 11:42, a warrior in King David's army.

Adir (אַדִּיר) From the Hebrew meaning "lord, noble, majestic." The exact Hebrew equivalent is Adir. The exact feminine equivalent is Adira. When spelled with an *a'yin* (עָדִיר), the meaning is "digging."

Adiv (אָדִיב) From the Hebrew and Arabic, meaning "pleasant, gentle-mannered." The exact Hebrew equivalent is Adiv. The exact feminine equivalent is Adiva.

Adlai (עֶדְלַי) From the Aramaic, meaning "refuge of God" or "God is witness." Also, from the Arabic, meaning "to act justly." The exact Hebrew equivalent is Adlai. FEMININE HEBREW EQUIVALENTS: Avigdora, Chasya, Chosa. In I Chronicles 27:29, the father of one of King David's officers.

Adler From the German, meaning "eagle." The exact Hebrew equivalent is Nesher. FEMININE HEBREW EQUIVALENTS: A'ya, Da'ya, Efrona.

Admon (אַדְמוֹן) From the Hebrew *adom*, meaning "red." The exact Hebrew equivalent is Admon. FEMININE HEBREW EQUIVALENTS: Almoga, Odem, Tzachara.

Adna, **Adnah** (עַדְנָה) From the Aramaic, meaning "good fortune" or "adorned." The exact Hebrew equivalent is Adna. FEMININE HEBREW EQUIVALENTS: Ashera, Asherit, Ashrat. In Nehemiah 12:15, the head of a priestly family.

Adni (עֶדְנִי) From the Hebrew, meaning "my delight." The exact Hebrew equivalent is Adni. FEMININE HEBREW EQUIVALENTS: Adina, Na'a, Na'ama.

Adolf, **Adolfo** Variant German forms of Adolph. *See* Adolph.

Adolph From the Old German, meaning "noble wolf" or "noble helper." HEBREW EQUIVALENTS: Elazar, Eli'ezer, Ezra. FEMININE HEBREW EQUIVALENTS: Aleksandra, Milka, Nediva.

Adolphe The French form of Adolph. *See* Adolph.

Adom (אָדוֹם) From the Hebrew, meaning "red, ruby." The exact Hebrew equivalent is Adom. The exact feminine equivalent is Aduma. Also, an African name meaning "red."

Adon (אָדוֹן) From the Hebrew and Phoenician, meaning "lord" or "master." The exact Hebrew equivalent is Adon. FEMININE HEBREW EQUIVALENTS: Adira, Malka, Yisra'ela.

Adoniya (אֲדוֹנִיָה) A unisex name. From the Hebrew meaning "the

Lord is my God." The exact Hebrew equivalent is Adoniya. In I Kings 1:5, the fourth son of King David.

Adoram (אֲדוֹרָם) A short form of Adoniram. From the Hebrew, meaning "God is exalted" or "my master is mighty." The exact Hebrew equivalent is Adoram. FEMININE HEBREW EQUIVALENTS: Ram, Rama, Rami.

Adrian A short form of the Latin name Hadrian. Also, from the Greek, meaning "rich." HEBREW EQUIVALENTS: Adar, Hotir, Huna. FEMININE HEBREW EQUIVALENTS: Adara, Ashira.

Adriel (אֲדְרִיאֵל) From the Hebrew, meaning "God is my majesty." The exact Hebrew equivalent is Adri'el. FEMININE HEBREW EQUIVALENTS: Adira, Ge'ona, Ge'onit. In I Samuel 18:19, King Saul's son-in-law.

Adrien A variant spelling of Adrian. *See* Adrian.

Aduk (אָדוּק) From the Hebrew, meaning "pious, zealous." The exact Hebrew equivalent is Aduk. The exact feminine equivalent is Aduka.

Afek (אָפֵק) From the Hebrew, meaning "horizon" or "water channel." The exact Hebrew equivalent is Afek. The exact feminine equivalent is Afeka.

Afik (אָפִיק) A variant form of Afek. The exact Hebrew equivalent is Afik. *See* Afek.

Afri A variant spelling of Ofri. *See* Ofri.

Aga A pet form of Hagai. *See* Hagai.

Agaf (אֲגָף) From the Hebrew, meaning "wing" or "branch." The exact Hebrew equivalent is Agaf. FEMININE HEBREW EQUIVALENTS: Anefa, Anufa, Zemora.

Agan (אַגָּן) From the Hebrew, meaning "basin, sink." The exact Hebrew equivalent is Agan.

Agas (אַגָּס) From the Hebrew, meaning "pear." The exact Hebrew equivalent is Agas.

Agel (אָגֵל) From the Hebrew, meaning "I will rejoice." The exact Hebrew equivalent is Agel. FEMININE HEBREW EQUIVALENTS: Aliza, Avigal, Aviga'yil.

Aggie A pet form of Augustus. *See* Augustus.

Agil (אֲגִיל) A variant form of Agel. The exact Hebrew equivalent is Agil. *See* Agel.

Agmon (אַגְמוֹן) From the Hebrew, meaning "reed." The exact Hebrew equivalent is Agmon. The feminine equivalent is Kani'ela.

Agnon A variant form of Ogen. *See* Ogen.

Agron (אַגְרוֹן) From the Hebrew, meaning "correspondence" or "vocabulary." The exact Hebrew equivalent is Agron. The feminine equivalent is Soferet.

Agur (אָגוּר) From the Hebrew, meaning "knowledgeable, learned." The exact Hebrew equivalent is Agur. FEMININE HEBREW EQUIVALENTS: Chochma, Da'at.

Ahab The Anglicized form of Achav. *See* Achav.

Aharon (אַהֲרֹן) From the Hebrew, meaning "teaching," "singing," "shining," or "mountain." Also, from the Arabic, meaning "messenger." The exact Hebrew equivalent is Aharon. The exact feminine equivalent is Aharona.

Ahava, **Ahavah** (אַהֲבָה) A unisex name. From the Hebrew, meaning "love." The exact Hebrew equivalent is Ahava.

Ahud (אָהוּד) From the Hebrew, meaning "liked, likable." The exact Hebrew equivalent is Ahud. The exact feminine equivalent is Ahuda.

Ahuv (אָהוּב) From the Hebrew, meaning "beloved." The exact Hebrew equivalent is Ahuv. The exact feminine equivalent is Ahuva.

Ain From the Scottish, meaning "belonging to one." HEBREW EQUIVALENTS: Achuzat, Ka'yin, Kenam. FEMININE HEBREW EQUIVALENTS: Achuza, Be'ula, Li.

Ainsley From the Scottish, meaning "one's own field." HEBREW EQUIVALENTS: Nir, Niram, Nirel. FEMININE HEBREW EQUIVALENTS: Achuza, Be'ula, Nir.

Aisik A variant spelling of Isaac. *See* Isaac.

Akavel A variant form of Akiva. *See* Akiva.

Akavya The Aramaic form of Akiva. *See* Akiva.

Akevy The Hungarian form of Jacob. *See* Jacob.

Aki A pet form of Yaakov (Jacob). *See* Jacob.

Akiba A variant spelling of Akiva. *See* Akiva.

Akim A Russian short form of Yehoyakim. *See* Yehoyakim.

Akiva (עֲקִיבָא) A variant form of the Hebrew name Ya'akov (Jacob), meaning to "hold by the heel." The exact Hebrew equivalent is Akiva. FEMININE HEBREW EQUIVALENTS: Efrat, Magena, Ya'akova.

Akki A variant spelling of Aki. *See* Aki.

Akom (עָקֹם) From the Hebrew, meaning "crooked, irregular." The exact Hebrew equivalent is Akom. The exact feminine equivalent is Akuma.

Aksel From the Old German, meaning "small oak tree." HEBREW EQUIVALENTS: Alon, Armon, Elon. FEMININE HEBREW EQUIVALENTS: Alona, Ela, Elona.

Al A pet form of many first names, including Alan, Albert, Alfred, and Alexander.

Alain From the Gaelic, meaning "bright, fair, handsome." Akin to Alan. *See* Alan.

Alan Of doubtful origin, but usually taken from the Celtic, meaning "harmony, peace," or from the Gaelic, meaning "fair, handsome." HEBREW EQUIVALENTS: Avshalom, Lavan, Na'aman. FEMININE HEBREW EQUIVALENTS: Achino'am, Na'ama, Na'omi.

Alard From the Old German, meaning "of noble ancestry." HEBREW EQUIVALENTS: Achinadav, Adon, Chirom. FEMININE HEBREW EQUIVALENTS: Adina, Adira, Adoniya.

Alastair From the Greek, meaning "avenger." The Hebrew equivalent is Elnakam.

Alban From the Latin, meaning "white." HEBREW EQUIVALENTS: Lavan, Levanon, Livna. FEMININE HEBREW EQUIVALENTS: Livnat, Levona, Malbina.

Albert A French form of the Old High German name Adelbrecht, meaning "noble, nobility." HEBREW EQUIVALENTS: Achinadav, Achiram, Adar. FEMININE HEBREW EQUIVALENTS: Adina, Adira, Adoniya.

Albie A pet form of Albert. *See* Albert.

Albin A variant spelling of Alban. *See* Alban.

Albion A variant form of Alban. *See* Alban.

Albrecht An early German form of Albert. *See* Albert.

Aldan A variant spelling of Alden. *See* Alden.

Alden From the Middle English, meaning "antiquated, aged." HEBREW EQUIVALENTS: Kadmi'el, Kedem, Saba. FEMININE HEBREW EQUIVALENTS: Bilha, Keshisha, Yeshana.

Alder From the Old English, meaning "old." Also, from Middle English, meaning "tree [of the birch family]." HEBREW EQUIVALENTS: Alon, Amir, Arzi. FEMININE HEBREW EQUIVALENTS: Alona, Ariza, Arzit.

Aldo An Old German and Italian form of Alder. *See* Alder.

Aldon A variant spelling of Alden. *See* Alden.

Aldous A variant spelling of Aldus. *See* Aldus.

Aldred From the Old English name Ealdred, meaning "old, wise counsel." HEBREW EQUIVALENTS: Bina, Buna, De'uel. FEMININE HEBREW EQUIVALENTS: Berura, Beruriya, Nevona.

Aldren Probably a variant form of Alder. *See* Alder.

Aldus A Latinized form of the Old German name Aldo. *See* Aldo.

Aldwin From the Old English, meaning "old friend." HEBREW EQUIVALENTS: Amit, Amitai, Amitan. FEMININE HEBREW EQUIVALENTS: Achava, Amit, Amita.

Alec, **Aleck** Short forms of Alexander, popular in Scotland. *See* Alexander.

Alef, **Aleph** (אָלֶף) From the Hebrew, meaning "number one" or "leader." The exact Hebrew equivalent is Alef. The exact feminine equivalent is Alufa.

Alejandro A Spanish form of Alexander. *See* Alexander.

Aleksandr A variant Russian spelling of Alexander. *See* Alexander.

Alemet (עֲלֶמֶת) From the Hebrew, meaning "concealed, hidden." The exact Hebrew equivalent is Alemet. FEMININE HEBREW EQUIVALENTS: Shemura, Tzofnat.

Alessandro A Spanish form of Alexander. *See* Alexander.

Alex A popular short form of Alexander. *See* Alexander.

Alexander From the Greek name Alexandros, meaning "protector of men." The exact Hebrew equivalent is Aleksander. The exact feminine equivalent is Aleksandra.

Alexandre A variant spelling of Alexander. *See* Alexander.

Alexandri A variant form of Alexander. *See* Alexander.

Alexis A variant form of Alexander. *See* Alexander.

Alf, **Alfeo**, **Alfie** Pet forms of Alfred. *See* Alfred.

Alfon (אַלְפוֹן) From the Hebrew, meaning "primer." The exact Hebrew equivalent is Alfon.

Alfonse, **Alfonso**, **Alfonzo** Variant spellings of Alphonso. *See* Alphonso.

Alfred From the Old English, meaning "old, wise counsel." HEBREW EQUIVALENTS: Avin, Bina, Buna. FEMININE HEBREW EQUIVALENTS: Berura, Beruriya, Ge'onit.

Alfredo The Spanish form of Alfred. *See* Alfred.

Alger From the Anglo-Saxon, meaning "noble spearman" or "warrior." HEBREW EQUIVALENTS: Avicha'yil, Ben-Cha'yil, Gad. FEMININE HEBREW EQUIVALENTS: Amtza, Gavri'ela, Gavrila.

Ali From the Arabic, meaning "exalted." HEBREW EQUIVALENTS: Atalya, Atlai, Ram. FEMININE HEBREW EQUIVALENTS: Ge'ona, Ge'onit, Rama.

Alis A short form of Alistair. *See* Alistair.

Alistair A variant spelling of Alastair. *See* Alastair. Also, perhaps derived from the Arabic, meaning "bird." HEBREW EQUIVALENTS: Deror, Efron, Gozal. FEMININE HEBREW EQUIVALENTS: A'ya, Da'ya, Efrona.

Alitz (עָלִיץ) From the Hebrew, meaning "joy." The exact Hebrew equivalent is Alitz. FEMININE HEBREW EQUIVALENTS: Alisa, Aliza, Aviga'yil.

Alix A variant spelling of Alex. *See* Alex.

Aliz (עָלִיז) A unisex name. From the Hebrew, meaning "joy, joyful, merry." The exact Hebrew equivalent is Aliz.

Allan A variant spelling of Alan. *See* Alan.

Allard A variant spelling of Alard. *See* Alard.

Allen A popular variant spelling of Alan. *See* Alan.

Allison A masculine name derived from Alice, meaning "Alice's son." *See* Alice (*feminine section*).

Allistair A variant spelling of Alastair. *See* Alastair.

Allister A variant form of Alastair. *See* Alastair.

Allix A variant spelling of Alex. *See* Alex.

Allon A variant spelling of Alon. *See* Alon.

Allyn A unisex name. A variant spelling of Alan. *See* Alan.

Almagor (אַלְמָגוֹר) From the Hebrew, meaning "fearless." The exact Hebrew equivalent is Almagor. FEMININE HEBREW EQUIVALENTS: No'aza, Odeda.

Alman (אַלְמָן) A variant form of Almon. *See* Almon. The exact Hebrew equivalent is Alman.

Almodad (אַלְמוֹדָד) From the Hebrew, meaning "God is a friend." The exact Hebrew equivalent is Almodad. FEMININE HEBREW EQUIVALENTS: Amit, Amita. In Genesis 10:26, a descendant of Shem, grandson of Noah.

Almog (אַלְמוֹג) From the Hebrew, meaning "coral." The exact Hebrew equivalent is Almog. The exact feminine equivalent is Almoga.

Almon (אַלְמוֹן) From the Hebrew, meaning "forsaken" or "widower." The exact Hebrew equivalent is Almon. The exact feminine equivalent is Almana.

Almoni (אַלְמוֹנִי) From the Hebrew, meaning "anonymous." The exact Hebrew equivalent is Almoni. The exact feminine equivalent is Almonit.

Alon (אַלוֹן) From the Hebrew, meaning "oak tree." The exact Hebrew equivalent is Alon. FEMININE HEBREW EQUIVALENTS: Alona, Eila, Eilona.

Alphonse The French form of Alphonso. *See* Alphonso.

Alphonso From the Old High German, meaning "of noble family." HEBREW EQUIVALENTS: Achiram, Adoniya, Aminadav, Chirom. FEMININE HEBREW EQUIVALENTS: Malka, Nediva, Ne'edara.

Alpin From the Latin name Alpes (Alps), meaning "high mountain." HEBREW EQUIVALENTS: Aharon, Harel, Sinai. FEMININE HEBREW EQUIVALENTS: Aharona, Chermona, Harela.

Alroy From the Latin and Old English, meaning "royalty, ruler." HEBREW EQUIVALENTS: Aluf, Avraham, Elrad. FEMININE HEBREW EQUIVALENTS: Alufa, Malka, Sara.

Alsie A pet form of Alson. *See* Alson.

Alson From the Anglo-Saxon, meaning "noble stone" or "son of Al." HEBREW EQUIVALENTS: Achitzur, Elitzur, Tzur. FEMININE HEBREW EQUIVALENTS: Avna, Avni'ela, Ritzpa.

Alta From the Latin and Spanish, meaning "tall, high." HEBREW EQUIVALENTS: Aharon, Aram. FEMININE HEBREW EQUIVALENTS: Aharona, Alya, Givat.

Alter From the Old English and the Old High German, meaning "old one." Popular as a Yiddish name. The exact Yiddish form is Alter. HEBREW EQUIVALENTS: Kadmi'el, Kedem, Yiftach. FEMININE HEBREW EQUIVALENTS: Bilha, Yeshana, Yeshisha.

Altie A pet form of Alta or Alastair. *See* Alta *and* Alastair.

Alto A variant form of Alta. *See* Alta.

Alton From the Old English, meaning "old town." HEBREW EQUIVALENTS: Chetzron, Kadmi'el, Kedem. FEMININE HEBREW EQUIVALENTS: Lina, Me'ona, Tira.

Altus A variant form of Alta. *See* Alta.

Aluf, Aluph (אַלוּף) From the Hebrew, meaning "master, prince, leader." The exact Hebrew equivalent is Aluf. The exact feminine equivalent is Alufa.

Aluv (עָלוּב) From the Hebrew, meaning "lonely, wretched, poor." The exact Hebrew equivalent is Aluv. The exact feminine equivalent is Aluva.

Alva From the Latin, meaning "white, bright." HEBREW EQUIVALENTS: Lavan, Livni, Me'ir. FEMININE HEBREW EQUIVALENTS: Levana, Levona, Me'ira.

Alvan From the Old English, meaning "beloved friend." HEBREW EQUIVALENTS: Ahuv, Ahuv-Am, Ahuvya. FEMININE HEBREW EQUIVALENTS: Ahava, Ahuva, Ahuvya.

Alvin A variant form of Alvan. *See* Alvan.

Alvis From the Old Norse, meaning "wise." HEBREW EQUIVALENTS: Avida, Bina, Chacham. FEMININE HEBREW EQUIVALENTS: Chanukah, Nevona, Tushiya.

Alwin, Alwyn From the Old English, meaning "old, noble friend." HEBREW EQUIVALENTS: Amitai, Amitan, Eldad. FEMININE HEBREW EQUIVALENTS: Achava, Amit, Rut.

Alyn A variant spelling of Alan. *See* Alan.

Amadore From the Greek and Italian, meaning "gift of love." HEBREW EQUIVALENTS: Achiman, Ahud, Ahuv. FEMININE HEBREW EQUIVALENTS: Dorona, Matana, Netanela.

Amal (עָמָל) A unisex name. From the Hebrew, meaning "work, toil." The exact Hebrew equivalent is Amal. In I Chronicles 7:35, a grandson of Asher.

Amali (עֲמָלִי) A variant form of Amal. From the Hebrew, meaning "my work, my toil." *See* Amal.

Amami (עֲמָמִי) From the Hebrew, meaning "popular, folksy, nationalistic." The exact Hebrew equivalent is Amami. FEMININE HEBREW EQUIVALENTS: Le'uma, Le'umi, Uma.

Aman (אָמָן) From the Hebrew, meaning "artist" or "expert." The exact Hebrew equivalent is Aman.

Amand A French form of the Latin name Amandus, meaning "worthy of love." HEBREW EQUIVALENTS: Ahud, Ahuv, Ahuvya. FEMININE HEBREW EQUIVALENTS: Ahava, Ahuva, Chaviva.

Amania, Amaniah, Amanya (אֲמַנְיָה) A unisex name. From the Hebrew, meaning "loyal to the Lord." The exact Hebrew equivalent is Amanya.

Amaria, Amariah, Amarya (אֲמַרְיָה) From the Hebrew, meaning "word of God." The exact Hebrew equivalent is Amarya. FEMININE HEBREW EQUIVALENTS: Amira, Doveva. In Nehemiah 12:2, a priest who returned to Palestine from the Babylonian exile.

Amasa, Amassa (עֲמָשָׂא) From the Hebrew, meaning "burdensome." The exact Hebrew equivalent is Amasa. Teruda is a feminine equivalent. In II Samuel 17:25, the son of Avigal (Abigal), King David's sister.

Amatzia, Amatziah, Amatzya (אֲמַצְיָה) From the Hebrew, meaning "strength of God." The exact Hebrew equivalent is Amatzya. FEMININE HEBREW EQUIVALENTS: Amitza, Amitzya, Amtza, Gibora. In II Kings 14:8, the son of King Joash of Judah. In I Chronicles 6:45, an ancestor of Ethan, King David's musician.

Ambler From the Old French, meaning "one who walks leisurely." HEBREW EQUIVALENTS: Darkon, Divon, Shu'ach. FEMININE HEBREW EQUIVALENTS: Nacha, Nachat, Yanocha.

Ambrose From the Greek, meaning "divine" or "immortal." HEBREW EQUIVALENTS: Ami'ad, Avi'ad, Chi'el. FEMININE HEBREW EQUIVALENTS: Cha'yuta, Chi'yuta, Nitzcha.

Amel (עָמֵל) A variant form of Amal. See Amal. The exact Hebrew equivalent is Amel.

Amery A variant spelling of Emory. See Emory.

Ami, Ammi (עַמִּי) A unisex name. From the Hebrew, meaning "my nation, my people." The exact Hebrew equivalent is Ami. In Ezra 2: 57, a servant of King Solomon.

Amiaz (עֲמִיעַז) From the Hebrew, meaning "my nation is mighty." The exact Hebrew equivalent is Ami'az. FEMININE HEBREW EQUIVALENTS: Amiya, Amtza, Ari'el.

Amichai (עֲמִיחַי) From the Hebrew, meaning "my nation lives." The exact Hebrew equivalent is Amichai. FEMININE HEBREW EQUIVALENTS: Cha'ya, Cha'yuta, Yechi'ela.

Amidan (עֲמִידָן) From the Hebrew, meaning "my people [nation] is just, righteous." The exact Hebrew equivalent is Amidan. FEMININE HEBREW EQUIVALENTS: Chasida, Dana, Danit.

Amidar (עֲמִידָר) From the Hebrew, meaning "my nation is alive." The exact Hebrew equivalent is Amidar. *See* Amichai *for additional equivalents.*

Amidor (עֲמִידוֹר) From the Hebrew, meaning "my generation of people." The exact Hebrew equivalent is Amidor. FEMININE HEBREW EQUIVALENTS: Dor, Dorit, Dorya.

Amidror (עֲמִידְרוֹר) From the Hebrew, meaning "my nation is free." The exact Hebrew equivalent is Amidror. FEMININE HEBREW EQUIVALENTS: Derora, Derorit, Deroriya.

Amiel (עֲמִיאֵל) From the Hebrew, meaning "God of my people." The exact Hebrew equivalent is Ami'el. FEMININE HEBREW EQUIVALENTS: Ami'or, Le'uma, Uma. In Numbers 13:12, one of the spies sent out by Moses.

Amihud (עֲמִיהוּד) From the Hebrew, meaning "my nation is glorious." The exact Hebrew equivalent is Amihud. FEMININE HEBREW EQUIVALENTS: Ami'eta, Ami'ora, Amya. In Numbers 34:20, a member of the tribe of Shimon (Simeon).

Amin (אָמִין) From the Hebrew, meaning "trustworthy." The exact Hebrew equivalent is Amin. The exact feminine equivalent is Amina.

Aminadav (עֲמִינָדָב) From the Hebrew, meaning "my people's pledge." The exact Hebrew equivalent is Aminadav. Nedava is a feminine equivalent. In Exodus 6:23, a leader of the tribe of Judah; father of Elisheva, Aaron's wife.

Amior (עֲמִיאוֹר) A unisex name. From the Hebrew, meaning "my nation is a light, a beacon." The exact Hebrew equivalent is Ami'or.

Amir (עָמִיר/אָמִיר) When spelled with an *alef*, from the Hebrew meaning "mighty, strong." When spelled with an *a'yin*, from the Hebrew meaning "sheaf of corn." The exact Hebrew equivalent is Amir. The exact feminine equivalent is Amira.

Amiram (עֲמִירָם) From the Hebrew, meaning "my nation is mighty" or "my nation is exalted." The exact Hebrew equivalent is Amiram. FEMININE HEBREW EQUIVALENTS: Amira, Amitza, Amtza.

Amiran (עֲמִירָן) A variant form of Amiron. The exact Hebrew equivalent is Amiran. *See* Amiron *for additional equivalents.*

Amiron (עֲמִירֹן) From the Hebrew, meaning "my nation is a song" or "my people sings." The exact Hebrew equivalent is Amiron. FEMININE HEBREW EQUIVALENTS: Negina, Shira, Zemira.

Amishaddai (עֲמִישַׁדָּי) From the Hebrew, meaning "my nation is God's." The exact Hebrew equivalent is Amishaddai. FEMININE HEBREW EQUIVALENTS: Le'uma, Uma. In Numbers 1:12, a member of the tribe of Dan.

Amit (עָמִית) A unisex name. From the Hebrew, meaning "upright, honest friend." The exact Hebrew equivalent is Amit.

Amitai (אֲמִיתַי) From the Aramaic, meaning "true, faithful." The exact Hebrew equivalent is Amitai. FEMININE HEBREW EQUIVALENTS: Amit, Amita. In Jonah 1:1, the father of the prophet Jonah.

Amitan (אֲמִיתָן) From the Hebrew, meaning "true, faithful." The exact Hebrew equivalent is Amitan. FEMININE HEBREW EQUIVALENTS: Amit, Amita.

Amiti A variant form of Amit. *See* Amit.

Amitz (אֲמִיץ) From the Hebrew, meaning "courageous." The exact Hebrew equivalent is Amitz. The exact feminine equivalent is Amitza.

Ammi A variant spelling of Ami. *See* Ami.

Ammiel A variant spelling of Amiel. *See* Amiel.

Ammos A variant spelling of Amos. *See* Amos.

Amnon (אַמְנוֹן) From the Hebrew, meaning "faithful." The exact Hebrew equivalent is Amnon. FEMININE HEBREW EQUIVALENTS: Amana, Amanya, Amina. In II Samuel 3:2, King David's eldest son.

Amok (עָמוֹק) From the Hebrew, meaning "deep, profound." The exact Hebrew equivalent is Amok. Bika is a feminine equivalent. In Nehemiah 12:7, a leader of a family of priests.

Amon (אָמוֹן) From the Hebrew meaning "hidden." The exact Hebrew equivalent is Amon. FEMININE HEBREW EQUIVALENTS: Razi'ela, Tzefuna, Tzofnat. In II Kings 21:18, the fifteenth king of Judah.

Amory A variant form of Emery. *See* Emery.

Amos (עָמוֹס) From the Hebrew, meaning "burdened, troubled." The exact Hebrew equivalent is Amos. FEMININE HEBREW EQUIVALENTS: Teruda, Tzara. In Amos 1:1, the first literary prophet.

Amotz (אָמוֹץ) From the Hebrew, meaning "strong." The exact Hebrew equivalent is Amotz. FEMININE HEBREW EQUIVALENTS: Amitza, Amtza, Atzma. In Isaiah 1:1, the father of the prophet Isaiah.

Amoz A variant spelling of Amotz. *See* Amotz.

Amram (עַמְרָם) From the Hebrew, meaning "mighty nation." The exact Hebrew equivalent is Amram. FEMININE HEBREW EQUIVALENTS: Amitzya, Avirama, Bat-Ami. In Exodus 6:20, the father of Moses.

Amtzi (אַמְצִי) A variant form of Amotz, meaning "my strength." The exact Hebrew equivalent is Amtzi. FEMININE HEBREW EQUIVALENTS: Amtza, Amitza, Atzma. In I Chronicles 6:31, a member of the Merari family.

Anan (עָנָן) From the Hebrew, meaning "cloud" or "soothsayer." The exact Hebrew equivalent is Anan. FEMININE HEBREW EQUIVALENTS: Chazona, Nevi'a. In Nehemiah 10:26, a leader of the tribe of Judah.

Anani (עֲנָנִי) A variant form of Anan. *See* Anan. The exact Hebrew equivalent is Anani. In I Chronicles 3:24, a member of the tribe of Judah.

Anastasia A unisex name. From the Russian, meaning "resurrection." HEBREW EQUIVALENTS: Avichai, Cha'yim, Yechi'el. FEMININE HEBREW EQUIVALENTS: Chava, Techiya, Yechi'ela.

Anat, Anath (עֲנָת) A unisex name. From the Hebrew, meaning "to sing" or "sound of victory." The exact Hebrew equivalent is Anat. In Judges 3:31, the father of the Israelite judge Shamgar.

Anatole From the Greek, meaning "rising of the sun" or "from the east." HEBREW EQUIVALENTS: Aharon, Kadmi'el, Kedem. FEMININE HEBREW EQUIVALENTS: Me'ira, Noga, Ora.

Anatoly A Russian form of Anatole. *See* Anatole.

Anatot (עֲנָתוֹת) From the Hebrew, meaning "answers." The exact Hebrew equivalent is Anatot. In I Chronicles 7:8, a leader of the tribe of Benjamin.

Anav (עָנָב) From the Hebrew, meaning "grape." The exact Hebrew equivalent is Anav. The exact feminine equivalent is Anava.

Anavi (עֲנָבִי) From the Hebrew, meaning "my grape." The exact Hebrew equivalent is Anavi. FEMININE HEBREW EQUIVALENTS: Anava, Eshkola.

Anaya (עֲנָיָה) From the Hebrew, meaning "God has answered." The exact Hebrew equivalent is Anaya. FEMININE HEBREW EQUIVALENTS: Amira, Doveva. In Nehemiah 8:4, one of Nehemiah's supporters.

Ancel From the Old German name Ansi, meaning "god, godlike." HEBREW EQUIVALENTS: Adi'el, Adon, Adoniya. FEMININE HEBREW EQUIVALENTS: Bat-El, Betu'el, Imanu'ela.

Anchel, Anchelle Variant spellings of Anshel. *See* Anshel.

Anders, Anderson Patronymic forms of Andrew, meaning "son of Andrew." *See* Andrew.

Andi, Andie *See* Andy.

Andor A variant form of Andrew. *See* Andrew. Akin to Anders.

André A French form of Andrew. *See* Andrew.

Andrew From the Greek, meaning "manly, strong, courageous." HE-BREW EQUIVALENTS: Ariav, Aryei, Avicha'yil. FEMININE HEBREW EQUIVA-LENTS: Nili, Odedya, Uzit.

Andy A pet form of Andrew. *See* Andrew.

Angel, Angell From the Greek, meaning "messenger" or "saintly person." HEBREW EQUIVALENTS: Arel, Devir, Kadosh. FEMININE HEBREW EQUIVALENTS: Arela, Malach, Serafina.

Angelo An Italian form of Angel. *See* Angel.

Angus From the Gaelic and Irish, meaning "exceptional, outstanding." HEBREW EQUIVALENTS: Adif, Aluf, Ben-Tziyon. FEMININE HEBREW EQUIVALENTS: Adifa, Alufa, Degula.

Anschel A variant spelling of Anshel. *See* Anshel.

Ansel, Anselm From the Old German, meaning "divine helmet," symbolizing protection. HEBREW EQUIVALENTS: Avigdor, Betzalel, Bitzaron. FEMININE HEBREW EQUIVALENTS: Avigdora, Magena, Megina.

Anshel (אַנְשֶׁעל/אַנְשֶׁל) A Yiddish form of Asher. *See* Asher. Also, a Yiddish form of Anselm. *See* Anselm.

Anson, Ansonia From the Anglo-Saxon, meaning "the son of Ann" or "the son of Hans." *See* Hans *and* Ann (*feminine section*).

Antal A form of Anatole. *See* Anatole.

Anthony From the Greek meaning "flourishing," and from the Latin meaning "worthy of praise." HEBREW EQUIVALENTS: Gedalya, Hillel, Nitzan. FEMININE HEBREW EQUIVALENTS: Nirit, Nitza, Yehudit.

Anton, Antone, Antonin Variant forms of Antony. *See* Antony.

Antony A variant form of Anthony. *See* Anthony.

Anuv (עָנוּב) From the Hebrew, meaning "tied, bound, joined." The exact Hebrew equivalent is Anuv. The exact feminine equivalent is Anuva. In I Chronicles 4:8, a member of the tribe of Judah.

Anwar From the Arabic, meaning "shaft of light." HEBREW EQUIVALENTS: Achiner, Ami'or, Nahor. FEMININE HEBREW EQUIVALENTS: Behira, Li'ora, Noga.

Aquila From the Latin, meaning "eagle." The exact Hebrew equivalent is Nesher. FEMININE HEBREW EQUIVALENTS: A'ya, Tzipora, Tziporit.

Arad (אֲרָד) From the Akkadian, meaning "bronze." The exact Hebrew equivalent is Arad. FEMININE HEBREW EQUIVALENTS: Arda, Ardona.

Arak (עֲרַק) From the Hebrew, meaning "desert, flee." The exact Hebrew equivalent is Arak. The feminine equivalent is Orpah.

Aram (אֲרָם) From the Assyrian, meaning "high, heights." HEBREW EQUIVALENTS: Aram, Marom, Ram, Rami. FEMININE HEBREW EQUIVALENTS: Meroma, Rama, Ramit. In Genesis 10:22, a grandson of Noah.

Aran (אֲרָן) From the Assyrian and Arabic, meaning "chest, sarcophagus." HEBREW EQUIVALENTS: Aran, Aron. The feminine equivalent is Arona. In Genesis 36:28, a leader of an Edomite clan.

Arba (אַרְבָּע) From the Hebrew, meaning "four." The exact Hebrew equivalent is Arba. The exact feminine equivalent is Arba'a.

Arbel (אַרְבֵּל) From the Hebrew, meaning "sieve." The exact Hebrew equivalent is Arbel. The exact feminine equivalent is Arbela.

Arbie Probably from the Old French, meaning "crossbow." HEBREW EQUIVALENTS: Kashti, Kish, Kishoni. The feminine equivalent is Keshet.

Arch A short form of Archibald. *See* Archibald.

Archer From the Old French, meaning "maker of bows." HEBREW EQUIVALENTS: Kashti, Kish, Kishoni. The feminine equivalent is Keshet.

Archibald From the Anglo-Saxon, meaning "bold" or "holy prince." HEBREW EQUIVALENTS: Aryei, Avinadav, Chagiga. FEMININE HEBREW EQUIVALENTS: Ari'el, Ari'ela, Chagiga, Devira, Malka, Sara.

Ard (אַרְד) From the Akkadian, meaning "bronze." The exact Hebrew equivalent is Ard. FEMININE HEBREW EQUIVALENTS: Arda, Ardona. In Genesis 46:21, a son of Benjamin; grandson of Jacob.

Arden From the Latin, meaning "to burn." HEBREW EQUIVALENTS: Nur, Nuriya, Udi. FEMININE HEBREW EQUIVALENTS: Uri'ela, Urit.

Ardon (אַרְדּוֹן) From the Hebrew, meaning "bronze." The exact Hebrew equivalent is Ardon. FEMININE HEBREW EQUIVALENTS: Arda, Ardona.

Arel (אַרְאֵל) From the Hebrew, meaning "lion of God." The exact Hebrew equivalent is Arel.

Areli (אַרְאֵלִי) A variant form of Arel. The exact Hebrew equivalent is Areli. FEMININE HEBREW EQUIVALENTS: Arela, Ari'el, Ari'ela. In Genesis 46:16, a son of Gad; grandson of Jacob.

Argus From the Greek, meaning "bright." HEBREW EQUIVALENTS: Avner, Bahir, Barak. FEMININE HEBREW EQUIVALENTS: Behira, Me'ira, Noga.

Ari (אֲרִי) From the Hebrew, meaning "lion." The exact Hebrew equivalent is Ari. FEMININE HEBREW EQUIVALENTS: Ari'el, Ari'ela, Kefira.

Aric, Arick Early German forms of Richard. *See* Richard.

Arie A variant spelling of Ari. *See* Ari.

Arieh A variant spelling of Arye. *See* Arye.

Ariel (אֲרִיאֵל) A unisex name. From the Hebrew, meaning "lion of God." The exact Hebrew equivalent is Ari'el. In Ezra 8:16, a leader of the tribe of Judah.

Arik (עֲרִיק) From the Hebrew, meaning "deserter." The exact Hebrew equivalent is Arik. The exact feminine equivalent is Arika. Also, a pet form of Ariel and Arye. *See* Ariel *and* Arye.

Ario A variant form of Ari. *See* Ari.

Arkadi, Arkady A Russian form of the Greek place-name Arkadios.

Arke A Yiddish pet form of Aaron. *See* Aaron.

Arky A pet form of Archibald. *See* Archibald.

Arlan A variant spelling of Arlen. *See* Arlen.

Arlando A variant form of Orlando. *See* Orlando.

Arlen The Celtic form of the name Arles, meaning "pledge." HEBREW EQUIVALENTS: Nidri, Sheva. FEMININE HEBREW EQUIVALENTS: Batsheva, Elisheva, Nedira, Nidra.

Arlin A variant spelling of Arlen. *See* Arlen.

Arlo Probably from the Old English, meaning "fortified hill." HEBREW EQUIVALENTS: Aharon, Bira, Biranit. FEMININE HEBREW EQUIVALENTS: Aharona, Gal, Gali.

Arlyn A variant spelling of Arlin. *See* Arlin.

Armand The French and Italian form of the Old German Hermann, meaning "warrior." HEBREW EQUIVALENTS: Gad, Gadi'el, Gavri'el. FEMININE HEBREW EQUIVALENTS: Merav, Tigra.

Armando The Spanish form of Armand. *See* Armand.

Armen, Armin Variant forms of Armand. *See* Armand.

Armon (עַרְמוֹן/אַרְמוֹן) When spelled with the letter *alef*, from the Hebrew meaning "castle, palace." When spelled with the letter *a'yin*, from the Hebrew meaning "chestnut tree." The exact Hebrew equivalent is Armon. The exact feminine equivalent is Armona.

Armond A variant spelling of Armand. *See* Armand.

Armoni (עַרְמוֹנִי) From the Hebrew, meaning "chestnut" or "reddish brown." *See* Armon.

Arnan (אַרְנָן) From the Arabic, meaning "lotus fruit." Also, from the Hebrew, meaning "roaring stream." The exact Hebrew equivalent is Arnan. The exact feminine equivalent is Arnona.

Arndt A variant form of Arnold. *See* Arnold.

Arne A variant form of Arnold. *See* Arnold.

Arnel A variant form of Arnold. *See* Arnold.

Arni, Arnie Pet forms of Arnold. *See* Arnold.

Arno A pet form of Arnold. *See* Arnold.

Arnold From the Old German, meaning either "honorable, honest ruler" or "the power of an eagle." HEBREW EQUIVALENTS: Avraham, Melech, Nesher. FEMININE HEBREW EQUIVALENTS: Sara, Tamar, Yisra'ela.

Arnon (אַרְנוֹן) From the Hebrew, meaning "roaring stream." The exact Hebrew equivalent is Arnon. The exact feminine equivalent is Arnona.

Arnoni (אַרְנוֹנִי) A variant form of Arnon. *See* Arnon. The exact Hebrew equivalent is Arnoni.

Arny A pet form of Arnold. *See* Arnold.

Arod (אֲרוֹד) From the Hebrew, meaning "bronze." The exact Hebrew equivalent is Arod. FEMININE HEBREW EQUIVALENTS: Arda, Nechusha.

Arodi (אֲרוֹדִי) From the Hebrew, meaning "wild ass." The exact Hebrew equivalent is Arodi. FEMININE HEBREW EQUIVALENTS: Arda, Nechusha. In Genesis 46:16, a son of Gad who went down to Egypt with his grandfather Jacob.

Aron A variant form of Aharon (Aaron). *See* Aharon.

Arsen From the Greek, meaning "manly, strong." HEBREW EQUIVALENTS: Amiram, Avi'az, Avicha'yil. FEMININE HEBREW EQUIVALENTS: Abira, Aza, Azri'ela.

Art A pet form of Arthur. *See* Arthur.

Arthur From the Gaelic, meaning "rock, rocky hill." Also, from the Celtic, meaning "bear." HEBREW EQUIVALENTS: Aharon, Haran, Mordechai. FEMININE HEBREW EQUIVALENTS: Avni'ela, Dova, Doveva.

Artie A pet form of Arthur. *See* Arthur.

Arturo A Spanish form of Arthur. *See* Arthur.

Arty A pet form of Arthur. *See* Arthur.

Artza (אַרְצָא) From the Hebrew, meaning "land." The exact Hebrew equivalent is Artza. FEMININE HEBREW EQUIVALENTS: Artzit, Eretz. In I Kings 16:9, a supervisor of the household of King Elah of Israel.

Artzi (אַרְצִי) A variant form of Artza. *See* Artza. The exact Hebrew equivalent is Artzi.

Arvid From the Anglo-Saxon, meaning "man of the people" or "friend of the people." HEBREW EQUIVALENTS: Aluf, Amit, Amitai. FEMININE HEBREW EQUIVALENTS: Achva, Amit, Amita.

Ary A variant spelling of Ari. *See* Ari.

Arye, Aryei, Aryeh (אַרְיֵה) From the Hebrew, meaning "lion." The exact Hebrew equivalent is Aryei. FEMININE HEBREW EQUIVALENTS: Ari'el, Ari'ela.

Aryel, Aryell Variant spellings of Ariel. *See* Ariel.

Arza A variant spelling of Artza. *See* Artza.

Arzi (אַרְזִי) From the Hebrew, meaning "my cedar." The exact Hebrew equivalent is Arzi. FEMININE HEBREW EQUIVALENTS: Ariza, Arzit.

Arzon (אַרְזוֹן) A variant form of Arzi. *See* Arzi. The exact Hebrew equivalent is Arzon.

Asa (אָסָא) From the Aramaic and Arabic, meaning "create" or "heal." The exact Hebrew equivalent is Asa. FEMININE HEBREW EQUIVALENTS: Asa'ela, Refa'ela, Refu'a. In II Chronicles 14:2, the third king of Judah.

Asael (עֲשָׂהאֵל) From the Hebrew, meaning "God created." The exact Hebrew equivalent is Asa'el. The exact feminine equivalent is Asa'ela. In II Samuel 2:18, one of the sons of David's sister.

Asaf (אָסָף) From the Hebrew, meaning "gather." The exact Hebrew equivalent is Asaf. The exact feminine equivalent is Asafa. In I Chronicles 9:15, one of David's musicians.

Asahel A variant spelling of Asael. *See* Asael.

Asaph A variant spelling of Asaf. *See* Asaf.

Ascher A variant spelling of Asher. *See* Asher.

Aser A variant spelling of Asser. *See* Asser.

Ash (עָשׁ) From the Hebrew, meaning "moth," or from the Middle English, referring to "a tree from the olive family." The exact Hebrew equivalents are Ash and Za'yit. FEMININE HEBREW EQUIVALENTS: Alona, Ariza, Etzyona.

Ashaf (אָשָׁף) From the Hebrew, meaning "wizard, magician." The exact Hebrew equivalent is Ashaf. The feminine equivalent is Kessim.

Asher (אָשֵׁר) From the Hebrew, meaning "blessed, fortunate, happy." The exact Hebrew equivalent is Asher. The exact feminine Hebrew equivalent is Ashera. In Genesis 30:13, the eighth son of Jacob.

Ashi (אַשִׁי) From the Hebrew, meaning "my fire, my passion." The exact Hebrew equivalent is Ashi. FEMININE HEBREW EQUIVALENTS: Uri'ela, Urit.

Ashir (עָשִׁיר) From the Hebrew, meaning "wealthy." The exact Hebrew equivalent is Ashir. The exact feminine equivalent is Ashira.

Ashleigh, Ashley From the Old English, meaning "field of ash trees." HEBREW EQUIVALENTS: Alon, Bar-Ilan, Shaked. FEMININE HEBREW EQUIVALENTS: Alona, Ariza, Ilana.

Ashton From the Old English, meaning "a town surrounded by ash trees." HEBREW EQUIVALENTS: Almog, Alon, Eshel. FEMININE HEBREW EQUIVALENTS: Alona, Ilana, Shikmona.

Asiel (עֲשִׂיאֵל) A variant form of Asael. The exact Hebrew equivalent is Asi'el. *See also* Asael.

Asif (אָסִיף) From the Hebrew, meaning "harvest, gathering." The exact Hebrew equivalent is Asif. The exact feminine equivalent is Asifa.

Asir (אָסִיר) From the Arabic and Aramaic, meaning "bound up, imprisoned." The exact Hebrew equivalent is Asir. The exact feminine equivalent is Asira. In Exodus 6:24, one of the sons of Korach.

Asis, Asiss (עָסִיס) From the Hebrew, meaning "juice." The exact Hebrew equivalent is Asis. The exact feminine equivalent is Asisa.

Asisi (עֲסִיסִי) A variant form of Asis. *See* Asis.

Askan (עַסְקָן) From the Hebrew, meaning "worker, volunteer." The exact Hebrew equivalent is Askan. FEMININE HEBREW EQUIVALENTS: Amal, Amalya, Amela.

Asriel (אַשְׂרִיאֵל) From the Hebrew, meaning "prince of God." The exact Hebrew equivalent is Asri'el. The exact feminine equivalent is Asri'ela. In Chronicles 7:4, a son of Manasseh, a grandson of Joseph.

Assa A variant spelling of Asa. *See* Asa.

Asser A variant form of Asher. *See* Asher.

Assi (אַסִי) From the Aramaic, meaning "doctor." The exact Hebrew equivalent is Assi. FEMININE HEBREW EQUIVALENTS: Asa'ela, Refa'ela, Refa'ya.

Asur, Assur (אָסוּר) From the Hebrew, meaning "imprisoned, chained." The exact Hebrew equivalent is Asur. FEMININE HEBREW EQUIVALENTS: Aguna, Rivka.

Atalia, Atalia, Atalya, Atalyah (עֲתַלְיָה) A unisex name. From the Hebrew, meaning "God is exalted." The exact Hebrew equivalent is Atalyah. In I Chronicles 8:26, a son of King Jeroboam.

Atar (עָתָר) From the Hebrew, meaning "to pray." The exact Hebrew equivalent is Atar. FEMININE HEBREW EQUIVALENTS: Ateret, Atira, Tehila.

Ater (אָטֵר) From the Hebrew, meaning "to seal, close." The exact Hebrew equivalent is Ater. FEMININE HEBREW EQUIVALENTS: Ne'ilah, Segura. In Ezra 2:16, a member of a family that returned to Palestine from Babylonian exile.

Athalia, Athaliah Anglicized forms of Atalia. *See* Atalia.

Atid (עָתִיד) From the Hebrew, meaning "timely, prepared, ready" or "the future." The exact Hebrew equivalent is Atid. The exact feminine equivalent is Atida.

Atif (עָטִיף) From the Hebrew, meaning "covered, bound up." The exact Hebrew equivalent is Atif. The exact feminine equivalent is Atifa.

Atik (עַתִּיק) From the Hebrew, meaning "ancient, old." The exact Hebrew equivalent is Atik. The exact feminine equivalent is Atika.

Atir (עָטִיר) From the Hebrew, meaning "wreath, crown, ornament." The exact Hebrew equivalent is Atir. FEMININE HEBREW EQUIVALENTS: Atara, Ateret.

Attai (עַתַּי) A unisex name. From the Hebrew, meaning "ready" or "seasonal." The exact Hebrew equivalent is Attai. In I Chronicles 2:35, the daughter of a leader of Judah. In I Chronicles 12:11, one of the warriors from the tribe of Gad.

Atzalyahu (אֲצַלְיָהוּ) From the Hebrew, meaning "God strengthens."

The exact Hebrew equivalent is Atzalyahu. FEMININE HEBREW EQUIVA-
LENTS: Amitza, Amtza, Avicha'yil. In II Kings 22:3, the father of Sha-
fan, King Josiah's secretary.

Atzil (אָצִיל) From the Hebrew, meaning "honorable, noble." The
exact Hebrew equivalent is Atzil. The exact feminine equivalent is
Atzila.

Atzmon (עַצְמוֹן) From the Hebrew, meaning "strength." The exact
Hebrew equivalent is Atzmon. The exact feminine equivalent is
Atzmona.

Aubrey From the Anglo-Saxon, meaning "[elf] ruler." HEBREW EQUIVALENTS:
Aluf, Avraham, Elrad. FEMININE HEBREW EQUIVALENTS: Alufa, Sara, Sarit.

August A variant form of Augustus. *See* Augustus.

Augustus From the Latin, meaning "revered, exalted." HEBREW EQUIVA-
LENTS: Atlai, Atalya, Avraham. FEMININE HEBREW EQUIVALENTS: Ge'ona,
Ge'onit, Ramit.

Aurel From the Latin and French, meaning "gold, golden." HEBREW
EQUIVALENTS: Elifaz, Ofar, Ofir. FEMININE HEBREW EQUIVALENTS: Ofira,
Paz, Paza.

Austen, Austin Variant Anglicized forms of Augustus. *See* Augustus.

Av (אָב) From the Hebrew, meaning "father." The exact Hebrew
equivalent is Av.

Avak (אָבָק) From the Hebrew, meaning "dust, powder." The exact
Hebrew equivalent is Avak. The feminine equivalent is Avka.

Avaz (אַוָז) From the Hebrew, meaning "goose." The exact Hebrew
equivalent is Avaz.

Avda (עַבְדָּא) From the Aramaic, meaning "servant" or "worshipper."
The exact Hebrew equivalent is Avda. FEMININE HEBREW EQUIVALENTS:
Ama'a, Shimsona. In I Kings 4:6, a member of King Solomon's
household.

Avdan (אַבְדָן) From the Hebrew, meaning "father is judge." The exact
Hebrew equivalent is Avdan. *See also* Avidan.

Avdel (עַבְדְּאֵל) From the Hebrew, meaning "servant of God." The exact Hebrew equivalent is Avdel. FEMININE HEBREW EQUIVALENTS: Ama'a, Shimshona. In Jeremiah 36:26, one of the officials in King Jehoiakim's court.

Avdi (עַבְדִּי) From the Hebrew meaning "my servant." The exact Hebrew equivalent is Avdi. FEMININE HEBREW EQUIVALENTS: Ama'a, Shimshona. In I Chronicles 6:29, a Levite belonging to the family of Merari.

Avdiel (עַבְדִּיאֵל) From the Hebrew, meaning "servant of God." The exact Hebrew equivalent is Avdi'el. FEMININE HEBREW EQUIVALENTS: Ama'a, Shimshona. In I Chronicles 5:15, the head of a family in the tribe of Gad.

Avdima (אַבְדִּימָא) From the Aramaic, meaning "destruction, loss." The exact Hebrew equivalent is Avdima.

Avdimi (אַבְדִּימִי) A variant form of Avdima. *See* Avdima.

Avdon (עַבְדּוֹן) From the Hebrew, meaning "servile." The exact Hebrew equivalent is Avdon. FEMININE HEBREW EQUIVALENTS: Ama'a, Shimshona. In Judges 12:13, one of the judges of Israel.

Averel, Averell From the Anglo-Saxon, meaning "to open," connoting springtime. HEBREW EQUIVALENTS: Aviv, Pesach, Pesachya. FEMININE HEBREW EQUIVALENTS: Aviva, Avivi, Avivit.

Averil, Averill Variant spellings of Averel. *See* Averel.

Avery A variant form of Aubrey. *See* Aubrey.

Avgar (אַבְגָּר) From the Hebrew, meaning "dwelling of the father" or "father of a stranger." The exact Hebrew equivalent is Avgar. FEMININE HEBREW EQUIVALENTS: Gershona, Gi'ora, Gi'oret.

Avi (אֲבִי) A unisex name. From the Hebrew, meaning "my father." The exact Hebrew equivalent is Avi. In II Kings 18:2, Avi is a feminine name.

Avia A variant spelling of Aviya. *See* Aviya.

Aviad (אֲבִיעַד) From the Hebrew, meaning "my father is witness" or "my father is eternal." The exact Hebrew equivalent is Avi'ad. FEMININE HEBREW EQUIVALENTS: Nitzcha, Nitzchiya, Nitzchona.

Aviah A variant spelling of Avia. *See* Avia.

Aviam (אֲבִיעָם) From the Hebrew, meaning "father of a nation." The exact Hebrew equivalent is Avi'am. FEMININE HEBREW EQUIVALENTS: Le'uma, Le'umi, Uma. In II Kings 14:31, a son of King Jeroboam.

Aviasaf (אֲבִיאָסָף) From the Hebrew, meaning "father of a multitude" or "my father has gathered." The exact Hebrew equivalent is Avi'asaf. FEMININE HEBREW EQUIVALENTS: Asafa, Ketifa. In Exodus 6:24, a descendant of Korach.

Aviav (אֲבִיאָב) From the Hebrew, meaning "grandfather." The exact Hebrew equivalent is Avi'av. FEMININE HEBREW EQUIVALENTS: Avi'em, Savta.

Aviaz (אֲבִיעַז) From the Hebrew, meaning "father of strength." The exact Hebrew equivalent is Avi'az. FEMININE HEBREW EQUIVALENTS: Aza, Azi'az, Aziza, Azri'ela, Me'uza, Uza, Uzit.

Avichayil (אֲבִיחַיִל) A unisex name. From the Hebrew, meaning "father of strength" or "my father is strong." The exact Hebrew equivalent is Avicha'yil. In Esther 2:15, the father of Queen Esther.

Avichai (אֲבִיחַי) From the Hebrew, meaning "my father lives" or "father of all living things." The exact Hebrew equivalent is Avichai. FEMININE HEBREW EQUIVALENTS: Achiya, Chava, Cha'ya.

Avichen (אֲבִיחֵן) From the Hebrew, meaning "father of grace." The exact Hebrew equivalent is Avichen. FEMININE HEBREW EQUIVALENTS: Chana, Chanina, Chanita.

Avida (אֲבִידָע) From the Hebrew, meaning "my father knows." The exact Hebrew equivalent is Avida. FEMININE HEBREW EQUIVALENTS: Da'at, Dati'ela, De'uela. In Genesis 25:4, a grandson of Abraham and Keturah.

Avidan (אֲבִידָן) From the Hebrew, meaning "my father is judge [or judgment]." The exact Hebrew equivalent is Avidan. FEMININE HEBREW EQUIVALENTS: Dana, Dani'ela, Danit.

Avideror A variant spelling of Avidror. *See* Avidror.

Avidor (אֲבִידוֹר) From the Hebrew, meaning "father of a generation."

The exact Hebrew equivalent is Avidor. FEMININE HEBREW EQUIVALENTS: Dor, Dorit, Dorya.

Avidror (אֲבִידְרוֹר) From the Hebrew, meaning "father of freedom." The exact Hebrew equivalent is Avidror. FEMININE HEBREW EQUIVALENTS: Derora, Derorit, Deroriya.

Aviel (אֲבִיאֵל) From the Hebrew, meaning "my father is God." The exact Hebrew equivalent is Avi'el. FEMININE HEBREW EQUIVALENTS: Avi, Avi'ela. In I Samuel 9:1, King Saul's grandfather.

Aviem (אֲבִיאָם) A unisex name. From the Hebrew meaning "father of mother, grandfather." The exact Hebrew equivalent is Avi'em.

Aviezer (אֲבִיעֶזֶר) From the Hebrew, meaning "God is help, salvation." The exact Hebrew equivalent is Avi'ezer. FEMININE HEBREW EQUIVALENTS: Ezra'ela, Ezri'ela, Sa'ada. In Joshua 17:2, a member of the tribe of Manasseh.

Aviezri (אֲבִיעֶזְרִי) A variant form of Aviezer. *See* Aviezer.

Avigal (אֲבִיגָל) A unisex name. From the Hebrew, meaning "father of the sea" or "father of joy." The exact Hebrew equivalent is Avigal. In II Samuel 17:25, King David's sister.

Avigdor (אֲבִיגְדוֹר) From the Hebrew, meaning "father protector." The exact Hebrew equivalent is Avigdor. The exact feminine Hebrew equivalent is Avigdora. In I Chronicles 4:18, the name Gedor is probably its origin.

Avihai A variant spelling of Avichai. *See* Avichai.

Avihu (אֲבִיהוּ) From the Hebrew, meaning "he is my father." The exact Hebrew equivalent is Avihu. FEMININE HEBREW EQUIVALENTS: Avi'el, Avramit, Avuya. A son of Aaron in Exodus 6:23.

Avihud (אֲבִיהוּד) From the Hebrew, meaning "my father is majestic." The exact Hebrew equivalent is Avihud. FEMININE HEBREW EQUIVALENTS: Adira, Ge'ona, Ge'onit. In I Chronicles 8:3, a grandson of Benjamin.

Avikam (אֲבִיקָם) From the Hebrew, meaning "my father arises." The exact Hebrew equivalent is Avikam. FEMININE HEBREW EQUIVALENTS: Asiya, Komema.

Avikar (אֲבִיקָר) From the Hebrew, meaning "my father is precious." The exact Hebrew equivalent is Avikar. FEMININE HEBREW EQUIVALENTS: Kevuda, Yakira, Yekara.

Avimael (אֲבִימָאֵל) From the Hebrew, meaning "God is my father." The exact Hebrew equivalent is Avima'el. FEMININE HEBREW EQUIVALENTS: Aviya, Avi'el, Avi'ela. In Genesis 10:28, a descendant of Shem, Noah's son.

Avimelech (אֲבִימֶלֶךְ) From the Hebrew, meaning "father of the king" or "my father is the king." The exact Hebrew equivalent is Avimelech. FEMININE HEBREW EQUIVALENTS: Avi'ela, Avigal, Avramit. A son of Gideon in Judges 9:1.

Avimi (אֲבִימִי) A contraction of *avi immi*, meaning "grandfather." The exact Hebrew equivalent is Avimi. FEMININE HEBREW EQUIVALENTS: Avi'em, Savta.

Avin (אָבִין) The Aramaic form of Av, meaning "father." The exact Hebrew equivalent is Avin. FEMININE HEBREW EQUIVALENTS: Avi, Avi'el, Avirama.

Avina (אֲבִינָא) From the Aramaic, meaning "father." The exact Hebrew equivalent is Avina. *See* Avin *for additional equivalents.*

Avinadav (אֲבִינָדָב) From the Hebrew, meaning "my father is noble." The exact Hebrew equivalent is Avinadav. FEMININE HEBREW EQUIVALENTS: Nedava, Nediva. In I Samuel 16:8, a brother of King David.

Avinatan (אֲבִינָתָן) From the Hebrew, meaning "my father has given, father's [God's] gift." The exact Hebrew equivalent is Avinatan. FEMININE HEBREW EQUIVALENTS: Netana, Netani'ela, Netanya.

Aviner (אֲבִינֵר) A variant form of Avner. *See* Avner.

Avinoam (אֲבִינֹעַם) From the Hebrew, meaning "father of delight." The exact Hebrew equivalent is Avino'am. FEMININE HEBREW EQUIVALENTS: Achino'am, Na'ama, Ne'ima. In Judges 4:6, the father of Barak.

Avira (אֲוִירָא) From the Aramaic, meaning "air, atmosphere, spirit." The exact Hebrew equivalent is Avira. The exact feminine equivalent is Avirit.

Aviram (אֲבִירָם) From the Hebrew, meaning "my father is mighty." The exact Hebrew equivalent is Aviram. The exact feminine equivalent is Avirama. In Numbers 16:1, a conspirator who sided with Korach.

Aviri (אֲוִירִי) From the Hebrew, meaning "air, atmosphere." The exact Hebrew equivalent is Aviri. The exact feminine equivalent is Avirit.

Avishai, **Avishay**, **Avishy** (אֲבִישַׁי) From the Hebrew, meaning "God is my gift." The exact Hebrew equivalent is Avishai. FEMININE HEBREW EQUIVALENTS: Darona, Teshura, Zevuda. In I Samuel 26:6, the son of Tzeruyah, Yoav's brother.

Avishalom (אֲבִישָׁלוֹם) From the Hebrew, meaning "father of peace." The exact Hebrew equivalent is Avishalom. FEMININE HEBREW EQUIVALENTS: Shalviya, Shlomit, Shulamit. In I Kings 15:2, the father-in-law of King Jeroboam of Judah.

Avishua (אֲבִישׁוּעַ) From the Hebrew, meaning "God is salvation." The exact Hebrew equivalent is Avishu'a. FEMININE HEBREW EQUIVALENTS: Shu'a, Teshu'a. In Ezra 7:5, an ancestor of Ezra; in I Chronicles 8:4, a grandson of Benjamin.

Avital (אֲבִיטַל) A unisex name. From the Hebrew, meaning "father of dew." The exact Hebrew equivalent is Avital. In I Chronicles 3:3, one of King David's sons.

Avitul (אֲבִיטוּל) A variant form of Avital. *See* Avital. The exact Hebrew equivalent is Avitul.

Avitus From the Latin, meaning "bird." HEBREW EQUIVALENTS: A'ya, Deror, Efron. FEMININE HEBREW EQUIVALENTS: A'ya, Da'ya, Salit, Tzipora, Tziporit.

Avituv (אֲבִיטוֹב) From the Hebrew, meaning "father of goodness." The exact Hebrew equivalent is Avituv. FEMININE HEBREW EQUIVALENTS: Tova, Tovat, Tovit.

Aviur (אֲבִיאוֹר) From the Hebrew, meaning "my father (God) is light." The exact Hebrew equivalent is Avi'ur. FEMININE HEBREW EQUIVALENTS: Ora, Orli, Urit, Zohar.

Aviv (אָבִיב) A unisex name. From the Hebrew, meaning "spring, springtime." The exact Hebrew equivalent is Aviv.

Avivi (אֲבִיבִי) From the Hebrew, meaning "springlike, springtime." The exact Hebrew equivalent is Avivi. FEMININE HEBREW EQUIVALENTS: Aviva, Avivit.

Aviya, Aviyah (אֲבִיָּה) A unisex name. From the Hebrew, meaning "God is my father." The exact Hebrew equivalent is Aviya. Used as a feminine name in I Chronicles 2:24.

Aviyam (אֲבִיָּם) From the Hebrew, meaning "father of the sea." The exact Hebrew equivalent is Aviyam. FEMININE HEBREW EQUIVALENTS: Bat-Yam, Yam, Yamit. In I Kings 14:31, a king of Judah, also known as Aviya.

Avizemer (אֲבִיזֶמֶר) From the Hebrew, meaning "father of song." The exact Hebrew equivalent is Avizemer. FEMININE HEBREW EQUIVALENTS: Zimra, Zimrat, Zimriya.

Avner (אַבְנֵר) From the Hebrew, meaning "father of light" or "father's candle," connoting strength and inspiration. The exact Hebrew equivalent is Avner. FEMININE HEBREW EQUIVALENTS: Ne'ira, Nera, Ner-Li. In I Samuel 17:55, an uncle of King Saul.

Avniel (אַבְנִיאֵל) From the Hebrew, meaning "God is my rock," signifying strength. The exact Hebrew equivalent is Avni'el. The exact feminine equivalent is Avni'ela.

Avraham (אַבְרָהָם) From the Hebrew, meaning "father of a mighty nation" or "father of a multitude." The exact Hebrew equivalent is Avraham. FEMININE HEBREW EQUIVALENTS: Avirama, Avrahamit, Avramit. The first Hebrew in the Bible (Genesis 11:26).

Avram (אַבְרָם) The exact Hebrew equivalent is Avram. *See also* Avraham. In Genesis 17:5, Avraham's original name.

Avrech (אַבְרֵךְ) From the Hebrew, meaning "tender, youngster." The exact Hebrew equivalent is Avrech. FEMININE HEBREW EQUIVALENTS: Ge'ona, Nevona. The salutation by which Joseph was greeted in Egypt (Genesis 41:43).

Avrom A variant Yiddish form of Avraham. *See* Avraham.

Avron (אַבְרוֹן) From the Hebrew, meaning "father of song." The exact Hebrew equivalent is Avron. FEMININE HEBREW EQUIVALENTS: Anat, Arni, Arninit.

Avrum A variant Yiddish form of Avraham. *See* Avraham.

Avrumi A pet form of Avrum. *See* Avrum.

Avshalom (אַבְשָׁלוֹם) From the Hebrew, meaning "father of peace." The exact Hebrew equivalent is Avshalom. FEMININE HEBREW EQUIVALENTS: Meshulemet, Shlomit, Shulamit. In II Samuel 14:25, the rebellious son of King David.

Avtalyon (אַבְטַלְיוֹן) From the Hebrew, meaning "father of dew." The exact Hebrew equivalent is Avtalyon. FEMININE HEBREW EQUIVALENTS: Avital, Avtalya, Talilia. A first-century B.C.E. talmudic scholar presumed to be a descendant of proselytes.

Avuya, Avuyah (אֲבוּיָה) From the Aramaic, meaning "God is our Father." The exact Hebrew equivalent is Avuya. FEMININE HEBREW EQUIVALENTS: Avi, Avi'el.

Axel, Axtel Swedish names of Germanic origin, meaning "divine source of life." HEBREW EQUIVALENTS: Amichai, Amram, Bachya. FEMININE HEBREW EQUIVALENTS: Achiya, Chava, Cha'ya.

Aya, Ayah (אַיָּה) A unisex name. From the Hebrew, meaning "vulture." The exact Hebrew equivalent is A'ya. In II Samuel 3:7, the father of one of King Saul's concubines.

Ayal (אַיָל) From the Hebrew, meaning "deer" or "ram." The exact Hebrew equivalent is A'yal. The exact feminine equivalent is A'yala.

Ayali (אַיָלִי) From the Hebrew, meaning "my deer" or "my ram." The exact Hebrew equivalent is A'yali. The exact feminine equivalent is A'yala.

Ayalon (אַיָלוֹן) A variant form of Ayal. *See* Ayal. The exact Hebrew equivalent is A'yalon. The feminine equivalent is A'yal.

Ayo An African name, meaning "happiness." Hebrew equivalents: Alitz, Avigal, Yagil. FEMININE HEBREW EQUIVALENTS: Aliza, Aviga'yil, Ditza.

Ayya An alternate spelling of Aya. *See* Aya.

Az (עַז) From the Hebrew, meaning "strong." The exact Hebrew equivalent is Az. The exact feminine equivalent is Aza.

Azai, Azzai (עַזַּאי) From the Aramaic, meaning "strength." The exact Hebrew equivalent is Azai. FEMININE HEBREW EQUIVALENTS: Aza, Azi'az, Aziza.

Azan (עַזָן) From the Hebrew, meaning "strength." The exact Hebrew equivalent is Azan. FEMININE HEBREW EQUIVALENTS: Aza, Azi'az, Azri'ela. In Numbers 34:26, a leader of the tribe of Issachar.

Azania, Azaniah, Azanya (אֲזַנְיָה) From the Hebrew, meaning "God listens." The exact Hebrew equivalent is Azanya. FEMININE HEBREW EQUIVALENTS: Shimat, Shimona, Shmu'ela. In Nehemiah 10:10, the name of the father of a Levite.

Azarel (עֲזַרְאֵל) From the Hebrew, meaning, "God helped." The exact Hebrew equivalent is Azarel. FEMININE HEBREW EQUIVALENTS: Eli'ezra, Ezra'ela, Ezri'ela. A warrior who defected from King Saul's army and joined David's forces (I Chronicles 12:7).

Azaria, Azariah, Azarya (עֲזַרְיָה) From the Hebrew, meaning "the help of God." The exact Hebrew equivalent is Azarya. FEMININE HEBREW EQUIVALENTS: Azri'ela, Eli'ezra, Ezr'ela. In I Chronicles 2:8, a leader of the tribe of Judah.

Azaryahu (עֲזַרְיָהוּ) A variant form of Azarya. *See* Azarya.

Azaz (עֲזָז) From the Hebrew, meaning "strength." The exact Hebrew equivalent is Azaz. FEMININE HEBREW EQUIVALENTS: Aza, Azi'az, Azri'ela. In I Chronicles 5:8, a leader of the tribe of Re'uven (Reuben).

Azazia, Azaziah, Azazyah (עֲזַזְיָה) From the Hebrew, meaning "strength of God." The exact Hebrew equivalent is Azazyah. FEMININE HEBREW EQUIVALENTS: Amitzu, Atzma, Uzi'ela. In I Chronicles 15:21, a musician in the court of King David.

Azi (עָזִי) From the Hebrew, meaning "strength." The exact Hebrew equivalent is Azi. FEMININE HEBREW EQUIVALENTS: Aza, Azi'az, Aziza.

Aziel (עֲזִיאֵל) From the Hebrew, meaning "God is my strength." The exact Hebrew equivalent is Azi'el. The exact feminine equivalent is Azi'ela.

Aziz (עָזִיז) From the Hebrew, meaning "strong." The exact Hebrew equivalent is Aziz. The exact feminine equivalent is Aziza.

Aziza, Azizah (עֲזִיזָא) A unisex name. From the Aramaic and Hebrew, meaning "strong." The exact Hebrew equivalent is Aziza. In Ezra 10:27, a man who divorced his non-Jewish wife, in accordance with Ezra's instructions.

Azizi From the Arabic, meaning "beloved, precious." HEBREW EQUIVALENTS: Ahuv, Chaviv, David. FEMININE HEBREW EQUIVALENTS: Ahava, Amita, Chaviva.

Azori (אֲזוֹרִי) From the Hebrew, meaning "regional." The exact Hebrew equivalent is Azori.

Azriel (עַזְרִיאֵל) From the Hebrew, meaning "God is my help." The exact equivalent is Azri'el. The exact feminine equivalent is Azri'ela. In I Chronicles 27:19, the father of a leader of the tribe of Naftali.

Azuv (עָזוּב) From the Hebrew, meaning "forsaken, lonely." The exact Hebrew equivalent is Azuv. The exact feminine equivalent is Azuva.

Azzi, Azzy Pet forms of Azarya or Azriel. *See* Azarya *and* Azriel.

❧ B ❧

Baba A variant spelling of Bava. *See* Bava.

Bahir (בָּהִיר) From the Hebrew, meaning "clear, bright." The exact Hebrew equivalent is Bahir. The exact feminine equivalent is Behira.

Bailey From the Old French, meaning "bailiff, guardian." HEBREW EQUIVALENTS: Eri, Shemarya, Shomer. FEMININE HEBREW EQUIVALENTS: Mishmeret, Noteret, Shomera.

Baldwin From the Middle High German, meaning "bold friend." HEBREW EQUIVALENTS: Bildad, Binyamin, David. FEMININE HEBREW EQUIVALENTS: Chaviva, Davida, Hadasa.

Balfour (בַּלְפוּר) From the Old English, meaning "hill along the way." The exact Hebrew equivalent is Balfur. FEMININE HEBREW EQUIVALENTS: Balfura, Balfuriya.

Banet A short form of Barnet and Benedict. *See* Barnet *and* Benedict.

Bani (בָּנִי) From the Aramaic, meaning "my son" or "build." The exact Hebrew equivalent is Bani. FEMININE HEBREW EQUIVALENTS: Bat, Batya, Bona. In II Samuel 23:36, a soldier in King David's army.

Barak (בָּרָק) From the Hebrew, meaning "flash of light." The exact Hebrew equivalent is Barak. FEMININE HEBREW EQUIVALENTS: Bareket, Behira, Me'ira. In Judges 4:12, the Israelite military commander.

65

Baram (בַּרְעָם) From the Aramaic, meaning "son of the nation." The exact Hebrew equivalent is Baram. FEMININE HEBREW EQUIVALENTS: Bat-Ami, Bat-Tziyon, Le'uma.

Bard From the Gaelic and Irish, meaning "minstrel" or "poet." HEBREW EQUIVALENTS: Liron, Ron, Ronen. FEMININE HEBREW EQUIVALENTS: Oda, Odiya, Ronit.

Bari A variant spelling of Barrie. *See* Barrie.

Barkan (בַּרְקָן) The name of a plant native to Israel. The exact Hebrew equivalent is Barkan. FEMININE HEBREW EQUIVALENTS: Alona, Ariza, Ilana.

Barker From the Old English, meaning "logger of birch trees." HEBREW EQUIVALENTS: Bar-Ilan, Bros, Ilan. FEMININE HEBREW EQUIVALENTS: Alona, Ariza, Arna.

Barnaby From the Aramaic, meaning "speech." HEBREW EQUIVALENTS: Amarya, Divri, Imri. FEMININE HEBREW EQUIVALENTS: Amira, Devora, Niva.

Barnard The French form of Bernard. *See* Bernard.

Barnet, Barnett Variant forms of Bernard. *See* Bernard.

Barney A pet form of Bernard or Barnaby. *See* Bernard *and* Barnaby.

Baron From the Old English, meaning "noble." HEBREW EQUIVALENTS: Achiram, Adon, Yonadav. FEMININE HEBREW EQUIVALENTS: Adina, Adira, Nagida.

Barr, Barre A short form of Bernard and Barnard. *See* Bernard *and* Barnard.

Barret, Barrett A short form of Barnet. *See* Barnet.

Barri, Barrie Variant spellings of Barry. *See* Barry.

Barry A Welsh patronymic form of Harry, meaning "son of Harry." *See* Harry. Also, a pet form of Baruch. *See* Baruch.

Bart A pet form of Barton and Bartholomew. *See* Barton *and* Bartholomew.

Barth A variant spelling of Bart. *See* Bart.

Bartholomew From the Greek and Aramaic, meaning "son of Talmai." *See* Talmai.

Bartlet, Bartlett Variant forms of Bartholomew. *See* Bartholomew.

Barton From the Anglo-Saxon, meaning "barley town." Also, from the Old English, meaning "bear town." HEBREW EQUIVALENTS: Dagan, Dov, Goren. FEMININE HEBREW EQUIVALENTS: Degana, Deganit, Duba.

Baruch, Barukh (בָּרוּךְ) From the Hebrew, meaning "blessed." The exact Hebrew equivalent is Baruch. FEMININE HEBREW EQUIVALENTS: Beracha, Berucha. In Jeremiah 32:12, the scribe of the prophet Jeremiah.

Barzilai (בַּרְזִילַי) From the Aramaic, meaning "man of iron." The exact Hebrew equivalent is Barzilai. FEMININE HEBREW EQUIVALENTS: Amtza, Ari'el, Atzma. In II Samuel 21:8, the father-in-law of King Saul's daughter.

Basil From the Greek, meaning "royal, kingly." HEBREW EQUIVALENTS: Adoniya, Avimelech, Katri'el. FEMININE HEBREW EQUIVALENTS: Atara, Malka, Yisra'ela.

Bava (בָּבָא) A unisex name. From the Aramaic, meaning "gate." The exact Hebrew equivalent is Bava.

Bayard From the Old English, meaning "red-haired." HEBREW EQUIVALENTS: Admon, Odem, Tzochar. FEMININE HEBREW EQUIVALENTS: Dala, Delila, Nima.

Baz (בַּז) From the Hebrew, meaning "falcon" or "booty." The exact Hebrew equivalent is Baz. FEMININE HEBREW EQUIVALENTS: Efrona, Tzipora.

Bazak (בָּזָק) From the Hebrew, meaning "flash of light." The exact Hebrew equivalent is Bazak. FEMININE HEBREW EQUIVALENTS: Bareket, Behira, Me'ira.

Bear From the German name Baer, meaning "bear." The exact Hebrew equivalent is Dov. FEMININE HEBREW EQUIVALENTS: Dova, Dovit, Duba.

Beau From the Latin and French, meaning "pretty, handsome." HEBREW

EQUIVALENTS: Adin, Hadar, Noi. FEMININE HEBREW EQUIVALENTS: Hadura, Na'a, Nava.

Beaumont From the French, meaning "beautiful mountain." HEBREW EQUIVALENTS: Adin, Aharon, Gal. FEMININE HEBREW EQUIVALENTS: Aharona, Chermona, Hadura.

Becher (בֶּכֶר) From the Hebrew, meaning "young camel." The exact Hebrew equivalent is Becher. In Numbers 26:35, a member of the tribe of Ephraim.

Beck From the Middle English and Old Norse, meaning "brook." HEBREW EQUIVALENTS: Afek, Arnon, Beri. FEMININE HEBREW EQUIVALENTS: Arona, Afeka, Bat-Yam.

Bede From the Middle English, meaning "prayer." HEBREW EQUIVALENTS: Eflal, Elipal, Pali'el. FEMININE HEBREW EQUIVALENTS: Ateret, Atira, Tachan.

Bedell A unisex name. From the Old French, meaning "messenger." The exact Hebrew equivalent is Malach.

Beebe From the Anglo-Saxon, meaning "one who lives on a bee farm." HEBREW EQUIVALENTS: Bustana'i, Chaklai, Yogev. FEMININE HEBREW EQUIVALENTS: Davrat, Devora, Devorit.

Be'eri (בְּאֵרִי) From the Hebrew, meaning "my well." The exact Hebrew equivalent is Be'eri. FEMININE HEBREW EQUIVALENTS: B'era, B'erit. In Hosea 1:1, the father of the prophet Hosea.

Beka (בֶּקַע) From the Hebrew, referring to a biblical coin mentioned in Exodus 38:26. The exact Hebrew equivalent is Beka. FEMININE HEBREW EQUIVALENTS: Agora, Dinar.

Bela (בֶּלַע) From the Hebrew, meaning "to swallow" or "confuse." The exact Hebrew equivalent is Bela. In Genesis 46:21, the eldest son of Benjamin; grandson of Jacob and Rachel.

Bell From the Latin and French, meaning "beautiful." HEBREW EQUIVALENTS: Adin, Hadar, Kalil. FEMININE HEBREW EQUIVALENTS: Hadura, Na'ama, Na'ami.

Bellamy From the Latin and French, meaning "beautiful friend."

HEBREW EQUIVALENTS: Avino'am, David, Na'ama. FEMININE HEBREW EQUIV-
ALENTS: Adina, Davida, Shifra.

Belmont From the Old French, meaning "beautiful mountain." HE-
BREW EQUIVALENTS: Aharon, Gal, Harel. FEMININE HEBREW EQUIVALENTS:
Aharona, Chermona, Harela.

Belton From the French and Anglo-Saxon, meaning "beautiful town."
HEBREW EQUIVALENTS: Avino'am, Chilkiya, David. FEMININE HEBREW
EQUIVALENTS: Adina, Galiliya, Nachala.

Ben (בֶּן) From the Hebrew, meaning "son." The exact Hebrew equivalent is Ben.

Ben-Ami (בֶּן-עַמִי) From the Hebrew, meaning "son of my people."
The exact Hebrew equivalent is Ben-Ami. The exact feminine equivalent is Bat-Ami. In Genesis 19:38, the son of Lot and his younger
daughter.

Ben-Chayil (בֶּן-חַיִל) From the Hebrew, meaning "son of valor." The
exact Hebrew equivalent is Ben-Cha'yil. FEMININE HEBREW EQUIVALENTS:
Abira, Avicha'yil, Gavri'ela. In II Chronicles 17:7, one of the countries of King Jehoshafat of Judah.

Bendit A short form of Benedict. *See* Benedict.

Benedict From the Latin, meaning "blessed." HEBREW EQUIVALENTS:
Asher, Baruch, Berachya. FEMININE HEBREW EQUIVALENTS: Ashra, Berakha.

Benek A Hungarian form of Benedict. *See* Benedict.

Benesh (בֶּענֶעש) A Yiddish form of Benedict. *See* Benedict.

Bengi A pet form of Benjamin. *See* Benjamin.

Ben-Gurion (בֶּן-גוּרְיוֹן) From the Hebrew, meaning "son of the lion"
or "son of might." The exact Hebrew equivalent is Ben-Guryon.
FEMININE HEBREW EQUIVALENTS: Gavrila, Gevura, Gibora.

Benish (בֶּענִיש) A Yiddish form of Benedict. *See* Benedict.

Benjamin The Anglicized form of Binyamin. *See* Binyamin.

Benji A pet form of Benjamin. *See* Benjamin.

Benli, Ben-Li (בֶּן־לִי/בְּנָלִי) From the Aramaic and Hebrew, meaning "I have a son." The exact Hebrew equivalent is Ben-Li. The feminine equivalent is Bat-Li.

Bennet, Bennett Variant English forms of the Latin Benedict. *See* Benedict.

Benor, Ben-Or (בֶּן־אוֹר/בְּנָאוֹר) From the Hebrew, meaning "son of light." The exact Hebrew equivalent is Benor. FEMININE HEBREW EQUIVALENTS: Behira, Eli'ora, Li'ora.

Benroy From the Gaelic and French, meaning "royal mountain." HEBREW EQUIVALENTS: Haran, Harel, Sinai. FEMININE HEBREW EQUIVALENTS: Aharona, Chermona, Harela.

Benson A patronymic form, meaning "son of Ben [Benjamin]." Also, a form of Ben Zion. *See* Ben Zion *and* Binyamin.

Bentley From the Old English, meaning "meadows of ben [grass]." HEBREW EQUIVALENTS: Gan, Rotem, Yarden. FEMININE HEBREW EQUIVALENTS: Ganit, Ginat, Yardeniya.

Benton From the Old English, meaning "Ben's town." *See* Ben.

Bentzi A pet form of Ben-Tziyon and Binyamin. *See* Ben-Tziyon *and* Binyamin.

Ben-Tziyon (בֶּן־צִיּוֹן) From the Hebrew, meaning "excellence" or "son of Zion." Ben Zion is a variant spelling. The exact Hebrew equivalent is Ben-Tziyon. The exact feminine equivalent is Bat-Tziyon.

Benzecry A patronymic form, meaning "son of Zecharia." *See* Zecharia.

Benzi A pet form of Ben Zion. *See* Zion.

Ben Zion The Anglicized form of Ben-Tziyon. *See* Ben-Tziyon.

Ber A Yiddish name derived from the German name Baer, meaning "bear." HEBREW EQUIVALENTS: Dov, Dubi. FEMININE HEBREW EQUIVALENTS: Doveva, Duba, Dubit.

Berel A pet form of Ber. *See* Ber.

Berg From the German, meaning "mountain." HEBREW EQUIVALENTS: Aharon, Haran, Harel. FEMININE HEBREW EQUIVALENTS: Aharona, Harela.

Bergen From the German, meaning "one who lives on a hill or mountain." HEBREW EQUIVALENTS: Aharon, Haran, Harel. FEMININE HEBREW EQUIVALENTS: Aharona, Harela, Horiya.

Berger A variant form of Burgess. *See* Burgess. Also, a form of Bergen. *See* Bergen.

Beril A variant spelling of Beryl. *See* Beryl.

Berish (בֶּעְרִישׁ) A variant Yiddish form of Ber. *See* Ber.

Berk, Berke Variant spellings of Burk. *See* Burk.

Berkeley, Berkley, Berkly From the Anglo-Saxon, meaning "from the birch meadow." HEBREW EQUIVALENTS: Amir, Bar-Ilan, Bros. FEMININE HEBREW EQUIVALENTS: Almuga, Alona, Arna.

Berlin, Berlyn From the German, meaning "boundary line." HEBREW EQUIVALENTS: Efes, Galil, Galili. FEMININE HEBREW EQUIVALENTS: Galila, Gedera, Gelila, Geliliya.

Bern, Berna From the German, meaning "bear." HEBREW EQUIVALENTS: Dov, Dubi. FEMININE HEBREW EQUIVALENTS: Dova, Doveva, Dubit.

Bernard From the Old High German, meaning "bold as a bear." HEBREW EQUIVALENTS: Barzilai, Binyamin, Bo'az, Dov. FEMININE HEBREW EQUIVALENTS: Ari'el, Atzma, Duba, Dubit, Gavrila, Gibora.

Bernardo The Spanish form of Bernard. *See* Bernard.

Bernarr A variant form of Bernard. *See* Bernard.

Bernd, Berndt Variant forms of Bernard. *See* Bernard.

Bernhard, Bernhardt Variant German forms of Bernard. *See* Bernard.

Berni, Bernie Pet forms of Bernard. *See* Bernard.

Bert, Bertie Pet forms of Albert, Berthold, Bertol, and Bertram.

Berthold From the German, meaning "bright." HEBREW EQUIVALENTS: Bahir, Barak, Bezek. FEMININE HEBREW EQUIVALENTS: Bareket, Behira, Me'ira.

Bertin A variant form of Bertram. *See* Bertram.

Bertol, Bertold Variant forms of Berthold. *See* Berthold.

Berton A variant form of Berthold. *See* Berthold.

Bertram From the Old High German, meaning "bright, illustrious one." HEBREW EQUIVALENTS: Barak, Bazak, Gedalya. FEMININE HEBREW EQUIVALENTS: Behira, Levana, Me'ira.

Bertran A variant form of Bertram. *See* Bertram.

Bertrand A variant form of Bertram. *See* Bertram.

Bertrem A variant spelling of Bertram. *See* Bertram.

Berwin From the Anglo-Saxon, meaning "powerful friend." HEBREW EQUIVALENTS: Regem, Re'uel, Yadid. FEMININE HEBREW EQUIVALENTS: Achva, Amit, Amita.

Beryl (בֶּעְרִיל) From the Greek, meaning "sea-green precious stone." Also, from the Yiddish, meaning "bear," connoting strength. HEBREW EQUIVALENTS: Barak, Bo'az, Dov. FEMININE HEBREW EQUIVALENTS: Bareket, Duba, Gavrila.

Betuel (בְּתוּאֵל) From the Hebrew, meaning "house of God." Bethuel is an Anglicized form. The exact Hebrew equivalent is Betu'el. FEMININE HEBREW EQUIVALENTS: Armona, Armonit. In Genesis 22:22, the father of Rebecca and Laban.

Betzalel (בְּצַלְאֵל) From the Hebrew, meaning "shadow of God," signifying God's protection. The exact Hebrew equivalent is Betzalel. FEMININE HEBREW EQUIVALENTS: Shimrit, Tzina, Ya'akova. In Exodus 31: 2, the architect of the Tabernacle.

Beverley, Beverly A unisex name. From the Old English, meaning "beaver meadow" or "field." HEBREW EQUIVALENTS: Carmel, Carmeli, Yara. FEMININE HEBREW EQUIVALENTS: Carmela, Gana, Nava.

Bezalel A variant spelling of Betzalel. *See* Betzalel.

Bibi (בִּיבִּי) A pet form of Binyamin. *See* Binyamin.

Bichri (בִּכְרִי) From the Hebrew, meaning "my eldest" or "youthful." The exact Hebrew equivalent is Bichri. FEMININE HEBREW EQUIVALENTS: Bekhira, Bekhora. In II Samuel 20:1, a Benjaminite who revolted against King David.

Biddie, Biddy Pet forms of Bridget. *See* Bridget.

Bil A pet form of William. *See* William.

Bildad (בִּלְדַד) From the Hebrew, meaning "Baal has loved." The exact Hebrew equivalent is Bildad. FEMININE HEBREW EQUIVALENTS: Ahuva, Davida, Rut. In Job 2:12, one of Job's friends.

Bilga, Bilgah (בִּלְגָה) From the Hebrew, meaning "joy, cheer." The exact Hebrew equivalent is Bilga. FEMININE HEBREW EQUIVALENTS: Avigal, Aviga'yil, Gil. In I Chronicles 24:14, a priest during King David's reign.

Bilgai (בִּלְגַי) From the Arabic and Aramaic meaning "joy, cheerfulness." The exact Hebrew equivalent is Bilgai. FEMININE HEBREW EQUIVALENTS: Aviga'yil, Bilga, Gila. In Nehemiah 10:8, one of Nehemiah's followers.

Bilguy A variant spelling of Bilgai. *See* Bilgai.

Billi, Billie, Billy, Billye Pet forms of William. *See* William.

Bilu (בִּילוּ) An acronym formed from the first letters of the Hebrew phrase *Beit Yisrael lechu ve-neilchah*, "O, House of Jacob, come, let us walk together" (Isaiah 2:5). The exact Hebrew equivalent is Bilu.

Bin A pet form of Binyamin. *See* Binyamin.

Bina (בִּינָה) A unisex name. From the Hebrew, meaning "understanding, intelligence, wisdom." The exact Hebrew equivalent is Bina.

Bing From the Old German, meaning "an area shaped like a pot." Kad is a Hebrew equivalent.

Binjamin A variant spelling of Binyamin. *See* Binyamin.

Binyamin (בִּנְיָמִין) From the Hebrew, meaning "son of my right hand," having the connotation of strength. The exact Hebrew equivalent is Binyamin. The exact feminine equivalent is Binyamina. In Genesis 35:18, the son of Jacob and Rachel.

Binyomin A variant spelling of Binyamin. *See* Binyamin.

Bird From the English and Anglo-Saxon *bridd*, which by metathesis became "bird." HEBREW EQUIVALENTS: Deror, Efron, Nesher. FEMININE HEBREW EQUIVALENTS: A'ya, Da'ya, Efrona.

Birdie, Birdye Variant pet forms of Bird. *See* Bird.

Birgit A variant form of Bridgit. *See* Bridgit.

Birk A variant form of Barker. *See* Barker.

Bitan From the Hebrew, meaning "temporary dwelling." The term is first mentioned in Esther 1:5. The exact Hebrew equivalent is Bitan. FEMININE HEBREW EQUIVALENTS: Me'ona, Shafrira, Zevula.

Biv (בִּיב) From the Hebrew, meaning "water canal, viaduct." The exact Hebrew equivalent is Biv. FEMININE HEBREW EQUIVALENTS: Afeka, Dalya.

Bivar (בִּיבָר) From the Hebrew, meaning "zoo." The exact masculine Hebrew equivalent is Bivar. FEMININE HEBREW EQUIVALENTS: Cha'ya, Duba.

Blair From the Scottish, meaning "dweller on the plain." HEBREW EQUIVALENTS: Avgar, Dar, Duri'el. FEMININE HEBREW EQUIVALENTS: Dira, Me'ona, Zevula.

Blake From the Anglo-Saxon, meaning "to whiten, to bleach." HEBREW EQUIVALENTS: Lavan, Livni. FEMININE HEBREW EQUIVALENTS: Levana, Levona, Tzechora.

Blanchard A variant form of Blake. *See* Blake.

Blane, Blaine From the Old English, meaning "the source of a river." HEBREW EQUIVALENTS: Afek, Beri, Chamat. FEMININE HEBREW EQUIVALENTS: Afeka, Bat-Yam, Miryam.

Bo, Bob, Bobbie, Bobby Pet forms of Robert. *See* Robert.

Boaz (בֹּעַז) From the Hebrew, meaning "strength" or "swiftness." The exact Hebrew equivalent is Bo'az. FEMININE HEBREW EQUIVALENTS: Azri'ela, Gavrila, Gibora. In Ruth 3:2, the husband of Ruth.

Bondi From the French, meaning "happy holiday." The exact Hebrew equivalent is Yom-Tov. FEMININE HEBREW EQUIVALENTS: Chagit, Chagiya.

Bonesh (בֹּונֶעש) From the Yiddish, meaning "good." HEBREW EQUIVALENTS: Bekhi'el, Ben-Tovim, Elituv. FEMININE HEBREW EQUIVALENTS: Tova, Tovit, Yatva.

Boni From the Italian, meaning "good." *See* Boniface.

Boniface From the Latin, meaning "well-doer." HEBREW EQUIVALENTS: Ben-Tovim, Litov, Tovi. FEMININE HEBREW EQUIVALENTS: Tova, Tovit, Tuvit.

Booker From the Anglo-Saxon, meaning "beech tree." An occupational name for one who copies books, since paper for books was made from the beech tree. HEBREW EQUIVALENTS: Bar-Ilan, Bros, Elon. FEMININE HEBREW EQUIVALENTS: Shikma, Shikmona, Soferet.

Boone From the Latin and the Old French, meaning "good." HEBREW EQUIVALENTS: Ben-Tov, Ben-Tovim, Tovi'el. FEMININE HEBREW EQUIVALENTS: Tiva, Tova, Tovat.

Borg From the Old Norse, meaning "castle." Also a variant form of the German name Berg, meaning "mountain." HEBREW EQUIVALENTS: Aharon, Armon, Armoni. FEMININE HEBREW EQUIVALENTS: Armonit, Harela, Hariya.

Boris From the Russian, meaning "fight" or "warrior." HEBREW EQUIVALENTS: Ben-Cha'yil, Gibor, Mordechai. FEMININE HEBREW EQUIVALENTS: Gavrila, Givora, Yisra'ela.

Bosem (בֹּשֶׂם) From the Hebrew, meaning "pleasant fragrance." The exact Hebrew equivalent is Bosem. FEMININE HEBREW EQUIVALENTS: Bosmat, Ketzi'a.

Bowen A Celtic patronymic, meaning "son [or descendant] of Owen." HEBREW EQUIVALENTS: Ben-Gever, Ben-Guryon, Ben-Oni. FEMININE HEBREW EQUIVALENTS: Bat-Ami, Bat-Galim, Bat-Tziyon.

Boyd From the Slavic, meaning "fighting warrior," or from the Celtic, meaning "yellow." HEBREW EQUIVALENTS: Ben-Azai, Ben-Cha'yil, Ben-Gever. FEMININE HEBREW EQUIVALENTS: Gevura, Gibora, Zehuva.

Brad A pet form of Braden and Bradley. *See* Braden *and* Bradley.

Braden From the Old English, meaning "broad, wide." HEBREW EQUIVALENTS: Nof, Rechavam, Rechavya. FEMININE HEBREW EQUIVALENTS: Artzit, Eretz, Merchava.

Bradford From the Old English, meaning "broad ford." HEBREW EQUIV-

ALENTS: Arnan, Arnon, Zerem. FEMININE HEBREW EQUIVALENTS: Afeka, Arnona, Arnonit.

Bradlee, Bradley From the Old English, meaning "broad lea, meadow." HEBREW EQUIVALENTS: Carmela, Ginat, Rechavam. FEMININE HEBREW EQUIVALENTS: Carmela, Carmelit, Gana.

Brady From the Anglo-Saxon, meaning "broad island." HEBREW EQUIVALENTS: Afek, Arnon, Rechavya. FEMININE HEBREW EQUIVALENTS: Afeka, Arnona, Arnonit.

Brahm, Bram Short form of Abraham or Abram. *See* Abraham *and* Abram.

Bran From the Irish, meaning "raven." HEBREW EQUIVALENTS: Efron, Orev, Tzipor. FEMININE HEBREW EQUIVALENTS: Efrona, Kanit, Tzipora.

Branch From the Late Latin, meaning "an extension from the tree trunk." HEBREW EQUIVALENTS: Bar-Ilan, Bros, Oren. FEMININE HEBREW EQUIVALENTS: Alona, Ilana, Shikma.

Brand A variant form of Bran. *See* Bran.

Brandan, Brandon Variant forms of Brand. *See* Brand.

Brandt A variant form of Brand. *See* Brand.

Brant From the Old English, meaning "firebrand" or "sword." HEBREW EQUIVALENTS: Avi'ur, Lahav, Udi. FEMININE HEBREW EQUIVALENTS: Uri'ela, Urit.

Bremel, Breml Yiddish pet forms of Avraham. *See* Avraham.

Brent From the Old English, meaning "mountain, hilltop." HEBREW EQUIVALENTS: Gali, Tivon, Talmai. FEMININE HEBREW EQUIVALENTS: Gal, Galit, Givona.

Bret, Brett English surnames, adopted as a unisex first name. From the Old French Bret, meaning "native of Brittany." MASCULINE HEBREW EQUIVALENTS: Ezrach, Nativ.

Brian From the Celtic and Gaelic, meaning "strength" or "one who is nobly born and eloquent." HEBREW EQUIVALENTS: Abir, Barzilai, Ben-Cha'yil. FEMININE HEBREW EQUIVALENTS: Abira, Amira, Doveva.

Briand From the French, meaning "castle." The Hebrew equivalent is Armoni. FEMININE HEBREW EQUIVALENTS: Armona, Armonit.

Bridge From the Old English, meaning "wooden causeway." HEBREW EQUIVALENTS: Gesher, Geshur.

Brion A variant spelling of Brian. *See* Brian.

Bris A variant spelling of Brit. *See* Brit.

Brit, Britt (בְּרִית) A short form of Briton. *See* Briton. Also, from the Hebrew meaning "covenant." HEBREW EQUIVALENTS: Brit, Brit-El.

Briton *Also spelled* Britain. An early name for Wales, a division of Great Britain.

Brock From the Anglo-Saxon and Gaelic, meaning "badger." Also, an early name for a "grain dealer." HEBREW EQUIVALENTS: Dagan, Goren, Kela'ya. FEMININE HEBREW EQUIVALENTS: Chita, Degana, Deganit.

Broderick A name compounded from Brad and Richard, meaning "rich, flat land." HEBREW EQUIVALENTS: Artzi, Rechavam, Rechavya. FEMININE HEBREW EQUIVALENTS: Artzit, Eretz, Merchavya.

Bromley From the Anglo-Saxon, meaning "meadow" or "field of brushwood." HEBREW EQUIVALENTS: Artza, Artzi, Nir. FEMININE HEBREW EQUIVALENTS: Artzit, Eretz, Nira.

Bronson From the Old English, meaning "son of the brown one." HEBREW EQUIVALENTS: Arad, Arod, Arodi. FEMININE HEBREW EQUIVALENTS: Nechushta.

Brook, Brooke From the Old English, meaning "stream." HEBREW EQUIVALENTS: Yoval, Yuval, Zerem. FEMININE HEBREW EQUIVALENTS: Afeka, Arnona, Arnonit.

Brooks A variant form of Brook. *See* Brook.

Bruce A Scottish name of French origin, probably meaning "woods, thicket." HEBREW EQUIVALENTS: Carmel, Carmeli, Yara. FEMININE HEBREW EQUIVALENTS: Artzit, Carmela, Carmelit.

Bruno From the Old German, meaning "brown, dark in appearance." Also, a form of the German name Brunn, meaning "fountain."

HEBREW EQUIVALENTS: Arnon, Kush, Pinchas. FEMININE HEBREW EQUIVALENTS: Arnona, Tzila.

Bry A short form of Bryan. *See* Bryan.

Bryan, Bryant Variant forms of Brian. *See* Brian.

Bub From the Old English, meaning "pal, friend." HEBREW EQUIVALENTS: Chovav, David, Yedida. FEMININE HEBREW EQUIVALENTS: Adina, Adira, Nagida.

Bubba From the German, meaning "boy." HEBREW EQUIVALENTS: Bachur, Ben, Na'arai.

Buck From the Anglo-Saxon and German, meaning "male deer" or "he-goat." HEBREW EQUIVALENTS: Ben-Tzvi, Efer, Tzevi. FEMININE HEBREW EQUIVALENTS: A'yala, A'yelet, Ofra.

Bucky A pet form of Buck. *See* Buck.

Bud, Budd From the Old English, meaning "messenger," or from the Welsh, meaning "rich, victorious." HEBREW EQUIVALENTS: Kalev, Mevaser, Yishai. FEMININE HEBREW EQUIVALENTS: Bat-Shu'a, Dafna, Hadasa.

Buddy A pet form of Budd. *See* Budd.

Buell A variant spelling of the British *bul*, meaning "bull." HEBREW EQUIVALENTS: Arad, Ard, Ardi.

Buki (בֻּקִי) From the Hebrew, meaning "bottle" or "test, investigate." The exact Hebrew equivalent is Buki. The feminine equivalent is Bakara. In Numbers 34:22, a leader of the tribe of Dan.

Buna, Bunah (בּוּנָה) A unisex name. From the Hebrew, meaning "understanding, intelligence." The exact Hebrew equivalent is Buna. In I Chronicles 2:25, a member of the tribe of Judah.

Buni, Bunni (בּוּנִי) From the Hebrew, meaning "built, constructed." The exact Hebrew equivalent is Buni. FEMININE HEBREW EQUIVALENTS: Bona, Buna, Yavnela. In Nehemiah 11:15, a Levite who settled in Jerusalem.

Bunim (בּוּנִים) From the Yiddish, meaning "good." HEBREW EQUIVA-

LENTS: Bechi'el, Ben-Tov, Ben-Tovim. FEMININE HEBREW EQUIVALENTS: Tiva, Tova, Tovat.

Burdette From the Middle English, meaning "small bird." HEBREW EQUIVALENTS: Deror, Efron, Gozal. FEMININE HEBREW EQUIVALENTS: Efrona, Gozala, Salit.

Burgess From the Middle English and Old French, meaning "shopkeeper," signifying a free man. HEBREW EQUIVALENTS: Avidror, Derori, Pesach. FEMININE HEBREW EQUIVALENTS: Derora, Ge'ula, Rachav.

Burk, Burke Old English forms of the German name Burg, meaning "castle." HEBREW EQUIVALENTS: Armon, Armoni. FEMININE HEBREW EQUIVALENTS: Armona, Armonit.

Burl, Burle From the Latin, meaning "coarse hair." Also, from the Middle English, meaning "tree knot." HEBREW EQUIVALENTS: Anuv, Esav, Isur. FEMININE HEBREW EQUIVALENTS: Delila, Nima, Rivka.

Burleigh From the Old English, meaning "field with prickly, burr-covered plants." HEBREW EQUIVALENTS: Avgar, Ezrach, Iris. FEMININE HEBREW EQUIVALENTS: Atzmonit, Iris, Marganit.

Burley A variant spelling of Burleigh. *See* Burleigh.

Burr A short form of Burleigh. *See* Burleigh.

Burt, Burte A short form of Burton. *See* Burton. Also, from the Anglo-Saxon meaning "bright, clear, excellent." HEBREW EQUIVALENTS: Ben-Tzion, Me'ir, Tuviya. FEMININE HEBREW EQUIVALENTS: Bat-Tziyon, Behira, Me'ira.

Burton From the Old English, meaning "town on a hill." HEBREW EQUIVALENTS: Aharon, Chaga, Gal. FEMININE HEBREW EQUIVALENTS: Aharona, Galit, Galya, Givona, Talma, Talmit.

Bustan (בּוּסתָן) From the Arabic and Hebrew, meaning "garden." The exact Hebrew equivalent is Bustan. FEMININE HEBREW EQUIVALENTS: Ganya, Ginat, Yardeniya.

Buz (בּוּז) From the Hebrew, meaning "shame" or "ridicule." The exact Hebrew equivalent is Buz. The exact feminine equivalent is Buza. In Genesis 22:21, the son of Nachor, brother of Abraham.

Buzi (בּוּזִי) From the Hebrew, meaning "my shame, embarrassment." The exact Hebrew equivalent is Buzi. The exact feminine equivalent is Buza. In Ezekiel 1:3, the father of the prophet Ezekiel.

Byk From the Polish, meaning "ox." HEBREW EQUIVALENTS: Arad, Ard, Ardi.

Byrd From the Anglo-Saxon, meaning "bird." HEBREW EQUIVALENTS: Derori, Efron, Nesher. FEMININE HEBREW EQUIVALENTS: Efrona, Tzipora, Tzipori.

Byron From the German, meaning "cottage," or from the Old English, meaning "bear." HEBREW EQUIVALENTS: Dov, Dubi. FEMININE HEBREW EQUIVALENTS: Dova, Dovit, Duba.

✐ C ✐

Cal A pet form of Caleb. *See* Caleb.

Calder From the Celtic, meaning "from the stony river." HEBREW EQUIV-
ALENTS: Chamat, Even, Regem. FEMININE HEBREW EQUIVALENTS: Afeka,
Gazit, Yaval.

Cale Possibly a pet form of Caleb. *See* Caleb.

Caleb An Anglicized form of Kalev. *See* Kalev.

Calev A variant spelling of Kalev. *See* Calev.

Calvert An Old English occupational name for a herdsman. HEBREW
EQUIVALENTS: Eder, Edri, Maron. FEMININE HEBREW EQUIVALENTS: Eder,
Merona.

Calvin From the Latin, meaning "bald." The exact Hebrew equivalent
is Korach.

Cameron A unisex name. From the Gaelic, meaning "crooked nose."
The Hebrew equivalent is Nachor.

Camillus From the Latin, meaning "attendant" or "messenger." HE-
BREW EQUIVALENTS: Azarya, Ezra, Kalev. FEMININE HEBREW EQUIVALENTS:
Aleksandra, Ozera, Sa'ada.

Capp A variant form of Chaplin. *See* Chaplin.

Carey From the Welsh or Cornish, meaning "rock island." HEBREW

EQUIVALENTS: Almog, Aviyam, Tzur. FEMININE HEBREW EQUIVALENTS: Avni'ela, Miryam, Ritzpa.

Carl A variant form of Charles. *See* Charles.

Carlos The Spanish form of Charles. *See* Charles.

Carlton From the Old English, meaning "Carl's town." *See* Carl.

Carmel (כַּרְמֶל) A unisex name. From the Hebrew, meaning "vineyard" or "garden." The exact Hebrew equivalent is Carmel. FEMININE HEBREW EQUIVALENTS: Carma, Carmiya, Carmit.

Carmeli (כַּרְמְלִי) A unisex name. From the Hebrew, meaning "my vineyard." The exact Hebrew equivalent is Carmeli. FEMININE HEBREW EQUIVALENTS: Carmela, Carmelit, Carmi'ela.

Carmen The Spanish form of Carmel. *See* Carmel.

Carmi (כַּרְמִי) From the Hebrew, meaning "my vineyard." The exact Hebrew equivalent is Carmi. FEMININE HEBREW EQUIVALENTS: Carmela, Carmi'ela. In Genesis 46:9, a son of Reuben and grandson of Jacob and Leah.

Carmiel (כַּרְמִיאֵל) From the Hebrew, meaning "the Lord is my vineyard." The exact Hebrew equivalent is Carmi'el. FEMININE HEBREW EQUIVALENTS: Carmela, Carmelit, Carmi'ela.

Carmine The Italian form of Carmen. *See* Carmen.

Carney, Carnie From the Celtic, meaning "fighter." HEBREW EQUIVALENTS: Gavri'el, Gevarya, Ish-Cha'yil. FEMININE HEBREW EQUIVALENTS: Gavri'ela, Gibora, Uzi'ela.

Carol, Caroll Variant forms of Charles. *See* Charles.

Carr From the Scandinavian and Old Norse, meaning "marshy land." HEBREW EQUIVALENTS: Aviyam, Beri, Dalfon. FEMININE HEBREW EQUIVALENTS: Bat-Yam, Miryam, Yaval.

Carrol, Carroll Variant spellings of Carol. *See* Carol.

Cary A variant spelling of Carey. *See* Carey.

Case From the Middle English and Old French, meaning "chest, box." HEBREW EQUIVALENTS: Aran, Aron. FEMININE HEBREW EQUIVALENTS: Arona.

Casey A unisex name. From the Celtic, meaning "valorous." Also, a pet form of Case. HEBREW EQUIVALENTS: Chason, Chutzpit, Yechezkel. FEMININE HEBREW EQUIVALENTS: Odeda, Uzit, Yechezkela.

Cash A short form of Cassius. *See* Cassius.

Caspar From the German, meaning "imperial." HEBREW EQUIVALENTS: Katri'el, Malkam, Melech. FEMININE HEBREW EQUIVALENTS: Atara, Malka, Tzefira.

Casper A variant spelling of Caspar. *See* Caspar.

Cassidy A unisex name. From the Irish/Gaelic, meaning "wise, clever." HEBREW EQUIVALENTS: Chacham, Chachmon, Haskel. FEMININE HEBREW EQUIVALENTS: Behira, Nevona.

Cassius From the Latin, meaning "vain, ostentatious." HEBREW EQUIVALENTS: Hadur, Hevel, Me'utar. FEMININE HEBREW EQUIVALENTS: Atura, Hadar, Pe'era.

Cato From the Latin, meaning "omniscient, all-knowing." HEBREW EQUIVALENTS: Bahir, Chachmon, Navon. FEMININE HEBREW EQUIVALENTS: Behira, Ge'ona, Tushiya.

Cecil From the Latin, meaning "blind." EUPHEMISTIC HEBREW EQUIVALENTS: Koresh, Me'ir, Shimshon. EUPHEMISTIC FEMININE HEBREW EQUIVALENTS: Me'ira, Noga, Ora.

Cedric A Welsh name meaning "bountiful" or "war chief." HEBREW EQUIVALENTS: Hotir, Huna, Yishai, Yitro. FEMININE HEBREW EQUIVALENTS: Ashira, Bat-Shu'a, Yitra.

Cerf From the French, meaning "hart, deer." HEBREW EQUIVALENTS: A'yal, Ben-Tzevi, Efer. FEMININE HEBREW EQUIVALENTS: A'yelet, Hertzeliya, Tzeviya.

Chad From the Celtic, meaning "battle" or "warrior." HEBREW EQUIVALENTS: Ben-Cha'yil, Gad, Gidon. FEMININE HEBREW EQUIVALENTS: Amitza, Gavrila, Gibora.

Chadad (חֲדַד) From the Hebrew, meaning "sharp." The exact Hebrew equivalent is Chadad. In Genesis 25:15, the sixth son of Ishmael.

Chag (חַג) From the Hebrew, meaning "holiday." The exact Hebrew equivalent is Chag. FEMININE HEBREW EQUIVALENTS: Chagit, Chagiga, Chagiya.

Chagai (חַגַי) *Also spelled* Haggai. From the Aramaic and Hebrew, meaning "my feast(s), festive." The exact Hebrew equivalent is Chagai. FEMININE HEBREW EQUIVALENTS: Chagiga, Chagit, Chagiya. In Chagai 1:1, one of the latter-day prophets.

Chagi (חַגִי) A variant form of Chagai. *See* Chagai. The exact Hebrew equivalent is Chagi. In Genesis 46:16, a son of Gad; grandson of Jacob.

Chai (חַי) From the Hebrew, meaning "life." The exact Hebrew equivalent is Chai. The exact feminine equivalent is Cha'ya.

Chaim (חַיִים) A variant spelling of Chayim. *See* Chayim.

Cham (חָם) From the Hebrew meaning "warm, hot." The exact Hebrew equivalent is Cham. FEMININE HEBREW EQUIVALENTS: Chamama, Chuma, Chumi. In Genesis 5:32, the second son of Noah.

Chami (חַמִי) A pet form of Nechemya. *See* Nechemya. The exact Hebrew equivalent is Chami.

Champ From the Latin *campus*, meaning "field, stadium where games are played." Also, from the Middle English and Old French, meaning "gladiator." HEBREW EQUIVALENTS: Gadi'el, Gevaryahu, Gidon. FEMININE HEBREW EQUIVALENTS: Gada, Gadit, Merav.

Champion A variant form of Champ. *See* Champ.

Chanan (חָנָן) A variant form of Chanina. The exact Hebrew equivalent is Chanan. *See* Chanina *and* Yochanan *for additional equivalents*. In I Chronicles 8:23, a chief of the tribe of Benjamin.

Chanani (חֲנָנִי) From the Hebrew, meaning "gracious." The exact Hebrew equivalent is Chanani. FEMININE HEBREW EQUIVALENTS: Chana, Chananya. In I Kings 16:1, a critic of King Asa of Judah.

Chanania, Chananiah, Chananya (חֲנַנְיָה) From the Hebrew, meaning "compassionate God" or "God is gracious." The exact Hebrew equivalent is Chananya. FEMININE HEBREW EQUIVALENTS: Chana, Chanita, Yochana. In I Chronicles 8:24, a leader of the tribe of Benjamin living in Jerusalem.

Chancellor From the Middle English and Old French, meaning "keeper of records" or "secretary." HEBREW EQUIVALENTS: Betach, Mivtach, Sofer. FEMININE HEBREW EQUIVALENTS: Mivtechet, Razi, Razi'ela.

Chandler From the French, meaning "maker or seller of candles." HEBREW EQUIVALENTS: Avner, Ner, Neri. FEMININE HEBREW EQUIVALENTS: Nehara, Nehira, Nehura.

Chaniel (חֲנִיאֵל) From the Hebrew, meaning "God is gracious." The exact Hebrew equivalent is Chani'el. FEMININE HEBREW EQUIVALENTS: Chana, Chanita, Yochana. In Numbers 34:23, a member of the tribe of Manasseh.

Chanina (חֲנִינָא) A unisex name. From the Aramaic, meaning "gracious" or "compassionate." The exact Hebrew equivalent is Chanina.

Chanoch (חֲנוֹךְ) From the Hebrew, meaning "dedicated" or "educated." The exact Hebrew equivalent is Chanoch. Chanukah is a feminine equivalent. In Genesis 25:4, a grandson of Abraham and Keturah. In Numbers 26:5, a son of Reuben; grandson of Jacob. Enoch is the Anglicized form. *See* Enoch.

Chapin A contracted form of the Old French, meaning "chaplain." *See* Chaplin.

Chaplin From the Middle English, meaning "chaplain." HEBREW EQUIVALENTS: Aharon, Moran, Rav. FEMININE HEBREW EQUIVALENTS: Aharona, Horiya, Mora.

Chapman From the Middle English, meaning "trader." HEBREW EQUIVALENTS: Amal, Amali, Mahir. FEMININE HEBREW EQUIVALENTS: Amal, Amalya, Amel.

Charan (חָרָן) From the Hebrew, meaning "mountainous." The exact Hebrew equivalent is Charan. FEMININE HEBREW EQUIVALENTS: Aharona, Chermona, Harela. In Genesis 11:26, a brother of Abraham.

Charle A variant spelling of Charley or Charlie. *See* Charley.

Charles A French form of the Anglo-Saxon, meaning "manly, strong" or "full-grown." HEBREW EQUIVALENTS: Abir, Ben-Cha'yil, Chizkiyahu. FEMININE HEBREW EQUIVALENTS: Abira, Ari'el, Ari'ela.

Charley, Charlie Pet forms of Charles. *See* Charles.

Charlton A French-German name, meaning "Charles's town." *See* Charles.

Charney From the Slavic, meaning "black." HEBREW EQUIVALENTS: Cham, Chumi, Pinchas. FEMININE HEBREW EQUIVALENTS: Adara, Laila, Shechora.

Chase From the Old French and Middle English, meaning "hunt." HEBREW EQUIVALENTS: Tzedani, Sheva'ya. Tzedanit is a feminine equivalent.

Chauncey, Chauncy Pet forms of Chancellor. *See* Chancellor.

Chavakuk (חֲבַקּוּק) From the Assyrian, meaning "garden plant." The exact Hebrew equivalent is Chavakuk. FEMININE HEBREW EQUIVALENTS: Chelmit, Chelmonit, Gana. In Chavakuk 1:1, a seventh-century B.C.E. Hebrew prophet in the kingdom of Judah.

Chaviv (חָבִיב) From the Hebrew, meaning "beloved." The exact Hebrew equivalent is Chaviv. The exact feminine equivalent is Chaviva.

Chavivi (חֲבִיבִי) From the Hebrew, meaning "my beloved" or "my friend." The exact Hebrew equivalent is Chavivi. FEMININE HEBREW EQUIVALENTS: Chaviva, Chavuka, Davida.

Chayim, Chayyim, Chayym (חַיִּים) From the Hebrew, meaning "life." The exact Hebrew equivalent is Cha'yim. The exact feminine equivalent is Cha'ya.

Chaziel (חֲזִיאֵל) From the Hebrew, meaning "vision of God." The exact Hebrew equivalent is Chazi'el. FEMININE HEBREW EQUIVALENTS: Nevi'a, Ro'a. In I Chronicles 23:9, an appointee of King David to minister in the Tabernacle.

Chazo (חֲזוֹ) From the Hebrew, meaning "to foresee, envision." The exact Hebrew equivalent is Chazo. FEMININE HEBREW EQUIVALENTS: Nevi'a, Ro'a. In Genesis 22:22, a son of Nachor and Milka, a nephew of Abraham.

Cheifer (חֵפֶר) From the Hebrew, meaning "pit." The exact Hebrew equivalent is Cheifer. In Numbers 26:33, the father of Tzelophchad of the tribe of Manasseh.

Chemdat (חֶמְדַּת) A unisex name. From the Hebrew, meaning "lovable, desirable." The exact Hebrew equivalent is Chemdat. FEMININE HEBREW EQUIVALENTS: Chamuda, Chemdiya.

Chemi (חֶמִי) A pet form of Nechemya. *See* Nechemya. The exact Hebrew equivalent is Chemi.

Chemia, Chemiah (חֶמְיָה) Pet forms of Nechemya. *See* Nechemya.

Chen (חֵן) A unisex name. From the Hebrew, meaning "graceful, gracious, charming." The exact Hebrew equivalent is Chen. FEMININE HEBREW EQUIVALENTS: Chana, Chanita, Yochana.

Chermon (חֶרְמוֹן) From the Hebrew, meaning "consecrated, sacred." The exact Hebrew equivalent is Chermon. The exact feminine equivalent is Chermona.

Chermoni (חֶרְמוֹנִי) A variant form of Chermon. *See* Chermon. The exact Hebrew equivalent is Chermoni.

Cheskie A pet form of Yechezkel (Ezekiel). *See* Yechezkel.

Chester From the Latin, meaning "fortress" or "camp." HEBREW EQUIVALENTS: Chosa, Chupma, Shemarya. FEMININE HEBREW EQUIVALENTS: Batzra, Efrat, Tzila.

Chet A pet form of Chester. *See* Chester.

Chetzron (חֶצְרוֹן) *Also spelled* Hezron. From the Hebrew, meaning "outsider, stranger." The exact Hebrew equivalent is Chetzron. FEMININE HEBREW EQUIVALENTS: Gershona, Gi'ora. In Numbers 26:6, a son of Reuben; grandson of Jacob.

Chevy From the British, meaning "hunt, chase." The Hebrew equivalent is Tzedani. The feminine equivalent is Tzedanit.

Chia A variant spelling of Chiya. *See* Chiya.

Chiel (חִיאֵל) From the Hebrew, meaning "God lives." A short form of Yechiel. The exact Hebrew equivalent is Chi'el. The feminine equivalent is Yechi'ela.

Chilton From the Anglo-Saxon, meaning "town by the river." HEBREW EQUIVALENTS: Aviyam, Beri, Chamat. FEMININE HEBREW EQUIVALENTS: Afeka, Bat-Yam, Miryam.

Chip, Chipper Pet forms of Charles. *See* Charles.

Chiram (חִירָם) *Also spelled* Hiram. From the Hebrew, meaning "lofty, exalted." The exact Hebrew equivalent is Chiram. FEMININE HEBREW EQUIVALENTS: Rami, Ramot, Romema. In II Samuel 5:11, a king of Tyre who assisted David in building his house.

Chirom (חִירוֹם) A variant spelling of Chiram (Hiram). *See* Chiram.

Chiya (חִיָּא) A short form of Yechiel. *See* Yechiel.

Chizkiya, Chizkiyah (חִזְקִיָּה) From the Hebrew, meaning "God is my strength." The exact Hebrew equivalent is Chizkiya. FEMININE HEBREW EQUIVALENTS: Chasna, Uzi'ela, Yechezkela. In II Kings 18:1, the thirteenth king of Judah after the kingdom was divided following the death of Solomon.

Chizkiyahu (חִזְקִיָּהוּ) A variant form of Chizkiya. Chizkiyahu is the exact Hebrew equivalent. *See* Chizkiya.

Choni (חוֹנִי) From the Hebrew, meaning "gracious." The exact Hebrew equivalent is Choni. FEMININE HEBREW EQUIVALENTS: Chana, Chanita, Chen.

Chor (חֹר) From the Hebrew, meaning "hollow, hole" or "cave." The exact Hebrew equivalent is Chor. Me'ara is a feminine equivalent.

Chori (חוֹרִי) From the Hebrew, meaning "nobility, honorable one" or "my cave." The exact Hebrew equivalent is Chori. FEMININE HEBREW EQUIVALENTS: Atzila, Nediva. In Numbers 13:5, the father of Shafat of the tribe of Shimon (Simeon).

Chovav (חוֹבָב) A variant form of Chovev. *See* Chovev. The exact Hebrew equivalent is Chovav.

Chovev (חוֹבֵב) From the Hebrew, meaning "friend" or "lover." The exact Hebrew equivalent is Chovev. FEMININE HEBREW EQUIVALENTS: Chaviva, Chiba, Chibat-Tziyon.

Chris A pet form of Christopher. *See* Christopher.

Christopher From the Greek and Latin, meaning "Christ-bearer." The Christian patron saint of travelers. HEBREW EQUIVALENTS: Mashi'ach, Orach. Yiska is a feminine equivalent.

Christy A Scottish pet form of Christopher. *See* Christopher.

Chuck A pet form of Charles. *See* Charles.

Chupah, Chuppah (חוּפָּה) From the Hebrew, meaning "covering." The exact Hebrew equivalent is Chupah. FEMININE HEBREW EQUIVALENTS: Talal, Talila, Telalit. In I Chronicles 24:13, a leader of a priestly family during the reign of King David.

Chur (חוּר) From the Akkadian, meaning "child." The exact Hebrew equivalent is Chur. FEMININE HEBREW EQUIVALENTS: Alma, Betula, Na'ara, Tze'ira.

Churi (חוּרִי) A variant form of Chur. *See* Chur. The exact Hebrew equivalent is Churi.

Cicero From the Latin, meaning "orator" or "guide." HEBREW EQUIVALENTS: Amarya, Amir, Divri. FEMININE HEBREW EQUIVALENTS: Amira, Doveva, Dovevet.

Cid A Spanish name derived from the Arabic, meaning "lord, sir." HEBREW EQUIVALENTS: Adoniya, Chirom, Yisra'el. FEMININE HEBREW EQUIVALENTS: Adira, Adonit, Yisra'ela.

Cimon A variant spelling of Simon. *See* Simon.

Claibe A short form of Claiborn. *See* Claiborn.

Claiborn, Claiborne Compounded from the German and French, meaning "boundary marked by clovers." HEBREW EQUIVALENTS: Chavakuk, Dashe, Narkis, Rotem, Shatil, Shatul. FEMININE HEBREW EQUIVALENTS: Chelmit, Chelmonit, Narkis.

Clancy From the Gaelic, meaning "red-haired child." HEBREW EQUIVALENTS: Adom, Edom, Odem. The feminine Hebrew equivalent is Aduma.

Clarence From the Latin, meaning "illustrious." HEBREW EQUIVALENTS: Katri'el, Melech, Shem-Tov. FEMININE HEBREW EQUIVALENTS: Malka, Sara, Yisra'ela.

Clark, Clarke From the Old English, meaning "clergyman, scholar, wise person." HEBREW EQUIVALENTS: Chanoch, Kalev, Kohen. FEMININE HEBREW EQUIVALENTS: Bina, Buna, Morit.

Claud, Claude From the French and Latin, meaning "lame." EUPHEMISTIC HEBREW EQUIVALENTS: Ben-Tzevi, Bo'az, Efer. EUPHEMISTIC FEMININE HEBREW EQUIVALENTS: A'yelet, Ofra, Tzivya.

Claudell A pet form of Claude. *See* Claude.

Claudio The Spanish form of Claud. *See* Claud.

Clay From the German and Indo-European, meaning "to stick together." The Hebrew equivalent is Levi. FEMININE HEBREW EQUIVALENTS: Leviya, Shelavya.

Clayton A variant form of Clay, meaning "town built upon clay." HEBREW EQUIVALENTS: Adam, Admata, Artza. FEMININE HEBREW EQUIVALENTS: Adama, Artzit, Eretz. *See* Clay.

Clem A pet form of Clement. *See* Clement.

Clement From the Latin, meaning "merciful" or "gracious." HEBREW EQUIVALENTS: Amichen, Chanan, Choni. FEMININE HEBREW EQUIVALENTS: Adiva, Chana, Chanita.

Clemmons A variant form of Clement. *See* Clement.

Clemon A variant form of Clement. *See* Clement.

Cleo A variant spelling of Clio. *See* Clio.

Cleon A variant form of Clio. *See* Clio.

Cleve A pet form of Cleveland. *See* Cleveland.

Cleveland From the Old English, meaning "land near a steep waterfall." HEBREW EQUIVALENTS: Afek, Arnon, Aviyam. FEMININE HEBREW EQUIVALENTS: Afeka, Eretz, Miryam.

Clever From the Old English, meaning "claw, hand." HEBREW EQUIVALENTS: Chofni, Yeda'ya.

Cliff, Cliffe From the Old English, meaning "steep, bank." HEBREW EQUIVALENTS: Givon, Givton, Talmai. FEMININE HEBREW EQUIVALENTS: Gali, Galit, Givona.

Clifford An English local name meaning "ford" or "crossing near the cliff." HEBREW EQUIVALENTS: Aharon, Talmai, Telem. FEMININE HEBREW EQUIVALENTS: Gali, Migdala, Timora.

Clifton From the Old English, meaning "town near the cliff." HEBREW EQUIVALENTS: Givon, Karmel, Tzuri. FEMININE HEBREW EQUIVALENTS: Givona, Karmela, Ritzpa.

Clint A pet form of Clinton. See Clinton.

Clinton From the Anglo-Saxon, meaning "town on a hill." HEBREW EQUIVALENTS: Aharon, Talmai, Talman. FEMININE HEBREW EQUIVALENTS: Aharona, Givona, Talma.

Clio From the Greek, meaning "to praise, to acclaim." HEBREW EQUIVALENTS: Hillel, Shevach, Yehuda. FEMININE HEBREW EQUIVALENTS: Hila, Hilana, Hillela.

Clive A variant form of Cliff. See Cliff.

Clovis From the Anglo-Saxon and German, meaning "clover." HEBREW EQUIVALENTS: Chavakuk, Rotem, Shatul. FEMININE HEBREW EQUIVALENTS: Chelmit, Chelmonit, Dalya.

Clyde From the Welsh, meaning "heard from afar." HEBREW EQUIVALENTS: Shemu'el, Shimi, Shimon. FEMININE HEBREW EQUIVALENTS: Kashuva, Shemu'ela, Shimat.

Clydell A variant form of Clyde. See Clyde.

Cobe, Cobi, Coby Variant spellings of Kobe. See Kobe.

Cochav, Cokhav Variant spellings of Kochav. See Kochav.

Cody From the Old English, meaning "pillow, cushion, comforter." HEBREW EQUIVALENTS: Latif, Menachem, Nachman. FEMININE HEBREW EQUIVALENTS: Nachmanit, Nechama, Ruchama.

Colby From the Old English and Danish, meaning "coal town." The Hebrew equivalent is Rishpon. FEMININE HEBREW EQUIVALENTS: Rishpa, Rishpona, Ritzpa.

Cole A pet form of Colby or Coleman. See Colby and Coleman.

Coleman Either from the Latin, meaning "dove"; the Icelandic, meaning "chief"; or the Middle English, meaning "charcoal maker" or "cabbage farmer." HEBREW EQUIVALENTS: Elimelech, Katri'el, Melech, Yona. FEMININE HEBREW EQUIVALENTS: Malka, Yemima, Yonina.

Colin Usually taken as a pet form of Nicholas, meaning "victory." Or, from the Celtic, meaning "cub, whelp." Some authorities describe it as a variant form of Coleman. *See* Coleman. HEBREW EQUIVALENTS: Ben-Guryon, Gover, Kefir. FEMININE HEBREW EQUIVALENTS: Kefira, Levi'a, Nitzcha.

Colvin From the Middle English, meaning "coal miner." The Hebrew equivalent is Rishpon. FEMININE HEBREW EQUIVALENTS: Rishpa, Rishpona, Ritzpa.

Conan, Conant From the Middle English, meaning "to be able" or "to be knowledgeable." Also, from the Celtic, meaning "chief, king." HEBREW EQUIVALENTS: Chashmon, Katri'el, Malki'el. FEMININE HEBREW EQUIVALENTS: Alufa, Gevira, Nevona.

Conrad From the Old High German, meaning "able counsellor." HEBREW EQUIVALENTS: Aleksander, Chachmoni, Eli'ezer. FEMININE HEBREW EQUIVALENTS: Aleksandra, Buna, Chochma.

Cook, Cooke, Cookie, Cooky From the Middle English, meaning "to cook, prepare food." The exact Hebrew equivalent is Ofeh. FEMININE HEBREW EQUIVALENTS: Uga, Ugit.

Cooper From the Latin, meaning "one who makes barrels and containers." HEBREW EQUIVALENTS: Akiva, Akuv, Yeho'achaz. The feminine equivalent is Akuva.

Corbet, Corbett From the Old French and the Middle English, meaning "raven." The exact Hebrew equivalent is Orev. FEMININE HEBREW EQUIVALENTS: Chagla, Da'ya, Efrona.

Corbin A variant form of Corbet. *See* Corbet.

Cord A pet form of Cordell. *See* Cordell.

Cordell From the Latin and Old French, meaning "cord, rope." The Hebrew equivalent is Petil. The feminine equivalent is Petila.

Corey A variant spelling of Cory. *See* Cory.

Corliss A variant form of Carl. *See* Carl.

Cornelius From the Norman-French, meaning "crow," or from the Latin, meaning "horn of the sun," a symbol of kingship and long life. HEBREW EQUIVALENTS: Cha'yim, Katri'el, Melech. FEMININE HEBREW EQUIVALENTS: Shekeda, Shikmona, Yechi'ela.

Cornell A French form of Cornelius. *See* Cornelius.

Corwin, Corwyn From the Latin, meaning "raven," and the Old English, meaning "friend, companion." HEBREW EQUIVALENTS: David, Orev, Yedid. FEMININE HEBREW EQUIVALENTS: Ahava, Davida.

Cory From the Latin, meaning "helmet," or from the Anglo-Saxon, meaning "chosen one." HEBREW EQUIVALENTS: Nivchar, Yivchar. FEMININE HEBREW EQUIVALENTS: Bara, Ila, Nivcheret.

Cosmo From the Greek, meaning "universe" and "order, peace, harmony." HEBREW EQUIVALENTS: Cheldai, Cheled, Sadir. FEMININE HEBREW EQUIVALENTS: Sedira, Shulamit, Sidra.

Craig From the Celtic and Gaelic, meaning "from the crag [rugged, rocky mass]." HEBREW EQUIVALENTS: Avitzur, Avni'el, Sela. FEMININE HEBREW EQUIVALENTS: Ritzpa, Tzurit, Tzuriya.

Crawford From the Old English, meaning "ford or stream where the crows flock." HEBREW EQUIVALENTS: Arnon, B'eri, Enan. FEMININE HEBREW EQUIVALENTS: Chasida, Dalia, Devora.

Cristofer, Cristopher Alternate spellings of Christopher. *See* Christopher.

Curt A pet form of Curtis. *See* Curtis. Kurt is a variant spelling.

Curtis From the Old French, meaning "courteous, polite" or "educated man." HEBREW EQUIVALENTS: Adiv, Chanoch, Maskil. FEMININE HEBREW EQUIVALENTS: Adiva, Na'amiya, Ne'ima.

Cy A pet form of Cyrus. *See* Cyrus.

Cyril From the Greek, meaning "lord, lordly." HEBREW EQUIVALENTS: Avimelech, Avraham, Katri'el. FEMININE HEBREW EQUIVALENTS: Alufa, Be'ula, Gevira.

Cyrus (כּוֹרֶשׁ) From the Persian, meaning "sun, brightness." The masculine Hebrew equivalent is Koresh. FEMININE HEBREW EQUIVALENTS: Chamaniya, Me'ira, Ora. In II Chronicles 36:22, the king of Persia who befriended the Jews.

~ D ~

Dab A variant form of David. *See* David.

Dabbey, Dabby A variant form of David. *See* David.

Dabney A variant form of David. *See* David.

Dael (דְעָאֵל) From the Hebrew, meaning "knowledge of God." The exact Hebrew equivalent is Da'el. FEMININE HEBREW EQUIVALENTS: De'a, De'uela, Dati'ela.

Dag (דָג) From the Danish and German, meaning "day." Also, from the Hebrew, meaning "fish." The exact Hebrew equivalent is Dag. FEMININE HEBREW EQUIVALENTS: Dagit, Dagiya, Yemu'ela.

Dagan (דָגָן) A unisex name. From the Hebrew, meaning "grain." The exact Hebrew equivalent is Dagan.

Daglan (דַגְלָן) From the Hebrew, meaning "flag carrier." The exact Hebrew equivalent is Daglan. The feminine Hebrew equivalent is Dagal.

Dagobert From the German, meaning "bright day." HEBREW EQUIVALENTS: Bahir, Barak, Zerachya. FEMININE HEBREW EQUIVALENTS: Behira, Me'ira, Tzelila.

Dagul (דָגוּל) From the Hebrew, meaning "flag emblem." The exact Hebrew equivalent is Dagul. FEMININE HEBREW EQUIVALENTS: Degula, Digla.

Dahn A variant spelling of Dan. *See* Dan.

Dahvid A variant spelling of David. *See* David.

Dale A unisex name. From the Old English and the Old Norse, meaning "valley." HEBREW EQUIVALENTS: Emek, Gai, Gechazi. The feminine equivalent is Ga'ya.

Daley, Daly From the Irish/Gaelic, meaning "assembly, gathering." HEBREW EQUIVALENTS: Ami'asaf, Kohelet, No'adya. FEMININE HEBREW EQUIVALENTS: Le'uma, Uma.

Dalin A variant spelling of Dallin. *See* Dallin.

Dall A variant form of Dale. *See* Dale.

Dallas From the Old English, meaning "dale, valley, hollow." HEBREW EQUIVALENTS: Guy, Gayora. Bika is a feminine equivalent.

Dallin From the Anglo-Saxon, meaning "from the dale, valley." HEBREW EQUIVALENTS: Emek, Gai, Ge'ora. Ga'ya is a feminine equivalent.

Dama (דָּמָה) From the Hebrew and Aramaic, meaning "to resemble." The exact Hebrew equivalent is Dama. FEMININE HEBREW EQUIVALENTS: Dumiya, Micha'ela, Michal.

Damon From the Latin, meaning "spirit, demon." Also, from the Danish and the Anglo-Saxon, meaning "day." HEBREW EQUIVALENTS: Aviri, Yemu'el. Yemu'ela is a feminine equivalent.

Dan (דָּן) From the Hebrew, meaning "judge." The exact Hebrew equivalent is Dan. FEMININE HEBREW EQUIVALENTS: Dana, Danit, Daniya. In Genesis 30:6, the fifth son of Jacob.

Dana A variant form of Dan. *See* Dan.

Dani A variant form of Dan or Daniel. *See* Dan *and* Daniel.

Daniel (דָּנִיאֵל) From the Hebrew, meaning "God is my judge." The exact Hebrew equivalent is Dani'el. The exact feminine equivalent is Dani'ela. In Daniel 1:6, a man selected to serve as a scribe in Nebuchadnezzar's court.

Danil, Danile, Danilo Variant forms of Daniel. *See* Daniel.

Dannie, Danny Pet forms of Daniel. *See* Daniel. Danilo is an Italian form.

Dante From the Latin, meaning "eternal, enduring, steadfast." HEBREW EQUIVALENTS: Ami'ad, Avi'ad, Nitzchi. FEMININE HEBREW EQUIVALENTS: Nitzcha, Nitzchiya, Nitzchona.

Dar (דָּר/דָּר) From the Hebrew, meaning "pearl, mother-of-pearl, marble" or "reside, sojourn." Also, from the British, meaning "oak." The exact Hebrew equivalent is Dar. FEMININE HEBREW EQUIVALENTS: Dara, Margalit, Penina.

Darbey, Darby A unisex name. From the Old English, meaning "deer meadow." HEBREW EQUIVALENTS: Ben-Tzevi, Ofer, Tzevi. FEMININE HEBREW EQUIVALENTS: Ofra, Re'eima, Tzivya.

Darcy From the Celtic, meaning "dark." HEBREW EQUIVALENTS: Adar, Chumi, Pinchas. FEMININE HEBREW EQUIVALENTS: Adara, Chachila, Laila.

Dardar (דַּרְדָּר) From the Aramaic, meaning "sticker, thorn." The exact Hebrew equivalent is Dardar. FEMININE HEBREW EQUIVALENTS: Akitza, Chochit.

Daren A variant form of Darius. *See* Darius.

Darian, Darien Variant forms of Darius. *See* Darius.

Darin, Darren Variant forms of Darius. *See* Darius.

Dario An Italian form of Darius. *See* Darius.

Darius (דָּרְיָוֶשׁ) From the Persian, meaning "king" or "rich." The Hebrew equivalent is Daryavesh. FEMININE HEBREW EQUIVALENTS: Bat-Shu'a, Negida, Yitra. In Ezra 6:3, King Darius of Persia orders the Temple in Jerusalem to be rebuilt.

Darlin From the British, meaning "grove of oak trees." HEBREW EQUIVALENTS: Alon, Armon, Elon. FEMININE HEBREW EQUIVALENTS: Alona, Ela, Elona.

Daro A variant form of Darrow. *See* Darrow.

Darold A variant form of Darrell and Darlin. *See* Darrell *and* Darlin.

Darom (דָרוֹם) From the Hebrew, meaning "south." The exact Hebrew equivalent is Darom. The exact feminine equivalent is Daroma.

Darrell From the Anglo-Saxon, meaning "dear, darling." HEBREW EQUIVALENTS: David, Dodi, Eldad. FEMININE HEBREW EQUIVALENTS: Davida, Doda, Yedida.

Darren, Darrin From the British, meaning "small, rocky hill." HEBREW EQUIVALENTS: Aharon, Chagai, Gal. FEMININE HEBREW EQUIVALENTS: Aharona, Gal, Gali.

Darrol, Darroll Variant forms of Darrell. *See* Darrell.

Darrow From the Old English, meaning "spear." HEBREW EQUIVALENTS: Sirya, Siryon. FEMININE HEBREW EQUIVALENTS: Chanit, Chinit, Moran.

Darry A pet form of Darren. *See* Darren. Also, from the French, meaning "from Harry." *See* Harry.

Darryl A variant form of Darren. *See* Darren.

Darwin From the British and Anglo-Saxon, meaning "lover of the sea." HEBREW EQUIVALENTS: Avigal, Aviyam, Dalfon. FEMININE HEBREW EQUIVALENTS: Bat-Galim, Bat-Yam, Miryam.

Dary A pet form of Daryl. *See* Daryl.

Daryl, Daryle Variant spellings of Darrell. *See* Darrell.

Datan (דָתָן) From the Hebrew, meaning "law, judgment." The exact Hebrew equivalent is Datan. FEMININE HEBREW EQUIVALENTS: Dati, Dina, Nadin. In Numbers 16:1, a conspirator who opposed Moses.

Dathan The Anglicized form of Datan. *See* Datan.

Daud The Arabic form of David. *See* David.

Dave A pet form of David. *See* David.

Davey A pet form of David. *See* David.

Davi A pet form of David. *See* David. Used also as a feminine name.

David (דָוִד) From the Hebrew, meaning "beloved." The exact Hebrew equivalent is David. The exact feminine equivalent is Davida. In I Samuel 17:12, the second king of Israel.

Davie A pet form of David. *See* David.

Daviel (דָּוִיאֵל) A variant form of David. *See* David. The exact Hebrew equivalent is Davi'el.

Davis A patronymic form of David, meaning "son of David." *See* David.

Davy A pet form of David. *See* David.

Davyd A variant spelling of David. *See* David.

Daw, Dawe From the Old English, meaning "doe." HEBREW EQUIVALENTS: Ayal, Efer, Efron, Ofar, Tzevi. FEMININE HEBREW EQUIVALENTS: A'yala, A'yelet, Tzivya. Also, a variant form of David. *See* David.

Dawson A patronymic form of David, meaning "son of David." *See* David.

Dawud The Arabic form of David. *See* David.

Dayan From the Hebrew, meaning "lawyer" or "judge." HEBREW EQUIVALENTS: Da'yan, Datan, Dati'el. FEMININE HEBREW EQUIVALENTS: Nadan, Nadin.

Dean, Deane A unisex name. From the Old French, meaning "head, leader." HEBREW EQUIVALENTS: Chanoch, Rabi, Rosh, Tana. FEMININE HEBREW EQUIVALENTS: Mori'el, Morit, Moriya, Rishona.

Dee A pet form of Dean. *See* Dean.

Degel (דֶּגֶל) From the Hebrew, meaning "flag" or "staff." The exact Hebrew equivalent is Degel. The exact feminine equivalent is Dagal.

Dekel (דֶּקֶל) From the Arabic and Hebrew, meaning "palm [date] tree." The exact Hebrew equivalent is Dekel. FEMININE HEBREW EQUIVALENTS: Dikla, Diklit.

Delano From the Old French, meaning "of the night," or from the Erse, meaning "healthy, dark man." HEBREW EQUIVALENTS: Adar, Chachalya, Chumi, Kedar, Pinchas. FEMININE HEBREW EQUIVALENTS: Adara, Efa, Laila, Layli, Tzila.

Delbert From the Old English, meaning "bright day." HEBREW EQUIVA-

LENTS: Bahir, Barak, Zerachya. FEMININE HEBREW EQUIVALENTS: Behira, Me'ira, Tzelila.

Delmor, Delmore From the Old French, meaning "of the sea." HEBREW EQUIVALENTS: Avigal, Aviyam, Yam. FEMININE HEBREW EQUIVALENTS: Bat-Galim, Bat-Yam, Yamit.

Demetrius From the Greek, meaning "lover of the earth." HEBREW EQUIVALENTS: Adam, Adamata, Artza, David, Regev. FEMININE HEBREW EQUIVALENTS: Adama, Ahuva, Chiba, Davida, Eretz.

Denis The French form of the Latin and Greek name Dionysius. In Greek mythology, the god of wine and revelry. HEBREW EQUIVALENTS: Anav, Efra'yim, Gefen, Karmel, Pura, Tzemach. FEMININE HEBREW EQUIVALENTS: Anava, Bikura, Gita, Gitit, Zimra.

Dennis A variant spelling of Denis. *See* Denis.

Deno An Italian form of Dean. *See* Dean.

Denys A variant spelling of Denis. *See* Denis.

Derek An English form of the Old High German name Hrodrich, meaning "famous." HEBREW EQUIVALENTS: Achimelech, Adoniya, El-rad, Katri'el, Melech, Nadav. FEMININE HEBREW EQUIVALENTS: Atara, Be'ula, Gevira, Nediva, Yisra'ela.

Derel A variant form of Darlin. *See* Darlin.

Deror (דְּרוֹר) A unisex name. From the Hebrew, meaning "bird [swallow]" or "free, freedom." The exact Hebrew equivalent is Deror.

Derori (דְּרוֹרִי) A variant form of Deror. The exact Hebrew equivalent is Derori. The exact feminine equivalent is Derorit.

Derorli, Deror-Li (דְּרוֹר-לִי/דְּרוֹרלִי) From the Hebrew, meaning "I am free." The exact Hebrew equivalent is Derorli. FEMININE HEBREW EQUIVALENTS: Derora, Derorit, Derorya.

Derrek, Derrick, Derrik, Derryk Variant spellings of Derek. *See* Derek.

Derry From the British, meaning "oak tree." The Hebrew equivalent is Alon. The feminine equivalent is Alona.

Desi A pet form of Desiderio. *See* Desiderio.

Desiderio From the Latin, meaning "desire." HEBREW EQUIVALENTS: Chamadel, Chamadya, Chemdan. FEMININE HEBREW EQUIVALENTS: Chamuda, Cheftzi-Ba, Chemda.

Desmond From the French and Latin, meaning "world" or "mankind." HEBREW EQUIVALENTS: Cheldai, Cheled, Enosh. FEMININE HEBREW EQUIVALENTS: Adama, Gavri'ela.

Deuel (דְעוּאֵל) From the Hebrew, meaning "knowledge of God." The exact Hebrew equivalent is De'uel. The exact feminine equivalent is De'uela.

Devin A variant spelling of Devon. *See* Devon.

Devir (דְבִיר) A unisex name. From the Hebrew, meaning "innermost room" or "sanctuary." The exact Hebrew equivalent is Devir.

Devlin From the Irish/Gaelic, meaning "extremely courageous." HEBREW EQUIVALENTS: Abir, Abiri, No'az. FEMININE HEBREW EQUIVALENTS: No'aza, Odeda.

Devon A unisex name. From the Gaelic, meaning "bard, poet." Pi'ut is the Hebrew equivalent. The feminine equivalent is Pi'uta.

Dewey A Welsh form of David. *See* David.

Dexter From the Latin, meaning "right, to the right." HEBREW EQUIVALENTS: Binyamin, Teman, Yamin. FEMININE HEBREW EQUIVALENTS: Binyamina, Yemina, Yimna.

Diamond From the Latin and Greek, meaning "precious stone." HEBREW EQUIVALENTS: Chamadel, Chamud, Chemed. FEMININE HEBREW EQUIVALENTS: Bareket, Chamuda, Kevuda.

Dick, Dickey, Dickie, Dicky Pet forms of Richard. *See* Richard.

Didi (דִידִי) From the Hebrew, meaning "beloved." A pet form of Yedidya. The exact Hebrew equivalent is Didi. FEMININE HEBREW EQUIVALENTS: Davida, Yedida.

Diego A Spanish form of Jacob or James. *See* Jacob *and* James.

Dietrich A variant form of Derek. *See* Derek.

Dimitry A variant form of Demetrius. *See* Demetrius.

Din (דִּין) From the Hebrew, meaning "law." The exact Hebrew equivalent is Din. FEMININE HEBREW EQUIVALENTS: Nadan, Nadin.

Dion, Dione, Dionne Variant forms of Dionysius, the Greek god of wine. HEBREW EQUIVALENTS: Gefanya, Giti, Sava. FEMININE HEBREW EQUIVALENTS: Gat, Gita, Gitit.

Dir (דִּיר) From the Hebrew, meaning "dwelling, shed" or "sheep pen." The exact Hebrew equivalent is Dir. The exact feminine equivalent is Dira.

Dirk An English form of the Old High German name Hrodrich, meaning "famous." HEBREW EQUIVALENTS: Hillel, Noda, Shevach. FEMININE HEBREW EQUIVALENTS: Degula, Hillela, Shavcha, Tehila, Yehudit, Yudit.

Divri (דִּבְרִי) From the Hebrew, meaning "orator." The exact Hebrew equivalent is Divri. FEMININE HEBREW EQUIVALENTS: Amira, Dovevet.

Dix A patronymic form of Dick, meaning "Dick's son." A pet form of Richard. *See* Richard.

Dixie A pet form of Dix. *See* Dix.

Dixon A patronymic form of Richard, meaning "Richard's [Dick's] son." *See* Richard.

Dob A variant form of Robert. *See* Robert.

Dodi From the Hebrew, meaning "my friend, my uncle." A variant form of Dodo. *See* Dodo.

Dodic, Dodick Pet forms of David. *See* David.

Dodo (דּוֹדוֹ) From the Hebrew meaning "his beloved" or "his uncle." The exact Hebrew equivalent is Dodo. The exact feminine equivalent is Doda.

Doeg (דֹּאֵג) From the Hebrew, meaning "anxious, concerned." The exact Hebrew equivalent is Do'eg. FEMININE HEBREW EQUIVALENTS: Letifa, Rachmi'ela, Ruchama.

Dolph A short form of Adolph. *See* Adolph.

Dom A pet form of Dominic. *See* Dominic.

Dominic, Dominick From the Latin, meaning "pertaining to God." HEBREW EQUIVALENTS: Ami'el, Dani'el, De'uel. FEMININE HEBREW EQUIVALENTS: Dani'ela, Michal, Yisra'ela.

Don A pet form of Donald. *See* Donald.

Donald From the Irish, meaning "brown stranger." Also, from the Celtic and Scottish, meaning "proud ruler." HEBREW EQUIVALENTS: Adoniya, Avinadav, Gershom. FEMININE HEBREW EQUIVALENTS: Atara, Be'ula, Gevira.

Donnie, Donny Pet forms of Donald. *See* Donald.

Donniel A variant form of Daniel. *See* Daniel.

Dor (דּוֹר) From the Hebrew, meaning "generation." Also, a French name derived from the Latin, meaning "of gold." The exact Hebrew equivalent is Dor. The exact feminine equivalent is Dorit.

Doran (דּוֹרָן) From the Hebrew and Greek, meaning "gift." *See* Doron. The exact Hebrew equivalent is Doran.

Dore From the Greek, meaning "gift." Also, a short form of Isidore. *See* Isidore. HEBREW EQUIVALENTS: Doran, Doron, Doroni. FEMININE HEBREW EQUIVALENTS: Dorina, Doriya, Dorona.

Dori (דּוֹרִי) A variant form of Dor, meaning "my generation." The exact Hebrew equivalent is Dori. The exact feminine equivalent is Dorit.

Dorian A Greek place-name, derived from Doris. *See* Doris (*feminine section*).

Doron (דּוֹרוֹן) From the Hebrew, meaning "gift, present." The exact Hebrew equivalent is Doron. FEMININE HEBREW EQUIVALENTS: Dorina, Doriya, Dorona.

Dorris The masculine form of the feminine name Doris. *See* Doris (*feminine section*).

Dotan (דּוֹתָן) A unisex name. From the Hebrew, meaning "law." The exact Hebrew equivalent is Dotan.

Dothan An Anglicized form of Dotan. *See* Dotan.

Doug A pet form of Douglas. *See* Douglas.

Douglas From the Celtic, meaning "gray." Also, from the Gaelic, meaning "black stream." HEBREW EQUIVALENTS: Adar, Aviyam, Aynan. FEMININE HEBREW EQUIVALENTS: Adara, Devora, Laila.

Dov (דוֹב) From the Hebrew, meaning "bear." The exact Hebrew equivalent is Dov. The exact feminine equivalent is Duba.

Dover (דוֹבֵר) From the Hebrew, meaning "speaker, spokesman." The exact Hebrew equivalent is Doveir. FEMININE HEBREW EQUIVALENTS: Amira, Doveva, Neva.

Dovev (דוֹבֵב) From the Hebrew, meaning "to speak, whisper." The exact Hebrew equivalent is Dovev. FEMININE HEBREW EQUIVALENTS: Doveva, Dovevit.

Dovid A variant spelling of David. *See* David.

Drew A unisex name. A short form of Andrew. *See* Andrew.

Dror A variant form of Deror. *See* Deror.

Drori A variant spelling of Derori. *See* Derori.

Dru A variant spelling of Drew. *See* Drew.

Duane From the Gaelic, meaning "dark, black." HEBREW EQUIVALENTS: Ashchur, Cham, Pinchas. FEMININE HEBREW EQUIVALENTS: Adara, Chama, Shechora.

Dubi (דוּבִּי) From the Hebrew, meaning "my bear." The exact Hebrew equivalent is Dubi. FEMININE HEBREW EQUIVALENTS: Duba, Dubit.

Dudi (דוּדִי) A variant form of Dudu. *See* Dudu.

Dudley From the Old English, meaning "Dodd's meadow [lea]" or "Duda's meadow." HEBREW EQUIVALENTS: Adam, Admata, Artza. FEMININE HEBREW EQUIVALENTS: Adama, Gana, Karmel.

Dudu (דוּדוּ) A pet form of David. *See* David. The exact Hebrew equivalent is Dudu.

Duff From the Celtic, meaning "dark, black-faced." HEBREW EQUIVA-

LENTS: Chumi, Kedar, Pinchas. FEMININE HEBREW EQUIVALENTS: Chachila, Laila, Tzila.

Duke From the Latin, meaning "leader." HEBREW EQUIVALENTS: Avraham, Raba, Rav. FEMININE HEBREW EQUIVALENTS: Alufa, Sara, Tzameret.

Duma (דּוּמָה) From the Hebrew, meaning "silence." The exact Hebrew equivalent is Duma. The exact feminine equivalent is Dumit.

Duncan From the Celtic, meaning "warrior with dark skin." HEBREW EQUIVALENTS: Adar, Chumi, Gavri'el. FEMININE HEBREW EQUIVALENTS: Adara, Chachila, Gavri'ela.

Dunn, Dunne From the Old English, meaning "brown." HEBREW EQUIVALENTS: Chum, Chumi. FEMININE HEBREW EQUIVALENTS: Chum, Chuma, Chumit.

Dunstan From the Old English, meaning "brown, rock quarry." HEBREW EQUIVALENTS: Chum, Chumi, Etan. FEMININE HEBREW EQUIVALENTS: Chum, Chumit, Etana.

Dur (דּוּר) From the Hebrew, meaning "to heap, pile up" or "to circle." Also, from the Old English, meaning "wild animal, deer." The exact Hebrew equivalent is Dur. FEMININE EQUIVALENTS: Bat-Galim, Talmit, Tzivya.

Durand The French form of the Latin, meaning "enduring." HEBREW EQUIVALENTS: Notzer, Oved, Shemaryahu. FEMININE HEBREW EQUIVALENTS: Notera, Noteret, Shimriya.

Durant, Durante Variant Italian forms of Durand. *See* Durand.

Duriel (דּוּרִיאֵל) From the Hebrew, meaning "God is my dwelling place." The exact Hebrew equivalent is Duri'el. FEMININE HEBREW EQUIVALENTS: Devira, Me'ona, Shafrira.

Durk A variant spelling of Dirk. *See* Dirk.

Duryea From the Latin, meaning "enduring, eternal." HEBREW EQUIVALENTS: Ami'ad, Netzach, Nitzchi. FEMININE HEBREW EQUIVALENTS: Chava, Cha'ya, Nitzchiya.

Dustin A variant form of Dunstan. *See* Dunstan.

Dusty A pet form of Dustin. *See* Dustin.

Duv A variant form of Dov. *See* Dov.

Dvir A variant spelling of Devir. *See* Devir.

Dwayne A variant spelling of Duane. *See* Duane. Also, a variant form of Wayne. *See* Wayne.

Dwight From the Anglo-Saxon, meaning "white, fair." HEBREW EQUIVALENTS: Ben-Chur, Churi, Lavan, Levanon, Livni. FEMININE HEBREW EQUIVALENTS: Levana, Levona, Tzechora.

Dyck A variant spelling of Dick. *See* Dick.

Dyke, Dykes Variant spellings of Dick and Dix. *See* Dick *and* Dix.

Dylan From the Welsh, meaning "sea." HEBREW EQUIVALENTS: Aviyam, Ma'ayan, Moshe. FEMININE HEBREW EQUIVALENTS: Michal, Miryam, Rut.

❧ E ❧

Earl, Earle From the Middle English, meaning "nobleman, well-bred, intelligent." HEBREW EQUIVALENTS: Achban, Buna, Maskil. FEMININE HEBREW EQUIVALENTS: Bina, Milka, Ne'ora.

Eban A variant form of Even. *See* Even.

Eben A variant spelling of Even. *See* Even.

Ebenezer The Anglicized form of Evenezer. *See* Evenezer.

Ebin A variant form of Even. *See* Even.

Ebril (עֶבְרִיל) A Yiddish form of Abraham. *See* Abraham.

Ed A pet form of Edward. *See* Edward.

Edan From the Celtic, meaning "fire, flame." HEBREW EQUIVALENTS: Lapid, Nur, Nuri. FEMININE HEBREW EQUIVALENTS: Avuka, Shalhevet, Urit.

Edd A pet form of Edward. *See* Edward.

Eddie A pet form of Edward. *See* Edward.

Eddy From the Middle English, meaning "whirlpool" or "energetic." HEBREW EQUIVALENTS: Arnon, Yaziz, Ziva. FEMININE HEBREW EQUIVALENTS: Charutza, Tirtza, Zeriza. Also, a pet form of Edward. *See* Edward.

Edel From the Old German, meaning "noble." HEBREW EQUIVALENTS: Adon, Ish-Hod, Nadiva. FEMININE HEBREW EQUIVALENTS: Adina, Nediva, Ne'edara.

Eden (עֵדֶן) A unisex name. Akin to Adina. From the Hebrew, meaning "pleasure, delight, paradise." The exact Hebrew equivalent is Eiden (Ayden). ADDITIONAL HEBREW EQUIVALENTS: Adin, Adiv, Na'im. The Garden of Eden is mentioned in Genesis 2:10. In II Chronicles 29:12, a Levite during the reign of King Hezekiah.

Eder (עֵדֶר) A unisex name. From the Hebrew, meaning "herd, flock." The exact Hebrew equivalent is Eder.

Edgar From the Anglo-Saxon, meaning "happy, blessed warrior." HEBREW EQUIVALENTS: Baruch, Gad, Gavri'el. FEMININE HEBREW EQUIVALENTS: Avicha'yil, Gibora, Gila.

Edison A patronymic form, meaning "son of Ed [Edward]." *See* Edward.

Edlow From the Old English, meaning "fruitful hill." HEBREW EQUIVALENTS: Bar-Ilan, Efra'yim, Merom. FEMININE HEBREW EQUIVALENTS: Gal, Givona, Pora.

Edmond From the Anglo-Saxon, meaning "rich, fortunate" or "happy warrior or protector." HEBREW EQUIVALENTS: Asher, Ashir, Gad. FEMININE HEBREW EQUIVALENTS: Ashera, Ashira, Gada.

Edmund A variant spelling of Edmond. *See* Edmond.

Edri (עֶדְרִי) From the Hebrew, meaning "my flock." The exact Hebrew equivalent is Edri. The feminine equivalent is Eder.

Edric From the Anglo-Saxon, meaning "rich ruler." HEBREW EQUIVALENTS: Aluf, Ba'al, Elrad. FEMININE HEBREW EQUIVALENTS: Sara, Sarit, Yisra'ela.

Edsel From the Anglo-Saxon, meaning "rich, prosperous." HEBREW EQUIVALENTS: Ashir, Hotir, Huna. FEMININE HEBREW EQUIVALENTS: Ashira, Yitra.

Edson A patronymic form, meaning "son of Ed [Edward]." *See* Edward.

Eduard A Spanish form of Edward. *See* Edward.

Edward From the Anglo-Saxon, meaning "blessed, happy guardian." HEBREW EQUIVALENTS: Avigdor, Mishmar, Noter. FEMININE HEBREW EQUIVALENTS: Efrat, Migdala, Notera.

Edwin   From the Anglo-Saxon, meaning "happy, blessed friend." HE-BREW EQUIVALENTS: Asher, Chovav, David. FEMININE HEBREW EQUIVALENTS: Doda, Liba, Yedida.

Edy   A variant spelling of Eddy. *See* Eddy.

Effi, Effie   (אֶפִּי)   Pet forms of Efrayim. *See* Efrayim.

Efod, Eifod   (אֵפֹד)   The name of a garment worn by the High Priest. From the Akkadian, meaning "garment, vest." The exact Hebrew equivalent is Eifod. FEMININE HEBREW EQUIVALENTS: Gelima, Salma. In Numbers 34:23, a member of the tribe of Manasseh.

Efraim   A variant spelling of Efrayim. *See* Efrayim.

Efrat   (אֶפְרָת)   A unisex name. From the Hebrew, meaning "honored, distinguished" or "fruitful." Also, from the Aramaic, meaning "mantle, turban." The exact Hebrew equivalent is Efrat. Akin to Efrayim.

Efrayim   (אֶפְרַיִם)   From the Hebrew, meaning "fruitful." The exact Hebrew equivalent is Efra'yim. FEMININE HEBREW EQUIVALENTS: Nitza, Pora, Poriya. In Genesis 41:52, the second son of Joseph.

Efrem   A unisex name. A variant form of Efrayim. *See* Efrayim.

Efron   (עֶפְרוֹן)   From the Hebrew, meaning "bird." The exact Hebrew equivalent is Efron. The exact feminine equivalent is Efrona.

Efry   A pet form of Efrayim. *See* Efrayim.

Egan   From the Anglo-Saxon, meaning "formidable, strong." HEBREW EQUIVALENTS: Gavri'el, Gever, Gibor. FEMININE HEBREW EQUIVALENTS: Gavri'ela, Gibora, Uzi'ela.

Egged   (אֶגֶד)   From the Hebrew, meaning "binding" or "association." The exact Hebrew equivalent is Egged. FEMININE HEBREW EQUIVALENTS: Aguda, Retem, Rivka.

Egon   A variant spelling of Egan. *See* Egan.

Egoz   (אֱגוֹז)   From the Hebrew, meaning "nut." The exact Hebrew equivalent is Egoz. The exact feminine equivalent is Egoza.

Ehud, Eihud   (אֵהוּד)   From the Hebrew, meaning "pleasant, beloved." The exact Hebrew equivalent is Eihud. FEMININE HEBREW EQUIVALENTS:

Adina, Ahuva, Davida. In I Chronicles 7:10, a leader of the tribe of Benjamin.

Eila, Eilah (אֵלָה) A unisex name. From the Hebrew, meaning "oak tree, terebinth tree." The exact Hebrew equivalent is Eila (Ayla).

Eilon A variant spelling of Elon. *See* Elon.

Eiphod An alternate spelling of Eifod. *See* Eifod.

Eiran A variant spelling of Eran. *See* Eran.

Eish A variant spelling of Esh. *See* Esh.

Eitan (אֵיתָן) From the Hebrew, meaning "strong, firm, permanent." The exact Hebrew equivalent is Eitan. The exact feminine equivalent is Etana. In I Chronicles 2:6, a grandson of Jacob.

Elad (אֶלְעָד) From the Hebrew, meaning "forever, eternal." The exact Hebrew equivalent is Elad. The exact feminine equivalent is Elada.

Elan A variant spelling of Ilan. *See* Ilan. Also, from the British, meaning "young deer." HEBREW EQUIVALENTS: A'yal, A'yalon, Efer. FEMININE HEBREW EQUIVALENTS: A'yala, A'yelet, Ofra.

Elazar (אֶלְעָזָר) From the Hebrew, meaning "God has helped." The exact Hebrew equivalent is Elazar. FEMININE HEBREW EQUIVALENTS: Azri'ela, Ezra, Ezr'ela. In Exodus 6:23, a son of Aaron.

Elbert A variant form of Albert. *See* Albert.

Elbie A pet form of Elbert. *See* Elbert.

Elchanan, Elchonon (אֶלְחָנָן) From the Hebrew, meaning "God is merciful." The exact Hebrew equivalent is Elchanan. FEMININE HEBREW EQUIVALENTS: Ruchama, Yeruchama. In II Samuel 21:19, a warrior in King David's army who slew the brother of Goliath.

Eldad (אֶלְדָּד) From the Hebrew, meaning "beloved of God." The exact Hebrew equivalent is Eldad. FEMININE HEBREW EQUIVALENTS: Amita, Chaviva, Davida. In Numbers 11:26, a person who prophesied.

Eldar (אֶלְדָּר) From the Hebrew, meaning "habitation of God." The exact Hebrew equivalent is Eldar. FEMININE HEBREW EQUIVALENTS: Devira, Me'ona, Zevula.

Elden From the Anglo-Saxon, meaning "older." HEBREW EQUIVALENTS: Kadmi'el, Kedem, Saba. FEMININE HEBREW EQUIVALENTS: Bilha, Yeshisha, Zekena.

Elder From the Old English, meaning "old, older." *See also* Elden.

Eleazar (אֶלְעָזָר) A variant spelling of Eliezer. *See* Eliezer.

Elem (עֶלֶם) From the Hebrew, meaning "youngster." The exact Hebrew equivalent is Elem. Alma is a feminine equivalent.

Elex A variant form of Alex. *See* Alex.

Elford From the Old English, meaning "old river crossing." HEBREW EQUIVALENTS: Aviyam, Chamat, Dalfon. FEMININE HEBREW EQUIVALENTS: Afeka, Bat-Yam, Miryam.

Elgin From the Old English, meaning "true nobility." HEBREW EQUIVALENTS: Adon, Aminadav, Nadav. FEMININE HEBREW EQUIVALENTS: Adina, Adira, Matrona.

Elhanan The Anglicized spelling of Elchanan. *See* Elchanan.

Eli (אֵלִי) From the Hebrew, meaning "ascend" or "uplift." The exact Hebrew equivalent is Eli. FEMININE HEBREW EQUIVALENTS: Aliya, Elya, Ya'el. Also, a short form of Eliyahu. *See* Eliyahu. In I Samuel 1:9, the High Priest who counseled Hannah.

Eliad (אֶלִיעַד) From the Hebrew, meaning "my God is eternal." The exact Hebrew equivalent is Eli'ad. FEMININE HEBREW EQUIVALENTS: Nitzcha, Nitzchiya, Nitzchona.

Eliada A variant spelling of Elyada. *See* Elyada.

Eliah A variant form of Eliyahu. *See* Eliyahu.

Eliahu A variant spelling of Eliyahu. *See* Eliyahu.

Eliakim A variant spelling of Elyakim. *See* Elyakim.

Eliam (אֱלִיעָם) From the Hebrew, meaning "God's people." The exact Hebrew equivalent is Eli'am. FEMININE HEBREW EQUIVALENTS: Le'uma, Le'umit, Uma. In II Samuel 11:13, the father of Bathsheba, King David's wife.

Elian A Spanish form of the Hebrew, meaning "God has answered." Also, a variant form of Elijah. *See* Elijah.

Elias The Greek form of Elijah. *See* Elijah.

Eliata (אֱלִיאָתָה) From the Hebrew, meaning "my God has come." The exact Hebrew equivalent is Eli'ata. FEMININE HEBREW EQUIVALENTS: Eliya, Imanu'ela, Yo'ela.

Eliav (אֱלִיאָב) From the Hebrew, meaning "my God is [my] Father." The exact Hebrew equivalent is Eli'av. FEMININE HEBREW EQUIVALENTS: Aviya, Avi'el, Avi'ela. In Numbers 26:8, the son of Palu of the tribe of Re'uven (Reuben).

Eliaz (אֱלִיעַז) From the Hebrew, meaning "my God is strong." The exact Hebrew equivalent is Eli'az. FEMININE HEBREW EQUIVALENTS: Azri'ela, Gamli'ela, Gavri'ela.

Elidad (אֱלִידָד) From the Hebrew, meaning "my God is a friend." The exact Hebrew equivalent is Elidad. FEMININE HEBREW EQUIVALENTS: Amit, Amita, Yedida. In Numbers 34:21, a member of the tribe of Benjamin.

Elie A form of Eliyahu. *See* Eliyahu.

Eliezer (אֱלִיעֶזֶר) A variant form of Elazar. From the Hebrew, meaning "my God has helped." The exact Hebrew equivalent is Eli'ezer. FEMININE HEBREW EQUIVALENTS: Azri'ela, Ezra, Ezri'ela. In Genesis 15:2, the steward of Abraham.

Elihu (אֱלִיהוּא) A variant form of Eliyahu. The exact Hebrew equivalent is Elihu. Akin to Eliyahu. In Job 32:2, one of Job's friends.

Elijah The Anglicized form of Eliyahu. *See* Eliyahu.

Elika A variant form of Elyakim. *See* Elyakim.

Elio A Spanish form of Elijah. *See* Elijah.

Elior (אֱלִיאוֹר) From the Hebrew, meaning "my God is light." The exact Hebrew equivalent is Eli'or. The exact feminine equivalent is Eli'ora.

Eliot A variant form of Elijah. *See* Elijah.

Eliram (אֱלִירָם) From the Hebrew, meaning "my God is mighty." The exact Hebrew equivalent is Eliram. FEMININE HEBREW EQUIVALENTS: Adira, Amtza, Ari'el.

Eliraz (אֱלִירָז) From the Hebrew, meaning "my God is joy." The exact Hebrew equivalent is Eliraz. FEMININE HEBREW EQUIVALENTS: Aliza, Ditza, Gila.

Eliseo A Spanish form of Elisha. *See* Elisha.

Elish A pet form of Elisha. *See* Elisha.

Elisha (אֱלִישָׁע) From the Hebrew meaning "my God is salvation." The exact Hebrew equivalent is Elisha. FEMININE HEBREW EQUIVALENTS: Aleksandra, Elisheva, Milka, Teshu'a. In II Kings 2:1, a disciple and successor of the prophet Elijah.

Elison A variant spelling of Ellison. *See* Ellison.

Elitzafan (אֱלִיצָפָן) From the Hebrew, meaning "God is my protector." The exact Hebrew equivalent is Elitzafan. FEMININE HEBREW EQUIVALENTS: Avigdora, Shimriya, Ya'akova. In Numbers 34:25, a member of the tribe of Zevulun (Zebulun).

Eliya A short form of Eliyahu. *See* Eliyahu.

Eliyahu (אֱלִיָהוּ) From the Hebrew, meaning "the Lord is my God." The exact Hebrew equivalent is Eliyahu. FEMININE HEBREW EQUIVALENTS: Avi'ela, Aviya, Elisheva. In I Kings 17:1, the prophet who reprimanded King Ahab.

Elkan (אֱלְקָאן) A Yiddish form of Elkanah. *See* Elkanah.

Elkana, Elkanah (אֱלְקָנָה) From the Hebrew, meaning "God has acquired." The exact Hebrew equivalent is Elkana. Be'ula is a feminine equivalent. In Exodus 6:24, one of the sons of Korach.

Elkin (אֱלְקִין) A variant spelling of Elkan. *See* Elkan.

Ellery From the Old English, meaning "alder tree," connoting growth. HEBREW EQUIVALENTS: Erez, Ilan, Luz. FEMININE HEBREW EQUIVALENTS: Ariza, Ilana, Ilanit.

Elliot, Elliott A variant spelling of Eliot. *See* Eliot.

Ellis A variant form of Elisha. *See* Elisha.

Ellison A patronymic form, meaning "son of Elijah." *See* Elijah.

Elly A pet form of Elijah. *See* Elijah.

Elmer From the Old English, meaning "noble, famous." HEBREW EQUIVALENTS: Gedalya, Hillel, Mehalel. FEMININE HEBREW EQUIVALENTS: Devora, Hila, Hillela.

Elmo A variant form of Elmer. *See* Elmer.

Elmor, Elmore Variant forms of Elmer. *See* Elmer.

Elnatan (אֶלְנָתָן) From the Hebrew, meaning "gift of God." The exact Hebrew equivalent is Elnatan. The exact feminine equivalent is Netanela.

Elon (אֵלוֹן) A variant form of Alon. *See* Alon. In Numbers 26:26, a member of the tribe of Zevulun (Zebulun).

Elrad (אֶלְרָד) From the Hebrew, meaning "God is the ruler." The exact Hebrew equivalent is Elrad. FEMININE HEBREW EQUIVALENTS: Alufa, Atara, Be'ula.

Elroy From the Latin, meaning "royal, king." HEBREW EQUIVALENTS: Avimelech, Elrad, Malki'el. FEMININE HEBREW EQUIVALENTS: Atara, Malka, Malkit.

Elsen A patronymic form, meaning "son of Elias" or "son of Ellis." *See* Elias *and* Ellis.

Elvin From the Anglo-Saxon, meaning "godly friend." HEBREW EQUIVALENTS: David, Eldad, Yedidya. FEMININE HEBREW EQUIVALENTS: Chaviva, Davida, Liba.

Elvis From the Scandinavian, meaning "all-wise." HEBREW EQUIVALENTS: Chacham, Elyada, Navon. FEMININE HEBREW EQUIVALENTS: Bina, Da'at, Nevona.

Elwin, Elwyn Variant forms of Elvin. *See* Elvin.

Ely A pet form of Eliyahu. *See* Eli.

Elyada (אֶלְיָדָע) From the Hebrew, meaning "God knows." The exact

Hebrew equivalent is Elyada. FEMININE HEBREW EQUIVALENTS: Bina, Da'at, Dei'a. In II Samuel 5:16, one of the sons of King David.

Elyakim (אֶלְיָקִים) From the Hebrew, meaning "God will establish." The exact Hebrew equivalent is Elyakim. FEMININE HEBREW EQUIVALENTS: Komeima, Mashena, Mosada, Sa'ada. In II Kings 18:18, the son of Chilkiah, who was in charge of the king's palace.

Elyakum (אֶלְיָקוּם) A variant form of Elyakim. *See* Elyakim. The exact Hebrew equivalent is Elyakum.

Emanuel (עִמָנוּאֵל) From the Hebrew, meaning "God is with us" or "God is our protector." The exact Hebrew equivalent is Imanu'el. The exact feminine equivalent is Imanu'ela.

Emerson A patronymic form, meaning "son of Emery." *See* Emery.

Emery From the Old High German, meaning "rich in accomplishments" or "industrious." HEBREW EQUIVALENTS: Arnon, Mahir, Yaziz. FEMININE HEBREW EQUIVALENTS: Amalya, Amela, Zeriza.

Emil From the Latin, meaning "industrious." HEBREW EQUIVALENTS: Arnon, Yaziz, Ziruz. FEMININE HEBREW EQUIVALENTS: Amalya, Amela, Zeriza.

Émile A French form of Emil. *See* Emil.

Emmanuel A variant spelling of Emanuel. *See* Emanuel.

Emmet, Emmett (אֱמֶת) A unisex name. From the Hebrew, meaning "truth," or from the Anglo-Saxon, meaning "ant." The exact Hebrew equivalent is Emmet.

Emory A variant spelling of Emery. *See* Emery.

Engelbert From the Old German, meaning "bright, shining angel." HEBREW EQUIVALENTS: Bahir, Barak, Malach. FEMININE HEBREW EQUIVALENTS: Behira, Me'ira, Tzelila.

Ennis A short form of Denis. *See* Denis.

Enoch (חֲנוֹך) An Anglicized form of the Hebrew name Chanoch, meaning "educated" or "dedicated." The exact Hebrew equivalent is Chanoch. Chanukah is a feminine equivalent.

Enos A variant form of Enosh. *See* Enosh.

Enosh (אֱנוֹשׁ) From the Hebrew, meaning "man." The exact Hebrew equivalent is Enosh. FEMININE HEBREW EQUIVALENTS: Adonit, Adoniya, Gevira. In Genesis 4:26, a son of Seth.

Ephraim A variant spelling of Efrayim. *See* Efrayim.

Er (עֵר) From the Hebrew, meaning "awake" or "guardian." The exact Hebrew equivalent is Er. FEMININE HEBREW EQUIVALENTS: Era, Erana, Eranit. In Genesis 38:7, the eldest son of Judah.

Eran (עֵרָן/עֵירָן) From the Hebrew, meaning "industrious, quick-minded, awake." The exact Hebrew equivalent is Eiran. FEMININE HEBREW EQUIVALENTS: Erana, Mahir, Ziruz, Ziza. In Numbers 26:36, a son of Shutelach of the tribe of Ephraim.

Erel (אֶרְאֵל) From the Hebrew, meaning "I will see God." The exact Hebrew equivalent is Erel. The exact feminine equivalent is Erela.

Erez (אֶרֶז) A unisex name. From the Hebrew, meaning "cedar tree," suggesting youthful sturdiness. The exact Hebrew equivalent is Erez. Also, a variant spelling of Eretz.

Eri (עֵרִי) From the Hebrew, meaning "my guardian." The exact Hebrew equivalent is Eri. FEMININE HEBREW EQUIVALENTS: Mishmeret, Nitzra, Notera.

Eric, Erich From the Old Norse, meaning "honorable ruler," and from the Anglo-Saxon, meaning "brave king." HEBREW EQUIVALENTS: Elitzur, Gur, Guryon. FEMININE HEBREW EQUIVALENTS: Atara, Gavrila, Gibora.

Erik A variant spelling of Eric. *See* Eric.

Erin A unisex name. *See* Erin (*feminine section*).

Ernest From the Old High German, meaning "resolute, earnest, sincere." HEBREW EQUIVALENTS: Amnon, Avishur, Yeshurun. FEMININE HEBREW EQUIVALENTS: Berura, Tamar, Temima.

Ernesto A Spanish form of Ernest. *See* Ernest.

Ernie A pet form of Ernest. *See* Ernest.

Erno A Hungarian form of Ernest. *See* Ernest.

Ernst A variant form of Ernest. *See* Ernest.

Errol From the Latin, meaning "to wander, wanderer," having the connotation of stranger. HEBREW EQUIVALENTS: Gershom, Golyat, Sarid. FEMININE HEBREW EQUIVALENTS: Avishag, Hagar, Sarida.

Erskine From the Scottish, meaning "high cliff, mountain." HEBREW EQUIVALENTS: Aharon, Gal, Tel. FEMININE HEBREW EQUIVALENTS: Aharona, Harela, Horiya.

Erv A variant spelling of Irv (Irving). *See* Irving.

Erve A short form of Herve. *See* Herve.

Ervin A variant form of Irvin. *See* Irvin.

Erving A variant spelling of Irving. *See* Irving.

Erwin A variant form of Ervin. *See* Ervin.

Eryk A variant spelling of Eric. *See* Eric.

Eryle A variant spelling of Errol. *See* Errol.

Esh (אֵשׁ) From the Hebrew, meaning "fire." The exact Hebrew equivalent is Eish. FEMININE HEBREW EQUIVALENTS: Uri'ela, Urit.

Eshed (אֶשֶׁד) From the Hebrew, meaning "waterfall." The exact Hebrew equivalent is Eshed. FEMININE HEBREW EQUIVALENTS: Ashdoda, Miryam.

Eshel (אֶשֶׁל) From the Hebrew, meaning "tamarisk [tree]." The exact Hebrew equivalent is Eshel. FEMININE HEBREW EQUIVALENTS: Ela, Shikma, Shikmona.

Eshkol (אֶשְׁכּוֹל) From the Hebrew, meaning "cluster of grapes." The exact Hebrew equivalent is Eshkol. The exact feminine equivalent is Eshkola. In Genesis 14:13, neighbors of Abraham.

Esmé From the French, meaning "loved, to love." HEBREW EQUIVALENTS: Ahud, Ahuv, Yedidya. FEMININE HEBREW EQUIVALENTS: Ahada, Ahava, Davida.

Esmond From the Anglo-Saxon, meaning "gracious protector." HEBREW EQUIVALENTS: Betzalel, Shimri, Sitri. FEMININE HEBREW EQUIVALENTS: Cha'ya, Setura, Shimra.

Esmund A variant spelling of Esmond. *See* Esmond.

Esteban A Spanish form of Stephen. *See* Stephen.

Etan A variant spelling of Eitan. *See* Eitan.

Etgar, Etgarr (אֶתְגָּר) From the Hebrew, meaning "to challenge, battle." The exact Hebrew equivalent is Etgar. FEMININE HEBREW EQUIVALENTS: Gidona, Merav, Tigra.

Ethan An Anglicized spelling of Eitan. *See* Eitan.

Ethelbert From the Old English, meaning "high-born, shining nobility." HEBREW EQUIVALENTS: Bahir, Barak, Nadiv. FEMININE HEBREW EQUIVALENTS: Behira, Meira, Ne'edara.

Eugen A variant form of Eugene. *See* Eugene.

Eugene From the Greek, meaning "well-born, born lucky, one of noble descent." HEBREW EQUIVALENTS: Aminadav, Mazal, Mazal-Tov. FEMININE HEBREW EQUIVALENTS: Malka, Mazal, Nediva.

Evan A Welsh form of John, meaning "gracious." Also, from the Celtic, meaning "young warrior." HEBREW EQUIVALENTS: Avi-Cha'yil, Ben-Cha'yil, Gad. FEMININE HEBREW EQUIVALENTS: Chana, Gavrila, Yochana.

Evander A variant form of Evan. *See* Evan.

Evans A patronymic form of Evan. *See* Evan.

Evelyn A unisex name. *See* Evelyn (*feminine section*).

Even (אֶבֶן) From the Hebrew, meaning "stone." The exact Hebrew equivalent is Even. FEMININE HEBREW EQUIVALENTS: Avna, Avni'ela, Gazit.

Evenezer (אֶבֶן-עֶזֶר) From the Hebrew, meaning "rock of salvation." The exact Hebrew equivalent is Even'ezer. Ebenezer is the Anglicized form. FEMININE HEBREW EQUIVALENTS: Avora, Teshu'a, Tzurit.

Everett, Everette From the Anglo-Saxon, meaning "boar." Also, from the Norse, meaning "warrior." HEBREW EQUIVALENTS: Avi-Cha'yil, Ben-Cha'yil, Gad. FEMININE EQUIVALENTS: Gibora, Merav, Tigra.

Evril (עֶבְרִיל) A Yiddish form of Avraham. *See* Avraham.

Evron (עֶבְרוֹן) From the Hebrew, meaning "overflowing anger, fury." The exact Hebrew equivalent is Evron. The exact feminine equivalent is Evrona.

Evyatar (אֶבְיָתָר) From the Hebrew, meaning "father of plenty" or "father of riches." The exact Hebrew equivalent is Evyatar. FEMININE HEBREW EQUIVALENTS: Ashira, Yerusha.

Ewen Probably a variant form of Evan, the Welsh form of John. *See* Evan and John.

Eyal (אֱיָל) From the Hebrew, meaning "strength." The exact Hebrew equivalent is E'yal. FEMININE HEBREW EQUIVALENTS: Abira, Amitzya, Gavri'ela.

Eytan A variant spelling of Eitan. *See* Eitan.

Ezekiel (יְחֶזְקֵאל) From the Hebrew, meaning "God will strengthen." The exact Hebrew equivalent is Yechezkel. The exact feminine equivalent is Yechezkela. In Ezekiel 1:3, one of the three major prophets.

Ezer (עֶזֶר) From the Hebrew, meaning "help." The exact Hebrew equivalent is Ezer. FEMININE HEBREW EQUIVALENTS: Ezra, Ezr'ela, Ezri'ela.

Ezra (עֶזְרָא) Used as a unisex name in Israel. From the Hebrew, meaning "help." The exact Hebrew equivalent is Ezra. In Nehemiah 12:1, a priest who returned to Judah from exile in Babylonia.

Ezri (עֶזְרִי) From the Hebrew, meaning "my help." The exact Hebrew equivalent is Ezri. FEMININE HEBREW EQUIVALENTS: Ezra, Ezr'ela, Ezri'ela. In I Chronicles 27:26, a supervisor of King David's estate.

F

Fabian A variant form of Fabius. *See* Fabius.

Fabius From the Latin, meaning "bean, bean farmer." HEBREW EQUIVA-LENTS: Adam, Karmel, Karmeli. FEMININE HEBREW EQUIVALENTS: Eretz, Karmela, Nava.

Fairchild From the Old English, meaning "fair-haired child." HEBREW EQUIVALENTS: Lavan, Livini, Tzachar. FEMININE HEBREW EQUIVALENTS: Delila, Nima, Yuta.

Fairley A variant form of Farleigh. *See* Farleigh.

Farleigh, Farley From the Anglo-Saxon, meaning "beautiful mead-ow." HEBREW EQUIVALENTS: Adam, Bustanai, Shifron. FEMININE HEBREW EQUIVALENTS: Shadmit, Shedema, Shifra.

Farrel, Farrell From the Celtic, meaning "valorous one." HEBREW EQUIVALENTS: Abir, Abiri, Chutzpit. FEMININE HEBREW EQUIVALENTS: Abira, Avni'ela, Azi'ela.

Feibush, Feivish Variant forms of Feivel. *See* Feivel.

Feivel (פֿײװל/פֿײװעל) The Yiddish form of Phoebus. From the Latin and Greek, meaning "bright one." HEBREW EQUIVALENTS: Avner, Bahir, Barak. FEMININE HEBREW EQUIVALENTS: Behira, Me'ira, Ora.

Feiwel A variant spelling of Feivel. *See* Feivel.

Feliks A Russian form of Felix. *See* Felix.

Felipe A Spanish form of Philip. *See* Philip.

Felix From the Latin, meaning "happy, fortunate, prosperous." HEBREW EQUIVALENTS: Asher, Mazal, Osher. FEMININE HEBREW EQUIVALENTS: Ashera, Gadi'ela, Gadit.

Ferd, Ferde A short form of Ferdinand. *See* Ferdinand.

Ferdie A pet form of Ferd. *See* Ferd.

Ferdinand From the German, meaning "to be bold, courageous." HEBREW EQUIVALENTS: Amotz, Kalev, Uzi'el. FEMININE HEBREW EQUIVALENTS: Gavrila, Gibora, Uzi'ela.

Ferdy A pet form of Ferd. *See* Ferd.

Fergus From the Irish and Gaelic, meaning "manly." HEBREW EQUIVALENTS: Ben-Azai, Ben-Cha'yil, Ben-Gever. FEMININE HEBREW EQUIVALENTS: Avicha'yil, Me'uza, Nili.

Ferrin A variant form of Ferris. *See* Ferris.

Ferris From the Latin, meaning "iron," symbolizing strength. HEBREW EQUIVALENTS: Barzilai, Ben-Azai, Ben-Cha'yil. FEMININE HEBREW EQUIVALENTS: Avni'ela, Chasina, Yechezkela.

Fidel From the Latin, meaning "faithful, trustworthy." HEBREW EQUIVALENTS: Amitai, Amnon. FEMININE HEBREW EQUIVALENTS: Amana, Emuna.

Filmore, Fillmore From the Old English, meaning "very famous." HEBREW EQUIVALENTS: Noda, Shevach. The feminine Hebrew equivalent is Degula.

Finian From the Irish/Gaelic, meaning "fair, white." HEBREW EQUIVALENTS: Lavan, Livini. FEMININE HEBREW EQUIVALENTS: Livnat, Livona, Malbina.

Fish From the German, meaning "fish." HEBREW EQUIVALENTS: Dag, Nun. FEMININE HEBREW EQUIVALENTS: Dagit, Dagiya.

Fishel (פִישֶׁעל/פִישְׁל) A Yiddish pet form of Fish. *See* Fish.

Fishke (פִישְׁקֶע) A Yiddish pet form of Fish. *See* Fish.

Fishkin A Slavic form of Fish. *See* Fish.

Fishlin A pet form of Fish. *See* Fish.

Fisk, Fiske From the Scandinavian, meaning "fish." *See* Fish.

Flint, Flynt From the Old English, meaning "stream." Also, the name of a fine-grained, very hard rock, usually gray. HEBREW EQUIVALENTS: Arnan, Arnon, Yuval. FEMININE HEBREW EQUIVALENTS: Afeka, Amona, Arnonit.

Floren, Florence, Florentz, Florenz From the Latin, meaning "blooming." HEBREW EQUIVALENTS: Pekach, Pekachya, Tzemach. FEMININE HEBREW EQUIVALENTS: Atalya, Perach, Pericha.

Floyd A corrupt form of Lloyd. *See* Lloyd.

Forest From the Latin, meaning "woods." HEBREW EQUIVALENTS: Karmel, Ya'ar, Ya'ari. FEMININE HEBREW EQUIVALENTS: Gana, Karmela, Ya'ara.

Forester An Old French occupational name for one who was in charge of a forest. *See* Forest.

Forrest A variant spelling of Forest. *See* Forest.

Foster A variant form of Forester. *See* Forester.

Fox From the German, meaning "fox." The Hebrew equivalent is Shu'al. Shu'ala is the feminine equivalent.

Fraime (פְרֵיימֶע) A Yiddish pet form of Ephraim. *See* Ephraim.

Franchot A variant French form of Francis. *See* Francis.

Francis From the Middle English, meaning "a free man." HEBREW EQUIVALENTS: Deror, Deror-Li, Pesach. FEMININE HEBREW EQUIVALENTS: Chufshit, Derora, Derorit.

Frank A pet form of Francis and Franklin. *See* Francis *and* Franklin.

Frankie A pet form of Frank. *See* Frank.

Franklin From the Old English, meaning "freeholder," connoting ownership and independence. HEBREW EQUIVALENTS: Elkana, Ka'yin, Pesach. FEMININE HEBREW EQUIVALENTS: Be'ula, Devora, Ge'ula.

Franklyn A variant spelling of Franklin. *See* Franklin.

Franz The German form of Francis. *See* Francis.

Fred, Freddie, Freddy Pet forms of Frederick. *See* Frederick.

Frederic A variant spelling of Frederick. *See* Frederick.

Frederic, Fredrick Variant spellings of Frederick. *See* Frederick.

Frederick From the Latin and Old High German, meaning "peaceful ruler." HEBREW EQUIVALENTS: Avshalom, Ish-Shalom, Katri'el. FEMININE HEBREW EQUIVALENTS: Rivka, Sha'anana, Shlomit.

Freed A variant form of Freeman. *See* Freeman.

Freeman From the Anglo-Saxon, meaning "one born free." HEBREW EQUIVALENTS: Amidror, Avidror, Cherut. FEMININE HEBREW EQUIVALENTS: Derora, Li-Dror, Serach.

Fremont From the French, meaning "freedom mountain." HEBREW EQUIVALENTS: Aharon, Avidror, Chagai. FEMININE HEBREW EQUIVALENTS: Aharona, Cheruta, Derora.

Frits A variant spelling of Fritz. *See* Fritz.

Fritz A German form of Frederick. *See* Frederick.

Froim, Froime (פְּרוֹימֶע/פְּרוֹיִים) Yiddish pet forms of Ephraim. *See* Ephraim.

From, Fromel, Frommel (פְּרָאמֶעל/פְּרָאם) Yiddish forms of Avraham (Abraham). *See* Abraham.

G

Gab A pet form of Gabriel. *See* Gabriel.

Gabai (גַּבַּאי/גַּבָּי) From the Hebrew, meaning "communal official." The exact Hebrew equivalent is Gabai. FEMININE HEBREW EQUIVALENTS: Alufa, Tzameret.

Gabby A pet form of Gabriel. *See* Gabriel.

Gabe A pet form of Gabriel. *See* Gabriel.

Gabel An Old French variant form of Gabriel. *See* Gabriel.

Gabi (גַּבִּי) A pet form of Gabriel. *See* Gabriel.

Gabriel (גַּבְרִיאֵל) From the Hebrew, meaning "God is my strength." The exact Hebrew equivalent is Gavri'el. FEMININE HEBREW EQUIVALENTS: Gavri'ela, Gavrila. In Daniel 8:16, the name of an archangel.

Gad (גָּד) From the Hebrew and Arabic, meaning "happy, fortunate, lucky" or "warrior." The exact Hebrew equivalent is Gad. FEMININE HEBREW EQUIVALENTS: Gada, Gadit. In Genesis 30:11, the seventh son of Jacob.

Gader (גָּדֵר) From the Hebrew, meaning "fence, boundary." The exact Hebrew equivalent is Gader. The exact feminine equivalent is Gedera.

Gadi, Gaddi (גָּדִי) Variant forms of Gad. *See* Gad. In II Kings 15:17, a king of Israel.

Gadiel (גַּדִיאֵל) From the Hebrew, meaning "God is my good fortune." The exact Hebrew equivalent is Gadi'el. The exact feminine equivalent is Gadi'ela. In Numbers 13:10, a leader of the tribe of Zevulun (Zebulun).

Gafni (גַּפְנִי) From the Hebrew, meaning "my vineyard." The exact Hebrew equivalent is Gafni. FEMININE HEBREW EQUIVALENTS: Gafna, Gafnit.

Gai (גַּיְא/גַּי) From the Hebrew, meaning "ravine, valley." The exact Hebrew equivalent is Gai. FEMININE HEBREW EQUIVALENTS: Bika, Ga'ya.

Gaia (גַּיְא) A variant form of Gai. *See* Gai.

Gal (גַּל) A unisex name. From the Hebrew, meaning "mound, hill" or "wave, fountain, spring." The exact Hebrew equivalent is Gal.

Gali (גַּלִי) A unisex name. From the Hebrew, meaning "my wave" or "my hill." *See* Gal. The exact Hebrew equivalent is Gali.

Galia A variant form of Galya. *See* Galya.

Galil (גָּלִיל) From the Hebrew, meaning "cylinder, roll" or "district, land area." The name of the northern part of Israel. The exact Hebrew equivalent is Galil. The exact feminine equivalent is Galila.

Galmud (גַּלְמוּד) From the Hebrew, meaning "lonely." The exact Hebrew equivalent is Galmud.

Galvin From the Irish, meaning "sparrow" or "brilliantly white." HEBREW EQUIVALENTS: A'ya, Gozal, Talvas. FEMININE HEBREW EQUIVALENTS: Da'ya, Efrona, Tziporit.

Galya (גַּלְיָה) A unisex name. From the Hebrew, meaning "wave of God" or "hill of God." The exact Hebrew equivalent is Galya.

Gamal (גָּמָל) From the Arabic and Hebrew, meaning "camel." The exact Hebrew equivalent is Gamal.

Gamaliel A variant spelling of Gamliel. *See* Gamliel.

Gamliel (גַּמְלִיאֵל) From the Hebrew, meaning "God is my reward." The exact Hebrew equivalent is Gamli'el. The exact feminine equivalent is Gamli'ela. In Numbers 1:10, a leader of the tribe of Manasseh.

Gan (גַן) From the Hebrew, meaning "garden." The exact Hebrew equivalent is Gan. The exact feminine equivalent is Gana.

Ganan (גַנָן) From the Hebrew, meaning "gardener." The exact Hebrew equivalent is Ganan. The exact feminine equivalent is Gana.

Gani (גַנִי) From the Hebrew, meaning "my garden." The exact Hebrew equivalent is Gani. FEMININE HEBREW EQUIVALENTS: Gana, Ganit, Gina.

Gaon (גָאוֹן) From the Hebrew, meaning "esteemed scholar." The exact Hebrew equivalent is Ga'on. The exact feminine equivalent is Ge'ona.

Garden From the Old High German and Danish, meaning "enclosure, garden." HEBREW EQUIVALENTS: Gan, Gani, Gina. FEMININE HEBREW EQUIVALENTS: Gana, Ganit, Ganya.

Gardener An occupational name for one who tends a garden. A variant form of Garden. *See* Garden.

Garfield From the Old English, meaning "promontory." HEBREW EQUIVALENTS: Aviyam, Dalfon, Dela'ya. FEMININE HEBREW EQUIVALENTS: Bat-Yam, Eretz, Yaval.

Garin (גַרְעִין) From the Hebrew, meaning "seed, kernel." The exact Hebrew equivalent is Garin.

Garner From the Latin, meaning "granary." HEBREW EQUIVALENTS: Dagan, Goren, Idra. FEMININE HEBREW EQUIVALENTS: Garna, Garnit, Garona.

Garnet, Garnett From the Latin, meaning "grain." Also, a precious jewel so named because of its deep red color. HEBREW EQUIVALENTS: Almog, Goren, Guni. FEMININE HEBREW EQUIVALENTS: Degana, Deganit, Deganya.

Garon (גָרוֹן) From the Hebrew, meaning "threshing floor [for grain]." The exact Hebrew equivalent is Garon. FEMININE HEBREW EQUIVALENTS: Garna, Garnit, Garona.

Garret From the Old French, meaning "to watch, guard." HEBREW EQUIVALENTS: Eri, Mishmar, Notzer. FEMININE HEBREW EQUIVALENTS: Mishmeret, Nitzra, Notera.

Garreth A variant form of Garret. *See* Garret.

Garrett A variant spelling of Garret. *See* Garret.

Garth From the Old English, meaning "garden, enclosed field." HE-BREW EQUIVALENTS: Gan, Gani, Ginat. FEMININE HEBREW EQUIVALENTS: Gana, Ganit, Ganya.

Garvey From the Anglo-Saxon, meaning "spearbearer, warrior." Also, a form of Garth. *See* Garth.

Gary, Garry Variant forms of Gerald and Gerard. *See* Gerald *and* Gerard.

Gaston Possibly a French form of the German *Gast*, meaning "guest" or "stranger." HEBREW EQUIVALENTS: Gershom, Gershon, Gi'ora. FEMININE HEBREW EQUIVALENTS: Gershona, Gi'oret.

Gavan A variant spelling of Gavin. *See* Gavin.

Gavin From the Welsh, meaning "little hawk." HEBREW EQUIVALENTS: Gozal, Orev, Tzipor. FEMININE HEBREW EQUIVALENTS: Chogla, Efrona, Tzipora.

Gavirol (גְּבִירוֹל) A Sephardic form of Gavriel. *See* Gavriel.

Gavra (גַּבְרָא) The Aramaic form of Gever. *See* Gever.

Gavri (גַּבְרִי) From the Hebrew, meaning "manly, virile." A variant form of Gever. *See* Gever.

Gavriel (גַּבְרִיאֵל) The Hebrew form of Gabriel. *See* Gabriel.

Gay (גֵּא) From the Hebrew, meaning "egocentric, self-centered." The exact Hebrew equivalent is Gay. The exact feminine equivalent is Ga'ya. In Job 40:11, an overly proud individual.

Gaylord From the Gaelic, meaning "son of the fair-skinned one." HEBREW EQUIVALENTS: Lavan, Levanon, Livini. FEMININE HEBREW EQUIVALENTS: Levana, Livnat, Malbina.

Gaziz (גָּזִיז) From the Hebrew, meaning "shearing" or "fragment." The exact Hebrew equivalent is Gaziz. The exact feminine equivalent is Geziza.

Gedalia, Gedaliah Variant spellings of Gedalya. *See* Gedalya.

Gedalya (גְּדַלְיָה) From the Hebrew, meaning "God is great." The exact Hebrew equivalent is Gedalya. FEMININE HEBREW EQUIVALENTS: Atalya, Gedola, Gedula.

Gedalyahu (גְּדַלְיָהוּ) A variant form of Gedalya. *See* Gedalya. The exact Hebrew equivalent is Gedalyahu.

Gedi (גְּדִי) From the Hebrew, meaning "goat." The exact Hebrew equivalent is Gedi. Gadya is the feminine equivalent.

Gefania, Gefaniah Variant spellings of Gefanya. *See* Gefanya.

Gefanya (גְּפַנְיָה) From the Hebrew, meaning "vineyard of the Lord." The exact Hebrew equivalent is Gefanya. FEMININE HEBREW EQUIVALENTS: Gafna, Gafnit, Gefen.

Gefen, Geffen (גֶּפֶן) A unisex name. From the Hebrew, meaning "vine." The exact Hebrew equivalent is Gefen.

Geled (גֶּלֶד) From the Hebrew, meaning "skin" or "leathery covering." The exact Hebrew equivalent is Geled. The exact feminine equivalent is Gilda.

Gemali (גְּמַלִי) From the Hebrew, meaning "my camel." The exact Hebrew equivalent is Gemali. In Numbers 13:12, the father of Ami'el of the tribe of Dan.

Gene A pet form of Eugene. *See* Eugene.

Geoff A pet form of Geoffrey. *See* Geoffrey.

Geoffrey From the Anglo-Saxon, meaning "gift of peace" or "God's peace." HEBREW EQUIVALENTS: Avshalom, Magdi'el, Natan. FEMININE HEBREW EQUIVALENTS: Menucha, Migdana, Shalva.

George From the Greek, meaning "farmer." HEBREW EQUIVALENTS: Adam, Bustenai, Choresh. FEMININE HEBREW EQUIVALENTS: Gana, Karmela, Nava.

Gerald An Old French and German form of Gerard. *See* Gerard.

Gerard From the Anglo-Saxon, meaning "spear" or "spearbearer, warrior." HEBREW EQUIVALENTS: Gad, Gadi'el, Gavri'el. FEMININE HEBREW EQUIVALENTS: Chanit, Chanita, Gibora.

Gerardo A Spanish variant form of Gerard. *See* Gerard.

Gerhard, Gerhardt, Gerhart Variant forms of Gerard. *See* Gerard.

Gerome From the Greek, meaning "holy fame" or "sacred name." HE-BREW EQUIVALENTS: Ben-Shem, Chagai, Devir. FEMININE HEBREW EQUIVA-LENTS: Bat-Shem, Chagit, Chagiya.

Gerre A variant spelling of Gerry. *See* Gerry.

Gerry A pet form of Gerome. *See* Gerome.

Gershom (גֵרְשֹׁם) From the Hebrew, meaning "stranger." The exact Hebrew equivalent is Gershom. The exact feminine equivalent is Ger-shoma. In Exodus 2:22, the first child born to Moses and Tziporah.

Gershon (גֵרְשׁוֹן) A variant form of Gershom. *See* Gershom. The exact Hebrew equivalent is Gershon. The exact feminine equivalent is Gershona. In Genesis 46:11, the eldest of Levi's three sons.

Gerson A variant form of Gershon. *See* Gershon.

Geshem (גֵשֵׁם) From the Hebrew, meaning "rain." The exact Hebrew equivalent is Geshem. FEMININE HEBREW EQUIVALENTS: Lital, Ravital, Reviva.

Getzel (גֵעֶצֶל/גֵעְצֶל) A Yiddish pet form of the German name Gott-fried. *See* Gottfried.

Geuel (גְאוּאֵל) From the Hebrew, meaning "God has saved, re-deemed." The exact Hebrew equivalent is Ge'uel. FEMININE HEBREW EQUIVALENTS: Ge'alya, Ge'ula, Yigala. In Numbers 13:15, the son of Machi of the tribe of Gad.

Geva (גֵבַע) From the Hebrew, meaning "hill." The exact Hebrew equivalent is Geva. FEMININE HEBREW EQUIVALENTS: Gal, Giva, Givona.

Gever (גֵבֵר) From the Hebrew, meaning "man, hero." The exact Hebrew equivalent is Gever. FEMININE HEBREW EQUIVALENTS: Gavi, Gavri'ela, Gevira.

Gevir (גְבִיר) From the Hebrew, meaning "man of wealth, lord, mas-ter." The exact Hebrew equivalent is Gevir. The exact feminine equivalent is Gevira.

Geza (גֶּזַע) From the Hebrew, meaning "stem, trunk" or "cutting." The exact Hebrew equivalent is Geza. FEMININE HEBREW EQUIVALENTS: Gitit, Giza.

Gezer (גֶּזֶר) From the Hebrew, meaning "clipping" or "carrot." The exact Hebrew equivalent is Gezer. The exact feminine equivalent is Gezira.

Ghary A variant spelling of Gary. *See* Gary.

Gian An Italian form of John. *See* John.

Gib A pet form of Gilbert. *See* Gilbert.

Gibor, Gibbor (גִּבּוֹר) From the Hebrew, meaning "strong person." The exact Hebrew equivalent is Gibor. The exact feminine equivalent is Gibora.

Gideon A variant spelling of Gidon. *See* Gidon.

Gidi A pet form of Gidon. *See* Gidon.

Gidon (גִּדְעוֹן) From the Hebrew, meaning "cut off, maimed" or "mighty warrior." The exact Hebrew equivalent is Gidon. The exact feminine equivalent is Gidona. In Judges 6:11, an Israelite judge and military commander.

Gidone A variant spelling of Gidon. *See* Gidon.

Gidoni (גִּדְעוֹנִי) A variant form of Gidon. *See* Gidon. The exact Hebrew equivalent is Gidoni.

Gifford From the Middle English, meaning "worthy gift." HEBREW EQUIVALENTS: Avishai, Doron, Elnatan. FEMININE HEBREW EQUIVALENTS: Dorona, Matana, Netanela.

Gil (גִּיל) From the Hebrew, meaning "joy." The exact Hebrew equivalent is Gil. The exact feminine equivalent is Gila. Also, a pet form of Gilbert. *See* Gilbert.

Gilad (גִּלְעָד) From the Hebrew, meaning "mound [hill] of testimony." The exact Hebrew equivalent is Gilad. The exact feminine equivalent is Gilada. In Numbers 26:29, a grandson of Manasseh.

Giladi (גִּלְעָדִי) A variant form of Gilad, meaning "man from Gilad [Gilead]." *See* Gilad. The exact Hebrew equivalent is Giladi.

Gilbert From the Anglo-Saxon, meaning "light of many," "bright promise," or "sword." HEBREW EQUIVALENTS: Barak, Eli-Or, Me'ir. FEMININE HEBREW EQUIVALENTS: Me'ira, Noga, Ora.

Gildor (גִּלְדּוֹר) From the Hebrew, meaning "generation of joy." The exact Hebrew equivalent is Gildor. FEMININE HEBREW EQUIVALENTS: Dor, Dorit, Doriya.

Giles From the Greek, meaning "goatskin," connoting a protective shield. HEBREW EQUIVALENTS: Efer, Ofri, Shaked. FEMININE HEBREW EQUIVALENTS: Gadya, Mishmeret, Nitzra.

Gili (גִּילִי) A unisex name. From the Hebrew, meaning "my joy." The exact Hebrew equivalent is Gili.

Gill A variant spelling of Gil. *See* Gil.

Gilli A variant spelling of Gili. *See* Gili.

Gilmore From the Celtic, meaning "valley near the sea." HEBREW EQUIVALENTS: Avigal, Aviyam, Emek. FEMININE HEBREW EQUIVALENTS: Miryam, Yama, Yamit.

Gimpel (גִּימְפֶּעל) A Yiddish form of the German Gumprecht, meaning "bright." HEBREW EQUIVALENTS: Me'ir, Or, Ori. FEMININE HEBREW EQUIVALENTS: Me'ira, Uri'ela, Urit.

Gina, Ginat (גִּינַת/גִּינָה) Unisex names. From the Hebrew, meaning "garden." The exact Hebrew equivalents are Gina and Ginat.

Ginson A variant form of Ginton. *See* Ginton.

Ginton (גִּינְתוֹן) From the Hebrew, meaning "garden, orchard." The exact Hebrew equivalent is Ginton. FEMININE HEBREW EQUIVALENTS: Gana, Ganit, Gina.

Giora (גִּיוֹרָא/גִּיוֹרָה) A unisex name. From the Hebrew, meaning "strong." The exact Hebrew equivalent is Gi'ora.

Girard A variant spelling of Gerard. *See* Gerard.

Gitai (גִּיתַּאי/גִּיתַּי) From the Aramaic, meaning "one who presses grapes." The exact Hebrew equivalent is Gitai. FEMININE HEBREW EQUIVALENTS: Gat, Gita, Gitit.

Giti (גִּיתִּי) A variant form of Gitai. *See* Gitai. The exact Hebrew equivalent is Giti.

Giva, Givah (גִּבְעָה/גִּבְעָא) A unisex name. From the Hebrew, meaning "hill, high place." The exact Hebrew equivalent is Giva.

Givol (גִּבְעוֹל) From the Hebrew, meaning "budding, blooming." The exact Hebrew equivalent is Givol. The exact feminine equivalent is Givola.

Givon (גִּבְעוֹן) From the Hebrew, meaning "hill, heights." The exact Hebrew equivalent is Givon. The exact feminine equivalent is Givona.

Glen, Glenn From the Celtic, meaning "glen, secluded mountain valley." HEBREW EQUIVALENTS: Gai, Ge'ora, Ginton. FEMININE HEBREW EQUIVALENTS: Gana, Ganit, Ginat.

Gluke (גְלוּקֶע) A unisex name. From the German and Yiddish, meaning "luck, good fortune." The exact Hebrew equivalent is Mazal.

Goddard From the Old English, meaning "good in counsel." HEBREW EQUIVALENTS: Bina, Buna, Navon. FEMININE HEBREW EQUIVALENTS: Ge'ona, Ge'onit, Tushiya.

Godfrey A variant form of Gottfried. *See* Gottfried.

Godwin From the Anglo-Saxon, meaning "friend of God." HEBREW EQUIVALENTS: Chovav, Chovev, Re'uel. FEMININE HEBREW EQUIVALENTS: Re'uela, Rut, Yedida.

Goel (גּוֹאֵל) From the Hebrew, meaning "redeemer." The exact Hebrew equivalent is Go'el. FEMININE HEBREW EQUIVALENTS: Galya, Ge'ula, Go'elet.

Golan (גּוֹלָן) From the Hebrew, meaning "refuge." The exact Hebrew equivalent is Golan. FEMININE HEBREW EQUIVALENTS: Chosa, Luz, Sarida.

Goliath (גָּלְיַת) From the Hebrew, meaning "exiled one, stranger."

The exact Hebrew equivalent is Golyat. FEMININE HEBREW EQUIVALENTS: Avishag, Hagar. In I Samuel 17:4, a Philistine slain by David.

Gomer (גֹּמֶר) A unisex name. From the Hebrew, meaning "ember" or "one who burns sweet-smelling spices." The exact Hebrew equivalent is Gomer. In Genesis 10:2, the eldest son of Japhet and a grandson of Noah.

Goral (גּוֹרָל) From the Hebrew, meaning "lot, lottery" or "fate." The exact Hebrew equivalent is Goral. The exact feminine equivalent is Gorala.

Goran From the British, meaning "cathedral." The Hebrew equivalent is Devir. The feminine equivalent is Devira.

Gordon From the Gaelic, meaning "hero, strongman." HEBREW EQUIVALENTS: Gavri'el, Gevaram, Gevarya. FEMININE HEBREW EQUIVALENTS: Gavri'ela, Gavrila, Gevura.

Gore A short form of either Goran or Gordon. *See* Goran *and* Gordon.

Goren (גּוֹרֶן) From the Hebrew, meaning "threshing floor." The exact Hebrew equivalent is Goren. The exact feminine equivalent is Garona.

Gorman From the British, meaning "member of a choir." HEBREW EQUIVALENTS: Amiron, Amishar, Liron, Meshorer. FEMININE HEBREW EQUIVALENTS: Arnit, Lirona, Mangina.

Gottfried From the German, meaning "peace of God." HEBREW EQUIVALENTS: Avshalom, Ish-Shalom, Mano'ach. FEMININE HEBREW EQUIVALENTS: Menucha, Sha'anana, Shalva.

Gozal (גּוֹזָל) From the Hebrew, referring to a young bird. The exact Hebrew equivalent is Gozal. The exact feminine equivalent is Gozala, a term introduced in Deuteronomy 32:11.

Graham From the Old English, meaning "gray dwelling place." HEBREW EQUIVALENTS: Avgar, Dur, Yeshavam. FEMININE HEBREW EQUIVALENTS: Lina, Me'ona, Tira.

Granger From the Old French, meaning "farm steward." HEBREW

EQUIVALENTS: Avdel, Avdi, Eved. FEMININE HEBREW EQUIVALENTS: Adama, Ama, Shimshona.

Grant From the Old French, meaning "to grant, bequeath." HEBREW EQUIVALENTS: Avishai, Doron, Elnatan. FEMININE HEBREW EQUIVALENTS: Matana, Migdana, Mincha.

Granville From the Old French, meaning "grand town" or "great city." HEBREW EQUIVALENTS: Bitan, Dur, Ir. FEMININE HEBREW EQUIVALENTS: Dira, Me'ona, Zevu'ala.

Gray From the Old English, meaning "to shine, gleam." HEBREW EQUIVALENTS: Hillel, Me'ir, Yitzhar, Zahir. FEMININE HEBREW EQUIVALENTS: Me'ira, Zehara, Zoheret.

Greeley, Greely Abbreviated forms of the Anglo-Saxon *greenlea*, meaning "green meadow." HEBREW EQUIVALENTS: Chaglai, Choresh, Shadmon. FEMININE HEBREW EQUIVALENTS: Shadmit, Shedema, Yarkona.

Greg, Gregg From the Anglo-Saxon, meaning "to shine." HEBREW EQUIVALENTS: Me'ir, Yitzhar, Yizrach. FEMININE HEBREW EQUIVALENTS: Korenet, Mazhira, Me'ira.

Gregory From the Greek, meaning "vigilant watchman." HEBREW EQUIVALENTS: Avigdor, Ginat, Shemarya. FEMININE HEBREW EQUIVALENTS: Avigdora, Botzra, Gana.

Griffin From the Welsh, meaning "strong in faith." HEBREW EQUIVALENTS: Amitai, Amnon, Buki. FEMININE HEBREW EQUIVALENTS: Emuna, Gavrila, Gibora.

Griffith A Welsh form of Griffin. *See* Griffin.

Grover From the Anglo-Saxon, meaning "one who grows trees." HEBREW EQUIVALENTS: Alon, Amir, Arzi. FEMININE HEBREW EQUIVALENTS: Alona, Ariza, Artzit.

Guni (גּוּנִי) From the Hebrew, meaning "tinge of color" or "reddish black." The exact Hebrew equivalent is Guni. FEMININE HEBREW EQUIVALENTS: Chachila, Efa, Laila. In Numbers 26:48, a member of the tribe of Naftali.

Gunther From the Old German, meaning "war" or "warrior." HEBREW EQUIVALENTS: Gera, Gibor, Gidon. FEMININE HEBREW EQUIVALENTS: Gavrila, Gibora, Tigra.

Gur (גוּר) From the Hebrew, meaning "young lion." The exact Hebrew equivalent is Gur. FEMININE HEBREW EQUIVALENTS: Ari'el, Ari'ela, Gurit.

Gur-Ari (גוּר־אֲרִי) A variant form of Gur-Arye. *See* Gur-Arye. The exact Hebrew equivalent is Gur-Ari.

Gur-Arye, Gur-Aryeh, Gur-Aryei (גוּר־אַרְיֵה) From the Hebrew, meaning "young lion, cub." The exact Hebrew equivalent is Gur-Aryei. FEMININE HEBREW EQUIVALENTS: Ari'el, Ari'ela, Gurit.

Guri (גוּרִי) From the Hebrew, meaning "my young lion." The exact Hebrew equivalent is Guri. FEMININE HEBREW EQUIVALENTS: Ari'el, Ari'ela, Gurit.

Guria A variant spelling of Gurya. *See* Gurya.

Guriel (גוּרִיאֵל) From the Hebrew, meaning "God is my lion" or "God is my refuge." The exact Hebrew equivalent is Guri'el. FEMININE HEBREW EQUIVALENTS: Gurit, Kefira, Leviya.

Gurion The popular spelling of Guryon. *See* Guryon.

Gurya (גוּרְיָה/גוּרְיָא) An Aramaic and Hebrew form of Gur. *See* Gur. The exact Hebrew equivalent is Gurya.

Guryon (גוּרְיוֹן) From the Hebrew, meaning "lion," signifying strength. The exact Hebrew equivalent is Guryon. FEMININE HEBREW EQUIVALENTS: Ari'el, Ari'ela, Gurit.

Gus A pet form of Gustavus. *See* Gustavus.

Gustaf The Swedish form of Gustavus. *See* Gustavus.

Gustav, Gustave, Gustavo German and Spanish forms of Gustavus. *See* Gustavus.

Gustavus From the German and Swedish, meaning "the staff [weapon] of the Goths," a symbol of authority. HEBREW EQUIVALENTS: Gad, Gera, Gidon. FEMININE HEBREW EQUIVALENTS: Gavri'ela, Gavrila, Gibora.

Guthrie From the Celtic, meaning "war serpent" or "war hero." HE-BREW EQUIVALENTS: Gad, Gadi, Gavri'el. FEMININE HEBREW EQUIVALENTS: Gada, Gadit, Gidona.

Guy From the Old French, meaning "a guide" or "rope [that guides]." Also, a variant spelling of Gai, meaning "valley." *See* Gai. HEBREW EQUIVALENTS: Aluf, Chanoch, Gai. FEMININE HEBREW EQUIVALENTS: Alufa, Petila, Rivka.

Gwynn, Gwynne From the Welsh, meaning "fair, white." HEBREW EQUIVALENTS: Lavon, Levanon, Malbin. FEMININE HEBREW EQUIVALENTS: Levana, Livna, Livnat.

Gyles A variant spelling of Giles. *See* Giles.

❧ H ❧

Habakuk, Habakkuk (חֲבַקּוּק) The Anglicized form of Chavakuk. *See* Chavakuk.

Habib A variant spelling of Chaviv. *See* Chaviv.

Habibi A variant spelling of Chavivi. *See* Chavivi.

Hada A variant form of Hadar. *See* Hadar.

Hadad (הָדַד) From the Hebrew, meaning "echo." The exact Hebrew equivalent is Hadad. The feminine equivalent is Kolya.

Hadar (הָדָר) From the Hebrew, meaning "beautiful, ornamented, honored." The exact Hebrew equivalent is Hadar.

Hadas (הֲדַס) From the Hebrew, meaning "myrtle." The exact Hebrew equivalent is Hadas. The exact feminine equivalent is Hadasa.

Hadrian From the Greek, meaning "rich." HEBREW EQUIVALENTS: Ashir, Hotir, Huna. FEMININE HEBREW EQUIVALENTS: Ashira, Bat-Shu'a, Yitra.

Hadriel (הַדְרִיאֵל) From the Hebrew, meaning "splendor of the Lord." The exact Hebrew equivalent is Hadri'el. FEMININE HEBREW EQUIVALENTS: Hadara, Yifa, Yifat.

Hag (חַג) The Anglicized form of Chag. *See* Chag.

Haga A pet form of Haggai. *See* Haggai.

Hagai, Haggai Anglicized forms of Chagai. *See* Chagai.

Hagi The Anglicized form of Chagi. *See* Chagi.

Hai The Anglicized form of Chai. *See* Chai.

Haim The Anglicized form of Chaim. *See* Chaim.

Hal A pet form of Harold or Haley. *See* Harold *and* Haley.

Hale A pet form of Haley. *See* Haley.

Haley From the Old English, meaning "healthy, whole" or "holy." HEBREW EQUIVALENTS: Rafi, Refa'el, Yekuti'el. FEMININE HEBREW EQUIVALENTS: Refu'a, Rofi, Terufa.

Hallel (הַלֵּל) From the Hebrew, meaning "praise." The exact Hebrew equivalent is Hallel. The exact feminine equivalent is Hallela.

Halley, Hallie Variant spellings of Haley. *See* Haley.

Ham The Anglicized form of Cham. Also, a short form of Hamilton. *See* Cham *and* Hamilton.

Hamilton A variant form of Hamlet and Hamlin. *See* Hamlet *and* Hamlin.

Hamish A variant form of the Gaelic name Seumas, which is a form of James. *See* James.

Hamlet From the Low German, meaning "enclosed area," or from the Old German, meaning "home." HEBREW EQUIVALENTS: Betzer, Bitzaron, Chetzrai. FEMININE HEBREW EQUIVALENTS: Gana, Ganit, Ganya.

Hamlin From the Old English, meaning "a brook near home." HEBREW EQUIVALENTS: Beri, Chamat, Dalfon. FEMININE HEBREW EQUIVALENTS: Arnona, Dalya, Miryam.

Hanan The Anglicized form of Chanan. *See* Chanan.

Hanania, Hananiah Anglicized forms of Chananiah. *See* Chananiah.

Hanina The Anglicized form of Chanina. *See* Chanina.

Hank A pet form of Henry. *See* Henry.

Hanley From the Old English, meaning "high meadow." HEBREW EQUIVALENTS: Hevel, Ya'ar, Ya'ari. FEMININE HEBREW EQUIVALENTS: Ya'ara, Ya'arit.

Hanoch The Anglicized form of Chanoch. *See* Chanoch.

Hans A short form of the German name Johannes (John). *See* John.

Hansel A Bavarian form of Hans. *See* John.

Hansen A variant spelling of Hanson. *See* Hanson.

Hanson A Bavarian form of Hans. *See* Hans.

Haran The Anglicized form of Charan. *See* Charan.

Harari (הֲרָרִי) From the Hebrew, meaning "mountainous." The exact Hebrew equivalent is Harari. FEMININE HEBREW EQUIVALENTS: Aharona, Harela.

Harel (הַר-אֵל/הַרְאֵל) From the Hebrew, meaning "mountain of God." The exact Hebrew equivalent is Harel. The exact feminine equivalent is Harela.

Harlan From the Middle English and the Low German, meaning "hemp" or "flax." Or from the Old English, meaning "warrior." HEBREW EQUIVALENTS: Amatzya, Ben-Cha'yil, Gavri'el. FEMININE HEBREW EQUIVALENTS: Amtza, Gavri'ela, Gavrila.

Harley From the Old English, meaning "field of plants." HEBREW EQUIVALENTS: Chavakuk, Ezrach, Narkis. FEMININE HEBREW EQUIVALENTS: Marganit, Marva, Ofrit.

Harlin, Harlyn Variant spellings of Harlan. *See* Harlan.

Harlow From the Old Norse, meaning "army leader." HEBREW EQUIVALENTS: Gad, Gadi'el, Gevarya. FEMININE HEBREW EQUIVALENTS: Chila, Gada, Gadit.

Harman From the Anglo-Saxon, meaning "soldier," or from the Old English, meaning "keeper of hares and deer." HEBREW EQUIVALENTS: A'yal, Mishmar, Nitron. FEMININE HEBREW EQUIVALENTS: Shimrit, Shomera, Tzivya.

Harmon From the Greek, meaning "peace, harmony." HEBREW EQUIVALENTS: Sha'anan, Shalom, Shelomo. FEMININE HEBREW EQUIVALENTS: Menucha, Meshulemet, Shalva.

Harold From the Old English, meaning "leader of the army" or "warrior." HEBREW EQUIVALENTS: Avicha'yil, Barzilai, Chizki. FEMININE HEBREW EQUIVALENTS: Gidona, Merav, Tigra.

Harris A patronymic form, meaning "Harry's son." *See* Harry.

Harrison A patronymic form, meaning "Harry's son." *See* Harry.

Harry From the Middle English, a variant form of Henry. *See* Henry.

Hart, Harte From the Middle English, meaning "deer, stag." HEBREW EQUIVALENTS: A'yal, Ben-Tzvi, Efer. FEMININE HEBREW EQUIVALENTS: Ofra, Re'ema, Tzivya.

Hartley From the Old English, meaning "field in which the deer roam." HEBREW EQUIVALENTS: Efer, Hertzel, Tzevi. FEMININE HEBREW EQUIVALENTS: Hertzela, Ofra, Tzivya.

Harvey From the Old High German, meaning "army battle." Also, from the Celtic, meaning "progressive, liberal, flourishing." HEBREW EQUIVALENTS: Gad, Gidoni, Meron. FEMININE HEBREW EQUIVALENTS: Amtza, Chila, Gada.

Harvi, Harvie Pet forms of Harvey. *See* Harvey.

Hasan, Hassan From the Arabic, meaning "handsome." HEBREW EQUIVALENTS: Adin, Hadar, Shapir. FEMININE HEBREW EQUIVALENTS: Hadura, Na'a, Yafa.

Haskel, Haskell (הַשְׂכֵּל) From the Hebrew, meaning "wise, wisdom." Also from the Anglo-Saxon, meaning "ash tree." Also, a Yiddish form of the Hebrew name Yechezkel, meaning "God is my strength." *See* Yechezkel. HEBREW EQUIVALENTS: Achban, Bina, Chanoch. FEMININE HEBREW EQUIVALENTS: Chochma, Ge'ona, Nevona.

Havel A Czech form of the Latin, meaning "small." HEBREW EQUIVALENTS: Katan, Yaktan, Ze'ira. FEMININE HEBREW EQUIVALENTS: Ketana, Ketina, Ze'ira.

Havelock From the Anglo-Saxon, meaning "dwelling near the lake." HEBREW EQUIVALENTS: Dur, Yeshevav, Zevulun. FEMININE HEBREW EQUIVALENTS: Lina, Me'ona, Tira.

Haven A unisex name. From the Old English, meaning "sanctuary, harbor." HEBREW EQUIVALENTS: Devir, Nemalya, Nemu'el. FEMININE HEBREW EQUIVALENTS: Cheifa, Devira.

Haviv The Anglicized form of Chaviv. *See* Chaviv.

Hayden From the Anglo-Saxon, meaning "hayfield, pasture land." HEBREW EQUIVALENTS: Bustanai, Chaklai, Choresh. FEMININE HEBREW EQUIVALENTS: Churshit, Shadmit, Shedma.

Haym, Hayyim, Hayym Anglicized forms of Chayim. *See* Chayim.

Hector From the Greek, meaning "anchor, protector." HEBREW EQUIVALENTS: Avigdor, Chetzron, Ginat. FEMININE HEBREW EQUIVALENTS: Batzra, Chasya, Chosa.

Hed (הֵד) From the Hebrew, meaning "echo." The exact Hebrew equivalent is Hed. The feminine equivalent is Hedya.

Hedley From the Old English, meaning "covering" or "covered meadow." HEBREW EQUIVALENTS: Chupam, Gidron, Shafrir. FEMININE HEBREW EQUIVALENTS: Shafrira, Talal, Talila.

Heinrich The German form of Henry. *See* Henry.

Heinz A pet form of Heinrich. *See* Heinrich.

Helem (הֶלֶם) From the Hebrew, meaning "hammer." The exact Hebrew equivalent is Helem. Makabit is a feminine equivalent.

Heller An Old High German form of the Latin, meaning "sun." HEBREW EQUIVALENTS: Charsom, Koresh, Shimshon. FEMININE HEBREW EQUIVALENTS: Chamaniya, Shimshona.

Helmut From the German, meaning "courageous protector." HEBREW EQUIVALENTS: Avigdor, Shemer, Shmarya. FEMININE HEBREW EQUIVALENTS: Avigdora, Chasya, Megina.

Heman (הֵימָן) From the Hebrew, meaning "faithful." The exact equivalent is Heman. FEMININE HEBREW EQUIVALENTS: Amana, Amanya, Emuna.

Hen The Anglicized form of Chen. *See* Chen.

Henech, Henoch Anglicized forms of Hanoch. *See* Hanoch.

Henri A French form of Henry. *See* Henry.

Henrique A French form of Henry. *See* Henry.

Henry From the Anglo-Saxon, meaning "ruler of the home, rich lord." HEBREW EQUIVALENTS: Adoniya, Aluf, Avraham. FEMININE HEBREW EQUIVALENTS: Alufa, Atara, Malka.

Heraldo, Heroldo Variant forms of Harold. *See* Harold.

Herbert From the Old High German, meaning "clever, smart" or "excellent ruler." HEBREW EQUIVALENTS: Adoniya, Avraham, Haskel. FEMININE HEBREW EQUIVALENTS: Alufa, Atara, Malka.

Hercules From the Greek, meaning "glory." HEBREW EQUIVALENTS: Hadar, Hod, Hodiya. FEMININE HEBREW EQUIVALENTS: Tifara, Tiferet, Yocheved.

Herman From the Old High German, meaning "army man, soldier." HEBREW EQUIVALENTS: Gibor, Mordechai, Yariv. FEMININE HEBREW EQUIVALENTS: Gavri'ela, Gavrila, Gibora.

Hermann A variant German spelling of Herman. *See* Herman.

Hermon The Anglicized form of Chermon. *See* Chermon.

Hermoni The Anglicized form of Chermoni. *See* Chermoni.

Hersch, Herschel Variant spellings of Hersh and Hershel. *See* Hersh *and* Hershel.

Hersh (הֶערְשׁ) From the Yiddish, meaning "deer." HEBREW EQUIVALENTS: A'yal, A'yalon, Efron, Tzevi. FEMININE HEBREW EQUIVALENTS: A'yala, A'yelet, Tzivya.

Hershel (הֶערְשֶׁל/הֶערְשְׁעל) A pet form of Hersh. *See* Hersh.

Hertz (הֶערְץ) A pet form of Hersh. *See* Hersh.

Hertzel (הֶערְצֶעל) A variant spelling of Herzl. *See* Herzl.

Hertzl (הֶערְצְל) A diminutive form of Hertz. *See* Hertz.

Herve A variant form of Harvey. Erve is a pet form.

Herz A variant spelling of Hertz. *See* Hertz.

Herzl (הֶרצֶל) A pet form of Hersh. *See* Hersh.

Heschel (הֶעשֶׁעל/הֶעשׁל) A variant form of Hershel. *See* Hershel.

Hesh (הֶעשׁ) A Yiddish pet form of Hersh. *See* Hersh.

Heshel A variant spelling of Heschel. *See* Heschel.

Heshi, Heshy Pet forms of Heschel. *See* Heschel.

Heske A pet form of Heskel. *See* Heskel.

Heskel (הֶעשׁקֶעל/הֶעשׁקֶל) A variant form of Haskel. *See* Haskel.

Hesketh Probably a variant form of Hezekia. *See* Hezekia.

Heskiah A variant spelling of Hezekia. *See* Hezekia.

Hevel (הֶבֶל) From the Hebrew, meaning "breath, vapor," or from the Assyrian, meaning "son." Abel is the Anglicized form. The exact Hebrew equivalent is Hevel. FEMININE HEBREW EQUIVALENTS: Bat, Batya, Nafshiya.

Heywood From the Old English, meaning "hayfield" or "dark forest." HEBREW EQUIVALENTS: Efa, Karmel, Kedar. FEMININE HEBREW EQUIVALENTS: Chachila, Tzila, Ya'ara.

Hezekia, Hezekiah Variant forms of Chizkiya. *See* Chizkiya.

Hezron A variant spelling of Chetzron. *See* Chetzron.

Hi A pet form for a variety of names, including Hilary, Hiram, and Hyman.

Hiam A variant form of Chaim. *See* Chaim.

Hiel A variant spelling of Chiel. *See* Chiel.

High From the Old English, meaning "high, a hillsite." *See* Hi.

Hila (הִילָה) A unisex name. From the Aramaic and Hebrew, meaning "praise." The exact Hebrew equivalent is Hila.

Hilary From the Greek and Latin, meaning "cheerful." Also, from the Anglo-Saxon, meaning "guardian, protector." HEBREW EQUIVALENTS: Avigdor, Shemaryahu, Simcha. FEMININE HEBREW EQUIVALENTS: Aviga'yil, Avigdora, Botzra.

Hili (הִילִי/הִלִי) A pet form of Hillel. *See* Hillel.

Hill From the Anglo-Saxon, meaning "hill, high place." HEBREW EQUIV-ALENTS: Aharon, Haran, Harel. FEMININE HEBREW EQUIVALENTS: Harela, Meroma, Talma.

Hillard A variant form of Hill. *See* Hill.

Hillary A variant spelling of Hilary. *See* Hilary.

Hillel (הִלֵּל) From the Hebrew, meaning "praised, famous." The exact Hebrew equivalent is Hillel. The exact feminine equivalent is Hillela.

Hilliard A variant form of Hill. *See* Hill.

Hiram A variant spelling of Chiram. *See* Chiram.

Hirsch A variant spelling of Hersh. *See* Hersh.

Hirsh, Hirshel Variant spellings of Hersh and Hershel. *See* Hersh *and* Hershel.

Hob A variant Middle English form of Rob and Robert. *See* Robert.

Hobart From the Danish, meaning "Bart's hill." *See* Bart *and* Hill.

Hobert A variant form of Hobart. *See* Hobart.

Hobs A variant form of Hob, meaning "son of Hob." *See* Hob.

Hod (הוֹד) From the Hebrew, meaning "splendor, vigor." The exact Hebrew equivalent is Hod. Hodiya is the feminine equivalent.

Hodia, Hodiah Variant spellings of Hodiya. *See* Hodiya.

Hodiya (הוֹדִיָה) A unisex name derived from the Hebrew, meaning "God is my splendor" or "praise the Lord." The exact equivalent is Hodiya.

Holden From the Old English *haldan*, meaning "to tend sheep." Also, from the Greek, meaning "swift horse." HEBREW EQUIVALENTS: Bo'az, Cha'yil, Maron, Sisera, Susi. FEMININE HEBREW EQUIVALENTS: Mahira, Marona.

Hollis A variant form of Haley. *See* Haley.

Holm From the Old Norse, meaning "island." HEBREW EQUIVALENTS: Avi-yam, Dalfon, Itamar. FEMININE HEBREW EQUIVALENTS: Afeka, Bat-Yam, Miryam.

Holmes A variant form of Holm. *See* Holm.

Holt From the Old English and the German, meaning "wood, wooded area." HEBREW EQUIVALENTS: Ya'ar, Ya'ari. FEMININE HEBREW EQUIVALENTS: Ya'ari, Ya'arit.

Homer From the Greek and Latin, meaning "hostage, one being led," hence, one who is blind. EUPHEMISTIC HEBREW EQUIVALENTS: Koresh, Me'ir, Shimshon. EUPHEMISTIC FEMININE HEBREW EQUIVALENTS: Noga, Ora, Zahara.

Hon (הוֹן) From the Hebrew, meaning "wealth." The exact Hebrew equivalent is Hon. FEMININE HEBREW EQUIVALENTS: Ashira, Yitra.

Honi The Anglicized form of Choni. *See* Choni.

Honor, Honore From the Middle English and the Latin, meaning "dignity, esteem." HEBREW EQUIVALENTS: Atzil, Efrat, Hadar. FEMININE HEBREW EQUIVALENTS: Atzila, Efrat, Efrata.

Hopkins A pet form of Hob and Hobs, which are pet forms of Robert. *See* Robert.

Horace From the Greek, meaning "to see, behold." HEBREW EQUIVALENTS: Achazya, Chaza'el, Chazon. FEMININE HEBREW EQUIVALENTS: Nevi'a, Ro'a, Re'uvena, Tzofi.

Horatio The Italian form of Horace. *See* Horace.

Hori A variant spelling of Chori. *See* Chori.

Horton From the Latin, meaning "garden." HEBREW EQUIVALENTS: Bustan, Bustanai, Gan. FEMININE HEBREW EQUIVALENTS: Gana, Ganit, Ganya.

Hosea The Anglicized form of Hosheia. *See* Hoshea.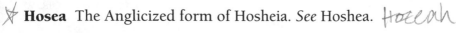

Hoshea (הוֹשֵׁעַ) From the Hebrew, meaning "salvation." The exact Hebrew equivalent is Hoshei'a. FEMININE HEBREW EQUIVALENTS: Matzila, Mosha'a, Teshu'a. In Hosea 1:1, a Hebrew prophet in the kingdom of Israel.

Howard From the Anglo-Saxon, meaning "watchman, protector." HE-BREW EQUIVALENTS: Avigdor, Chetzron, Gina. FEMININE HEBREW EQUIVA-LENTS: Botzra, Chasya, Chosa.

Howe From the Anglo-Saxon, meaning "hill." HEBREW EQUIVALENTS: Gali, Harel, Talmi. FEMININE HEBREW EQUIVALENTS: Aharona, Galit, Galya.

Howel, Howell From the Old English, meaning "well on the hill." HE-BREW EQUIVALENTS: Aharon, Be'er, Harel. FEMININE HEBREW EQUIVALENTS: Be'erit, Galit, Harela.

Howie A pet form of Howard. *See* Howard.

Hubert A variant form of Herbert. *See* Herbert.

Huey A pet form of Hubert. *See* Hubert.

Hugh A pet form of Hubert. *See* Hubert.

Hugo A pet form of Hubert. *See* Hubert.

Humphrey, Humphry From the Anglo-Saxon, meaning "protector of the home," or from the Old German, meaning "man of peace." HE-BREW EQUIVALENTS: Akiva, Meshulam, Shalem. FEMININE HEBREW EQUIVA-LENTS: Avigdora, Chasya, Magena.

Hur The Anglicized form of Chur. *See* Chur.

Hussein From the Arabic, meaning "small, handsome one." HEBREW EQUIVALENTS: Hadar, Katan, Zutra. FEMININE HEBREW EQUIVALENTS: Ha-dura, Ketana, Ketina.

Hy A pet form of Hyland and Hyman. *See* Hyland *and* Hyman.

Hyland From the Anglo-Saxon, meaning "one who lives on high land." Akin to Hyman. *See* Hyman.

Hyman From the Anglo-Saxon, meaning "one who lives in a high place." HEBREW EQUIVALENTS: Aharon, Givon, Harel. FEMININE HEBREW EQUIVALENTS: Harela, Talma, Talmit.

~ I ~

Iaacov A Russian form of Isaac, meaning "Isaac's son." *See* Isaac.

Ian The Scottish form of John. *See* John.

Ibrahim The Arabic form of Abraham. *See* Abraham.

Idan (עִדָן) From the Hebrew, meaning "era, period of time." The exact Hebrew equivalent is Idan. FEMININE HEBREW EQUIVALENTS: Itai, Iti'el, Itiya.

Idi A variant form of Ido. *See* Ido.

Ido, Iddo (עְדוֹא/עְדוֹ) From the Hebrew and Aramaic, meaning "to rise up [like a cloud]" or "to reckon time." The exact Hebrew equivalent is Ido. FEMININE HEBREW EQUIVALENTS: Alita, Aliya, Ya'el. In I Kings 4:14, the father of one of King Solomon's officers in the royal household.

Idra (אִדְרָא) From the Aramaic, meaning "granary." The exact Hebrew equivalent is Idra. FEMININE HEBREW EQUIVALENTS: Degana, Garna, Garnit.

Iezer An abbreviated form of Aviezer. *See* Aviezer.

Igael A variant spelling of Yigael. *See* Yigael.

Igal A variant spelling of Yigal. *See* Yigal.

Iggud (אָגוּד) From the Hebrew, meaning "binding" or "association."

The exact Hebrew equivalent is Iggud. FEMININE HEBREW EQUIVALENTS: Aguda, Retem, Rivka.

Iggy A pet form of Yigael. *See* Yigael.

Igor From the Scandinavian, meaning "hero." HEBREW EQUIVALENTS: Gavri, Gavri'el, Gevaram. FEMININE HEBREW EQUIVALENTS: Avigdora, Magena, Megina.

Igul (עָגוּל) From the Hebrew, meaning "circle." The exact Hebrew equivalent is Igul. FEMININE HEBREW EQUIVALENTS: Akifa, Gal, Seviva.

Ike A pet form of Isaac. *See* Isaac.

Ila (עִילָא) From the Aramaic, meaning "exalted," or from the Arabic, meaning "noble cause." The exact Hebrew equivalent is Ila. FEMININE HEBREW EQUIVALENTS: Ge'ona, Ge'onit, Ramit.

Ilai (עִילָאִי) From the Hebrew and Aramaic, meaning "superior." The exact Hebrew equivalent is Ila'i. FEMININE HEBREW EQUIVALENTS: Ram, Romema, Romit.

Ilan (אִילָן) From the Hebrew, meaning "tree." The exact Hebrew equivalent is Ilan. The exact feminine equivalent is Ilana.

Ili (עִילִי/עָלִי) A variant form of Ila. *See* Ila. The exact Hebrew equivalent is Ili.

Ilie A variant form of Elijah or Elisha. *See* Elijah *and* Elisha.

Ilija A variant Slavic form of Elijah. *See* Elijah.

Iliya A variant form of Elijah and Elisha. *See* Elijah *and* Elisha.

Ilya A variant spelling of Ilija. *See* Ilija.

Imanuel, Immanuel (עִמָּנוּאֵל) From the Hebrew, meaning "God is with us." The exact Hebrew equivalent is Imanu'el. The exact feminine equivalent is Imanu'ela.

Imri, Imrie (אִמְרִי) From the Hebrew, meaning "my utterance." The exact Hebrew equivalent is Imri. FEMININE HEBREW EQUIVALENTS: Amira, Doveva, Dovevet.

Inbal (עִנְבָּל) A unisex name. Probably from the Greek, referring to the metallic clapper in a bell that creates the ringing sound. The exact Hebrew equivalent is Inbal.

Ingmar From the Old English, meaning "meadow near the sea." HEBREW EQUIVALENTS: Nir, Nirel, Sharon. FEMININE HEBREW EQUIVALENTS: Nira, Nirit, Sharona.

Ir (עִיר) From the Hebrew, meaning "city, town." The exact Hebrew equivalent is Ir. The exact feminine equivalent is Irit.

Ira (עִירָא) From the Hebrew and Arabic, meaning "to escape [by being swift]." The exact Hebrew equivalent is Ira. FEMININE HEBREW EQUIVALENTS: Mahira, Sarid, Tzivya.

Iran A variant form of Ira. *See* Ira.

Iri A variant form of Ira. *See* Ira.

Irvin From the Gaelic, meaning "beautiful, handsome, fair." HEBREW EQUIVALENTS: Shapir, Shefer, Shifron. FEMININE HEBREW EQUIVALENTS: Ra'anana, Rivka, Yafa.

Irvine A variant form of Irvin.

Irving A variant form of Irvin.

Irwin, Irwyn Variant spellings of Irvin. *See* Irvin.

Is A short form of Isaiah. *See* Isaiah.

Isa A short form of Isaac and Isaiah. *See* Isaac *and* Isaiah.

Isaac (יִצְחָק) From the Hebrew, meaning "he will laugh." The exact Hebrew equivalent is Yitzchak. The exact feminine equivalent is Yitzchaka.

Isador, Isadore Variant spellings of Isidor. *See* Isidor.

Isaiah (יְשַׁעְיָהוּ/יְשַׁעְיָה) From the Hebrew, meaning "God is salvation." HEBREW EQUIVALENTS: Yesha'ya, Yesha'yahu. FEMININE HEBREW EQUIVALENTS: Teshu'a, Yesha, Yeshu'a.

Isak A variant form of Isaac. *See* Isaac.

Isea A variant form of Yitzchak. *See* Yitzchak.

Iser A variant spelling of Isser. *See* Isser.

Ishmael (יִשְׁמָעֵאל) An Anglicized form of the Hebrew name Yishma'el, meaning "God will hear." The exact Hebrew equivalent is Yishma'el. FEMININE HEBREW EQUIVALENTS: Shimat, Shimona, Shmu'ela.

Ish-Shalom (אִישׁ-שָׁלוֹם) From the Hebrew, meaning "man of peace." The exact Hebrew equivalent is Ish-Shalom. FEMININE HEBREW EQUIVALENTS: Shelom-Tziyon, Shlomit, Shulamit.

Ish-Tov (אִישׁ-טוֹב) From the Hebrew, meaning "good man." The exact Hebrew equivalent is Ish-Tov. FEMININE HEBREW EQUIVALENTS: Tova, Tovit, Tuvit, Yatva.

Isidor, Isidore From the Greek, meaning "gift of Isis," the Egyptian moon-goddess. HEBREW EQUIVALENTS: Avishai, Elnatan, Yonatan. FEMININE HEBREW EQUIVALENTS: Sahara, Zevida, Zevuda.

Isidoro The Spanish form of Isidor. *See* Isidor.

Ismar A variant form of Itamar. *See* Itamar.

Israel (יִשְׂרָאֵל) The Anglicized form of the Hebrew, meaning "prince of God" or "wrestled with God." The exact Hebrew equivalent is Yisra'el. The exact feminine equivalent is Yisra'ela.

Issa A short form of Isaac and Isaiah. *See* Isaac *and* Isaiah.

Issachar (יִשָּׂשכָר) From the Hebrew, meaning "there is a reward." The exact Hebrew equivalent is Yisachar. FEMININE HEBREW EQUIVALENTS: Ashera, Beracha, Gamli'ela.

Isser (אִיסֶער/אִיסֶר) A Yiddish form of Yisrael (Israel). *See* Yisrael *and* Israel.

Issi (אִיסִי) A pet form of Isser. *See* Isser.

Isur (אָסוּר) From the Hebrew, meaning "prohibition, ban." The exact Hebrew equivalent is Isur.

Itai (אִיתַּי) A unisex name. From the Hebrew, meaning "friendly, compassionate" or literally, "God is with me." The exact Hebrew equivalent is Itai.

Itamar (אִיתָמָר) From the Hebrew, meaning "island of palms." The exact Hebrew equivalent is Itamar. FEMININE HEBREW EQUIVALENTS: Tamar, Timora.

Itiel (אִיתִיאֵל) From the Hebrew, meaning "God is with me." The exact Hebrew equivalent is Iti'el. FEMININE HEBREW EQUIVALENTS: Eli'ezra, Eli'ora, Itai.

Ittai A variant spelling of Itai. *See* Itai.

Ittamar A variant spelling of Itamar. *See* Itamar.

Itzhak A variant spelling of Yitzchak. *See* Yitzchak.

Itzig, Itzik (אִיצִיק/אִיצִיג) Yiddish forms of Yitzchak (Isaac). *See* Yitzchak.

Ivan The Russian form of John, meaning "grace." *See* John.

Ivri (עִבְרִי) From the Hebrew, meaning "cross over," referring to the patriarch Abraham, who crossed the Euphrates River. In Jonah 1:9, Jonah is referred to as an Ivri, meaning "Hebrew." The exact Hebrew equivalent is Ivri. The exact feminine equivalent is Ivriya.

Iyov The Hebrew form of Job. *See* Job.

Iz A pet form of Isidor. *See* Isidor.

Izzie, Izzy Pet forms of Isidor. *See* Isidor.

ꙮ J ꙮ

Jack A pet form of Jacob. *See* Jacob. Also, a nickname for John. *See* John.

Jackie A pet form of Jack. *See* Jack.

Jackson A patronymic form, meaning "son of Jack" or "son of Jacob." *See* Jack and Jacob.

Jacob (יַעֲקֹב) The Anglicized form of Ya'akov. From the Hebrew, meaning "held by the heel, supplanted, or protected." The exact Hebrew equivalent is Ya'akov. The exact feminine equivalent is Ya'akova.

Jacobo A Spanish form of Jacob. *See* Jacob.

Jacque, Jacques French forms of Jacob. *See* Jacob.

Jael A variant spelling of Yael. *See* Yael.

Jaime A Spanish form of Chayim. *See* Chayim.

Jaimie A pet form of James. *See* James.

Jair The Anglicized form of Yair. *See* Yair.

Jake A pet form of Jacob. *See* Jacob.

Jakob A variant spelling of Jacob. *See* Jacob.

Jamal From the Arabic, meaning "handsome." HEBREW EQUIVALENTS:

Kalil, Noi, Yefet. FEMININE HEBREW EQUIVALENTS: Na'ama, Nava, No-fiya.

James The Middle English form of Jacob. *See* Jacob.

Jamie A pet form of James. *See* James.

Jamin A short form of Benjamin. *See* Benjamin.

Jan A variant form of John. *See* John. Also, a pet form of James. *See* James.

Janus From the Latin, meaning "gate, passageway" or "opening, beginning," from which the month January takes its name. HEBREW EQUIVALENTS: Bava, Rav, Rosh. FEMININE HEBREW EQUIVALENTS: Bava, Rishona.

Japhet, Japheth English forms of Yefet. *See* Yefet.

Jardine From the Anglo-Saxon and French, meaning "garden." HEBREW EQUIVALENTS: Gan, Gani, Gina. FEMININE HEBREW EQUIVALENTS: Ganya, Gina, Yardena.

Jared The Anglicized form of Yared. *See* Yared.

Jaron An English form of Yaron. *See* Yaron.

Jarrett A variant form of Garrett. *See* Garrett.

Jarrod A variant spelling of Jared, the Anglicized form of Yared. *See* Yared. ⊹ Jareth –

Jarvis From the Old English, meaning "battle spear" or "conqueror." HEBREW EQUIVALENTS: Gavri'el, Gevarya, Gidoni. FEMININE HEBREW EQUIVALENTS: Chanit, Chanita, Chinanit.

Jascha A Russian form of Jacob and James. *See* Jacob *and* James.

Jason From the Greek, meaning "healer." HEBREW EQUIVALENTS: Assi, Rafa, Refa'el. FEMININE HEBREW EQUIVALENTS: Asa'ela, Refa'ela, Refa'ya.

Jaspar, Jasper From the Greek, meaning "precious stone." Also, from the Persian, meaning "secret." HEBREW EQUIVALENTS: Safir, Sapir, Shoham. FEMININE HEBREW EQUIVALENTS: Sapira, Sapirit, Yahaloma.

Jay From the Old French and Latin, referring to a bird in the crow family. Also, from the Anglo-Saxon, meaning "happy." HEBREW EQUIV-

ALENTS: A'ya, Efron, Gil. FEMININE HEBREW EQUIVALENTS: A'ya, Gozala, Kanarit.

Jayson A patronymic form, meaning "Jay's son." Also, a variant spelling of Jason. *See* Jay *and* Jason.

Jean The French form of John. *See* John.

Jeb From the Arabic, meaning "hand." HEBREW EQUIVALENTS: Chofni, Yeda'ya. Also, a pet form of Jedediah. *See* Jedediah.

Jed A pet form of Jared or Jedediah. *See* Jared *and* Jedediah.

Jedediah An English form of Yedidya. *See* Yedidya.

Jef, Jeff Short forms of Jeffrey. *See* Jeffrey.

Jeffers A patronymic form, meaning "son of Jeffrey." *See* Jeffrey.

Jefferson A patronymic form, meaning "son of Jeffers." *See* Jeffers.

Jeffery, Jefferey, Jeffrey, Jeffry Variant spellings of Geoffrey. *See* Geoffrey.

Jehiel A variant spelling of Yechiel. *See* Yechiel.

Jehoiakim A variant spelling of Yehoyakim. *See* Yehoyakim.

Jekuthiel, Jekutiel Variant forms of Yekutiel. *See* Yekutiel.

Jephtah, Jephthah Variant forms of Yiftach. *See* Yiftach.

Jerald A variant spelling of Gerald. *See* Gerald.

Jere A variant spelling of Jerry. *See* Jerry. Also, a short form of Jeremiah. *See* Jeremiah.

Jered A variant spelling of Yered. *See* Yered.

Jeremais The Greek form of Jeremiah. *See* Jeremiah.

Jeremiah (יִרְמְיָהוּ/יִרְמְיָה) From the Hebrew, meaning "God will loosen [the bonds]" or "God will uplift [the spirit]." The exact Hebrew equivalent is Yirmeyahu. *See* Yirmeyahu.

Jeremy A pet form of Jeremiah. *See* Jeremiah.

Jeroboam The Anglicized form of Yeravam. *See* Yeravam.

Jerold A variant spelling of Gerald. *See* Gerald.

Jerome A variant spelling of Gerome, meaning "holy person" or "sacred name." HEBREW EQUIVALENTS: Shem-Tov, Tamir, Zakai. FEMININE HEBREW EQUIVALENTS: Chagit, Chagiya, Devira.

Jeromy A pet form of Jeremiah or Jerome. *See* Jeremiah *and* Jerome.

Jerrald A variant spelling of Jerold. *See* Jerold.

Jerrem A pet form of Jeremiah or Jerome. *See* Jeremiah *and* Jerome.

Jerrold A variant spelling of Jerold. *See* Jerold.

Jerry A pet form of Jeremiah, Jerold, and Jerome. *See* Jeremiah, Jerold, *and* Jerome.

Jess A short form of Jesse. *See* Jesse.

Jesse (יִשַׁי) From the Hebrew, meaning "wealthy" or "gift." The exact Hebrew equivalent is Yishai. FEMININE HEBREW EQUIVALENTS: Ashira, Dorona, Matana, Netanela, Yitra.

Jethro (יִתְרוֹ) From the Hebrew, meaning "abundance, riches." The exact Hebrew equivalent is Yitro. The exact feminine equivalent is Yitra.

Jibril The Arabic form of Gabriel. *See* Gabriel.

Jim A pet form of James. *See* James.

Jimbo A pet form of James, probably a short form of Jimboy. *See* James.

Jimm A variant spelling of Jim.

Jimmie, Jimmy Pet forms of James. *See* James.

Jiri A Czech form of George. *See* George.

Joab The Anglicized form of Yoav. *See* Yoav. or Joeb

Joash The Anglicized form of Yoash. *See* Yoash.

Job (אִיּוֹב) From the Hebrew, meaning "enemy, hated one." The exact Hebrew equivalent is Iyov. FEMININE HEBREW EQUIVALENTS: Talmona, Talmonit. The name given to a book of the Bible whose title character's loyalty to God was being tested.

Joce A variant form of Joseph. *See* Joseph.

Jochanan A variant spelling of Yochanan. *See* Yochanan.

Jody A pet form of Joseph. *See* Joseph.

Joe, Joey Pet forms of Joseph. *See* Joseph.

Joel (יוֹאֵל) From the Hebrew, meaning "God is willing." The exact Hebrew equivalent is Yo'el. The exact feminine equivalent is Yo'ela.

Joelle A unisex name. A variant form of Joel or Joela. *See* Joel (*masculine section*) and Joela (*feminine section*).

Johan A Czech form of John. *See* John.

Johanan A variant spelling of Yochanan. *See* Yochanan.

Johannes A Latin form of John. *See* John.

John (יְהוֹחָנָן/יוֹחָנָן) The Anglicized form of Yochanan, meaning "God is gracious." HEBREW EQUIVALENTS: Yehochanan, Yochanan. The feminine equivalent is Yochana.

Johnnie, Johnny Pet forms of John. *See* John.

Jojo A pet form of Joseph. *See* Joseph.

Jon A pet form of John or Jonathan. *See* John *and* Jonathan.

Jona, Jonah (יוֹנָה) A unisex name. From the Hebrew, meaning "dove." The exact masculine and feminine Hebrew equivalent is Yona.

Jonas The Greek and Latin form of Jonah. *See* Jonah.

Jonathan (יְהוֹנָתָן/יוֹנָתָן) From the Hebrew, meaning "God has given" or "gift of God." The exact Hebrew equivalent is Yehonatan. FEMININE HEBREW EQUIVALENTS: Netanela, Netanya, Netina.

Jonji A pet form of Jonathan. *See* Jonathan.

Jon-Jon A pet form of Jonathan. *See* Jonathan.

Jonni, Jonnie, Jonny Pet forms of Jonathan. *See* Jonathan.

Jordan The Anglicized form of Yarden. *See* Yarden.

Jordy A pet form of Jordan. *See* Jordan.

Jori, Jory Pet forms of Jordan. *See* Jordan.

Jose An Aramaic form of Joseph. *See* Joseph.

José A Spanish form of Joseph. *See* Joseph.

Joseph (יוֹסֵף) From the Hebrew, meaning "He [God] will add, increase." The exact Hebrew equivalent is Yosef. FEMININE HEBREW EQUIVALENTS: Yosefa, Yosifa.

Josephus (יוֹסִיפוֹס) The Latin form of Joseph. The exact Hebrew equivalent is Yosifus.

Josh A pet form of Joshua. *See* Joshua.

Joshua (יְהוֹשֻׁעַ) From the Hebrew, meaning "the Lord is salvation." The exact Hebrew equivalent is Yehoshu'a. FEMININE HEBREW EQUIVALENTS: Mosha'a, Shu'a, Teshu'a.

Josiah The Anglicized form of Yoshiyahu. *See* Yoshiyahu.

Jotham A variant spelling of Yotam. *See* Yotam.

Juan A Spanish form of John. *See* John.

Jubal The Anglicized form of Yuval. *See* Yuval.

Jud A variant spelling of Judd. *See* Judd.

Juda A variant spelling of Judah. *See* Judah.

Judah (יְהוּדָה) From the Hebrew, meaning "praise." The exact Hebrew equivalent is Yehuda. The exact feminine equivalent is Yehudit.

Judas The Latin form of Judah. *See* Judah.

Judd A variant form of Judah. *See* Judah.

Jude A variant form of Judah. *See* Judah.

Judea A variant form of Judah. *See* Judah.

Judel A Yiddish form of Judah. *See* Judah.

Judson A patronymic form of Judah, meaning "Judah's [or Judd's] son." *See* Judah.

Jule, Jules Variant forms of Julian or Julius. *See* Julian *and* Julius.

Julian From the Greek, meaning "soft-haired, mossy-bearded," symbolizing youth. HEBREW EQUIVALENTS: Aviv, Avrech, Elino'ar. FEMININE HEBREW EQUIVALENTS: Aviva, Dala, Delila.

Julius A variant form of Julian. *See* Julian.

Junior From the Latin, meaning "young." HEBREW EQUIVALENTS: Aviv, Avrech, Bachur. FEMININE HEBREW EQUIVALENTS: Aviva, Gurit.

Junius From the Latin, meaning "young lion." HEBREW EQUIVALENTS: Gur-Aryei, Kefir, Lavi. FEMININE HEBREW EQUIVALENTS: Gurit, Kefira, Levi'a.

Justin A variant form of Justus. *See* Justus.

Justice A variant spelling of Justus. *See* Justus.

Justus From the Latin, meaning "just, honest." HEBREW EQUIVALENTS: Yadon, Yehoshafat, Yudan. FEMININE HEBREW EQUIVALENTS: Dani'ela, Danit, Danya.

❦ K ❧

Kad (כַּד) From the Hebrew, meaning "pitcher, jug, pot." The exact Hebrew equivalent is Kad. The exact feminine equivalent is Kada.

Kaddish A variant spelling of Kadish. *See* Kadish.

Kadi (כַּדִי) From the Hebrew, meaning "my pitcher." The exact Hebrew equivalent is Kadi. The exact feminine equivalent is Kadya.

Kadish (קָדִישׁ) From the Hebrew, meaning "sanctification." The exact Hebrew equivalent is Kadish. FEMININE HEBREW EQUIVALENTS: Chermona, Devira, Kedosha.

Kadmiel (קַדְמִיאֵל) From the Hebrew, meaning "the Ancient One is my God." The exact Hebrew equivalent is Kadmi'el. FEMININE HEBREW EQUIVALENTS: Bilha, Kadmi'ela, Keshisha.

Kadosh (קָדוֹשׁ) From the Hebrew, meaning "holy, holy one." The exact Hebrew equivalent is Kadosh. The exact feminine equivalent is Kedosha.

Kailil A variant form of Kalil. *See* Kalil.

Kal (קָל) A short form of Kalman. *See* Kalman.

Kalev (כָּלֵב) *Also spelled* Calev. From the Hebrew, meaning "dog" or "heart." Also, from the Assyrian, meaning "messenger" or "priest," and from the Arabic, meaning "bold, brave." Caleb is the Anglicized form. The exact Hebrew equivalent is Kalev. FEMININE HEBREW EQUIVALENTS: Libi, No'aza, Odeda.

Kalil (כָּלִיל) From the Greek, meaning "beautiful." Also, from the Hebrew, meaning "crown, wreath." The exact Hebrew equivalent is Kalil. The exact feminine equivalent is Kelila.

Kalman A short form of Kalonymos. *See* Kalonymos.

Kalonymos, Kalonymus (קָלוֹנִימוּס) Variant forms of the Latin name Clement, meaning "merciful" or "gracious." Also, from the Greek, meaning "beautiful name." The exact Hebrew equivalent is Kalonimos. FEMININE HEBREW EQUIVALENTS: Bat-Shem, Tova, Tovit.

Kanai (קָנָאי) From the Hebrew, meaning "zealous." The exact Hebrew equivalent is Kana'i. The feminine equivalent is Chasida.

Kane A variant form of Keene. *See* Keene.

Kani (קָנִי) A pet form of Kaniel. *See* Kaniel.

Kaniel (קָנִיאֵל) From the Hebrew, meaning "reed [support]." Also, from the Arabic, meaning "spear." The exact Hebrew equivalent is Kani'el. The exact feminine equivalent is Kani'ela.

Kareem From the Arabic, meaning "noble, exalted." HEBREW EQUIVALENTS: Achiram, Adonikam, Atlai. FEMININE HEBREW EQUIVALENTS: Ge'ona, Ge'onit, Ramit.

Karel A variant form of Carol. *See* Carol.

Karim A variant spelling of Kareem. *See* Kareem.

Karin (קָרִין) From the Arabic, meaning "horn." The exact Hebrew equivalent is Karin. FEMININE HEBREW EQUIVALENTS: Karnay, Karni'el, Karniya, Ya'el.

Karl A variant spelling of Carl. *See* Carl.

Karmel (כַּרְמֶל) A variant spelling of Carmel. *See* Carmel.

Karmeli (כַּרְמְלִי) A variant spelling of Carmeli. *See* Carmeli.

Karna (קַרְנָא) From the Aramaic, meaning "horn." The Hebrew equivalent is Karna. FEMININE HEBREW EQUIVALENTS: Karni'ela, Karnit, Karniya.

Karni (קַרְנִי) From the Hebrew, meaning "my horn." The exact Hebrew equivalent is Karni. FEMININE HEBREW EQUIVALENTS: Karni'ela, Karnit, Karniya.

Karniel (קַרְנִיאֵל) From the Hebrew, meaning "God is my horn." The exact Hebrew equivalent is Karni'el. The exact feminine equivalent is Karni'ela.

Karol, Karole Variant spellings of Carol. *See* Carol.

Kashti (קַשְׁתִּי) From the Hebrew, meaning "my rainbow." The exact Hebrew equivalent is Kashti. Keshet is a feminine equivalent.

Kaski (קַסְקִי) A Yiddish pet form of Yechezkel. *See* Yechezkel.

Kasriel A variant spelling of Katriel. *See* Katriel.

Kati (כַּתִּי) A short form of Katriel. *See* Katriel. The exact Hebrew equivalent is Kati.

Katriel (כַּתְרִיאֵל) From the Hebrew, meaning "God is my crown." The exact Hebrew equivalent is Katri'el. The exact feminine equivalent is Katri'ela.

Katzin (קָצִין) From the Hebrew, meaning "prince, officer, leader." The exact Hebrew equivalent is Katzin. FEMININE HEBREW EQUIVALENTS: Nagida, Sara, Yisra'ela.

Kaufman, Kaufmann From the German, meaning "buyer." *See* Yaakov.

Kay From the Greek, meaning "rejoicing," or from the Anglo-Saxon, meaning "warden of a fortified place." HEBREW EQUIVALENTS: Akiva, Avigdor, Lotan. FEMININE HEBREW EQUIVALENTS: Avigdora, Magena, Marnina.

Kedem (קֶדֶם) From the Hebrew, meaning "east." The exact Hebrew equivalent is Kedem. The exact feminine equivalent is Kedma.

Kedma (קֶדְמָה) A unisex name. From the Hebrew, meaning "east, eastward." The exact Hebrew equivalent is Kedma.

Keenan A variant form of Keene. *See* Keene.

Keene From the Old English, meaning "wise, learned," or from the

German, meaning "bold." HEBREW EQUIVALENTS: Navon, No'az, Utz. FEMININE HEBREW EQUIVALENTS: Ge'onit, No'aza, Tushiya.

Kefir (כְּפִיר) From the Hebrew, meaning "young lion cub." The exact Hebrew equivalent is Kefir. The exact feminine equivalent is Kefira.

Keith From the Old Gaelic, meaning "wood, woody area." HEBREW EQUIVALENTS: Adam, Ya'ar, Ya'ari. FEMININE HEBREW EQUIVALENTS: Adama, Ya'ara, Ya'arit.

Kelley, Kelly A unisex name. From the Cornish, meaning "wood grove," or from the Irish, meaning "warlike." Also, a variant form of Kelsey. HEBREW EQUIVALENTS: Erez, Efyon, Ilan. FEMININE HEBREW EQUIVALENTS: Arza, Ilana, Livnat.

Kelsey A unisex name. A variant form of Kelson. *See* Kelson.

Kelson From the Middle Dutch, meaning "boat." The Hebrew equivalent is Sira. Aniya is a feminine equivalent.

Kelsy A variant form of Kelson. *See* Kelson.

Kelvin, Kelwin, Kelwyn From the Anglo-Saxon, meaning "lover of ships." HEBREW EQUIVALENTS: Ahuv, Bildad, Narkis. FEMININE HEBREW EQUIVALENTS: Ahuva, Aniya, Chiba.

Kemuel (קְמוּאֵל) From the Hebrew, meaning "raised by God." The exact Hebrew equivalent is Kemu'el. FEMININE HEBREW EQUIVALENTS: Komema, Uzi'ela. In Numbers 34:24, a member of the tribe of Ephraim.

Ken A pet form of Kenneth. *See* Kenneth.

Kendal, Kendall From the Celtic, meaning "ruler of the valley." HEBREW EQUIVALENTS: Emek, Katri'el, Melech, Moshel, Yamlech, Yisra'el. FEMININE HEBREW EQUIVALENTS: Ga'ya, Malka, Sara.

Kendrick From the Anglo-Saxon, meaning "royal." HEBREW EQUIVALENTS: Katri'el, Malkam, Malki. FEMININE HEBREW EQUIVALENTS: Alufa, Malka, Sara.

Kene A variant spelling of Kenny. *See* Kenny.

Kenen From the Old English and German, meaning "to know." HEBREW

EQUIVALENTS: Bina, Buna, Yavin. FEMININE HEBREW EQUIVALENTS: Bina, Buna, Dati'ela.

Kenneth From the Celtic and Scottish, meaning "beautiful, handsome." HEBREW EQUIVALENTS: Adin, Hadar, Kalil. FEMININE HEBREW EQUIVALENTS: Na'a, Na'ama, Nava.

Kennie, Kenny Pet forms of Kenneth. *See* Kenneth.

Kent A variant form of Kenneth. *See* Kenneth.

Kerby A variant spelling of Kirby. *See* Kirby.

Kerem (כֶּרֶם) A unisex name. From the Hebrew, meaning "vineyard." The exact Hebrew equivalent is Kerem.

Keren (קֶרֶן) From the Hebrew, meaning "horn." The exact Hebrew equivalent is Keren. FEMININE HEBREW EQUIVALENTS: Karni'ela, Karnit, Karniya.

Kermit From the Dutch, meaning "church." HEBREW EQUIVALENTS: Devir, Kadosh. FEMININE HEBREW EQUIVALENTS: Devira, Kedosha.

Kern From the Old Irish, meaning "band of soldiers." HEBREW EQUIVALENTS: Gad, Gadi'el, Gavri'el. FEMININE HEBREW EQUIVALENTS: Gibora, Gidona, Tigra.

Kerr From the Norse, meaning "marshland." HEBREW EQUIVALENTS: Aviyam, Beri, Dalfon. FEMININE HEBREW EQUIVALENTS: Afeka, Bat-Yam, Miryam.

Kerry From the Gaelic, meaning "black, black-haired person." HEBREW EQUIVALENTS: Cham, Kush, Pinchas. FEMININE HEBREW EQUIVALENTS: Dala, Delila, Shechora.

Kesem (קֶסֶם) From the Hebrew, meaning "magic, witchcraft." The exact Hebrew equivalent is Kesem. The exact feminine equivalent is Kesima.

Kesher (קֶשֶׁר) From the Hebrew, meaning "knot, tie." The exact Hebrew equivalent is Kesher. FEMININE HEBREW EQUIVALENTS: Keshira, Keshura.

Keta (קֶטַע) From the Hebrew, meaning "section, excerpt, portion."

The exact Hebrew equivalent is Keta. FEMININE HEBREW EQUIVALENTS: Chelkat, Mana, Menat.

Keter (כֶּתֶר) From the Hebrew, meaning "crown." The exact Hebrew equivalent is Keter. FEMININE HEBREW EQUIVALENTS: Katri'ela, Kelila, Kelula.

Ketina (קְטִינָא) A unisex name. From the Aramaic, meaning "small." The exact Hebrew equivalent is Ketina.

Kevin From the Gaelic, meaning "handsome, beautiful." HEBREW EQUIVALENTS: Hadar, Kalil, Nechmad. FEMININE HEBREW EQUIVALENTS: Hadura, Na'ama, Na'omi.

Khalil From the Arabic, meaning "friend." HEBREW EQUIVALENTS: Amitan, Chovav, Yedidya. FEMININE HEBREW EQUIVALENTS: Achva, Amit, Amita.

Kibby From the British, meaning "cottage by the water." HEBREW EQUIVALENTS: Aviyam, Avgar, Betu'el. FEMININE HEBREW EQUIVALENTS: Afeka, Bat-Yam, Molada.

Kidd From the British, meaning "strong." HEBREW EQUIVALENTS: Amitz, Azi'el, Chizkiya, Yechezkel. FEMININE HEBREW EQUIVALENTS: Adira, Amitza, Avni'ela.

Kiel A short form of Ezekiel. *See* Ezekiel.

Kile A variant spelling of Kyle. *See* Kyle.

Kimberley, Kimberly A unisex name derived from "kimberlite," a type of rock formation that sometimes contains diamonds. The exact masculine Hebrew equivalent is Yahalom. FEMININE HEBREW EQUIVALENTS: Yahaloma, Yahalomit.

Kin A pet form of Kingsley and Kingston. *See* Kingsley *and* Kingston.

King From the Anglo-Saxon, meaning "ruler." The exact Hebrew equivalent is Melech. The exact feminine equivalent is Malka.

Kingsley From the Anglo-Saxon, meaning "from the king's meadow." HEBREW EQUIVALENTS: Ben-Carmi, Carmel, Gan. FEMININE HEBREW EQUIVALENTS: Gana, Ginat, Katri'ela.

Kingston From the Old English, meaning "king's town." HEBREW EQUIV-
ALENTS: Avimelech, Elimelech, Malkam. FEMININE HEBREW EQUIVALENTS:
Malka, Malkit, Sara.

Kinori (כְּנוֹרִי) From the Hebrew, meaning "my lyre, my harp." The
exact Hebrew equivalent is Kinori. The feminine equivalent is Kinneret.

Kinsey From the British, meaning "royal." HEBREW EQUIVALENTS: Elrad,
Melech, Moshel, Rozen, Yisra'el. FEMININE HEBREW EQUIVALENTS: Malka,
Sara, Sarit.

Kip, Kipp Pet forms of Kipling. *See* Kipling.

Kipling Probably from the Old English, meaning "pointed hill." HE-
BREW EQUIVALENTS: Aharon, Gal, Harel. FEMININE HEBREW EQUIVALENTS:
Galit, Galya, Talmi.

Kirby From the Old English and Middle English, meaning "church."
Also, from the British, meaning "cottage by the water." HEBREW
EQUIVALENTS: Aviyam, Kadish, Kadosh. FEMININE HEBREW EQUIVALENTS:
Devira, Kedosha, Miryam.

Kirk From the Old Norse and Old English, meaning "church." HEBREW
EQUIVALENTS: Devir, Kadish, Kadosh. FEMININE HEBREW EQUIVALENTS: Devira, Kedosha.

Kislon (כִּסְלוֹן) From the Hebrew, meaning "nonsensical." The exact
Hebrew equivalent is Kislon. In Numbers 34:21, a member of the
tribe of Simeon.

Kitron (כִּתְרוֹן) A unisex name. From the Hebrew, meaning "crown."
The exact Hebrew equivalent is Kitron.

Kiva, Kive, Kivi (קִיבִי/קִיבָא) Pet forms of Akiva and Yaakov. *See*
Akiva *and* Yaakov.

Kliel (כְּלִיאֵל) From the Hebrew, meaning "vessel of God." The exact
Hebrew equivalent is Kli'el. Yora is a feminine equivalent.

Kobe, Kobi, Koby Pet forms of Jacob. *See* Jacob.

Kochav, Kokhav (כּוֹכָב) From the Hebrew, meaning "star." The exact Hebrew equivalent is Kochav. The exact feminine equivalent is Kochava.

Kochavi (כּוֹכָבִי) From the Hebrew, meaning "my star." The exact Hebrew equivalent is Kochavi. FEMININE HEBREW EQUIVALENTS: Kochava, Mazal, Mazalit.

Konrad A variant spelling of Conrad. *See* Conrad.

Koppel (קָאפֶּעל/קָאפֶּל) A Yiddish form of Yaakov. *See* Yaakov.

Korach (קֹרַח) From the Hebrew, meaning "bald." The exact Hebrew equivalent is Korach.

Korah An Anglicized form of Korach. *See* Korach.

Kornell A variant spelling of Cornell. *See* Cornell.

Kotz (קוֹץ) From the Hebrew, meaning "thorn." The exact Hebrew equivalent is Kotz. FEMININE HEBREW EQUIVALENTS: Akitza, Chochit.

Kovi (קוֹבִי) A pet form of Yaakov. *See* Yaakov.

Kris A pet form of Kristofer. *See* Kristofer.

Kristofer A variant spelling of Christopher. *See* Christopher.

Kubi A pet form of Jacob. *See* Jacob.

Kunama (קוּנָמָא) From the Aramaic form of the Hebrew words *kinman* and *kinamon*, meaning "cinnamon." In Exodus 30:23, the spice is referred to as *kinman*; in Proverbs 7:17, as *kinamon*. The exact Hebrew equivalent is Kunama.

Kurt A pet form of Konrad. *See* Konrad.

Kus (קוּת) A short form of Yekusiel (Yekutiel). *See* Yekutiel.

Kyle A Gaelic form of the Old English, meaning "hill where the cattle graze." Also from the Scottish, meaning "narrow channel." HEBREW EQUIVALENTS: Aharon, Emek, Gain, Gal, Gali. FEMININE HEBREW EQUIVALENTS: Bika, Geva, Gilada, Talma.

✌ L ✌

Laban A variant spelling of Lavan. *See* Lavan.

Label (לֵייבֶעל/לֵייבְּל) A pet form of the Yiddish name Leib, meaning "lion." HEBREW EQUIVALENTS: Ari, Ari'el, Lavi. FEMININE HEBREW EQUIVALENTS: Ari'ela, Kefira, Levi'a.

Lad, Ladd From the Middle English, meaning "boy, young man." HEBREW EQUIVALENTS: Bachur, Na'ari, Na'arya. FEMININE HEBREW EQUIVALENTS: Alma, Betula, Na'ara.

Lahat (לַהַט) From the Hebrew, meaning "flame" or "sword." The exact Hebrew equivalent is Lahat. FEMININE HEBREW EQUIVALENTS: Avuka, Shalhevet, Uri'ela.

Lahav (לַהַב) A unisex name. From the Hebrew, meaning "flame, fire." The exact Hebrew exquivalent is Lahav. The exact feminine Hebrew equivalent is Lehava.

Lamar, Lamarr From the Latin and French, meaning "of the sea." HEBREW EQUIVALENTS: Aviyam, Chaifa, Shuni. FEMININE HEBREW EQUIVALENTS: Bat-Galim, Bat-Yam, Miryam.

Lambert From the German and French, meaning "brightness of the land." HEBREW EQUIVALENTS: Avner, Hillel, Lapidot. FEMININE HEBREW EQUIVALENTS: Hila, Hillela, Levana.

Lamed (לָמֵד) From the Hebrew, meaning "learning, knowledge."

The exact Hebrew equivalent is Lamed. FEMININE HEBREW EQUIVALENTS: Da'at, Dei'a.

Lance From the Latin, meaning "servant, spear carrier." HEBREW EQUIVALENTS: Avda, Avdel, Avdi. FEMININE HEBREW EQUIVALENTS: Aleksandra, Ama, Ezr'ela.

Lancelot A variant form of Lance. *See* Lance.

Landan From the Anglo-Saxon, meaning "open, grassy area; lawn." HEBREW EQUIVALENTS: Bustan, Desheh, Gan. FEMININE HEBREW EQUIVALENTS: Ginat, Yardeniya.

Landis A variant form of Landan. *See* Landan.

Lane From the Old English, meaning "to move ahead," hence, "a path." HEBREW EQUIVALENTS: Nativ, Shovav, Solel. FEMININE HEBREW EQUIVALENTS: Netiva, Selila.

Lang From the German, meaning "long, tall." HEBREW EQUIVALENTS: Aram, Aricha, Aryoch. Meroma is a feminine Hebrew equivalent.

Lapid (לַפִּיד) From the Hebrew, meaning "flame, torch." The exact Hebrew equivalent is Lapid. FEMININE HEBREW EQUIVALENTS: Avuka, Shalhevet, Uri'ela.

Lapidos A variant form of Lapidot. *See* Lapidot.

Lapidot (לַפִּידוֹת) From the Hebrew, meaning "flame, torch." The exact Hebrew equivalent is Lapidot. FEMININE HEBREW EQUIVALENTS: Avuka, Bareket, Shalhevet.

Larry A pet form of Laurence. *See* Laurence.

Lars A Swedish pet form of Laurence. *See* Laurence.

Laurence From the Latin, meaning "laurel, crown." HEBREW EQUIVALENTS: Atir, Kalil, Katri'el. FEMININE HEBREW EQUIVALENTS: Katri'ela, Kelila, Malka.

Laurie A pet form of Laurence. *See* Laurence.

Lavan (לָבָן) From the Hebrew, meaning "white." The exact Hebrew equivalent is Lavan. The exact feminine equivalent is Levana.

Lavi (לָבִיא) From the Hebrew, meaning "lion." The exact Hebrew equivalent is Lavi. FEMININE HEBREW EQUIVALENTS: Ari'el, La'yish, Levi'a.

Lavey A variant spelling of Lavi or Levi. *See* Lavi *and* Levi.

Lavid (לָבִיד) From the Hebrew, meaning "plywood." The exact Hebrew equivalent is Lavid. FEMININE HEBREW EQUIVALENTS: Ilana, Ilanit, Livnat.

Lavlar (לַבְלָר) From the Hebrew, meaning "writer, clerk." The exact Hebrew equivalent is Lavlar.

Lawrence A variant spelling of Laurence. *See* Laurence.

Layil (לַיִל) A unisex name. From the Hebrew, meaning "night, nocturnal." The exact Hebrew equivalent is La'yil.

Layser A variant form of Layzer. *See* Layzer.

Layzer An alternate spelling of Lazar. *See* Lazar.

Lazar (לָאזַר) A Yiddish form of Eliezer. *See* Eliezer. Also, a short form of Lazarus. *See* Lazarus.

Lazarus The Greek form of Elazar and Eliezer. *See* Elazar *and* Eliezer.

Leander From the Greek, meaning "like a lion." HEBREW EQUIVALENTS: Ari, Aryei, Lavi. FEMININE HEBREW EQUIVALENTS: Ari'el, Ari'ela, Kefira.

Lebush A variant spelling of Leibush. *See* Leibush.

Lee A pet form of Leo, Leon, Leonard, or Leslie. *See* Leonard. Also, from the Anglo-Saxon, meaning "meadow." HEBREW EQUIVALENTS: Bustenai, Carmel, Lavi. FEMININE HEBREW EQUIVALENTS: Ganit, Levi'a, Yizr'ela.

Leeber A variant spelling of Lieber. *See* Lieber.

Leeser (לִיסֶער) A Yiddish form of Eliezer. *See* Eliezer.

Leib (לֵיב) A Yiddish form of the German name Loeb, meaning "lion." HEBREW EQUIVALENTS: Gur, Lavi, La'yish. FEMININE HEBREW EQUIVALENTS: Ari'el, Ari'ela, Levi'a.

Leibel (לֵייבֶּעל) A pet form of Leib. *See* Leib.

Leibush (לֵייבּוּש) A variant form of Leib. *See* Leib.

Leif An Old Norse form of Lief. *See* Lief.

Leigh A variant spelling of Lee. *See* Lee.

Leiser A Yiddish form of the Hebrew names Elazar and Eliezer. *See* Elazar *and* Eliezer.

Lemuel (לְמוּאֵל) From the Hebrew, meaning "a nation dedicated to God." The Hebrew equivalent is Chanoch. The feminine Hebrew equivalent is Chanukah. In Proverbs 3:21, the king of Massa.

Len A pet form of Leonard. *See* Leonard.

Lenn A variant spelling of Len. *See* Len.

Lennard, Lennart Variant forms of Leonard. *See* Leonard.

Lennie A pet form of Leonard. *See* Leonard.

Leo From the Latin, meaning "lion" or "the lion's nature." *See* Leonard.

Leon The Greek form of Leo, meaning "lion." *See* Leo.

Leonard A French form of the Old High German, meaning "strong as a lion." HEBREW EQUIVALENTS: Aryei, Lavi, La'yish. FEMININE HEBREW EQUIVALENTS: Ari'ela, Gavrila, Levi'a.

Leonardo A Spanish and Italian form of Leonard. *See* Leonard.

Leopold From the Old High German and the Old English, meaning "bold, free man" and "defender of people." HEBREW EQUIVALENTS: Ya'akov, Zimri. FEMININE HEBREW EQUIVALENTS: Shimrit, Tzila, Ya'akova.

Leor, Le-or Variant spelling of Lior. *See* Lior.

Leron, Lerone Variant spellings of Liron. *See* Liron.

LeRoy, Leroy A French form of the Latin, meaning "the king, royalty." HEBREW EQUIVALENTS: Katri'el, Melech, Yisra'el. FEMININE HEBREW EQUIVALENTS: Laya, Malka, Yisra'ela.

Les A pet form of Leslie and Lester. *See* Leslie *and* Lester.

Leser A variant spelling of Lesser. *See* Lesser.

Leshem (לֶשֶׁם) From the Hebrew, meaning "precious stone." The exact Hebrew equivalent is Leshem. FEMININE HEBREW EQUIVALENTS: Yahaloma, Yakira, Yekara.

Lesley A variant spelling of Leslie. *See* Leslie.

Leslie From the Anglo-Saxon, meaning "meadowlands." HEBREW EQUIVALENTS: Karmel, Karmeli, Sharon. FEMININE HEBREW EQUIVALENTS: Karmela, Sharona, Ya'ara.

Lesser (לֶעסר/לֶעסֶער) A Yiddish form of Eliezer. *See* Eliezer.

Lester Originally Leicester, an English place-name. From the Latin and the Old English, meaning "camp, protected area." HEBREW EQUIVALENTS: Latan, Lot, Tzilai. FEMININE HEBREW EQUIVALENTS: Avigdora, Chasya, Magena.

Leumi (לְאוּמִי) A unisex name. From the Hebrew, meaning "nation, national." The exact Hebrew equivalent is Le'umi.

Lev (לֵב) Either from the Hebrew, meaning "heart," or from the Yiddish, meaning "lion." The exact Hebrew equivalent is Lev. FEMININE HEBREW EQUIVALENTS: Arela, Ari'ela, Kefira, Levi'a.

Levanon (לְבָנוֹן) From the Hebrew, meaning "white" or "moon, month." The exact Hebrew equivalent is Levanon. The exact feminine equivalent is Levana.

Levi (לֵוִי) From the Hebrew, meaning "joined to" or "attendant upon." The exact Hebrew equivalent is Levi. The exact feminine equivalent is Levi'a.

Levitas (לְוִיטַס) A variant form of Levi. *See* Levi.

Leviva (לְבִיבָה) A unisex name. From the Hebrew, meaning "pancake." The exact Hebrew equivalent is Leviva.

Lew A pet form of Lewis. *See* Lewis.

Lewes A variant spelling of Lewis. *See* Lewis.

Lewi The Hawaiian form of Levi. *See* Levi.

Lewis An English form of the French name Louis. *See* Louis.

Lezer (לֶעזֶר) A Yiddish form of Eliezer. *See* Eliezer.

Li (לִי) A unisex name. From the Hebrew, meaning "me" or "to me." The exact Hebrew equivalent is Li.

Liam (לִי-עָם) From the Hebrew, meaning "my nation." Also, a variant form of William. The exact Hebrew equivalent is Li'am. FEMININE HEBREW EQUIVALENTS: Le'uma, Le'umi, Uma.

Liba (לִיבָּא) A variant spelling of Lieber. *See* Lieber.

Lieb (לִיב) A short form of Lieber. *See* Lieber.

Lieber (לִיבֶּער) A Yiddish form of the German, meaning "beloved." Akin to Lief. *See* Lief.

Lief From the Middle English and the Old English, meaning "beloved, dear." HEBREW EQUIVALENTS: Bildad, Eldad, Chavivel. FEMININE HEBREW EQUIVALENTS: Davida, Liba, Yedida.

Liel, Li-El (לִי-אֵל/לִיאֵל) From the Hebrew, meaning "God is mine" or "I have [faith in] God." The exact Hebrew equivalent is Li'el. FEMININE HEBREW EQUIVALENTS: Bat-El, Betu'el, Imanu'ela.

Liezer (לִי-עֶזֶר/לִיעֶזֶר) A short form of Eliezer. *See* Eliezer.

Limon (לִימוֹן) From the Hebrew, meaning "lemon." The exact Hebrew equivalent is Limon.

Linc A pet form of Lincoln. *See* Lincoln.

Lincoln From the Old English and the German, meaning "lithe, flexible," referring to the trees of the linden family. Also, from the Old English and Latin, meaning "camp near the stream." HEBREW EQUIVALENTS: Dalfon, Dela'ya, Miklos. FEMININE HEBREW EQUIVALENTS: Tirza, Tzeruya, Yaval.

Lindsay, Lindsey Unisex names. From the Old English, meaning "linden trees near the water [sea]." HEBREW EQUIVALENTS: Dalfon, Ilan, Raviv. FEMININE HEBREW EQUIVALENTS: Miryam, Reviva, Yaval.

Lindsy A variant spelling of Lindsay. *See* Lindsay.

Link From the Old English, meaning "enclosure." HEBREW EQUIVALENTS: Avigdor, Gidron, Lotan. FEMININE HEBREW EQUIVALENTS: Afeka, Avigdora, Efrat.

Lion A variant spelling of Leon. *See* Leon.

Li-On (לִי-אוֹן/לִיאוֹן) From the Hebrew, meaning "I have strength." The exact Hebrew equivalent is Li'on. FEMININE HEBREW EQUIVALENTS: Gavri'ela, Gavrila, Nili.

Lionel A variant form of Lion. *See* Lion.

Lior, Li-Or (לִי-אוֹר/לִיאוֹר) A unisex name. From the Hebrew, meaning "light is mine." The exact Hebrew equivalent is Li'or.

Lipman, **Lipmann** (לִיפְּמַן/לִיפְּמַאן) A Yiddish form of the German name Liebman, meaning "lover of man." HEBREW EQUIVALENTS: Chaviv, David, Eldad. FEMININE HEBREW EQUIVALENTS: Davida, Liba, Yedida.

Liran (לִירָן) From the Hebrew, meaning "joy is mine." The exact Hebrew equivalent is Liran. FEMININE HEBREW EQUIVALENTS: Ron, Roni, Ronli.

Liron, Li-Ron (לִי-רוֹן/לִירוֹן) A unisex name. From the Hebrew, meaning "song is mine." The exact Hebrew equivalent is Liron.

Litov, Li-Tov (לִי-טוֹב/לִיטוֹב) A unisex name. From the Hebrew, meaning "I am good, doing well." The exact Hebrew equivalent is Li'tov.

Livni (לִבְנִי) From the Hebrew, meaning "white" or "frankincense [because of its white color]." The exact Hebrew equivalent is Livni. FEMININE HEBREW EQUIVALENTS: Levona, Livnat, Malbina.

Llewellyn From the Welsh, meaning "in the likeness of a lion." HEBREW EQUIVALENTS: Ari, Ari'el, Lavi. FEMININE HEBREW EQUIVALENTS: Ari'ela, Kefira, Levi'a.

Lloyd From the Celtic or Welsh, meaning "grey" or "brown" or "a dark-complexioned person." HEBREW EQUIVALENTS: Adar, Kedar, Pinchas. FEMININE HEBREW EQUIVALENTS: Efa, Laila, Tzila.

Loeb (לויב) From the German, meaning "lion." HEBREW EQUIVALENTS: Aryei, Lavi, La'yish. FEMININE HEBREW EQUIVALENTS: Ari'ela, Kefira, Levi'a.

Loel A variant spelling of Lowell. *See* Lowell.

Lon, Lonnie, Lonny Pet forms of Alphonso. *See* Alphonso.

Lorence A variant spelling of Laurence. *See* Laurence.

Lorn, Lorne Variant forms of Laurence. *See* Laurence.

Lorry A variant spelling of Laurie and a pet form of Laurence. *See* Laurie *and* Laurence.

Lot (לוט) From the Hebrew, meaning "envelop, protect." The exact Hebrew equivalent is Lot. FEMININE HEBREW EQUIVALENTS: Afeka, Avigdora, Efrat.

Lotan (לוטן) From the Hebrew, meaning "envelop, protect." The exact Hebrew equivalent is Lotan. Akin to Lot. *See* Lot *for feminine equivalents.*

Lothar From the Anglo-Saxon, meaning "renowned warrior" or "hero of the people." HEBREW EQUIVALENTS: Abir, Amitz, Ben-Cha'yil. FEMININE HEBREW EQUIVALENTS: Amtza, Avicha'yil, Avirama.

Lother, Lothur Variant spellings of Lothar. *See* Lothar.

Louis From the Old French and the Old High German, meaning "famous in battle" or "refuge of the people." HEBREW EQUIVALENTS: Avicha'yil, Ben-Cha'yil, Ish-Cha'yil. FEMININE HEBREW EQUIVALENTS: Gavri'ela, Gavrila, Gibora.

Lovell A variant form of Lowell. *See* Lowell.

Lowe A variant form of the German name Loeb. *See* Loeb.

Lowell From the Old English, meaning "beloved" or "hill." HEBREW EQUIVALENTS: Bildad, Eldad, David. FEMININE HEBREW EQUIVALENTS: Liba, Talma, Yedida.

Loy A pet form of Loyal. *See* Loyal.

Loyal From the Old French and the Latin, meaning "faithful, true."

HEBREW EQUIVALENTS: Amanya, Amitai, Amitan. FEMININE HEBREW EQUIV-
ALENTS: Amana, Emuna, Ne'emana.

Lucas A variant form of Lucius. *See* Lucius.

Lucian A variant form of Lucius. *See* Lucius.

Lucius From the Latin, meaning "light." HEBREW EQUIVALENTS: Avner,
Eli'or, Li'or, Ma'or. FEMININE HEBREW EQUIVALENTS: Behira, Eli'ora,
Li'ora.

Lucky From the Middle English, meaning "good fortune." HEBREW
EQUIVALENTS: Mazal, Mazal-Tov, Siman-Tov. FEMININE HEBREW EQUIVA-
LENTS: Mazal, Mazala, Mazalit.

Ludwig A German form of Louis. *See* Louis.

Luke The English form of Lucius. *See* Lucius.

Lupo From the Latin, meaning "wolf." The Hebrew equivalent is
Ze'ev. The feminine equivalent is Ze'eva.

Lupus A variant form of Lupo. *See* Lupo.

Luz (לוז) From the Hebrew, meaning "almond tree." The exact Hebrew equivalent is Luz. The exact feminine Hebrew equivalent is
Luza.

Lyall, Lyell Variant forms of Lyle. *See* Lyle.

Lyle A French form of the Latin, meaning "from the island." Also, a
Scottish name meaning "little." HEBREW EQUIVALENTS: Moshe, Peleg,
Ze'ira. FEMININE HEBREW EQUIVALENTS: Arnona, Devora, Gali.

Lyn A pet form of Lyndon. *See* Lyndon.

Lyndon From the Old English, meaning "the hill with the linden
trees." HEBREW EQUIVALENTS: Aharon, Ilan, Luz. FEMININE HEBREW EQUIV-
ALENTS: Alona, Ilana, Shikma.

Lyndy A pet form of Lyndon. *See* Lyndon.

Lynn From the Old English and Welsh, meaning "cataract, lake,
brook." HEBREW EQUIVALENTS: Arnon, Aviyam, Dela'ya. FEMININE HEBREW
EQUIVALENTS: Reviva, Silona, Silonit.

Lyon The French form of Lion. *See* Lion.

Lyonell A variant form of Lyon. *See* Lyon.

Lyor A variant spelling of Lior. *See* Lior.

Lyron A variant spelling of Liron. *See* Liron.

~ M ~

Maagal (מַעֲגָל) From the Hebrew, meaning "circle." The exact Hebrew equivalent is Ma'agal. Akifa is a feminine Hebrew equivalent.

Maaseiyahu (מַעֲשֵׂיָהוּ) From the Hebrew, meaning "work of God." The exact Hebrew equivalent is Ma'aseiyahu. FEMININE HEBREW EQUIVALENTS: Amal, Amalya. In I Chronicles 15:18, a Levite who played a musical instrument.

Maazya, Maazyah (מַעַזְיָה) From the Hebrew, meaning "God is a refuge." The exact Hebrew equivalent is Ma'azya. FEMININE HEBREW EQUIVALENTS: Avigdora, Chasya, Shimriya. In Nehemiah 10:9, the name of a Levite.

Mac From the Gaelic, meaning "son of." The exact Hebrew equivalent is Ben.

Macabee, Maccabee (מַכַּבִּי) From the Hebrew, meaning "hammer." The exact Hebrew equivalent is Makabi. The exact feminine Hebrew equivalent is Makabiya.

Macdonald From the Scottish, meaning "son of Donald." *See* Donald.

Mace An English form of the Old French, meaning "club, hammer." The Hebrew equivalent is Makabi. The feminine Hebrew equivalent is Makabiya.

Macey A variant form of Mace. *See* Mace.

Machir (מָכִיר) From the Hebrew, meaning "sold." The exact Hebrew equivalent is Machir. In Genesis 50:23, a son of Manasseh.

Mack A variant spelling of Mac. *See* Mac.

Mackenzie A unisex name. From the Irish/Gaelic, meaning "son of a wise ruler." HEBREW EQUIVALENTS: Melech, Moshel, Sar. FEMININE HEBREW EQUIVALENTS: Alufa, Sara, Sarit.

Mackey A variant form of Mack. *See* Mack.

Macy A variant spelling of Macey. *See* Macey.

Madon (מָדוֹן) From the Hebrew, meaning "strife, conflict." The exact Hebrew equivalent is Madon.

Magen (מָגֵן) From the Hebrew, meaning "protector." The exact Hebrew equivalent is Magen. The exact feminine Hebrew equivalent is Magena.

Magnus From the Latin, meaning "great." HEBREW EQUIVALENTS: Gedalya, Gedalyahu, Gidel. FEMININE HEBREW EQUIVALENTS: Atalya, Gedola, Gedula.

Maher (מַהֵר) From the Hebrew, meaning "quick, industrious, expert." HEBREW EQUIVALENTS: Maher, Mahir. The feminine equivalent is Mehira.

Maimon (מַיְמוֹן) From the Arabic, meaning "luck, good fortune." The exact Hebrew equivalent is Maimon. FEMININE HEBREW EQUIVALENTS: Mazal, Mazala, Mazalit.

Maimun A variant spelling of Maimon. *See* Maimon.

Major From the Latin, meaning "great." Akin to Magnus. *See* Magnus.

Makabi A variant spelling of Macabee. *See* Macabee.

Machi (מָכִי) From the Hebrew, meaning "decrease." The exact Hebrew equivalent is Machi. In Numbers 13:15, the father of Ge'uel of the tribe of Gad.

Maks A variant spelling of Max. *See* Max.

Maksim (מַקְסִים) From the Hebrew, meaning "charming." The exact Hebrew equivalent is Maksim. The exact feminine equivalent is Maksima.

Mal A pet form of Malcolm. *See* Malcolm.

Malach (מַלָח) From the Hebrew, meaning "sailor." The exact Hebrew equivalent is Malach.

Malachai A variant spelling of Malachi. *See* Malachi.

Malachi (מַלְאָכִי) From the Hebrew, meaning "my messenger, my minister" or "my servant." The exact Hebrew equivalent is Malachi. FEMININE HEBREW EQUIVALENTS: Ama, Milka, Sa'ada.

Malachy A variant spelling of Malachi. *See* Malachi.

Malbin (מַלְבִּין) From the Hebrew, meaning "to whiten," signifying embarrassment. The exact Hebrew equivalent is Malbin. The exact feminine equivalent is Malbina.

Malcam A variant spelling of Malkam. *See* Malkam.

Malcolm From the Arabic, meaning "dove," or from the Gaelic, meaning "servant of St. Columba." HEBREW EQUIVALENTS: Ovadya, Oved, Yona. FEMININE HEBREW EQUIVALENTS: Malka, Malkit, Sa'ada, Yonina.

Malkam (מַלְכָּם) From the Hebrew, meaning "God is their King." The exact Hebrew equivalent is Malkam. The feminine equivalent is Malka.

Malki (מַלְכִּי) From the Hebrew, meaning "my king." The exact Hebrew equivalent is Malki. Malka is the feminine equivalent.

Malkiel (מַלְכִּיאֵל) From the Hebrew, meaning "God is my King." The exact Hebrew equivalent is Malki'el. FEMININE HEBREW EQUIVALENTS: Malka, Malki'ela, Malkit. In Numbers 26:44, a member of the tribe of Asher.

Malkosh (מַלְקוֹשׁ) From the Hebrew, meaning "rain." The exact Hebrew equivalent is Malkosh. The exact feminine equivalent is Malkosha.

Malon (מָלוֹן) From the Hebrew, meaning "lodge, inn." The exact Hebrew equivalent is Malon. FEMININE HEBREW EQUIVALENTS: Magena, Magina, Mishan.

Malvin A variant spelling of Melvin. *See* Melvin.

Manashi A variant spelling of Menashi. *See* Menashi.

Manasseh An Anglicized form of Menashe. *See* Menashe.

Mandel, Mandell From the Old French and the Middle Latin, meaning "almond." HEBREW EQUIVALENTS: Luz, Shaked. FEMININE HEBREW EQUIVALENTS: Luza, Shekeda.

Mandy A pet form of Manfred. *See* Manfred.

Manford From the Anglo-Saxon, meaning "small bridge over a brook." HEBREW EQUIVALENTS: Arnon, Geshur. Arnona is a feminine Hebrew equivalent.

Manfred From the German, meaning "man of peace." HEBREW EQUIVALENTS: Ish-Shalom, Shlomo. FEMININE HEBREW EQUIVALENTS: Meshulemet, Shlomit, Shulamit.

Mani A pet form of Emanuel, Manasseh, Manfred, and Manuel.

Manin A variant form of Mann. *See* Mann.

Manis A variant form of Mann. *See* Mann.

Manish (מַאֲנִישׁ) A Yiddish form of Mann. *See* Mann.

Manley, Manly From the Old English, meaning "protected field." HEBREW EQUIVALENTS: Gonen, Niram, Nirel. FEMININE HEBREW EQUIVALENTS: Magena, Niriya, Shemura.

Mann From the German, meaning "man." HEBREW EQUIVALENTS: Ben-Azai, Ben-Gever, Enosh. FEMININE HEBREW EQUIVALENTS: Adama, Gavri'ela. Also, a variant form of Menachem. *See* Menachem.

Mannes, Mannis (מַאֲנִיס/מַאֲנֶעס) Variant Yiddish forms of Mann. *See* Mann.

Manni A variant spelling of Mani and Manny. *See* Mani *and* Manny.

Manny, Mannye Pet forms of Emanuel, Manasseh, Manfred, and Manuel.

Manoach (מָנוֹחַ) The Anglicized form is Manoah. From the Hebrew, meaning "rest, peace." The exact Hebrew equivalent is Mano'ach. FEMININE HEBREW EQUIVALENTS: Menucha, Shelomit, Shulamit. In Judges 13:2, the father of Samson, whose birth was foretold by an angel.

Mansur From the Arabic, meaning "victorious." HEBREW EQUIVALENTS: Gavri'el, Gover, Netzach. FEMININE HEBREW EQUIVALENTS: Atara, Ateret, Dafina.

Manu A pet form of Manuel. *See* Manuel.

Manuel A short form of Emanuel. *See* Emanuel.

Manus A variant form of Magnus. *See* Magnus.

Maon (מָעוֹן) From the Hebrew, meaning "dwelling." The exact Hebrew equivalent is Ma'on. The exact feminine Hebrew equivalent is Me'ona.

Maor (מָאוֹר) From the Hebrew, meaning "light." The exact Hebrew equivalent is Ma'or. The exact feminine Hebrew equivalent is Me'ora.

Maoz (מָעוֹז) From the Hebrew, meaning "strength" or "fortress." The exact Hebrew equivalent is Ma'oz. FEMININE HEBREW EQUIVALENTS: Me'uza, Uza, Uzi'ela.

Mar From the Aramaic, meaning "master" or "lord." The exact Hebrew equivalent is Mar. FEMININE HEBREW EQUIVALENTS: Sara, Yisra'ela.

Maran (מָרָן) From the Aramaic, meaning "teacher, master." The exact Hebrew equivalent is Maran. FEMININE HEBREW EQUIVALENTS: Mora, Moran, Moriya.

Marc A short form of Marcus. *See* Marcus.

Marcel A popular French pet form of Marcus. *See* Marcus.

Marcelo, Marcello Pet forms of Marcus. *See* Marcus.

March A variant form of Marcus. *See* Marcus.

Marchall A variant spelling of Marshall. *See* Marshall.

Marco, Marcos Variant forms of Marcus. *See* Marcus.

Marcus From the Latin name Mars, meaning "warlike." HEBREW EQUIV-ALENTS: Makabi, Medan, Mordechai. FEMININE HEBREW EQUIVALENTS: Amtza, Atzma, Gavri'ela.

Marcy A variant form of Marcus. *See* Marcus.

Marek A Polish form of Marcus. *See* Marcus.

Mari A pet form of Marius. *See* Marius.

Marian A unisex name. *See* Marian (*feminine section*).

Marin From the Latin, meaning "small harbor." HEBREW EQUIVALENTS: Moshe, Nemali, Nemalya. FEMININE HEBREW EQUIVALENTS: Chaifa, Yama, Yamit.

Marino From the Greek, meaning "sea." HEBREW EQUIVALENTS: Avigal, Aviyam, Yam. FEMININE HEBREW EQUIVALENTS: Bat-Galim, Bat-Yam, Yama.

Mario A variant form of Marcus. *See* Marcus.

Maris From the Old English and French, meaning "sea, lake." HEBREW EQUIVALENTS: Avigal, Aviyam, Moshe. FEMININE HEBREW EQUIVALENTS: Bat-Yam, Miryam, Yama.

Marish (מָרִישׁ) From the Hebrew, meaning "beam, rafter." The exact Hebrew equivalent is Marish.

Marius A variant form of Marcus. *See* Marcus.

Mark A variant spelling of Marcus. *See* Marcus.

Marko, Markos Variant forms of Marcus. *See* Marcus.

Marlin From the Latin, Old English, and French, meaning "sea." HEBREW EQUIVALENTS: Avigal, Dalfon, Moshe. FEMININE HEBREW EQUIVA-LENTS: Bat-Galim, Bat-Yam, Yama.

Marlo A variant form of Marlin. *See* Marlin.

Marlow, Marlowe A variant form of Marlin. *See* Marlin.

Marne From the Latin, Old English, and French, meaning "sea." HEBREW EQUIVALENTS: Aviyam, Livyatan, Moshe. FEMININE HEBREW EQUIVALENTS: Bat-Galim, Miryam, Yamit.

Marnin (מַרְנִין) From the Hebrew, meaning "one who creates joy" or "one who sings." The exact Hebrew equivalent is Marnin. The exact feminine Hebrew equivalent is Marnina.

Marom (מָרוֹם) From the Hebrew, meaning "lofty, exalted." The exact Hebrew equivalent is Marom. The exact feminine Hebrew equivalent is Meroma.

Maron (מָרוֹן) From the Hebrew, meaning "flock of sheep." The exact Hebrew equivalent is Maron. The exact feminine Hebrew equivalent is Marona.

Marshal, Marshall From the Old English, meaning "one who grooms a horse, one who masters a horse" or "an officer in charge of military matters." HEBREW EQUIVALENTS: Ben-Cha'yil, Cha'yil, Ish-Cha'yil. FEMININE HEBREW EQUIVALENTS: Amtza, Gavrila, Gavri'ela.

Marshe A variant form of Marcus and Marshal. *See* Marcus *and* Marshal.

Martin A French form of the Latin name Martinus. Akin to Marcus, meaning "warlike." *See* Marcus.

Marvin From the Old English, meaning "friend of the sea" or "friendly sea." Also, from the Celtic, meaning "white sea," and from the Gaelic, meaning "mountainous area." HEBREW EQUIVALENTS: Medan, Moshe, Talmai. FEMININE HEBREW EQUIVALENTS: Marata, Migdala, Miryam.

Marwin A variant form of Marvin. *See* Marvin.

Masad (מַסָד) From the Hebrew, meaning "foundation, support." The exact Hebrew equivalent is Masad. The exact feminine Hebrew equivalent is Masada.

Mashiach (מָשִׁיחַ) From the Hebrew, meaning "Messiah, anointed one." The exact Hebrew equivalent is Mashi'ach. FEMININE HEBREW EQUIVALENTS: Mosha'a, Yiska.

Maskil (מַשְׂכִּיל) From the Hebrew, meaning "enlightened, educated." The exact Hebrew equivalent is Maskil. The exact feminine Hebrew equivalent is Maskila.

Mason From the Anglo-Saxon, meaning "mason, worker in stone." HEBREW EQUIVALENTS: Even, Shamir, Tzeror. FEMININE HEBREW EQUIVALENTS: Gazit, Ritzpa, Tzurel.

Masoor A variant spelling of Masur. *See* Masur.

Masos (מָשׂוֹשׂ) From the Hebrew, meaning "joy, happiness." The exact Hebrew equivalent is Masos. FEMININE HEBREW EQUIVALENTS: Aliza, Ditza, Mitzhala.

Masur (מָסוּר) From the Hebrew, meaning "transmitted" or "inherited." The exact Hebrew equivalent is Masur. The exact feminine Hebrew equivalent is Mesora.

Mat A pet form of Matthew. *See* Matthew.

Matan (מַתָּן) From the Hebrew, meaning "gift." The exact Hebrew equivalent is Matan. The exact feminine Hebrew equivalent is Matana.

Matania, Mataniah Variant spellings of Matanya. *See* Matanya.

Matanya, Matanyah (מַתַּנְיָה) From the Hebrew, meaning "gift of God." The exact Hebrew equivalent is Matanya. FEMININE HEBREW EQUIVALENTS: Matana, Matat.

Matanyahu (מַתַּנְיָהוּ) From the Hebrew, meaning "gift of God." The exact Hebrew equivalent is Matanyahu. FEMININE HEBREW EQUIVALENTS: Matana, Matat, Netanela.

Matat (מַתַּת) A unisex name. From the Hebrew, meaning "gift." The exact Hebrew equivalent is Matat. Also, a short form of Matityahu. *See* Matityahu.

Matel A Yiddish pet form of Mordechai. *See* Mordechai.

Mateo A Spanish form of Matthew. *See* Matthew.

Mati (מַתִּי) A pet form of Matanya and Mattathias. *See* Matanya *and* Mattathias.

Matia, Matiah Variant spellings of Matya. *See* Matya.

Matif (מַטִיף) From the Hebrew, meaning "preacher, teacher." The exact Hebrew equivalent is Matif. FEMININE HEBREW EQUIVALENTS: Mora, Moran, Moriya.

Matis (מַתִּית) A short form of Matisyahu, the Ashkenazic pronunciation of Matityahu. *See* Matityahu.

Matitya, Matityahu (מַתִּתְיָהוּ/מַתִּתְיָה) From the Hebrew, meaning "gift of God." Mattathias is a Greek form. *See* Mattathias.

Matmon (מַטְמוֹן) From the Hebrew, meaning "treasure, wealth." The exact Hebrew equivalent is Matmon. The exact feminine equivalent is Matmona.

Matok (מָתוֹק) From the Hebrew, meaning "sweet." The exact Hebrew equivalent is Matok. The exact feminine equivalent is Metuka.

Matri (מַטְרִי) From the Hebrew, meaning "rain, my rain." The exact Hebrew equivalent is Matri. FEMININE HEBREW EQUIVALENTS: Malkosha, Ravital, Reviva.

Matt A pet form of Matthew. *See* Matthew.

Matti, Mattie Pet forms of Matanya and Mattathias. *See* Matanya *and* Mattathias.

Mattathias (מַתִּתְיָהוּ) From the Greek, meaning "gift of God." The exact Hebrew equivalent is Matityahu. FEMININE HEBREW EQUIVALENTS: Matana, Matat, Migdana.

Matthew, Matthue Variant forms of Mattathias. *See* Mattathias.

Mattie, Matty, Mattye Pet forms of Matthew. *See* Matthew.

Matya (מַתְיָה) A short form of Matityahu. *See* Matityahu.

Maurey A pet form of Maurice. *See* Maurice.

Maurice From the Greek, Latin, and Middle English, meaning "moorish, dark-skinned." HEBREW EQUIVALENTS: Cham, Kedar, Pinchas. FEMININE HEBREW EQUIVALENTS: Ayfa, Chachila, Tzila.

Mauricio A Spanish form of Maurice. *See* Maurice.

Maurie A pet form of Maurice. *See* Maurice.

Maury A pet form of Maurice. *See* Maurice.

Max A short form of Maximilian. *See* Maximilian.

Maximilian From the Latin, meaning "great" or "famous." HEBREW EQUIVALENTS: Hillel, Migdal, Mehulal. FEMININE HEBREW EQUIVALENTS: Migdala, Ya'el, Zimra.

Maxwell An English form of Maximilian. *See* Maximilian.

Mayan (מַעְיָן) From the Hebrew, meaning "spring, fountain." The exact Hebrew equivalent is Mayan. FEMININE HEBREW EQUIVALENTS: Silona, Silonit.

Mayer A variant spelling of Meir. *See* Meir.

Maynard From the Old High German, meaning "powerful, strong," or from the Latin and the French, meaning "hand." HEBREW EQUIVALENTS: Amotz, Aryei, Binyamin. FEMININE HEBREW EQUIVALENTS: Amtza, Ari'el, Ari'ela.

Mazal (מַזָל) A unisex name. From the Hebrew, meaning "star" or "luck." The exact Hebrew equivalent is Mazal.

Mazal-Tov (מַזָל-טוֹב) From the Hebrew, meaning "good star, lucky star." The exact Hebrew equivalent is Mazal-Tov. FEMININE HEBREW EQUIVALENTS: Mazal, Mazala, Mazalit.

Medad (מֵידָד) From the Hebrew, meaning "measurement." The exact Hebrew equivalent is Medad.

Meged (מֶגֶד) From the Hebrew, meaning "goodness, sweetness, excellence." The exact Hebrew equivalent is Meged. FEMININE HEBREW EQUIVALENTS: Migda, Migdana.

Meir (מֵאִיר) From the Hebrew, meaning "one who brightens or shines." The exact Hebrew equivalent is Me'ir. The exact feminine Hebrew equivalent is Me'ira.

Meiri (מְאִירִי) A variant form of Meir. *See* Meir. The exact Hebrew equivalent is Me'iri.

Meitav (מֵיטָב) From the Hebrew, meaning "best, choicest." The exact

Hebrew equivalent is Meitav. FEMININE HEBREW EQUIVALENTS: Bechira, Mishbachat, Nivchara.

Mel A pet form of Melvin. *See* Melvin.

Melchior A variant form of the Latin name Melchita. Derived from the Hebrew *melech*, meaning "king." Melech is the Hebrew equivalent. Malka is the feminine Hebrew equivalent.

Melech, Melekh (מֶלֶךְ) From the Hebrew, meaning "king." The exact Hebrew equivalent is Melech. The exact feminine Hebrew equivalent is Malka.

Mell A pet form of Melvin. *See* Melvin.

Melton A variant form of Milton. *See* Milton.

Meltzar (מֶלְצָר) From the Hebrew, meaning "waiter" or "guard." The exact Hebrew equivalent is Meltzar. FEMININE HEBREW EQUIVALENTS: Mishmeret, Shimrit, Shomrona. The term was introduced in Daniel 1:11.

Melville From the Old English, meaning "village near the mill." HEBREW EQUIVALENTS: Goren, Ir, Kimchi. FEMININE HEBREW EQUIVALENTS: Degana, Deganiya, Keret.

Melvin From the Celtic, meaning "leader" or "chief." Also, from the Anglo-Saxon, meaning "friendly toiler" or "famous friend." HEBREW EQUIVALENTS: Amel, Amit, David. FEMININE HEBREW EQUIVALENTS: Amalya, Amita, Atara.

Melvyn A variant spelling of Melvin. *See* Melvin.

Menachem (מְנַחֵם) From the Hebrew, meaning "comforter." The exact Hebrew equivalent is Menachem. FEMININE HEBREW EQUIVALENTS: Menachema, Nechama.

Menahem A variant spelling of Menachem. *See* Menachem.

Menas An abbreviated form of Menashe. *See* Menashe.

Menashe, Menasheh (מְנַשֶּׁה) From the Hebrew, meaning "causing to forget." The Anglicized form is Manasseh. The exact Hebrew equivalent is Menashe.

Menashi (מְנַשִׁי) A variant form of Menashe. *See* Menashe. The exact Hebrew equivalent is Menashi.

Mendel (מֶענדל) From the Middle English *menden*, meaning "to repair." Also, a Yiddish name derived from Menachem. *See* Menachem.

Mendi, Mendy Pet forms of Mendel. *See* Mendel.

Mendl A variant spelling of Mendel. *See* Mendel.

Mercer From the Old French and Latin, meaning "wares, merchandise" or "a dealer in dry goods." HEBREW EQUIVALENTS: Avitagar, Machir. Sechora is a feminine equivalent.

Mered (מֶרֶד) From the Hebrew, meaning "revolt, feud." The exact Hebrew equivalent is Mered. The exact feminine Hebrew equivalent is Merida.

Meredith From the Anglo-Saxon, meaning "sea dew" or "sea defender." Also, from the Welsh, meaning "great chief, defender of the people." HEBREW EQUIVALENTS: Arnon, Gedalya, Melech. FEMININE HEBREW EQUIVALENTS: Atara, Malka, Mara.

Merek (מֶרֶק) From the Hebrew meaning "putty." The exact Hebrew equivalent is Merek.

Meretz (מֶרֶץ) From the Hebrew, meaning "energetic, vigorous." The exact Hebrew equivalent is Meretz. FEMININE HEBREW EQUIVALENTS: Mirtza, Zariza, Zeriza.

Meri (מְרִי) From the Hebrew, meaning "rebellion, revolt." The exact Hebrew equivalent is Meri. FEMININE HEBREW EQUIVALENTS: Merida, Meriva.

Merom (מֵרוֹם) From the Hebrew, meaning "heights." The exact Hebrew equivalent is Merom. The exact feminine Hebrew equivalent is Meroma.

Meron (מֵרוֹן) From the Hebrew, meaning "sheep." The exact Hebrew equivalent is Meron. The exact feminine Hebrew equivalent is Merona.

Merrill From the Old English, meaning "sea, pool, river" or "famous."

HEBREW EQUIVALENTS: Gedalya, Hillel, Mehulal. FEMININE HEBREW EQUIVALENTS: Hillela, Miryam, Tehila.

Merton From the Anglo-Saxon, meaning "from the farm by the sea." HEBREW EQUIVALENTS: Avigal, Aviyam, Livyatan. FEMININE HEBREW EQUIVALENTS: Bat-Galim, Bat-Yam, Miryam.

Mervin A Welsh form of Marvin. *See* Marvin.

Mervyn A variant spelling of Mervin. *See* Mervin.

Merwin, Merwyn Variant forms of Marvin. *See* Marvin.

Mesek (מֶתֶק) From the Hebrew, meaning "sweetness." The exact Hebrew equivalent is Mesek. Metuka is the feminine equivalent.

Meshi (מֶשִׁי) From the Hebrew, meaning "silk." The exact Hebrew equivalent is Meshi.

Mevorach (מְבוֹרָךְ) From the Hebrew, meaning "blessed." The exact Hebrew equivalent is Mevorach. FEMININE HEBREW EQUIVALENTS: Beracha, Berucha, Bracha.

Meyer A variant spelling of Meir. *See* Meir.

Mica, Micah Anglicized forms of Micha. *See* Micha.

Micha (מִיכָה) From the Hebrew, meaning "Who is like God?" A short form of Michael. The exact Hebrew equivalent is Micha. The exact feminine Hebrew equivalent is Michal. In Micha 1:1, one of the twelve minor prophets.

Michael (מִיכָאֵל) From the Hebrew, meaning "Who is like God?" The exact Hebrew equivalent is Micha'el. FEMININE HEBREW EQUIVALENTS: Micha'ela, Michal. In Numbers 13:13, the father of Setur of the tribe of Naftali.

Michal (מִיכַל) A short form of Michael. *See* Michael. Also, the feminine form of Micha and Micha'el. *See* Michal *(feminine section)*.

Michel A variant form of Michael. *See* Michael.

Mickey, Mickie, Micky Pet forms of Michael. *See* Michael.

Miguel A Spanish form of Michael. *See* Michael.

Mika A variant spelling of Micah. *See* Micah.

Mike A pet form of Michael. *See* Michael.

Mikel A pet form of Michael. *See* Michael.

Mikhail A Russian form of Michael. *See* Michael.

Miki A pet form of Michael. *See* Michael.

Miles From the Greek and Latin, meaning "warrior, soldier," or from the Old German, meaning "beloved." Used in England as a short form of Michael. HEBREW EQUIVALENTS: Gidon, Mordechai, Medan. FEMININE HEBREW EQUIVALENTS: Amtza, Gibora, Yedida. *See* Michael *for additional equivalents.*

Milford From the Old English, meaning "a mill near a stream." HEBREW EQUIVALENTS: Arnon, Yuval, Zerem. FEMININE HEBREW EQUIVALENTS: Afeka, Arnona, Arnonit.

Milton From the Old English, meaning "mill town." HEBREW EQUIVALENTS: Adam, Shadmon, Yizr'el. FEMININE HEBREW EQUIVALENTS: Adama, Shadmit, Shedema.

Miri (מִירִי) The name of a resident of (or one associated with) Mir, a small town in Belorussia once famous for its outstanding *yeshivah.* The exact Hebrew equivalent is Miri.

Misha A Russian form of Michael. *See* Michael. Also, a pet form of Moshe. *See* Moshe.

Mishael (מִישָׁאֵל) From the Hebrew, meaning "borrowed." The exact Hebrew equivalent is Misha'el. FEMININE HEBREW EQUIVALENTS: Misha'ela, Sha'ula, Sha'ulit.

Mitch A pet form of Mitchel. *See* Mitchel.

Mitchel, Mitchell Variant forms of Michael. *See* Michael.

Mo A pet form of Morris. *See* Morris.

Modi A pet form of Mordechai. *See* Mordechai.

Moe A pet form of Morris. *See* Morris.

Moise, Moises French forms of Moses. *See* Moses.

Moishe, Moisheh Yiddish forms of Moshe. *See* Moshe.

Monroe From the Celtic, meaning "red marsh." HEBREW EQUIVALENTS: Arnon, Aviyam, Moshe. FEMININE HEBREW EQUIVALENTS: Arnona, Mara, Miryam.

Montague The French form of the Latin, meaning "from the pointed mountain." HEBREW EQUIVALENTS: Amir, Harel, Marom. FEMININE HEBREW EQUIVALENTS: Meroma, Talma, Talmit.

Monte A pet form of Montague and Montgomery. *See* Montague *and* Montgomery.

Montgomery The English form of the French name Montague. *See* Montague.

Monty A variant spelling of Monte. *See* Monte.

Mor (מֹר) A unisex name. From the Hebrew, meaning "myrrh, spice." The exact Hebrew equivalent is Mor.

Moran (מוֹרָן) A unisex name. From the Aramaic, meaning "our teacher." Akin to Morenu. *See* Morenu. The exact Hebrew equivalent is Moran.

Mordecai The Anglicized form of Mordechai. *See* Mordechai.

Mordechai (מָרְדְּכַי) From the Persian and Babylonian, meaning "warrior, warlike." The exact Hebrew equivalent is Mordechai. FEMININE HEBREW EQUIVALENTS: Amtza, Atzma, Gavri'ela.

Mordicai A variant spelling of Mordecai. *See* Mordecai.

Mordke A Yiddish form of Mordechai. *See* Mordechai.

Mordy A pet form of Mordechai. *See* Mordechai.

Moreg (מוֹרֵג) From the Hebrew, meaning "grain thresher." The exact Hebrew equivalent is Moreg. The exact feminine Hebrew equivalent is Morega.

Morenu (מוֹרֵנוּ) From the Hebrew, meaning "our teacher." The exact Hebrew equivalent is Morenu. FEMININE HEBREW EQUIVALENTS: Moran, Morit, Moriya.

Morey A pet form of Maurice. *See* Maurice.

Morgan From the Celtic, meaning "one who lives near the sea." HEBREW EQUIVALENTS: Arnon, Avigal, Aviyam. FEMININE HEBREW EQUIVALENTS: Miryam, Yama, Yamit.

Mori, Morie From the Hebrew, meaning "my teacher." Also, variant spellings of Morey. *See* Morey.

Moriel (מוֹרִיאֵל) From the Hebrew, meaning "God is my teacher." The exact Hebrew equivalent is Mori'el. FEMININE HEBREW EQUIVALENTS: Mora, Morit, Moriya.

Moritz A variant form of Maurice. *See* Maurice.

Morrey, Morrie Variant spellings of Morey. *See* Morey.

Morris A variant form of Maurice. *See* Maurice. Also, from the Gaelic, meaning "great warrior." HEBREW EQUIVALENTS: Gavri'el, Meron, Mordechai. FEMININE HEBREW EQUIVALENTS: Gavrila, Merav, Merona.

Morrison A patronymic form, meaning "son of Morris." *See* Morris.

Morry A variant spelling of Morey. *See* Morey.

Morse A variant form of Maurice. *See* Maurice.

Mortimer From the Anglo-French, meaning "one who lives near the sea" or "one who dwells near still water." HEBREW EQUIVALENTS: Aviyam, Moshe. FEMININE HEBREW EQUIVALENTS: Bat-Yam, Miryam, Yamit.

Morton From the Old English, meaning "town near the sea" or "farm on the moor." HEBREW EQUIVALENTS: Adam, Aviyam, Ma'ayan. FEMININE HEBREW EQUIVALENTS: Adama, Miryam, Shadmit.

Mosad, Mossad (מוֹסָד) From the Hebrew, meaning "establishment." The exact Hebrew equivalent is Mosad. The exact feminine Hebrew equivalent is Mosada.

Mose A pet form of Moses. *See* Moses.

Moses The Anglicized form of Moshe. *See* Moshe.

Mosha (מוֹשָׁע) From the Hebrew, meaning "salvation." The exact Hebrew equivalent is Mosha. The exact feminine Hebrew equivalent is Mosha'a.

Moshael (מוֹשָׁעֵאל) From the Hebrew, meaning "God saves." The exact Hebrew equivalent is Mosha'el. FEMININE HEBREW EQUIVALENTS: Mosha'a, Shu'a, Teshu'a.

Moshe (מֹשֶׁה) From the Hebrew, meaning "drawn out [of the water]." Also, from the Egyptian, meaning "son, child." The exact Hebrew equivalent is Moshe. FEMININE HEBREW EQUIVALENTS: Matzila, Miryam, Mosha'a.

Moss An English variant form of Moses. *See* Moses.

Motel (מָאטְל/מָאטְעל) A Yiddish pet form of Mordechai. *See* Mordechai.

Moti, Motti (מָתִי) Nicknames for Mordechai. *See* Mordechai. The exact Hebrew equivalent is Moti.

Moy, Moyse Variant English forms of Moses. *See* Moses.

Muki A pet form of Mordecai. *See* Mordecai.

Murray From the Celtic and Welsh, meaning "sea" or "seaman." HEBREW EQUIVALENTS: Aviyam, Moshe, Peleg. FEMININE HEBREW EQUIVALENTS: Bat-Yam, Mara, Miryam. Also, a variant form of Maurice. *See* Maurice.

Mychal A variant spelling of Michael. *See* Michael.

Myer A variant form of Mayer. *See* Mayer.

Myles A variant spelling of Miles. *See* Miles.

Myron From the Greek, meaning "fragrant, sweet, pleasant." HEBREW EQUIVALENTS: Achino'am, Avino'am, Na'aman. FEMININE HEBREW EQUIVALENTS: Metuka, Na'ama, Na'amana.

Myrtle A unisex name. From the Persian, meaning "myrtle tree," a symbol of victory. The masculine Hebrew equivalent is Hadas. The feminine Hebrew equivalent is Hadasa.

Myrton A variant spelling of Merton. *See* Merton.

⌁ N ⌁

Naam (נַעַם/נָעַם) From the Hebrew, meaning "sweet, pleasant." The exact Hebrew equivalent is Na'am. FEMININE HEBREW EQUIVALENTS: Na'ama, Na'omi.

Naaman (נַעֲמָן) From the Hebrew, meaning "sweet, beautiful, pleasant, good." The exact Hebrew equivalent is Na'aman. The exact feminine Hebrew equivalent is Na'amana. In Numbers 26:40, a member of the tribe of Benjamin.

Naar (נַעַר) From the Hebrew, meaning "boy, youngster." The exact Hebrew equivalent is Na'ar. The exact feminine Hebrew equivalent is Na'ara.

Nachbi (נַחְבִּי) From the Hebrew, meaning "hidden." The exact Hebrew equivalent is Nachbi. FEMININE HEBREW EQUIVALENTS: Shemura, Tzafnat. In Numbers 13:14, the son of Vofsi of the tribe of Naftali.

Nachman (נַחְמָן) From the Hebrew, meaning "comforter." HEBREW EQUIVALENTS: Nachman, Nachmani. FEMININE HEBREW EQUIVALENTS: Nachmana, Nechama.

Nachmani (נַחְמָנִי) A variant form of Nachman. *See* Nachman.

Nachshon (נַחְשׁוֹן) From the Hebrew, meaning "snake" or "one who divines." The exact Hebrew equivalent is Nachshon. In Exodus 6:23, a brother-in-law of Aaron.

Nachum (נָחוּם) From the Hebrew, meaning "comfort." The exact Hebrew equivalent is Nachum. The exact feminine Hebrew equivalent is Nechama.

Nadav (נָדָב) From the Hebrew, meaning "generous, noble." The exact Hebrew equivalent is Nadav. The exact feminine Hebrew equivalent is Nedava.

Nadim (נָדִים) From the Hebrew, meaning "friend." HEBREW EQUIVALENTS: Amita, Elidad, Yedid. FEMININE HEBREW EQUIVALENTS: Achava, Amita, Davida.

Nadir (נָדִיר) From the Hebrew, meaning "rare, scarce, precious." The exact Hebrew equivalent is Nadir. The exact feminine Hebrew equivalent is Nedira.

Nadiv (נָדִיב) From the Hebrew, meaning "princely, generous." The exact Hebrew equivalent is Nadiv. FEMININE HEBREW EQUIVALENTS: Nedava, Nediva.

Naf A pet form of Naftali. *See* Naftali.

Naftali, Naftalie (נַפְתָּלִי) From the Hebrew, meaning "to wrestle" or "to be crafty." Also, from the Hebrew, meaning "likeness, comparison." The exact Hebrew equivalent is Naftali. FEMININE HEBREW EQUIVALENTS: Naftala, Naftalya.

Nagid (נָגִיד) From the Hebrew, meaning, "ruler, prince." The exact Hebrew equivalent is Nagid. The exact feminine Hebrew equivalent is Negida.

Nagiv (נָגִיב) From the Hebrew, meaning "pertaining to the south." Akin to Negev. The exact Hebrew equivalent is Nagiv. FEMININE HEBREW EQUIVALENTS: Deroma, Deromit.

Nahir (נָהִיר) A variant form of Nahor. *See* Nahor. The exact Hebrew equivalent is Nahir.

Nahor (נָהוֹר) From the Aramaic, meaning "light." The exact Hebrew equivalent is Nahor. FEMININE HEBREW EQUIVALENTS: Nehara, Nehira, Nurya.

Nahum An Anglicized form of Nachum. *See* Nachum.

Naim (נָעִים) From the Hebrew, meaning "pleasant." The exact Hebrew equivalent is Na'im. FEMININE HEBREW EQUIVALENTS: Na'omi, Na'ama, Ne'ima.

Nalim From the Hindi, referring to the lotus plant. HEBREW EQUIVALENTS: Admon, Narkis, Nufar. FEMININE HEBREW EQUIVALENTS: Atzmoni, Chelmonit, Kalanit.

Namer (נָמֵר) From the Hebrew, meaning "leopard, tiger." The exact Hebrew equivalent is Namer. The exact feminine Hebrew equivalent is Nemera.

Namir (נָמִיר) A variant form of Namer. *See* Namer.

Nanod (נָנוֹד) From the Hebrew, meaning "wanderer." The exact Hebrew equivalent is Nanod. FEMININE HEBREW EQUIVALENTS: Gershona, Gerusha, Gi'ora, Hagar, Zara.

Naom (נָעֹם) A variant form of Naaman. *See* Naaman. The exact Hebrew equivalent is Na'om.

Naor (נָאוֹר) From the Hebrew, meaning "light" or "enlightened." The exact Hebrew equivalent is Na'or. The exact feminine Hebrew equivalent is Ne'ora.

Naphtali, Naphthali Variant spelling of Naftali. *See* Naftali.

Nasi (נָשִׂיא) From the Hebrew, meaning "prince, leader." The exact Hebrew equivalent is Nasi. The exact feminine Hebrew equivalent is Nesi'a.

Nason A variant form of Natan. *See* Natan.

Natan (נָתָן) From the Hebrew, meaning "gift." The exact Hebrew equivalent is Natan. The exact feminine Hebrew equivalent is Netana.

Nate A pet form of Nathan. *See* Nathan.

Nathan An Anglicized form of Natan. *See* Natan.

Nathanel, Nathaniel Variant spellings of Netanel. *See* Netanel.

Nati A pet form of Nathan. *See* Nathan.

Natik (נָתִיק) From the Hebrew, meaning "detachable, removable."

Natin (נַתִּין) From the Hebrew, meaning "citizen" or "bestower of a gift." The exact Hebrew equivalent is Natin. The exact feminine Hebrew equivalent is Netina.

Nativ (נָתִיב) From the Hebrew, meaning "path, road." The exact Hebrew equivalent is Nativ. The exact feminine Hebrew equivalent is Netiva.

Naveh (נָאוֶה) From the Hebrew, meaning "beautiful." The exact Hebrew equivalent is Naveh. FEMININE HEBREW EQUIVALENTS: Na'ama, Nava, Nofiya.

Navi (נָבִיא) From the Hebrew, meaning "prophet." The exact Hebrew equivalent is Navi. The exact feminine Hebrew equivalent is Nevi'a.

Navon (נָבוֹן) From the Hebrew, meaning "wise." The exact Hebrew equivalent is Navon. The exact feminine Hebrew equivalent is Nevona.

Neal, Neale From the Middle English and the Gaelic, meaning "champion, courageous person" or "dark-complexioned." HEBREW EQUIVALENTS: Gibor, Kedar, Pinchas. FEMININE HEBREW EQUIVALENTS: No'aza, Odeda, Shechora.

Nechemia, Nechemiah Variant spellings of Nechemya. *See* Nechemya.

Nechemya (נְחֶמְיָה) From the Hebrew, meaning "comforted by the Lord." The exact Hebrew equivalent is Nechemya. FEMININE HEBREW EQUIVALENTS: Menachema, Nachmaniya, Nechama.

Ned A pet form of Edmond and Edward. *See* Edmond *and* Edward.

Nedar (נֶאְדָּר) From the Hebrew, meaning "adored, exalted." The exact Hebrew equivalent is Nedar. The exact feminine Hebrew equivalent is Nedara.

Nedavia, Nedaviah, Nedavya (נְדַבְיָה) A unisex name. From the Hebrew, meaning "generosity of the Lord." The exact Hebrew equivalent is Nedavya.

Neddy A pet form of Edmond and Edward. *See* Edmond *and* Edward.

Neder (נֶדֶר) From the Hebrew, meaning "oath, promise." The exact Hebrew equivalent is Neder. FEMININE HEBREW EQUIVALENTS: Bat-Sheva, Elisheva, Yehosheva.

Negev (נֶגֶב) From the Hebrew, meaning "south, southerly." Akin to Nagiv. The exact Hebrew equivalent is Negev. FEMININE HEBREW EQUIVALENTS: Deroma, Deromit.

Nehemia, Nehemiah Anglicized forms of Nechemya. *See* Nechemya.

Neil A variant spelling of Neal. *See* Neal.

Neilson A patronymic form of Neil, meaning "son of Neil." *See* Neil.

Nelson A patronymic form of Neal, meaning "son of Neal." *See* Neal.

Nemuel (נְמוּאֵל) From the Hebrew, meaning "ant," hence, industrious. The exact Hebrew equivalent is Nemuel. FEMININE HEBREW EQUIVALENTS: Amalya, Amela, Charutza. *See also* Yemuel.

Ner (נֵר) From the Hebrew, meaning "light." The exact Hebrew equivalent is Ner. The exact feminine Hebrew equivalent is Nera. In I Chronicles 8:33, the father of Kish and grandfather of Saul.

Neri (נֵרִי) From the Hebrew, meaning "my light." The exact Hebrew equivalent is Neri. FEMININE HEBREW EQUIVALENTS: Ne'ira, Ne'ora, Nera.

Nerli, Ner-Li (נֵר-לִי/נֵרְלִי) A unisex name. From the Hebrew, meaning "I have [a] light." The exact masculine and feminine Hebrew equivalent is Nerli.

Nes (נֵס) From the Hebrew, meaning "miracle." The exact Hebrew equivalent is Nes. FEMININE HEBREW EQUIVALENTS: Nasya, Nesya, Nisya.

Nesher (נֶשֶׁר) From the Hebrew, meaning "eagle" or "vulture." The exact Hebrew equivalent is Nesher. FEMININE HEBREW EQUIVALENTS: A'ya, A'yit, Tzipora.

Ness A variant spelling of Nes. *See* Nes.

Netanel (נְתַנְאֵל) From the Hebrew, meaning "gift of God." The exact

Hebrew equivalent is Netanel. The exact feminine Hebrew equivalent is Netanela.

Netaniel (נְתַנִיאֵל) A variant form of Netanel. *See* Netanel. The exact Hebrew equivalent is Netani'el. The exact feminine Hebrew equivalent is Netani'ela.

Netanya (נְתַנְיָה) A unisex name. From the Hebrew, meaning "gift of God." The exact Hebrew equivalent is Netanya.

Netanyahu (נְתַנְיָהוּ) A variant form of Netanya. *See* Netanya. The exact Hebrew equivalent is Netanyahu.

Nethanel An Anglicized form of Netanel. *See* Netanel.

Nethaniel An Anglicized form of Netanel. *See* Netanel.

Netzer (נֵצֶר) From the Hebrew, meaning "sprout, branch." The exact Hebrew equivalent is Netzer. FEMININE HEBREW EQUIVALENTS: Anefa, Anufa, Zemora.

Nevat (נְבָט) From the Hebrew, meaning "sprout, blossom." The exact Hebrew equivalent is Nevat. FEMININE HEBREW EQUIVALENTS: Pericha, Pirchit, Semadar. In I Kings 11:26, the father of the wicked Jeroboam.

Neve, Nevei (נְבֵה) From the Hebrew, meaning "desert oasis, resting place." The exact Hebrew equivalent is Nevei. FEMININE HEBREW EQUIVALENTS: Afeka, Bat-Yam, Einat.

Nevil, Nevile, Nevill, Neville From the French, meaning "new town." HEBREW EQUIVALENTS: Yeshavam, Zevul, Zevulun. FEMININE HEBREW EQUIVALENTS: Keret, Lina, Shafrira.

Newbold From the Old English, meaning "new town [beside the tree]." Akin to Newton. *See* Newton.

Newman From the Anglo-Saxon, meaning "new man." HEBREW EQUIVALENTS: Adam, Chadash. FEMININE HEBREW EQUIVALENTS: Adama, Chadasha.

Newt An abbreviated form of Newton. *See* Newton.

Newton From the Old English, meaning "from the new farmstead" or "new town." Akin to Newbold. HEBREW EQUIVALENTS: Adam, Bustena'i, Karmel, Yizr'el. FEMININE HEBREW EQUIVALENTS: Nava, Shedema, Yizr'ela.

Niall A British form of Neil. *See* Neil.

Nicholas From the Greek, meaning "victory of the people." HEBREW EQUIVALENTS: Gavri'el, Netzach, Yatzli'ach. FEMININE HEBREW EQUIVALENTS: Nitzcha, Nitzchiya, Nitzchona.

Nicolas A variant spelling of Nicholas. *See* Nicholas.

Nidri (נִדְרִי) From the Hebrew, meaning "my oath." The exact Hebrew equivalent is Nidri. FEMININE HEBREW EQUIVALENTS: Batsheva, Elisheva, Sheva.

Niel A variant Norse form of Nicholas. *See* Nicholas.

Nigel From the Irish/Gaelic, meaning "champion, saver." HEBREW EQUIVALENTS: Atzalya, Hosha'ya, Yoshiya. FEMININE HEBREW EQUIVALENTS: Matzila, Shu'a, Teshu'a.

Nike, Niko Pet forms of Nicholas. *See* Nicholas.

Niles A patronymic form of Neal, meaning "son of Neal." *See* Neal.

Nili (נִילִי) A unisex name. An acronym of the Hebrew words "the glory (or eternity) of Israel will not lie," found in I Samuel 15:29. The exact Hebrew equivalent is Nili.

Nils A patronymic form of Neal, meaning "son of Neal." *See* Neal.

Nimrod (נִמְרוֹד) From the Hebrew, meaning "we shall rebel." The exact Hebrew equivalent is Nimrod. FEMININE HEBREW EQUIVALENTS: Mardut, Meri. In Genesis 10:9, a renowned hunter, the son of Cush and grandson of Noah.

Nir (נִיר) From the Hebrew, meaning "to plough, to cultivate a field." The exact Hebrew equivalent is Nir. The exact feminine Hebrew equivalent is Nira.

Nirel, Nir-El (נִיר-אֵל/נִירְאֵל) A unisex name. From the Hebrew, meaning "cultivated field of the Lord" or "light of God." The exact Hebrew equivalent is Nirel.

Niria, Niriah Variant spellings of Niriya. *See* Niriya.

Niriel (נִירִיאֵל) A variant form of Nirel. *See* Nirel. The exact Hebrew equivalent is Niri'el.

Niriya (נִירִיָה) From the Hebrew, meaning "cultivated field of the Lord." The exact Hebrew equivalent is Niriya. FEMININE HEBREW EQUIVALENTS: Nira, Nirit, Odera.

Nirya (נִירִיָה) A variant form of Niriya. *See* Niriya. The exact Hebrew equivalent is Nirya.

Nisan, Nissan (נִיסָן) From the Hebrew, meaning "banner, emblem" or "miracle." The exact Hebrew equivalent is Nissan. FEMININE HEBREW EQUIVALENTS: Digla, Nasya, Nesya.

Nisim, Nissim (נִסִים) From the Hebrew, meaning "miracles." The exact Hebrew equivalent is Nisim. FEMININE HEBREW EQUIVALENTS: Nasya, Nesya, Nisya.

Nison, Nisson Variant spellings of Nisan. *See* Nisan.

Nissi (נִסִי) A variant form of Nisim. *See* Nisim. The exact Hebrew equivalent is Nissi.

Nitai (נִיתַּאי) An Aramaic form of Natan. *See* Natan.

Nitza, Nitzah (נִיצָה) A unisex name. From the Hebrew, meaning "flower bud, blossom." The exact Hebrew equivalent is Nitza.

Nitzan (נִיצָן) From the Hebrew, meaning "flower bud, blossom." The exact Hebrew equivalent is Nitzan. The exact feminine Hebrew equivalent is Nitzana.

Niv (נִיב) From the Hebrew, meaning "speech, expression." The exact Hebrew equivalent is Niv. FEMININE HEBREW EQUIVALENTS: Amira, Dovevet, Neva, Niva.

Nivchar (נִבְחַר) From the Hebrew, meaning "chosen, elected." The exact Hebrew equivalent is Nivchar. The exact feminine Hebrew equivalent is Nivchara.

Noach (נֹחַ) From the Hebrew, meaning "rest, quiet, peace." The exact Hebrew equivalent is No'ach. FEMININE HEBREW EQUIVALENTS: Menucha, Meshulemet, Shulamit.

Noah The Anglicized form of Noach. *See* Noach.

Noam (נֹעַם) From the Hebrew, meaning "sweetness" or "friendship." The exact Hebrew equivalent is No'am. FEMININE HEBREW EQUIVALENTS: Na'ama, Na'omi.

Noaz (נֹעַז) From the Hebrew, meaning "daring, bold." The exact Hebrew equivalent is No'az. The exact feminine Hebrew equivalent is No'aza.

Noble From the Latin, meaning "well-known, famous." HEBREW EQUIVALENTS: Hillel, Noda, Shevach. FEMININE HEBREW EQUIVALENTS: Degula, Hillela, Yehudit.

Noda (נוֹדָע) From the Hebrew, meaning "famous, well-known." The exact Hebrew equivalent is Noda. FEMININE HEBREW EQUIVALENTS: Hillela, Tishbacha, Yehudit.

Noel An Old French form of the Latin name Natalis, meaning "to be born" or "birthday." HEBREW EQUIVALENTS: Aharon, Amiram, Amiron. FEMININE HEBREW EQUIVALENTS: Aharona, Lirit, Liron.

Nof (נוֹף) From the Hebrew, meaning "beautiful landscape." The exact Hebrew equivalent is Nof. The exact feminine Hebrew equivalent is Nofiya.

Noga, Nogah (נֹגַה) A unisex name. From the Hebrew, meaning "morning light, brightness." The exact Hebrew equivalent is Noga.

Noi (נוֹי) From the Hebrew, meaning "beautiful, ornamented." The exact Hebrew equivalent is Noi. The exact feminine Hebrew equivalent is Noi'a.

Nolan From the Celtic, meaning "noble" or "famous." HEBREW EQUIVALENTS: Hillel, Noda, Shevach. FEMININE HEBREW EQUIVALENTS: Degula, Hillela, Yehudit.

Noland A variant form of Nolan. *See* Nolan.

Nomar Ramon in reverse. *See* Ramon.

Noni A pet form of Arnon. *See* Arnon.

Nora (נוֹרָא) From the Aramaic, meaning "awesome, great, mind-boggling." The exact Hebrew equivalent is Nora. FEMININE HEBREW EQUIVALENTS: Gedula, Rachav.

Norbert From the German, meaning "divine brightness." HEBREW EQUIVALENTS: Avner, Me'ir, Uri'el. FEMININE HEBREW EQUIVALENTS: Behira, Me'ira, Noga.

Norland From the Anglo-Saxon, meaning "person from the northland." HEBREW EQUIVALENTS: Tzefanya, Tzefanyahu. The feminine Hebrew equivalent is Tzafona.

Norman, Normann From the Anglo-Saxon, meaning "man from the north." HEBREW EQUIVALENTS: Tzefanya, Tzefanyahu. Tzafona is a feminine Hebrew equivalent.

Norris From the Anglo-Saxon, meaning "the dwelling place of a man from the north." Also, from the French-Latin, meaning "caretaker." HEBREW EQUIVALENTS: Ovadya, Oved, Tzefanya, Tzefanyahu. FEMININE HEBREW EQUIVALENTS: Magena, Tzafona.

North From the Anglo-Saxon, meaning "[a] man from the north." HEBREW EQUIVALENTS: Tzefanya, Tzefanyahu. The feminine equivalent is Tzafona.

Norton From the Anglo-Saxon, meaning "town in the north." HEBREW EQUIVALENTS: Avgar, Dor, Ma'on. FEMININE HEBREW EQUIVALENTS: Devira, Me'ona, Tzafona.

Norvin From the Old English, meaning "friend from the north." HEBREW EQUIVALENTS: David, Tzefanya. FEMININE HEBREW EQUIVALENTS: Davida, Tzafona.

Norwood From the Old English, meaning "woods in the north." HEBREW EQUIVALENTS: Artzi, Tzefanya, Ya'ari. FEMININE HEBREW EQUIVALENTS: Tzafona, Ya'ara, Ya'arit.

Noson, Nosson Variant Yiddish forms of Natan. *See* Natan.

Notza, Notzah (נוֹצָה) A unisex name. From the Hebrew, meaning "feather." The exact Hebrew equivalent is Notza.

Noy A variant spelling of Noi. *See* Noi.

Nufar (נוּפָר) From the Hebrew, referring to a water-plant with large leaves. HEBREW EQUIVALENTS: Neta, Netiya, Tzemach. FEMININE HEBREW EQUIVALENTS: Narkis, Nurit, Yasmin.

Nun (נוּן) From the Hebrew, meaning "fish." The exact Hebrew equivalent is Nun. FEMININE HEBREW EQUIVALENTS: Dagit, Dagiya. In Numbers 13:8, the father of Hosea of the tribe of Ephraim.

Nuphar A variant spelling of Nufar. *See* Nufar.

Nur (נוּר) From the Hebrew and Aramaic, meaning "fire, light." The exact Hebrew equivalent is Nur. The exact feminine Hebrew equivalent is Nura.

Nuri (נוּרִי) From the Hebrew and Aramaic, meaning "my fire, my light." The exact Hebrew equivalent is Nuri. FEMININE HEBREW EQUIVALENTS: Ne'ira, Ne'ora, Nera.

Nuria, Nuriah Variant spellings of Nuriya. *See* Nuriya.

Nuriel (נוּרִיאֵל) From the Aramaic and Hebrew, meaning "fire of the Lord." The exact Hebrew equivalent is Nuri'el. The exact feminine Hebrew equivalent is Nuri'ela.

Nuriya (נוּרְיָה) From the Aramaic and Hebrew, meaning "fire of the Lord." The exact Hebrew equivalent is Nuriya. FEMININE HEBREW EQUIVALENTS: Nehira, Nehura, Ner-Li.

Nurya (נוּרְיָה) A unisex name. A variant form of Nuriya. *See* Nuriya. The exact Hebrew equivalent is Nurya.

Nyle A variant Irish form of Neal. *See* Neal.

❦ O ❧

Oakleigh A variant spelling of Oakley. *See* Oakley.

Oakley From the Old English, meaning "field of oak trees." HEBREW EQUIVALENTS: Alon, Elon. FEMININE HEBREW EQUIVALENTS: Alona, Elona.

Obadiah The Anglicized form of Ovadya. *See* Ovadya.

Obe A pet form of Obadiah. *See* Obadiah.

Oded (עוֹדֵד) From the Hebrew, meaning "to encourage." The exact Hebrew equivalent is Oded. The exact feminine Hebrew equivalent is Odeda.

Odem (אֹדֶם) From the Hebrew, meaning "red, ruby." The exact Hebrew equivalent is Odem. Aduma is a feminine Hebrew equivalent.

Odo From the Old German and the Old English, meaning "rich." HEBREW EQUIVALENTS: Ashir, Oshri, Yitro. FEMININE HEBREW EQUIVALENTS: Ashira, Batshu'a, Yitra.

Ofan (אוֹפָן) From the Hebrew, meaning "wheel." The exact Hebrew equivalent is Ofan.

Ofar (עוֹפָר) From the Hebrew, meaning "young deer." The exact Hebrew equivalent is Ofar. The exact feminine Hebrew equivalent is Ofra.

Ofeh (אוֹפֶה) From the Hebrew, meaning "baker, cook." The exact Hebrew equivalent is Ofeh. FEMININE HEBREW EQUIVALENTS: Uga, Ugit.

Ofek (אֹפֶק) From the Hebrew, meaning "horizon." The exact Hebrew equivalent is Ofek. The exact feminine equivalent is Afeka.

Ofer (עוֹפֶר) From the Hebrew, meaning "young mountain goat" or "young deer." The exact Hebrew equivalent is Ofer. The feminine equivalent is Ofra.

Ofir A variant spelling of Ophir. *See* Ophir.

Ofra (עָפְרָה) A unisex name, although primarily feminine. From the Hebrew, meaning "young mountain goat" or "young deer." The exact Hebrew equivalent is Ofra. In I Chronicles 4:14, the father of a leader of the tribe of Judah.

Ofri (עָפְרִי) From the Hebrew, meaning "my goat" or "my deer." The exact Hebrew equivalent is Ofri. The feminine equivalent is Ofra.

Og (עוֹג) From the Hebrew, meaning "giant." The exact Hebrew equivalent is Og. FEMININE HEBREW EQUIVALENTS: Atalya, Gedola, Rachav.

Ogden From the Old English, meaning "valley with oak trees." HEBREW EQUIVALENTS: Alon, Armon, Eila. FEMININE HEBREW EQUIVALENTS: Alona, Eila, Eilona.

Ogen (עוֹגֶן) From the Hebrew, meaning "to imprison" or "to chain, anchor." The exact Hebrew equivalent is Ogen. The exact feminine Hebrew equivalent is Aguna.

Ohev (אוֹהֵב) From the Hebrew, meaning "lover." The exact Hebrew equivalent is Ohev. Ahuva is a feminine Hebrew equivalent.

Olaf From the Norse and Danish, meaning "ancestor." HEBREW EQUIVALENTS: Kadmi'el, Kedem. FEMININE HEBREW EQUIVALENTS: Kadmi'ela, Kedma, Yeshisha.

Oleg From the Norse, meaning "holy." HEBREW EQUIVALENTS: Chaga, Devir, Kadish. FEMININE HEBREW EQUIVALENTS: Chagit, Kadisha, Kedosha.

Olin From the Old English and the Middle English, meaning "holy." HEBREW EQUIVALENTS: Chaga, Devir, Kadish. FEMININE HEBREW EQUIVALENTS: Chagit, Chagiya, Devira.

Oliver From the Latin, meaning "man of peace." HEBREW EQUIVALENTS: Avshalom, Mano'ach, No'ach. FEMININE HEBREW EQUIVALENTS: Menucha, Shlomit, Shulamit.

Olivier The French form of Oliver. *See* Oliver.

Ollie A pet form of Oliver. *See* Oliver.

Omar From the Arabic, meaning "elevated." HEBREW EQUIVALENTS: Gidel, Yarom, Yirmeya. FEMININE HEBREW EQUIVALENTS: Merima, Meroma.

Omen (אֹמֵן) From the Hebrew, meaning "to rear, bring up faithfully." The exact Hebrew equivalent is Omein. FEMININE HEBREW EQUIVALENTS: Amana, Amanya, Ne'emana, Omenet.

Omer (עוֹמֵר) From the Hebrew, meaning "sheaf." The exact Hebrew equivalent is Omer. FEMININE HEBREW EQUIVALENTS: Omrit, Umarit.

Ometz (אֹמֶץ) From the Hebrew, meaning "strength, courage." The exact Hebrew equivalent is Ometz. The exact feminine Hebrew equivalent is Amtza.

Omri (עָמְרִי) From the Hebrew, meaning "my sheaf." Also, from the Arabic, meaning "long life." The exact Hebrew equivalent is Omri. FEMININE HEBREW EQUIVALENTS: Chava, Cha'ya, Yechi'ela.

Onan (אוֹנָן) From the Hebrew, meaning "one who spills semen needlessly." The exact Hebrew equivalent is Onan. In Genesis 38:4, a son of Judah; grandson of Jacob.

Opher A variant spelling of Ofer. *See* Ofer.

Ophir (אוֹפִיר) From the Hebrew, meaning "darkness, blackness." The exact Hebrew equivalent is Ofir. FEMININE HEBREW EQUIVALENTS: Adara, Chachila, Laila. In Genesis 10:29, a descendant of Shem.

Or (אוֹר) From the Hebrew, meaning "light." When spelled with an *a'yin* (עוֹר), it means "skin." The exact Hebrew equivalent is Or. FEMININE HEBREW EQUIVALENTS: Ora, Orali, Ornina.

Orde From the Latin, meaning "order," and from the Old English, meaning "beginning." HEBREW EQUIVALENTS: Rishon, Sadir, Sidra. FEMININE HEBREW EQUIVALENTS: Rishona, Sidra.

Oreb The Anglicized form of Orev. *See* Orev.

Oreg (אוֹרֵג) From the Hebrew, meaning "weaver." The exact Hebrew equivalent is Oreg. Rikma is a feminine equivalent.

Oreiv A variant spelling of Orev. *See* Orev.

Oren (אוֹרֶן) From the Hebrew, meaning "a tree [cedar or fir]." The exact Hebrew equivalent is Oren. FEMININE HEBREW EQUIVALENTS: Arza, Ayla, Ilana.

Orev (עוֹרֵב) A unisex name. From the Hebrew, meaning "raven." In Judges 7:25, a Midianite leader when Gideon was judge. The exact Hebrew equivalent is Oreiv.

Orez (אֹרֶז) From the Hebrew, meaning "rice." The exact Hebrew equivalent is Orez.

Ori (אוֹרִי) A unisex name. From the Hebrew, meaning "my light." The exact Hebrew equivalent is Ori.

Orin, Orrin Variant spellings of Oren. *See* Oren.

Orland A variant form of Roland and Rolando by reversal of letters. *See* Roland.

Orlando A variant form of Orland. *See* Orland.

Orli, Or-Li (אוֹר-לִי/אוֹרְלִי) A unisex name. From the Hebrew, meaning "light is mine." The exact Hebrew equivalent is Orli.

Oron (אוֹרוֹן) From the Hebrew, meaning "light." The exact Hebrew equivalent is Oron. FEMININE HEBREW EQUIVALENTS: Or, Orna, Ornina. Also, a variant form of Oren. *See* Oren.

Orson From the Latin, meaning "bear." HEBREW EQUIVALENTS: Dov, Dubi. FEMININE HEBREW EQUIVALENTS: Dova, Dovit, Duba.

Orval A variant form of Orville. *See* Orville.

Orven A variant spelling of Orvin. *See* Orvin.

Orville From the French, meaning "golden city." HEBREW EQUIVALENTS: Elifaz, Ofar, Ofir. FEMININE HEBREW EQUIVALENTS: Ofira, Paziya, Zehava.

Orvin From the Old French, meaning "warrior." HEBREW EQUIVALENTS: Gibor, Sirya, Siryon. FEMININE HEBREW EQUIVALENTS: Chanita, Meirav, Tigra.

Osbert From the Anglo-Saxon and German, meaning "famous [bright] god." HEBREW EQUIVALENTS: Bahir, Hillel, Noda. FEMININE HEBREW EQUIVALENTS: Behira, Tehila, Yehudit.

Oscar From the Anglo-Saxon, meaning "divine spear" or "divine strength." Also, from the Celtic, meaning "leaping warrior." HEBREW EQUIVALENTS: Gad, Gidon, Kani'el. FEMININE HEBREW EQUIVALENTS: Amtza, Chanita, Gavrila.

Osher (עוֹשֶׁר) From the Hebrew, meaning "wealth." The exact Hebrew equivalent is Osher. FEMININE HEBREW EQUIVALENTS: Ashira, Oshra, Yitra.

Oshri (אָשְׁרִי) From the Hebrew, meaning "my good fortune." The exact Hebrew equivalent is Oshri. The exact feminine equivalent is Oshrat.

Osman From the Anglo-Saxon, meaning "servant of God" or "protected by God." HEBREW EQUIVALENTS: Avigdor, Avdi, Betzalel. FEMININE HEBREW EQUIVALENTS: Magena, Shamira, Ya'akova.

Osmand A variant form of Osman. *See* Osman.

Osmond, Osmund Variant spellings of Osmand. *See* Osmand.

Ossie A pet form of Oscar or Oswald. *See* Oscar *and* Oswald.

Oswald From the Old English, meaning "god of the forest" or "house steward." HEBREW EQUIVALENTS: Avdi, Ovadya, Ya'ari. FEMININE HEBREW EQUIVALENTS: Aleksandra, Amitza, Amtza.

Otis From the Greek, meaning "one who hears well." HEBREW EQUIVALENTS: Oz, Ozni, Shmu'el. FEMININE HEBREW EQUIVALENTS: Kashuva, Shimona, Shmu'ela.

Otniel (עָתְנִיאָל) From the Hebrew, meaning "strength of God" or "God is my strength." The exact Hebrew equivalent is Otni'el. FEMININE HEBREW EQUIVALENTS: Amitza, Atzmona, Odedya.

Otto From the Old High German, meaning "prosperous, wealthy."

HEBREW EQUIVALENTS: Hotir, Huna, Yishai. FEMININE HEBREW EQUIVALENTS: Bat-Shu'a, Matzlicha, Yitra.

Otzar (אוֹצָר) From the Hebrew, meaning "treasure." The exact Hebrew equivalent is Otzar. The exact feminine equivalent is Otzara.

Ovadya (עֹבַדְיָה) From the Hebrew, meaning "servant of God." The exact Hebrew equivalent is Ovadya. FEMININE HEBREW EQUIVALENTS: Ama, Shimshona.

Ovadyahu (עֹבַדְיָהוּ) A variant form of Ovadya. *See* Ovadya. The exact Hebrew equivalent is Ovadyahu.

Oved (עוֹבֵד) From the Hebrew, meaning "servant." The exact Hebrew equivalent is Oveid. FEMININE HEBREW EQUIVALENTS: Ama'a, Da'yelet, Shimshona.

Owen From the Latin, meaning "well-born," or from the Welsh, meaning "young warrior." HEBREW EQUIVALENTS: Avicha'yil, Avinadav, Ben-Cha'yil. FEMININE HEBREW EQUIVALENTS: Amtza, Gavri'ela, Gavrila.

Oz (עֹז) From the Hebrew, meaning "strength." The exact Hebrew equivalent is Oz. FEMININE HEBREW EQUIVALENTS: Odedya, Uza, Uzi'ela.

Ozar A variant spelling of Otzar. *See* Otzar.

Ozer (עוֹזֵר) From the Hebrew, meaning "strength" or "helper." The exact Hebrew equivalent is Ozer. FEMININE HEBREW EQUIVALENTS: Eli'ezra, Ezr'ela, Ozera.

Ozni (אָזְנִי) From the Hebrew, meaning "my ear" or "my hearing." The exact Hebrew equivalent is Ozni. FEMININE HEBREW EQUIVALENTS: Kashuva, Shimat, Shimona.

Ozri (עוֹזְרִי) From the Hebrew, meaning "my helper." The exact Hebrew equivalent is Ozri. FEMININE HEBREW EQUIVALENTS: Ezra, Ezr'ela, Ezri'ela.

Ozzi A pet form of Oswald. *See* Oswald.

⁓ P–Q ⁓

Pablo A variant Spanish form of Paul. *See* Paul.

Paddy A pet form of Patrick. *See* Patrick.

Page From the Italian, meaning "boy attendant, servant." HEBREW EQUIVALENTS: Avda, Ovadya, Shimshon. FEMININE HEBREW EQUIVALENTS: Ama, Shimshona.

Paine From the Latin, meaning "countryman." The masculine Hebrew equivalent is Artzi. FEMININE HEBREW EQUIVALENTS: Artzit, Eretz, Medina.

Palmer From the Middle English, meaning "pilgrim who carries a palm leaf [as proof of having been to the Holy Land]." HEBREW EQUIVALENTS: Dekel, Itamar, Tamar. FEMININE HEBREW EQUIVALENTS: Dikla, Diklit, Lulava.

Palti (פַּלְטִי) From the Hebrew, meaning "my escape, my deliverance." The exact Hebrew equivalent is Palti. FEMININE HEBREW EQUIVALENTS: Sarid, Teshu'a, Yeshu'a. In Numbers 13:9, the son of Rafu of the tribe of Benjamin.

Paltiel (פַּלְטִיאֵל) From the Hebrew, meaning "God is my savior." The exact Hebrew equivalent is Palti'el. FEMININE HEBREW EQUIVALENTS: Teshu'a, Yisha. In Numbers 34:26, a member of the tribe of Issachar.

Palu, Pallu (פַּלּוּא) From the Hebrew, meaning "wondrous, famous."

The exact Hebrew equivalent is Palu. FEMININE HEBREW EQUIVALENTS: Pelia, Tama. In Numbers 26:5, a son of Reuben; grandson of Jacob.

Parker An occupational name for one who tends a park. HEBREW EQUIVALENTS: Ben-Carmi, Gani, Kerem. FEMININE HEBREW EQUIVALENTS: Carma, Carmelit, Gana.

Parnell A variant form of Peter. *See* Peter.

Pat A pet form of Patrick. *See* Patrick.

Patrick From the Latin, meaning "patrician, one of noble descent." HEBREW EQUIVALENTS: Chirom, Nadav, Yisra'el. FEMININE HEBREW EQUIVALENTS: Nediva, Sara, Yisra'ela.

Paul From the Latin, meaning "small." HEBREW EQUIVALENTS: Katan, Tzu'ar, Vofsi, Ze'ira, Zutra. FEMININE HEBREW EQUIVALENTS: Delila, Ketina, Pe'uta.

Pauley A variant form of Paul. *See* Paul.

Pavel A Czech form of Paul. *See* Paul.

Paxton From the Latin, meaning "town of peace." HEBREW EQUIVALENTS: Avshalom, Meshulam, Shalem. FEMININE HEBREW EQUIVALENTS: Sha'anana, Shalva, Shulamit.

Payne A variant spelling of Paine. *See* Paine.

Payton The Scottish form of Patrick. *See* Patrick.

Paz (פָּז) A unisex name. From the Hebrew, meaning "gold, golden, sparkling." The exact Hebrew equivalent is Paz.

Pazi (פָּזִי) From the Hebrew, meaning "my gold." The exact Hebrew equivalent is Pazi. FEMININE HEBREW EQUIVALENTS: Paz, Pazit, Paziya.

Pedro A Spanish and Portuguese form of Peter. *See* Peter.

Pe'er (פְּאֵר) From the Hebrew, meaning "glory, splendor." The exact Hebrew equivalent is Pe'er. FEMININE HEBREW EQUIVALENTS: Tifara, Tiferet, Yocheved.

Pekach (פֶּקַח) From the Hebrew, meaning "opening." The exact Hebrew equivalent is Pekach. In II Kings 15:25, one of the sons of Remaliah, an army officer.

Pele, Peleh (פֶּלֶא) From the Hebrew, meaning "miracle." The exact Hebrew equivalent is Peleh. FEMININE HEBREW EQUIVALENTS: Peliya, Pili.

Peleg (פֶּלֶג) From the Hebrew, meaning "stream, brook." The exact Hebrew equivalent is Peleg. FEMININE HEBREW EQUIVALENTS: Afeka, Arnona, Dalya.

Peli (פְּלָאִי) A variant form of Pele. *See* Pele. The exact Hebrew equivalent is Peli.

Peniel (פְּנִיאֵל) A variant form of Penuel. *See* Penuel.

Penini (פְּנִינִי) A unisex name. From the Hebrew, meaning "pearl" or "precious stone." The exact Hebrew equivalent is Penini.

Penuel (פְּנוּאֵל) From the Hebrew, meaning "face of God" or "sight of God." The exact Hebrew equivalent is Penu'el. FEMININE HEBREW EQUIVALENTS: Mofa'at, Nevi'a, Shechina.

Per A Swedish form of Peter. Akin to the English Piers. *See* Peter.

Perach (פֶּרַח) A unisex name. From the Hebrew, meaning "flower, blossom." The exact Hebrew equivalent is Perach.

Peretz (פֶּרֶץ) From the Hebrew, meaning "burst open." The exact Hebrew equivalent is Peretz. FEMININE HEBREW EQUIVALENTS: Nitza, Nitzana. In Numbers 26:20, a member of the tribe of Judah.

Perez A variant spelling of Peretz. *See* Peretz.

Perry A French form of Peter. *See* Peter.

Pesach (פֶּסַח) From the Hebrew, meaning "to pass over" or "to limp." The Hebrew name for the Passover (freedom) holiday. The exact Hebrew equivalent is Pesach. FEMININE HEBREW EQUIVALENTS: Derora, Derorit, Ge'ula.

Pete A pet form of Peter. *See* Peter.

Peter From the Greek and the Latin, meaning "rock." HEBREW EQUIVALENTS: Achitzur, Avitzur, Avni'el, Sela. FEMININE HEBREW EQUIVALENTS: Avni'ela, Ritzpa, Tzuriya.

Phelps A variant form of Philip. *See* Philip.

Phil A pet form of Philip. *See* Philip.

Philip A variant spelling of Phillip. *See* Phillip.

Phill A pet form of Phillip. *See* Phillip.

Phillip From the Greek, meaning "lover of horses." HEBREW EQUIVA-LENTS: Avicha'yil, Ben-Cha'yil, Peresh, Susi. FEMININE HEBREW EQUIVA-LENTS: Ahada, Ahava, Chiba.

Phillipe A French form of Phillip. *See* Phillip.

Phillipp A Scottish spelling of Phillip. *See* Phillip.

Philo From the Greek, meaning "loving." HEBREW EQUIVALENTS: Bildad, David, Yedidya. FEMININE HEBREW EQUIVALENTS: Ahuva, Chiba, Davida.

Phineas The Anglicized form of Pinchas. *See* Pinchas.

Phoebus In Greek mythology, the god of light and sun. HEBREW EQUIVA-LENTS: Bahir, Me'ir, Shimshon. FEMININE HEBREW EQUIVALENTS: Behira, Me'ira, Noga.

Pierce A form of Peter, meaning "rock." *See* Peter.

Pierre A French form of Peter. *See* Peter.

Piers A variant English form of Peter. *See* Peter.

Pinchas (פִּנְחָס) From the Egyptian, meaning "Negro, dark-complex-ioned." Also, from the Hebrew, meaning "mouth of a snake." The exact Hebrew equivalent is Pinchas. FEMININE HEBREW EQUIVALENTS: Shechora, Tzila.

Pinchos A variant spelling of Pinchas. *See* Pinchas.

Pincus An Anglicized form of Pinchas. *See* Pinchas.

Pinhas A variant spelling of Pinchas. *See* Pinchas.

Pini (פִּינִי) A pet form of Pinchas. *See* Pinchas.

Pinkas A variant form of Pinchas. *See* Pinchas.

Pinkie A pet form of Pinchas. *See* Pinchas.

Pinkus A variant spelling of Pincus. *See* Pincus.

Pinky A pet form of Pinchas. *See* Pinchas.

Pinnie, Pinny Pet forms of Pinchas. *See* Pinchas.

Pip A pet form of Philip. *See* Philip.

Pirchoni (פִּרְחוֹנִי) From the Hebrew, meaning "flowery." The exact Hebrew equivalent is Pirchoni. FEMININE HEBREW EQUIVALENTS: Perach, Pericha, Pirchiya.

Placid From the Latin, meaning "placid, tranquil, at peace." HEBREW EQUIVALENTS: Avshalom, Meshulam, Shalem. FEMININE HEBREW EQUIVALENTS: Menucha, Sha'anana, Shalva.

Placido From the Spanish, meaning "placid, peaceful." HEBREW EQUIVALENTS: Amishalom, Shalom, Shlomo. FEMININE HEBREW EQUIVALENTS: Menucha, Sha'anana, Shulamit.

Pol (פוֹל) From the Hebrew, meaning "bean." The exact Hebrew equivalent is Pol.

Porter From the Latin, meaning "carrier" or "attendant." HEBREW EQUIVALENTS: Ovadya, Puti'el, Sabal. FEMININE HEBREW EQUIVALENTS: Ama'a, Da'yelet, Shimshona.

Poul A variant spelling of Paul. *See* Paul.

Powell A variant form of Paul. *See* Paul.

Prentice From the Middle English, meaning "beginner, learner." HEBREW EQUIVALENTS: Chadash, Petachya, Yiftach. FEMININE HEBREW EQUIVALENTS: Chadasha, Chadusha.

Prentiss A variant spelling of Prentice. *See* Prentice.

Presley A unisex name. From the Old English, meaning "priest's meadow." HEBREW EQUIVALENTS: Hevel, Kahana, Kohen, Ya'ar. FEMININE HEBREW EQUIVALENTS: Adama, Ya'ara, Ya'arit.

Preston An Old English name, meaning "priest's town." HEBREW EQUIVALENTS: Devir, Kadish, Yekuti'el. FEMININE HEBREW EQUIVALENTS: Buna, Devira, Kedosha.

Price From the Middle English and Old French, meaning "price, value." HEBREW EQUIVALENTS: Yakar, Yakir. FEMININE HEBREW EQUIVALENTS: Yakira, Yakara.

Primo From the Italian, meaning "firstborn." HEBREW EQUIVALENTS: Bechor, Rishon, Yiftach. FEMININE HEBREW EQUIVALENTS: Bechora, Rishona.

Prince From the Latin, meaning "prince." HEBREW EQUIVALENTS: Sar, Sarel, Sar-Shalom. FEMININE HEBREW EQUIVALENTS: Nagida, Sara, Yisr'ela.

Princeton Literally, "town of the prince." HEBREW EQUIVALENTS: Nagid, Nasi, Yisra'el. FEMININE HEBREW EQUIVALENTS: Nagida, Sara, Yisr'ela.

Prosper From the Latin, meaning "prosperous, favorable, fortunate." HEBREW EQUIVALENTS: Asher, Matzli'ach, Yatzli'ach, Yitzlach. FEMININE HEBREW EQUIVALENTS: Ashira, Hatzlacha, Matzlicha, Tzalcha.

Pryor From the Latin, referring to the head of a priory or other religious house. HEBREW EQUIVALENTS: Aluf, Raba, Solel. FEMININE HEBREW EQUIVALENTS: Alufa, Sara, Tzameret.

Quentin From the Latin, meaning "fifth." There are no Hebrew equivalents.

Quenton A variant spelling of Quentin. *See* Quentin.

Quincy A variant form of Quentin. *See* Quentin.

Quinn A variant form of Quentin. *See* Quentin.

☙ R ❧

Raam (רַעַם) From the Hebrew, meaning "thunder, noise." The exact Hebrew equivalent is Ra'am. Kolya is a feminine equivalent.

Raamya (רַעַמְיָה) From the Hebrew, meaning "God's thunder." The exact Hebrew equivalent is Ra'amya. Kolya is a feminine equivalent.

Raanan (רַעֲנָן) From the Hebrew, meaning "fresh, luxuriant, beautiful." The exact Hebrew equivalent is Ra'anan. The exact feminine equivalent is Ra'anana.

Rabi (רַבִּי) From the Hebrew, meaning "my teacher." The exact Hebrew equivalent is Rabi. FEMININE HEBREW EQUIVALENTS: Aharona, Mora, Morit.

Rachaman (רַחֲמָן) From the Hebrew, meaning "compassionate One [God]." The exact Hebrew equivalent is Rachaman. FEMININE HEBREW EQUIVALENTS: Rachmi'ela, Ruchama.

Rachamim (רַחֲמִים) From the Hebrew, meaning "compassion, mercy." The exact Hebrew equivalent is Rachamim. FEMININE HEBREW EQUIVALENTS: Rachmi'ela, Ruchama.

Rachman A variant form of Rachaman. The exact Hebrew equivalent is Rachman. *See* Rachaman.

Rafa (רָפָא) From the Hebrew, meaning "heal." The exact Hebrew equivalent is Rafa. FEMININE HEBREW EQUIVALENTS: Rafya, Refa'ela, Refu'a.

Rafael A Spanish form of Refael. *See* Refael.

Rafe, Rafei, Rafi (רָפִי) Pet forms of Refael. *See* Refael.

Rafu (רָפוּא) From the Hebrew, meaning "healing." The exact Hebrew equivalent is Rafu. FEMININE HEBREW EQUIVALENTS: Refa'ela, Refu'a, Rofi. In Numbers 13:9, the father of Palti of the tribe of Benjamin.

Raleigh From the Old French, meaning "field of wading birds," or from the Old English, meaning "deer meadow." HEBREW EQUIVALENTS: Efer, Gozal, Karmel. FEMININE HEBREW EQUIVALENTS: Karmela, Nava, Tzivya.

Ralph From the Old Norse and Anglo-Saxon, meaning "courageous advice" or "fearless advisor." HEBREW EQUIVALENTS: Aleksander, Azarya, Azri'el, Bina, Eli'ezer. FEMININE HEBREW EQUIVALENTS: Aleksandra, Buna, Ge'ona.

Ram (רָם) From the Hebrew, meaning "high, exalted, mighty." The exact Hebrew equivalent is Ram. The exact feminine equivalent is Rama.

Rama (רָמָה) A unisex name. From the Hebrew, meaning "lofty, exalted." The exact Hebrew equivalent is Rama.

Rami (רָמִי) A variant form of Ram. The exact Hebrew equivalent is Rami. FEMININE HEBREW EQUIVALENTS: Meroma, Rama, Roma.

Ramon A Spanish form of Raymond. *See* Raymond.

Ramsay A variant spelling of Ramsey. *See* Ramsey.

Ramsey From the Old English, meaning "ram's island." HEBREW EQUIVALENTS: Itamar, Meron, Zimri. FEMININE HEBREW EQUIVALENTS: Merona, Tamar, Timora.

Ran (רָן) From the Hebrew, meaning "joy" or "song." The exact Hebrew equivalent is Ran. The exact feminine equivalent is Ranit.

Ranan A variant spelling of Raanan. *See* Raanan.

Randal, Randall From the Anglo-Saxon, meaning "superior, protection." HEBREW EQUIVALENTS: Shomer, Ya'akov, Zahir. FEMININE HEBREW EQUIVALENTS: Chasya, Ya'akova, Zehira.

Randell A variant form of Randall. *See* Randall.

Randi A variant spelling of Randy. *See* Randy.

Randolph From the Anglo-Saxon, meaning "good counsel." HEBREW EQUIVALENTS: Bina, Navon, Yo'etz. FEMININE HEBREW EQUIVALENTS: Aleksandra, Buna, Ge'ona.

Randy A pet form of Randal or Randolph. *See* Randal *and* Randolph.

Ranen (רָנֶן) From the Hebrew, meaning "to sing, to be joyous." The exact Hebrew equivalent is Ranen. The exact feminine equivalent is Renana.

Rani (רָנִי) From the Hebrew, meaning "my joy" or "my song." The exact Hebrew equivalent is Rani. The exact feminine equivalent is Ranit.

Ranier A French variant form of Reginald. *See* Reginald.

Ranon (רָנוֹן) A variant form of Ranen. *See* Ranen. The exact Hebrew equivalent is Ranon. FEMININE HEBREW EQUIVALENTS: Ranit, Ranita, Ranya.

Raoul A French form of Ralph and Randolph. *See* Ralph *and* Randolph.

Raphael A variant spelling of Refael. *See* Refael.

Raphu A variant spelling of Rafu. *See* Rafu.

Raul A variant spelling of Raoul. *See* Raoul.

Rav (רָב) From the Hebrew, meaning "great" or "teacher." The exact Hebrew equivalent is Rav. FEMININE HEBREW EQUIVALENTS: Mora, Moran, Mori'el.

Rava (רָבָא) A variant form of Rav. *See* Rav.

Raven From the Old English, meaning "raven," a bird in the crow family. Orev is the Hebrew equivalent. FEMININE HEBREW EQUIVALENTS: Gozala, Tzipora, Tziporit.

Ravi A variant form of Rabi. *See* Rabi.

Ravid (רָבִיד) A unisex name. From the Hebrew, meaning "necklace." The exact Hebrew equivalent is Ravid.

Raviv (רָבִיב) From the Hebrew, meaning "rain" or "dew." The exact Hebrew equivalent is Raviv. The exact feminine equivalent is Reviva.

Ray From the Old English, meaning "stream," or from the Celtic, meaning "grace." HEBREW EQUIVALENTS: Arnon, Yuval, Zerem. FEMININE HEBREW EQUIVALENTS: Arnona, Arnonit, Chana. Also, a pet form of Raymond. *See* Raymond.

Raya (רֵעַ) A unisex name. From the Hebrew, meaning "friend." The exact Hebrew equivalent is Raya.

Raymond From the Old French, meaning "mighty protector," or from the German, meaning "quiet, peaceful." HEBREW EQUIVALENTS: Avigdor, Magen, Shemaryahu. FEMININE HEBREW EQUIVALENTS: Avigdora, Botzra, Efrat.

Raymund A variant spelling of Raymond. *See* Raymond.

Raz (רָז) A unisex name. From the Aramaic, meaning "secret." The exact Hebrew equivalent is Raz.

Razi (רָזִי) A unisex name. From the Hebrew, meaning "my secret." The exact Hebrew equivalent is Razi.

Raziel (רָזִיאֵל) From the Aramaic, meaning "God is my secret" or "secret of the Lord." The exact Hebrew equivalent is Razi'el. The exact feminine equivalent is Razi'ela.

Read, Reade From the Old English, meaning "reed." The Hebrew equivalent is Kani'el. The feminine equivalent is Kani'ela.

Reagan, Regan From the Gaelic, meaning "little king." HEBREW EQUIVALENTS: Avimelech, Malki'el, Melech. FEMININE HEBREW EQUIVALENTS: Malka, Malkit, Malkiya.

Redd A variant form of Read. *See* Read.

Reece A Welsh form of the Old English, meaning "stream." HEBREW

EQUIVALENTS: Arnon, Yuval, Zerem. FEMININE HEBREW EQUIVALENTS: Arnona, Arnonit, Miryam.

Reed A variant spelling of Read. *See* Read.

Rees, Reese An Anglicized form of a Welsh name meaning "ardor, fiery, passionate." HEBREW EQUIVALENTS: Lahav, Reshef, Uri. FEMININE HEBREW EQUIVALENTS: Avuka, Uri'ela, Urit.

Refael (רְפָאֵל) From the Hebrew, meaning "God has healed." The exact Hebrew equivalent is Refa'el. The exact feminine equivalent is Refa'ela.

Refi (רְפִי) A pet form of Refael. *See* Refael.

Reg, Reggie Pet forms of Reginald. *See* Reginald.

Regem (רֶגֶם) From the Hebrew, meaning "to stone." Also, from the Arabic, meaning "friend." The exact Hebrew equivalent is Regem. FEMININE HEBREW EQUIVALENTS: Amita, Avni'el, Davida.

Reginald From the Old High German, meaning "wise, judicious" or "powerful ruler." HEBREW EQUIVALENTS: Barzilai, Gavri'el, Gibor. FEMININE HEBREW EQUIVALENTS: Gavri'ela, Gevira, Gibora.

Regis From the Latin, meaning "regal, royal." HEBREW EQUIVALENTS: Avimelech, Malki'el, Melech. FEMININE HEBREW EQUIVALENTS: Malka, Malkit, Malkiya.

Reid A variant spelling of Read. *See* Read.

Reinhard, Reinhart Variant forms of Reynard. *See* Reynard.

Reinhold A variant German form of Reginald. *See* Reginald.

Remez (רֶמֶז) From the Hebrew, meaning "sign" or "signal." The exact Hebrew equivalent is Remez. The exact feminine equivalent is Remiza.

René A French name from the Latin, meaning "to be reborn, renew." HEBREW EQUIVALENTS: Chadash, Cha'yim. FEMININE HEBREW EQUIVALENTS: Cha'ya, Techiya, Tekuma.

Renay A variant spelling of René. *See* René.

Renen (רֶנֶן) From the Hebrew, meaning "song." The exact Hebrew equivalent is Renen. The exact feminine equivalent is Renana.

Rennie A pet form of Reginald. *See* Reginald.

Reo A variant form of the Old English *rae*, meaning "stream." HEBREW EQUIVALENTS: Arnan, Arnon, Zerem. FEMININE HEBREW EQUIVALENTS: Arnona, Arnonit, Miryam.

Rephael A variant spelling of Refael. *See* Refael.

Rephi A variant spelling of Refi. *See* Refi.

Reuben, Reubin Variant forms of Reuven. *See* Reuven.

Reuel (רְעוּאֵל) From the Hebrew, meaning "friend of God." The exact Hebrew equivalent is Re'uel. The exact feminine equivalent is Re'uela.

Reuvain A variant spelling of Reuven. *See* Reuven.

Reuven (רְאוּבֵן) From the Hebrew, meaning "behold, a son." The exact Hebrew equivalent is Re'uven. The exact feminine equivalent is Re'uvena.

Rex From the Latin, meaning "king." HEBREW EQUIVALENTS: Malkam, Razin, Rozen. FEMININE HEBREW EQUIVALENTS: Atara, Malka, Malki'ela.

Reynard A variant German form of Richard. *See* Richard.

Reynold A variant French form of Reginald. *See* Reginald.

Rhett From the Old English, meaning "small stream." HEBREW EQUIVALENTS: Arnan, Arnon, Moshe. FEMININE HEBREW EQUIVALENTS: Arnona, Arnonit, Miryam.

Rhys From the Welsh, meaning "zealous." Elkana is a Hebrew equivalent.

Ric A pet form of Richard. *See* Richard.

Ricardo, Riccardo Spanish and Italian forms of Richard. *See* Richard.

Ricci A pet form of Richard. *See* Richard.

Ricco A pet form of Richard. *See* Richard.

Rice A variant spelling of Rhys. *See* Rice.

Rich, Richie Pet forms of Richard. *See* Richard.

Richard A French form of the Old High German Reynard, meaning "powerful, rich ruler" or "valiant rider." HEBREW EQUIVALENTS: Ben-Cha'yil, Gavri'el. FEMININE HEBREW EQUIVALENTS: Amtza, Ashira, Gavri'ela.

Richardo A Spanish form of Richard. *See* Richard.

Richie A pet form of Richard. *See* Richard.

Rici, Ricci Pet forms of Richard. *See* Richard.

Rick, **Ricki**, **Rickie**, **Ricky** Pet forms of Richard. *See* Richard.

Riley From the Irish/Gaelic, meaning "courageous." HEBREW EQUIVALENTS: Abir, Chutzpit, No'az. FEMININE HEBREW EQUIVALENTS: No'aza, Odeda.

Rimon, Rimmon (רִמּוֹן) From the Hebrew, meaning "pomegranate." The exact Hebrew equivalent is Rimon. The exact feminine equivalent is Rimona.

Rio From the Spanish, meaning "river." HEBREW EQUIVALENTS: Aviyam, Ye'or, Ye'ori. FEMININE HEBREW EQUIVALENTS: Bat-Yam, Einat, Ga'yil.

Rip From the Latin, meaning "river bank." HEBREW EQUIVALENTS: Arnon, Ye'or, Ye'ori. FEMININE HEBREW EQUIVALENTS: Arnona, Arnonit.

Rishon (רִאשׁוֹן) From the Hebrew, meaning "first." The exact Hebrew equivalent is Rishon. The exact feminine equivalent is Rishona.

Rob A pet form of Robert. *See* Robert.

Robard, Robart Variant French forms of Robert. *See* Robert.

Robert From the Anglo-Saxon, meaning "bright, wise counsel." HEBREW EQUIVALENTS: Azri'el, Bahir, Barak. FEMININE HEBREW EQUIVALENTS: Ezr'ela, Hillela, Me'ira.

Roberto A Spanish form of Robert. *See* Robert.

Robin A pet form of Robert popular in France. *See* Robert.

Robson A patronymic form, meaning "son of Rob [Robert]." *See* Robert.

Robyn A variant spelling of Robin. *See* Robin.

Rocco A pet form of Richard or Rockne. *See* Richard *and* Rockne.

Rock From the Old English, meaning "rock." A short form of Rockne. *See* Rockne.

Rockne From the Old English, meaning "rock." HEBREW EQUIVALENTS: Avni'el, Sela, Shamir. FEMININE HEBREW EQUIVALENTS: Avna, Avni'ela, Ritzpa.

Rockwell From the Old English, meaning "the well near the rock." HEBREW EQUIVALENTS: Arnon, Avitzur, Avni'el. FEMININE HEBREW EQUIVALENTS: Arnona, Avni'ela, Tzurit.

Rocky A pet form of Rockne and Rockwell. *See* Rockne *and* Rockwell.

Rod, Rodd A pet form of Roderick. *See* Roderick.

Roddy A pet form of Roderick. *See* Roderick.

Roderic, Roderick From the Old High German, meaning "famous ruler." HEBREW EQUIVALENTS: Gedalya, Hillel, Rosh. FEMININE HEBREW EQUIVALENTS: Hillela, Malka, Sara.

Rodger A variant spelling of Roger. *See* Roger.

Rodgers A patronymic form of Roger. *See* Roger.

Rodman From the Old German, meaning "respected man." HEBREW EQUIVALENTS: Ben-Shem, Mokir. FEMININE HEBREW EQUIVALENTS: Ahada, Kevuda.

Rodney From the Old English, meaning "cleared land near the water" or "one who carries a leveling rod, a surveyor." HEBREW EQUIVALENTS: Artzi, Aryoch, Beri. FEMININE HEBREW EQUIVALENTS: Artzit, Bat-Yam, Miryam.

Rofi (רֹפִי) A pet form of Refael (Rephael). The exact Hebrew equivalent is Rofi. *See* Refael.

Roger From the Old French and the Anglo-Saxon, meaning "famous, noble warrior" or "honorable man." HEBREW EQUIVALENTS: Efrat, Hillel, Mordechai. FEMININE HEBREW EQUIVALENTS: Hillela, Tigra, Yehudit.

Rohn From the Greek, meaning "rose." The masculine and feminine Hebrew equivalent is Vered.

Roi (רֹעִי) From the Hebrew, meaning "shepherd, overseer, guardian." A name probably based on a word found in the first verse of Psalm 23. The exact Hebrew equivalent is Ro'i. FEMININE HEBREW EQUIVALENTS: Shamira, Shimra, Shimriya.

Roland A French form of the Old High German, meaning "fame of the land." HEBREW EQUIVALENTS: Gedalya, Hillel, Shevach. FEMININE HEBREW EQUIVALENTS: Hillela, Tehila, Yehudit.

Rolando An Italian and Portuguese form of Roland. *See* Roland.

Rolf, Rolfe Pet forms of Rudolph. *See* Rudolph.

Rolland A variant spelling of Roland. *See* Roland.

Rollen, Rollin Variant forms of Roland. *See* Roland.

Rollo A pet form of Roland. *See* Roland.

Rom (רוֹם) From the Hebrew, meaning "heights." The exact Hebrew equivalent is Rom. The exact feminine equivalent is Roma.

Roman From the Old French, meaning "to write, scribe" words reflecting romance and love. HEBREW EQUIVALENTS: Amarya, Sofer.

Romem (רוֹמֵם) A variant form of Rom. *See* Rom. The exact Hebrew equivalent is Romem.

Romi, Romie (רוֹמִי) From the Hebrew, meaning "heights" or "nobility." The exact Hebrew equivalent is Romi. FEMININE HEBREW EQUIVALENTS: Rama, Ramit, Roma, Romit.

Romney From the Welsh, meaning "winding river." HEBREW EQUIVALENTS: Aviyam, Ye'or, Ye'ori. FEMININE HEBREW EQUIVALENTS: Bat-Yam, Einat, Ga'yil.

Ron (רוֹנִית) A unisex name. From the Hebrew, meaning "joy" or "song." The exact Hebrew equivalent is Ron. Also, a pet form of Ronald. *See* Ronald.

Ronald The Scottish form of Reginald. *See* Reginald.

Rondell A variant pet form of Ronald. *See* Ronald.

Ronel (רוֹנְאֵל) From the Hebrew, meaning "song of the Lord" or "joy of the Lord." The exact Hebrew equivalent is Ronel. The exact feminine equivalent is Ronela.

Ronen (רוֹנֵן) From the Hebrew, meaning "song" or "joy." The exact Hebrew equivalent is Ronen. The exact feminine equivalent is Ronena.

Roni (רוֹנִי) A unisex name. A variant form of Ron. *See* Ron. The exact Hebrew equivalent is Roni.

Ronli, Ron-Li (רוֹן-לִי/רוֹנְלִי) A unisex name. From the Hebrew, meaning "song is mine." The exact Hebrew equivalent is Ronli.

Ronnie, Ronny Pet forms of Ronald. *See* Ronald.

Rophi A variant spelling of Rofi. *See* Rofi.

Rory An Irish form of Roderick. *See* Roderick. Also, from the Celtic, meaning "the ruddy one." HEBREW EQUIVALENTS: Admon, Almog, Guni. FEMININE HEBREW EQUIVALENTS: Almoga, Odem, Tzachara.

Roscoe A variant form of Ross. *See* Ross.

Rosh (רֹאשׁ) From the Hebrew, meaning "head, leader." The exact Hebrew equivalent is Rosh. FEMININE HEBREW EQUIVALENTS: Alufa, Sara.

Ross From the Anglo-Saxon, meaning "woods, meadows." HEBREW EQUIVALENTS: Artza, Karmel, Yara. FEMININE HEBREW EQUIVALENTS: Eretz, Karmela, Ya'ari.

Rotem (רֹתֶם) A unisex name. From the Hebrew, meaning "to bind." Also, a plant found in southern Israel. The exact Hebrew equivalent is Rotem.

Rowe A short form of Rowland. *See* Rowland.

Rowland From the Old English, meaning "rugged land." Also, a variant form of Roland. *See* Roland.

Rowle A variant form of Ralph. *See* Ralph.

Roy From the Old French, meaning "king." HEBREW EQUIVALENTS: Katri'el, Yisra'el. FEMININE HEBREW EQUIVALENTS: Atara, Katri'ela, Yisra'ela.

Royal From the Middle English and the Latin, meaning "king." HEBREW EQUIVALENTS: Katri'el, Malki, Yisrael. FEMININE HEBREW EQUIVALENTS: Atara, Gavrila, Yisra'ela.

Royce A form of Roy, meaning "Roy's son." *See* Roy.

Roye A variant spelling of Roy. *See* Roy.

Rube A pet form of Reuben. *See* Reuben.

Ruben A variant spelling of Reuben. *See* Reuben.

Rubens A patronymic form of Reuben, meaning "son of Reuben." *See* Reuben.

Rubin A variant spelling of Reuben. *See* Reuben.

Ruby A pet form of Reuben. *See* Reuben.

Rudd From the Anglo-Saxon, meaning "red." HEBREW EQUIVALENTS: Admon, Almog, Edom. FEMININE HEBREW EQUIVALENTS: Almoga, Odem, Tzachara.

Rudolph A variant form of Ralph and Randolph. *See* Ralph *and* Randolph.

Rueben A variant spelling of Reuben. *See* Reuben.

Ruel A variant spelling of Reuel. *See* Reuel.

Rufus From the Latin, meaning "red, red-haired." HEBREW EQUIVALENTS: Admon, Almog, Guni. FEMININE HEBREW EQUIVALENTS: Delila, Nima, Odem.

Rupert A variant English, French, and German form of Robert. *See* Robert.

Russ   A pet form of Russell. *See* Russell.

Russel, Russell French forms of the Latin, meaning "rusty-haired." Also, from the Anglo-Saxon, meaning "horse." HEBREW EQUIVALENTS: Admon, Peresh, Susi. FEMININE HEBREW EQUIVALENTS: Avicha'yil, Delila, Nima.

Rusty A pet name, usually for a person with red or reddish-brown hair. Akin to Russel. *See* Russel.

Ruvane A variant spelling of Reuven. *See* Reuven.

Ruvik A pet form of Reuven. *See* Reuven.

Ryan Probably a pet form of Richard and Roy, meaning "little king." *See* Roy. Also, a variant form of Bryan. *See* Bryan.

Ryne A variant form of Ryan. *See* Ryan.

✒ S ✒

Sa'ar (סַעַר) From the Hebrew, meaning "storm, upheaval." The exact Hebrew equivalent is Sa'ar. The exact feminine equivalent is Se'ara.

Saad (סַעַד) From the Aramaic, meaning "support." The exact Hebrew equivalent is Sa'ad. The exact feminine equivalent is Sa'ada.

Saada (סַעְדָה) A unisex name. A variant form of Saad. *See* Saad. The exact Hebrew equivalent is Sa'ada.

Saadi (סַעְדִי) From the Hebrew, meaning "my support." The exact Hebrew equivalent is Sa'adi. FEMININE HEBREW EQUIVALENTS: Mosada, Sa'ada.

Saadia, Saadiah Variant spellings of Saadya. *See* Saadya.

Saadli (סַעְדְלִי) A variant form of Saadi. *See* Saadi. The exact Hebrew equivalent is Sa'adli.

Saadya (סַעְדְיָה) From the Hebrew, meaning "God is my support." The exact Hebrew equivalent is Sa'adya. The exact feminine equivalent is Sa'ada.

Saba (סָבָא) A unisex name. From the Aramaic and Hebrew, meaning "old, aged" or "grandfather." The exact Hebrew equivalent is Saba.

Sabal (סַבָּל) From the Hebrew, meaning "porter." The exact Hebrew equivalent is Sabal. FEMININE HEBREW EQUIVALENTS: Ama'a, Da'yelet, Shimshona.

Sabra (סַבְּרָה) A unisex name. From the Arabic, meaning "cactus, prickly pear." The exact Hebrew equivalent is Sabra. Akin to Tzabar. *See* Tzabar.

Sacha *Also spelled* Sasha. A Russian pet form of Alexander. *See* Alexander.

Sachar (שָׂכָר) A short form of Issachar. *See* Issachar. The exact Hebrew equivalent is Sachar.

Sadir (סָדִיר) From the Aramaic, meaning "order." The exact Hebrew equivalent is Sadir. The exact feminine equivalent is Sadira.

Safran (סַפְרָן) From the Hebrew, meaning "librarian." The exact Hebrew equivalent is Safran.

Sage A unisex name. From the Latin, meaning "wise." HEBREW EQUIVALENTS: Ish-Sechel, Navon, Zavin. FEMININE HEBREW EQUIVALENTS: Chochma, Ge'ona, Ge'onit.

Sagi (שַׂגִיא/סַגִיא) From the Aramaic and Hebrew, meaning "sufficient" or "strong, mighty." The exact Hebrew equivalent is Sagi. FEMININE HEBREW EQUIVALENTS: Amitza, Aza, Gibora.

Sagiv (סָגִיב) From the Aramaic and Hebrew, meaning "tall, noble" or "strong, mighty." The exact Hebrew equivalent is Sagiv. The exact feminine equivalent is Sagiva.

Sagy A variant spelling of Sagi. *See* Sagi.

Said From the Arabic, meaning "happy." HEBREW EQUIVALENTS: Gad, Gadi, Masos, Simcha. FEMININE HEBREW EQUIVALENTS: Gila, Rona, Simchit.

Sal From the Latin, meaning "salt," or from the Old English, meaning "willow." Also, a pet form of Salvador. *See* Salvador.

Salem (שָׁלֵם) The English form of the Hebrew *shalom*, meaning "peace." The exact Hebrew equivalent is Shalem. FEMININE HEBREW EQUIVALENTS: Shlomit, Shlom-Tzion, Shulamit.

Sali (סַלִי) From the Hebrew, meaning "my basket." Also, a pet form of Yisrael, a name popular among the Jews of Morocco. *See* Yisrael. The exact Hebrew equivalent is Sali. FEMININE HEBREW EQUIVALENTS: Salit, Yisra'ela.

Salil (סָלִיל) From the Hebrew, meaning "path." The exact Hebrew equivalent is Salil. The exact feminine equivalent is Selila.

Salim From the Arabic, meaning "peace, tranquility." Akin to Shalom. HEBREW EQUIVALENTS: Shalom, Shlomi, Shlomo. FEMININE HEBREW EQUIVALENTS: Sha'anana, Shlomit, Shulamit.

Salman A variant spelling of Salmon. *See* Salmon.

Salmon (שַׁלְמוֹן) From the Aramaic, meaning "garment." Also, a variant form of Solomon. HEBREW EQUIVALENTS: Salmon, Shlomo. FEMININE HEBREW EQUIVALENTS: Salma, Shlomit, Shulamit.

Salo A short form of Saloman. *See* Saloman.

Saloman, Salomon Variant forms of Solomon. *See* Solomon.

Salu (סָלוּ) From the Aramaic, meaning "basket." The exact Hebrew equivalent is Salu. The feminine equivalent is Salit.

Salvador, Salvatore From the Latin, meaning "to be saved." HEBREW EQUIVALENTS: Elisha, Elishu'a, Ezra. FEMININE HEBREW EQUIVALENTS: Mosha'a, Teshu'a, Yeshu'a.

Sam A pet form of Samuel. *See* Samuel.

Samal (סָמָל) From the Aramaic, meaning "sign, symbol." Also, from the modern Hebrew, meaning "sergeant." The exact Hebrew equivalent is Samal. FEMININE HEBREW EQUIVALENTS: Remazya, Simona.

Sami From the Arabic, meaning "exalted, on high." HEBREW EQUIVALENTS: Amram, Ram, Romem. FEMININE HEBREW EQUIVALENTS: Rama, Romit, Romiya.

Samm A variant spelling of Sam. *See* Sam.

Sammy A pet form of Samuel. *See* Samuel.

Sampson A variant spelling of Samson. *See* Samson.

Samson (שִׁמְשׁוֹן) From the Hebrew, meaning "sun." The exact Hebrew equivalent is Shimshon. The exact feminine equivalent is Shimshona.

Samuel (שְׁמוּאֵל) From the Hebrew, meaning "His name is God" or

"God has dedicated." The exact Hebrew equivalent is Shemu'el. The exact feminine equivalent is Shemu'ela.

Samy A pet form of Samuel. *See* Samuel.

Sander A short form of Alexander. *See* Alexander.

Sanders A patronymic form of Sander. *See* Sander.

Sandor A variant spelling of Sander, a pet form of Alexander. *See* Alexander.

Sandy A pet form of Alexander and Sanford. *See* Alexander *and* Sanford.

Sanford From the Old English, meaning "sandy river crossing" or "peaceful counsel." HEBREW EQUIVALENTS: Avshalom, Shlomo, Ye'or. FEMININE HEBREW EQUIVALENTS: Aleksandra, Bina, Shulamit.

Sapan (סַפָּן) From the Hebrew, meaning "sailor." The exact Hebrew equivalent is Sapan.

Sapir (סַפִּיר) A unisex name. From the Greek, meaning "precious stone." The exact Hebrew equivalent is Sapir.

Sar (שַׂר) From the Hebrew, meaning "prince." The exact Hebrew equivalent is Sar. FEMININE HEBREW EQUIVALENTS: Sara, Yisra'ela.

Sarag (סָרָג) From the Hebrew, meaning "tailor, weaver of cloth." The exact masculine Hebrew equivalent is Sarag. FEMININE HEBREW EQUIVALENTS: Adra, Rikma.

Sargeant From the Old French, referring to an officer, a leader. HEBREW EQUIVALENTS: Aluf, Katzin, Solel. FEMININE HEBREW EQUIVALENTS: Alufa, Sara, Tzameret.

Sari An Arabic name meaning "prince." Akin to Sar. *See* Sar.

Sarid (שָׂרִיד) From the Hebrew, meaning "remnant." The exact Hebrew equivalent is Sarid. The exact feminine equivalent is Sarida.

Sarug (סָרוּג) From the Hebrew, meaning "knitted." The exact Hebrew equivalent is Sarug. Keshira is a feminine equivalent.

Sasha *Also spelled* Sacha. A Russian pet form of Alexander. *See* Alexander.

Sason, Sasson (שָׂשׂוֹן) From the Hebrew, meaning "joy." The exact Hebrew equivalent is Sason. FEMININE HEBREW EQUIVALENTS: Aliza, Simchon, Sisa.

Saul (שָׁאוּל) From the Hebrew, meaning "borrowed." The Anglicized form of Shaul. *See* Shaul.

Saunders A variant spelling of Sanders. *See* Sanders.

Sava (סָבָא) From the Aramaic, meaning "grandfather" or "old man." The exact Hebrew equivalent is Sava. The exact feminine equivalent is Savta.

Savir (סָבִיר) From the Hebrew, meaning "learned, reasonable, rational." The exact Hebrew equivalent is Savir. The exact feminine equivalent is Sevira.

Saviv (סָבִיב) From the Hebrew, meaning "around, round." The exact Hebrew equivalent is Saviv. The exact feminine equivalent is Seviva.

Savyon (סַבְיוֹן) From the Hebrew, referring to a plant with white and yellow daisylike flowers. The exact Hebrew equivalent is Savyon. FEMININE HEBREW EQUIVALENTS: Savyona, Shetila, Yenika.

Saxby From the Old English, meaning "resident of Saxony."

Saxe A variant form of the Old English name Saxony. *See* Saxony.

Saxony The name of a region in Germany known for its production of a fine wool fabric with a soft finish. Sarag is a Hebrew equivalent. FEMININE HEBREW EQUIVALENTS: Adra, Rikma.

Sayer From the Old German, meaning "victory of the people." HEBREW EQUIVALENTS: Gevarya, Gover, Shu'a. FEMININE HEBREW EQUIVALENTS: Nitzcha, Nitzchiya, Nitzchona.

Scott The Late Latin form of the term Scotchman, meaning "tattooed one." A Hebrew equivalent is Sofer. A feminine equivalent is Soferet.

Scottie, Scotty Pet forms of Scott. *See* Scott.

Seamus An Irish/Gaelic form of James. *See* James.

Sean A popular Gaelic form of John. *See* John.

Seder (סֵדֶר) From the Hebrew, meaning "order." The exact Hebrew equivalent is Seder. The feminine Hebrew equivalent is Sedira.

Seely From the Old English, meaning "blessed." HEBREW EQUIVALENTS: Baruch, Berachya, Mevorach. FEMININE HEBREW EQUIVALENTS: Barucha, Beruchya, Mevorechet.

Seff (סֶעף) A Yiddish form of Ze'ev (Zev), meaning "wolf." *See* Ze'ev.

Sefi (סֶפִי) A pet form of Yosef (Joseph). *See* Yosef.

Segel (סֶגֶל) From the Hebrew, meaning "treasure." The exact Hebrew equivalent is Segel. The exact feminine equivalent is Segula.

Segev (שֶׂגֶב) From the Hebrew, meaning "glory, majesty, exalted." The exact Hebrew equivalent is Segev. FEMININE HEBREW EQUIVALENTS: Atara, Malka, Sara.

Seguv (שְׂגוּב) From the Hebrew, meaning "exalted." The exact Hebrew equivalent is Seguv. FEMININE HEBREW EQUIVALENTS: Atalya, Atara, Malka.

Seker (סֶקֶר) From the Hebrew, meaning "surveyor of land." The exact Hebrew equivalent is Seker.

Sela (סֶלַע) A unisex name. From the Hebrew, meaning "stone, rock." The exact Hebrew equivalent is Sela.

Selby A variant form of Shelby. *See* Shelby.

Selden, Seldon From the Middle English, meaning "rare," connoting an article of value. HEBREW EQUIVALENTS: Avikar, Chamdi'el, Chemed. FEMININE HEBREW EQUIVALENTS: Sapira, Sapirit, Yekara.

Seled (סֶלֶד) From the Hebrew, meaning "leap for joy" or "praise." The exact Hebrew equivalent is Seled. FEMININE HEBREW EQUIVALENTS: Hillela, Sasona, Simcha.

Selek (סֶלֶק) From the Hebrew, meaning "beet." The exact Hebrew equivalent is Selek.

Selig (סֶעלִיג) A Yiddish name, from the German and Old English, meaning "blessed, holy." HEBREW EQUIVALENTS: Asher, Baruch, Kadosh. FEMININE HEBREW EQUIVALENTS: Kedosha, Oshra.

Selwyn From the Anglo-Saxon, meaning "holy place" or "friend at court." HEBREW EQUIVALENTS: Bildad, David, Eldad. FEMININE HEBREW EQUIVALENTS: Chaviva, Davida, Devira.

Semadar (סְמָדַר) From the Hebrew, meaning "blossom." The exact Hebrew equivalent is Semadar. FEMININE HEBREW EQUIVALENTS: Perach, Pircha, Porachat.

Semel (סֶמֶל) From the Hebrew, meaning "sign, symbol." The exact equivalent is Semel. FEMININE HEBREW EQUIVALENTS: Remazya, Simona.

Sender (סֶנְדֶר) A Yiddish form of Sander, a form of Alexander. *See* Alexander.

Senior From the Latin, meaning "elder." Shneur is a Yiddish variant form. HEBREW EQUIVALENTS: Yeshishai, Zaken. FEMININE HEBREW EQUIVALENTS: Bilha, Kedma, Yeshana.

Sered (סֶרֶד) Of unknown derivation. The exact Hebrew equivalent is Sered. In Numbers 26:26, a member of the tribe of Zebulun.

Seren (סֶרֶן) From the Hebrew, meaning "captain, leader." The exact Hebrew equivalent is Seren. FEMININE HEBREW EQUIVALENTS: Alufa, Sarah.

Serge From the Old French and the Latin, meaning "serve." HEBREW EQUIVALENTS: Eved, Ovadya, Oved. FEMININE HEBREW EQUIVALENTS: Ezra, Ezri'ela.

Sergei A Russian form of Serge. *See* Serge.

Sergio A Spanish and Italian form of Serge. *See* Serge.

Seth The Anglicized form of Shet, the son of Adam. *See* Shet.

Seton From the Anglo-Saxon, meaning "town near the sea." HEBREW EQUIVALENTS: Aviyam, Livyatan, Moshe. FEMININE HEBREW EQUIVALENTS: Bat-Yam, Miryam, Yamit.

Setur (סְתוּר) From the Hebrew, meaning "closed, hidden." The exact Hebrew equivalent is Setur. FEMININE HEBREW EQUIVALENTS: Shemura, Tzafnat. In Numbers 13:13, the son of Michael of the tribe of Asher.

Seward From the Anglo-Saxon, meaning "defender of the sea coast." HEBREW EQUIVALENTS: Aviyam, Moshe, Shemer. FEMININE HEBREW EQUIVALENTS: Bat-Galim, Bat-Yam, Miryam.

Sewell From the Old English, meaning "well near the sea." HEBREW EQUIVALENTS: Arnon, Aviyam, Moshe. FEMININE HEBREW EQUIVALENTS: Bat-Galim, Bat-Yam, Miryam.

Seymore A variant spelling of Seymour. *See* Seymour.

Seymour From the Old English, meaning "marshy land near the sea." HEBREW EQUIVALENTS: Arnon, Aviyam, Dalfon. FEMININE HEBREW EQUIVALENTS: Arnona, Nava, Yizr'ela.

Shaanan (שַׁאֲנָן) From the Hebrew, meaning "peaceful." The exact Hebrew equivalent is Sha'anan. The exact feminine equivalent is Sha'anana.

Shabbetai, Shabetai Variant spellings of Shabtai. *See* Shabtai.

Shabbtai, Shabtai (שַׁבְּתַאי/שַׁבְּתַי) From the Hebrew and Aramaic, meaning "rest, sabbath." The exact Hebrew equivalent is Shabtai. FEMININE HEBREW EQUIVALENTS: Mashen, Menucha, Shalva.

Shabtiel (שַׁבְּתִיאֵל) A variant form of Shabtai. *See* Shabbtai. The exact Hebrew equivalent is Shabti'el.

Shachar (שַׁחַר) A unisex name. From the Hebrew, meaning "morning." The exact Hebrew equivalent is Shachar.

Shachna, Shachne Yiddish names derived from the Hebrew, meaning "neighbor."

Shael (שָׁאֵל) A pet form of Mishael. *See* Mishael.

Shafat, Shaphat (שָׁפָט) From the Hebrew, meaning "judge." The exact Hebrew equivalent is Shafat. FEMININE HEBREW EQUIVALENTS: Dani'ela, Danit, Dina. In Numbers 13:5, the son of Chori of the tribe of Shimon (Simeon).

Shai (שַׁי) From the Hebrew and Aramaic, meaning "gift." Also, a pet form of Yesha'ya (Isaiah). The exact Hebrew equivalent is Shai. FEMININE HEBREW EQUIVALENTS: Matana, Teruma, Teshura.

Shaked (שָׁקֵד) A unisex name. From the Hebrew, meaning "almond." The exact Hebrew equivalent is Shaked.

Shalem (שָׁלֵם) From the Hebrew, meaning "whole." The exact Hebrew equivalent is Shalem. FEMININE HEBREW EQUIVALENTS: Shlomit, Shulamit, Temima.

Shalev (שָׁלֵו) From the Hebrew, meaning "peaceful." The exact Hebrew equivalent is Shalev. The exact feminine equivalent is Shalva.

Shalman (שַׁלְמָן) From the Assyrian, meaning "to be complete" or "to be rewarded." The exact Hebrew equivalent is Shalman. FEMININE HEBREW EQUIVALENTS: Gomer, Shlomit, Shulamit.

Shalom (שָׁלוֹם) From the Hebrew, meaning "peace." The exact Hebrew equivalent is Shalom. FEMININE HEBREW EQUIVALENTS: Shlomit, Shulamit, Za'yit.

Shalum, Shallum (שָׁלוּם) From the Hebrew, meaning "whole, complete peace" or "reward." The exact Hebrew equivalent is Shalum. FEMININE HEBREW EQUIVALENTS: Gemula, Shlomit, Shulamit.

Shalvi (שַׁלְוִי) A variant form of Shalev. See Shalev. The exact Hebrew equivalent is Shalvi. FEMININE HEBREW EQUIVALENTS: Shalva, Shalviya.

Shamai (שַׁמַּאי) From the Hebrew and Aramaic, meaning "name." The exact Hebrew equivalent is Shamai. FEMININE HEBREW EQUIVALENTS: Shimat, Shimona, Shmu'ela.

Shamir (שָׁמִיר) From the Aramaic and Hebrew, meaning "diamond" or "flint." The exact Hebrew equivalent is Shamir. FEMININE HEBREW EQUIVALENTS: Ritzpa, Tzuri'el, Tzuriya.

Shamma (שַׁמָּא) A variant form of Shamai. See Shamai.

Shammai A variant spelling of Shamai. See Shamai.

Shamu'a (שָׁמוּעַ) From the Hebrew, meaning "that which is noted, listened to." The exact Hebrew equivalent is Shamu'a. FEMININE HEBREW EQUIVALENTS: Shimat, Shimona. In Numbers 13:4, the son of Zakur of the tribe of Re'uven (Reuben).

Shanan A variant spelling of Shaanan. See Shaanan.

Shane A variant form of Sean. See Sean.

Shani, Shanie (שָׁנִי) A unisex name. From the Hebrew, meaning "scarlet [thread]." The exact Hebrew equivalent is Shani.

Shanon, Shannon A variant form of Sean. *See* Sean.

Shapir (שַׁפִּיר) From the Aramaic, meaning "beautiful." The exact Hebrew equivalent is Shapir. FEMININE HEBREW EQUIVALENTS: Na'omi, Nava, Nofiya, Shifra.

Sharon (שָׁרוֹן) A unisex name. From the Hebrew, meaning "a plain." The Sharon is an area of ancient Palestine extending from Mount Carmel south to Jaffa where roses grew in abundance. The exact Hebrew equivalent is Sharon.

Sharp, Sharpe From the Old English, meaning "clever, perceptive." HEBREW EQUIVALENTS: Avida, Bina, Navon. FEMININE HEBREW EQUIVALENTS: Bina, Buna, Ge'ona.

Shatil (שָׁתִיל) From the Hebrew, meaning "plant." The exact Hebrew equivalent is Shatil. The exact feminine equivalent is Shatila.

Shatul (שָׁתוּל) A variant form of Shatil. *See* Shatil. The exact Hebrew equivalent is Shatul.

Shaul (שָׁאוּל) From the Hebrew, meaning "asked" or "borrowed." The Anglicized form is Saul. The exact Hebrew equivalent is Sha'ul. The exact feminine equivalent is Sha'ula. In I Samuel 9:1–2, the son of Kish; the first king of Israel.

Shaun A variant spelling of Sean. *See* Sean.

Shaw From the Middle English, meaning "wood grove, forest." HEBREW EQUIVALENTS: Arzi, Bar-Ilan, Etzyon. FEMININE HEBREW EQUIVALENTS: Ariza, Etzyona, Ilana.

Shawn A unisex name. A variant spelling of Sean, a variant form of John. *See* John.

Shay A variant spelling of Shai. *See* Shai.

Shaya, Shaye (שַׁעְיָה) A short form of Yeshaya (Isaiah). *See* Yeshaya. The exact Hebrew equivalent is Sha'ya.

Shea, Sheah Variant spellings of Shia. *See* Shia.

Shebsel, Shebsil (שֶׁעְבְּתֵל) Variant forms of Shepsel and Shepsil. *See* Shepsel *and* Shepsil.

Shefer (שֶׁפֶר) From the Hebrew, meaning "pleasant, beautiful." The exact Hebrew equivalent is Shefer. The exact feminine equivalent is Shifra.

Shela, Sheila (שֵׁלָה) From the Hebrew, meaning "prayer, petition." The exact Hebrew equivalent is Sheila. FEMININE HEBREW EQUIVALENTS: Techina, Tehila. In Genesis 38:5, a son of Judah; grandson of Jacob.

Shelby A unisex name. From the Anglo-Saxon, meaning "sheltered town." HEBREW EQUIVALENTS: Chasun, Eltzafun, Gonen. FEMININE HEBREW EQUIVALENTS: Setura, Shamira, Shimriya.

Sheldon From the Old English, meaning "shepherd's hut on a hill" or "protected hill." HEBREW EQUIVALENTS: Aharon, Avigdor, Shemarya. FEMININE HEBREW EQUIVALENTS: Migdala, Shimrit, Tira.

Shelet (שֶׁלֶט) From the Hebrew, meaning "sign, shield, coat of arms." The exact Hebrew equivalent is Shelet. FEMININE HEBREW EQUIVALENTS: Remazya, Simona.

Sheli (שֶׁל-לִי/שֶׁלִי) From the Hebrew, meaning "mine, belonging to me." The exact Hebrew equivalent is Sheli. Also, a variant spelling of Shelley. *See* Shelley.

Shelley From the Old English, meaning "island of shells." HEBREW EQUIVALENTS: Aviyam, Aynan, Deror. FEMININE HEBREW EQUIVALENTS: Derora, Miryam, Rachel.

Shelly A variant spelling of Shelley. *See* Shelley.

Shelomi A variant spelling of Shlomi. *See* Shlomi.

Shelomo A variant spelling of Shlomo. *See* Shlomo.

Shelton From the Old English, meaning "a town near the shelf [cliff]." HEBREW EQUIVALENTS: Aharon, Gal, Harel. FEMININE HEBREW EQUIVALENTS: Gal, Kaf, Talma.

Shelumiel, Shlumiel (שְׁלוּמִיאֵל) From the Hebrew, meaning "God is my peace." In Jewish folklore the name appears as Shlemiel and represents a ne'er-do-well. The exact Hebrew equivalent is Shlumi'el. In Numbers 1:6, a member of the tribe of Simeon.

Shem (שֵׁם) From the Hebrew, meaning "name," connoting reputation. The exact Hebrew equivalent is Shem. FEMININE HEBREW EQUIVALENTS: Bat-Shem, Hila, Hillela.

Shemaia, Shemaiah Variant spellings of Shemaya. *See* Shemaya.

Shemaria, Shemariah Variant spellings of Shemarya. *See* Shemarya.

Shemarya (שְׁמַרְיָה) From the Hebrew, meaning "protection of God." The exact Hebrew equivalent is Shemarya. FEMININE HEBREW EQUIVALENTS: Shamira, Shemura, Shimra.

Shemaryahu (שְׁמַרְיָהוּ) A variant form of Shemarya. *See* Shemarya. The exact Hebrew equivalent is Shemaryahu.

Shemaya (שְׁמַעְיָה) From the Hebrew, meaning "God has heard." The exact Hebrew equivalent is Shemaya. FEMININE HEBREW EQUIVALENTS: Shimat, Shimona, Shmuda.

Shemer (שֶׁמֶר) From the Hebrew, meaning "to guard, watch" or "preserve." The exact Hebrew equivalent is Shemer. FEMININE HEBREW EQUIVALENTS: Shemura, Shimra, Shimriya.

Shemuel A variant spelling of Shmuel. *See* Shmuel.

Shepard From the Anglo-Saxon, meaning "shepherd." HEBREW EQUIVALENTS: Meron, Ro'i, Talya. FEMININE HEBREW EQUIVALENTS: Merona, Rachel.

Shepherd From the Old English, meaning "one who tends sheep, one who protects." HEBREW EQUIVALENTS: Ro'i, Shemarya, Shermaryahu. FEMININE HEBREW EQUIVALENTS: Botzra, Magena, Migdala.

Shepley From the Old English, meaning "sheep meadow." HEBREW EQUIVALENTS: Ro'i, Talya, Zimri. FEMININE HEBREW EQUIVALENTS: Merona, Rachel.

Sheppard A variant spelling of Shepherd. *See* Shepherd.

Shepsel, Shepsil (שֶׁעפְּסֶעל/שֶׁעפְּסִיל) From the Yiddish, meaning "sheep." *See* Shepherd *and* Shepley *for equivalents.*

Sheraga, Sheragai (שְׁרָגָא) From the Aramaic, meaning "light." HEBREW EQUIVALENTS: Sheraga, Sheragai. FEMININE HEBREW EQUIVALENTS: Behira, Me'ira, Nahara.

Sherira (שְׁרִירָא) From the Aramaic, meaning "strong." The exact Hebrew equivalent is Sherira. FEMININE HEBREW EQUIVALENTS: Abira, Adira, Gavri'ela.

Sherman From the Old English, meaning "servant [or resident] of the shire [district]" or "one who shears [sheep]." HEBREW EQUIVALENTS: Avdi, Avdon, Shimshon. FEMININE HEBREW EQUIVALENTS: Merona, Rachel, Shimshona.

Sherry A pet form of Sherman. *See* Sherman.

Sherwin From the Anglo-Saxon, meaning "one who shears the wind." Also, from the Old English, meaning "shining friend." HEBREW EQUIVALENTS: Amit, Amitai, David. FEMININE HEBREW EQUIVALENTS: Ahuva, Amita, Davida.

Sherwood An Old English name referring to one who shears (cuts) wood in a forest. HEBREW EQUIVALENTS: Karmel, Karmeli, Ya'ar. FEMININE HEBREW EQUIVALENTS: Gana, Karmela, Nava.

Shet (שֵׁת) From the Hebrew, meaning "garment" or "appointed." Also, from the Syriac, meaning "appearance." The exact Hebrew equivalent is Shet. FEMININE HEBREW EQUIVALENTS: Mofa'at, No'ada, Salma.

Sheva (שְׁבַע) A unisex name. From the Hebrew, meaning "oath." The exact Hebrew equivalent is Sheva.

Shevach (שֶׁבַח) From the Hebrew, meaning "praise." The exact Hebrew equivalent is Shevach. FEMININE HEBREW EQUIVALENTS: Hillela, Tehila, Tishbacha.

Shia, Shiah (שַׁעְיָה) Short forms of Yeshaya (Isaiah). *See* Yeshaya. The exact Hebrew equivalent is Shia.

Shibi A modern Hebrew nickname formed from Shimon (Simeon) and Binyamin (Benjamin). *See* Shimon *and* Binyamin.

Shiftan (שִׁפְטָן) From the Hebrew, meaning "judge, judgment." The exact Hebrew equivalent is Shiftan. FEMININE HEBREW EQUIVALENTS: Dani'ela, Danit, Dina. In Numbers 34:24, a member of the tribe of Ephraim.

Shilem, Shillem (שָׁלֵם) From the Hebrew, meaning "paid" or "made peace." The exact Hebrew equivalent is Shilem. FEMININE HEBREW EQUIVALENTS: Shlomit, Shulamit. In Numbers 26:49, a member of the tribe of Naftali.

Shimi (שִׁמְעִי) A pet form of Shimon. *See* Shimon.

Shimke A Lithuanian pet form of Shimon. *See* Shimon.

Shimmel (שִׁימְעֶל) A Yiddish form of Shimon. *See* Shimon.

Shimon (שִׁמְעוֹן) From the Hebrew, meaning "to hear, to be heard" or "reputation." Simon and Simeon are Anglicized forms. The exact Hebrew equivalent is Shimon. The exact feminine equivalent is Shimona.

Shimri (שִׁמְרִי) From the Hebrew, meaning "my guard." The exact Hebrew equivalent is Shimri. FEMININE HEBREW EQUIVALENTS: Shamira, Shemura, Shimriya.

Shimron (שִׁמְרוֹן) From the Hebrew, meaning "guard house." The exact Hebrew equivalent is Shimron. FEMININE HEBREW EQUIVALENTS: Shomera, Shomrit, Shomrona. In Numbers 26:24, a member of the tribe of Issachar.

Shimshon (שִׁמְשׁוֹן) From the Hebrew, meaning "sun." The exact Hebrew equivalent is Shimshon. The exact feminine equivalent is Shimshona.

Shipley A variant form of Shepley. *See* Shepley.

Shir (שִׁיר) A unisex name. From the Hebrew, meaning "song." The exact Hebrew equivalent is Shir.

Shiri (שִׁירִי) A unisex name. From the Hebrew, meaning "my song." The exact Hebrew equivalent is Shiri.

Shirley A unisex name. From the Old English, meaning "from the white meadow." HEBREW EQUIVALENTS: Gani, Sharon, Yarden. FEMININE HEBREW EQUIVALENTS: Ginat, Sharona, Yardeniya.

Shiron (שִׁירוֹן) From the Hebrew, meaning "song, songfest." The exact Hebrew equivalent is Shiron. FEMININE HEBREW EQUIVALENTS: Shir, Shira, Shiri, Shir-Li.

Shlomi (שְׁלוֹמִי) From the Hebrew, meaning "my peace." The exact Hebrew equivalent is Shlomi. The exact feminine equivalent is Shlomit. In Numbers 34:27, a member of the tribe of Asher.

Shlomo (שְׁלֹמֹה) From the Hebrew, meaning "his peace." The exact Hebrew equivalent is Shlomo. FEMININE HEBREW EQUIVALENTS: Shlomit, Shulamit.

Shlomy A variant spelling of Shlomi. *See* Shlomi.

Shmuel (שְׁמוּאֵל) From the Hebrew, meaning "His name is God." The exact Hebrew equivalent is Shmu'el. The exact feminine equivalent is Shmu'ela.

Shmuli, Shmulik (שְׁמוּלִיק/שְׁמוּלִי) Yiddish forms of Shmuel. *See* Shmuel.

Shneur (שְׁנִיאוּר) A Yiddish form of Senior. *See* Senior.

Sholom A variant spelling of Shalom. *See* Shalom.

Shomer (שׁוֹמֵר) From the Hebrew, meaning "watchman, guardian." The exact Hebrew equivalent is Shomer. FEMININE HEBREW EQUIVALENTS: Notzeret, Shimrit, Shomeret.

Shor (שׁוֹר) From the Hebrew, meaning "ox." The exact Hebrew equivalent is Shor.

Shoshan (שׁוֹשָׁן) A unisex name. From the Hebrew, meaning "lily," or from the Egyptian and Coptic, meaning "lotus." The exact Hebrew equivalent is Shoshan.

Shoshi, Shoshie Pet forms of Shoshana. *See* Shoshana.

Shoval (שׁוֹבָל) From the Hebrew, meaning "path." The exact Hebrew equivalent is Shoval. FEMININE HEBREW EQUIVALENTS: Netiva, Selila, Mesilla. In I Chronicles 4:1, the youngest son of Judah and a grandson of Jacob.

Shraga (שְׁרָגָא) A Yiddish form of Sheraga. *See* Sheraga.

Shushan (שׁוּשָׁן) From the Hebrew, meaning "lily." The exact Hebrew equivalent is Shushan. The exact feminine equivalent is Shoshana.

Shutelach (שׁוּתֶּלַח) From the Hebrew, meaning "strife." The exact

Hebrew equivalent is Shutelach. FEMININE HEBREW EQUIVALENTS: Gidona, Meirav, Tigra. In Numbers 26:35, a member of the tribe of Ephraim.

Si A pet form of Seymour, Simeon, and Simon. *See* Seymour, Simeon, *and* Simon.

Sid (סִיד) From the Hebrew, meaning "plaster." The exact Hebrew equivalent is Sid. Also, a short form of Sidney. *See* Sidney.

Sidney A contracted form of Saint Denys. The original form of Denys is Dionysius, the Greek god of wine, drama, and fruitfulness. HEBREW EQUIVALENTS: Efra'yim, Gefanya, Gefen. FEMININE HEBREW EQUIVALENTS: Gat, Gitit, Zimra.

Sidra (סִדְרָה) A unisex name. From the Latin, meaning "starlike." Also, from the Hebrew, meaning "order, sequence." The exact Hebrew equivalent is Sidra.

Siegfried From the German, meaning "victorious peace." HEBREW EQUIVALENTS: Netzach, Shlomo, Yatzli'ach. FEMININE HEBREW EQUIVALENTS: Hadasa, Shlomit, Shulamit.

Siegmond, Siegmund From the German, meaning "victory" and "protection." HEBREW EQUIVALENTS: Avigdor, Chosa, Shemarya. FEMININE HEBREW EQUIVALENTS: Efrat, Magena, Shimrit.

Sig (סִיג) From the Hebrew, meaning "dross," signifying evil. The exact Hebrew equivalent is Sig. Also, a short form of Sigmond. *See* Sigmond.

Siggi, Sigi A pet form of Sigmond. *See* Sigmond.

Sigmond, Sigmund Variant spellings of Siegmond and Siegmund. *See* Siegmond *and* Siegmund.

Silas A variant form of Sylvan. *See* Sylvan.

Sili (סִלְעִי) From the Hebrew, meaning "rocky." The exact Hebrew equivalent is Sili. The exact feminine equivalent is Silit.

Silvan A variant spelling of Sylvan. *See* Sylvan.

Silvester A variant spelling of Sylvester. *See* Sylvester.

Siman (סִימָן) From the Hebrew, meaning "sign, symbol, mark, omen." The exact Hebrew equivalent is Siman. Remazya is a feminine equivalent.

Siman-Tov (סִימָן-טוֹב) From the Hebrew, meaning "good sign, good omen." The exact Hebrew equivalent is Siman-Tov. FEMININE HEBREW EQUIVALENTS: Mazal, Mazala, Mazalit, Tova, Tovit, Yatva.

Simcha (שִׂמְחָה) A unisex name. From the Hebrew, meaning "joy." The exact Hebrew equivalent is Simcha.

Simeon An Anglicized form of Shimon. *See* Shimon.

Simha A variant spelling of Simcha. *See* Simcha.

Simi, Simie Pet forms of Simeon and Simon. *See* Simeon *and* Simon.

Simkha A variant spelling of Simcha. *See* Simcha.

Simmie A pet form of Simeon and Simon. *See* Simeon *and* Simon.

Simon (שִׁמְעוֹן) A Greek form of Shimon. *See* Shimon.

Simpson A patronymic form, meaning "son of Simon." *See* Simon.

Sinai (סִינַי) A unisex name sometimes given to a person steeped in Torah learning. In Exodus 19:20, the name of the mountain on which the Torah was given. The exact Hebrew equivalent is Sinai.

Sinclair From the Latin, meaning "shining" or "sanctified." HEBREW EQUIVALENTS: Aharon, Chagai, Devir. FEMININE HEBREW EQUIVALENTS: Aharona, Behira, Me'ira.

Singer From the Old English, meaning "one who sings, a poet." HEBREW EQUIVALENTS: Amishar, Shir, Zemira. FEMININE HEBREW EQUIVALENTS: Liron, Ranit, Shira.

Sion A variant form of Zion (Tziyon). *See* Zion.

Sisi (שִׂישִׂי) From the Hebrew, meaning "my joy." The exact Hebrew equivalent is Sisi. FEMININE HEBREW EQUIVALENTS: Alisa, Alitza, Rina.

Sivan (סִיוָן) The third month of the Jewish year, corresponding to May–June. Its zodiacal sign is Gemini ("twins"). The exact Hebrew equivalent is Sivan. The exact feminine equivalent is Sivana.

Sloan From the Celtic, meaning "warrior." HEBREW EQUIVALENTS: Gibor, Ish-Cha'yil, Nimrod. FEMININE HEBREW EQUIVALENTS: Gavri'ela, Gibora, Gidona.

Smadar (סְמָדָר) A unisex name. From the Hebrew, meaning "blossom." The exact Hebrew equivalent is Smadar.

Sodi (סוֹדִי) From the Hebrew, meaning "my secret." The exact Hebrew equivalent is Sodi. FEMININE HEBREW EQUIVALENTS: Eliraz, Liraz, Raz. In Numbers 13:11, the father of Gaddi'el of the tribe of Zevulun (Zebulun).

Sol From the Latin, meaning "sun." The exact Hebrew equivalent is Shimshon. The exact feminine equivalent is Shimshona. Also, a pet form of Solomon. *See* Solomon.

Solomon (שְׁלֹמֹה) From the Hebrew, meaning "peace." The exact Hebrew equivalent is Shlomo. FEMININE HEBREW EQUIVALENTS: Shlomit, Shulamit.

Solon From the Greek, meaning "wise lawmaker." HEBREW EQUIVALENTS: Dan, Dani'el, Dotan. FEMININE HEBREW EQUIVALENTS: Dani'ela, Nadan, Nadin.

Somers Probably derived from the Old English place-name Somerset, meaning "summer settlement." HEBREW EQUIVALENTS: Charshom, Shamash, Shimshon. FEMININE HEBREW EQUIVALENTS: Chamaniya, Shimshona.

Sonny A popular nickname meaning "son" or "boy." The exact Hebrew equivalent is Ben.

Sorrell From the Old French, meaning "reddish-brown." HEBREW EQUIVALENTS: Admon, Adom, Tzochar. The feminine Hebrew equivalent is Aduma.

Sos (שׂוֹשׂ) From the Hebrew, meaning "joy, joyous." The exact Hebrew equivalent is Sos. FEMININE HEBREW EQUIVALENTS: Sasona, Simchona.

Spencer From the Anglo-Saxon, meaning "steward, administrator, guardian." HEBREW EQUIVALENTS: Avdi, Avigdor, Ovadya. FEMININE HEBREW EQUIVALENTS: Avigdora, Efrat, Tira.

Sruli, Srulik Yiddish pet forms of Yisrael (Israel). *See* Yisrael.

Stacey, Stacy From the Latin, meaning "firmly established." HEBREW EQUIVALENTS: Elyakim, Sa'adya, Yeho'yakim. FEMININE HEBREW EQUIVALENTS: Amitza, Kana, Sa'ada.

Stan A pet form of Stanley. *See* Stanley.

Stanford From the Old English, meaning "from the stone [or paved] ford." HEBREW EQUIVALENTS: Achitzur, Avitzur, Avni'el, Elitzur. FEMININE HEBREW EQUIVALENTS: Tzur-El, Tzurit, Tzuriya.

Stanley From the Old English, meaning "from the stony field." HEBREW EQUIVALENTS: Achitzur, Avitzur, Avni'el. FEMININE HEBREW EQUIVALENTS: Tzur-El, Tzurit, Tzuriya.

Stansfield From the Old English, meaning "field of stone." HEBREW EQUIVALENTS: Avni'el, Even, Regem. FEMININE HEBREW EQUIVALENTS: Avna, Avni'ela, Gazit.

Stefan A variant spelling of the German Stephan. *See* Stephan.

Stefano An Italian form of Stefan. *See* Stefan.

Stephan The German form of Stephen. *See* Stephen.

Stephen From the Greek, meaning "crown." HEBREW EQUIVALENTS: Katri'el, Kitron, Malkam. FEMININE HEBREW EQUIVALENTS: Atara, Ateret, Tzefira.

Sterling From the Old English name for a species of bird (starling). Also, from the Old English, meaning "one of noble character." HEBREW EQUIVALENTS: Adir, Gozal, Tzipor. FEMININE HEBREW EQUIVALENTS: Efrona, Gozala, Sara.

Stevan A variant form of Stephen. *See* Stephen.

Steven A variant form of Stephen. *See* Stephen.

Stewart From the Anglo-Saxon, meaning "guardian, keeper of the estate." HEBREW EQUIVALENTS: Shemarya, Shemaryahu, Ya'akov. FEMININE HEBREW EQUIVALENTS: Efrat, Tira, Tzila.

Stodard, Stoddard From the Old English, meaning "horse herder." HEBREW EQUIVALENTS: Cha'yil, Ish-Cha'yil, Sisera. The feminine Hebrew equivalent is Susi.

Stone From the Old English, meaning "stone, rock." HEBREW EQUIVA-
LENTS: Avni'el, Regem, Sapir. FEMININE HEBREW EQUIVALENTS: Avna, Gazit, Tzuriya.

Storm From the Old English, meaning "to whirl, move about quick-
ly." Sa'ar is a Hebrew equivalent. Sufa is a feminine equivalent.

Stu A pet form of Stuart. *See* Stuart.

Stuart A variant form of Stewart. *See* Stewart.

Sullivan From the Irish/Gaelic, meaning "black-eyed." HEBREW EQUIVA-
LENTS: Cham, Einan, Shachor. The feminine Hebrew equivalent is
Shechora.

Sumner From the French and Latin, meaning "one who summons a
messenger," or from the Old English, meaning "one who serves a
summons." HEBREW EQUIVALENTS: Mevaser, Shemarya. FEMININE HEBREW
EQUIVALENTS: Shomera, Shomrona.

Sus, Suss (סוּס) From the Hebrew, meaning "horse." The exact Hebrew equivalent is Sus. The exact feminine equivalent is Susa.

Susi (סוּסִי) From the Hebrew, meaning "my horse." The exact Hebrew equivalent is Susi. In Numbers 13:11, the father of Gaddi.

Sy A pet form of Seymour and Sylvan. *See* Seymour *and* Sylvan.

Sydney A variant spelling of Sidney. *See* Sidney.

Sylvan From the Latin, meaning "forest, woods." HEBREW EQUIVALENTS:
Ya'ar, Ya'ari. FEMININE HEBREW EQUIVALENTS: Ya'ara, Ya'arit.

Sylvester A variant form of Sylvan. *See* Sylvan.

Symon A variant spelling of Simon. *See* Simon.

Syshe (סִישֶׁע) From the Yiddish, meaning "sweet." Zushe, Zusye, and
Zisya are variant forms. HEBREW EQUIVALENTS: Avino'am, Magdi'el, Matok. FEMININE HEBREW EQUIVALENTS: Achino'am, Metuka, Na'ama.

T

Tab A pet form of David. *See* David.

Tabai, Tabbai (טַבַּאי) From the Aramaic, meaning "good." The exact Hebrew equivalent is Tabai. FEMININE HEBREW EQUIVALENTS: Tova, Tovit.

Tabur (טַבּוּר) From the Hebrew, meaning "navel, center, hub." The exact Hebrew equivalent is Tabur. FEMININE HEBREW EQUIVALENTS: Akifa, Seviva.

Taburi (טַבּוּרִי) A variant form of Tabur. *See* Tabur.

Tachan (תַּחַן) From the Hebrew word *techina*, meaning "prayer, petition." The exact Hebrew equivalent is Tachan. The exact feminine equivalent is Techina. In Numbers 26:35, a member of the tribe of Ephraim.

Tad, Tadd A pet form of Thaddeus. *See* Thaddeus.

Tadir (תָּדִיר) From the Hebrew, meaning "frequent, regular." The exact Hebrew equivalent is Tadir.

Tal (טַל) A unisex name. From the Hebrew, meaning "dew." The exact Hebrew equivalent is Tal.

Tali (טַלִי) A unisex name. From the Hebrew, meaning "my dew." A variant form of Tal. *See* Tal. The exact Hebrew equivalent is Tali.

Talia, Taliah Variant spellings of Talya. *See* Talya.

Talmai (תַּלְמַי) From the Aramaic, meaning "mound" or "hill." The exact Hebrew equivalent is Talmai. FEMININE HEBREW EQUIVALENTS: Talma, Talmi.

Talmi (תַּלְמִי) A unisex name. From the Hebrew, meaning "spring of water." The exact Hebrew equivalent is Talmi.

Talmon (תַּלְמוֹן) A unisex name. From the Aramaic, meaning "furrow." The exact Hebrew equivalent is Talmon.

Talor, Tal-Or (טַל-אוֹר/טַלְאוֹר) A unisex name. From the Hebrew, meaning "dew of the light [morning]." The exact Hebrew equivalent is Tal-Or.

Tal-Shachar (טַל-שַׁחַר) From the Hebrew, meaning "morning dew." The exact Hebrew equivalent is Tal-Shachar. FEMININE HEBREW EQUIVALENTS: Tal, Tali, Talya.

Taly A variant spelling of Tali. *See* Tali.

Talya (טַלְיָא) A unisex name. From the Hebrew, meaning "God's dew," and from the Aramaic, meaning "young lamb." The exact Hebrew equivalent is Talya.

Tam (תָּם) From the Hebrew, meaning "complete, whole" or "honest." The exact Hebrew equivalent is Tam. The exact feminine equivalent is Temima. In Genesis 25:27, a nickname for Jacob.

Tami (תָּמִי) A variant form of Tam. *See* Tam. The exact Hebrew equivalent is Tami.

Tamir (תָּמִיר) From the Hebrew, meaning "tall, stately, like the palm tree." The exact Hebrew equivalent is Tamir. The exact feminine equivalent is Temira.

Tamur (תָּמוּר) A variant form of Tamir. *See* Tamir. The exact Hebrew equivalent is Tamur.

Tanchum (תַּנְחוּם) From the Hebrew, meaning "comfort, consolation." The exact Hebrew equivalent is Tanchum. FEMININE HEBREW EQUIVALENTS: Nachmanit, Nachmaniya, Ruchama.

Tanhum The Anglicized form of Tanchum. *See* Tanchum.

Tate From the Old English, meaning "tenth, tithing" or "to be cheerful." HEBREW EQUIVALENTS: Simcha, Yachdi'el, Yagil. FEMININE HEBREW EQUIVALENTS: Aliza, Chedva, Ditza.

Tavas (טָוַס) From the Hebrew, meaning "peacock." The exact Hebrew equivalent is Tavas.

Tavi (טָבִי) From the Aramaic, meaning "good." The exact Hebrew equivalent is Tavi. FEMININE HEBREW EQUIVALENTS: Tova, Tovit.

Taylor From the Late Latin, meaning "to split, cut," referring specifically to one who cuts garments. Originally a surname. HEBREW EQUIVALENTS: Bavai, Gidon, Salmai. FEMININE HEBREW EQUIVALENTS: Gitit, Giza, Salma.

Ted, Teddy Pet forms of Theodor. *See* Theodor.

Tel (תֵּל) A variant form of Telem. *See* Telem. The exact Hebrew equivalent is Tel.

Telem (תֶּלֶם) From the Hebrew, meaning "mound" or "furrow." Also, from the Aramaic, meaning "oppress, injure." The exact Hebrew equivalent is Telem. FEMININE HEBREW EQUIVALENTS: Talma, Talmi.

Tema, Temah (תֵּימָא) From the Hebrew and Aramaic, meaning "astonishment, wonder." The exact Hebrew equivalent is Tema. FEMININE HEBREW EQUIVALENTS: Peliya, Tama.

Teman (תֵּימָן) From the Hebrew, meaning "right side," denoting the south. (When facing east, toward Jerusalem, south is to the right). The exact Hebrew equivalent is Teman. The feminine equivalent is Deromit.

Temani (תֵּימָנִי) A variant form of Teman. The exact Hebrew equivalent is Temani.

Tene, Teneh (טֶנֶא) From the Hebrew, meaning "basket." The exact Hebrew equivalent is Teneh. Salit is a feminine equivalent.

Teom (תְּאוֹם) From the Hebrew, meaning "twin." The exact Hebrew equivalent is Te'om. FEMININE HEBREW EQUIVALENTS: Sivan, Sivana.

Terence, Terrance, Terrence From the Latin, meaning "tender, good, gracious." HEBREW EQUIVALENTS: Na'aman, Tuviya, Yochanan. FEMININE HEBREW EQUIVALENTS: Na'ami, Tova, Tziyona.

Terri, Terry A pet form of Terence. *See* Terence.

Teruma, Terumah (תְּרוּמָה) A unisex name. From the Hebrew meaning "offering, gift." The exact Hebrew equivalent is Teruma.

Teva (טֶבַע) From the Hebrew, meaning "nature." The exact Hebrew equivalent is Teva. FEMININE HEBREW EQUIVALENTS: Tivona, Tivoni.

Tewel, Tewele Yiddish forms of David. *See* David.

Thaddeus, Thadeus From the Greek, meaning "gift of God." HEBREW EQUIVALENTS: Avi-Natan, Avishai, Hadar. FEMININE HEBREW EQUIVALENTS: Matana, Teruma, Teshura.

Than From the Greek, meaning "death." Originally a surname. EUPHEMISTIC HEBREW EQUIVALENTS: Chai, Cha'yim, Yechi'el. EUPHEMISTIC FEMININE HEBREW EQUIVALENTS: Chava, Cha'ya.

Thane A Danish form of Than. *See* Than.

Theo A pet form of Theobald and Theodore. *See* Theobald *and* Theodore.

Theobald, Theobold From the Old German, meaning "brave people." HEBREW EQUIVALENTS: Abir, Bo'az. FEMININE HEBREW EQUIVALENTS: Abira, Abiri, Atzmona.

Theodor, Theodore From the Greek, meaning "divine gift." HEBREW EQUIVALENTS: Elnatan, Matanya, Matityahu. FEMININE HEBREW EQUIVALENTS: Deronit, Matana, Teshura.

Thom A pet form of Thomas. *See* Thomas.

Thomas (תְּאוֹם) From the Hebrew and Aramaic, meaning "twin." Also, from the Phoenician, meaning "sun god." The exact Hebrew equivalent is Te'om. FEMININE HEBREW EQUIVALENTS: Behira, Ora, Orit.

Tibon, Tibbon Variant spellings of Tivon. *See* Tivon.

Tiger From the Greek, Latin, and Old French, meaning "tiger." The Hebrew equivalent is Namer. The feminine equivalent is Nemera.

Tikva (תִּקְוָה) A unisex name. From the Hebrew, meaning "hope." The exact Hebrew equivalent is Tikva.

Tilden From the Old English, meaning "fertile valley." HEBREW EQUIVA-
LENTS: Emek, Geichazi, Guy. FEMININE HEBREW EQUIVALENTS: Bik'a.

Tim A pet form of Timothy. *See* Timothy.

Timo A short form of Timothy. *See* Timothy.

Timothy From the Greek, meaning "to honor [or fear] God." HEBREW
EQUIVALENTS: Hadar, Hadaram, Sered. FEMININE HEBREW EQUIVALENTS:
Hadura, Kevuda, Nichbada.

Timur (תִּימוּר) From the Hebrew, meaning "tall, stately" or "to rise
up." The exact Hebrew equivalent is Timur. The exact feminine
equivalent is Timora.

Tip A nickname for Thomas. *See* Thomas.

Tiv (טִיב) From the Hebrew and Aramaic, meaning "good, goodness."
The exact Hebrew equivalent is Tiv. The exact feminine equivalent
is Tova.

Tivi (טִיבְעִי) From the Hebrew, meaning "natural." The exact Hebrew
equivalent is Tivi. FEMININE HEBREW EQUIVALENTS: Tivona, Tivoni.

Tivon (טִבְעוֹן) From the Hebrew, meaning "natural." The exact Hebrew equivalent is Tivon. The exact feminine equivalent is Tivona.

Tobe, Tobey, Tobi Variant spellings of Toby. *See* Toby.

Tobiah A variant form of Tuviya. *See* Tuviya.

Tobias The Greek form of Tobiah. *See* Tobiah.

Toby A pet form of Tobias. *See* Tobias.

Tod From the Old English, meaning "thicket." Also, from the Scottish
and Norse, meaning "fox." HEBREW EQUIVALENTS: Ilan, Kotz, Shu'al.
FEMININE HEBREW EQUIVALENTS: Shu'ala, Ya'ara, Ya'arit.

Toda, Todah (תּוֹדָה) A unisex name. From the Hebrew, meaning
"thanks, thankfulness." The exact Hebrew equivalent is Toda.

Todd A variant spelling of Tod. *See* Tod.

Todros From the Greek, meaning "gift." Akin to Theodor. *See* Theodor.

Tola (תּוֹלָע) From the Hebrew, meaning "maggot." The exact Hebrew equivalent is Tola. In Numbers 26:23, a member of the tribe of Issachar.

Tolya A variant form of Anatoly (Anatole). *See* Anatole.

Tom A pet form of Thomas. *See* Thomas.

Tomer (תּוֹמֶר) A unisex name. A variant form of Tamar. *See* Tamar (*feminine section*). The exact Hebrew equivalent is Tomer.

Tommi, Tommie, Tommy A pet form of Thomas. *See* Thomas.

Toni, Tony Pet forms of Anthony. *See* Anthony.

Toolie A pet form of Naftali.

Tor (תּוֹר) From the Hebrew, meaning "investigate, scout." The exact Hebrew equivalent is Tor. Bakara is a feminine equivalent.

Tov (טוֹב) From the Hebrew, meaning "good." The exact Hebrew equivalent is Tov. The exact feminine equivalent is Tova.

Tovi (טוֹבִי) A variant form of Tov, meaning "my good." The exact Hebrew equivalent is Tovi. *See also* Tov.

Tovia, Toviah Variant spellings of Toviya. *See* Toviya.

Toviel (טוֹבִיאֵל) From the Hebrew, meaning "my God is goodness." The exact Hebrew equivalent is Tovi'el. FEMININE HEBREW EQUIVALENTS: Tova, Tovat, Tovit.

Toviya (טוֹבִיָה) From the Hebrew, meaning "goodness of God." The exact Hebrew equivalent is Toviya. FEMININE HEBREW EQUIVALENTS: Tova, Tovit, Yatvata.

Trace A variant form of Tracey. *See* Tracey.

Tracee A variant spelling of Tracey. *See* Tracey.

Tracey, Tracy From the Old French, meaning "path" or "road." HEBREW EQUIVALENTS: Nativ, Shoval, Solel. FEMININE HEBREW EQUIVALENTS: Netiva, Selila.

Travis An English form of the Old French, meaning "to traverse, cross over." The exact Hebrew equivalent is Ivri. Avira is a feminine equivalent.

Trent From the Latin, meaning "moving water." HEBREW EQUIVALENTS: Aviyam, Chamat, Dela'ya. FEMININE HEBREW EQUIVALENTS: Afeka, Bat-Yam, Yaval.

Trevor From the Welsh, meaning "large homestead." HEBREW EQUIVALENTS: Artzi, Choresh, Shadmon, Yagev. FEMININE HEBREW EQUIVALENTS: Artzit, Molada, Moledet.

Tristan From the Old French and Gaelic, meaning "tumult, uproar." Sa'ar is a masculine Hebrew equivalent. Se'ara is a feminine equivalent.

Troy From the Gaelic, meaning "foot soldier." HEBREW EQUIVALENTS: Gad, Gevarya, Ish-Cha'yil. FEMININE HEBREW EQUIVALENTS: Gidona, Meirav, Tigra.

Truman From the Old English, meaning "a truthful and loyal person." HEBREW EQUIVALENTS: Amit, Amitai. FEMININE HEBREW EQUIVALENTS: Amita, Emet.

Trygve From the British, meaning "town by the water." HEBREW EQUIVALENTS: Beri, Chamat, Moshe. FEMININE HEBREW EQUIVALENTS: Bat-Yam, Miryam, Yaval.

Tsvi A variant spelling of Tzevi. *See* Tzevi.

Tucker An Old English occupational name for a fabric pleater. HEBREW EQUIVALENTS: Aman, Asa'el, Sarag.

Tudor A variant Welsh form of Theodore. *See* Theodore.

Tully From the Irish/Gaelic, meaning "mighty people." HEBREW EQUIVALENTS: Amiram, Amram, Ben-Guryon. FEMININE HEBREW EQUIVALENTS: Amtza, Ari'ela.

Tuvia, Tuviah Variant spellings of Tuviya. *See* Tuviya.

Tuviya (טוּבִיָה) From the Hebrew, meaning "God is good" or "the goodness of God." The exact Hebrew equivalent is Tuviya. FEMININE HEBREW EQUIVALENTS: Bat-Tziyon, Tova, Tovit.

Tuviyahu (טוּבִיָהוּ) A variant form of Tuviya. *See* Tuviya. The exact Hebrew equivalent is Tuviyahu.

Ty A pet form of Tyron. *See* Tyron.

Tyler An Old English occupational name for a maker of tiles.

Tyron, Tyrone From the Greek, meaning "lord, ruler." Also, from the Latin, meaning "young soldier." HEBREW EQUIVALENTS: Avraham, Gavri'el, Katri'el, Yisra'el. FEMININE HEBREW EQUIVALENTS: Atara, Be'ula, Gevira.

Tyson A patronymic form, meaning "son of Ty." *See* Ty.

Tzabar (צָבָּר) From the Aramaic, meaning "to gather, assemble." Also, from the Arabic, meaning "cactus, prickly pear." The exact Hebrew equivalent is Tzabar. The exact feminine equivalent is Tzabara.

Tzachi (צָחִי) A pet form of Yitzchak. *See* Yitzchak.

Tzadok (צָדוֹק) From the Hebrew, meaning "just, righteous." The exact Hebrew equivalent is Tzadok. FEMININE HEBREW EQUIVALENTS: Chasida, Tamar. In II Samuel 8:17, a High Priest during the reign of King David.

Tzafreer, Tzafrir (צְפְרִיר) From the Hebrew, meaning "morning," with special reference to demons that come to life during the morning hours. The exact Hebrew equivalent is Tzafrir. FEMININE HEBREW EQUIVALENTS: Tzafra, Tzafrira, Tzafririt.

Tzahi An Anglicized form of Tzachi. *See* Tzachi.

Tzarua (צָרוּעַ) From the Hebrew, meaning "blemished, diseased." The exact Hebrew equivalent is Tzaru'a. A feminine equivalent is Tzeru'a.

Tzefania, Tzefaniah, Tzefanya (צְפַנְיָה) From the Hebrew, meaning "God has treasured." The exact Hebrew equivalent is Tzefanya. FEMININE HEBREW EQUIVALENTS: Adiya, Otzara, Segula.

Tzefaniahu, Tzefanyahu (צְפַנְיָהוּ) A variant form of Tzefania. *See* Tzefania. The exact Hebrew equivalent is Tzefanyahu.

Tzemach (צֶמַח) From the Hebrew, meaning "plant, growth." The exact Hebrew equivalent is Tzemach. FEMININE HEBREW EQUIVALENTS: Narkis, Nurit, Yasmin.

Tzevi (צְבִי) From the Hebrew, meaning "deer, gazelle." The exact Hebrew equivalent is Tzevi. The feminine equivalent is Tzivya.

Tzelophchad (צְלָפְחָד) From the Hebrew, meaning "protection from fear." The exact Hebrew equivalent is Tzelophchad. In Numbers 26: 33, the son of Cheifer and father of five daughters.

Tzi (צִי) From the Hebrew, meaning "ship" or "navy." The exact Hebrew equivalent is Tzi. The feminine equivalent is Aniya.

Tzidkiah, Tzidkiya (צִדְקִיָּה) From the Hebrew, meaning "God is my righteousness." The exact Hebrew equivalent is Tzidkiya. FEMININE HEBREW EQUIVALENTS: Chisda, Tamar. In Kings 22:11 one of the four hundred "prophets" of King Ahab of Israel.

Tzidkiyahu (צִדְקִיָּהוּ) A variant form of Tzidkiya. *See* Tzidkiya.

Tzipor, Tzippor (צִפּוֹר) From the Hebrew, meaning "bird." The exact Hebrew equivalent is Tzipor. The exact feminine equivalent is Tzipora. In Numbers 22:2, the father of Balak, king of Moab.

Tziyon (צִיּוֹן) The Hebrew form of Zion. *See* Zion.

Tzofi (צוֹפִי) From the Hebrew, meaning "scout, guard, protector." The exact Hebrew equivalent is Tzofi. The exact feminine equivalent is Tzofiya.

Tzur (צוּר) From the Hebrew, meaning "rock." The exact Hebrew equivalent is Tzur. FEMININE HEBREW EQUIVALENTS: Tzurit, Tzuriya. In Numbers 25:15, the father of Cozbi, a Midianite woman.

Tzuri (צוּרִי) From the Hebrew, meaning "my rock." The exact Hebrew equivalent is Tzuri. FEMININE HEBREW EQUIVALENTS: Tzurit, Tzuriya.

Tzuriel (צוּרִיאֵל) From the Hebrew, meaning "God is my rock." The exact Hebrew equivalent is Tzuri'el. FEMININE HEBREW EQUIVALENTS: Avna, Tzur-El, Tzuriya. In Numbers 3:35, the son of the Levite Avi'chayil.

Tzvee A variant spelling of Tzevi. *See* Tzevi.

Tzvi A variant spelling of Tzevi. *See* Tzevi.

Tzvika (צְבִיקָה) A pet form of Tzevi. *See* Tzevi.

~ U ~

Ud (אוּד) From the Hebrew, meaning "flame, fire." The exact Hebrew equivalent is Ud. FEMININE HEBREW EQUIVALENTS: Uri'ela, Urit.

Udi (אוּדִי) From the Hebrew, meaning "my flame, my torch." The exact Hebrew equivalent is Udi. FEMININE HEBREW EQUIVALENTS: Uri'ela, Urit. Also, a pet form of Ehud. *See* Ehud.

Uel A short form of Samuel. *See* Samuel.

Uri (אוּרִי) From the Hebrew, meaning "my flame" or "my light." The exact Hebrew equivalent is Uri. FEMININE HEBREW EQUIVALENTS: Uri'ela, Urit.

Uria, Uriah Variant spellings of Uriya. *See* Uriya.

Uriel (אוּרִיאֵל) From the Hebrew, meaning "God is my light" or "God is my flame." The exact Hebrew equivalent is Uri'el. The exact feminine equivalent is Uri'ela.

Uriya (אוּרִיָה) From the Hebrew, meaning "God is my flame." The exact Hebrew equivalent is Uriya. FEMININE HEBREW EQUIVALENTS: Uri'ela, Urit. In II Samuel 11:15, King David sends Uriya to the battlefront.

Uza (עֻזָה/עֻזָא) A unisex name. From the Hebrew, meaning "strength." The exact Hebrew equivalent is Uza.

Uzi (עֻזִי) From the Hebrew, meaning "my strength." The exact Hebrew equivalent is Uzi. FEMININE HEBREW EQUIVALENTS: Uza, Uzi'ela, Uzit.

Uziel (עֻזִיאֵל) From the Hebrew, meaning "God is my strength." The exact Hebrew equivalent is Uzi'el. The exact feminine equivalent is Uzi'ela.

Uziya (עֻזִיָה) From the Hebrew, meaning "God is my strength." The exact Hebrew equivalent is Uziya. FEMININE HEBREW EQUIVALENTS: Uza, Uzi'ela, Uzit.

Uzza A variant spelling of Uza. *See* Uza.

Uzzi A variant spelling of Uzi. *See* Uzi.

Uzziah A variant spelling of Uziya. *See* Uziya.

~ V ~

Vail From the Latin, meaning "valley." HEBREW EQUIVALENTS: Gai, Gayora, Gaychazi. Ga'ya is a feminine equivalent.

Val A French form of Vail. Also, a pet form of Valentine. *See* Valentine.

Vale A variant spelling of Vail. *See* Vail.

Valentine From the Latin, meaning "strong, valorous." HEBREW EQUIVALENTS: Abir, Abiri, Gever. FEMININE HEBREW EQUIVALENTS: Amitza, Gavrila, Gibora.

Valerie A unisex name. An English form of the French (derived from the Latin name Valeria), meaning "healthy, strong, courageous." HEBREW EQUIVALENTS: Gavri'el, Oz, Uzi'el. FEMININE HEBREW EQUIVALENTS: Abira, Eitana, Gavri'ela.

Valery A variant form of Valerie. *See* Valerie.

Vasily, Vassily From the Greek and Russian, meaning "king, royalty." HEBREW EQUIVALENTS: Aluf, Melech, Yisra'el. FEMININE HEBREW EQUIVALENTS: Alufa, Malka, Sara.

Vaughan, Vaughn From the Celtic, meaning "small." HEBREW EQUIVALENTS: Katan, Ze'ira, Zutra. FEMININE HEBREW EQUIVALENTS: Ketana, Ketina, Pe'uta.

Velvel (וֶעלוֶעל) A pet form of the Yiddish name Volf. *See* Volf.

Vered (וֶרֶד) A unisex name. From the Hebrew, meaning "rose." The exact Hebrew equivalent is Vered.

Vern From the British, meaning "alder tree." Also, a pet form of Vernon. *See* Vernon.

Vernon From the Latin, meaning "belonging to spring, springtime," hence, flourishing. HEBREW EQUIVALENTS: Aviv, Avivi, Perach. FEMININE HEBREW EQUIVALENTS: Pericha, Tifracha, Yarkona.

Vic, Vickie Pet forms of Victor. *See* Victor.

Victor From the Latin, meaning "victor, conqueror." HEBREW EQUIVALENTS: Gavri'el, Gover, Katri'el. FEMININE HEBREW EQUIVALENTS: Dafnit, Gevira, Hadasa.

Vida A variant form of Vitas. *See* Vitas.

Vince A pet form of Vincent. *See* Vincent.

Vincent From the Latin, meaning "victor, conqueror." HEBREW EQUIVALENTS: Gevarya, Gevaryahu, Netzach. FEMININE HEBREW EQUIVALENTS: Nitzcha, Nitzchiya, Nitzchona.

Virgil From the Latin, meaning "flourishing, youthful." HEBREW EQUIVALENTS: Admon, Nitzan, Perach. FEMININE HEBREW EQUIVALENTS: Kalanit, Nirit, Pericha.

Vitas From the Latin, meaning "life." HEBREW EQUIVALENTS: Avichai, Cha'yim, El-Chai, Yechi'el. FEMININE HEBREW EQUIVALENTS: Chava, Cha'ya, Techiya.

Vitya A Russian form of Vitas. *See* Vitas.

Vivian, Vivien Used only occasionally as a masculine name. *See* Vivian (*feminine section*).

Vladimir A Slavonic/Russian name, meaning "famous ruler." HEBREW EQUIVALENTS: Aluf, Avimelech, Nagid. FEMININE HEBREW EQUIVALENTS: Alufa, Degula, Malka.

Volf (וֶאלְף) A Yiddish form of Wolf. *See* Wolf.

Vyvyan A variant spelling of Vivian. *See* Vivian.

❧ W ❧

Wade From the Old English, meaning "river ford." HEBREW EQUIVA-LENTS: Dela'ya, Silon, Yuval. FEMININE HEBREW EQUIVALENTS: Afeka, Bat-Yam, Silonit.

Wal A short form of Wallace and Walter. *See* Wallace *and* Walter.

Walbert From the Old English, meaning "secure fortification." HEBREW EQUIVALENTS: Eltzafan, Lot, Magen. FEMININE HEBREW EQUIVALENTS: Magena, Megina, Tzina.

Walden From the Old English, meaning "wooded valley." HEBREW EQUIVALENTS: Emek, Guy, Ya'ar. FEMININE HEBREW EQUIVALENTS: Bik'a, Ya'ara, Ya'arit.

Waldo A variant form of Walden. *See* Walden.

Walker From the Greek, meaning "to roll up," and from the Old English, meaning "to journey." HEBREW EQUIVALENTS: Aminad, Darkon, Divon. FEMININE HEBREW EQUIVALENTS: Gershona, Gi'oret, Hagar.

Wallace From the Anglo-French and the Middle English, meaning "foreigner, stranger." HEBREW EQUIVALENTS: Gershom, Gershona, Gi'ora. FEMININE HEBREW EQUIVALENTS: Avishag, Gershona, Gerusha.

Wallie A pet form of Walter. *See* Walter.

Wally A pet form of Wallace and Walter. *See* Wallace *and* Walter.

Walt A short form of Walter. *See* Walter.

Walter From the Old English, meaning "woods" or "master of the woods." Also, from the Old French, meaning "army general," and the Welsh-Latin, meaning "pilgrim, stranger." HEBREW EQUIVALENTS: Gavri'el, Gershom, Gershon. FEMININE HEBREW EQUIVALENTS: Avishag, Gavrila, Gerusha.

Ward From the Old English, meaning "to guard, guardian." HEBREW EQUIVALENTS: Natron, Noter, Shimron. FEMININE HEBREW EQUIVALENTS: Mishmeret, Shimra, Shimrit.

Warner A variant form of Warren. *See* Warren.

Warren From the Middle English and the Old French, meaning "to protect, preserve" or "enclosure, park." HEBREW EQUIVALENTS: Gina, Shemarya, Shomer. FEMININE HEBREW EQUIVALENTS: Gana, Karmela, Shimriya.

Wayne From the British, meaning "meadow," or from the Old English, meaning "maker of wagons." HEBREW EQUIVALENTS: Adam, Artzi, Eglon. FEMININE HEBREW EQUIVALENTS: Adama, Agala, Arzit.

Webster From the Old English, meaning "tailor" or "weaver." HEBREW EQUIVALENTS: Arig, Oreg, Rekem, Sarag. Rikma is a feminine Hebrew equivalent.

Weld A unisex name. A pet form of Weldon. *See* Weldon.

Weldon From the Middle English, meaning "to weld, bring together, unite." HEBREW EQUIVALENTS: Chever, Chevron, Yachad. FEMININE HEBREW EQUIVALENTS: Leviya, Shelavya.

Wendel, Wendell From the British, meaning "good dale or pleasant valley," or from the Old English, meaning "wanderer, stranger." HEBREW EQUIVALENTS: Gershom, Gershon, Gi'ora. FEMININE HEBREW EQUIVALENTS: Avishag, Gershona, Hagar.

Werner A variant form of Warren. *See* Warren.

Wesley From the Old English, meaning "west meadow." HEBREW EQUIVALENTS: Ma'arav, Sharon. FEMININE HEBREW EQUIVALENTS: Sharona, Yama.

Whitney A unisex name. From the Old English, meaning "land near the water" or "white palace." HEBREW EQUIVALENTS: Armon, Armoni, Bitan. FEMININE HEBREW EQUIVALENTS: Armona, Bat-Yam, Levana.

Wilber, Wilbert Variant forms of Walbert. *See* Walbert.

Wilbur A variant spelling of Wilber. *See* Wilber.

Wiley, Willy Pet forms of William. *See* William.

Wilfred, Wilfrid, Wilfried From the Old English, meaning "hope for peace." HEBREW EQUIVALENTS: Sha'anan, Shalev, Shalom. FEMININE HEBREW EQUIVALENTS: Menucha, Meshulemet, Shalva.

Wilhelm The German form of William. *See* William.

Will A pet form of William. *See* William.

Willard From the Old English, meaning "yard of willow trees." HEBREW EQUIVALENTS: Almog, Alon, Ilan. FEMININE HEBREW EQUIVALENTS: Almona, Almuga, Ilanit.

Willi A pet form of William. *See* William.

William A variant form of the Old French name Willaume and the Old High German name Willehelm, meaning "resolute protector." HEBREW EQUIVALENTS: Betzalel, Gad, Gavri'el. FEMININE HEBREW EQUIVALENTS: Chasya, Chosa, Magena.

Willie A pet form of William. *See* William.

Willis A patronymic form, meaning "son of William." *See* William.

Willoughby From the Old English, meaning "place by the willows." Akin to Willard. *See* Willard.

Willy A pet form of William. *See* William.

Willmer, Wilmar, Wilmer From the Old English, meaning "willows near the sea." Akin to Willard. *See* Willard.

Wilt A variant form of Walt (Walter). *See* Walter.

Wilton From the Old English, meaning "from the farmstead by the spring." HEBREW EQUIVALENTS: Aviyam, Moshe, Peleg. FEMININE HEBREW EQUIVALENTS: Derora, Marata, Miryam.

Win A short form of Winston. *See* Winston.

Winston From the Old English, meaning "victory town" or "a friend firm as a stone." HEBREW EQUIVALENTS: No'am, Shamir, Tzur. FEMININE HEBREW EQUIVALENTS: Amita, Avna, Davida.

Winthrop From the Old English, meaning "victory at the crossroads" or "friendly village." HEBREW EQUIVALENTS: No'am, Rayi, Regem. FEMININE HEBREW EQUIVALENTS: Ahuva, Chaviva, Davida.

Wolf, Wolfe From the Anglo-Saxon, meaning "wolf," connoting strength. HEBREW EQUIVALENTS: Ben-Cha'yil, Gavri'el, Ze'ev. FEMININE HEBREW EQUIVALENTS: Amtza, Ari'el, Gavri'ela.

Wolfgang From the German, meaning "path of the wolf." HEBREW EQUIVALENTS: Zev, Ze'evi. The feminine Hebrew equivalent is Ze'eva.

Wood, Woods From the Anglo-Saxon, meaning "from the wooded area." HEBREW EQUIVALENTS: Adam, Artza, Ilan. FEMININE HEBREW EQUIVALENTS: Eretz, Ilana, Yara.

Woodie A pet form of Woodrow. *See* Woodrow.

Woodrow From the Anglo-Saxon, meaning "wooded hedge." *See* Wood.

Woody A pet form of Woodrow. *See* Woodrow.

Wyn, Wynn From the British, meaning "white, fair." HEBREW EQUIVALENTS: Lavan, Levanon, Livni. FEMININE HEBREW EQUIVALENTS: Livnat, Levona, Malbina.

❧ X–Y ❧

Xander A pet form of Alexander. *See* Alexander.

Xavier From the Latin, meaning "savior," or from the Arabic, meaning "bright." HEBREW EQUIVALENTS: Bahir, Mashi'ach, Me'ir. FEMININE HEBREW EQUIVALENTS: Behira, Me'ira, Zahara.

Xeno From the Greek, meaning "sign, symbol." HEBREW EQUIVALENTS: Nisan, Samal, Siman. FEMININE HEBREW EQUIVALENTS: Simana, Simona.

Yaacov A variant spelling of Yaakov. *See* Yaakov.

Yaakov (יַעֲקֹב) From the Hebrew, meaning "supplanted" or "held by the heel." Jacob is the Anglicized form. The exact Hebrew equivalent is Ya'akov. The exact feminine equivalent is Ya'akova.

Yaar (יַעַר) From the Hebrew, meaning "forest." The exact Hebrew equivalent is Ya'ar. FEMININE HEBREW EQUIVALENTS: Ya'ara, Ya'arit.

Yachin (יָכִין) From the Hebrew, meaning "prepare, establish." The exact Hebrew equivalent is Yachin. FEMININE HEBREW EQUIVALENTS: No'ada, Techuna. In Numbers 26:12, a member of the tribe of Shimon (Simeon).

Yachlel (יַחְלְאֵל) From the Hebrew, meaning "faith in God" or "yearning for God." The exact Hebrew equivalent is Yachl'el. FEMININE HEBREW EQUIVALENTS: Tikva, Tzipiya. In Numbers 26:26, a member of the tribe of Zevulun (Zebulun).

Yadid (יָדִיד) From the Hebrew, meaning "beloved, friend." The exact Hebrew equivalent is Yadid. The exact feminine equivalent is Yedida.

Yadin (יָדִין) A variant form of Yadon. *See* Yadon. The exact Hebrew equivalent is Yadin.

Yadon (יָדוֹן) From the Hebrew, meaning "He [God] will judge." The exact Hebrew equivalent is Yadon. FEMININE HEBREW EQUIVALENTS: Dani'ela, Danit, Nadin.

Yadua (יָדוּעַ) From the Hebrew, meaning "celebrity" or "that which is known." The exact Hebrew equivalent is Yadu'a. FEMININE HEBREW EQUIVALENTS: Bina, Buna, Yedi'ela.

Yael (יָעֵל) A unisex name. From the Hebrew, meaning "mountain goat" or "to ascend." The exact Hebrew equivalent is Ya'el.

Yafet (יָפֶת) A variant form of Yefet. *See* Yefet. The exact Hebrew equivalent is Yafet.

Yagel A variant form of Yagil. *See* Yagil.

Yagil (יָגִיל) From the Hebrew, meaning "to rejoice." The exact Hebrew equivalent is Yagil. FEMININE HEBREW EQUIVALENTS: Gila, Gili, Giliya.

Yagli (יָגְלִי) From the Hebrew, meaning "wanderer" or "exiled." The exact Hebrew equivalent is Yagli. FEMININE HEBREW EQUIVALENTS: Galuta, Gola, No'a. In Numbers 34:22, a member of the tribe of Dan.

Yair (יָאִיר) From the Hebrew, meaning "to light up" or "to enlighten." The exact Hebrew equivalent is Ya'ir. Jair is the Anglicized form. FEMININE HEBREW EQUIVALENTS: Me'ira, Nurya, Uranit, Urit, Ya'ira. In Numbers 32:41, a son of Manesseh and grandson of Joseph.

Yakar (יָקָר) From the Hebrew, meaning "precious, dear, beloved, honorable." The exact Hebrew equivalent is Yakar. FEMININE HEBREW EQUIVALENTS: Yakira, Yekara, Yikrat.

Yaki (יָקִי) A pet form of Yaakov. *See* Yaakov.

Yakim (יָקִים) A short form of Yehoyakim (Jehoiakim). *See* Yehoyakim. The exact Hebrew equivalent is Yakim.

Yakir (יָקִיר) A variant form of Yakar. *See* Yakar. The exact Hebrew equivalent is Yakir.

Yale From the Anglo-Saxon, meaning "one who yields [pays]." HEBREW EQUIVALENTS: Efra'yim, Porat, Pura. FEMININE HEBREW EQUIVALENTS: Bikura, Porat, Poriya.

Yam (יָם) From the Hebrew, meaning "sea." The exact Hebrew equivalent is Yam. FEMININE HEBREW EQUIVALENTS: Yama, Yamit.

Yamin (יָמִין) From the Hebrew, meaning "right, right-handed." The exact Hebrew equivalent is Yamin. The exact feminine equivalent is Yemina. In Numbers 26:12, a member of the tribe of Shimon (Simeon).

Yancy A variant form of the Danish name Jon (John). *See* John.

Yaniv (יָנִיב) From the Hebrew, meaning "grow." The exact Hebrew equivalent is Yaniv. FEMININE HEBREW EQUIVALENTS: Tenuva, Tzemicha.

Yankel (יַאנְקעל) A Yiddish form of Yaakov (Jacob). *See* Yaakov.

Yarden (יַרְדֵן) From the Hebrew, meaning "to flow down, descend." The exact Hebrew equivalent is Yarden. The exact feminine equivalent is Yardena.

Yardeni (יַרְדֵנִי) A variant form of Yarden. *See* Yarden. The exact Hebrew equivalent is Yardeni.

Yared (יָרֵד) From the Hebrew, meaning "descend, descendant." The exact Hebrew equivalent is Yared. Jared is the Anglicized form. FEMININE HEBREW EQUIVALENTS: Tzelila, Yardena, Yardeniya. In Genesis 5: 15-20, the grandfather of Methusaleh.

Yariv (יָרִיב) From the Hebrew, meaning "he will quarrel, contend." The exact Hebrew equivalent is Yariv. Tigra is a feminine equivalent.

Yarkon (יַרְקוֹן) From the Hebrew, meaning "green." The exact Hebrew equivalent is Yarkon. The exact feminine equivalent is Yarkona.

Yarom (יָרוֹם) From the Hebrew, meaning "He [God] will raise up." The exact Hebrew equivalent is Yarom. FEMININE HEBREW EQUIVALENTS: Merima, Meroma.

Yaron (יָרוֹן) From the Hebrew, meaning "he will sing, cry out." The exact Hebrew equivalent is Yaron. The exact feminine equivalent is Yarona.

Yashar (יָשָׁר) A variant form of Yesher. *See* Yesher. The exact Hebrew equivalent is Yashar. The exact feminine equivalent is Yeshara.

Yashish (יָשִׁישׁ) From the Hebrew, meaning "old." The exact Hebrew equivalent is Yashish. The exact feminine equivalent is Yeshisha.

Yashuv (יָשׁוּב) From the Hebrew, meaning "return." The exact Hebrew equivalent is Yashuv. In Numbers 26:24, a member of the tribe of Issachar.

Yavin (יָבִין) From the Hebrew, meaning "he will understand." The exact Hebrew equivalent is Yavin. FEMININE HEBREW EQUIVALENTS: Bina, Buna.

Yavneel (יַבְנְאֵל) From the Hebrew, meaning "God builds." The exact Hebrew equivalent is Yavne'el. The exact feminine equivalent is Yavne'ela.

Yavniel (יַבְנִיאֵל) A variant form of Yavne'el. *See* Yavne'el. The exact Hebrew equivalent is Yavni'el.

Yaziz (יָזִיז) From the Assyrian and Hebrew, meaning "to move, to rise up" or "to be agitated, angry." The exact Hebrew equivalent is Yaziz. FEMININE HEBREW EQUIVALENTS: Evrona, Tigra.

Yechezkel (יְחֶזְקֵאל) From the Hebrew, meaning "God is my strength." The exact Hebrew equivalent is Yechezkel. The exact feminine equivalent is Yechezkela.

Yechiam (יְחִיעָם) From the Hebrew, meaning "may the nation live, survive." The exact Hebrew equivalent is Yechi'am. FEMININE HEBREW EQUIVALENTS: Cha'ya, Chayuta, Yechi'ela.

Yechiel (יְחִיאֵל) From the Hebrew, meaning "May God live." The exact Hebrew equivalent is Yechi'el. The exact feminine equivalent is Yechi'ela.

Yechieli (יְחִיאֵלִי) A variant form of Yechiel. *See* Yechiel. The exact Hebrew equivalent is Yechi'eli.

Yechiya, Yechiyah (יְחִיָה) A Yemenite name, meaning "life." The exact Hebrew equivalent is Yechiya. FEMININE HEBREW EQUIVALENTS: Techiya, Yechi'ela.

Yedid (יְדִיד) A variant form of Yadid.

Yedidia, Yedidiah, Yedidya (יְדִידְיָה) A unisex name. From the Hebrew, meaning "friend of God" or "beloved of God." The exact Hebrew equivalent is Yedidya.

Yediel (יְדִיאֵל) From the Hebrew, meaning "knowledge of the Lord." The exact Hebrew equivalent is Yedi'el. The exact feminine equivalent is Yedi'ela.

Yefet (יֶפֶת) From the Hebrew, meaning "beautiful," or from the Aramaic, meaning "abundant, spacious." The exact Hebrew equivalent is Yefet. FEMININE HEBREW EQUIVALENTS: Yafa, Yafit.

Yefuneh (יְפֻנֶה) From the Hebrew, meaning "regarded with favor." The exact Hebrew equivalent is Yefuneh. In Numbers 13:6, the father of Kalev of the tribe of Judah.

Yehiel A variant spelling of Yechiel. *See* Yechiel.

Yehieli A variant spelling of Yechieli. *See* Yechieli.

Yehochanan (יְהוֹחָנָן) From the Hebrew, meaning "God is compassionate." The exact Hebrew equivalent is Yehochanan. FEMININE HEBREW EQUIVALENTS: Chanita, Ruchama, Yeruchama. In I Chronicles 26:3, a Levite who served in the Tabernacle during the reign of King David. Yochanan is a variant form. *See* Yochanan.

Yehonatan (יְהוֹנָתָן) From the Hebrew, meaning "God has given" or "gift of God." The exact Hebrew equivalent is Yehonatan. FEMININE HEBREW EQUIVALENTS: Dorona, Matana, Migda.

Yehoram (יְהוֹרָם) From the Hebrew, meaning "God is exalted." The exact Hebrew equivalent is Yehoram. FEMININE HEBREW EQUIVALENTS: Ram, Rama, Ramit.

Yehoshua (יְהוֹשֻׁעַ) From the Hebrew, meaning "the Lord is salvation" The exact Hebrew equivalent is Yehoshu'a. FEMININE HEBREW EQUIVALENTS: Mosha'a, Shu'a, Teshu'a.

Yehoyakim (יְהוֹיָקִים) From the Hebrew, meaning "God will establish." The exact Hebrew equivalent is Yehoyakim. FEMININE HEBREW EQUIVALENTS: Asa'el, Mosada, Sa'ada.

Yehuda, Yehudah (יְהוּדָה) From the Hebrew, meaning "praise." The exact Hebrew equivalent is Yehuda. The exact feminine equivalent is Yehudit.

Yehudi A variant form of Yehuda. *See* Yehuda.

Yekev (יֶקֶב) From the Hebrew, meaning "wine press." The exact Hebrew equivalent is Yekev. FEMININE HEBREW EQUIVALENTS: Gat, Gitit.

Yekusiel The Ashkenazic form of Yekutiel. *See* Yekutiel.

Yekutiel (יְקוּתִיאֵל) From the Hebrew, meaning "God will nourish." The exact Hebrew equivalent is Yekuti'el. FEMININE HEBREW EQUIVALENTS: Mashena, Mosada, Sa'ada.

Yemin (יְמִין) From the Hebrew, meaning "right, right-handed." The exact Hebrew equivalent is Yemin. The exact feminine equivalent is Yemina.

Yemuel (יְמוּאֵל) From the Hebrew, meaning "God's day." The exact Hebrew equivalent is Yemu'el. In Genesis 46:10, the son of Eliav of the tribe of Re'uven (Reuben). In Numbers 26:9, Yemuel appears as Nemuel.

Yeravam (יְרָבְעָם) From the Hebrew, meaning "a nation in conflict." The exact Hebrew equivalent is Yeravam. Jeroboam is the Anglicized form. FEMININE HEBREW EQUIVALENTS: Gidona, Meirav, Tigra. In I Kings 11:26ff., the first king of Israel after the split in the monarchy.

Yered (יֶרֶד) From the Hebrew, meaning "descend." The exact Hebrew equivalent is Yered. FEMININE HEBREW EQUIVALENTS: Yardena, Yardeniya.

Yermi (יְרְמִי) A pet form of Yirmeyahu. *See* Yirmeyahu.

Yerusha, Yerushah (יְרוּשָׁה) A unisex name. From the Hebrew, meaning "inheritance." The exact Hebrew equivalent is Yerusha.

Yeshaya (יְשַׁעְיָה) From the Hebrew, meaning "God is salvation." The exact Hebrew equivalent is Yesha'ya. FEMININE HEBREW EQUIVALENTS: Mosha'a, Shu'a, Teshu'a.

Yeshayahu (יְשַׁעְיָהוּ) A variant form of Yesha'ya. *See* Yesha'ya. The exact Hebrew equivalent is Yesha'yahu.

Yesher (יֶשֶׁר) From the Hebrew, meaning "upright, honest." The exact Hebrew equivalent is Yesher. The exact feminine equivalent is Yeshara.

Yeshurun (יְשׁוּרוּן) From the Hebrew, meaning "upright." The exact Hebrew equivalent is Yeshurun. FEMININE HEBREW EQUIVALENTS: Amida, Tamar, Yeshara.

Yiftach (יִפְתָּח) From the Hebrew, meaning "he will open." The exact Hebrew equivalent is Yiftach.

Yigael (יִגְאָל) From the Hebrew, meaning "he will be redeemed, saved." The exact Hebrew equivalent is Yiga'el. The exact feminine equivalent is Yiga'ela.

Yigal (יִגְאָל) From the Hebrew, meaning "he will redeem." The exact Hebrew equivalent is Yigal. The exact feminine equivalent is Yigala. In Numbers 13:7, a son of Yosef of the tribe of Issachar.

Yigdal (יִגְדַּל) From the Hebrew, meaning "he will grow" or "he will be exalted." The exact Hebrew equivalent is Yigdal. FEMININE HEBREW EQUIVALENTS: Atalya, Atlit, Ge'ona.

Yimna (יִמְנָא) A unisex name. From the Hebrew and Arabic, meaning "right side," signifying good fortune. The exact Hebrew equivalent is Yimna.

Yirmeya (יִרְמְיָה) From the Hebrew, meaning "God will raise up." The exact Hebrew equivalent is Yirmeya. FEMININE HEBREW EQUIVALENTS: Rama, Ramit, Romema.

Yirmeyahu (יִרְמְיָהוּ) A variant form of Yirmeya. *See* Yirmeya. The exact Hebrew equivalent is Yirmeyahu.

Yirmi (יִרְמִי) A pet form of Yirmeya. The exact Hebrew equivalent is Yirmi. FEMININE HEBREW EQUIVALENTS: Rama, Ramit.

Yishai (יִשַׁי) From the Hebrew, meaning "gift." The exact Hebrew equivalent is Yishai. FEMININE HEBREW EQUIVALENTS: Matana, Netana, Netanela.

Yishi (יִשְׁעִי) From the Hebrew, meaning "my deliverer, savior." The exact Hebrew equivalent is Yishi. FEMININE HEBREW EQUIVALENTS: Matzlicha, Mosha'a.

Yishmael (יִשְׁמָעֵאל) From the Hebrew, meaning "God will hear." The exact Hebrew equivalent is Yishma'el. The exact feminine equivalent is Shmu'ela.

Yisrael (יִשְׂרָאֵל) From the Hebrew, meaning "prince of God" or "to contend, fight." The exact Hebrew equivalent is Yisra'el. The exact feminine equivalent is Yisra'ela.

Yisroel A variant spelling of Yisrael. *See* Yisrael.

Yitzchak (יִצְחָק) From the Hebrew, meaning "he will laugh." The exact Hebrew equivalent is Yitzchak. The exact feminine equivalent is Yitzchaka.

Yitzchok A variant spelling of Yitzchak. *See* Yitzchak.

Yitzhak, Yizhak Variant spellings of Yitzchak. *See* Yitzchak.

Yitz, Yitzi Pet forms of Yitzchak. *See* Yitzchak.

Yizkor (יִזְכּוֹר) From the Hebrew, meaning "remember." The exact Hebrew equivalent is Yizkor. FEMININE HEBREW EQUIVALENTS: Zichriya, Zichrona.

Yoash (יוֹעָשׁ) From the Hebrew, meaning "heavenly star." The exact Hebrew equivalent is Yo'ash. Joash is the Anglicized form. FEMININE HEBREW EQUIVALENTS: Ester, Kochava, Mazala. In I Chronicles 7:8, a grandson of Benjamin.

Yoav (יוֹאָב) From the Hebrew, meaning "God is father" or "God is willing." The exact Hebrew equivalent is Yo'av. FEMININE HEBREW EQUIVALENTS; Avi, Avi'ela, Aviya.

Yochai (יוֹחָאִי) From the Aramaic, meaning "God lives." The exact Hebrew equivalent is Yocha'i. FEMININE HEBREW EQUIVALENTS: Chava, Cha'ya, Yechi'ela.

Yochanan (יוֹחָנָן)   A variant form of Yehochanan. From the Hebrew, meaning "God's mercy" or "compassionate God." The exact Hebrew equivalent is Yochanan. FEMININE HEBREW EQUIVALENTS: Rachmona, Ruchama, Yeruchama. In I Chronicles 12:4, a member of the tribe of Benjamin.

Yoel (יוֹאֵל)   From the Hebrew, meaning "God is willing" or "the Lord is God." The exact Hebrew equivalent is Yo'el. FEMININE HEBREW EQUIVALENTS: Yo'ela, Yo'elit.

Yohanan   A variant spelling of Yochanan. *See* Yochanan.

Yom Tov (יוֹם טוֹב)   From the Hebrew, meaning "good, happy holiday." The exact Hebrew equivalent is Yom Tov. FEMININE HEBREW EQUIVALENTS: Chagit, Chagiya.

Yon (יוֹן)   A variant form of Yona or Yonatan. *See* Yona *and* Yonatan.

Yona, Yonah (יוֹנָה)   A unisex name. From the Hebrew, meaning "dove." The exact Hebrew equivalent is Yona.

Yonat (יוֹנַת)   A pet form of Yonatan. *See* Yonatan. The exact Hebrew equivalent is Yonat.

Yonatan (יוֹנָתָן)   From the Hebrew, meaning "God's gift." The exact Hebrew equivalent is Yonatan. FEMININE HEBREW EQUIVALENTS: Netani'ela, Netanya, Netina. Yehonatan is a variant form.

Yoni   A pet form of Yonatan. *See* Yonatan.

Yora, Yorah (יוֹרָה)   A unisex name. From the Hebrew, meaning "teach" or "shoot" or "kettle, pot." The exact Hebrew equivalent is Yora.

Yoram (יוֹרָם)   From the Hebrew, meaning "God is exalted." The exact Hebrew equivalent is Yoram. FEMININE HEBREW EQUIVALENTS: Atalya, Malka, Roma.

Yoran (יוֹרָן)   From the Hebrew, meaning "sing." The exact Hebrew equivalent is Yoran. FEMININE HEBREW EQUIVALENTS: Rani, Shira, Yarona.

Yos (יָאס)   A Yiddish pet form of Yosef. *See* Yosef.

Yosef (יוֹסֵף) From the Hebrew, meaning "God will add, increase." Joseph is the Anglicized form. The exact Hebrew equivalent is Yosef. The exact feminine equivalent is Yosifa.

Yosei An Aramaic form of Yosi. The exact Hebrew equivalent is Yosei. *See* Yosi.

Yosel, Yossel (יָאסֶעל) Yiddish pet forms of Yosef. *See* Yosef.

Yoshiya (יֹאשִׁיָה) A variant form of Yoshiyahu. *See* Yoshiyahu.

Yoshiyahu (יֹאשִׁיָהוּ) From the Hebrew, meaning "despair of the Lord." The exact Hebrew equivalent is Yoshiyahu. In II Kings 22:1, the king who reigned in Jerusalem for thirty-one years.

Yosi, Yossi (יָאסִי) Pet forms of Yosef. *See* Yosef.

Yotam (יוֹתָם) From the Hebrew, meaning "God is perfect." The exact Hebrew equivalent is Yotam. FEMININE HEBREW EQUIVALENTS: Ne'etzala, Nitzalov, Nitzelet.

Yotan (יוֹתָן) An abbreviated form of Yehonatan. *See* Yehonatan.

Yovel (יוֹבֵל) A unisex name. From the Hebrew, meaning "ram." The exact Hebrew equivalent is Yovel. The name is mentioned in Joshua 6:5.

Yuda, Yudah (יוּדָה) Variant forms of Yehuda. *See* Yehuda.

Yudan (יוּדָן) From the Hebrew, meaning "will be judged." The exact Hebrew equivalent is Yudan. FEMININE HEBREW EQUIVALENTS: Dani'ela, Danya, Dina.

Yuki (יוּקִי) A pet form of Yaakov. *See* Yaakov.

Yummy A pet form of Binyamin. *See* Binyamin.

Yuri (יוּרִי) A pet form of Uriah. *See* Uriah.

Yuval (יוּבָל) From the Hebrew, meaning "stream, brook." The exact Hebrew equivalent is Yuval. FEMININE HEBREW EQUIVALENTS: Afeka, Armonit, Bat-Yam.

Yves A French variation of the Old German, meaning "yew wood," used in making archery bows. HEBREW EQUIVALENTS: Ilan, Oren, Ya'ar. FEMININE HEBREW EQUIVALENTS: Alona, Livnat, Ya'arit.

~ Z ~

Zac A variant spelling of Zak. *See* Zak.

Zacharia, Zachariah Anglicized forms of Zecharia. *See* Zecharia.

Zachary A variant form of Zecharia. *See* Zecharia.

Zackary A variant spelling of Zachary. *See* Zachary.

Zadok The Anglicized form of Tzadok. *See* Tzadok.

Zahar (זַהַר) An Arabic form of the Hebrew name Zohar. *See* Zohar.

Zahir (זָהִיר) From the Hebrew, meaning "clear, shining, bright." Akin to Zohar. The exact Hebrew equivalent is Zahir. FEMININE HEBREW EQUIVALENTS: Behira, Zaka, Zivit.

Zak (זַק) A pet form of Yitzchak and Zecharya. *See* Yitzchak *and* Zecharya.

Zakai, Zakkai (זַכַּאי/זַכַּי) From the Aramaic and Hebrew, meaning "pure, clean, innocent." The exact Hebrew equivalent is Zakai. The exact feminine equivalent is Zaka.

Zaken (זָקֵן) From the Hebrew, meaning "old." The exact Hebrew is Zaken. The exact feminine equivalent is Zakena.

Zaki From the Arabic, meaning "pure, virtuous." Akin to the Hebrew name Zakai. The exact Hebrew equivalent is Zaki. FEMININE HEBREW EQUIVALENTS: Berura, Berurya, Zakiya.

Zakur (זָכוּר) From the Hebrew, meaning "mindful" or "remembered." The exact Hebrew equivalent is Zakur. FEMININE HEBREW EQUIVALENTS: Zichriya, Zichrona, Zichroni. In Numbers 13:4, the father of Shamu'a of the tribe of Re'uven (Reuben).

Zal A pet form of Zalman. *See* Zalman.

Zalki A pet form of Zalkin. *See* Zalkin.

Zalkin Yiddish pet forms of Solomon. *See* Solomon.

Zalman, Zalmen, Zalmon Yiddish short forms of Solomon. *See* Solomon.

Zamir (זָמִיר) From the Hebrew, meaning "song, singing." The exact Hebrew equivalent is Zamir. FEMININE HEBREW EQUIVALENTS: Zimra, Zemira.

Zan (זָן) From the Hebrew, meaning "nourish, sustain." The exact Hebrew equivalent is Zan. FEMININE HEBREW EQUIVALENTS: Mashena, Mosada, Sa'ada.

Zanav (זָנָב) From the Hebrew, meaning "tail." The exact Hebrew equivalent is Zanav. Alya is a feminine equivalent.

Zander A variant form of Sander. *See* Sander.

Zane A variant form of Zan. *See* Zan.

Zanvil, Zanvyl A Yiddish form of Shemuel. *See* Shemuel.

Zavad (זָבָד) From the Hebrew, meaning "gift, portion, dowry." The exact Hebrew equivalent is Zavad. The exact feminine equivalent is Zevuda.

Zavdi (זַבְדִי) A variant form of Zavad. *See* Zavad. The exact Hebrew equivalent is Zavdi.

Zavdiel (זַבְדִיאֵל) A variant form of Zavad. From the Hebrew, meaning "God is my gift." The exact Hebrew equivalent is Zavdi'el. FEMININE HEBREW EQUIVALENTS: Matana, Zevida, Zevuda.

Zayde, Zaydeh (זיידע) From the Yiddish, meaning "grandfather." *See* Aviav.

Zaydel (זײַדֶעל) A pet form of Zayde. *See* Zayde.

Zayit (זַיִת) A unisex name. From the Hebrew, meaning "olive." The exact Hebrew equivalent is Za'yit.

Zeb A pet form of Zebulun. *See* Zebulun.

Zebulon, Zebulun Variant spellings of Zevulun. *See* Zevulun.

Zecharia, Zechariah, Zecharya (זְכַרְיָה) From the Hebrew, meaning "memory" or "remembrance of the Lord." Zacharia and Zachariah are Anglicized forms. The exact Hebrew equivalent is Zecharya. FEMININE HEBREW EQUIVALENTS: Zichrini, Zichriya, Zichrona.

Zechariahu, Zecharyahu (זְכַרְיָהוּ) A variant form of Zecharia. *See* Zecharia. The exact Hebrew equivalent is Zecharyahu.

Zedekiah (צְדְקִיָה) The Anglicized form of Tzidkiah. *See* Tzidkiah.

Ze'ev (זְאֵב) From the Hebrew, meaning "wolf." The exact Hebrew equivalent is Ze'ev. The exact feminine equivalent is Ze'eva. In Judges 7:25, a Midianite prince.

Zefania, Zefaniah Anglicized forms of Tzefania. *See* Tzefania.

Zehavi (זְהָבִי) A unisex name. From the Hebrew, meaning "gold." The exact Hebrew equivalent is Zehavi.

Zeide, Zeideh Variant spellings of Zayde and Zaydeh. *See* Zayde *and* Zaydeh.

Zeidel A variant spelling of Zaydel. *See* Zaydel.

Zeira (זְעִירָא) A unisex name. From the Aramaic, meaning "small, junior." The exact Hebrew equivalent is Ze'ira.

Zeke A pet form of Zecharia. *See* Zecharia.

Zelig (זֶעלִיג) A variant form of Selig. *See* Selig.

Zelophehad An Anglicized form of Tzelophchad. *See* Tzelophchad.

Zemach A variant spelling of Tzemach. *See* Tzemach.

Zemel (זֶעמֶעל) From the Yiddish, meaning "bread." HEBREW EQUIVALENTS: Lachma, Lachmi, Lechem. FEMININE HEBREW EQUIVALENTS: Bat-Lechem.

Zemer (זֶמֶר) From the Hebrew, meaning "song." The exact Hebrew equivalent is Zemer. The exact feminine equivalent is Zimra.

Zemira, Zemirah (זְמִירָה) A unisex name. From the Hebrew, meaning "song, melody." The exact Hebrew equivalent is Zemira.

Zeno A variant spelling of Xeno. *See* Xeno.

Zeph A short form of Zephania. *See* Zephania.

Zephania, Zephaniah Variant spellings of Zefania. *See* Zefania.

Zer (זֵר) From the Hebrew, meaning "wreath" or "crown." The exact Hebrew equivalent is Zer. FEMININE HEBREW EQUIVALENTS: Atara, Ateret, Tzefira.

Zera (זֶרַע) From the Hebrew, meaning "seed." The exact Hebrew equivalent is Zera. FEMININE HEBREW EQUIVALENTS: Yizr'ela, Zeru'a.

Zerach (זֶרַח) From the Hebrew, meaning "to shine." The exact Hebrew equivalent is Zerach. FEMININE HEBREW EQUIVALENTS: Mazhira, Zahara, Zaharit. In Numbers 26:12, a member of the tribe of Shimon (Simeon).

Zerachya (זְרַחְיָה) From the Hebrew, meaning "light of the Lord." The exact Hebrew equivalent is Zerachya. FEMININE HEBREW EQUIVALENTS: Me'ira, Uri'ela, Urit.

Zerah A variant spelling of Zerach. *See* Zerach.

Zerem (זֶרֶם) From the Hebrew, meaning "stream." The exact Hebrew equivalent is Zerem. FEMININE HEBREW EQUIVALENTS: Arnona, Arnonit.

Zero A French and Italian form of the Arabic, meaning "cipher." The Hebrew equivalent is Sofer. The feminine equivalent is Sofera.

Zetan (זֵיתָן) From the Hebrew, meaning "olive tree." The exact Hebrew equivalent is Zetan. The exact feminine equivalent is Zetana.

Zev A variant spelling of Zeev. *See* Zeev.

Zevadia, Zevadiah, Zevadya (זְבַדְיָה) From the Hebrew, meaning "God has bestowed." FEMININE HEBREW EQUIVALENTS: Yehava, Zevida, Zevuda.

Zeved (זֶבֶד) From the Hebrew, meaning "gift." The exact Hebrew equivalent is Zeved. The exact feminine equivalent is Zevuda.

Zevi (צְבִי) From the Hebrew, meaning "deer." The exact Hebrew equivalent is Tzevi. The feminine equivalent is Tzivya.

Zeviel (צְבִיאֵל) From the Hebrew, meaning "gazelle of the Lord." The exact Hebrew equivalent is Tzevi'el. The exact feminine equivalent is Tzevi'ela.

Zevulun (זְבוּלֻן) From the Hebrew, meaning "to exalt" or "lofty house." The exact Hebrew equivalent is Zevulun. The exact feminine equivalent is Zevula.

Zichri (זִכְרִי) From the Hebrew, meaning "my memorial." The exact Hebrew equivalent is Zichri. FEMININE HEBREW EQUIVALENTS: Zichriya, Zichrona, Zichroni. In Exodus 6:21, a leader of the tribe of Levi.

Zik (זִיק) A Yiddish pet form of Itzik (Isaac). *See* Isaac. Also, from the Hebrew, meaning "spark."

Zim (זִים) From the Hebrew, meaning "gill." The exact Hebrew equivalent is Zim. FEMININE HEBREW EQUIVALENTS: Binit, Idna.

Zimra (זִמְרָא/זִמְרָה) A unisex name. From the Hebrew and Aramaic, meaning "song, tune" and "choice fruit." The exact Hebrew equivalent is Zimra.

Zimran (זִמְרָן) A variant form of Zimri. *See* Zimri. The exact Hebrew equivalent is Zimran.

Zimri (זִמְרִי) From the Hebrew, meaning "mountain-sheep" or "goat." The exact Hebrew equivalent is Zimri. FEMININE HEBREW EQUIVALENTS: Chosa, Ya'el, Zehira.

Zindel (זִינְדֵל) A variant form of Zundel. *See* Zundel.

Zion (צִיּוֹן) From the Hebrew, meaning "a sign" or "excellent." The exact Hebrew equivalent is Tziyon. The exact feminine equivalent is Tziyona.

Ziony A pet form of Zion. *See* Zion.

Ziv (זִיו) From the Hebrew, meaning "shine, brilliance" or "gazelle."

The exact Hebrew equivalent is Ziv. The exact feminine equivalent is Ziva.

Ziz (זִיז) From the Hebrew, meaning "balcony." The exact Hebrew equivalent is Ziz. Bima is a feminine equivalent.

Zizi (זִיזִי) A variant form of Ziz. *See* Ziz.

Zofi A variant spelling of Tzofi. *See* Tzofi.

Zohar (זֹהַר) A unisex name. From the Hebrew, meaning "light, brilliance." The exact Hebrew equivalent is Zohar.

Zoltan From the Hungarian, meaning "life." HEBREW EQUIVALENTS: Chai, Cha'yim, Yechi'el. FEMININE HEBREW EQUIVALENTS: Chava, Cha'ya, Techiya.

Zundel (זוּנְדֶעל) From the Yiddish, meaning "son, sonny." *See* Ben.

Zur A variant spelling of Tzur. *See* Tzur.

Zuri An Anglicized form of Tzuri. *See* Tzuri.

Zuriel A variant spelling of Tzuriel. *See* Tzuriel.

Zusman, Zussmann (זוּסְמַאן) Yiddish forms of the German, meaning "sweet man." HEBREW EQUIVALENTS: Avino'am, Na'am, Yivsam. FEMININE HEBREW EQUIVALENTS: Metuka, Mirit.

Zuta, Zutah (זוּטָא/זוּטָה) From the Aramaic and Hebrew, meaning "small." The exact Hebrew equivalent is Zuta. FEMININE HEBREW EQUIVALENTS: Ketana, Ketina, Ze'ira.

Zvi, Zwi A variant spelling of Zevi. *See* Zevi.

Zvulun A variant spelling of Zevulun. *See* Zevulun.

FEMININE
NAMES

✧ A ✧

Aaliya A variant spelling of Aliya. *See* Aliya.

Aarona A variant form of Aharona. *See* Aharona.

Abbe A pet form of Abigail. *See* Abigail.

Abbey A pet form of Abigail. *See* Abigail.

Abbie A pet form of Abigail. *See* Abigail.

Abby A variant spelling of Abbey. *See* Abbey.

Abela From the Latin, meaning "beautiful." HEBREW EQUIVALENTS: Adina, Rivka, Shifra. MASCULINE HEBREW EQUIVALENTS: Adin, Avino'am, Chemdan.

Abibi A variant spelling of Avivi. *See* Avivi.

Abibit A variant spelling of Avivit. *See* Avivit.

Abiela, Abiella Variant spellings of Aviela. *See* Aviela.

Abigail The Anglicized form of Aviga'yil. *See* Aviga'yil.

Abira (אַבִּירָה) From the Hebrew, meaning "strong." The exact Hebrew equivalent is Abira. The exact masculine equivalent is Abir.

Abiri (אַבִּירִי) A unisex name. From the Hebrew, meaning "my hero, gallant one." The exact Hebrew equivalent is Abiri.

Abital A variant spelling of Avital. *See* Avital.

Abra A feminine form of Abraham. *See* Abraham (*masculine section.*)

Achinoam (אֲחִינֹעַם) A unisex name. From the Hebrew, meaning "my brother is pleasing, sweet." The exact Hebrew equivalent is Achino'am. In I Samuel 14:50, a wife of King Saul; in I Samuel 25: 43, a wife of King David.

Achsa, Achsah (עַכְסָה) From the Hebrew, meaning "anklet, ornament," referred to in Isaiah 3:18. The exact Hebrew equivalent is Achsa. MASCULINE HEBREW EQUIVALENTS: Adi, Adin, Ravid. In I Joshua 15:16, a daughter of Caleb.

Ada, Adah (עָדָה) From the Hebrew, meaning "adorned, beautiful." Also, from the Latin and German, meaning "of noble birth." The exact Hebrew equivalent is Ada. MASCULINE HEBREW EQUIVALENTS: Adin, Adir, Aminadav.

Adaline A pet form of Adelaide. *See* Adelaide.

Adama, Adamah From the Hebrew, meaning "earth, soil." The exact Hebrew equivalent is Adama. The exact masculine equivalent is Adam.

Adamina A feminine pet form of Adam. *See* Adam (*masculine section*).

Adara From the Greek, meaning "beautiful," or from the Arabic, meaning "virgin." HEBREW EQUIVALENTS: Hadura, Na'ama, Zakit. MASCULINE HEBREW EQUIVALENTS: Adin, Hadar, Zakai.

Adasha, Adashah (עֲדָשָׁה) From the Hebrew, meaning "lentil" or "lens." The exact Hebrew equivalent is Adasha.

Adda A variant spelling of Ada. *See* Ada.

Addie A pet form of Adelaide. *See* Adelaide.

Adeena A variant spelling of Adina. *See* Adina.

Adela A variant form of Adelaide. *See* Adelaide.

Adelaide A French form of the German name Adelheid, meaning "of noble birth." HEBREW EQUIVALENTS: Adina, Malka, Ne'edara. MASCULINE HEBREW EQUIVALENTS: Adir, Adiv, Adoniya.

Adele A variant form of Adelaide. *See* Adelaide.

Adelia A variant form of Adelaide. *See* Adelaide.

Adelina A pet form of Adele and Adelaide. *See* Adelaide.

Adeline A pet form of Adelaide. *See* Adelaide.

Adella A variant form of Adelaide. *See* Adelaide.

Adelle A variant form of Adelaide. *See* Adelaide.

Adelyn A variant spelling of Adeline. *See* Adeline.

Adena, Adenah Variant spellings of Adina. *See* Adina.

Aderet (אַדֶּרֶת) From the Hebrew, meaning "cape, cloak." The exact Hebrew equivalent is Aderet. MASCULINE HEBREW EQUIVALENTS: Salma, Shet.

Adi (עֲדִי) A unisex name. From the Hebrew, meaning "ornament." The exact Hebrew equivalent is Adi.

Adie A variant spelling of Adi. *See* Adi.

Adiel (עֲדִיאֵל) A unisex name. From the Hebrew, meaning "ornament of the Lord." The exact Hebrew equivalent is Adi'el.

Adiela, Adiella (עֲדִיאֵלָה) A variant form of Adiel. The exact Hebrew equivalent is Adi'ela. *See* Adiel.

Adika (אֲדִיקָה) From the Hebrew, meaning "pious one." Among African tribes, the name given to the first child of a woman's second husband. The exact Hebrew equivalent is Adika. The exact masculine equivalent is Adik.

Adina, Adinah (עֲדִינָה) A unisex name. From the Hebrew, meaning "delicate." The exact Hebrew equivalent is Adina. In I Chronicles 11:42, a warrior in King David's army.

Adira, Adirah (עֲדִירָה) From the Hebrew, meaning "digging, hoeing." The exact Hebrew equivalent is Adira. MASCULINE HEBREW EQUIVALENTS: Chefer, Cheifer, Koresh. When spelled with an *alef* (אֲדִירָה), the meaning is "noble, majestic, powerful."

Adiva (אֲדִיבָה) From the Hebrew and Arabic, meaning "gracious, pleasant." The exact Hebrew equivalent is Adiva. The exact masculine equivalent is Adiv.

Adiya (עֲדִיָה) From the Hebrew, meaning "God's treasure, God's ornament." The exact Hebrew equivalent is Adiya. MASCULINE HEBREW EQUIVALENTS: Adi, Adi'el, Adin.

Adolpha A feminine form of Adolph. *See* Adolph (*masculine section*).

Adoniya (אֲדוֹנִיָה) A unisex name. From the Hebrew, meaning "my Lord is God." The exact Hebrew equivalent is Adoniya.

Adora From the Latin, meaning "one who is adored or loved." HEBREW EQUIVALENTS: Ahada, Ahava, Ahuva. MASCULINE HEBREW EQUIVALENTS: Ahud, Ahuv, Bildad.

Adorna From the Anglo-Saxon, meaning "to adorn." HEBREW EQUIVALENTS: Adi'el, Adina, Hadara. MASCULINE HEBREW EQUIVALENTS: Adi'el, Adin, Hadar.

Adra A variant form of Adara. *See* Adara.

Adria, Adrian From the Greek, meaning "rich." HEBREW EQUIVALENTS: Ashira, Bat-Shu'a, Negida, Yitra. MASCULINE HEBREW EQUIVALENTS: Hotir, Huna, Yishai.

Adriana, Adrianna Variant forms of Adrian. *See* Adrian.

Adriane A variant spelling of Adrian. *See* Adrian.

Adrien, Adrienne Variant spellings of Adrian. *See* Adrian.

Aduka, Adukah (אֲדוּקָה) From the Hebrew, meaning "pious, zealous." The exact Hebrew equivalent is Aduka. The exact masculine equivalent is Aduk.

Aduma, Adumah From the Hebrew, meaning "red, reddish." The exact Hebrew equivalent is Aduma. The exact masculine equivalent is Odem.

Adva, Advah (אַדְוָה) From the Aramaic, meaning "wave, ripple." The exact Hebrew equivalent is Adva. MASCULINE HEBREW EQUIVALENTS: Aviyam, Be'eri, Gal, Moshe.

Aerin A variant spelling of Erin. *See* Erin.

Afeka (אֲפֵקָה) From the Hebrew, meaning "horizon." The exact Hebrew equivalent is Afeka. The exact masculine equivalent is Ofek.

Afra, Afrah (עָפְרָה) From the Hebrew, meaning "dust." The exact Hebrew equivalent is Afra. MASCULINE HEBREW EQUIVALENTS: Adam, Artzi.

Agala (עֲגָלָה) From the Hebrew, meaning "wagon." The exact Hebrew equivalent is Agala. MASCULINE HEBREW EQUIVALENTS: Eglon, Tzoveva.

Agatha From the Greek, meaning "good." HEBREW EQUIVALENTS: Bat-Tziyon, Shifra, Tova. MASCULINE HEBREW EQUIVALENTS: Achituv, Ben-Tziyon, Na'aman.

Agil (עָגִיל) From the Hebrew, meaning "earring." The exact Hebrew equivalent is Agil. MASCULINE HEBREW EQUIVALENTS: Adi, Adin, Eter, Ozri.

Agnes From the Greek and Latin, meaning "lamb," symbolizing purity and chastity. HEBREW EQUIVALENTS: Berura, Rachel, Talya, Teli, Zaka. MASCULINE HEBREW EQUIVALENTS: Amitai, Amnon, Barur, Tzadok, Yesher.

Agora, Agorah (אֲגוֹרָה) An Israeli coin. The exact Hebrew equivalent is Agora. Zara is a masculine equivalent.

Aguda, Agudah (אֲגֻדָה) From the Hebrew, meaning "bundle, group, association." The exact Hebrew equivalent is Aguda. MASCULINE HEBREW EQUIVALENTS: Amir, Omer, Omri.

Aharona (אַהֲרוֹנָה) The feminine form of Aharon (Aaron). *See* Aharon (*masculine section*). The exact Hebrew equivalent is Aharona.

Aharonit (אַהֲרוֹנִית) A feminine form of Aharon (Aaron). *See* Aharon (*masculine section*). The exact Hebrew equivalent is Aharonit.

Ahava, Ahavah (אַהֲבָה) A unisex name. From the Hebrew, meaning "love." The exact Hebrew equivalent is Ahava.

Ahavat (אַהֲבַת) From the Hebrew, meaning "love [of]." The exact Hebrew equivalent is Ahavat. MASCULINE HEBREW EQUIVALENTS: Ahava, Ahuv, Ohev.

Ahavia, Ahavya (אֲהַבְיָה) Variant forms of Ahuviya. *See* Ahuviya. The exact Hebrew equivalent is Ahavya.

Ahuda, Ahudah (אֲהוּדָה) From the Hebrew, meaning "adored." The exact Hebrew equivalent is Ahuda. The exact masculine equivalent is Ahud.

Ahuva, Ahuvah (אֲהוּבָה) From the Hebrew, meaning "beloved." The exact Hebrew equivalent is Ahuva. The exact masculine equivalent is Ahuv.

Ahuvia, Ahuviah Variant spellings of Ahuviya. *See* Ahuviya.

Ahuviya (אֲהוּבִיָה) From the Hebrew, meaning "beloved of God." The exact Hebrew equivalent is Ahuviya. MASCULINE HEBREW EQUIVALENTS: Ahava, Ahuv, Ohev.

Aida From the Latin and Old French, meaning "to help." HEBREW EQUIVALENTS: Eli'ezra, Ezra, Ezr'ela. MASCULINE HEBREW EQUIVALENTS: Achi'ezer, Avi'ezer, Eli'ezer, Ezra.

Aidel A variant spelling of Eidel. *See* Eidel.

Aileen From the Greek, meaning "light." HEBREW EQUIVALENTS: Eli'ora, Li'ora, Li'orit. MASCULINE HEBREW EQUIVALENTS: Eli'or, Li'or, Ma'or, Me'ir.

Ailene A variant spelling of Aileen. *See* Aileen.

Aimee From the French and Latin, meaning "love, friendship." HEBREW EQUIVALENTS: Ahada, Ahava, Ahavat. MASCULINE HEBREW EQUIVALENTS: Ahud, Bildad, David.

Akifa, Akifah (עֲקִיפָה) From the Hebrew, meaning "encircling" or "enclosure." The exact Hebrew equivalent is Akifa. MASCULINE HEBREW EQUIVALENTS: Bitzaron, Gedor, Lotan, Ma'agal.

Akitza (עֲקִיצָה) From the Hebrew, meaning "stinging" or "sarcasm." The exact Hebrew equivalent is Akitza. MASCULINE HEBREW EQUIVALENTS: Kotz, Dardar.

Akuma, Akumah (עֲקֻמָה) From the Hebrew, meaning "curved, crooked, irregular." The exact Hebrew equivalent is Akuma. The exact masculine equivalent is Akum.

Alaina, Alaine   Variant feminine forms of Alan. *See* Alan (*masculine section*).

Alanna   A hybrid name formed from Allison and Anna. *See* Allison *and* Anna.

Alata, Alatah (עֲלָטָה)   From the Hebrew, meaning "darkness." The exact Hebrew equivalent is Alata. MASCULINE HEBREW EQUIVALENTS: Adar, Ard, Pinchas.

Alba   From the Latin, meaning "white." HEBREW EQUIVALENTS: Livnat, Malbina, Tzechora. MASCULINE HEBREW EQUIVALENTS: Lavan, Livni, Malbin.

Alberta   The feminine form of Albert. *See* Albert (*masculine section*).

Albertina, Albertine   Pet forms of Alberta. *See* Alberta.

Albina   From the Latin, meaning "white." HEBREW EQUIVALENTS: Levana, Malbina, Tzechora. MASCULINE HEBREW EQUIVALENTS: Alvan, Lavan, Malbin.

Alcina   A pet form of Alice. *See* Alice.

Alcinda   A variant form of Lucinda. *See* Lucinda.

Alda   From the Old German, meaning "old" or "rich." HEBREW EQUIVALENTS: Ashira, Negida, Keshisha. MASCULINE HEBREW EQUIVALENTS: Ashir, Hotir, Huna.

Aldora   From the Anglo-Saxon, meaning "noble gift." HEBREW EQUIVALENTS: Darona, Matana, Migdana. MASCULINE HEBREW EQUIVALENTS: Doran, Doron, Elinatan.

Aleeza (עֲלִיזָה)   From the Hebrew, meaning "joy, joyous one." The exact Hebrew equivalent is Aliza. MASCULINE HEBREW EQUIVALENTS: Alitz, Aliz, Gilam.

Aleksandra   A variant spelling of Alexandra. *See* Alexandra.

Alena, Alene   Variant forms of Allene. *See* Allene.

Aletta   From the Latin, meaning "the winged one." HEBREW EQUIVALENTS: A'ya, Senunit, Tzipora. MASCULINE HEBREW EQUIVALENTS: Orev, Gozal, Tzipor.

Alexa A variant form of Alexandra. *See* Alexandra.

Alexandra (אֲלֶכְּסַנְדְרָה) A feminine form of the Greek name Alexander, meaning "protector of man." The exact Hebrew equivalent is Aleksandra. The exact masculine equivalent is Aleksander.

Alexandrina A pet form of Alexandra. *See* Alexandra.

Alexia A variant form of Alexandra. *See* Alexandra.

Alexis A variant form of Alexandra. *See* Alexandra.

Alfreda The feminine form of Alfred, meaning "all peace" or "wise counsellor." HEBREW EQUIVALENTS: Aleksandra, Bina, Buna. MASCULINE HEBREW EQUIVALENTS: Aleksander, Avshalom, Eflal.

Ali A pet form of Alice and Alison. *See* Alice *and* Alison.

Alice From the Middle English and the Old French, meaning "of noble birth." HEBREW EQUIVALENTS: Malka, Matana, Nediva. MASCULINE HEBREW EQUIVALENTS: Adar, Adoniya, Elinatan.

Alicen A variant spelling of Alison. *See* Alison.

Alicia A Spanish form of Alice. *See* Alice.

Alila, Alilah (עֲלִילָה) From the Hebrew, meaning "deed" or "libel." The exact Hebrew equivalent is Alila. MASCULINE HEBREW EQUIVALENTS: Amana, Ma'aseiya.

Aliliya, Aliliyah (עֲלִילְיָה) From the Hebrew, meaning "deed." The exact Hebrew equivalent is Aliliya. MASCULINE HEBREW EQUIVALENTS: Amasa, Ma'aseiya.

Alina A Slavic form of Helen. *See* Helen.

Aline A pet form of Gwendaline. *See* Gwendaline.

Alisa A variant form of Alice. *See* Alice.

Alisia From the Greek, meaning "enchanting, endearing." Also, a variant form of Alicia. *See* Alicia. HEBREW EQUIVALENTS: Chaviva, Maksima, Yokara. MASCULINE HEBREW EQUIVALENTS: Chaviv, Maksim, Yakar.

Alison A matronymic form, meaning "son of Alice." *See* Alice.

Alissa A variant form of Alice. *See* Alice.

Alissyn, Alisyn Variant spellings of Alison. *See* Alison.

Alita (עֲלִיתָה) From the Hebrew, meaning "high, above" or "excellent." The exact Hebrew equivalent is Alita. MASCULINE HEBREW EQUIVALENTS: Aharon, Ben-Tziyon, Marom.

Alitza, Alitzah (עֲלִיצָה) From the Hebrew, meaning "joy, happiness." The exact Hebrew equivalent is Alitza. The exact masculine equivalent is Alitz.

Alix A pet form of Alexandra. *See* Alexandra.

Aliya, Aliyah (עֲלִיָה) From the Hebrew, meaning "to ascend, go up." The exact Hebrew equivalent is Aliya. MASCULINE HEBREW EQUIVALENTS: Atlai, Ram, Rama.

Aliz (עַלִיז) A unisex name. From the Hebrew, meaning "joy, joyful, merry." The exact Hebrew equivalent is Aliz.

Aliza, Alizah Variant spellings of Aleeza and Alitza. *See* Aleeza *and* Alitza.

Alla (עָלָה) From the Hebrew, meaning "to ascend." The exact Hebrew equivalent is Alla. MASCULINE HEBREW EQUIVALENTS: Eli, Ya'al, Yaziz.

Allegra From the Latin, meaning "cheerful." HEBREW EQUIVALENTS: Alisa, Aliza, Aviga'yil, Elza, Ronli. MASCULINE HEBREW EQUIVALENTS: Alitz, Aliz, Eletz.

Allena, Allene Variant feminine forms of Allen. *See* Allen (*masculine section*).

Alleyne A variant spelling of Allene. *See* Allene.

Allison A variant spelling of Alison. *See* Alison.

Ally A variant spelling of Ali. *See* Ali.

Allyn A unisex name. A variant spelling of Alan. *See* Alan (*masculine section*).

Allysin A variant spelling of Alison. *See* Alison.

Alma (עַלְמָה) From the Hebrew, meaning "maiden." The exact Hebrew equivalent is Alma. MASCULINE HEBREW EQUIVALENTS: Elam, Cha'yim, Na'aman.

Almana (אַלְמָנָה) From the Hebrew, meaning "alone, lonely, widow." The exact Hebrew equivalent is Almana. The exact masculine equivalent is Alman.

Almonit (אַלְמוֹנִית) From the Hebrew, meaning "anonymous." The exact Hebrew equivalent is Almonit. The exact masculine equivalent is Almoni.

Alona (אַלוֹנָה) From the Hebrew, meaning "oak tree." The exact Hebrew equivalent is Alona. The exact masculine equivalent is Alon.

Alta From the Latin, meaning "elevated, exalted." HEBREW EQUIVALENTS: Merima, Meroma. MASCULINE HEBREW EQUIVALENTS: Gidel, Yirmeyahu.

Althea From the Greek and Latin, meaning "to heal" or "healer." HEBREW EQUIVALENTS: Refu'a, Rofi, Terufa. MASCULINE HEBREW EQUIVALENTS: Asa, Asa'el, Marpay.

Alufa (אַלוּפָה) From the Hebrew, meaning "leader" or "princess." The exact Hebrew equivalent is Alufa. The exact masculine equivalent is Aluf.

Aluma, Alumah (עֲלוּמָה) From the Hebrew, meaning "maiden" or "secret." The exact Hebrew equivalent is Aluma. MASCULINE HEBREW EQUIVALENTS: Bachur, Elam, Na'arai.

Aluva (עֲלוּבָה) From the Hebrew, meaning "lonely, wretched, poor." The exact Hebrew equivalent is Aluva. The exact masculine equivalent is Aluv.

Alva From the Spanish, meaning "blond, fair-skinned." HEBREW EQUIVALENTS: Livnat, Malbina, Zehuva. MASCULINE HEBREW EQUIVALENTS: Lavan, Zahavi, Zahuv.

Alvina A feminine form of Alvin. *See* Alvin (*masculine section*).

Alvita From the Latin, meaning "lively." HEBREW EQUIVALENTS: Chava, Cha'ya, Yechi'ela. MASCULINE HEBREW EQUIVALENTS: Avichai, Cha'yim, Yechi'eli.

Alya, Alyah (אַלְיָה) From the Hebrew, meaning "fat of the tail." The exact Hebrew equivalent is Alya. MASCULINE HEBREW EQUIVALENTS: Achlav, Cheilev, Chelbo.

Alyce A variant spelling of Alice. *See* Alice.

Alyna A variant spelling of Alina. *See* Alina.

Alyonna A feminine form of Elon. *See* Elon (*masculine section*).

Alysa A variant spelling of Alisa. *See* Alisa.

Alysha A feminine form of Elisha. *See* Elisha (*masculine section*).

Alyson A variant spelling of Alison. *See* Alison.

Alyssa, Alysse Variant spellings of Alissa. *See* Alissa.

Alyza A variant spelling of Aleeza. *See* Aleeza.

Amabel Compounded from the Latin *amor*, meaning "love," and the French *belle*, meaning "beautiful." HEBREW EQUIVALENTS: Ahuva, Chaviva, Davida. MASCULINE HEBREW EQUIVALENTS: Ahuv, Chaviv, David.

Amada From the Latin, meaning "loved one." HEBREW EQUIVALENTS: Ahada, Ahuva, Chiba. MASCULINE HEBREW EQUIVALENTS: Ahava, Ahuv, Ehud.

Amadea From the Latin, meaning "God's beloved." HEBREW FQUIVALENTS: Ahavam, Ahavat, Chibat-Tziyon. MASCULINE HEBREW EQUIVALENTS: Ahuv, Bildad, Yedidya.

Amal (עָמָל) A unisex name, but more common among males. From the Hebrew, meaning "work, toil." The exact Hebrew equivalent is Amal.

Amala, Amalah (עֲמָלָה) From the Hebrew, meaning "fee, commission." The exact Hebrew equivalent is Amala.

Amalia, Amaliah A variant spelling of Amalya. *See* Amalya.

Amalie A German variant form of Amelia. *See* Amelia.

Amalya (עֲמַלְיָה) From the Hebrew, meaning "work of the Lord." The exact Hebrew equivalent is Amalya. The exact masculine equivalent is Amel.

Amana (אֲמָנָה) From the Hebrew, meaning "faithful." The exact Hebrew equivalent is Amana. MASCULINE HEBREW EQUIVALENTS: Amitai, Amitan, Amnon.

Amanda From the Latin, meaning "love." HEBREW EQUIVALENTS: Ahada, Ahava, Ahuda. MASCULINE HEBREW EQUIVALENTS: Ahuv, Ahuviya, Chovev.

Amandalina A pet form of Amanda. *See* Amanda.

Amania, Amaniah, Amanya (אֲמַנְיָה) A unisex name. From the Hebrew, meaning "loyal to the Lord." The exact Hebrew equivalent is Amanya.

Amber From the Old French and Arabic, meaning "amber" or "golden, brownish-yellow." HEBREW EQUIVALENTS: Ofira, Paza, Pazit. MASCULINE HEBREW EQUIVALENTS: Elifaz, Ofir, Paz.

Amberlee A hybrid name formed from Amber and Lee. *See* Amber *and* Lee.

Amela (עֲמֵלָה) From the Hebrew, meaning "labor, toil." The exact Hebrew equivalent is Amela. The exact masculine equivalent is Amel.

Amelia From the Latin, meaning "to work, to be industrious." HEBREW EQUIVALENTS: Amalya, Arnona, Zeriza. MASCULINE HEBREW EQUIVALENTS: Amel, Arnon, Ovadya.

Ami, Amie, Ammi (עַמִי) A unisex name. From the Hebrew, meaning "my nation, my people." The exact Hebrew equivalent is Ami. In Ezra 2:57, a servant of King Solomon. Also, a variant spelling of Amy. *See* Amy.

Amila (עֲמִילָה) A variant form of Amela. *See* Amela. The exact Hebrew equivalent is Amila.

Amilie A variant French form of Amelia. *See* Amelia.

Amina (אֲמִינָה/אֲמִינָא) From the Hebrew and Arabic, meaning "trusted, faithful." The exact Hebrew equivalent is Amina. MASCULINE HEBREW EQUIVALENTS: Amitai, Amitan, Amnon.

Amior (עֲמִיאוֹר) A unisex name. From the Hebrew, meaning "my nation is a light, a beacon." The exact Hebrew equivalent is Ami'or.

Amira (אֲמִירָה) From the Hebrew, meaning "speech, utterance." The exact Hebrew equivalent is Amira. The exact masculine equivalent is Amir.

Amit (אָמִית) A unisex name. From the Hebrew, meaning "upright, honest, friend." The exact Hebrew equivalent is Amit.

Amita (אֲמִיתָה) A variant form of Amit. The exact Hebrew equivalent is Amita. *See* Amit.

Amity From the Latin, meaning "love, friendship." HEBREW EQUIVALENTS: Ahava, Chiba, Davida. MASCULINE HEBREW EQUIVALENTS: Ahud, Ahuv, Bildad.

Amitza, Amitzah (אֲמִיצָה) From the Hebrew, meaning "strong, powerful." The exact Hebrew equivalent is Amitza. The exact masculine equivalent is Amitz.

Amitzia, Amitziah, Amitzya (אֲמִיצְיָה) From the Hebrew, meaning "strength of God." The exact Hebrew equivalent is Amitzyah. MASCULINE HEBREW EQUIVALENTS: Amitz, Gavri'el, Gibor.

Amiza, Amizza Variant spellings of Amitza. *See* Amitza.

Amtza, Amtzah (אַמְצָה) From the Hebrew, meaning "strength, courage." The exact Hebrew equivalent is Amtza. The exact masculine equivalent is Amotz.

Amy A variant spelling of Aimee. *See* Aimee.

Ana A variant spelling of Anna. *See* Anna.

Anabella, Annabelle Variant forms of Annabel. *See* Annabel.

Anabeth, Annabeth Hybrid names formed from Anna and Beth. *See* Anna *and* Beth.

Anastasia A unisex name. From the Russian, meaning "resurrection." HEBREW EQUIVALENTS: Chava, Techiya, Yechi'ela. MASCULINE HEBREW EQUIVALENTS: Avichai, Cha'yim, Yechi'el.

Anat, Anath (עֲנָת) A unisex name. From the Hebrew, meaning "to sing" or "sound of victory." The exact Hebrew equivalent is Anat. In Judges 3:31, the father of the Israelite judge Shamgar.

Anava, Anavah (עֲנָבָה) From the Hebrew, meaning "grape." The exact Hebrew equivalent is Anava. The exact masculine equivalent is Anav.

Anchelle A feminine form of Anshel. *See* Anshel (*masculine section*).

Andra From the Old Norse, meaning "breath." HEBREW EQUIVALENTS: Chava, She'ifa. MASCULINE HEBREW EQUIVALENTS: Hevel, Terach.

Andrea, Andria The feminine form of the Greek name Andrew, meaning "valiant, strong, courageous." HEBREW EQUIVALENTS: Amitza, Amtza, Odeda. MASCULINE HEBREW EQUIVALENTS: Abir, Abiri, Amotz.

Andye A feminine form of Andy. *See* Andy (*masculine section*).

Anett A variant spelling of Annette. *See* Annette.

Angel From the Greek, meaning "messenger." HEBREW EQUIVALENTS: Ama'a, Shimshona. MASCULINE HEBREW EQUIVALENTS: Avdon, Malach, Malachi.

Angela, Angella From the Latin, meaning "angel," or from the Greek, meaning "messenger." HEBREW EQUIVALENTS: Aharona, Erela. MASCULINE HEBREW EQUIVALENTS: Aharon, Kalev, Mevaser-Tov.

Angelica The Latin form of Angela. *See* Angela.

Angelina A pet form of Angela. *See* Angela.

Angeline A pet form of Angela. *See* Angela.

Angelique A pet form of Angela. *See* Angela.

Angelita A pet form of Angela. *See* Angela.

Angie A pet form of Angela. *See* Angela.

Angilee A variant form of Angela. *See* Angela.

Aniela, Aniella Pet forms of Ann and Annie. *See* Ann *and* Annie.

Anina (עֲנִינָא) A pet form of Anna. *See* Anna. Also, from the Aramaic, meaning "answer my prayer."

Anita A pet form of Anna. *See* Anna.

Aniya (אֲנִיָּה) From the Hebrew, meaning "boat, ship." The exact Hebrew equivalent is Oniya. The masculine equivalent is Sira.

Ann A variant form of Anna. *See* Anna.

Anna (חַנָה) The Greek form of the Hebrew name Chana, meaning "gracious." The exact Hebrew equivalent is Chana.

Annabel A hybrid name formed from Anna and Bela, meaning "gracious, beautiful." Also, a variant form of the Latin name Amabel, meaning "lovable." HEBREW EQUIVALENTS: Ahuva, Chana, Davida. MASCULINE HEBREW EQUIVALENTS: Ahuv, Bildad, David.

Annabeth A hybrid name formed from Anna and Beth. *See* Anna *and* Beth.

Annalisa A hybrid name formed from Anna and Lisa. *See* Anna *and* Lisa.

Anne (חַנָה) A French form of Hannah, meaning "gracious." *See* Hannah. Anna is a variant form. *See* Anna.

Annetta A pet form of Anna. *See* Anna.

Annette A French form of Anna. *See* Anna.

Annice A variant spelling of Annis. *See* Annis.

Annie A pet form of Anna. *See* Anna.

Annika A Swedish form of Ann. *See* Ann.

Annis A Scottish form of Agnes. *See* Agnes.

Antia A pet form of Antoinette. *See* Antoinette.

Antoina The Italian and Swedish form of Antoinette. *See* Antoinette.

Antoinette From the Greek and Latin, meaning "of high esteem, revered." HEBREW EQUIVALENTS: Adonit, Ahuda, Atalya. MASCULINE HEBREW EQUIVALENTS: Aminadav, Gedalya, Hillel.

Antonella A pet form of Anton. *See* Anton (*masculine section*).

Anuva (עֲנוּבָה) The feminine form of Anuv. *See* Anuv (*masculine section*).

Anya A pet form of Anna. *See* Anna.

Aphra, Aphrah Variant spellings of Afra. *See* Afra.

Aphrodite In Greek mythology, the goddess of love. HEBREW EQUIVALENTS: Ahada, Ahava, Ahuva. MASCULINE HEBREW EQUIVALENTS: Ahuv, Bildad, Yedidya.

April From the Latin, meaning "to open," symbolic of springtime. HE-BREW EQUIVALENTS: Aviva, Avivi, Avivit. MASCULINE HEBREW EQUIVALENTS: Aviv, Avivi.

Arabel From the German *ara*, meaning "eagle," and the Latin *bella*, meaning "beautiful." HEBREW EQUIVALENTS: Gozala, Hadura, Na'ama. MASCULINE HEBREW EQUIVALENTS: Adin, Hadar, Nechmad.

Arabela, Arabella Variant forms of Arabel. *See* Arabel.

Arabelle A variant spelling of Arabel. *See* Arabel.

Arava, Aravah (עֲרָבָה) From the Hebrew, meaning "willow." The exact Hebrew equivalent is Arava. MASCULINE HEBREW EQUIVALENTS: Alon, Bar-Ilan, Etzion, Luz.

Arda, Ardah (אַרְדָה) From the Hebrew, meaning "bronze." The exact Hebrew equivalent is Arda. MASCULINE HEBREW EQUIVALENTS: Arad, Ardi, Arod.

Ardra From the Celtic, meaning "high, high one." HEBREW EQUIVALENTS: Aharona, Gali, Galit. MASCULINE HEBREW EQUIVALENTS: Aharon, Amir, Givon.

Arela, Arella (אַרְאֵלָה) From the Hebrew, meaning "angel, messenger." The exact Hebrew equivalent is Arela. The exact masculine equivalent is Arel.

Ari A pet form of Ariel. *See* Ariel.

Arian A variant form of Ariana. *See* Ariana.

Ariana, Arianna, Arianne From the Latin, meaning "song," or from the Welsh, meaning "silvery." HEBREW EQUIVALENTS: Kaspit, Shira, Yarona. MASCULINE HEBREW EQUIVALENTS: Aharon, Amiran, Ana.

Ariel (אֲרִיאָל) A unisex name. From the Hebrew, meaning "lioness of God." The exact Hebrew equivalent is Ari'el.

Ariela, Ariella (אֲרִיאֵלָה) Variant forms of Ariel. *See* Ariel. The exact Hebrew equivalent is Ari'ela.

Arielle A variant spelling of Ariel. *See* Ariel.

Arika (עֲרִיקָה) From the Hebrew, meaning "deserter." The exact Hebrew equivalent is Arika. The exact masculine equivalent is Arik.

Ariri (עֲרִירִי) From the Hebrew, meaning "barren" or "lonely." The exact Hebrew equivalent is Ariri. Yachid is a masculine equivalent.

Arista From the Greek, meaning "the best, excellent." HEBREW EQUIVALENTS: Adifa, Degula, Idit. MASCULINE HEBREW EQUIVALENTS: Ben-Tziyon, Mehudar, Meshubach.

Ariza (אֲרִיזָה) From the Hebrew, meaning "cedar panels" and "to package." The exact Hebrew equivalent is Ariza. MASCULINE HEBREW EQUIVALENTS: Arzi, Erez.

Arleen A variant spelling of Arlene. *See* Arlene.

Arlene A variant spelling of Arline. *See* Arline.

Arlett A pet form of Arlene. *See* Arlene.

Arline From the German, meaning "girl," and from the Celtic, meaning "pledge, oath." HEBREW EQUIVALENTS: Alma, Bat-Sheva, Betula, Tze'ira. MASCULINE HEBREW EQUIVALENTS: Moshe, Na'arai, Na'arya.

Arlyne A variant spelling of Arline. *See* Arline.

Armina From the Old German, meaning "soldier." HEBREW EQUIVALENTS: Gidona, Meirav, Tigra. MASCULINE HEBREW EQUIVALENTS: Gad, Gidon, Ish-Cha'yil.

Armona (אַרְמוֹנָה) From the Hebrew, meaning "castle" or "fortress." The exact Hebrew equivalent is Armona. The exact masculine equivalent is Armon.

Armonit (אַרְמוֹנִית) A variant form of Armona. *See* Armona. The exact Hebrew equivalent is Armonit.

Arnett From the German, meaning "strong as an eagle." Akin to Arnold. *See* Arnold (*masculine section*).

Arni (אַרְנִי) A pet form of Aharona. *See* Aharona.

Arnina (אַרְנִינָה) A pet form of Arni. *See* Arni.

Arninit (אַרְנִינִית) A variant form of Arni. *See* Arni.

Arnit (אַרְנִית) A variant form of Arni. *See* Arni.

Arnolde A feminine form of Arnold. *See* Arnold (*masculine section*).

Arnoldine A French variant form of Arnold, meaning "eagle's rule," signifying power. HEBREW EQUIVALENTS: Adira, Amitza, Etana. MASCULINE HEBREW EQUIVALENTS: Chaltzon, Nesher, Uzi'el.

Arnona (אַרְנוֹנָה) From the Hebrew, meaning "roaring stream." The exact Hebrew equivalent is Arnona. The exact masculine equivalent is Arnon.

Arnonit (אַרְנוֹנִית) A pet form of Arnona. *See* Arnona.

Arona (אֲרוֹנָה) A variant form of Aharona, the feminine form of Aharon (Aaron). *See* Aharona.

Artia, Artina Feminine forms of Arthur. *See* Arthur (*masculine section*).

Aruga, Arugah (עֲרוּגָה) From the Hebrew, meaning "flower bed." The exact Hebrew equivalent is Aruga. MASCULINE HEBREW EQUIVALENTS: Mifrach, Perach, Perachya.

Aryn A feminine form of Aaron. *See* Aaron (*masculine section*).

Arza (אַרְזָה) From the Hebrew, meaning "cedar panels." The exact Hebrew equivalent is Arza. MASCULINE HEBREW EQUIVALENTS: Arzi, Erez, Oren.

Arzit (אַרְזִית) A variant form of Arza. *See* Arza. The exact Hebrew equivalent is Arzit.

Asaela (עֲשָׂהאֵלָה) From the Hebrew, meaning "God has created." The exact Hebrew equivalent is Asa'ela. The exact masculine equivalent is Asa'el.

Asefa (אֲסִיפָה) From the Hebrew, meaning "gathering." The exact Hebrew equivalent is Asifa. The exact masculine equivalent is Asif.

Ashby From the Old English, meaning "ash tree on the meadow." HEBREW EQUIVALENTS: Arza, Ilana, Shikma. MASCULINE HEBREW EQUIVALENTS: Arzi, Bar-Ilan, Eshel.

Asenath The Anglicized form of Osnat. *See* Osnat.

Ashera (אֲשֵׁרָה) From the Hebrew, meaning "blessed, fortunate" or "idol." The exact Hebrew equivalent is Ashera. The exact masculine equivalent is Asher.

Ashira (עֲשִׁירָה) From the Hebrew, meaning "wealthy." The exact Hebrew equivalent is Ashira. The exact masculine equivalent is Ashir.

Ashirut (עֲשִׁירוּת) From the Hebrew, meaning "wealth, riches." A variant form of Ashira. *See* Ashira.

Ashleigh, Ashley From the Old English, meaning "grove of ash trees." HEBREW EQUIVALENTS: Alona, Ilana, Ilanit. MASCULINE HEBREW EQUIVALENTS: Eshel, Pardes.

Asia, Asiah Variant spellings of Asiya. *See* Asiya.

Asifa, Asifah Variant spellings of Asefa. *See* Asefa.

Asisa (עֲסִיסָה) From the Hebrew, meaning "juicy, ripe." The exact Hebrew equivalent is Asisa. The exact masculine equivalent is Asis.

Asisya (עֲסִיסְיָה) From the Hebrew, meaning "juice [fruit] of the Lord." A variant form of Asisa. *See* Asisa. The exact Hebrew equivalent is Asisya.

Asiya, Asiyah (עֲשִׂיָּה) From the Hebrew, meaning "deed" or "God's creation." The exact Hebrew equivalent is Asiya. MASCULINE HEBREW EQUIVALENTS: Asa'el, Asaya, Ya'asiel.

Asnat A variant spelling of Osnat. *See* Osnat.

Assia, Assya (אָסְיָא) From the Aramaic, meaning "doctor." The exact Hebrew equivalent is Assia. MASCULINE HEBREW EQUIVALENTS: Rafa, Raji, Refa'el.

Asta A variant form of Astera. *See* Astera.

Astera, Asteria From the Persian and Greek, meaning "star." Akin to Esther. *See* Esther.

Astra From the Latin, meaning "starlike." HEBREW EQUIVALENTS: Ayelet-Hashachar, Ester, Mazalit. MASCULINE HEBREW EQUIVALENTS: Bar-Kochva, Kochav, Mazal-Tov.

Atalia, Atalia, Atalya, Atalyah (עֲתַלְיָה) A unisex name. From the Hebrew, meaning "God is exalted." The exact Hebrew equivalent is Atalyah. In II Kings 8:26, a queen of Israel.

Atara (עֲטָרָה) From the Hebrew, meaning "crown, wreath." The exact

Hebrew equivalent is Atara. MASCULINE HEBREW EQUIVALENTS: Atur, Katri'el, Kitron.

Ateret (עֲטֶרֶת) A variant form of Atara. *See* Atara. The exact Hebrew equivalent is Ateret. When spelled with a *tav* (עֲתֶרֶת), Ateret means "riches."

Athalia, Athaliah Anglicized forms of Atalia. *See* Atalia.

Athena From the Greek, meaning "wisdom." HEBREW EQUIVALENTS: Chochma, Ge'oga, Nevona. MASCULINE HEBREW EQUIVALENTS: Bina, Navon, Zavin.

Atida, Atidah (עֲתִידָה) From the Hebrew, meaning "future." The exact Hebrew equivalent is Atida. The exact masculine equivalent is Atid.

Atifa, Atifah (עֲטִיפָה) From the Hebrew, meaning "covering, bound up." The exact Hebrew equivalent is Atifa. The exact masculine equivalent is Atif.

Atika, Atikah (עַתִּיקָה) From the Hebrew, meaning "old, ancient." The exact Hebrew equivalent is Atika. The exact masculine equivalent is Atik.

Atira (עֲתִירָה) From the Hebrew, meaning "prayer." The exact Hebrew equivalent is Atira. The exact masculine equivalent is Atir.

Atlit (עַתְלִית) A variant form of Atalya. *See* Atalya. The exact Hebrew equivalent is Atlit.

Attai (עַתַּי) A unisex name. From the Hebrew, meaning "ready" or "seasonal." The exact Hebrew equivalent is Attai. In I Chronicles 2:35, the daughter of a leader of Judah. In I Chronicles 12:11, one of the warriors from the tribe of Gad.

Atura (עֲטוּרָה) From the Hebrew, meaning "ornamented, adorned with a crown." The exact Hebrew equivalent is Atura. The exact masculine equivalent is Atur.

Atzila (אֲצִילָה) From the Hebrew, meaning "honorable, noble." The exact Hebrew equivalent is Atzila. The exact masculine equivalent is Atzil.

Atzili (אֲצִילִי) From the Hebrew, meaning "noble." The exact Hebrew equivalent is Atzili. The exact masculine equivalent is Atzil.

Atzira, Atzirah (אֲצִירָה) From the Hebrew, meaning "gathering, assembly." The exact Hebrew equivalent is Atzira. MASCULINE HEBREW EQUIVALENTS: Asaf, Asif. When spelled with an *a'yin* (עֲצִירָה), Atzira means "withholding, hoarding."

Atzma, Atzmah (עָצְמָה) From the Hebrew, meaning "strength." The exact Hebrew equivalent is Atzma. MASCULINE HEBREW EQUIVALENTS: Amitz, Atzmon, Gavri'el.

Audra A variant form of Audrey. *See* Audrey.

Audrey From the Old English, meaning "noble strength." HEBREW EQUIVALENTS: Abira, Ari'el, Malka. MASCULINE HEBREW EQUIVALENTS: Adir, Adoniya, Adiv.

Audrina A pet form of Audrey. *See* Audrey.

Audris From the Old German, meaning "fortunate" or "wealthy." HEBREW EQUIVALENTS: Asher, Asherit, Ashira. MASCULINE HEBREW EQUIVALENTS: Asher, Ashir, Oshri.

Augusta From the Latin, meaning "revered, sacred." HEBREW EQUIVALENTS: Atalya, Chermona, Sara. MASCULINE HEBREW EQUIVALENTS: Aviram, Chermon, Gedalya.

Augustina A German form of Augusta. *See* Augusta.

Augustine A French form of Augusta. *See* Augusta.

Aura From the Greek, meaning "air, atmosphere." HEBREW EQUIVALENTS: Avirit, She'ifa. MASCULINE HEBREW EQUIVALENTS: Avira, Hevel, Nafish.

Aurea A variant form of Aurelia. *See* Aurelia.

Aurelia A feminine form of the Latin name Aurelius, meaning "gold." HEBREW EQUIVALENTS: Ofira, Paza, Pazit, Paziya. MASCULINE HEBREW EQUIVALENTS: Ofir, Paz, Upaz.

Auriel From the Latin, meaning "golden." HEBREW EQUIVALENTS: Ofira, Paz, Zehava. MASCULINE HEBREW EQUIVALENTS: Ofir, Pazi, Zehavi.

Aurora From the Latin, meaning "dawn." HEBREW EQUIVALENTS: Shachar, Shacharit, Tzefira. MASCULINE HEBREW EQUIVALENTS: Ben-Shachar, Shacharya.

Aury A pet form of Aurelia. *See* Aurelia.

Autumn The season of the year between summer and winter. There are no Hebrew equivalents. S'tav is an Aramaic masculine equivalent.

Ava From the Latin, meaning "bird," Also, from the Hebrew, meaning "to desire" or "to agree." HEBREW EQUIVALENTS: A'ya, Chasida, Derora. MASCULINE HEBREW EQUIVALENTS: Gozal, Orev, Tzipor.

Aveline From the French, meaning "hazelnut." Egoza is a Hebrew equivalent. The masculine Hebrew equivalent is Egoz.

Avella A pet form of Aveline. *See* Aveline.

Avi (אֲבִי) A unisex name. From the Assyrian and Hebrew, meaning "progenitor." The exact Hebrew equivalent is Avi. In II Kings 18:2, the wife of Ahaz, king of Judah.

Avia, Aviah Variant spellings of Aviya. *See* Aviya.

Avichayil (אֲבִיחַיִל) A unisex name. From the Hebrew, meaning "my father is strength." The exact Hebrew equivalent is Avicha'yil. In I Chronicles 2:29, the wife of Avishur of the tribe of Judah.

Aviela, Aviella (אֲבִיאֶלָה) From the Hebrew, meaning "God is my father." The exact Hebrew equivalent is Avi'ela. The exact masculine equivalent is Avi'el.

Avigal (אֲבִיגַל) A unisex name. From the Hebrew, meaning "father of joy." The exact Hebrew equivalent is Avigal.

Avigayil (אֲבִיגַיִל) From the Hebrew, meaning "father's joy" or "my father is joy." Abigail is the popular English form. The exact Hebrew equivalent is Aviga'yil. MASCULINE HEBREW EQUIVALENTS: Agil, Avuya, Bilgai. In I Samuel 25:39, a woman King David seeks to marry.

Avigdora (אֲבִיגְדוֹרָה) The feminine form of the masculine name Avigdor. *See* Avigdor (*masculine section*). The exact Hebrew equivalent is Avigdora.

Avira, Avirah (עֲבִירָה) From the Hebrew, meaning "cross over." The exact Hebrew equivalent is Avira. Aviri is a masculine equivalent.

Avirit (אֲוִירִית) From the Hebrew, meaning "air, atmosphere, spirit." The exact Hebrew equivalent is Avirit. The exact masculine equivalent is Aviri.

Avis An Old German name meaning "refugee, fortress." Also, from the Latin, meaning "bird." HEBREW EQUIVALENTS: Armona, Metzada, Migdala. MASCULINE HEBREW EQUIVALENTS: Armon, Armoni, Betzer.

Avishag (אֲבִישַׁג) Of doubtful origin. In I Kings 1:3, a beautiful young Shunamite girl who tended to David in his old age.

Avit (עֲוִית) From the Hebrew, meaning "spasm, convulsion." The exact Hebrew equivalent is Avit.

Avital (אֲבִיטַל) A unisex name. From the Hebrew, meaning "father of dew," referring to God as sustainer. The exact Hebrew equivalent is Avital. In II Samuel 3:4, a wife of King David.

Aviv (אָבִיב) A unisex name. From the Hebrew, meaning "spring, springtime." The exact Hebrew equivalent is Aviv.

Aviva, Avivah (אֲבִיבָה) From the Hebrew, meaning "springtime," connoting youthfulness. The exact Hebrew equivalent is Aviva. The exact masculine equivalent is Aviv.

Avivi (אֲבִיבִי) A unisex name. From the Hebrew, meaning "springlike." The exact Hebrew equivalent is Avivi.

Avivia A variant spelling of Aviviya. *See* Aviviya.

Avivit (אֲבִיבִית) A variant form of Aviva. *See* Aviva. The exact Hebrew equivalent is Avivit.

Avivith A variant spelling of Avivit. *See* Avivit.

Aviviya (אֲבִיבִיָה) A variant form of Aviya. *See* Aviya. The exact Hebrew equivalent is Aviviya.

Aviya (אֲבִיָה) A unisex name. From the Hebrew, meaning "God is my father." The exact Hebrew equivalent is Aviya.

Avka, Avkah (אֲבְקָה) From the Hebrew, meaning "powder, dust." The exact Hebrew equivalent is Avka. The exact masculine equivalent is Avak.

Avna (אַבְנָה) From the Hebrew, meaning "stone, rock." The exact Hebrew equivalent is Avna. MASCULINE HEBREW EQUIVALENTS: Avni'el, Even, Tzur.

Avrasha (אַבְרָשָׁא) A Sephardic form of Avraham (Abraham). *See* Avraham.

Avril The French word for the month of April. *See* April. Also, from the Old English, meaning "battle warrior." Akin to Hildegard. HEBREW EQUIVALENTS: Gidona, Merav, Tigra. MASCULINE HEBREW EQUIVALENTS: Gavri'el, Gevarya, Gidon.

Avuka (אֲבוּקָה) From the Hebrew, meaning "torch, flame." The exact Hebrew equivalent is Avuka. MASCULINE HEBREW EQUIVALENTS: Lapid, Lapidot, Nur.

Aya, Ayah (אַיָּה) A unisex name. From the Hebrew, meaning "vulture." The exact Hebrew equivalent is A'ya.

Ayala, Ayalah (אַיָּלָה) From the Hebrew, meaning "deer, gazelle." The exact Hebrew equivalent is A'yala. The exact masculine equivalent is A'yal.

Ayelet (אַיֶּלֶת) From the Hebrew, meaning "deer, gazelle." The exact Hebrew equivalent is A'yelet. MASCULINE HEBREW EQUIVALENTS: A'yal, A'yalon, Tzevi.

Ayit (עַיִט) From the Hebrew, meaning "eagle." The exact Hebrew equivalent is A'yit. The exact masculine equivalent is Nesher.

Ayla (אֵלָה) From the Hebrew, meaning "oak tree." The exact Hebrew equivalent is Ayla (Eila). The exact masculine equivalent is Aylon (Eilon).

Ayya An alternate spelling of Aya. *See* Aya.

Aza, Azah (עַזָּה) From the Hebrew, meaning "strong, powerful." The exact Hebrew equivalent is Aza. MASCULINE HEBREW EQUIVALENTS: Az, Azai, Azan, Oz, Uzi.

Aziela (עֲזִיאֵלָה) The feminine equivalent of Aziel. The exact Hebrew equivalent is Azi'ela. The exact masculine equivalent is Azi'el. *See* Aziel (*masculine section*).

Aziva, Azivah (עֲזִיבָה) From the Hebrew, meaning "abandonment" or "departure." The exact Hebrew equivalent is Aziva. The masculine equivalent is Azuv.

Aziza, Azizah (עֲזִיזָה) A unisex name. From the Aramaic and Hebrew, meaning "strong." The exact Hebrew equivalent is Aziza.

Azuva, Azuvah (עֲזוּבָה) From the Hebrew, meaning "forsaken, lonely, desolate." The exact Hebrew equivalent is Azuva. The exact masculine equivalent is Azuv.

❦ B ❦

Bab A pet form of Barbara and Elizabeth. *See* Barbara *and* Elizabeth.

Babette A pet form of Barbara. *See* Barbara.

Babs A variant form of Bab. *See* Bab.

Baila, **Baile** Variant spellings of Bayla and Bayle. *See* Bayla *and* Bayle.

Bama (בָּמָה) From the Hebrew, meaning "platform, high place." The exact Hebrew equivalent is Bama. MASCULINE HEBREW EQUIVALENTS: Ram, Rami, Rom.

Bambi A pet form of the Italian name Bambalina, meaning "little doll" or "boy." HEBREW EQUIVALENTS: Alumit, Bat-Tziyon, Buba. MASCULINE HEBREW EQUIVALENTS: Ben, Ben-Tziyon, Na'arai.

Bara (בָּרָה) From the Hebrew, meaning "to choose." The exact Hebrew equivalent is Bara. MASCULINE HEBREW EQUIVALENTS: Bachir, Nivchar, Yivchar.

Barbara From the Greek, meaning "strange, stranger, foreign." HEBREW EQUIVALENTS: Avishag, Hagar, Sarida. MASCULINE HEBREW EQUIVALENTS: Gershom, Gershon, Golyat.

Barbi, **Barbie** A pet form of Barbara. *See* Barbara.

Bareket (בָּרֶקֶת) From the Hebrew, referring to a precious stone, first mentioned in Exodus 28:17. The exact Hebrew equivalent is Bareket. MASCULINE HEBREW EQUIVALENTS: Barak, Chemed, Leshem, Safir.

Bari A feminine form of Barry. *See* Barry (*masculine section*).

Barrie Used primarily as a masculine name. *See* Barrie (*masculine section*).

Basha A Yiddish form of Basya (Batya) and Bas-Sheva (Bat-Sheva). *See* Batya *and* Bat-Sheva.

Bashe A variant form of Basha. *See* Basha.

Basmat (בָּשְׂמַת) From the Hebrew and Aramaic *bosem*, meaning "sweet-smelling [spices]." The exact Hebrew equivalent is Basmat. A masculine Hebrew equivalent is Mor. In I Kings 4:15, a daughter of King Solomon.

Bas-Sheva The Ashkenazic pronunciation of Bat-Sheva. *See* Bat-Sheva.

Basya The Ashkenazic pronunciation of Batya. *See* Batya.

Bat-Ami (בַּת-עַמִי) From the Hebrew, meaning "daughter of my people." The exact Hebrew equivalent is Bat-Ami. The exact masculine equivalent is Ben-Ami.

Bat-El (בַּת-אֵל) From the Hebrew, meaning "daughter of God." The exact Hebrew equivalent is Bat-El.

Bathsheba The Anglicized form of Bat-Sheva. *See* Bat-Sheva.

Batli, Bat-Li (בַּת-לִי/בַּתְלִי) From the Hebrew, meaning "I have a daughter." The exact Hebrew equivalent is Bat-Li. The masculine equivalent is Ben-Li.

Bat-Sheva, Batsheva (בַּת-שֶׁבַע) From the Hebrew, meaning "daughter of an oath." The exact Hebrew equivalent is Bat-Sheva. MASCULINE HEBREW EQUIVALENTS: Amarya, Ela, Sheva. In II Samuel 11:3, the wife of King David and mother of Solomon.

Bat-Shir (בַּת-שִׁיר) From the Hebrew, meaning "songbird." The exact Hebrew equivalent is Bat-Shir. MASCULINE HEBREW EQUIVALENTS: Shir, Shiron, Yashir.

Bat-Shua, Batshua (בַּת-שׁוּעַ) A biblical variant spelling of Bat-Sheva. *See* Bat-Sheva. The exact Hebrew equivalent is Bat-Shu'a. In Genesis 38:2, the wife of Judah.

Bat-Tziyon (בַּת-צִיּוֹן) From the Hebrew, meaning "daughter of Zion" or "daughter of excellence." The exact Hebrew equivalent is Bat-Tziyon. The exact masculine equivalent is Ben-Tziyon.

Batya (בַּתְיָה) From the Hebrew, meaning "daughter of God." The exact Hebrew equivalent is Batya. MASCULINE HEBREW EQUIVALENTS: Ben-Shem, Ben-Tziyon, Binyamin.

Bat-Yam (בַּת-יָם) From the Hebrew, meaning "daughter of the sea." The exact Hebrew equivalent is Bat-Yam. MASCULINE HEBREW EQUIVALENTS: Aviyam, Dalfon, Dela'ya.

Bat-Zion A variant spelling of Bat-Tziyon. *See* Bat-Tziyon.

Bavua (בָּבוּאָה) From the Hebrew, meaning "mirage." The exact Hebrew equivalent is Bavu'a. MASCULINE HEBREW EQUIVALENTS: Betzalel, Micha'el.

Bay From the Middle English and Old French, meaning "wreath of bay leaves." HEBREW EQUIVALENTS: Eila, Ilana, Shalechet. MASCULINE HEBREW EQUIVALENTS: Alei, Ilan, Tzameret.

Bayla (בֵּיילָא) A Yiddish form of the Hebrew name Bilha. *See* Bilha. Also, a Yiddish form of Bela. *See* Bela.

Bayle (בֵּיילֶע) A variant spelling of Bayla. *See* Bayla.

Bea, Beah Pet forms of Beatrice. *See* Beatrice.

Beata From the Latin, meaning "blessed." A variant form of Beatrice. *See* Beatrice.

Beate A short form of Beatrice. *See* Beatrice.

Beatrice From the Latin, meaning "one who brings happiness and blessing." HEBREW EQUIVALENTS: Ashera, Ashra, Aviga'yil, Beracha. MASCULINE HEBREW EQUIVALENTS: Asher, Baruch, Berachya.

Beatrix The original form of Beatrice. *See* Beatrice.

Beca, Becca Pet forms of Rebecca. *See* Rebecca.

Beccie A variant spelling of Beckie. *See* Beckie.

Bechira (בְּחִירָה) From the Hebrew, meaning "chosen one." The exact Hebrew equivalent is Bechira. MASCULINE HEBREW EQUIVALENTS: Adef, Mivchar, Yivchar.

Beckie, Becky Pet forms of Rebecca. *See* Rebecca.

Behira (בְּהִירָה) From the Hebrew, meaning "light, clear, brilliant." The exact Hebrew equivalent is Behira. The exact masculine equivalent is Bahir.

Beka, Bekah Pet forms of Rebekah. *See* Rebekah.

Bela Either a form of Isabella, meaning "God's oath," or from the Hungarian, meaning "nobly bright." Also, from the Latin, meaning "beautiful one." HEBREW EQUIVALENTS: Achino'am, Bat-Sheva, Behira. MASCULINE HEBREW EQUIVALENTS: Avino'am, Bahir, Barak.

Belinda An Old Germanic name derived from the Latin, meaning "beautiful serpent," having the connotation of shrewdness. HEBREW EQUIVALENTS: Buna, Ge'ona, Rivka. MASCULINE HEBREW EQUIVALENTS: Achban, Bina, Buna.

Belita A Spanish pet form of Belle. *See* Belle.

Bella A short form of Isabella. *See* Isabella.

Belle A variant form of Bella. *See* Bella.

Belva From the Latin, meaning "beautiful view." HEBREW EQUIVALENTS: Adina, Na'ama, Na'omi. MASCULINE HEBREW EQUIVALENTS: Adin, Hadar, Naveh.

Benedicta A feminine form of the Latin name Benedict, meaning "blessed." HEBREW EQUIVALENTS: Ashera, Berakha, Berucha. MASCULINE HEBREW EQUIVALENTS: Asher, Baruch, Berachya.

Benette A feminine form of Ben and Benjamin. *See* Ben *and* Benjamin (*masculine section*).

Benita A Spanish form of Benedicta. *See* Benedicta.

Benjamina (בִּנְיָמִינָה) A feminine form of Benjamin. *See* Benjamin (*masculine section*). The exact Hebrew equivalent is Binyamina.

Beracha (בְּרָכָה) From the Hebrew, meaning "blessing." The exact Hebrew equivalent is Beracha. The masculine equivalent is Baruch.

Berenice From the Greek, meaning "bringer of victory." HEBREW EQUIVALENTS: Dafna, Dafnit, Hadasa. MASCULINE HEBREW EQUIVALENTS: Gavri'el, Gibor, Gover.

Bernadette From the French and German, meaning "bold as a bear." HEBREW EQUIVALENTS: Dova, Doveva, Duba. MASCULINE HEBREW EQUIVALENTS: Dov, Dubi, Kalev.

Bernadina A pet form of Bernadette. *See* Bernadette.

Bernadine A pet form of Bernadette. *See* Bernadette.

Bernarda A feminine form of Bernard. *See* Bernard.

Bernette A variant form of Bernadette. *See* Bernadette.

Bernice A variant form of Berenice. *See* Berenice.

Bernine A pet form of Berenice and Bernadette. *See* Berenice *and* Bernadette.

Bernita A pet form of Berenice. *See* Berenice.

Berta A variant form of Bertha. *See* Bertha.

Bertha From the Anglo-Saxon, meaning "bright, beautiful, famous." HEBREW EQUIVALENTS: Behira, Hillela, Me'ira. MASCULINE HEBREW EQUIVALENTS: Avino'am, Avner, Bahir.

Bertina, Bertine Feminine pet forms of Bert. *See* Bert (*masculine section*).

Berucha (בְּרוּכָה) From the Hebrew, meaning "blessed." The exact Hebrew equivalent is Berucha. The exact masculine equivalent is Baruch.

Beruchiya (בְּרוּכִיָה) A variant form of Beruchya. *See* Beruchya.

Beruchya (בְּרוּכְיָה) From the Hebrew, meaning "blessed of the Lord." The exact Hebrew equivalent is Beruchya. MASCULINE HEBREW EQUIVALENTS: Baruch, Mevorach.

Berura (בְּרוּרָה) From the Hebrew, meaning "pure, clean." The exact

Hebrew equivalent is Berura. The exact masculine equivalent is Barur.

Berurit (בְּרוּרִית) A variant form of Berura. *See* Berura. The exact Hebrew equivalent is Berurit.

Beruriya (בְּרוּרְיָה) A variant form of Berura. *See* Berura. The exact Hebrew equivalent is Beruriya.

Berurya (בְּרוּרְיָה) A variant form of Berura. *See* Berura. The exact Hebrew equivalent is Berurya.

Beryl From the Greek and the Sanskrit, meaning "precious stone." Also, from the Persian and Arabic, meaning "crystal clear." HEBREW EQUIVALENTS: Ada, Bahat, Berura. MASCULINE HEBREW EQUIVALENTS: Leshem, Nofach, Sapir.

Bess A popular pet form of Elizabeth. *See* Elizabeth.

Bessie A pet form of Elizabeth. *See* Elizabeth.

Bet A variant form of Beth. *See* Beth.

Beta A pet form of Elizabeth. *See* Elizabeth.

Beth A short form of Elizabeth. *See* Elizabeth.

Beth-Ami, Bethamie (בַּת-עַמִי) Anglicized forms of Bat-Ami. *See* Bat-Ami.

Bethany From the Hebrew, meaning "house of figs [*bet te'einim*]." HEBREW EQUIVALENTS: Divla, Divlata, Te'eina. Divla'yim is a masculine equivalent.

Bethe A variant spelling of Beth. *See* Beth.

Bethel (בֵּית-אֵל) An Anglicized feminine form of the masculine name Betuel, meaning "house of God." *See* Betuel (*masculine section*).

Betsey, Betsy Pet forms of Elizabeth. *See* Elizabeth.

Bette A pet form of Elizabeth. *See* Elizabeth.

Bettina A pet form of Elizabeth. *See* Elizabeth.

Betty, Bettye Pet forms of Elizabeth. *See* Elizabeth.

Betula, Betulah (בְּתוּלָה) From the Hebrew, meaning "maiden." The exact Hebrew equivalent is Betula. MASCULINE HEBREW EQUIVALENTS: Ben, Ben-Gover, Ben-Tziyon.

Beula, Beulah (בְּעוּלָה) From the Hebrew, meaning "married" or "possessed." The exact Hebrew equivalent is Be'ula. MASCULINE HEBREW EQUIVALENTS: Raba, Rav, Zimri.

Beverlee, **Beverley** Variant spellings of Beverly. *See* Beverly.

Beverly A unisex name. From the Old English, meaning "beaver's meadow." HEBREW EQUIVALENTS: Carmela, Gana, Nava. MASCULINE HEBREW EQUIVALENTS: Carmel, Carmeli, Ya'ari.

Bevya A pet form of Beverly. *See* Beverly.

Bianca From the Italian, meaning "white, fair." HEBREW EQUIVALENTS: Livnat, Livona, Malbina. MASCULINE HEBREW EQUIVALENTS: Lavan, Livni, Malbin.

Bika (בִּקְעָה) From the Hebrew, meaning "valley." The exact Hebrew equivalent is Bika. MASCULINE HEBREW EQUIVALENTS: Emek, Gai.

Bilha, Bilhah (בִּלְהָה) From the Hebrew, meaning "old, weak, troubled." The exact Hebrew equivalent is Bilha. MASCULINE HEBREW EQUIVALENTS: Kedma, Yiftach, Zaken. In Genesis 29:29, the maidservant of Rachel, the father of Dan and Naftali.

Billie A feminine pet form of William. *See* William (*masculine section*). Also, a pet form of Wilhelmina. *See* Wilhelmina.

Bima, Bimah (בִּימָה) From the Hebrew, meaning "platform, podium." The exact Hebrew equivalent is Bima. MASCULINE HEBREW EQUIVALENTS: Merom, Ram, Rom.

Bina (בִּינָה) A unisex name. From the Hebrew, meaning "understanding, intelligence, wisdom." The exact Hebrew equivalent is Bina.

Binit (בִּינִית) The Hebrew name for a species of sweetwater fish native to Israel. The exact Hebrew equivalent is Binit. Dag is a masculine equivalent.

Binyamina (בִּנְיָמִינָה) A feminine form of Binyamin (Benjamin). *See* Binyamin (*masculine section*). The exact Hebrew equivalent is Binyamina.

Bira (בִּירָה) From the Hebrew, meaning "fortified city" or "capital." The exact Hebrew equivalent is Bira. MASCULINE HEBREW EQUIVALENTS: Armon, Armoni.

Biranit (בִּירָנִית) A variant Hebrew form of Bira. *See* Bira. The exact Hebrew equivalent is Biranit.

Bird, Birdie From the English, meaning "bird." HEBREW EQUIVALENTS: A'ya, Efrona, Gozala, Tzipora. MASCULINE HEBREW EQUIVALENTS: Efron, Gozal, Tzipor.

Blair, Blaire From the Gaelic, meaning "field" or "battle." HEBREW EQUIVALENTS: Nira, Nirit, Odera. MASCULINE HEBREW EQUIVALENTS: Nir, Niram, Nirel.

Blanca The Spanish form of the Old French *blanc*, meaning "white, fair," or from the Latin, meaning "pure." HEBREW EQUIVALENTS: Yafa, Zahara, Zaka. MASCULINE HEBREW EQUIVALENTS: Lavan, Livni, Zakai.

Blanch, Blanche Variant forms of Blanca. *See* Blanca.

Blima (בְּלִימָא) A variant form of Bluma. *See* Bluma.

Blossom From the Old English, meaning "blooming flower." HEBREW EQUIVALENTS: Nirit, Nitza, Ofrit. MASCULINE HEBREW EQUIVALENTS: Efra'yim, Nitzan, Perach.

Blu, Blue Pet forms of Bluma. *See* Bluma.

Bluma (בְּלוּמָא) From the German and Yiddish, meaning "flower." *See* Blossom *for equivalents.*

Blume (בְּלוּמֶע) A variant form of Bluma. *See* Bluma.

Blythe From the Anglo-Saxon, meaning "happy." HEBREW EQUIVALENTS: Aliza, Aviga'yil, Gila, Rina. MASCULINE HEBREW EQUIVALENTS: Bilgai, Gilon, Ron.

Bo From the Chinese, meaning "precious." HEBREW EQUIVALENTS: Chemda, Kevuda, Yakira. MASCULINE HEBREW EQUIVALENTS: Amikar, Chamdi'el, Chemdai.

Bobbe, Bobbi, Bobby Pet forms of Babette, Barbara, and Roberta. *See* Babette, Barbara *and* Roberta.

Bona (בּוֹנָה) From the Hebrew, meaning "builder." The exact Hebrew equivalent is Bona. MASCULINE HEBREW EQUIVALENTS: Bena'ya, Bena'yahu, Yavni'el.

Bonita A Spanish form of Bonnie. *See* Bonnie.

Bonnie, Bonny From the Latin and the French, meaning "good" or "pretty." HEBREW EQUIVALENTS: Na'ama, Na'omi, Nofiya. MASCULINE HEBREW EQUIVALENTS: Achituv, Ben-Tziyon, Na'aman.

Bosmat A variant spelling of Basmat. *See* Basmat.

Bracha A variant spelling of Beracha. *See* Beracha.

Bree A pet form of Gabriela. *See* Gabriela.

Breindel (בּרײנדל) A pet form of the Yiddish name Bruna. *See* Bruna.

Brenda From the Celtic, meaning "dark-haired." HEBREW EQUIVALENTS: Dala, Delila, Tzila. MASCULINE HEBREW EQUIVALENTS: Adar, Kedar, Pinchas.

Briana, Brianna A feminine form of the masculine Brian, meaning "strength," and Anna, meaning "grace." HEBREW EQUIVALENTS: Abira, Abiri, Azri'ela. MASCULINE HEBREW EQUIVALENTS: Abir, Azri'el, Yechezkel.

Bridget From the Celtic, meaning "strong" or "lofty." HEBREW EQUIVALENTS: Abira, Adira, Amitza. MASCULINE HEBREW EQUIVALENTS: Abir, Abiri, Barzilai.

Bridgit, Bridgitte Variant forms of Bridget. *See* Bridget.

Brigida A variant form of Bridget. *See* Bridget.

Brigit, Brigitte Variant spellings of Bridget. *See* Bridget.

Brin A variant spelling of Bryn. *See* Bryn.

Brina, Brine (בּרײנֶע/בּרײנָא) Variant forms of Bruna and Brune. *See* Bruna *and* Brune.

Brit, Brita Pet forms of Bridget. *See* Bridget.

Brittany From the Latin name Brito, referring to a Celtic people living in Britian in Roman times. *See* Brett (*masculine section*).

Brook, Brooke From the Old English and Middle English, meaning "to break out," referring to a stream of water. HEBREW EQUIVALENTS: Arnona, Bat-Yam, Nadyan. MASCULINE HEBREW EQUIVALENTS: Arnon, Aviyam, Peretz.

Brucha (בְּרוּכָה) From the Hebrew, meaning "blessed." The exact Hebrew equivalent is Brucha. The exact masculine equivalent is Baruch.

Bruna, Brune (ברונָא/ברונֶע) Yiddish forms, from the German, meaning "brunette" or "brown." HEBREW EQUIVALENTS: Chuma, Chumit. MASCULINE HEBREW EQUIVALENTS: Chum, Chumi.

Bryn From the Welsh, meaning "hill." HEBREW EQUIVALENTS: Gal, Galit, Talma. MASCULINE HEBREW EQUIVALENTS: Aharon, Gal, Harel.

Bryna A variant form of Bruna. *See* Bruna.

Buba (בֻּבָּה) From the Hebrew, meaning "doll." The exact Hebrew equivalent is Buba.

Bubati (בֻּבָּתִי) From the Hebrew, meaning "my doll." The exact Hebrew equivalent is Bubati.

Buna, Bunah (בּוּנָה) A unisex name. From the Hebrew, meaning "understanding, intelligence." The exact Hebrew equivalent is Buna.

Buni, Bunie Variant forms of Buna. *See* Buna. The exact Hebrew equivalent is Buni.

Bunny A nickname for Barbara and Roberta. *See* Barbara *and* Roberta.

Buza, Buzah (בּוּזָה) From the Hebrew, meaning "shame." The exact Hebrew equivalent is Buza. The exact masculine equivalent is Buz.

Byrd A variant spelling of Bird. *See* Bird.

Byrdie A variant spelling of Birdie. *See* Birdie.

❧ C ❧

Caasi A variant form of Cassandra or Catherine. *See* Cassandra *and* Catherine.

Caitlin A variant Irish form of Catherine or Cathleen. *See* Catherine *and* Cathleen.

Calla, Callie From the Greek, meaning "beautiful." HEBREW EQUIVALENTS: Na'ama, Na'omi, Ranana. MASCULINE HEBREW EQUIVALENTS: Hadar, Na'eh, Yefet.

Cameron A unisex name. From the Gaelic, meaning "crooked nose." The Hebrew equivalent is Nachor.

Camilla, Camille From the Latin, meaning "servant, helper" or "virgin of unblemished character." HEBREW EQUIVALENTS: Ezri'ela, Sa'ada, Zaka. MASCULINE HEBREW EQUIVALENTS: Ovadyahu, Sa'adya, Zakai.

Camillia A variant form of Camilla. *See* Camilla.

Candace From the Greek, meaning "fire-white, incandescent." Also, from the Latin, meaning "pure, unsullied." HEBREW EQUIVALENTS: Avuka, Levana, Ora. MASCULINE HEBREW EQUIVALENTS: Ud, Uri, Zakai.

Candance A variant form of Candace. *See* Candace.

Candice A variant spelling of Candace. *See* Candace.

Candida, Candide Variant forms of Candace. *See* Candace.

Candy A pet form of Candace. *See* Candace.

Candyce A variant spelling of Candace. *See* Candace.

Cara From the Latin, meaning "darling." HEBREW EQUIVALENTS: Chaviva, Tziporet. MASCULINE HEBREW EQUIVALENTS: Chaviv, Yakar, Yakir. Also, a pet form of Caroline and Charlotte. *See* Caroline *and* Charlotte.

Careena A variant spelling of Carina. *See* Carina.

Caren A pet form of Catherine. *See* Catherine.

Caressa From the Latin, meaning "caring, loving." HEBREW EQUIVALENTS: Ahuva, Chiba, Davida. MASCULINE HEBREW EQUIVALENTS: Ahuv, Bildad, David.

Carina From the Italian, meaning "dear little one." HEBREW EQUIVALENTS: Chaviva, Davida. MASCULINE HEBREW EQUIVALENTS: Chaviv, David, Yakar.

Carita A variant form of Carina. *See* Carina.

Carla, Carlana Feminine forms of Carl or Charles. Also, pet forms of Caroline. *See* Caroline.

Carlena, Carlene Pet forms of Caroline. *See* Caroline.

Carley A pet form of Caroline. *See* Caroline.

Carlina A pet form of Caroline. *See* Caroline.

Carlita An Italian pet form of Caroline. *See* Caroline.

Carlotta An Italian diminutive form of Carla. *See* Carla.

Carly A variant spelling of Carley. *See* Carley.

Carma A variant form of Carmel. *See* Carmel.

Carmel (כַּרְמֶל) A unisex name. From the Hebrew, meaning "vineyard" or "garden." The exact Hebrew equivalent is Carmel.

Carmela (כַּרְמֶלָה) From the Hebrew, meaning "garden, orchard." The exact Hebrew equivalent is Carmela. The exact masculine equivalent is Carmel.

Carmeli (כַּרְמֶלִי) A unisex name. From the Hebrew, meaning "my vineyard." The exact Hebrew equivalent is Carmeli.

Carmelit (כַּרְמֶלִית) A variant form of Carmela. *See* Carmela. The exact Hebrew equivalent is Carmelit.

Carmen The Spanish form of Carmel. *See* Carmel.

Carmia A variant spelling of Carmiya. *See* Carmiya.

Carmiela (כַּרְמִיאֶלָה) A variant form of Carmiya. *See* Carmiya. The exact Hebrew equivalent is Carmi'ela.

Carmit (כַּרְמִית) A variant form of Carmiya. *See* Carmiya. The exact Hebrew equivalent is Carmit.

Carmiya (כַּרְמִיָה) From the Hebrew, meaning "vineyard of the Lord." The exact Hebrew equivalent is Carmiya. MASCULINE HEBREW EQUIVALENTS: Carmi, Carmi'el.

Carna (קַרְנָה) From the Aramaic, meaning "horn," symbolizing strength. The exact Hebrew equivalent is Carna. The exact masculine equivalent is Keren.

Carni (קַרְנִי) A variant form of Carna. *See* Carna. The exact Hebrew equivalent is Carni.

Carnia A variant form of Carniya. *See* Carniya.

Carniela, Carniella (קַרְנִיאֶלָה) Variant forms of Carniya. *See* Carniya. The exact Hebrew equivalent is Carni'ela.

Carniya (קַרְנִיָה) From the Hebrew, meaning "horn of God." A variant form of Carna. *See* Carna. The exact Hebrew equivalent is Carniya. The exact masculine equivalent is Carni'el.

Carol From the Gaelic, meaning "melody, song." Also, a pet form of Caroline. *See* Caroline. HEBREW EQUIVALENTS: Lirona, Rani, Ranit. MASCULINE HEBREW EQUIVALENTS: Aharon, Amiran, Eliran.

Caroline From the French, meaning "strong, virile." HEBREW EQUIVALENTS: Gavri'ela, Gibora, Uzi'ela. MASCULINE HEBREW EQUIVALENTS: Uzi, Uzi'el, Yo'az.

Carolyn A variant spelling of Caroline. *See* Caroline.

Caron A variant spelling of Caren. *See* Caren.

Carren A variant spelling of Caren. *See* Caren.

Carrie A pet form of Caroline. *See* Caroline.

Carroll A variant spelling of Carol. *See* Carol.

Carry, Cary Pet forms of Caroline. *See* Caroline.

Caryl A variant spelling of Carol. *See* Carol.

Casey A unisex name. *See* Casey (*masculine section*).

Cassandra A character in Greek mythology who was gifted with pro- phetic powers. The exact Hebrew equivalent is Nevi'a. The mascu- line equivalent is Navi.

Cassi, Cassie Pet forms of Cassandra or Catherine. *See* Cassandra *and* Catherine.

Cassidy A unisex name. From the Irish/Gaelic, meaning "wise, clev- er." HEBREW EQUIVALENTS: Behira, Nevona. MASCULINE HEBREW EQUIVA- LENTS: Chacham, Chachmon, Haskel.

Cathay A variant form of Cathy. *See* Cathy.

Cathi A variant spelling of Cathy. *See* Cathy.

Catherin A variant spelling of Catherine. *See* Catherine.

Catherine From the Greek, meaning "pure, unsullied." HEBREW EQUIV- ALENTS: Zaka, Zakit, Zakiya. MASCULINE HEBREW EQUIVALENTS: Amizakai, Barur, Tzach.

Cathleen A variant form of Catherine. *See* Catherine.

Cathryn A variant spelling of Catherine. *See* Catherine.

Cathy A pet form of Catherine and Cathleen. *See* Catherine *and* Cathleen.

Cecelia From the Latin, meaning "blind" or "dim-sighted." EUPHEMIS- TIC HEBREW EQUIVALENTS: Behira, Me'ira, Zahara. EUPHEMISTIC MASCULINE HEBREW EQUIVALENTS: Me'ir, Shimshon, Uri'el.

Ceci A pet form of Cicely. *See* Cicely.

Cecil A variant form of Cecelia. *See* Cecelia.

Cecile, Cecille Variant spellings of Cecil. *See* Cecil.

Cecilia A variant spelling of Cecelia. *See* Cecelia.

Cecily A variant form of Cecilia. *See* Cecilia.

Ceil A pet form of Cecelia. *See* Cecelia.

Cele A variant spelling of Ceil. *See* Ceil.

Celeste From the Latin, meaning "heavenly." HEBREW EQUIVALENTS: Ester, Kochava, Kochevet. MASCULINE HEBREW EQUIVALENTS: Mazal, Shimshon.

Celia A variant form of Cecelia. *See* Cecelia.

Cerena A variant spelling of Serena. *See* Serena.

Chagit (חֲגִית) From the Aramaic, meaning "feast, festival, festive celebration." The exact Hebrew equivalent is Chagit. MASCULINE HEBREW EQUIVALENTS: Chag, Chagai, Chagi.

Chagiya (חַגִיָה) From the Hebrew, meaning "God's festival." The exact Hebrew equivalent is Chagiya. MASCULINE HEBREW EQUIVALENTS: Chagai, Chagi, Chagiga.

Chamuda (חֲמוּדָה) From the Hebrew, meaning "desired one." The exact Hebrew equivalent is Chamuda. The exact masculine equivalent is Chamud.

Chamutal (חֲמוּטַל) From the Hebrew, meaning "warmth" or "protective dew." The exact Hebrew equivalent is Chamutal. MASCULINE HEBREW EQUIVALENTS: Avigdor, Shemaryahu. In II Kings 23:31, the mother of King Jehoahaz.

Chana, Chanah (חַנָה) From the Hebrew, meaning "grace, gracious, merciful." Hannah is the Anglicized form. The exact Hebrew equivalent is Chana. MASCULINE HEBREW EQUIVALENTS: Chanan, Elchanan, Yochanan. In I Samuel 1:2, one of the two wives of Elkanah.

Chandler From the Middle English, meaning "candle handler." HEBREW EQUIVALENTS: Ora, Menora, Nura. MASCULINE HEBREW EQUIVALENTS: Avner, Me'ir, Ori.

Chandra From the Sanskrit, meaning "illustrious, eminent." HEBREW EQUIVALENTS: Adira, Adiva, Ge'ona. MASCULINE HEBREW EQUIVALENTS: Adir, Adiv, Ga'on.

Chani A pet form of Chana. *See* Chana.

Chaniette A pet form of Chana. *See* Chana

Chanit, Chanita (חֲנִיתָה/חֲנִית) Variant forms of Chana. *See* Chana.

Chantal From the French, meaning "stone, rock, boulder." HEBREW EQUIVALENTS: Avna, Salit, Tzuriya. MASCULINE HEBREW EQUIVALENTS: Amitzur, Even, Sela.

Chantel, Chantelle Various forms of Chantal. *See* Chantal.

Chanukah A feminine form of Chanoch. *See* Chanoch (*masculine section*).

Charissa From the Greek, meaning "grace." HEBREW EQUIVALENTS: Chana, Chanita, Chenya. MASCULINE HEBREW EQUIVALENTS: Adiv, Chanan, Yochanan.

Charity From the Latin, meaning "love, affection." HEBREW EQUIVALENTS: Ahuva, Chaviva, Tzedaka, Yedida. MASCULINE HEBREW EQUIVALENTS: Tzadik, Tzadok, Yedidya.

Charlayne A variant form of Charlene. *See* Charlene.

Charleen A variant spelling of Charlene. *See* Charlene.

Charlene A variant form of Caroline, meaning "strong, valiant." HEBREW EQUIVALENTS: Gavrila, Gibora, Uzit. MASCULINE HEBREW EQUIVALENTS: Gibor, Uzi, Uzi'el.

Charlet A variant form of Charlotte. *See* Charlotte.

Charlot A variant spelling of Charlotte. *See* Charlotte.

Charlotta A variant form of Charlotte. *See* Charlotte.

Charlotte The feminine form of Charles, meaning "strong." HEBREW EQUIVALENTS: Azri'ela, Chasina, Gavri'ela. MASCULINE HEBREW EQUIVALENTS: Cheletz, Gavri'el, Gur.

Chase A unisex name. *See* Chase (*masculine section*).

Chasia, Chasiah Variant spellings of Chasya. *See* Chasya.

Chasida, Chasidah (חֲסִידָה) From the Hebrew, meaning "stork" or "righteous." The exact Hebrew equivalent is Chasida. The exact masculine equivalent is Chasid.

Chasina (חֲסִינָה) From the Aramaic, meaning "strong, powerful." The exact Hebrew equivalent is Chasina. The exact masculine equivalent is Chasin.

Chasna (חַסְנָא) From the Aramaic, meaning "strong, powerful." The exact Hebrew equivalent is Chasna. MASCULINE HEBREW EQUIVALENTS: Chasin, Chason, Cheletz.

Chastity From the Old English, meaning "modesty, purity." HEBREW EQUIVALENTS: Anuva, Tehora, Zaka. MASCULINE HEBREW EQUIVALENTS: Anuv, Tzach, Zakai.

Chasya, Chasyah (חַסְיָה) From the Hebrew, meaning "protected by God." The exact Hebrew equivalent is Chasya. MASCULINE HEBREW EQUIVALENTS: Chaltzon, Chasin, Cha'yil.

Chava (חַוָה) From the Hebrew, meaning "life." The exact Hebrew equivalent is Chava. The masculine equivalent is Cha'yim.

Chavatzelet (חֲבַצֶלֶת) From the Akkadian word for the narcissus flower. The exact Hebrew equivalent is Chavatzelet.

Chavi A variant form of Chava. *See* Chava.

Chaviva (חֲבִיבָה) From the Hebrew, meaning "beloved." The exact Hebrew equivalent is Chaviva. The exact masculine equivalent is Chaviv.

Chaya, Chayah (חָיָה) From the Hebrew, meaning "alive, living." The exact Hebrew equivalent is Cha'ya. The masculine equivalent is Cha'yim.

Chayie A pet form of Chaya. *See* Chaya.

Chedva, Chedvah (חֶדְוָה) From the Hebrew, meaning "joy, happiness." The exact Hebrew equivalent is Chedva. MASCULINE HEBREW EQUIVALENTS: Chedvi, Gil, Gildad.

Cheftzi-Ba (חֶפְצִי-בָה) From the Hebrew, meaning "she is my desire." The exact Hebrew equivalent is Cheftzi-Ba. MASCULINE HEBREW EQUIVALENTS: Chamadel, Chamud, Chefetz. In II Kings 21:1, the wife of King Hezekiah.

Chel'a, Chel'ah (חֶלְאָה) From the Hebrew, meaning "unclean." The exact Hebrew equivalent is Chel'a. In I Chronicles 4:5, one of the two wives of Ashur of the tribe of Judah.

Chelsea From the Old English, meaning "port of ships." HEBREW EQUIVALENTS: Aniya, Bat-Yam, Yamit. MASCULINE HEBREW EQUIVALENTS: Aviyam, Chaifa, Cheifa.

Chelsea From the Old English, meaning "port, harbor." HEBREW EQUIVALENTS: Chaifa, Shu'a, Teshu'a. MASCULINE HEBREW EQUIVALENTS: Nemala, Nemalya, Yo'ezer.

Chemda (חֶמְדָה) From the Hebrew, meaning "desirable, charming." The exact Hebrew equivalent is Chemda. MASCULINE HEBREW EQUIVALENTS: Chamdel, Chamadya, Chamud.

Chemdat (חֶמְדַת) A unisex name. From the Hebrew, meaning "lovable, desirable." The exact Hebrew equivalent is Chemdat. FEMININE HEBREW EQUIVALENTS: Chamuda, Chemdiya.

Chen (חֵן) *Also spelled* Chein. From the Hebrew, meaning "graceful, gracious, charming." The exact Hebrew equivalent is Chein. MASCULINE HEBREW EQUIVALENTS: Chanina, Chanun, Yochanan.

Cher, Chere Pet forms of Cheryl. *See* Cheryl.

Cheri, Cherie French pet forms of Cheryl. *See* Cheryl.

Cherilynn A hybrid name formed from Cheryl and Lynn. *See* Cheryl *and* Lynn.

Cherlene A variant form of Charlene. *See* Charlene.

Cherri, Cherrie Pet forms of Cheryl. *See* Cheryl.

Cheryl, Cheryle From the French, meaning "dear, beloved." HEBREW EQUIVALENTS: Chaviva, Chiba, Davida. MASCULINE HEBREW EQUIVALENTS: Chovav, David, Yedidya.

Chesna From the Slavic, meaning "peaceful." HEBREW EQUIVALENTS: Meshulemet, Shlomit, Shulamit. MASCULINE HEBREW EQUIVALENTS: Ish-Shalom, Shabtai, Shalom.

Chita (חִיטָה/חִיטָא) From the Aramaic and Hebrew, meaning "grain, wheat." The exact Hebrew equivalent is Chita. MASCULINE HEBREW EQUIVALENTS: Dagan, Goren.

Chloe From the Greek, meaning "blooming" or "verdant." HEBREW EQUIVALENTS: Perach, Pericha, Smadar. MASCULINE HEBREW EQUIVALENTS: Pekach, Perachya, Tzemach.

Chloris A variant form of Chloe. *See* Chloe.

Chogla, Choglah (חָגְלָה) From the Hebrew, meaning "partridge." The exact Hebrew equivalent is Chogla. A masculine Hebrew equivalent is Tzipor. In Numbers 26:33, one of Tzelophchad's five daughters.

Chrissy, Christa Pet forms of Christina or Christine. *See* Christina *and* Christine.

Christina, Christine Feminine forms of the masculine name Christopher. *See* Christopher (*masculine section*).

Chryssa A pet form of Christina or Christine. *See* Christina *and* Christine.

Chrystal A variant spelling of Crystal. *See* Crystal.

Chulda, Chuldah (חֻלְדָה) From the Hebrew, meaning "weasel." The exact Hebrew equivalent is Chulda. In II Kings 22:14, a prophetess, the wife of Shallum.

Cicely, Cicily Variant forms of Cecelia. *See* Cecelia.

Cindy A pet form of Cynthia. *See* Cynthia.

Cipora A variant spelling of Tzipora. *See* Tzipora.

Ciporit A variant spelling of Tziporit. *See* Tziporit.

Cis, Ciss, Cissy Pet forms of Cecilia. *See* Cecilia.

Civia A variant spelling of Tzivya. *See* Tzivya.

Claire A French form of Clara. *See* Clara.

Clara From the Latin, meaning "clear, bright." HEBREW EQUIVALENTS: Behira, Me'ira, Noga, Ora. MASCULINE HEBREW EQUIVALENTS: Bahir, Barak, Me'ir.

Clarabella, Clarabelle Hybrid names formed from Clara and Bella or

Belle, both from the Latin, respectively meaning "bright" and "beautiful." HEBREW EQUIVALENTS: Behira, Keshet, Me'ira. MASCULINE HEBREW EQUIVALENTS: Avner, Bahir, Barak.

Clare A variant spelling of Claire. *See* Claire.

Clarette A variant form of Clara. *See* Clara.

Clarice A variant form of Clara. *See* Clara.

Clarissa, Clarisse Italian forms of Clara. *See* Clara.

Claudette A French pet form of Claudia. *See* Claudia.

Claudia From the Latin, meaning "lame." EUPHEMISTIC HEBREW EQUIVALENTS: A'yelet, Mehira, Ofra. EUPHEMISTIC MASCULINE HEBREW EQUIVALENTS: Bo'az, Efer, Gidon.

Claudine A French pet form of Claudia. *See* Claudia.

Clementine A French form of the Latin, meaning "merciful." HEBREW EQUIVALENTS: Chana, Chanina, Ruchama. MASCULINE HEBREW EQUIVALENTS: Rachmi'el, Yerachmi'el, Yerucham.

Cleo A variant spelling of Clio. *See* Clio.

Clio From the Greek, meaning "to celebrate, glorify." HEBREW EQUIVALENTS: Adra, Chagiga, Hadara. MASCULINE HEBREW EQUIVALENTS: Amihod, Chag, Hadar.

Cloe A variant spelling of Chloe. *See* Chloe.

Cochava A variant spelling of Kochava. *See* Kochava.

Colette From the Latin, meaning "victorious." HEBREW EQUIVALENTS: Gavri'ela, Gibora, Nitzcha. MASCULINE HEBREW EQUIVALENTS: Gevarya, Gevaryahu, Gover.

Colleen From the Irish, meaning "girl." HEBREW EQUIVALENTS: Bat, Bat-Sheva, Betula, Na'ara. MASCULINE HEBREW EQUIVALENTS: Bachur, Ben, Ben-Guryon.

Collette A variant spelling of Colette. *See* Colette.

Concetta From the Latin, meaning "conception." HEBREW EQUIVALENTS: Chavah, Cha'yah. MASCULINE HEBREW EQUIVALENTS: Chai, Cha'yim.

Condi A pet form of Condoleeza. *See* Condoleeza.

Condoleeza From the Italian, meaning "[to play] with sweetness." HEBREW EQUIVALENTS: Metuka, Mirit. MASCULINE HEBREW EQUIVALENTS: Matok, Na'am.

Connie A pet form of Constance. *See* Constance.

Constance From the Latin, meaning "constant, firm, faithful." HEBREW EQUIVALENTS: Bitcha, Emuna, Tama. MASCULINE HEBREW EQUIVALENTS: Amitai, Amnon, Tikva.

Cora From the Greek, meaning "maiden." HEBREW EQUIVALENTS: Aluma, Betula, Na'ara. MASCULINE HEBREW EQUIVALENTS: Bachur, Na'arai, Na'arya.

Coral (גּוֹרְלָה) From the Hebrew and Greek, meaning "small stone, pebble." The exact Hebrew equivalent is Gorala. The exact masculine equivalent is Goral.

Coralee, Coralie Variant forms of Coral. *See* Coral.

Cordelia A feminine form of Cordell. *See* Cordell *(masculine section)*

Cordis From the Latin, meaning "heart." The feminine Hebrew equivalent is Libi. MASCULINE HEBREW EQUIVALENTS: Kalev, Lev.

Coreen A pet form of Cora. *See* Cora.

Coretta A pet form of Cora. *See* Cora.

Corette A variant form of Coretta. *See* Coretta.

Corey From the Gaelic, meaning "ravine, enclosed place." HEBREW EQUIVALENTS: Afeka, Bik'a, Efrat. MASCULINE HEBREW EQUIVALENTS: Gaychazi, Gidron, Lotan.

Cori, Corie Variant spellings of Corey. *See* Corey.

Corinna, Corinne From the Greek, meaning "hummingbird." Also, French forms of Cora. *See* Cora.

Corita A pet form of Cora. *See* Cora.

Corna A pet form of Cornelia. *See* Cornelia.

Cornelia From the Greek, meaning "cornell tree," or from the Latin, meaning "horn of the sun," symbol of royalty. HEBREW EQUIVALENTS: Ilana, Malka, Malki'ela. MASCULINE EQUIVALENTS: Ilan, Malki'el, Melech.

Correy A variant spelling of Corey. *See* Corey.

Corri, Corrie Variant spellings of Corey. *See* Corey.

Corry, Cory Variant spellings of Corey. *See* Corey.

Cosima A feminine form of Cosmo. From the Greek, meaning "order, organization, unity." HEBREW EQUIVALENTS: Margei'a, Shalva, Shlomit. MASCULINE HEBREW EQUIVALENTS: Chever, Chevron, Shalom.

Courteny, Courtney Variant forms of Corey. *See* Corey.

Cozbi (כָּזְבִּי) From the Hebrew, meaning "prevaricator." The exact Hebrew equivalent is Cozbi. In Numbers 25:15, the daughter of a Midianite chief.

Crystal From the Greek, meaning "clear glass." HEBREW EQUIVALENTS: Ora, Zaka, Zivit. MASCULINE HEBREW EQUIVALENTS: Me'iri, Noga, Zerachya.

Cybil, Cybill From the Latin, meaning "soothsayer." HEBREW EQUIVALENTS: Amira, Doveva, Dovevet. MASCULINE HEBREW EQUIVALENTS: Amir, Anan, Anani.

Cyma From the Greek and Latin, meaning "to sprout, grow, flourish." HEBREW EQUIVALENTS: Carmel, Nitza, Shoshana. MASCULINE HEBREW EQUIVALENTS: Efra'yim, Pekach, Tzemach.

Cyndi A pet form of Cynthia. *See* Cynthia.

Cynthia From the Greek, meaning "from the cynthus." In Greek mythology, a mountain on which Artemis, goddess of the moon, was born. Hence, Cynthia came to mean the moon personified. HEBREW EQUIVALENTS: Chodesh, Levana, Me'ira. MASCULINE HEBREW EQUIVALENTS Me'ir, Yerach, Zerachya.

❧ D ❧

Dafna A variant spelling of Daphna. *See* Daphna.

Dafne A variant spelling of Daphne. *See* Daphne.

Dafnit (דָּפְנִית) The Hebrew form of the Greek name Daphne. *See* Daphne. The exact Hebrew equivalent is Dafnit.

Dagal (דָּגָל) From the Hebrew, meaning "flag carrier." The exact Hebrew equivalent is Dagal. MASCULINE HEBREW EQUIVALENTS: Dagal, Degel.

Dagan (דָּגָן) A unisex name. From the Hebrew, meaning "grain." The exact Hebrew equivalent is Dagan.

Daganit (דָּגָנִית) A variant feminine form of Dagan. *See* Dagan.

Daganya A variant spelling of Deganya. *See* Deganya.

Dagen A variant form of Dagan. *See* Dagan.

Dahlia A variant spelling of Dalya. *See* Dalya.

Daisy Often used as a nickname for Margaret. *See* Margaret.

Dale A unisex name. From the Old English and the Old Norse, meaning "valley." The feminine Hebrew equivalent is Ga'ya. MASCULINE HEBREW EQUIVALENTS: Emek, Gai, Gechazi.

Dalgia A variant spelling of Dalgiya. *See* Dalgiya.

Dalgiya (דַלְגִיָה) From the Hebrew, meaning "rope." The exact Hebrew equivalent is Dalgiya. Petil is a masculine equivalent.

Dalia A variant spelling of Daliya and Dalya. *See* Daliya *and* Dalya.

Dalit (דָלִית) From the Hebrew, meaning "to draw water" or "bough, branch." The exact Hebrew equivalent is Dalit. MASCULINE HEBREW EQUIVALENTS: Chamat, Dela'ya, Silon.

Daliya (דַלִיָה) A variant form of Dalya. *See* Dalya. The exact Hebrew equivalent is Daliya.

Dalya (דַלְיָה) From the Hebrew, meaning "branch, bough" or "to draw water." The exact Hebrew equivalent is Dalya. The exact masculine equivalent is Dela'ya.

Dama From the Latin, meaning "lady." HEBREW EQUIVALENTS: Adiva, Gevira, Sara. MASCULINE HEBREW EQUIVALENTS: Adoniya, Adoniram, Yisra'el.

Dame A variant form of Dama. *See* Dama.

Damita A Spanish form of Dama. *See* Dama.

Dana (דָנָה) From the Latin, meaning "bright, pure as day." Also, from the Hebrew, meaning "to judge." The exact Hebrew equivalent is Dana. The exact masculine equivalent is Dan.

Danette A feminine form of the masculine Dan. Also, a variant form of the feminine Dana. *See* Dan (*masculine section*) and Dana (*feminine section*).

Dani A feminine form of the masculine Dan. *See* Dan (*masculine section*).

Dania, Daniah Variant spellings of Danya. *See* Danya.

Danie A variant spelling of Dani. *See* Dani.

Daniela, Daniella (דָנִיאֵלָה) Feminine forms of the masculine Daniel, meaning "God is my judge." The exact Hebrew equivalent is Dani'ela. The exact masculine equivalent is Dani'el.

Daniele, Danielle Variant forms of Daniela. *See* Daniela.

Danit (דָּנִית) A variant form of Daniela. *See* Daniela. The exact Hebrew equivalent is Danit.

Danita (דָּנִיתָה) A variant form of Daniela. *See* Daniela. The exact Hebrew equivalent is Danita.

Danna A variant spelling of Dana. *See* Dana.

Danya (דַּנְיָה) A feminine form of the masculine Dan, meaning "judgment of the Lord." The exact Hebrew equivalent is Danya. MASCULINE HEBREW EQUIVALENTS: Dan, Dani'el.

Daphna, Daphne (דַּפְנָה) From the Greek, meaning "laurel" or "bay tree," symbols of victory. The exact Hebrew equivalent is Dafna. MASCULINE HEBREW EQUIVALENTS: Gover, Netzi'ach, Yatzli'ach.

Daphnit A variant spelling of Dafnit. *See* Dafnit.

Dapna A variant spelling of Daphne. *See* Daphne.

Dara, Darah (דָּרָה) From the Hebrew, meaning "reside, sojourn." Also, from the Old English, meaning "to dare, to be bold." The exact Hebrew equivalent is Dara. The exact masculine equivalent is Dar.

Darbey, Darby A unisex name. From the Old English, meaning "deer meadow." HEBREW EQUIVALENTS: Ofra, Re'eima, Tzivya. MASCULINE HEBREW EQUIVALENTS: Ben-Tzevi, Ofer, Tzevi.

Darcie From the Celtic, meaning "dark." HEBREW EQUIVALENTS: Chachila, Laila, Tzila. MASCULINE HEBREW EQUIVALENTS: Adar, Ashchur, Efai.

Dari, Daria, Darie Feminine forms of the Persian name Darius, meaning "wealth." *See* Darius (*masculine section*).

Darla From the Middle English, meaning "dear, loved one." HEBREW EQUIVALENTS: Chiba, Davida, Yedida. MASCULINE HEBREW EQUIVALENTS: Bildad, Chovav, David.

Darleen, Darlene, Darline Pet forms of Darla. *See* Darla.

Daroma (דָּרוֹמָה) From the Hebrew, meaning "south, southward." The exact Hebrew equivalent is Daroma. The exact masculine equivalent is Darom.

Darona (דָּרוֹנָה) A Hebrew form of the Greek, meaning "gift." The exact Hebrew equivalent is Darona. Akin to Dorona. The exact masculine equivalent is Daron.

Darrene A feminine form of Darren. *See* Darren (*masculine section*).

Daryl From the Old English, meaning "dear, beloved." Used also as a masculine name. HEBREW EQUIVALENTS: Chaviva, Davida, Dodi. MASCULINE HEBREW EQUIVALENTS: Chaviv, David, Dodo.

Dasa A short form of Hadassah. *See* Hadassah.

Dasi A variant spelling of Dassi. *See* Dassi.

Dassa, Dassah Variant short forms of Hadassah. *See* Hadassah.

Dassi, Dassy (דַּסִי) Pet forms of Hadassah. *See* Hadassah. The exact Hebrew equivalent is Dassi.

Dati (דָתִי) From the Hebrew, meaning "religious, observant." The exact Hebrew equivalent is Dati. MASCULINE HEBREW EQUIVALENTS: Datan, Dati'el, Da'yan.

Datit (דָתִית) A variant form of Dati. *See* Dati. The exact Hebrew equivalent is Datit.

Datya (דַתְיָה) From the Hebrew, meaning "faith in God" or "law of the Lord." The exact Hebrew equivalent is Datya. MASCULINE HEBREW EQUIVALENTS: Datan, Dati'el, Da'yan.

Davene A feminine form of David, meaning "beloved, friend." *See* David (*masculine section*).

Davida, Davide (דָוִידָה) Feminine forms of David. *See* David (*masculine section*). The exact Hebrew equivalent is Davida.

Davina A Scottish form of David used in the seventeenth century. *See* David (*masculine section*).

Davita A Spanish form of David. *See* David (*masculine section*).

Dawn, Dawna, Dawne From the Old Norse and Old English, meaning "dawn." HEBREW EQUIVALENTS: Bat-Shachar, Tzafra, Tzafrira. MASCULINE HEBREW EQUIVALENTS: Avi-Shachar, Tzafrir, Tzafriri.

Daya (דַיָּה) The Hebrew name for a bird of prey. The exact Hebrew equivalent is Da'ya. MASCULINE HEBREW EQUIVALENTS: Gozal, Orev, Tzipor.

Dayana (דַיָנָה) From the Hebrew, meaning "judge." The exact Hebrew equivalent is Da'yana. The exact masculine equivalent is Da'yan.

Da'yelet (דַיֶּלֶת) From the Hebrew, meaning "hostess, stewardess, server." The exact Hebrew equivalent is Da'yelet. MASCULINE HEBREW EQUIVALENTS: Avdon, Ovadya, Shamash.

Dayle A variant feminine spelling of Dale. *See* Dale.

Dean, Deane A unisex name. From the Old French, meaning "head, leader." HEBREW EQUIVALENTS: Mori'el, Morit, Moriya, Rishona. MASCULINE HEBREW EQUIVALENTS: Chanoch, Rabi, Rosh, Tana.

Deanna, Deanne Variant forms of Diana or Dinah. *See* Diana *and* Dinah.

Deb, Debbe, Debbi, Debby, Debi Pet forms of Deborah. *See* Deborah.

Debora A variant spelling of Deborah. *See* Deborah.

Deborah The Anglicized form of the Hebrew name Devora. *See* Devora.

Debra A variant form of Deborah. *See* Deborah.

Dee A coined name derived from the English letter *d*. Also, a river in northeast Scotland that flows into the North Sea. HEBREW EQUIVALENTS: Afeka, Bat-Yam, Einat. MASCULINE HEBREW EQUIVALENTS: Aviyam, Ye'or, Ye'ori.

Deena From the Anglo-Saxon, meaning "from the valley." Also, a variant spelling of Dinah. *See* Dinah.

Deenie A pet form of Dinah. *See* Dinah.

Degania, Deganiah Variant spellings of Deganya. *See* Deganya.

Deganit (דְגָנִית) A variant form of Deganya. *See* Deganya. The exact Hebrew equivalent is Deganit.

Deganya (דְּגָנְיָה) From the Hebrew, meaning "grain." The exact Hebrew equivalent is Deganya. The exact masculine equivalent is Dagan.

Degula (דְּגוּלָה) From the Hebrew, meaning "honored, famous." The exact Hebrew equivalent is Degula. MASCULINE HEBREW EQUIVALENTS: Ben-Tziyon, Dagul, Hillel.

Deidra A variant spelling of Deidre. *See* Deidre.

Deidre From the Middle Irish, meaning "young girl." HEBREW EQUIVALENTS: Alma, Aluma, Betu'el. MASCULINE HEBREW EQUIVALENTS: Na'arai, Na'ari, Na'arya.

Deirdre A variant form of Deidre. *See* Deidre.

Delia A pet form of Adelia. *See* Adelia.

Delicia From the Latin, meaning "delight" or "delicate." HEBREW EQUIVALENTS: Adina, Na'a, Na'ama. MASCULINE HEBREW EQUIVALENTS: Avino'am, Eiden, No'am.

Delila, Delilah (דְּלִילָה) From the Hebrew, meaning "hair" or "poor." The exact Hebrew equivalent is Delila. MASCULINE HEBREW EQUIVALENTS: Micha, Se'orim.

Dell, Della, Delle Variant pet forms of Adela and Adeline. *See* Adela *and* Adeline.

Delta A Greek and Latin form of the Hebrew *delet*, meaning "door." The Hebrew equivalent is Delet. MASCULINE HEBREW EQUIVALENTS: Bava, Sha'arya.

Dena A variant spelling of Dinah. *See* Dinah.

Denice, Deniece, Deniese Variant spellings of Denise. *See* Denise.

Denise A feminine form of the masculine name Denis, derived from Dionysius, the Greek god of wine and drama. *See* Denis (*masculine section*).

Denna From the Anglo-Saxon, meaning "valley." The Hebrew equivalent is Ga'ya. The masculine equivalent is Gai.

Denyce, Denyse Variant spellings of Denise. *See* Denise.

Deon, Deone Variant spellings of Dion. *See* Dion.

Deror (דְּרוֹר) A unisex name. From the Hebrew, meaning "bird [swallow]" or "free, freedom" or "flowing stream." The exact Hebrew equivalent is Deror.

Derora, Derorah (דְּרוֹרָה) From the Hebrew, meaning "bird [swallow]" or "freedom, liberty" or "flowing stream." The exact Hebrew equivalent is Derora. The exact masculine equivalent is Deror.

Deuela, Deuella (דְּעוּאֵלָה) From the Hebrew, meaning "knowledge of the Lord." The exact Hebrew equivalent is De'uela. The exact masculine equivalent is De'uel.

Deva A pet form of Devorah. *See* Devorah.

Devera A variant spelling of Devira or Devora. *See* Devira *and* Devora.

Devir (דְּבִיר) A unisex name. From the Hebrew, meaning "sanctuary." The exact Hebrew equivalent is Devir.

Devira (דְּבִירָה) A variant form of Devir. *See* Devir. The exact Hebrew equivalent is Devira.

Devon A unisex name. From the Gaelic, meaning "poet." Pi'ut is the Hebrew equivalent.

Devora, Devorah (דְּבוֹרָה) From the Hebrew, meaning "swarm of bees" or "to speak kind words." The exact Hebrew equivalent is Devora. MASCULINE HEBREW EQUIVALENTS: Amarya, Imri, Niv. In Genesis 35:8, Rebecca's nurse; in Judges 4:4, a prophetess.

Devorit (דְּבוֹרִית) A variant form of Devora. *See* Devora. The exact Hebrew equivalent is Devorit.

Devra A variant form of Devora. *See* Devora.

Di A pet form of Diana. *See* Diana.

Diana, Diane, Dianne From the Latin, meaning "bright, pure as a day." HEBREW EQUIVALENTS: Behira, Me'ira, Noga. MASCULINE HEBREW EQUIVALENTS: Aharon, Bahir, Me'ir, Neri.

Didi A pet form of Deidre and Diana. *See* Deidre *and* Diana.

Diedre A variant spelling of Deidre. *See* Deidre.

Digla (דִּגְלָה) From the Hebrew, meaning "flag." The exact Hebrew equivalent is Digla. MASCULINE HEBREW EQUIVALENTS: Dagul, Diglai.

Diglat (דִּגְלַת) A variant form of Digla. *See* Digla. The exact Hebrew equivalent is Diglat.

Dikla, Diklah (דִּקְלָה) The Aramaic form of the Hebrew word meaning "palm [date] tree." The exact Hebrew equivalent is Dikla. The exact masculine equivalent is Dekel.

Diklit (דִּקְלִית) A variant form of Dikla. *See* Dikla. The exact Hebrew equivalent is Diklit.

Dila, Dilah Pet forms of Delilah. *See* Delilah.

Dimples From the Middle English, meaning "deep hollow." Popular in India. The Hebrew equivalent is Me'arah. MASCULINE HEBREW EQUIVALENTS: Chor, Chori.

Dina, Dinah (דִּינָה) From the Hebrew, meaning "judgment." The exact Hebrew equivalent is Dina. The exact masculine equivalent is Dan. In Genesis 34:1, the daughter of Leah and Jacob.

Dion, Dione, Dionne Variant forms of Diana, Diane, and Dianne. *See* Diana.

Dira, Dirah (דִּירָה) From the Hebrew, meaning "dwelling." The exact Hebrew equivalent is Dira. The exact masculine equivalent is Dir.

Disa, Dissa (דִּיתָה) Yiddish pet forms of Yehudit (Judith). *See* Yehudit.

Ditza, Ditzah (דִּיצָה) From the Hebrew, meaning "joy." The exact Hebrew equivalent is Ditza. The exact masculine equivalent is Ditz.

Divan From the Arabic and Persian, meaning "a group of poems by a single poet." HEBREW EQUIVALENTS: Pi'uta, Shira. MASCULINE HEBREW EQUIVALENTS: Ronen, Shir, Shiron.

Divina From the Italian, meaning "divine." HEBREW EQUIVALENTS: Betu'el, Imanu'ela, Micha'ela. MASCULINE HEBREW EQUIVALENTS: Adoniya, Azri'el, Eliyahu.

Dixie A name adopted from a post-Civil War song identifying the southern Confederate states. Daroma is a Hebrew equivalent. Darom is the masculine Hebrew equivalent. Also, from the French, meaning "tenth."

Diza, Dizah Variant spellings of Ditza. *See* Ditza.

Dobe A pet form of Devora. *See* Devora.

Dobra, Dobrah (דָאבְּרָא) Variant Yiddish forms of Deborah. *See* Deborah. Also, from the Slavic, meaning "good." The exact Hebrew equivalent is Tova.

Doda, Dodah (דּוֹדָה) From the Hebrew, meaning "friend, beloved" or "aunt." The exact Hebrew equivalent is Doda.

Dodi, Dodie (דּוֹדִי) A unisex name. From the Hebrew, meaning "my friend, my beloved." The exact Hebrew equivalent is Dodi.

Dodo (דּוֹדוֹ) A pet form of Dorothy. *See* Dorothy. Also, a variant form of Doda. *See* Doda.

Dody A variant spelling of Dodi. *See* Dodi.

Doe From the Old English, meaning "female deer." The exact Hebrew equivalent is Tzivya. The exact masculine equivalent is Tzevi.

Dolley, Dollie Variant spellings of Dolly. *See* Dolly.

Dolly A variant form of Dorothy. *See* Dorothy.

Dolores A Christian name derived from the Latin, meaning "lady of sorrows."

Dona A variant spelling of Donna. *See* Donna.

Donabella A hybrid name formed from Donna and Bella. *See* Donna *and* Bella.

Donita A pet form of Donna. *See* Donna.

Donna From the Latin and Italian, meaning "lady of nobility." HEBREW EQUIVALENTS: Adina, Adoniya, Matrona. MASCULINE HEBREW EQUIVALENTS: Achinadav, Adon, Aminadav.

Donya A pet form of Donna. *See* Donna.

Dora A diminutive form of Dorothy. *See* Dorothy.

Doraleen, Doralene Pet forms of Dora. *See* Dora.

Dore A German form of Dorothea. *See* Dorothea.

Dorea A variant form of Doris. *See* Doris.

Doreen A pet form of Dorothy and its diminutive Dora. *See* Dorothy.

Doreet A variant spelling of Dorit. *See* Dorit.

Dorene A variant spelling of Doreen. *See* Doreen.

Doretha A variant form of Dorothy. *See* Dorothy.

Doretta, Dorette A French form of Dorothy. *See* Dorothy.

Doria, Dorie Variant feminine forms of Dorian. *See* Dorian (*masculine section*).

Dorina A pet form of Dora. *See* Dora.

Doris From the Greek, meaning "sacrificial knife." In Greek mythology, the mother of sea gods. HEBREW EQUIVALENTS: Afeka, Bat-Yam, Miryam. MASCULINE HEBREW EQUIVALENTS: Aviyam, Beri, Chamat.

Dorit (דוֹרִית) From the Greek, meaning "to heap, pile" or "dwelling place." Also, from the Hebrew, meaning "generation." The exact Hebrew equivalent is Dorit. The exact masculine equivalent is Dor.

Dorona (דוֹרוֹנָה) From the Greek, meaning "gift." The exact Hebrew equivalent is Dorona. The exact masculine equivalent is Doron.

Doronit (דוֹרוֹנִית) A variant form of Dorona. *See* Dorona. The exact Hebrew equivalent is Doronit.

Dorota A feminine form of the masculine name Dorot, meaning "generations." *See* Dorot (*masculine section*).

Dorothea A variant form of Dorothy. *See* Dorothy.

Dorothy From the Greek, meaning "gift of God." HEBREW EQUIVALENTS: Doronit, Matana, Matat. MASCULINE HEBREW EQUIVALENTS: Avishai, Doron, Doroni.

Dorri, Dorrie Pet forms of Dorothy. *See* Dorothy.

Dorris A variant spelling of Doris. *See* Doris.

Dorrit A variant spelling of Dorit. *See* Dorit.

Dot, Dottie, Dotty Pet forms of Dorothy. *See* Dorothy.

Dotan (דּוֹתָן) A unisex name. From the Hebrew, meaning "law." The exact Hebrew equivalent is Dotan.

Dovrat (דָּבְרַת) A variant form of Devora. *See* Devora. The exact Hebrew equivalent is Dovrat.

Drew A unisex name. A short form of Andrew. *See* Andrew (*masculine section*).

Drora A variant spelling of Derora. *See* Derora.

Dru An alternate spelling of Drew. *See* Drew.

Duba (דֻּבָּה) From the Hebrew, meaning "bear." The exact Hebrew equivalent is Duba. The exact masculine equivalent is Dov.

Dulcia, Dulcie From the Latin, meaning "charming, sweet." HEBREW EQUIVALENTS: Achino'am, Metuka, Na'ama. MASCULINE HEBREW EQUIVALENTS: Avino'am, Magdi'el, Matok.

Durene From the Latin, meaning "enduring, lasting." HEBREW EQUIVALENTS: Nitzcha, Nitzchiya, Nitzchona. MASCULINE HEBREW EQUIVALENTS: Elad, Netzach, Nitzchi.

Dvir A variant spelling of Devir. *See* Devir.

Dvora, Dvorah A variant spelling of Devora. *See* Devora.

Dvorit A variant spelling of Devorit. *See* Devorit.

Dyan A variant spelling of Diane. *See* Diane.

Dyana A variant spelling of Diana. *See* Diana.

∽ E ∽

Earla A feminine form of Earl. *See* Earl (*masculine section*).

Earlene A feminine form of Earl. *See* Earl (*masculine section*).

Eartha From the Old English, meaning "ground, land." HEBREW EQUIVALENTS: Adama, Artzit. MASCULINE HEBREW EQUIVALENTS: Adam, Artzi.

Eda, Edda From the Icelandic, meaning "poet" or "songwriter." HEBREW EQUIVALENTS: Aharona, Lirit, Ne'ima. MASCULINE HEBREW EQUIVALENTS: Aharon, Amiran, Amishar.

Ede A pet form of Edith. *See* Edith.

Edel A variant spelling of Eidel. *See* Eidel.

Eden (עֵדֶן) A unisex name. Akin to Adina. From the Hebrew, meaning "pleasure, delight, paradise." The exact Hebrew equivalent is Eiden (Ayden). MASCULINE HEBREW EQUIVALENTS: Adin, Adiv, Na'im. The Garden of Eden is mentioned in Genesis 2:10.

Eder (עֵדֶר) A unisex name. From the Hebrew, meaning "herd, flock." The exact Hebrew equivalent is Eder.

Edia, Ediah Variant spellings of Edya. *See* Edya.

Edie A popular Scottish pet form of Edith. *See* Edith.

Edina From the Anglo-Saxon, meaning "rich friend." HEBREW EQUIVALENTS: Chaviva, Rut, Yedida. MASCULINE HEBREW EQUIVALENTS: David, Tzefanya, Yedidya.

343

Edita A Spanish pet form of Edith. *See* Edith.

Edith From the Anglo-Saxon, meaning "rich, prosperous, happy warrior." HEBREW EQUIVALENTS: Ashira, Bat-Shu'a, Matzlicha. MASCULINE HEBREW EQUIVALENTS: Ashir, Etzer, Matzli'ach.

Edna, Ednah (עֶדְנָה) From the Hebrew, meaning "delight, desired, adorned, voluptuous." Also, a contracted form of the Anglo-Saxon name Edwina, meaning "rich friend." HEBREW EQUIVALENTS: Amita, Chaviva, Davida, Yedida. MASCULINE HEBREW EQUIVALENTS: David, Eden, Yedidya.

Edwina A feminine form of Edwin. *See* Edwin (*masculine section*).

Edya, Edyah (עֶדְיָה) From the Hebrew, meaning "adornment of the Lord." The exact Hebrew equivalent is Edya. MASCULINE HEBREW EQUIVALENTS: Ada'ya, Adi, Adi'el.

Edyth, Edythe Variant spellings of Edith. *See* Edith.

Eedit A variant spelling of Idit. *See* Idit.

Eetta A variant spelling of Ita. *See* Ita.

Effi, Effie Pet forms of Elfreda. *See* Elfreda.

Efrat (אֶפְרָת) A unisex name. From the Hebrew, meaning "honored, distinguished" or "fruitful." Also, from the Aramaic, meaning "mantle, turban." The exact Hebrew equivalent is Efrat.

Efrata (אֶפְרָתָה) A variant form of Efrat. *See* Efrat. The exact Hebrew equivalent is Efrata. In I Chronicles 2:19, the second wife of Caleb.

Efrem A unisex name. A variant form of the masculine Efrayim. *See* Efrayim (*masculine section*).

Efrona (עֶפְרוֹנָה) From the Hebrew, meaning "bird." The exact Hebrew equivalent is Efrona. The exact masculine equivalent is Efron.

Efroni (עֶפְרוֹנִי) From the Hebrew, meaning "bird, lark." The exact Hebrew equivalent is Efroni. MASCULINE HEBREW EQUIVALENTS: Deror, Efron, Gozal.

Eidel (אײדְל) From the Yiddish, meaning "delicate, gentle." HEBREW EQUIVALENTS: Adina, Adiva, Anuga. MASCULINE HEBREW EQUIVALENTS: Adin, Adiv, Chananel.

Eila, Eilah (אֵלָה) A unisex name. From the Hebrew, meaning "oak tree, terebinth tree." The exact Hebrew equivalent is Eila.

Eilat (אֵילַת) A unisex name. From the Hebrew, meaning "gazelle" or "tree." The exact Hebrew equivalent is Eilat.

Eileen A popular Irish form of Helen. *See* Helen.

Einat (עֵינַת) From the Hebrew, meaning "water well." The exact Hebrew equivalent is Einat. MASCULINE HEBREW EQUIVALENTS: Aviyam, Be'eri, Ma'ayan.

Elain, Elaine French forms of Helen, meaning "light." *See* Helen.

Elana A variant spelling of Ilana, meaning "tree." *See* Ilana.

Elayne A variant spelling of Elaine. *See* Elaine.

Elberta The feminine form of Elbert. *See* Elbert (*masculine section*).

Eldora From the Spanish, meaning "gilded." HEBREW EQUIVALENTS: Ofira, Paza, Zehava. MASCULINE HEBREW EQUIVALENTS: Elifaz, Ofir, Pazi, Zehavi.

Ele A pet form of Eleanor. *See* Eleanor.

Eleanor A German form of Helen, from the Greek, meaning "light." HEBREW EQUIVALENTS: Behira, Me'ira, Nitza. MASCULINE HEBREW EQUIVALENTS: Bahir, Me'ir, Neriya.

Eleanora A variant form of Eleanor. *See* Eleanor.

Eleanore A variant spelling of Eleanor. *See* Eleanor.

Electra From the Greek, meaning "shining, brightness." HEBREW EQUIVALENTS: Behira, Me'ira, Ora. MASCULINE HEBREW EQUIVALENTS: Avner, Barak, Me'ir.

Elen, Elene Variant spellings of Ellen. *See* Eleanor.

Elena From the Greek, meaning "light." The Italian form of Helen. *See* Helen.

Elenne, Ellenne Modern spellings of Ellen. *See* Ellen.

Elenor A variant spelling of Eleanor. *See* Eleanor.

Eleora A variant spelling of Eliora. *See* Eliora.

Elfreda An Anglicized form of the German name Elfrieda, meaning "supernatural strength." HEBREW EQUIVALENTS: Abira, Ertana, Gavri'ela. MASCULINE HEBREW EQUIVALENTS: Amitz, Azri'el, Gavri'el.

Eliana, Eliane, Elianna (אֱלִיעָנָה) From the Hebrew, meaning "my God has answered." The exact Hebrew equivalent is Eliana.

Eliava, Eliavah (אֱלִיאָבָה) From the Hebrew, meaning "my God is willing." The exact Hebrew equivalent is Eliava. The exact masculine equivalent is Eliav.

Elie A pet form of Eleanor. *See* Eleanor.

Eliezra (אֱלִיעֶזְרָה) From the Hebrew, meaning "my God is salvation." The exact Hebrew equivalent is Eli'ezra. The exact masculine equivalent is Eli'ezer.

Elin A variant spelling of Ellen. *See* Ellen.

Elinoar (אֱלִינֹעַר) From the Hebrew, meaning "God is my youth." The exact Hebrew equivalent is Elino'ar. MASCULINE HEBREW EQUIVALENTS: Aviv, Elam, Na'arai, Na'arya.

Elinoor, Elinor Variant spellings of Eleanor. *See* Eleanor.

Elinora A variant spelling of Eleanora. *See* Eleanora.

Elinore A variant spelling of Eleanor. *See* Eleanor.

Eliora (אֱלִיאוֹרָה) From the Hebrew, meaning "my God is light." The exact Hebrew equivalent is Eli'ora. The exact masculine equivalent is Eli'or.

Eliraz (אֱלִירָז) From the Hebrew, meaning "my God is my secret." The exact Hebrew equivalent is Eliraz. MASCULINE HEBREW EQUIVALENTS: Raz, Razi, Razi'el.

Elisa A short form of Elisabeth. *See* Elisabeth.

Elisabeta The Hawaiian form of Elisabeth. *See* Elisabeth.

Elisabeth A variant spelling of Elizabeth. *See* Elizabeth.

Elise A pet form of Elisabeth. *See* Elisabeth.

Elisheva (אֱלִישֶׁבַע) From the Hebrew, meaning "God is my oath." Elizabeth and Elisabeth are Anglicized forms. The exact Hebrew equivalent is Elisheva. MASCULINE HEBREW EQUIVALENTS: Amarya, Ela, Sheva. In Exodus 6:23, the wife of Aaron, the High Priest.

Elissa A pet form of Elisabeth. *See* Elisabeth.

Eliya, Eliyah Feminine forms of Elijah. *See* Elijah (*masculine section*).

Eliza A short form of Elizabeth. *See* Elizabeth.

Elizabeta A Spanish form of Elizabeth. *See* Elizabeth.

Elizabeth (אֱלִישֶׁבַע) From the Hebrew, meaning "God's oath." The exact Hebrew equivalent is Elisheva. MASCULINE HEBREW EQUIVALENTS: Amarya, Ela, Sheva.

Elize A short form of Elizabeth. *See* Elizabeth.

Elka, Elke Pet forms of Alice and Alexandra. *See* Alice *and* Alexandra.

Elki, Elkie, Elky Variant forms of Elka. *See* Elka.

Ella From the Old German, meaning "all." Also, a variant form of Eleanor. *See* Eleanor.

Ellen, Ellenne Short forms of Eleanor. *See* Eleanor.

Ellette A pet form of Ella. *See* Ella.

Ellie A pet form of Eleanor. *See* Eleanor.

Ellin A variant spelling of Ellen. *See* Ellen.

Ellis A variant spelling of Elyse. *See* Elyse.

Elly A pet form of Eleanor. *See* Eleanor.

Ellyn, Ellynne Variant spellings of Ellen. *See* Ellen.

Elma From the Greek and Latin, meaning "pleasant, fair, kind." HEBREW EQUIVALENTS: Achino'am, Adiva, Na'ama. MASCULINE HEBREW EQUIVALENTS: Achino'am, Adin, Na'im.

Eloise A variant form of Louise. *See* Louise.

Elona (אֵלוֹנָה) From the Hebrew, meaning "oak tree." The exact Hebrew equivalent is Eilona. The exact masculine equivalent is Eilon.

Elouise A variant spelling of Eloise. *See* Eloise.

Elsa, Else German pet forms of Elizabeth. *See* Elizabeth.

Elsie A variant form of Elisabeth. *See* Elisabeth.

Elvera, Elvira From the Latin, meaning "noble truth." HEBREW EQUIVALENTS: Amita, Emet. MASCULINE HEBREW EQUIVALENTS: Amit, Amitai, Amitana.

Elvita From the Latin, meaning "noble life." HEBREW EQUIVALENTS: Achiya, Chava, Cha'ya, Yechi'ela. MASCULINE HEBREW EQUIVALENTS: Amichai, Bar-Yocha'i, Cha'yim, Yechi'el.

Elyce A variant spelling of Elysa. *See* Elysa.

Elyn, Elynn Variant spellings of Ellen. *See* Ellen.

Elysa, Elyssa, Elysse Variant forms of Elisabeth. *See* Elisabeth.

Elza (עֶלְזָה) A pet form of Elizabeth. *See* Elizabeth. Also, from the Hebrew, meaning "joy." The exact Hebrew equivalent is Elza. The exact masculine equivalent is Elez.

Em A pet form of Emma. *See* Emma.

Emanuela, Emanuella (עִמָּנוּאֵלָה) Feminine forms of Emanuel, meaning "God is with us." The exact Hebrew equivalent is Imanu'ela. The exact masculine equivalent is Imanu'el.

Emeralda A variant form of Esmeralda. *See* Esmeralda.

Emilia A variant Spanish spelling of Amelia. *See* Amelia.

Emilie From the Anglo-Saxon, meaning "flatterer." Also, a variant spelling of Emily. *See* Emily.

Emily From the Latin, meaning "industrious, ambitious." HEBREW EQUIVALENTS: Charutza, Tirtza, Zeriza. MASCULINE HEBREW EQUIVALENTS: Amel, Mahir, Meretz.

Emma From the Anglo-Saxon, meaning "big one" or "grandmother."

HEBREW EQUIVALENTS: Atalya, Gedula, Ima. MASCULINE HEBREW EQUIVA-
LENTS: Abba, Gedalya, Raba.

Emmie A pet form of Emma. *See* Emma.

Emmy A pet form of Emily and Emma. *See* Emily *and* Emma.

Emmylou A hybrid name formed from Emmy and Lou. *See* Emmy *and* Lou.

Emuna, Emunah (אֱמוּנָה) From the Hebrew, meaning "faith, faithful." The exact Hebrew equivalent is Emuna. MASCULINE HEBREW EQUIVA-LENTS: Amit, Amitai, Amitan.

Ena A variant spelling of Ina. Also, a pet form of Eugenia. *See* Ina *and* Eugenia.

Enia From the Irish/Gaelic, meaning "fire." HEBREW EQUIVALENTS: Avuka, Shalhevet, Uri'ela. MASCULINE HEBREW EQUIVALENTS: Lahav, Lapid, Uri'el.

Enid From the Anglo-Saxon, meaning "fair," or from the Celtic, meaning "soul, life." HEBREW EQUIVALENTS: Chava, Cha'ya, Nafshiya. MASCULINE HEBREW EQUIVALENTS: Amichai, Chai, Cha'yim.

Enya A variant spelling of Enia. *See* Enia.

Erela (אֶרְאֶלָה) From the Hebrew, meaning "angel, messenger." The exact Hebrew equivalent is Erela. The exact masculine equivalent is Erel.

Eretz (אֶרֶץ) From the Hebrew, meaning "land, earth." The exact Hebrew equivalent is Eretz. MASCULINE HEBREW EQUIVALENTS: Artza, Artzi.

Erez (אֶרֶז) A unisex name. From the Hebrew, meaning "cedar tree," suggesting youthful sturdiness. The exact equivalent is Erez. Also, a variant spelling of Eretz.

Erga From the Hebrew, meaning "yearning, hope, longing." The exact Hebrew equivalent is Erga. MASCULINE HEBREW EQUIVALENTS: Tikva, Yachil, Yachl'el.

Erica The feminine form of Eric, meaning "ever-kingly, brave, powerful." *See* Eric (*masculine section*).

Erika A variant spelling of Erica. *See* Erica.

Erin From the Irish, meaning "peace." HEBREW EQUIVALENTS: Menucha, Meshulemet, Shalviya. MASCULINE HEBREW EQUIVALENTS: Avishalom, Sar-Shalom, Shalem.

Erma A variant spelling of Irma. *See* Irma.

Erna From the Anglo-Saxon, meaning "retiring, shy, reserved, peaceful." HEBREW EQUIVALENTS: Achishalom, Margaya, Menucha, Sha'anana. MASCULINE HEBREW EQUIVALENTS: Avishalom, Ish-Shalom, Shalev.

Ernesta, Ernestine Feminine forms of Ernest. *See* Ernest (*masculine section*).

Erwina A feminine form of Erwin. *See* Erwin (*masculine section*).

Esmeralda From the Spanish, meaning "jewel." HEBREW EQUIVALENTS: Margalit, Penina, Peninit. MASCULINE HEBREW EQUIVALENTS: Dar, Penini, Tzedef.

Essa, Essie Pet forms of Esther. *See* Esther.

Esta, Estee Variant forms of Esther. *See* Esther.

Estefania A Spanish form of Stephanie. *See* Stephanie.

Estella A Spanish form of Esther. *See* Esther.

Estelle A variant form of Esther. *See* Esther.

Ester, Esther (אֶסְתֵּר) From the Persian, meaning "star." The commonly used Hebrew equivalent is Ester, although the exact equivalent is Hadasa. *See* Hadasa. MASCULINE HEBREW EQUIVALENTS: Mazal, Oran, Zik. In Esther 1:7, Mordecai's young cousin, whom he raised.

Esti A pet form of Esther. *See* Esther.

Eta A variant spelling of Ita. *See* Ita.

Etana (אֵיתָנָה) From the Hebrew, meaning "strong." The exact Hebrew equivalent is Eitana. The exact masculine equivalent is Eitan. The Anglicized masculine form is Ethan.

Ethel From the Anglo-Saxon, meaning "noble." HEBREW EQUIVALENTS: Adina, Adira, Adoniya. MASCULINE HEBREW EQUIVALENTS: Achiram, Adar, Adir.

Eti A pet form of Esther. *See* Esther.

Etka (עֶטְקֶא) The Yiddish pet form of Ita and Yetta. *See* Ita *and* Yetta.

Etta A pet form of Harriet and Henrietta, meaning "mistress of the house, lord, ruler." *See* Harriet *and* Henrietta.

Etti, Etty Pet forms of Esther. *See* Esther.

Eudice A variant form of Eudit. *See* Eudit.

Eudit A variant spelling of Yudit. *See* Yudit.

Eudora From the Greek, meaning "good gift." HEBREW EQUIVALENTS: Dorona, Doronit, Matana. MASCULINE HEBREW EQUIVALENTS: Doran, Doron, Doroni.

Eugenia From the Greek, meaning "well-born." HEBREW EQUIVALENTS: Adina, Adira, Malka. MASCULINE HEBREW EQUIVALENTS: Adin, Adir, Adiv.

Eugenie The French form of Eugenia. *See* Eugenia.

Eulalia From the Greek, meaning "good talk, eulogy." HEBREW EQUIVALENTS: Amira, Doveva, Hillela. MASCULINE HEBREW EQUIVALENTS: Amarya, Dover, Hillel.

Eunice From the Greek, meaning "happy victory." HEBREW EQUIVALENTS: Dafna, Hadasa, Nitzcha. MASCULINE HEBREW EQUIVALENTS: Gevarya, Nitzchi, Yatzli'ach.

Eva A variant form of Eve. *See* Eve.

Evangeline From the Greek, meaning "bearer of glad tidings, messenger." HEBREW EQUIVALENTS: Ditza, Gila, Sisa. MASCULINE HEBREW EQUIVALENTS: Simcha, Yagil, Yitzchak.

Eve A Latin and German form, from the Hebrew, meaning "life." The exact Hebrew equivalent is Chava. MASCULINE HEBREW EQUIVALENTS: Chai, Cha'yim. In Genesis 2:23, the wife of Adam.

Eveline A variant spelling of Evelyn. *See* Evelyn.

Evelyn A pet form of Eve. *See* Eve. Also, from the Celtic, meaning "pleasant, good." HEBREW EQUIVALENTS: Achino'am, Na'ama, Na'omi. MASCULINE HEBREW EQUIVALENTS: Avino'am, Ben-Tziyon, Na'aman.

Evelyne A variant spelling of Evelyn. *See* Evelyn.

Evita A Spanish pet form of Eve. *See* Eve.

Evonne A pet form of Eva and Evelyn. *See* Eva and Evelyn. Or, a variant form of Yvonne. *See* Yvonne.

Evrona (עֶבְרוֹנָה) From the Hebrew, meaning "overflowing anger, fury." The exact Hebrew equivalent is Evrona. The exact masculine equivalent is Evron.

Evy A short form of Evelyn. *See* Evelyn.

Ezra (עֶזְרָא/עֶזְרָה) Most commonly a masculine name, but used in Israel as a unisex name. *See* Ezra (*masculine section*).

Ezraela, Ezraella (עֶזְרָאֵלָה) Variant forms of Ezra, meaning "God is my help." *See* Ezra. The exact Hebrew equivalent is Ezra'ela.

Ezriela, Ezriella (עֶזְרִיאֵלָה) Variant forms of Ezra, meaning "God is my help." *See* Ezra.

✎ F ✎

Fabia From the Greek, meaning "bean farmer." HEBREW EQUIVALENTS: Adama, Karmela, Nava. MASCULINE HEBREW EQUIVALENTS: Adam, Karmel, Karmeli.

Fabiana A feminine form of the masculine Fabian. *See* Fabian (*masculine section*).

Faga A variant spelling of Feiga. *See* Feiga.

Faiga, Faige Variant spellings of Feiga and Feige. *See* Feiga.

Faigel (פֵּייגֵל) A Yiddish pet form of Faiga. *See* Faiga.

Faith From the Anglo-Saxon, meaning "unswerving trust, hope." HEBREW EQUIVALENTS: Amana, Bitcha, Emuna. MASCULINE HEBREW EQUIVALENTS: Amitai, Amnon, Buki.

Falice, Falicia Variant spellings of Felice and Felicia. *See* Felice *and* Felicia.

Fani A variant spelling of Fannie. *See* Fannie.

Fania A pet form of Frances. *See* Frances.

Fannie, Fanny, Fannye Pet forms of Frances. *See* Frances.

Fanya A variant spelling of Fania. *See* Fania.

Farrah From the Latin, meaning "grain, fodder for cattle," or from the Old French, meaning "iron worker, blacksmith." HEBREW EQUIVA-

LENTS: Chita, Deganit, Deganya. MASCULINE HEBREW EQUIVALENTS: Barzilai, Peled, Pildash.

Fauna A variant form of Fawn. *See* Fawn.

Fawn From the Latin, meaning "young deer," or from the Middle English, meaning "friendly." HEBREW EQUIVALENTS: Amita, A'yala, A'yelet, Davida. MASCULINE HEBREW EQUIVALENTS: Amit, Amitai, Efer.

Fawna A variant form of Fawn. *See* Fawn.

Fawne A variant spelling of Fawn. *See* Fawn.

Fawnia A variant form of Fawn. *See* Fawn.

Fay, Faye From the Old French, meaning "fidelity." HEBREW EQUIVALENTS: Amana, Bitcha, Emuna. MASCULINE HEBREW EQUIVALENTS: Amit, Amitai, Amnon.

Fayette A pet form of Fay. *See* Fay.

Faygie A variant pet form of Faiga. *See* Faiga.

Feiga, Feige (פֵּייגָא/פֵּייגֶע) A Yiddish form of the German *Vogel*, meaning "bird." Also, from the Yiddish *feig*, meaning "fig." HEBREW EQUIVALENTS: Divla, Gozala, Tzipora. MASCULINE HEBREW EQUIVALENTS: Divla'yim, Tzipor, Yarkon.

Feigel (פֵּייגֶל) A variant spelling of Faigel. *See* Faigel.

Feigi A variant pet form of Feiga. *See* Feiga.

Felecia A variant spelling of Felicia. *See* Felicia.

Felecie A variant form of Felice. *See* Felice.

Felice, Felicia From the Latin, meaning "happy, fortunate." HEBREW EQUIVALENTS: Ashera, Gada, Mazal. MASCULINE HEBREW EQUIVALENTS: Adna, Asher, Gad.

Feliciana A Spanish form of Felice. *See* Felice.

Felicite, Felicity French and Spanish forms of Felice. *See* Felice.

Felisa, Felise, Felisse Variant spellings of Felice. *See* Felice.

Ferida A pet form of Frederica. *See* Frederica.

Fern, Ferne From the Anglo-Saxon, meaning "strong, brave." Also, a plant name. HEBREW EQUIVALENTS: Amitza, Ari'el, Gavri'ela, Savyon. MASCULINE HEBREW EQUIVALENTS: Amotz, Gavri'el, Narkis.

Fidelia From the Latin, meaning "faithful." HEBREW EQUIVALENTS: Amana, Bitcha, Emuna. MASCULINE HEBREW EQUIVALENTS: Amitai, Amnon, Buki.

Fidella A variant form of Fidelia. *See* Fidelia.

Fifi An African unisex name meaning "born of Friday," the sixth day of the week. Shishi is a Hebrew equivalent. Also, a pet form of Fiorella. *See* Fiorella.

Fiona From the Celtic, meaning "white." The feminine and masculine Hebrew equivalent is Livna.

Fiorella From the Italian, meaning "little flower." HEBREW EQUIVALENTS: Irit, Nitza, Shoshana. MASCULINE HEBREW EQUIVALENTS: Efra'yim, Nitzan, Shoshan.

Flavia From the Latin, meaning "yellow-haired, blond." HEBREW EQUIVALENTS: Paz, Zehava, Zahuv.

Fleur A French form of the Latin, meaning "flower." *See* Florence.

Fleurette A pet form of Fleur. *See* Fleur.

Flora From the Latin, meaning "flower." *See* Florence.

Floreen A variant form of Florence. *See* Florence.

Florella A pet form of Florence. *See* Florence.

Floren A short form of Florence. *See* Florence.

Florence From the Latin, meaning "blooming, flowery, flourishing." HEBREW EQUIVALENTS: Irit, Nitza, Pericha. MASCULINE HEBREW EQUIVALENTS: Efra'yim, Pekach, Perach.

Florentina A pet form of Florence. *See* Florence.

Floria A variant form of Flora. *See* Flora.

Floriane A hybrid name formed from Flora and Anne. *See* Flora *and* Anne.

Florrie A pet form of Flora and Florence. *See* Flora *and* Florence.

Floryn A pet form of Flora and Florence. *See* Flora *and* Florence.

Flossie A pet form of Flora and Florence. *See* Flora *and* Florence.

Fontana From the Latin, meaning "spring, fountain." HEBREW EQUIVA-
LENTS: Yam, Silona, Silonit. MASCULINE HEBREW EQUIVALENTS: Aviyam,
Ma'ayan, Silon.

Fortuna From the Latin, meaning "fate, fortune." HEBREW EQUIVALENTS:
Ashera, Gadi'ela, Me'usheret. MASCULINE HEBREW EQUIVALENTS: Asher,
Gadi'el, Mazal-Tov.

Fradel, Fradl (פְרֵיידל) A pet form of Frayda. *See* Frayda.

Fran A pet form of Frances. *See* Frances.

Francene A pet form of Frances. *See* Frances.

Frances From the Anglo-Saxon, meaning "free, liberal." HEBREW EQUIV-
ALENTS: Cheruta, Chufshit, Derora. MASCULINE HEBREW EQUIVALENTS:
Amidror, Avideror, Cherut.

Francesca An Italian form of Frances. *See* Frances.

Franci A pet form of Francine. *See* Francine.

Francine A pet form of Frances. *See* Frances.

Frani A pet form of Frances. *See* Frances.

Frankie A pet form of Frances. *See* Frances.

Frayda, Frayde Variant spellings of Freida and Freide. *See* Freida.

Freda A variant form of Frieda. *See* Frieda.

Fredda A pet form of Frederica and Frieda. *See* Frederica *and* Frieda.

Frederica The feminine form of the masculine Frederick, meaning
"peaceful ruler." HEBREW EQUIVALENTS: Malka, Menucha, Sha'anana.
MASCULINE HEBREW EQUIVALENTS: Avshalom, Ish-Shalom, Malkam.

Freida, Freide (פרֵיידְע/פרֵיידָא) From the Yiddish meaning "joy." HE-
BREW EQUIVALENTS: Aliza, Aviga'yil, Ditza. MASCULINE HEBREW EQUIVA-
LENTS: Alitz, Gil, Gili.

Frida A variant spelling of Frieda. *See* Frieda.

Frieda From the Old High German, meaning "peace." HEBREW EQUIVA-LENTS: Menucha, Sha'anana, Shalva. MASCULINE HEBREW EQUIVALENTS: Avshalom, Ish-Shalom, No'ach.

Friedel A pet form of Frieda. *See* Frieda.

Frimcha A Yiddish pet form of Fruma. *See* Fruma.

Fritzi A pet form of Frederica and Frieda. *See* Frederica *and* Frieda.

Fromet A variant spelling of Frumet. *See* Frumet.

Fruma (פְרוּמָא) From the Yiddish, meaning "pious one." HEBREW EQUIV-ALENTS: Chasida, Chasuda, Tzadika. MASCULINE HEBREW EQUIVALENTS: Chasdi'el, Chasid, Tzadik.

Frume (פרוּמֶע) A variant spelling of Fruma. *See* Fruma.

Frumet, Frumeth Variant forms of Frume. *See* Frume.

✌ G ✌

Gabi (גַּבִּי) A pet form of Gabriella. *See* Gabriella. The exact Hebrew equivalent is Gabi.

Gabriela, Gabriella Anglicized forms of Gavriela and Gavriella. *See* Gavriela.

Gabriele, Gabrielle Variant French forms of Gabriela and Gabriella. *See* Gabriela.

Gada (גָּדָה) The feminine form of Gad. *See* Gad (*masculine section*). The exact Hebrew equivalent is Gada.

Gadiela, Gadiella (גַּדִיאֵלָה) Feminine forms of Gadiel. *See* Gadiel (*masculine section*).

Gadit (גָּדִית) A variant form of Gada. *See* Gada. The exact Hebrew equivalent is Gadit.

Gafna (גַּפְנָה) The Aramaic form of Gefen. *See* Gefen. The exact Hebrew equivalent is Gafna.

Gafnit (גַּפְנִית) A variant form of Gafna. *See* Gafna. The exact Hebrew equivalent is Gafnit.

Gail A short form of Abigail. *See* Abigail.

Gal (גַּל) A unisex name. From the Hebrew, meaning "mound, hill" or "wave, fountain, spring." The exact Hebrew equivalent is Gal.

Gala A variant form of Gal. *See* Gal.

Gale A variant spelling of Gail. *See* Gail.

Gali (גְלִי) A unisex name. From the Hebrew, meaning "my wave" or "my hill." *See* Gal. The exact Hebrew equivalent is Gali.

Galia A variant spelling of Galya. *See* Galya.

Galila (גְלִילָה) From the Hebrew, meaning "roll up, roll away." The exact Hebrew equivalent is Galila. The exact masculine equivalent is Galil.

Galina The Russian form of Helen. *See* Helen.

Galit (גָלִית) A variant form of Gal. *See* Gal. The exact Hebrew equivalent is Galit.

Galiya (גְלִיָה) A variant form of Galya. *See* Galya. The exact Hebrew equivalent is Galiya.

Galya (גַלְיָה) A unisex name. From the Hebrew, meaning "wave of God" or "hill of God." The exact Hebrew equivalent is Galya.

Gamliela (גַמְלִיאֵלָה) The feminine form of Gamliel. *See* Gamliel (*masculine section*). The exact Hebrew equivalent is Gamli'ela.

Gana (גַנָה) From the Hebrew, meaning "garden." The exact Hebrew equivalent is Gana. MASCULINE HEBREW EQUIVALENTS: Ginat, Ginton.

Gania A variant spelling of Ganya. *See* Ganya.

Ganit (גַנִית) A variant form of Gana. *See* Gana. The exact Hebrew equivalent is Ganit.

Ganya (גַנְיָה) From the Hebrew, meaning "garden of the Lord." The exact Hebrew equivalent is Ganya. MASCULINE HEBREW EQUIVALENTS: Gan, Gani, Ginton.

Garnit (גָרְנִית) From the Hebrew, meaning "granary." The exact Hebrew equivalent is Garnit. MASCULINE HEBREW EQUIVALENTS: Dagan, Goren.

Garret, Garrett Used primarily as a masculine name. *See* Garret (*masculine section*).

Gat (גַּת) From the Hebrew, meaning "wine press." The exact Hebrew equivalent is Gat. MASCULINE HEBREW EQUIVALENTS: Gefanya, Giti, Yekev.

Gavi (גַּבִּי) A pet form of Gavriela. *See* Gavriela. The exact Hebrew equivalent is Gavi.

Gavriela, Gavriella (גַּבְרִיאֵלָה) From the Hebrew, meaning "heroine." The exact Hebrew equivalent is Gavri'ela. The exact masculine equivalent is Gavri'el.

Gavrila (גַּבְרִילָה) A variant form of Gavriela. *See* Gavriela. The exact Hebrew equivalent is Gavrila.

Gay From the Anglo-Saxon, meaning "gay, merry." HEBREW EQUIVA-LENTS: Aviga'yil, Gila, Giliya. MASCULINE HEBREW EQUIVALENTS: Bilgai, Gil, Gilam.

Gaya (גֵּאָה) From the Hebrew, meaning "proud." Adapted from a term used in Proverbs 8:13. The exact Hebrew equivalent is Gay'a. MASCU-LINE HEBREW EQUIVALENTS: Atzil, Efrat.

Gaye A variant spelling of Gay. *See* Gay.

Gayil (גַּיִל) From the Hebrew, meaning "wave." HEBREW EQUIVALENTS: Afeka, Bat-Yam, Einat. MASCULINE HEBREW EQUIVALENTS: Aviyam, Dal-fon, Yuval.

Gayle A variant spelling of Gail. *See* Gail.

Gayora (גֵּיאוֹרָה) From the Hebrew, meaning "valley of light." The exact Hebrew equivalent is Gayora. MASCULINE HEBREW EQUIVALENTS: Eli'or, Li'or, Me'ir.

Gazella From the Latin, meaning "gazelle, deer." HEBREW EQUIVALENTS: A'yala, A'yelet, Tzivya. MASCULINE HEBREW EQUIVALENTS: A'yal, A'yalon, Tzevi.

Gazit (גָּזִית) From the Hebrew, meaning "hewn stone." The exact Hebrew equivalent is Gazit. MASCULINE HEBREW EQUIVALENTS: Elitzur, Even, Tzuriya.

Ge'ula, Ge'ulah (גְּאוּלָה) From the Hebrew, meaning "redemption." The exact Hebrew equivalent is Ge'ula. MASCULINE HEBREW EQUIVA-LENTS: Ge'alya, Go'el, Yiga'el.

Gedera, Gederah (גְדֵרָה) From the Hebrew, meaning "fence, boundary." The exact Hebrew equivalent is Gedera. The exact masculine equivalent is Gader.

Geela, Geelah Variant spellings of Gila. *See* Gila.

Gefen, Geffen (גֶּפֶן) A unisex name. From the Hebrew, meaning "vine." The exact Hebrew equivalent is Gefen.

Gelila, Gelilah (גְלִילָה) From the Hebrew, meaning "rolling up." The exact Hebrew equivalent is Gelila. The exact masculine equivalent is Galil.

Gelima, Gelimah (גְלִימָה) From the Hebrew, meaning "cloak, mantle." The exact Hebrew equivalent is Gelima. MASCULINE HEBREW EQUIVALENTS: Salma, Simla.

Gemma From the Latin, meaning "swelling bud" or "precious stone." HEBREW EQUIVALENTS: Bareket, Chemda, Sapirit. MASCULINE HEBREW EQUIVALENTS: Avikar, Penini, Sapir.

Gena A variant spelling of Gina. *See* Gina.

Gene A pet form of Genevieve. *See* Genevieve.

Geneva From the Old French, meaning "juniper berry." Also, a variant form of Genevieve. *See* Genevieve. HEBREW EQUIVALENTS: Pora, Pori'el, Poriya. MASCULINE HEBREW EQUIVALENTS: Bar-Ilan, Efra'yim, Peri'el.

Genevieve From the Celtic, meaning "white wave." HEBREW EQUIVALENTS: Bat-Galim, Levana, Miryam. MASCULINE HEBREW EQUIVALENTS: Avigal, Lavan, Livni.

Geniza, Genizah (גְנִיזָה) From the Hebrew, meaning "hidden, storage." The exact Hebrew equivalent is Geniza. MASCULINE HEBREW EQUIVALENTS: Amon, Lot, Tzefanya.

Geona (גְאוֹנָה) From the Hebrew, meaning "esteemed scholar." The exact Hebrew equivalent is Ge'ona. The exact masculine equivalent is Ga'on.

Georgeanne A hybrid name formed from George and Anne. *See* George (*masculine section*) *and* Anne (*feminine section*).

Georgette A pet form of Georgia. *See* Georgia.

Georgia From the Greek, meaning "husbandman, farmer." HEBREW EQUIVALENTS: Gana, Karmela, Nava. MASCULINE HEBREW EQUIVALENTS: Adam, Karmel, Yizr'el.

Georgiana A variant form of Georgeanne. *See* Georgeanne.

Georgina, Georgine Pet forms of Georgia. *See* Georgia.

Geraldene, Geraldine From the Old High German, meaning "spear-wielder, warrior." HEBREW EQUIVALENTS: Gavrila, Gibora, Tigra. MASCULINE HEBREW EQUIVALENTS: Gad, Gera, Gidon.

Geralyn A hybrid name formed from Geraldine and Lyn. *See* Geraldine *and* Lyn.

Gerda From the Old High German, meaning "protected one." HEBREW EQUIVALENTS: Gana, Magena, Migdala. MASCULINE HEBREW EQUIVALENTS: Magen, Sa'adya, Shemarya.

Geri, Gerie, Gerrie, Gerry Pet forms of Geraldine. *See* Geraldine.

Gershoma (גֵּרְשׁוֹמָה) The feminine form of Gershom. *See* Gershom (*masculine section*). The exact Hebrew equivalent is Gershoma.

Gershona (גֵּרְשׁוֹנָה) The feminine form of Gershon. *See* Gershon (*masculine section*). The exact Hebrew equivalent is Gershona.

Gertrude From the Old High German, meaning "battlemaid" or "adored warrior." HEBREW EQUIVALENTS: Gada, Gavrila, Gibora. MASCULINE HEBREW EQUIVALENTS: Gad, Gera, Gevarya.

Gevira, Gevirah (גְּבִירָה) From the Hebrew, meaning "lady" or "queen." The exact Hebrew equivalent is Gevira. MASCULINE HEBREW EQUIVALENTS: Adiv, Adoniya, Gavra.

Gevura, Gevurah (גְּבוּרָה) From the Hebrew, meaning "strength." The exact Hebrew equivalent is Gevura. MASCULINE HEBREW EQUIVALENTS: Gavri'el, Gever, Gibor.

Gezira, Gezirah (גְּזִירָה) From the Hebrew, meaning "cutting, clipping." The exact Hebrew equivalent is Gezira. MASCULINE HEBREW EQUIVALENTS: Gidon, Gidoni.

Geziza, Gezizah (גְּזִיזָה) From the Hebrew, meaning "shearing" or "fragment." The exact Hebrew equivalent is Geziza. The exact masculine equivalent is Gaziz.

Ghila A variant spelling of Gila. *See* Gila.

Ghity, Ghitty Pet forms of Gitel. *See* Gitel.

Gianina An Italian form of Joanna. *See* Joanna.

Gibora, Giborah (גְּבוֹרָה) From the Hebrew, meaning "strong, heroine." The exact Hebrew equivalent is Gibora. The exact masculine equivalent is Gibor.

Gidona (גִּדְעוֹנָה) The feminine form of Gidon. *See* Gidon (*masculine section*). The exact Hebrew equivalent is Gidona.

Gidron (גִּדְרוֹן) From the Hebrew, referring to a short-tailed songbird. The exact Hebrew equivalent is Gidron. MASCULINE HEBREW EQUIVALENTS: Gozal, Tzipor, Zamir.

Gigi A pet form of Georgina. *See* Georgina.

Gigit (גִּיגִת) From the Hebrew, meaning "large bowl." The exact Hebrew equivalent is Gigit. MASCULINE HEBREW EQUIVALENTS: Kad, Kadi.

Gila, Gilah (גִּילָה) From the Hebrew, meaning "joy." The exact Hebrew equivalent is Gila. The exact masculine equivalent is Gil.

Gilada, Giladah (גִּלְעָדָה) From the Hebrew, meaning "[the] hill is [my] witness" or "joy is forever." The exact Hebrew equivalent is Gilada. The exact masculine equivalent is Gilad.

Gilana, Gilanah (גִּילָנָה) From the Hebrew, meaning "joy" or "stage of life." A variant form of Gila. *See* Gila. The exact Hebrew equivalent is Gilana.

Gilat (גִּילַת) A variant form of Gilana. *See* Gilana. The exact Hebrew equivalent is Gilat.

Gilberta, Gilberte Feminine forms of Gilbert. *See* Gilbert (*masculine section*).

Gilda (גִּלְדָה) From the Celtic, meaning "servant of God," or from the Old English, meaning "coated with gold." HEBREW EQUIVALENTS: Aleksandra, Shimshona, Zehava. MASCULINE HEBREW EQUIVALENTS: Ovadya, Shimshon, Zehavi.

Gili (גִּילִי) A unisex name. From the Hebrew, meaning "my joy." The exact Hebrew equivalent is Gili.

Gilit (גִּילִית) A variant form of Gilana. *See* Gilana. The exact Hebrew equivalent is Gilit.

Gill From the Old English, meaning "girl." HEBREW EQUIVALENTS: Alma, Betula, Na'ara. MASCULINE HEBREW EQUIVALENTS: Ben, Ben-Tziyon, Na'arai.

Gilla A variant form of Gill. *See* Gill.

Gillian A variant form of the Latin name Juliana, the feminine form of Julian. *See* Julian (*masculine section*).

Gina, Ginat (גִּינַת/גִּינָה) Unisex names. From the Hebrew, meaning "garden." The exact Hebrew equivalents are Gina and Ginat.

Ginger A pet form of Virginia. *See* Virginia.

Ginnie, Ginny Pet forms of Virginia. *See* Virginia. Also, variant forms of Jennie and Jenny. *See* Jennie *and* Jenny.

Giora (גִּיאוֹרָה) A unisex name. From the Hebrew, meaning "strong." The exact Hebrew equivalent is Gi'ora.

Giri (גִּירִי) From the Hebrew, meaning "chalky." The exact Hebrew equivalent is Giri.

Girit (גִּירִית) From the Hebrew, meaning "badger, groundhog." The exact Hebrew equivalent is Girit.

Gisa From the Anglo-Saxon, meaning "gift." HEBREW EQUIVALENTS: Dorona, Matana, Migdana. MASCULINE HEBREW EQUIVALENTS: Elnatan, Matityahu, Natan.

Gisela, Gisella From the Anglo-Saxon, meaning "bright hope of the people" or "sword." HEBREW EQUIVALENTS: Behira, Me'ira, Noga. MASCULINE HEBREW EQUIVALENTS: Uri, Uri'el, Zakai.

Giselle A variant form of Gisela. *See* Gisela.

Gita (גִיתָה) A variant form of Gitit. *See* Gitit. The exact Hebrew equivalent is Gita. *See also* Gitel.

Gitel, Gitele (גִיטְל) From the Yiddish, meaning "good." The exact Hebrew equivalent is Tova. MASCULINE HEBREW EQUIVALENTS: Achituv, Amituv, Ben-Tziyon.

Gitit (גִיתִּית) From the Hebrew, meaning "wine press." The exact Hebrew equivalent is Gitit. The masculine equivalent is Gitai.

Gittel A variant spelling of Gitel. *See* Gitel.

Gittie, Gitty Pet forms of Gitel. *See* Gitel.

Giva, Givah (גִבְעָה) A unisex name. From the Hebrew, meaning "hill, high place." The exact Hebrew equivalent is Giva.

Givona (גִבְעוֹנָה) A variant form of Giva. *See* Giva. The exact Hebrew equivalent is Givona.

Giza (גִיזָה) From the Hebrew, meaning "cut stone." The exact Hebrew equivalent is Giza. MASCULINE HEBREW EQUIVALENTS: Even, Gidon, Gidoni.

Gizela A variant spelling of Gisela. *See* Gisela.

Gladyce A variant spelling of Gladys.

Gladys A Welsh form of the Latin name Claudia, meaning "lame." Also, from the Celtic, meaning "brilliant, splendid." HEBREW EQUIVALENTS: Behira, Me'ira, Noga. MASCULINE HEBREW EQUIVALENTS: Bahir, Me'ir, Shimshon.

Glenda A variant form of Glendora or Glenna. *See* Glendora *and* Glenna.

Glendora A hybrid name formed from Glenna and Dora. *See* Glenna *and* Dora.

Glenna The feminine form of Glenn. *See* Glenn (*masculine section*).

Glikel, Glikl (גְלִיקְל) A pet form of Gluke. *See* Gluke.

Glora A variant form of Gloria. *See* Gloria.

Gloria From the Latin, meaning "glory, glorious." HEBREW EQUIVALENTS: Ahuda, Devora, Hillela. MASCULINE HEBREW EQUIVALENTS: Ahud, Gedalya, Hadar.

Gloriana A variant form of Gloria. *See* Gloria.

Glory A variant form of Gloria. *See* Gloria.

Gloryette A pet form of Glory. *See* Glory.

Gluke (גְלוּקֶע) A unisex name. From the German and Yiddish, meaning "luck, good fortune." The exact Hebrew equivalent is Mazal.

Glynda A variant form of Glenda. *See* Glenda.

Glynis, Glynnis From the British, meaning "glen, narrow valley." The Hebrew equivalent is Ga'ya. MASCULINE HEBREW EQUIVALENTS: Emek, Gai, Ge'ora.

Golda (גּוֹלְדָה) A popular Yiddish name, from the Old English and German, meaning "gold, golden." HEBREW EQUIVALENTS: Delila, Ofira, Paza. MASCULINE HEBREW EQUIVALENTS: Upaz, Zahav, Zehavi.

Goldie, Goldy Pet forms of Golda. *See* Golda.

Gomer (גֹּמֶר) A unisex name. From the Hebrew, meaning "ember" or "one who burns sweet-smelling spices." In Hosea 1:3, the wife of the prophet.

Gorala (גּוֹרָלָה) From the Hebrew, meaning "lot, lottery." The exact Hebrew equivalent is Gorala. The exact masculine equivalent is Goral.

Gozala (גּוֹזָלָה) From the Hebrew, meaning "young bird." The exact Hebrew equivalent is Gozala. The exact masculine equivalent is Gozal.

Grace From the Latin, meaning "grace." HEBREW EQUIVALENTS: Chana, Chanita, Chanya. MASCULINE HEBREW EQUIVALENTS: Elchanan, Chanan, Chanina.

Gracia The Italian form of Grace. *See* Grace.

Graciela A variant Spanish form of Grace. *See* Grace.

Greer From the Greek and Latin, meaning "guard, guardian." HEBREW EQUIVALENTS: Mishmeret, Nitzra, Notera. MASCULINE HEBREW EQUIVALENTS: Eri, Gonen, Mishmar.

Greta A Swedish pet form of Margaret. *See* Margaret.

Gretchen A German pet form of Margaret. *See* Margaret.

Gretel A variant form of Gretchen. *See* Gretchen.

Gurit (גוּרִית) From the Hebrew, meaning "young lion." The exact Hebrew equivalent is Gurit. The exact masculine equivalent is Gur.

Gussie, Gussy Popular pet forms of Augusta. *See* Augusta.

Gustine A variant form of Augusta. *See* Augusta.

Gwen From the Welsh, meaning "white, fair" or "beautiful, blessed." HEBREW EQUIVALENTS: Achino'am, Na'ama, Na'omi. MASCULINE HEBREW EQUIVALENTS: Livni, Na'aman, Yafeh.

Gwendaline, Gwendolen, Gwendoline, Gwendolyn From the Welsh, meaning "blessed ring" or "bow." HEBREW EQUIVALENTS: Beracha, Beruchya, Keshet. MASCULINE HEBREW EQUIVALENTS: Baruch, Kashti, Kish.

Gwenn, Gwenne Variant spellings of Gwen. *See* Gwen.

Gwyn A variant form of Gwen. *See* Gwen.

Gwyneth From the Welsh, meaning "happiness." HEBREW EQUIVALENTS: Aliza, Avi'gayil, Ronli. MASCULINE HEBREW EQUIVALENTS: Rani, Simcha, Yitzchak.

Gwynn, Gwynne Variant spellings of Gwyn. *See* Gwyn.

✌ H ✌

Hada A pet form of Hadasa. *See* Hadasa.

Hadar (הָדָר) A unisex name. From the Hebrew, meaning "ornamented, beautiful, honored." The exact Hebrew equivalent is Hadar.

Hadara (הֲדָרָה) A variant form of Hadar. *See* Hadar. The exact Hebrew equivalent is Hadara.

Hadarit (הֲדָרִית) A variant form of Hadar. *See* Hadar. The exact Hebrew equivalent is Hadarit.

Hadas (הֲדָס) A short form of Hadasa. *See* Hadasa. The exact Hebrew equivalent is Hadas.

Hadasa, Hadasah, Hadassa, Hadassah (הֲדַסָה) From the Hebrew, meaning "myrtle tree," a symbol of victory. The exact Hebrew equivalent is Hadasa. The exact masculine equivalent is Hadas. In Esther 2:7, the Hebrew name of Queen Esther.

Hadura (הֲדוּרָה) From the Hebrew, meaning "ornamented, beautiful." The exact Hebrew equivalent is Hadura. The exact masculine equivalent is Hadur.

Hagar (הָגָר) From the Hebrew, meaning "emigration, forsaken, stranger." The exact Hebrew equivalent is Hagar. MASCULINE HEBREW EQUIVALENTS: Gershom, Gershon, Golyat. In Genesis 16:1, the handmaid of Sarah, mother of Ishmael.

Hagia, Haggiah Variant spellings of Chagiya. *See* Chagiya.

Hagit A variant spelling of Chagit. *See* Chagit.

Haley From the Norse, meaning "hero." HEBREW EQUIVALENTS: Gavri'ela, Gavrila, Gibora. MASCULINE HEBREW EQUIVALENTS: Gavri, Gavri'el, Gever.

Halie A variant spelling of Haley. *See* Haley.

Halina From the Hawaiian, meaning "resemblance." Also, a Polish form of Helen. *See* Helen.

Halle A variant spelling of Haley. *See* Haley.

Hallela (הַלְלָה) A feminine form of Hillel. From the Hebrew, meaning "praise." The exact Hebrew equivalent is Hallela. The masculine equivalent is Hillel.

Halleli (הַלְלִי) A feminine form of Hillel. From the Hebrew, meaning "praise." The exact Hebrew equivalent is Halleli. The masculine Hebrew equivalent is Hillel.

Hallie, Hally Variant spellings of Haley. *See* Haley.

Hamisi An African unisex name, meaning "born on Thursday," the fifth day of the week. The exact Hebrew equivalent is Chamishi.

Hamutal A variant spelling of Chamutal. *See* Chamutal.

Hana A variant spelling of Chana. *See* Chana.

Hani A variant pet form of Chana. *See* Chana.

Hanit, Hanita Variant spellings of Chanit and Chanita. *See* Chanit *and* Chanita.

Hanna, Hannah Variant spellings of Hana. *See* Hana.

Happy A modern English name, meaning "joyful." HEBREW EQUIVALENTS: Aliza, Aviga'yil, Ditza, Gila. MASCULINE HEBREW EQUIVALENTS: Aliz, Eliran, Gili.

Harela (הַרְאֵלָה) The feminine form of Harel. *See* Harel (*masculine section*). The exact Hebrew equivalent is Harela.

Harmony From the Greek, meaning "unity, peace." HEBREW EQUIVALENTS: Shlomit, Shulamit, Temima. MASCULINE HEBREW EQUIVALENTS: Avshalom, Chever, Chevron.

Haron Norah spelled backwards.

Harriet, Harriette From the Old English, meaning "mistress of the house, ruler, lord." HEBREW EQUIVALENTS: Adonit, Alufa, Malka. MASCULINE HEBREW EQUIVALENTS: Adon, Adoniya, Aluf.

Hasia, Hasiah Variant spellings of Chasia. *See* Chasia.

Hasida A variant spelling of Chasida. *See* Chasida.

Hasina A variant spelling of Chasina. *See* Chasina.

Hasna A variant spelling of Chasna. *See* Chasna.

Hasya A variant spelling of Chasya. *See* Chasya.

Hava A variant spelling of Chava. *See* Chava.

Haven A unisex name. From the Old English, meaning "sanctuary, harbor." HEBREW EQUIVALENTS: Cheifa, Devira. MASCULINE HEBREW EQUIVALENTS: Devir, Nemalya, Nemu'el.

Havi A pet form of Hava. *See* Hava.

Haviva, Havivah Variant spellings of Chaviva. *See* Chaviva.

Haya A variant spelling of Chaya. *See* Chaya.

Haylee A variant spelling of Haley. *See* Haley.

Hazel From the Old English, meaning "hazel tree," connoting protection and authority. HEBREW EQUIVALENTS: Magena, Shimrit, Tzila. MASCULINE HEBREW EQUIVALENTS: Asaf, Chetzron, Lot.

Hazelbelle A hybrid name formed from Hazel and Belle. *See* Hazel *and* Belle.

Heather From the Anglo-Saxon, meaning "heath, plant, shrub." HEBREW EQUIVALENTS: Ketzi'a, Neta, Neti'a. MASCULINE HEBREW EQUIVALENTS: Narkis, Shatil, Shatul.

Heaven From the Old English, meaning "to cover," referring to the space that surrounds or seems to overarch the earth, in which the stars and planets appear. HEBREW EQUIVALENTS: Talal, Talila, Tzina. MASCULINE HEBREW EQUIVALENTS: Chupa, Shafrir.

Hedda From the German, meaning "strife, warfare." HEBREW EQUIVA-
LENTS: Amtza, Gavri'ela, Gavrila. MASCULINE HEBREW EQUIVALENTS:
Avicha'yil, Ben-Cha'yil, Naftali.

Hedi A pet form of Hedya. *See* Hedya.

Hedva, Hedvah Variant spellings of Chedva. *See* Chedva.

Hedy, Heddy Pet forms of Hedda, Hester, and Esther. *See* Hedda, Hester, *and* Esther.

Hedya (הֶדְיָה) From the Hebrew, meaning "echo [voice] of the Lord."
The exact Hebrew equivalent is Hedya. MASCULINE HEBREW EQUIVA-
LENTS: Amarya, Divri, Imri.

Hefziba, Hefzibah Anglicized forms of Cheftzi-Ba. *See* Cheftzi-Ba.

Heidi Probably a variant form of Helen and Esther. *See* Helen *and*
Esther.

Helaine A variant form of Helen. *See* Helen.

Helen From the Greek, meaning "light, bright torch." HEBREW EQUIVA-
LENTS: Ami'or, Behira, Me'ira. MASCULINE HEBREW EQUIVALENTS: Barak,
Barkai, Me'ir.

Helena A variant form of Helen. *See* Helen.

Helene The French form of Helen. *See* Helen.

Heleni A variant form of Helene. *See* Helene.

Helenmae A hybrid name formed from Helen and Mae. *See* Helen *and*
Mae.

Helga From the Old English, meaning "holy, sacred, blessed." HEBREW
EQUIVALENTS: Ashera, Beracha, Berucha. MASCULINE HEBREW EQUIVALENTS:
Asher, Baruch, Mevorach.

Heline The Hawaiian form of Helen. *See* Helen.

Hella A pet form of Helen. *See* Helen.

Helmni A pet form of Wilhelmina. *See* Wilhelmina.

Heloise A variant form of Louise. *See* Louise.

Helyne A variant form of Helen. *See* Helen.

Hemda A variant spelling of Chemda. *See* Chemda.

Hemdat A variant spelling of Chemdat. *See* Chemdat.

Hen A variant spelling of Chen. *See* Chen.

Henda, Hende (הֶענְדָע/הֶענְדָא) Variant Yiddish forms of Hene. *See* Hene.

Hendel (הֶנְדְל) A Yiddish pet form of Chana. *See* Chana.

Hene, Heneh (הֶענֶע) Yiddish pet forms of Chana. *See* Chana.

Heneleh (הֶענֶעלֶע) A Yiddish pet form of Chana. *See* Chana.

Henia (הֶענִיָא) A variant spelling of Henya. *See* Henya.

Henna (הֶענָא) A Yiddish form of Hannah. *See* Hannah.

Henrietta, Henriette Variant forms of Harriet. *See* Harriet.

Henya (הֶענִיָא) A Yiddish pet form of Henrietta. *See* Henrietta.

Hephziba, Hephzibah Variant spellings of Hefziba. *See* Hefziba.

Hepzi, Hepzia Pet forms of Hephziba. *See* Hephziba.

Hepziba, Hepzibah Variant forms of Hefziba. *See* Hefziba.

Hera From the Greek, meaning "protectress, queen." In Greek mythology, Hera was the sister and wife of Zeus, queen of the gods, and goddess of women and marriage. HEBREW EQUIVALENTS: Malka, Malki'ela, Malkiya. MASCULINE HEBREW EQUIVALENTS: Achimelech, Malki'el, Melech.

Heralda, Herolda Feminine forms of Harold. *See* Harold (*masculine section*).

Herma From the Latin, meaning "stone pillar, signpost." HEBREW EQUIVALENTS: Gal, Gilada, Giva. MASCULINE HEBREW EQUIVALENTS: Gal, Gali, Gilad, Talmai.

Hermine A variant form of Hermione. *See* Hermione.

Hermione In Greek mythology, the messenger and servant of gods. HEBREW EQUIVALENTS: Aharona, Shimshona. MASCULINE HEBREW EQUIVALENTS: Avda, Ovadya, Shimshon.

Hermona A feminine form of Hermon. *See* Hermon (*masculine section*).

Hertzela (הֶרְצֶלָה) The feminine form of Herzl. *See* Herzl (*masculine section*). The exact Hebrew equivalent is Hertzela.

Hertzliya (הֶרְצְלִיָה) A variant form of Hertzela. *See* Hertzela. The exact Hebrew equivalent is Hertzliya.

Herzlia, Herzliah Variant spellings of Hertzliya. *See* Hertzliya.

Hester The Latin form of Esther. *See* Esther.

Hesther A variant form of Hester. *See* Hester.

Hetta, Hetty Pet forms of Harriet. *See* Harriet.

Hila, Hilah (הִילָה) From the Hebrew, meaning "praise." The exact Hebrew equivalent is Hila. The masculine equivalent is Hillel. *See also* Tehila.

Hilaire The French form of Hilary. *See* Hilary.

Hilana (הִלָנָה) A variant form of Hila. *See* Hila. The exact Hebrew equivalent is Hilana.

Hilary, Hillary From the Greek and the Latin, meaning "cheerful." HEBREW EQUIVALENTS: Aviga'yil, Gilana, Gilit. MASCULINE HEBREW EQUIVALENTS: Roni, Simcha, Yitzchak.

Hilda, Hilde Short forms of Hildegard. *See* Hildegard.

Hildegard, Hildegarde, Hildergarde From the German, meaning "warrior, battlemaid." HEBREW EQUIVALENTS: Alma, Amtza, Gavri'ela. MASCULINE HEBREW EQUIVALENTS: Amotz, Gavri'el, Mordechai.

Hildi, Hildy Pet forms of Hildegard. *See* Hildegard.

Hili A pet form of Hilda and Hillela. *See* Hilda *and* Hillela.

Hilla, Hillah Variant spellings of Hila. *See* Hila.

Hillary A variant spelling of Hilary. *See* Hilary.

Hillela (הִלֶלָה) The feminine form of Hillel, meaning "praise." The exact Hebrew equivalent is Hillela. The exact masculine equivalent is Hillel.

Hillula (הִילוּלָה) From the Aramaic, meaning "joyful celebration." The exact Hebrew equivalent is Hillula. The exact feminine equivalent is Hillel.

Hilma Probably a variant form of Wilhelmina. *See* Wilhelmina.

Hinda (הִינְדָא) From the German and Yiddish, meaning "hind, deer." HEBREW EQUIVALENTS: A'yala, A'yelet, Ofra. MASCULINE HEBREW EQUIVALENTS: A'yal, Ben-Tzevi, Efer.

Hindel, Hindelle (הִינְדְל) Yiddish pet forms of Hinda. *See* Hinda.

Hindi, Hindie, Hindy (הִינְדִי) Pet forms of Hinda. *See* Hinda.

Hode, Hodeh (הָאדֶע) Yiddish forms of Hadasa. *See* Hadasa.

Hodel (הָאדְל) A Yiddish pet form of Hadasa. *See* Hadasa.

Hodi (הָאדִי) A Yiddish form of Hadasa. *See* Hadasa.

Hodia, Hodiah Variant spellings of Hodiya. *See* Hodiya.

Hodiya (הוֹדִיָה) A unisex name. From the Hebrew, meaning "God is my splendor" or "praise the Lord." The exact Hebrew equivalent is Hodiya.

Hogla, Hoglah Variant spellings of Chogla. *See* Chogla.

Holiday From the Anglo-Saxon, meaning "festive day, holiday." HEBREW EQUIVALENTS: Chagit, Chagiya, Kedosha. MASCULINE HEBREW EQUIVALENTS: Chag, Simcha, Yom-Tov.

Holis A variant spelling of Hollace. *See* Hollace.

Hollace A variant form of Haley. *See* Haley.

Holli A variant spelling of Holly. *See* Holly.

Hollis A variant spelling of Hollace. *See* Hollace.

Holly, Hollye From the Anglo-Saxon, meaning "holy." HEBREW EQUIVALENTS: Chagit, Chagiya, Devira. MASCULINE HEBREW EQUIVALENTS: Kadish, Kadosh, Yom-Tov.

Honey From the Anglo-Saxon, meaning "honey." The exact feminine and masculine equivalent is Devash.

Honor From the Latin, meaning "glory" or "respect." HEBREW EQUIVA-LENTS: Tifara, Tiferet, Yocheved. MASCULINE HEBREW EQUIVALENTS: Ami-hod, Hadar, Hod.

Honora A variant form of Honor. *See* Honor.

Honorine A pet form of Honor. *See* Honor.

Hope From the Anglo-Saxon, meaning "trust, faith." HEBREW EQUIVA-LENTS: Bitcha, Emuna, Tzipiya. MASCULINE HEBREW EQUIVALENTS: Amitai, Amnon, Ne'eman.

Horia, Horiah Variant spellings of Horiya. *See* Horiya.

Horiya, Horiyah (הוֹרִיָה) From the Hebrew, meaning "teaching of the Lord." The exact Hebrew equivalent is Horiya. MASCULINE HEBREW EQUIVALENTS: Aharon, Moran, Mori.

Hortense From the Latin, meaning "gardener." HEBREW EQUIVALENTS: Adama, Gana, Karmela. MASCULINE HEBREW EQUIVALENTS: Adam, Ginat, Karmel.

Hude, Hudes (הוּדְעַס/הוּדְע) Yiddish forms of Hadasa. *See* Hadasa. Also used as nicknames for Yehudit. *See* Yehudit.

Hudel (הוּדל) A pet form of Hude. *See* Hude.

Hulda, Huldah Variant spellings of Chulda. *See* Chulda.

Hyacinth A plant of the lily family, with narrow leaves and bell-shaped fragrant flowers. HEBREW EQUIVALENTS: Chavatzelet, Perach, Yasmina. MASCULINE HEBREW EQUIVALENTS: Nitzan, Perachya, Yasmin.

Ida From the Old English, meaning "fortunate warrior," or from the Old Norse, meaning "industrious." Also, from the Greek, meaning "happy." HEBREW EQUIVALENTS: Aliza, Aviga'yil, Ditza. MASCULINE HEBREW EQUIVALENTS: Amel, Simcha, Yachdi'el.

Idalee A hybrid name formed from Ida and Lee. *See* Ida *and* Lee.

Idel, Idella, Idelle Pet forms of Ida. *See* Ida.

Idena A hybrid name formed from Ida and Dena (Dinah). *See* Ida *and* Dena.

Idette A pet form of Ida. *See* Ida.

Idit (אִידִית) From the Hebrew, meaning "superior, choicest." The exact Hebrew equivalent is Idit. MASCULINE HEBREW EQUIVALENTS: Adif, Mivchar, Nivchar. Also, a Yiddish form of the Hebrew name Yehudit (Judith).

Idra (אִדְרָא/אִדְרָה) From the Aramaic, meaning "bone of a fish" or "fig tree," a symbol of scholarship. The exact Hebrew equivalent is Idra. MASCULINE HEBREW EQUIVALENTS: Aluf, Divla'yim, Mori'el.

Idria A variant spelling of Idriya. *See* Idriya.

Idrit (אִדְרִית) A variant form of Idriya. *See* Idriya. The exact Hebrew equivalent is Idrit.

Idriya (אִדְרִיָה) From the Hebrew, meaning "duck." The exact Hebrew equivalent is Idriya. The masculine equivalent is Barvaz.

Ieda A variant spelling of Ida. *See* Ida.

Ila A variant form of Ilit. *See* Ilit.

Ilana (אִילָנָה) From the Hebrew, meaning "tree." The exact Hebrew equivalent is Ilana. The exact masculine equivalent is Ilan.

Ilanit (אִלָנִית) A variant form of Ilana. *See* Ilana. The exact Hebrew equivalent is Ilanit.

Ileana A hybrid name formed from Ilene and Ana. *See* Ilene *and* Ana.

Ilene A variant spelling of Eileen. *See* Eileen.

Ilisa, Ilise Variant forms of Elisabeth. *See* Elisabeth.

Ilit (עָלִית) From the Aramaic, meaning "uppermost, superlative." The exact Hebrew equivalent is Ilit. MASCULINE HEBREW EQUIVALENTS: Adif, Ula.

Ilita (עָלִיתָה) A variant form of Ilit. *See* Ilit. The exact Hebrew equivalent is Ilita.

Ilona A Hungarian variant form of the Greek name Helen, meaning "light, bright torch." *See* Helen.

Ilsa, Ilse Variant forms of Elisabeth. *See* Elisabeth.

Ilyse A variant form of Elisabeth. *See* Elisabeth.

Ima, Imma (אִמָא) From the Hebrew, meaning "mother." The exact Hebrew equivalent is Imma.

Imogen, Imogene From the Latin, meaning "image, likeness." HEBREW EQUIVALENTS: Michal, Micha'ela. MASCULINE HEBREW EQUIVALENTS: Micha, Micha'el.

Imra (אִמְרָה) From the Hebrew, meaning "motto, statement" or "hem, border." The exact Hebrew equivalent is Imra. MASCULINE HEBREW EQUIVALENTS: Amarya, Dovev, Imri.

Ina, Inna From the Latin, meaning "mother." The exact Hebrew equivalent is Imma.

Inbal (אִנְבָּל) A unisex name. Probably from the Greek, referring to the metallic clapper in a bell that creates the ringing sound. The exact Hebrew equivalent is Inbal.

Indira From the Sanskrit, meaning "beauty." HEBREW EQUIVALENTS: Hadura, Na'ama, Nava. HEBREW EQUIVALENTS: Adin, Hadar, Ne'edar.

Inez From the Greek and Portuguese, meaning "pure." HEBREW EQUIVALENTS: Penuya, Zaka, Zakit. MASCULINE HEBREW EQUIVALENTS: Amizakai, Tzach, Tzachai.

Inga, Inge From the Old English, meaning "meadow." HEBREW EQUIVALENTS: Gana, Ganit, Sharona, Yardena. MASCULINE HEBREW EQUIVALENTS: Gani, Sharon, Yarden.

Inger A variant form of Inga. *See* Inga.

Ingrid From the Old English, meaning "Ing's ride." In Norse mythology, Ing is the god of fertility and peace. HEBREW EQUIVALENTS: Pora, Poriya, Shulamit. MASCULINE HEBREW EQUIVALENTS: Efra'yim, Shalom, Shlomo.

Iola From the Greek, meaning "morning clouds." HEBREW EQUIVALENTS: Anana, Tzafra, Tzefira. MASCULINE HEBREW EQUIVALENTS: Anan, Anani, Hevel.

Iora From the Latin, meaning "gold." HEBREW EQUIVALENTS: Ofira, Paz, Zehava. MASCULINE HEBREW EQUIVALENTS: Elifaz, Ofar, Zehavi.

Irena A Polish form of Irene. *See* Irene.

Irene From the Greek, meaning "peace." HEBREW EQUIVALENTS: Margaya, Rivka, Sha'anana, Shlomit. MASCULINE HEBREW EQUIVALENTS: Avshalom, Sha'anan, Shalom, Shelomo.

Irenee A variant form of Irene. *See* Irene.

Irina A variant form of Irena. *See* Irena.

Iris In Greek mythology, the goddess of the rainbow. From the Latin, meaning "faith, hope." HEBREW EQUIVALENTS: Amana, Bitcha, Emuna. MASCULINE HEBREW EQUIVALENTS: Amitai, Amnon, Ne'eman.

Irit (עִירִית) From the Hebrew, meaning "animal fodder." The exact Hebrew equivalent is Irit. MASCULINE HEBREW EQUIVALENTS: Garnit, Goren, Shachat.

Irma From the Anglo-Saxon, meaning "noble maid." HEBREW EQUIVALENTS: Alma, Batya, Nediva. MASCULINE HEBREW EQUIVALENTS: Aminadav, Nadav, Yisra'el.

Isa A pet form of Isabel, used chiefly in Scotland. *See* Isabel.

Isaaca (יִצְחָקָה) The feminine form of Isaac, meaning "laughter." *See* Isaac (*masculine section*). The exact Hebrew equivalent is Yitzchaka.

Isabel, Isabele, Isabella, Isabelle Variant forms of Elisabeth, meaning "God's oath." *See* Elisabeth.

Isadora, Isidora Feminine forms of the masculine name Isadore. *See* Isadore (*masculine section*).

Iscah A variant spelling of Yiscah. *See* Yiscah.

Isobel A variant Scottish spelling of Isabel. *See* Isabel.

Israela An Anglicized spelling of Yisraela. *See* Yisraela.

Ita (אִיטָא) From the Celtic, meaning "thirsty." Also, a corrupt Yiddish form of Yehudit (Judith) and a variant form of Yetta. *See* Yehudit *and* Yetta.

Iti (אִתִּי) From the Hebrew, meaning "with me." The exact Hebrew equivalent is Iti. MASCULINE HEBREW EQUIVALENTS: Itai, Iti'el.

Itia A variant spelling of Itiya. *See* Itiya.

Itiya (אִיתִּיָה) From the Hebrew, meaning "God is with me." The exact Hebrew equivalent is Itiya. MASCULINE HEBREW EQUIVALENTS: Itai, Iti'el.

Itka A pet form of Ita. *See* Ita.

Itta A variant spelling of Ita. *See* Ita.

Itti A variant spelling of Iti. *See* Iti.

Ivana, Ivanna Feminine forms of Ivan, the Russian form of John. *See* John (*masculine section*).

Ivette A variant spelling of Yvette. *See* Yvette.

Ivria, Ivriah Variant spellings of Ivriya. *See* Ivriya.

Ivrit (עִבְרִית) From the Hebrew, meaning "Hebrew [language]." The exact Hebrew equivalent is Ivrit. The exact masculine equivalent is Ivri.

Ivrita A variant form of Ivrit. *See* Ivrit.

Ivriya (עִבְרִיָה) The feminine form of Ivri. *See* Ivri (*masculine section*). The exact Hebrew equivalent is Ivriya. The exact masculine equivalent is Ivri.

Ivy From the Middle English, meaning "vine." HEBREW EQUIVALENTS: Gafna, Gafnit, Gefen. MASCULINE HEBREW EQUIVALENTS: Carmel, Gafni, Kerem.

❦ J ❦

Jackee A pet form of Jacoba and Jacqueline. *See* Jacoba *and* Jacqueline.

Jacklyn A variant form of Jacqueline. *See* Jacqueline. Also, a hybrid name formed from Jack and Lyn. *See* Jack (*masculine section*) *and* Lyn.

Jacky A pet form of Jacqueline. *See* Jacqueline.

Jaclyn, Jaclynn Variant forms of Jacqueline. *See* Jacqueline.

Jacoba (יַעֲקֹבָה) The feminine form of Jacob. *See* Jacob (*masculine section*). The exact Hebrew equivalent is Ya'akova. The exact masculine equivalent is Ya'akov.

Jacque A pet form of Jacqueline. *See* Jacqueline.

Jacqueline A French form of Jacoba. *See* Jacoba.

Jacquelyn, Jacquelyne, Jacquelynne Variant spellings of Jacqueline. *See* Jacqueline.

Jacqui, Jacquie Pet forms of Jacqueline. *See* Jacqueline.

Jade From the French and Spanish, referring to a "stone of the side," so called because it was thought to cure pains in the side. Jade is a hard stone, usually green or white, used in jewelry and artistic carvings. HEBREW EQUIVALENTS: Adi, Adi'ela, Hadara. MASCULINE HEBREW EQUIVALENTS: Adin, Atir, Ravid.

Jael A variant spelling of Yael. *See* Yael.

Jaen A variant spelling of Yaen. *See* Yaen.

Jaffa A variant spelling of Yafa. *See* Yafa.

Jafit A variant spelling of Yafit. *See* Yafit.

Jaime, Jaimee, Jaimie, Jami, Jamie Feminine forms of James, derived from Jacob, meaning "to supplant" or "to protect." The exact Hebrew equivalent is Ya'akova. The exact masculine equivalent is Ya'akov.

Jan A pet form of Janice or Jeanette. *See* Janice *and* Jeanette.

Jane A variant English form of Johanna. *See* Johanna. Also, a feminine form of John. *See* John (*masculine section*).

Janel, Janell, Janelle Pet forms of Jane. *See* Jane.

Janet An English and Scottish form of Johanna. *See* Johanna.

Janetta An English form of Johanna. *See* Johanna.

Janette A variant spelling of Janet. *See* Janet.

Jani A pet form of Jane. *See* Jane.

Janice A variant form of Jane. *See* Jane.

Janie A pet form of Jane. *See* Jane.

Janiece A variant spelling of Janice. *See* Janice.

Janina, Janine Pet forms of Jane. *See* Jane.

Janis A variant spelling of Janice. *See* Janice.

Janita A Spanish pet form of Jane. *See* Jane.

Janlori A hybrid name formed from Jan and Lori. *See* Jan *and* Lori.

Janna A pet form of Johanna. *See* Johanna.

Jardena A variant spelling of Yardena. *See* Yardena.

Jardenia A variant spelling of Yardeniya. *See* Yardeniya.

Jasmina (יַסְמִינָה) A variant form of Jasmine. *See* Jasmine. The exact Hebrew equivalent is Yasmina.

Jasmine (יַסְמִין) A Persian flower-name, usually referring to a flower in the olive family. The exact Hebrew equivalent is Yasmin. MASCULINE HEBREW EQUIVALENTS: Za'yit, Zefan.

Jaymee A variant spelling of Jamie. *See* Jamie.

Jean, Jeane, Jeanee Scottish forms of Johanna. *See* Johanna.

Jeanetta, Jeanette French forms of Johanna. *See* Johanna.

Jeanice A variant form of Jean. *See* Jean.

Jeanie A variant form of Jean. *See* Jean.

Jeanine A pet form of Jean. *See* Jean.

Jeanne A French form of Johanna. *See* Johanna.

Jeannette A variant spelling of Jeanette. *See* Jeanette.

Jeannine A variant spelling of Jeanine. *See* Jeanine.

Jedida, Jedidah Variant spellings of Yedida. *See* Yedida.

Jehane, Jehanne French forms of Johanna. *See* Johanna.

Jemima A variant spelling of Yemima. *See* Yemima.

Jemina A variant spelling of Yemina. *See* Yemina.

Jen A short form of Jeanette. *See* Jeanette. Also, a pet form of Jennifer. *See* Jennifer.

Jena From the Arabic, meaning "little bird." HEBREW EQUIVALENTS: Da'ya, Gozala, Tzipora. MASCULINE HEBREW EQUIVALENTS: A'ya, Gozal, Tzipor.

Jenat A variant form of Jeanette. *See* Jeanette.

Jene A variant spelling of Jean. *See* Jean.

Jenerette A pet form of Jane. *See* Jane.

Jenessa A variant form of Jeanette. *See* Jeanette.

Jenine A pet form of Jane. *See* Jane.

Jenna A variant form of Jeanette. *See* Jeanette.

Jennie A pet form of Jean, Jeanette, or Jennifer. *See* Jean, Jeanette, *and* Jennifer.

Jennifer From the Welsh, meaning "friend of peace." HEBREW EQUIVA-LENTS: Menucha, Sha'anana, Shalviya. MASCULINE HEBREW EQUIVALENTS: Avshalom, Ish-Shalom, Shalom.

Jennilee A hybrid name formed from Jennifer and Lee. *See* Jennifer *and* Lee.

Jenny A variant spelling of Jennie. *See* Jennie.

Jeralee A pet form of Geraldine. *See* Geraldine.

Jeralyn A variant spelling of Geralyn. *See* Geralyn.

Jeri, Jerri Pet forms of Geraldene. *See* Geraldene.

Jerriann A hybrid name formed from Jerri (Jerry) and Ann. *See* Jerry (*masculine section*) *and* Ann.

Jerrilyn A hybrid name formed from Jerri (Jerry) and Lyn. *See* Jerry (*masculine section*) *and* Lyn.

Jessica A variant form of Jessie. *See* Jessie.

Jessie, Jessye A Scottish form of Johanna. *See* Johanna. Also, a feminine form of Jesse. *See* Jesse (*masculine section*).

Jethra (יִתְרָה) A feminine form of Jethro, meaning "abundance, riches." *See* Jethro (*masculine section*). The exact Hebrew equivalent is Yitra.

Jewel, Jewell From the Old French, meaning "joy." HEBREW EQUIVA-LENTS: Aliza, Ditza, Gila, Rina. MASCULINE HEBREW EQUIVALENTS: Simcha, Yagil, Yitzchak.

Jewelia, Jewlia Variant spellings of Julia. *See* Julia.

Jill A variant spelling of Gill. *See* Gill.

Jillian A variant spelling of Gillian. *See* Gillian.

Jo A pet form of Josephine. *See* Josephine.

Joal A feminine form of Joel. *See* Joel (*masculine section*).

Joan A variant form of Johanna. *See* Johanna.

Joann, Jo Ann Short forms of Joanna. *See* Joanna.

Joanna A short form of Johanna. *See* Johanna.

Jo-Anne A hybrid name formed from Jo (Josephine) and Ann (e). *See* Josephine *and* Ann (e).

Joanne A variant spelling of Joann. *See* Joann.

Jocelin, Joceline German forms of the name Jacoba, the feminine form of Jacob, meaning "supplant" or "protect." The exact Hebrew equivalent is Ya'akova. The exact masculine equivalent is Ya'akov.

Jocelyn, Jocelyne Variant spellings of Jocelin. *See* Jocelin.

Jodeth A variant form of Yehudit (Judith). *See* Judith.

Jodette A French form of Jocelin or Jodi. *See* Jocelin *and* Jodi.

Jodi, Jodie, Jody Pet forms of Judith. *See* Judith. Also, pet forms of Josephine. *See* Josephine.

Joei A variant spelling of Joey, a pet form of Josephine. *See* Josephine.

Joela, Joella (יוֹאֵלָה) Feminine forms of Joel, meaning "God is willing." The exact Hebrew equivalent is Yo'ela. The exact masculine equivalent is Yo'el.

Joelle A unisex name. A variant form of Joel or Joela. *See* Joel (*masculine section*) *and* Joela (*feminine section*).

Joellen A variant form of Joelynn. *See* Joelynn.

Joely A feminine form of Joel. *See* Joel (*masculine section*).

Joelynn A hybrid name formed from Joela and Lynn. *See* Joela *and* Lynn.

Joette A feminine pet form of the masculine name Joseph. *See* Joseph (*masculine section*).

Joey A pet form of Josephine. *See* Josephine.

Johan, Johanna, Johanne German and English forms of the Hebrew masculine name Yochanan, meaning "God is gracious." HEBREW EQUIVALENTS: Chana, Yochana. The exact masculine Hebrew equivalent is Yochanan.

Johanne, Johnelle Variant forms of Johanna. *See* Johanna.

Johnetta A pet form of John. *See* John (*masculine section*).

Johnna A variant form of Johanna. *See* Johanna.

Joice A variant spelling of Joyce. *See* Joyce.

Jolanda, Jolanta Variant spellings of Yolande. *See* Yolande.

Jolene A pet form of Jolie. *See* Jolie.

Joletta A pet form of Jolie. *See* Jolie.

Jolie From the French, meaning "high spirits, good humor, pleasant." HEBREW EQUIVALENTS: Achino'am, Adina, Adiva. MASCULINE HEBREW EQUIVALENTS: Achino'am, Adin, Adiv.

Joliet A variant form of Jolie or Juliet. *See* Jolie *and* Juliet.

Jonina A variant spelling of Yonina. *See* Yonina.

Jonit, Jonita Variant spellings of Yonit and Yonita. *See* Yonit.

Jordana, Jordena Feminine forms of Jordan. *See* Jordan (*masculine section*).

Jordi, Jordie, Jordyn Pet forms of Jordana. *See* Jordana.

Joscelin An Old French form of Jocelin. *See* Jocelin.

Joscelind A variant form of Jocelin. *See* Jocelin.

Josefa, Josepha Variant spellings of Yosifa. *See* Yosifa.

Josephine A feminine French form of Joseph. *See* Joseph (*masculine section*).

Josetta, Josette Pet forms of Jocelyn and Josephine. *See* Jocelyn *and* Josephine.

Joslyn A variant spelling of Jocelyn. *See* Jocelyn.

Jovita A Spanish pet form of Joy. *See* Joy.

Joy A short form of Joyce. *See* Joyce.

Joya A variant form of Joy. *See* Joy.

Joyce From the Latin, meaning "jovial, merry." HEBREW EQUIVALENTS: Avigal, Aviga'yil, Gila. MASCULINE HEBREW EQUIVALENTS: Ranon, Yagil, Yitzchak.

Judi, Judie Pet forms of Judith. *See* Judith.

Judith An Anglicized form of Yehudit. *See* Yehudit.

Judy A pet form of Judith. *See* Judith.

Judythe A variant spelling of Judith. *See* Judith.

Jule A variant form of Julia. *See* Julia.

Julee A variant spelling of Julie. *See* Julie.

Juleen A variant form of Julia. *See* Julia.

Jules A variant form of Julia. *See* Julia.

Julia From the Greek, meaning "soft-haired," symbolizing youth. HEBREW EQUIVALENTS: Alma, Aviva, Delila. MASCULINE HEBREW EQUIVALENTS: Aviv, Elam, Se'orim.

Julian, Juliana Variant forms of Julia. *See* Julia.

Julianne A hybrid name formed from Julie and Anne. *See* Julie *and* Anne.

Julie A pet form of Julia. *See* Julia.

Julienne A French form of Julia. *See* Julia.

Juliet A French pet form of Julia. *See* Julia.

Julieta A pet form of Julia. *See* Julia.

Juliette A French pet form of Julia. *See* Julia.

June From the Latin, meaning "ever youthful." HEBREW EQUIVALENTS: Aviva, Tze'ira, Yenika. MASCULINE HEBREW EQUIVALENTS: Aviv, Avrech, Elino'ar.

Justina, Justine Feminine forms of Justin. *See* Justin (*masculine section*).

～ K ～

Kada, Kadda (כַּדָה) Feminine forms of the masculine name Kad. *See* Kad (*masculine section*).

Kadia A variant spelling of Kadiya. *See* Kadiya.

Kadisha (קְדִישָׁה) From the Hebrew, meaning "holy." The exact Hebrew equivalent is Kadisha. The exact masculine equivalent is Kadish.

Kadit (כַּדִּית) From the Hebrew, meaning "small jug." The exact Hebrew equivalent is Kadit. MASCULINE HEBREW EQUIVALENTS: Kad, Kadi.

Kadiya (כַּדְיָה) From the Hebrew, meaning "pitcher." The exact Hebrew equivalent is Kadiya. The exact masculine equivalent is Kadi.

Kadya A variant form of Kadiya. *See* Kadiya.

Kaethe A variant form of Kathy. *See* Kathy.

Kaf (כַּף) From the Hebrew, meaning "spoon" or "cliff." The exact Hebrew equivalent is Kaf. MASCULINE HEBREW EQUIVALENTS: Gal, Harel, Talmai.

Kai A variant spelling of Kay. *See* Kay.

Kaile, Kaille Variant forms of Kelila. *See* Kelila.

Kalanit (כַּלָּנִית) A cup-shaped plant with colorful flowers, grown in Israel. The exact Hebrew equivalent is Kalanit. MASCULINE HEBREW EQUIVALENTS: Chavakuk, Shatil, Tzemach.

Kalee, Kaley Variant forms of Kelli. *See* Kelli.

Kalia A variant form of Kelila. *See* Kelila.

Kalila From the Arabic, meaning "beloved." HEBREW EQUIVALENTS: Ahava, Ahuva, Chaviva. MASCULINE HEBREW EQUIVALENTS: Ahuv, Chaviva, Dodi.

Kamilla A variant spelling of Camilla. *See* Camilla.

Kanaf (כָּנָף) From the Hebrew, meaning "wing" or "fringe." The exact Hebrew equivalent is Kanaf.

Kara A pet form of Katherine. *See* Katherine.

Karan A variant spelling of Karen. *See* Karen.

Karen A Danish form of Katherine. *See* Katherine.

Kari A variant spelling of Carrie. *See* Carrie.

Karin, Karine A variant spelling of Karen. *See* Karen.

Karina A pet form of Karen. *See* Karen.

Karla A feminine form of Karl. *See* Karl (*masculine section*).

Karleen A pet form of Karla. *See* Karla.

Karlene A pet form of Karla. *See* Karla.

Karlyn A diminutive form of Karla. *See* Karla.

Karma A variant spelling of Carma. *See* Carma.

Karmel A variant spelling of Carmel. *See* Carmel.

Karmela A variant spelling of Carmela. *See* Carmela.

Karmeli A variant spelling of Carmeli. *See* Carmeli.

Karmelit A variant spelling of Carmelit. *See* Carmelit.

Karmit A variant spelling of Carmit. *See* Carmit.

Karmiya A variant spelling of Carmia. *See* Carmia.

Karna A variant spelling of Carna. *See* Carna.

Karni A variant spelling of Carni. *See* Carni.

Karnia A variant spelling of Carnia. *See* Carnia.

Karniela, Karniella Variant spellings of Carniela. *See* Carniela.

Karnit A variant form of Carna. *See* Carna.

Karol, Karole Variant spellings of Carol. *See* Carol.

Karolina The Polish form of Karolyn. *See* Karolyn.

Karolyn A variant spelling of Carolyn and Caroline. *See* Caroline.

Karon A variant spelling of Karen. *See* Karen.

Karyl A variant spelling of Carol. *See* Carol.

Karyn A variant spelling of Karen. *See* Karen.

Kaspit (כַּסְפִּית) From the Hebrew, meaning "mercury, quicksilver." The exact Hebrew equivalent is Kaspit. MASCULINE HEBREW EQUIVALENTS: Kaspi, Kesef.

Katania, Kataniya (קְטַנְיָה) From the Hebrew, meaning "small." The exact Hebrew equivalent is Kataniya. The exact masculine equivalent is Katan.

Kate, Katee Pet forms of Katherine. *See* Katherine.

Katharine A variant spelling of Katherine. *See* Katherine.

Kathe A pet form of Katherine. *See* Katherine.

Katherine From the Greek, meaning "pure, unsullied." Catherine is the more popular spelling. HEBREW EQUIVALENTS: Berura, Penuya, Zaka. MASCULINE HEBREW EQUIVALENTS: Amizakai, Barur, Tzach.

Kathie A pet form of Katherine. *See* Katherine.

Kathleen A variant spelling of Cathleen. *See* Cathleen.

Kathryn A variant spelling of Katherine. *See* Katherine.

Kathy A pet form of Katherine. *See* Katherine.

Kati, Katie Pet forms of Katherine. *See* Katherine.

Katrin, Katrina, Katrine Variant forms of Katherine. *See* Katherine.

Katy A pet form of Katherine. *See* Katherine.

Kay From the Greek, meaning "rejoice." *See* Joyce. Also, a variant form of Katherine. *See* Katherine.

Kayla, Kayle (קיילע/קיילא) Variant forms of Kelila. Also, a Yiddish form of Celia. *See* Celia *and* Kelila.

Kedma (קֶדְמָה) A unisex name. From the Hebrew, meaning "east, eastward." The exact Hebrew equivalent is Kedma.

Kedusha, Kedushah (קְדוּשָׁה) From the Hebrew, meaning "holy." The exact Hebrew equivalent is Kedusha. MASCULINE HEBREW EQUIVALENTS: Devir, Kadosh, Yom-Tov.

Kefira (כְּפִירָה) From the Hebrew, meaning "young lioness." The exact Hebrew equivalent is Kefira. The exact masculine equivalent is Kefir.

Kelci A variant spelling of Kelsey. *See* Kelsey.

Kelila (כְּלִילָה) From the Hebrew, meaning "crown" or "laurels." The exact Hebrew equivalent is Kelila. MASCULINE HEBREW EQUIVALENTS: Kalil, Kalul.

Kelley A unisex name. From the Cornish, meaning "wood grove," or from the Irish, meaning "warlike." Also, a variant form of Kelsey. HEBREW EQUIVALENTS: Arza, Ilana, Livnat. MASCULINE HEBREW EQUIVALENTS: Efyon, Erez, Ilan.

Kelli, Kellie, Kelly Variant spellings of Kelley. *See* Kelley.

Kelsey A unisex name. *See* Kelsey (*masculine section*).

Kelula (כְּלוּלָה) A variant form of Kelila. *See* Kelila. The exact Hebrew equivalent is Kelula.

Kendra A feminine form of Kendrick. *See* Kendrick (*masculine section*). Also, a modern creation from the Old English, meaning "knowledge, learning." HEBREW EQUIVALENTS: Da'at, Dei'a. MASCULINE HEBREW EQUIVALENTS: Bina, Dati'el, Yedi'el.

Kenna From the Old Norse, meaning "to have knowledge." HEBREW EQUIVALENTS: Buna, Chochma, Ge'ona. MASCULINE HEBREW EQUIVALENTS: Bina, Buna, Navon.

Kerem (כֶּרֶם) A unisex name. From the Hebrew, meaning "vineyard." The exact Hebrew equivalent is Kerem.

Keren (קֶרֶן) From the Hebrew, meaning "horn." The exact Hebrew equivalent is Keren.

Keret (קֶרֶת) From the Hebrew, meaning "city, settlement." The exact Hebrew equivalent is Keret. MASCULINE HEBREW EQUIVALENTS: Dur, Devir, Zevul, Zevulun.

Kerry From the Gaelic, meaning "black-haired person." Also, a county in southwest Ireland after which a breed of dairy cattle is named. HEBREW EQUIVALENTS: Adara, Dala, Nima, Shechora. MASCULINE HEBREW EQUIVALENTS: Adar, Cham, Guni, Pinchas.

Keryn A variant spelling of Keren. *See* Keren.

Keset (כֶּסֶת) From the Hebrew, meaning "quilt, featherbed." The exact Hebrew equivalent is Keset.

Keshet (קֶשֶׁת) From the Hebrew, meaning "bow, rainbow." The exact Hebrew equivalent is Keshet. MASCULINE HEBREW EQUIVALENTS: Kashti, Raviv, Tal.

Keshira, Keshirah (קְשִׁירָה) From the Hebrew, meaning "knot, tie." The exact Hebrew equivalent is Keshira. The masculine equivalent is Kesher.

Keshisha, Keshishah (קְשִׁישָׁה) From the Hebrew, meaning "old, elder." The exact Hebrew equivalent is Keshisha. MASCULINE HEBREW EQUIVALENTS: Yashish, Yeshishai, Zaken.

Keshura, Keshurah (קְשׁוּרָה) From the Hebrew, meaning "tied." The exact Hebrew equivalent is Keshura. The exact masculine equivalent is Kesher.

Kesima, Kesimah (קְסִימָה) From the Hebrew, meaning "enchantment, magic, witchcraft." The exact Hebrew equivalent is Kesima. The exact masculine equivalent is Kesem.

Ketana (קְטַנָה) From the Hebrew, meaning "small." The exact Hebrew equivalent is Ketana. The exact masculine equivalent is Katan.

Ketaniya (קְטַנְיָה) A variant form of Kataniya. *See* Kataniya. The exact Hebrew equivalent is Ketaniya.

Ketifa (קְטִיפָה) From the Hebrew and Arabic, meaning "picking [flowers, fruit]." The exact Hebrew equivalent is Ketifa. MASCULINE HEBREW EQUIVALENTS: Achazya, Gidon, Kotz.

Ketina (קְטִינָה/קְטִינָא) From the Aramaic, meaning "minor" or "small child." The exact Hebrew equivalent is Ketina. The exact masculine equivalent is Katan.

Ketura, Keturah (קְטוּרָה) From the Hebrew, meaning "spice, incense." The exact Hebrew equivalent is Ketura. MASCULINE HEBREW EQUIVALENTS: Mivsam, Mov, Tzeri. In Genesis 25:1, Abraham's third wife, whom he married after Sarah's death.

Ketzia, Ketziah (קְצִיעָה) From the Hebrew, meaning "a powdered, fragrant, cinnamon-like bark." The exact Hebrew equivalent is Ketzi'a. The masculine equivalent is Bosem. In Job 22:14, the second daughter of Job.

Kevuda, Kevudah (כְּבוּדָה) From the Hebrew, meaning "precious" or "respected." The exact Hebrew equivalent is Kevuda. The exact masculine equivalent is Kavud.

Kezi A pet form of Ketzia. *See* Ketzia.

Kezia, Keziah Variant spellings of Ketzia. *See* Ketzia.

Kezzi, Kezzie, Kezzy Pet forms of Ketzia. *See* Ketzia.

Kicki, Kiki Pet forms of Kristina. *See* Kristina.

Kiley From the Gaelic, meaning "graceful, beautiful." HEBREW EQUIVALENTS: Na'ama, Nava, Noya. MASCULINE HEBREW EQUIVALENTS: Adin, Hadar, Shapir.

Kim A pet form of Kimberly. *See* Kimberly.

Kimberley, Kimberly A unisex name derived from "kimberlite," a type of rock formation that sometimes contains diamonds. HEBREW EQUIVALENTS: Yahaloma, Yahalomit. The masculine equivalent is Yahalom.

Kinneret (כִּנֶּרֶת) From the Hebrew, meaning "harp." The name given to the harp-shaped lake (Sea of Galilee) in Israel. The exact Hebrew equivalent is Kinneret. The masculine equivalent is Kinori.

Kira, Kirah (כִּירָה) From the Hebrew, meaning "stove." The exact Hebrew equivalent is Kira. Also, a variant spelling of Kyra. *See* Kyra.

Kirsten, Kirstin From the Old English, meaning "stone, church." HE-BREW EQUIVALENTS: Devira, Gazit. MASCULINE HEBREW EQUIVALENTS: Devir, Even-Ezer.

Kit A pet form of Katherine. *See* Katherine.

Kitra (כִּתְרָא) From the Aramaic, meaning "crown." The exact Hebrew equivalent is Kitra. The masculine equivalent is Kitron.

Kitrit (כִּתְרִית) A variant form of Kitra. *See* Kitra. The exact Hebrew equivalent is Kitrit.

Kitron (כִּתְרוֹן) A unisex name. From the Hebrew, meaning "crown." The exact Hebrew equivalent is Kitron.

Kitty A pet form of Katherine. *See* Katherine.

Klara A variant spelling of Clara. *See* Clara.

Kobi, Koby Pet forms of the Hebrew name Yaakova. *See* Yaakova.

Kochava (כּוֹכָבָה) From the Hebrew, meaning "star." The exact Hebrew equivalent is Kochava. The exact masculine equivalent is Kochav.

Kochavit (כּוֹכָבִית) A variant form of Kochava. *See* Kochava.

Kokhava A variant spelling of Kochava. *See* Kochava.

Komema (קוֹמֶמָה) From the Hebrew, meaning "independent, well-established, upright." The exact Hebrew equivalent is Komema. The exact masculine equivalent is Komem.

Koranit (קוֹרָנִית) From the Hebrew, meaning "thistle." The exact Hebrew equivalent is Koranit. The masculine equivalent is Kotz.

Korenet (קוֹרֶנֶת) From the Hebrew, meaning "to shine, emit rays." The exact Hebrew equivalent is Korenet. MASCULINE HEBREW EQUIVALENTS: Karin, Karni, Karni'el.

Kori A variant spelling of Corey. *See* Corey.

Kozbi (כָּזְבִּי) From the Hebrew, meaning "lie, falsehood." The exact Hebrew equivalent is Kozbi. The masculine equivalent is Mirma.

Krayna, Krayne (קְרֵיינָא) Variant forms of Kreine. *See* Kreine.

Kreindel (קְרֵיינְדֶעל) A pet form of Kreine. *See* Kreine.

Kreine (קְרֵיינֶע) A Yiddish form of the German *Krone*, meaning "crown." HEBREW EQUIVALENTS: Atara, Ateret, Kitra. MASCULINE HEBREW EQUIVALENTS: Katri'el, Keter, Kitron.

Kristin A variant spelling of Christine. *See* Christine.

Kristina A variant spelling of Christina. *See* Christina.

Kristine A variant spelling of Christine. *See* Christine.

Kryna A variant spelling of Kreine. *See* Kreine.

Krystal A variant spelling of Crystal. *See* Crystal.

Kyla, Kyle (קיילָא) Variant forms of Kelila. *See* Kelila.

Kyra From the Greek, meaning "lady, mistress." HEBREW EQUIVALENTS: Adina, Adira, Nagida. MASCULINE HEBREW EQUIVALENTS: Adir, Adon, Mar.

⚍ L ⚎

Lacey A pet form of Lucille. *See* Lucille.

Laetitia A variant spelling of Letitia. *See* Letitia.

Lahav (לַהַב) A unisex name. From the Hebrew, meaning "flame, fire." The exact Hebrew exquivalent is Lahav.

Laila A variant spelling of Leila. *See* Leila.

Laili, Lailie Variant spellings of Leili and Leilie. *See* Leili.

Lana From the Latin, meaning "woolly." The Hebrew equivalent is Tzameret. The masculine equivalent is Tzemari.

Lane A variant spelling of Layne. *See* Layne.

Lani From the Hawaiian, meaning "sky, heaven." HEBREW EQUIVALENTS: Meroma, Rama, Ramit. MASCULINE HEBREW EQUIVALENTS: Ram, Rami, Romem. Also, a pet form of Ilana. *See* Ilana.

Lara A variant form of Laura. *See* Laura.

Laraine, Larainne From the Latin, meaning "sea bird." HEBREW EQUIVALENTS: A'ya, Tzipora, Tziporiya. MASCULINE HEBREW EQUIVALENTS: Gozal, Tzipor.

Laris, Larisa, Larissa From the Latin, meaning "cheerful." HEBREW EQUIVALENTS: Aviga'yil, Gilit, Rina. MASCULINE HEBREW EQUIVALENTS: Eliran, Gilon, Yagil.

Lark From the Old English, meaning "old" or "large." Also, a name applied to a large family of songbirds. HEBREW EQUIVALENTS: A'ya, Da'a, Tzipora. MASCULINE HEBREW EQUIVALENTS: Gozal, Tzipor, Zaken.

Lata From the Hindi, meaning "beautiful vine." HEBREW EQUIVALENTS: Gafna, Karmit, Soreka. MASCULINE HEBREW EQUIVALENTS: Carmel, Carmi, Gefen.

Latasha A Russian pet form of Natalie. *See* Natalie.

Latifa, Latifah From the Arabic, meaning "gentle, pleasant." HEBREW EQUIVALENTS: Achino'am, Adiva, Ne'ima. MASCULINE HEBREW EQUIVALENTS: Adiv, Na'aman, No'am.

Laura A variant form of the masculine name Laurel, meaning "laurel," a symbol of victory. HEBREW EQUIVALENTS: Dafna, Gavri'ela, Hadasa. MASCULINE HEBREW EQUIVALENTS: Gavri'el, Gever, Yatzli'ach.

Lauraine A variant form of Laura. *See* Laura.

Lauralee A hybrid name formed from Laura and Lee. *See* Laura *and* Lee.

Lauralynn A hybrid name formed from Laura and Lynn. *See* Laura *and* Lynn.

Laure A variant form of Laura. *See* Laura.

Laurel A variant form of Laura. *See* Laura.

Lauren A variant form of Laura. *See* Laura.

Laurene A variant form of Laura. *See* Laura.

Lauretta, Laurette Pet forms of Laura. *See* Laura.

Lauri, Laurie Pet forms of Laura. *See* Laura.

Laurice A variant form of Laurel. *See* Laurel.

Laverne From the Latin and French, meaning "spring, springlike" or "verdant." HEBREW EQUIVALENTS: Aviva, Silonit, Yarkona. MASCULINE HEBREW EQUIVALENTS: Aviv, Silon, Yarkon.

Lavina A variant form of Lavinia. *See* Lavinia.

Lavinia From the Latin, meaning "women of Rome," symbolizing sophistication. HEBREW EQUIVALENTS: Adoniya, Bina, Sara. MASCULINE HEBREW EQUIVALENTS: Ga'on, Navon, Zavin.

Lavita From the Latin, meaning "life." HEBREW EQUIVALENTS: Chava, Cha'ya, Techiya. MASCULINE HEBREW EQUIVALENTS: Chai, Cha'yim, Yechi'el.

Laya A variant spelling of Leah. *See* Leah.

Layil (לַיִל) A unisex name. From the Hebrew, meaning "night, nocturnal." The exact Hebrew equivalent is La'yil.

Laylie A variant spelling of Leili. *See* Leili.

Layne A feminine form of the masculine name Lane. *See* Lane (*masculine section*).

Lea A French form of Leah. *See* Leah. Also, a variant spelling of Lee. *See* Lee.

Leah (לֵאָה) From the Hebrew, meaning "to be weary." The exact Hebrew equivalent is Lei'ah.

Leann, Leanne A hybrid name formed from Leah and Anne. *See* Leah *and* Anne.

Leanor, Leanore Variant forms of Eleanor. *See* Eleanor.

Leatrice A hybrid name formed from Leah and Beatrice. *See* Leah *and* Beatrice.

Lee From the Anglo-Saxon, meaning "field, meadow," or from the Old English, meaning "shelter." HEBREW EQUIVALENTS: Nira, Nirit, Sharona. MASCULINE HEBREW EQUIVALENTS: Carmel, Hevel, Sharon. Also, a pet form of Leah. *See* Leah.

Leeba A variant spelling of Liba. *See* Liba.

Leena A variant spelling of Lena or Lina. *See* Lena *and* Lina.

Leesa, Leeza Variant spellings of Lisa. *See* Lisa.

Lehava, Lehavah (לֶהָבָה) From the Hebrew, meaning "flame, fire." The exact Hebrew equivalent is Lehava. The masculine equivalent is Lahav.

Leiah A variant spelling of Leah. *See* Leah.

Leila, Leilah (לַיְלָה) From the Arabic and Hebrew, meaning "night" or "dark, oriental beauty." The exact Hebrew equivalent is Laila. MASCULINE HEBREW EQUIVALENTS: Kalil, Nechmad, Ra'anan.

Leilani From the Hawaiian, meaning "heavenly flower." HEBREW EQUIVALENTS: Chelmit, Chelmonit, Kalanit. MASCULINE HEBREW EQUIVALENTS: Perach, Shoshan, Yasmin.

Leili, Leilie (לֵילִי) From the Hebrew, meaning "nocturnal." The exact Hebrew equivalent is Leili. The masculine equivalent is La'yil.

Lela From the Anglo-Saxon, meaning "loyal, faithful." HEBREW EQUIVALENTS: Amnona, Emuna, Tikva. MASCULINE HEBREW EQUIVALENTS: Amitai, Amnon, Buki.

Leland From the Old English, meaning "meadowland." HEBREW EQUIVALENTS: Gana, Ganit, Ganya. MASCULINE HEBREW EQUIVALENTS: Ginton, Sharon, Yarden.

Lelani A variant spelling of Leilani. *See* Leilani.

Lelia A variant form of Lela. *See* Lela.

Lena (לִינָה) A pet form of Eleanor, Helen, or Magdalene. *See* Eleanor, Helen, *and* Magdalene. Also, from the Hebrew, meaning "lodging, dwelling place," or from the Old English, meaning "farm." The exact Hebrew equivalent is Lina. MASCULINE HEBREW EQUIVALENTS: Dur, Malon, Zevulun.

Lennie A pet form of Eleanor. *See* Eleanor.

Lenora, Lenore Pet forms of Eleanor. *See* Eleanor.

Leola From the Anglo-Saxon, meaning "deer," connoting swiftness. HEBREW EQUIVALENTS: A'yelet, Ya'ala, Ya'alit. MASCULINE HEBREW EQUIVALENTS: Tzevi, Tzevi'el, Tzivyon.

Leona From the Greek, meaning "lion-like," connoting strength. HEBREW EQUIVALENTS: Ari'el, Ari'ela, Gavrila. MASCULINE HEBREW EQUIVALENTS: Ari, Ari'el, Aryei.

Leonia A variant form of Leona. *See* Leona.

Leonie A pet form of Leona. *See* Leona.

Leonora, Leonore Variant forms of Eleanor. *See* Eleanor.

Leontine, Leontyne From the Latin, meaning "lion-like." HEBREW EQUIVALENTS: Ari'el, Ari'ela, Gurit. MASCULINE HEBREW EQUIVALENTS: Ari'el, Gur, Gur-Aryei.

Leora A variant spelling of Liora. *See* Liora.

Leorit A variant spelling of Liorit. *See* Liorit.

Leron, Lerone Variant spellings of Liron. *See* Liron.

Lesley, Leslie From the Anglo-Saxon, meaning "meadowland." HEBREW EQUIVALENTS: Gana, Karmela, Nava. MASCULINE HEBREW EQUIVALENTS: Karmeli, Ya'ari, Yarden.

Leta Probably a form of Elizabeth. *See* Elizabeth. Also, a short form of Letitia. *See* Letitia.

Leticia A variant spelling of Letitia. *See* Letitia.

Letifa, Letipha (לְטִיפָה) From the Hebrew, meaning "caress." The exact Hebrew equivalent is Letifa. The exact masculine equivalent is Latif.

Letitia From the Latin, meaning "joy." HEBREW EQUIVALENTS: Aliza, Gila, Gilana. MASCULINE HEBREW EQUIVALENTS: Eliran, Yachdi'el, Yitzchak.

Lettie, Letty Pet forms of Elizabeth. *See* Elizabeth.

Leuma (לְאוּמָה) From the Hebrew, meaning "nation." The exact Hebrew equivalent is Le'uma. The exact masculine equivalent is Le'umi.

Leumi (לְאוּמִי) A unisex name. From the Hebrew, meaning "nation, national." The exact Hebrew equivalent is Le'umi.

Levana (לְבָנָה) From the Hebrew, meaning "white" or "moon." The exact Hebrew equivalent is Levana. The exact masculine equivalent is Lavan.

Levani (לְבָנִי) From the Fijian, meaning "anointed with oil." Also, a variant form of Levana. *See* Levana. The exact Hebrew equivalent is Levani. MASCULINE HEBREW EQUIVALENTS: Lavan, Levana, Mashi'ach.

Levia, Leviah (לְבִיאָה) From the Hebrew, meaning "lioness of the Lord." The exact Hebrew equivalent is Levi'a. The exact masculine equivalent is Lavi.

Levina From the Middle English, meaning "to shine." HEBREW EQUIVALENTS: Hillela, Korenet, Levana. MASCULINE HEBREW EQUIVALENTS: Hillel, Me'ir, Yizrach.

Leviva (לְבִיבָה) A unisex name. From the Hebrew, meaning "pancake." The exact Hebrew equivalent is Leviva.

Levona (לְבוֹנָה) From the Hebrew, meaning "frankincense," so called because of its white color. The exact Hebrew equivalent is Levona. The exact masculine equivalent is Lavan.

Leya A variant spelling of Leah. *See* Leah.

Leyla A variant spelling of Leila. *See* Leila.

Li (לִי) From the Hebrew, meaning "to me." *See also* Lee.

Lia, Liah Variant spellings of Leah. *See* Leah.

Lian A variant form of Liana. *See* Liana.

Liana, Lianna (לִיעָנָה) From the Hebrew, meaning "[God] answered me." The exact Hebrew equivalent is Li'ana.

Liat, Li-At (לִי-אַת/לִיאַת) From the Hebrew, meaning "you are mine." The exact Hebrew equivalent is Li'at.

Liba (לִיבָּא) A variant Yiddish form of Libe. *See* Libe.

Libbie, Libby Diminutive forms of Elizabeth. *See* Elizabeth.

Libe (לִיבֶּע) A Yiddish form of the German *Liebe*, meaning "loved one, dear one." Also, from the Hebrew *lev*, meaning "heart." HEBREW EQUIVALENTS: Ahava, Chaviva, Chiba. MASCULINE HEBREW EQUIVALENTS: Chaviv, David, Ehud.

Liberty From the Latin, meaning "freedom." HEBREW EQUIVALENTS:

Chafshiya, Cheruta, Derora. MASCULINE HEBREW EQUIVALENTS: Deror, Rechavam, Rechavya.

Libi (לִבִּי) A variant form of Liba. *See* Liba.

Libida From the Latin, meaning "love, pleasure." HEBREW EQUIVALENTS: Ahava, Ahuva, Yedida. MASCULINE HEBREW EQUIVALENTS: Bildad, David, Yedidya.

Libke, Libkeh (לִיבְקֶע) Yiddish pet forms of Libe. *See* Libe.

Lieba (לִיבָּא) A variant Yiddish form of Liebe. *See* Liebe.

Liebe A variant spelling of Libe. *See* Libe.

Lila, Lilac, Lilah (לִילָךְ) Flower names of Persian origin. The exact Hebrew equivalent is Lilach. MASCULINE HEBREW EQUIVALENTS: Efra'yim, Perachya, Tzemach.

Lili, Lilia Variant forms of Lilian. *See* Lilian.

Lilian From the Greek and Latin, meaning "lily." HEBREW EQUIVALENTS: Nitza, Shoshan, Shoshana. MASCULINE HEBREW EQUIVALENTS: Efra'yim, Perachya, Shushan.

Lilibet A pet form of Elizabeth. *See* Elizabeth.

Lilit, Lilith (לִילִית) From the Akkadian, meaning "owl" or "winged-woman demon [who menaces children at night]." The exact Hebrew equivalent is Lilit. The name of a creature mentioned in Isaiah 34: 14.

Lilita A pet form of Lilian. *See* Lilian.

Lilli, Lillia Pet forms of Lillian. *See* Lillian.

Lillian A variant spelling of Lilian. *See* Lilian.

Lilly A pet form of Lillian. *See* Lillian.

Lilo, Li-Lo (לִי־לוֹ/לֵילוֹ) From the Hebrew, meaning "from me to him," connoting selflessness. HEBREW EQUIVALENTS: Nedavya, Nediva. MASCULINE HEBREW EQUIVALENTS: Nadav, Nadiv, Nedavya.

Lily A pet form of Lilian. *See* Lilian.

Lilyan A variant spelling of Lilian. *See* Lilian.

Lilybeth A hybrid name formed from Lily (Lilian) and Beth (Elizabeth). *See* Lilian *and* Elizabeth.

Lina A pet form of Adelina or Caroline. *See* Adelina *and* Caroline. Also, a variant spelling of Lena. *See* Lena.

Linda From the Latin and Spanish, meaning "handsome, pretty," or from the Anglo-Saxon, meaning "lovely or gentle maid." HEBREW EQUIVALENTS: Alma, Na'ama, Na'omi. MASCULINE HEBREW EQUIVALENTS: Binyamin, Chemdan, Nun.

Lindsay, Lindsey Unisex names. From the Old English, meaning "the linden tree near the brook." HEBREW EQUIVALENTS: Alona, Eila, Ilana. MASCULINE HEBREW EQUIVALENTS: Ilan, Elon, Oren.

Linn, Linne From the Welsh, meaning "waterfall, lake." HEBREW EQUIVALENTS: Arnona, Miryam, Silona. MASCULINE HEBREW EQUIVALENTS: Moshe, Peleg, Silon.

Linnet From the Latin, meaning "flaxen or golden-haired." HEBREW EQUIVALENTS: Paziya, Pazit, Zehuva. MASCULINE HEBREW EQUIVALENTS: Elifaz, Paz, Zahavi.

Lior, Li-Or (לִי-אוֹר/לִיאוֹר) A unisex name. From the Hebrew, meaning "light is mine." The exact Hebrew equivalent is Li'or.

Liora, Li-Ora (לִי-אוֹרָה/לִיאוֹרָה) From the Hebrew, meaning "light is mine." The exact Hebrew equivalent is Li'ora. The exact masculine equivalent is Li'or.

Liorit (לִיאוֹרִית) A variant form of Liora. *See* Liora. Li'orit is the exact Hebrew equivalent.

Lipke, Lipkeh (לִיפְקֶע) Variant forms of the Yiddish name Libke. *See* Libke.

Lirit (לִירִית) A Hebrew form of the Greek, meaning "lyrical, musical, poetic." The exact Hebrew equivalent is Lirit. MASCULINE HEBREW EQUIVALENTS: Amiram, Liron, Yaron.

Liron, Li-Ron (לִי-רוֹן/לִירוֹן) A unisex name. From the Hebrew, meaning "song is mine." The exact Hebrew equivalent is Liron.

Lirona (לִירוֹנָה) A variant form of Liron. *See* Liron.

Lirone A variant spelling of Liron. *See* Liron.

Lisa A pet form of Elizabeth. *See* Elizabeth.

Lisi A pet form of Elisabeth. *See* Elisabeth.

Lissa A pet form of Melissa. *See* Melissa.

Lissie, Lissy Pet forms of Elisabeth. *See* Elisabeth.

Lital (לִיטַל) From the Hebrew, meaning "dew [rain] is mine." The exact Hebrew equivalent is Lital. MASCULINE HEBREW EQUIVALENTS: Tal, Tal-Or, Tal-Shachar.

Litov, Li-Tov (לִי-טוֹב/לִיטוֹב) A unisex name. From the Hebrew, meaning "I am good, doing well." The exact Hebrew equivalent is Li'tov.

Livana A variant spelling of Levana. *See* Levana.

Livia, Liviya Short forms of Olivia. *See* Olivia.

Livna (לִבְנָה) From the Hebrew, meaning "white." The exact Hebrew equivalent is Livna. The exact masculine equivalent is Lavan.

Livnat (לִבְנָת) A variant form of Livna. *See* Livna. The exact Hebrew equivalent is Livnat.

Livvie, Livvy Pet forms of Elizabeth. *See* Elizabeth.

Livya (לִוְיָה) From the Hebrew, meaning "crown." The exact Hebrew equivalent is Livya. MASCULINE HEBREW EQUIVALENTS: Kalil, Katri'el, Keter.

Liya A variant spelling of Leah. *See* Leah.

Liza A pet form of Elizabeth. *See* Elizabeth.

Lizbeth A pet form of Elizabeth. *See* Elizabeth.

Lize A variant spelling of Liza. *See* Liza.

Lizette A pet form of Elizabeth. *See* Elizabeth.

Lizzie, Lizzy Pet forms of Elizabeth. *See* Elizabeth.

Lois From the Greek, meaning "good, desirable." HEBREW EQUIVALENTS: Bat-Tziyon, Shifra, Tova. MASCULINE HEBREW EQUIVALENTS: Ben-Tziyon, Na'am, Na'aman.

Lola A pet form of the Italian name Carlotta. *See* Carlotta.

Lolli, Lollie, Lolly Variant forms of Lola. *See* Lola.

Lora From the Latin, meaning "she who weeps, sorrowful," or from the Old High German, meaning "famous warrior."

Lorac Carol spelled backwards. *See* Carol.

Loraine A variant form of Lora. *See* Lora.

Loran, Lorann Hybrid names formed from Laura and Ann. *See* Laura *and* Ann.

Loree A variant spelling of Laurie. *See* Laurie.

Lorelei From the German, meaning "melody, sing." HEBREW EQUIVALENTS: Lirit, Rina, Tehila. MASCULINE HEBREW EQUIVALENTS: Liron, Yaron, Zemer.

Loren From the Latin, meaning "crowned with laurel," connoting victory. HEBREW EQUIVALENTS: Kelila, Kelula, Livya, Taga. MASCULINE HEBREW EQUIVALENTS: Katri'el, Kitron, Yatzli'ach.

Loretta, Lorette From the Anglo-Saxon, meaning "ignorant." EUPHEMISTIC HEBREW EQUIVALENTS: Da'at, Dati'ela, Milka. EUPHEMISTIC MASCULINE HEBREW EQUIVALENTS: Chanoch, Yavin, Yosha.

Lori A pet form of Lora. *See* Lora.

Lorna From the Anglo-Saxon, meaning "lost, forlorn, forsaken." HEBREW EQUIVALENTS: Azuva, Hagar, Sarida. MASCULINE HEBREW EQUIVALENTS: Gershom, Gershon, Sarid.

Lorraine A variant spelling of Loraine. *See* Loraine.

Lorri A pet form of Laura. *See* Laura.

Lorrin A variant form of Lora. *See* Lora.

Loryn A variant spelling of Loren. *See* Loren.

Lotta, Lotte, Lottie Pet forms of Charlotte. *See* Charlotte.

Lotus In Greek legend, a fruit that was supposed to induce a dreamy languor and forgetfulness. Also, the name of a plant of the legume family, with irregular leaves and yellow, purple or white flowers.

HEBREW EQUIVALENTS: Chamaniya, Chelmit, Nurit. MASCULINE HEBREW EQUIVALENTS: Nitzan, Perach, Savyon.

Lou A pet form of Louise. *See* Louise.

Louella A hybrid name formed from Louise and Ella. *See* Louisa *and* Ella.

Louisa From the Anglo-Saxon, meaning "refuge of the people, warrior-prince." HEBREW EQUIVALENTS: Gavri'ela, Gavrila, Sara. MASCULINE HEBREW EQUIVALENTS: Avicha'yil, La'yish, Naftali.

Louise A French form of Louisa. *See* Louisa.

Loura A variant spelling of Laura. *See* Laura.

Luan, Luann, Luanne Hybrid names formed from Laura and Ann. *See* Laura *and* Ann.

Luba (לוּבָּא) A variant Yiddish form of Liba. *See* Liba.

Lucette A pet form of Lucile. *See* Lucile.

Luci A pet form of Lucile. *See* Lucile.

Lucia A diminutive form of Lucile. *See* Lucile.

Lucie A pet form of Lucile. *See* Lucile.

Lucile, Lucille From the Latin, meaning "light" or "daybreak." HEBREW EQUIVALENTS: Behira, Me'ira, Li'ora. MASCULINE HEBREW EQUIVALENTS: Lapidos, Li'or, Uri'el.

Lucinda An English form of Lucia. *See* Lucia.

Lucy An English form of Lucia. *See* Lucia.

Luella A hybrid name formed from Louise and Ella. *See* Louise *and* Ella.

Luisa An Italian and Spanish form of Louise. *See* Louise.

Luise A variant French form of Louise. *See* Louise.

Lula A pet form of Louise. *See* Louise.

Lulu A pet form of Louise. *See* Louise.

Luna From the Latin, meaning "moon" or "shining one." The exact Hebrew equivalent is Levana. MASCULINE HEBREW EQUIVALENTS: Eli'or, Lavan, Li'or.

Lunetta, Lunette Pet forms of Luna. *See* Luna.

Lupita From the Latin, meaning "wolf." The Hebrew equivalent is Ze'eva. MASCULINE HEBREW EQUIVALENTS: Ze'ev, Zev.

Lyda A Greek place-name, meaning "maiden from Lydia." HEBREW EQUIVALENTS: Alma, Bat-Tziyon, Tze'ira. MASCULINE HEBREW EQUIVALENTS: Ben, Binyamin, Re'uven.

Lydia A variant form of Lyda. *See* Lyda.

Lyn A variant spelling of Linn. *See* Linn.

Lyna A variant spelling of Lina. *See* Lina.

Lynda A variant spelling of Linda. *See* Linda.

Lynette A pet form of Lyn. *See* Lyn.

Lynn, Lynne Variant spellings of Linn. *See* Linn.

Lyor A variant spelling of Lior. *See* Lior.

Lyric From the Greek and Latin, meaning "a poem, words suitable for singing." HEBREW EQUIVALENTS: Ariana, Bat-Shir, Shira, Zimra. MASCULINE HEBREW EQUIVALENTS: Zamir, Zemer, Zimroni.

Lys A pet form of Elisabeth. *See* Elisabeth.

❦ M ❧

Mabel From the Latin, meaning "my beautiful one," or from the Old Irish, meaning "merry." HEBREW EQUIVALENTS: Gila, Na'omi, Shifra. MASCULINE HEBREW EQUIVALENTS: Avino'am, Chemdan, Na'aman.

Mabella, Mabelle Variant forms of Mabel. *See* Mabel.

Mable A variant spelling of Mabel. *See* Mabel.

Mackenzi, Mackenzie A unisex name. From the Irish/Gaelic, meaning "son of a wise ruler." HEBREW EQUIVALENTS: Alufa, Sara, Sarit. MASCULINE HEBREW EQUIVALENTS: Melech, Moshel, Sar.

Machla, Machlah (מַחְלָה) From the Hebrew, meaning "sickness." The exact Hebrew equivalent is Machla. EUPHEMISTIC MASCULINE HEBREW EQUIVALENTS: Rafi, Refa'el. In Numbers 26:33, the eldest of Tzelophchad's five daughters.

Madalyne A variant spelling of Madelyn. *See* Madelyn.

Madelaine A variant form of Magdalene. *See* Magdalene.

Madeleine, Madeline French forms of Magdalene. *See* Magdalene.

Madelon A variant form of Magdalene. *See* Magdalene.

Madelyn A variant form of Magdalene. *See* Magdalene.

Madge A pet form of Margaret. *See* Margaret.

Mady A pet form of Madge or Magdalene. *See* Madge *and* Magdalene.

Madylin A variant spelling of Madeline. *See* Madylin.

Mae A variant form of Mary and a variant spelling of May. *See* Mary *and* May.

Mag A pet form of Magdalene or Margaret. *See* Magdalene *and* Margaret.

Magda A pet form of Magdalene. *See* Magdalene.

Magdalen A variant spelling of Magdalene. *See* Magdalene.

Magdalene A Greek form of the Hebrew *migdal*, meaning "high tower." The exact Hebrew equivalent is Migdala. The exact masculine equivalent is Migdal.

Magdaline A variant spelling of Magdalene. *See* Magdalene.

Magena (מָגֵנָה) From the Hebrew, meaning "covering" or "protector." The exact Hebrew equivalent is Magena. The exact masculine equivalent is Magen.

Maggie A pet form of Margaret. *See* Margaret.

Magina (מָגִינָה) A variant form of Magena. *See* Magena. Magina is the exact Hebrew equivalent.

Magna From the Latin, meaning "great." HEBREW EQUIVALENTS: Atalya, Gedola, Gedula. MASCULINE HEBREW EQUIVALENTS: Gadol, Gedalya, Gedula.

Magnolia From Modern Latin, meaning "big laurel tree," a symbol of victory. HEBREW EQUIVALENTS: Dafna, Hadasa. MASCULINE HEBREW EQUIVALENTS: Hadas, Matzli'ach, Netzi'ach.

Mahira A variant spelling of Mehira. *See* Mehira.

Maia In Roman mythology, goddess of the earth and growth. The month of May was named in her honor. *See* May.

Maida, Maide From the Anglo-Saxon, meaning "maiden." HEBREW EQUIVALENTS: Alma, Na'ara, Riva. MASCULINE HEBREW EQUIVALENTS: Bachur, Na'arai, Na'arya.

Maira, Maire Irish forms of Mary. *See* Mary.

Maisie From the British, meaning "field." Also, a Scottish pet form of Margaret. *See* Margaret.

Maital A variant spelling of Meital. *See* Meital.

Maksima (מַקְסִימָה) From the Hebrew, meaning "charming." The exact Hebrew equivalent is Maksima. The exact masculine equivalent is Maksim.

Malbina (מַלְבִּינָה) From the Hebrew, meaning "to whiten" or "embarrass." The exact Hebrew equivalent is Malbina. The exact masculine equivalent is Malbin.

Malca A variant spelling of Malka. *See* Malka.

Malia The Hawaiian form of Mary. *See* Mary.

Malinda A variant spelling of Melinda. *See* Melinda.

Malka, Malkah (מַלְכָּה) From the Hebrew, meaning "queen." The exact Hebrew equivalent is Malka. The exact masculine equivalent is Melech.

Malke, Malkeh Variant spellings of Malka. *See* Malka.

Malki A pet form of Malka. *See* Malka.

Malkia, Malkiah Variant spellings of Malkiya. *See* Malkiya.

Malkit (מַלְכִּית) From the Hebrew, meaning "queen, queenly." The exact Hebrew equivalent is Malkit. The exact masculine equivalent is Melech.

Malkiya (מַלְכִּיָה) From the Hebrew, meaning "God is my king." The exact Hebrew equivalent is Malkiya. The exact masculine equivalent is Melech.

Mallory From the Old French, meaning "unlucky." The Hebrew equivalent is Asnat. MASCULINE HEBREW EQUIVALENTS: Asna, Tavor.

Malvina A variant form of Melvina. *See* Melvina.

Mamie A pet form of Mary. *See* Mary.

Mana (מָנָה) From the Hebrew, meaning "share, portion, gift." The exact Hebrew equivalent is Mana. MASCULINE HEBREW EQUIVALENTS: Matan, Matanya, Natan.

Manda A pet form of Amanda. *See* Amanda.

Mandy A pet form of Amanda. *See* Amanda.

Manette A pet form of Marion. *See* Marion.

Mangena A variant spelling of Mangina. *See* Mangina.

Mangina (מַנְגִּינָה) From the Hebrew, meaning "song, melody." The exact Hebrew equivalent is Mangina. MASCULINE HEBREW EQUIVALENTS: Zamir, Zemarya, Zemer.

Manuela A feminine form of the masculine name Manuel. *See* Manuel (*masculine section*).

Maor (מָאוֹר) From the Hebrew, meaning "light." The exact Hebrew equivalent is Ma'or. MASCULINE HEBREW EQUIVALENTS: Me'ir, Ori, Zerachya.

Mara, Marah (מָרָה) From the Hebrew, meaning "bitter, bitterness." The exact Hebrew equivalent is Mara. MASCULINE HEBREW EQUIVALENTS: Merari, Mera'ya.

Maralee A hybrid name formed from Mara and Lee. *See* Mara *and* Lee.

Maralyn A variant spelling of Marilyn. *See* Marilyn.

Marata (מָרָתָה) The Aramaic form of Mara. *See* Mara. The exact Hebrew equivalent is Marata.

Marcella From the Latin, meaning "brave, martial" or "hammer." HEBREW EQUIVALENTS: Amtza, Gada, Gavri'ela. MASCULINE HEBREW EQUIVALENTS: Makabi, Medan, Mordechai.

Marcelle A variant form of Marcella. *See* Marcella.

Marcelyn A variant form of Marcella. *See* Marcella.

Marcia A variant form of Marcella. *See* Marcella.

Marcie A variant form of Marcia. *See* Marcia.

Marcilen A variant form of Marcella. *See* Marcella.

Marcy A variant form of Marcia. *See* Marcia.

Mardi From the French, meaning "Tuesday." Also, a pet form of Martha. *See* Martha.

Mare A pet form of Marie and Mary. *See* Mary.

Maree A variant spelling of Marie. *See* Marie.

Mareea A variant spelling of Maria. *See* Maria.

Maren, Marena From the Latin, meaning "sea." HEBREW EQUIVALENTS: Bat-Galim, Bat-Yam, Miryam. MASCULINE HEBREW EQUIVALENTS: Avigal, Aviyam, Moshe.

Marenda A variant form of Miranda. *See* Miranda.

Margalit (מַרְגָּלִית) A Hebrew form of the Greek, meaning "pearl." The exact Hebrew equivalent is Margalit. MASCULINE HEBREW EQUIVALENTS: Dar, Penini, Tarshish.

Margalita (מַרְגָּלִיתָה) A variant form of Margalit. *See* Margalit. The exact Hebrew equivalent is Margalita.

Marganit (מַרְגָּנִית) A plant with blue, gold, and red flowers, common in Israel. The exact Hebrew equivalent is Marganit. MASCULINE HEBREW EQUIVALENTS: Chavakuk, Neti'a, Shatil.

Margaret From the Greek, meaning "pearl" or "child of light." HEBREW EQUIVALENTS: Margalit, Me'ira, Penina. MASCULINE HEBREW EQUIVALENTS: Dar, Me'ir, Penini.

Margarete A German form of Margaret. *See* Margaret.

Margaretta A Spanish pet form of Margaret. *See* Margaret.

Margarita A Spanish form of Margaret. *See* Margaret.

Marge A pet form of Margaret. *See* Margaret.

Margene A variant form of Margaret. *See* Margaret.

Margerie A variant spelling of Margery. *See* Margery.

Margery, Margerry Variant forms of Margaret. *See* Margaret.

Marget A pet form of Margaret. *See* Margaret.

Margi, Margie Pet forms of Margaret or Margery. *See* Margaret *and* Margery.

Margit A pet form of Margalit or Margaret. *See* Margalit *or* Margaret.

Margo A variant form of Margaret. *See* Margaret.

Margy A pet form of Margaret. *See* Margaret.

Mari A variant spelling of Mary. *See* Mary.

Maria A variant form of Mary. *See* Mary.

Mariah A variant spelling of Maria. *See* Maria.

Mariamne An early form of Mary. *See* Mary.

Marian, Mariane, Marianne Hybrid names formed from Mary and Ann. *See* Mary *and* Ann.

Maribel A variant form of Mary, meaning "beautiful Mary." *See* Mary.

Marie The French and Old German form of Mary. *See* Mary.

Mariel A Dutch form of Mary. *See* Mary.

Mariele A variant form of Mary. *See* Mary.

Marien, Marienne Variant forms of Marion. *See* Marion.

Marietta An Italian pet form of Mary. *See* Mary.

Mariette A French pet form of Mary. *See* Mary.

Marilee A hybrid name formed from Mary and Lee. *See* Mary *and* Lee.

Marily A variant spelling of Marilee. *See* Marilee.

Marilyn, Marilynn Variant forms of Mary, meaning "Mary's line, descendants of Mary." Also, a hybrid name formed from Mary and Lynn. *See* Mary *and* Lynn.

Marina, Marinna From the Latin, meaning "sea." HEBREW EQUIVALENTS: Bat-Galim, Bat-Yam, Miryam. MASCULINE HEBREW EQUIVALENTS: Aviyam, Moshe, Livyatan.

Marion A pet form of the French name Marie. Also, a variant form of Mary. *See* Mary.

Maris From the Latin, meaning "sea." HEBREW EQUIVALENTS: Miryam, Yama, Yamit. MASCULINE HEBREW EQUIVALENTS: Aviyam, Moshe, Peleg.

Marisa, Marise Variant forms of Maris. *See* Maris.

Marissa A variant spelling of Marisa. *See* Marisa.

Marit (מַרְאִית) From the Hebrew, meaning "sight, appearance." The exact Hebrew equivalent is Marit. MASCULINE HEBREW EQUIVALENTS: Peni'el, Re'uven.

Marita A pet form of Martha. *See* Martha.

Mariya A variant spelling of Maria. *See* Maria.

Marji, Marjie Pet forms of Marjorie. *See* Marjorie.

Marjorie, Marjory Variant spellings of Margery, popular in Scotland. *See* Margery.

Marla A short form of Marleen. *See* Marleen.

Marlee A pet form of Marleen. *See* Marleen.

Marleen A Slavic form of Magdalene. *See* Magdalene.

Marlena A variant form of Marleen. *See* Marleen.

Marlene A variant spelling of Marleen. *See* Marleen.

Marley A variant spelling of Marlee. *See* Marlee.

Marli, Marlie Pet forms of Marleen. *See* Marleen.

Marlo A variant form of Marleen. *See* Marleen.

Marlyn, Marlynn Contracted forms of Marilyn. *See* Marilyn.

Marna, Marne Variant forms of Marina. *See* Marina.

Marni A pet form of Marina. *See* Marina.

Marnina (מַרְנִינָה) From the Hebrew, meaning "rejoice." The exact Hebrew equivalent is Marnina. The exact masculine equivalent is Marnin.

Marona (מָרוֹנָה) From the Hebrew, meaning "flock of sheep." The exact Hebrew equivalent is Marona. The exact masculine equivalent is Maron.

Marsha, Marshe Variant spellings of Marcia. *See* Marcia.

Marta A variant form of Martha. *See* Martha.

Martelle A feminine French form of Martin. *See* Martin (*masculine section*).

Martha (מָרְתָה) From the Aramaic, meaning "sorrowful" or "mistress." The Hebrew equivalent is Marata. MASCULINE HEBREW EQUIVALENTS: Avimelech, Malkam, Merari.

Marthe A French form of Martha. *See* Martha.

Marti A pet form of Martina. *See* Martina.

Martina, Martine Feminine forms of Martin. *See* Martin (*masculine section*).

Marva (מַרְוָה) From the Hebrew, referring to a plant of the mint family. The exact Hebrew equivalent is Marva. MASCULINE HEBREW EQUIVALENTS: Neta, Neti'a, Tzemach.

Marvel, Marvella From the Middle English and the Latin, meaning "to wonder, admire." HEBREW EQUIVALENTS: Maksima, Nasya, Nesya. MASCULINE HEBREW EQUIVALENTS: Nisan, Nisim, Tema.

Mary The Greek form of the Hebrew name Miryam (Miriam), meaning "sea of bitterness." The exact Hebrew equivalent is Miryam. MASCULINE HEBREW EQUIVALENTS: Aviyam, Moshe, Peleg.

Marya A Russian and Polish form of Mary. *See* Mary.

Maryam A variant form of Mary or Miriam. *See* Mary *and* Miriam.

Maryan A hybrid name formed from Mary and Ann. *See* Mary *and* Ann.

Maryanne A hybrid name formed from Mary and Anne. *See* Mary *and* Anne.

Maryashe (מַרִיאַשֶׁע) A Yiddish form of Miriam. *See* Miriam.

Maryetta A hybrid name formed from Mary and Etta. *See* Mary *and* Etta.

Marylin, Maryline Variant spellings of Marilyn. *See* Marilyn.

Masada, Massada (מַסָדָה) From the Hebrew, meaning "foundation, support." The exact Hebrew equivalent is Masada. MASCULINE HEBREW EQUIVALENTS: Sa'ad, Sa'adya, Sa'id.

Masha A Russian form of Mary. *See* Mary.

Mashe A variant form of the Yiddish name Mariashe, a variant form of Miriam. *See* Miriam.

Maskit (מַשְׂכִּית) From the Hebrew, meaning "picture, ornament." The exact Hebrew equivalent is Maskit. MASCULINE HEBREW EQUIVALENTS: Adin, Atir, Ravid.

Masoret (מָסֹרֶת) From the Hebrew, meaning "tradition." The exact Hebrew equivalent is Masoret. The exact masculine equivalent is Masur.

Matana (מַתָּנָה) From the Hebrew, meaning "gift." The exact Hebrew equivalent is Matana. The exact masculine equivalent is Matan.

Matat (מַתָּת) A unisex name. From the Hebrew, meaning "gift." The exact Hebrew equivalent is Matat.

Matea (מַתְיָה) A feminine form of the masculine name Matityahu. *See* Matityahu (*masculine section*).

Mathilda, Mathilde From the Old High German and Anglo-Saxon, meaning "powerful in battle" or "battlemaid." HEBREW EQUIVALENTS: Alma, Gada, Gavri'ela. MASCULINE HEBREW EQUIVALENTS: Makabi, Medan, Mordechai.

Matilda A variant spelling of Mathilda. *See* Mathilda.

Matlit (מַטְלִית) From the Hebrew, meaning "cloth patch." The exact Hebrew equivalent is Matlit.

Matti, Mattie Pet forms of Mathilda. *See* Mathilda.

Matty, Mattye Pet forms of Mathilda. *See* Mathilda.

Matya (מַתְיָה) A Yiddish pet form of Mathilda. *See* Mathilda.

Maud, Maude French pet forms of Mathilda. *See* Mathilda.

Maura A form of Mary commonly used in Ireland. *See* Mary. Also, from the Celtic, meaning "dark." HEBREW EQUIVALENTS: Efa, Miryam, Tzila. MASCULINE HEBREW EQUIVALENTS: Adar, Kedar, Pinchas.

Maureen, Maurine Variant forms of Maura. *See* Maura.

Mavis A bird-name that evolved in France from an Old English word meaning "song thrush." HEBREW EQUIVALENTS: Derora, Efrona, Gozala. MASCULINE HEBREW EQUIVALENTS: Deror, Efron, Gozal.

Maxa A feminine form of Max. *See* Max (*masculine section*).

Maxene A variant spelling of Maxine. *See* Maxine.

Maxima A variant spelling of Maksima. *See* Maksima.

Maxime A feminine form of Maximilian. *See* Maximilian (*masculine section*).

Maxine A variant form of Maxime. *See* Maxime.

May, Maye Pet forms of Mary and Margaret. *See* Mary *and* Margaret. Also, a month of the year connoting spring, youth, growth. *See* Maia. HEBREW EQUIVALENTS: Alma, Na'ara, Shoshana. MASCULINE HEBREW EQUIVALENTS: Efra'yim, Gedalya, Perachya.

Maya A variant spelling of Maia. *See* Maia.

Mayim (מַיִם) From the Hebrew, meaning "water." The exact Hebrew equivalent is Ma'yim. MASCULINE HEBREW EQUIVALENTS: Aviyam, Dela'ya, Yuval.

Mayrav A variant spelling of Meirav. *See* Meirav.

Maytal A variant spelling of Meital. *See* Meital.

Mazal (מַזָּל) A unisex name. From the Hebrew, meaning "star" or "luck." The exact Hebrew equivalent is Mazal.

Mazala (מַזָּלָה) A variant form of Mazal. *See* Mazal. The exact Hebrew equivalent is Mazala.

Mazalit (מַזָּלִית) A variant form of Mazal. *See* Mazal. The exact Hebrew equivalent is Mazalit.

Mazhira (מַזְהִירָה) From the Hebrew, meaning "shining." The exact Hebrew equivalent is Mazhira. MASCULINE HEBREW EQUIVALENTS: Me'ir, Yitzhar, Zerach.

Meadow From the Old English, meaning "a piece of grassland." HEBREW EQUIVALENTS: Adama, Artzit, Eretz. MASCULINE HEBREW EQUIVALENTS: Adam, Artzi, Ya'ar.

Meara From the Irish, meaning "joy, happiness." HEBREW EQUIVALENTS: Aliza, Ditza, Ronit. MASCULINE HEBREW EQUIVALENTS: Aliz, Eliran, Marnin.

Me'ara, Me'arah (מְעָרָה) From the Hebrew, meaning "cave, hiding place." The exact Hebrew equivalent is Me'ara. MASCULINE HEBREW EQUIVALENTS: Chor, Chori.

Medura, Medurah (מְדוּרָה) From the Hebrew, meaning "fire, flame, conflagration." The exact Hebrew equivalent is Medura. MASCULINE HEBREW EQUIVALENTS: Lahat, Lahav, Lapid.

Meerit A variant spelling of Mirit. *See* Mirit.

Meg A pet form of Margaret. *See* Margaret.

Megan A Welsh form of Margaret. *See* Margaret.

Mehira (מְהִירָה) From the Hebrew, meaning "swift, energetic." The exact Hebrew equivalent is Mehira. The exact masculine equivalent is Mahir.

Meira, Meirah (מְאִירָה) From the Hebrew, meaning "light." The exact Hebrew equivalent is Me'ira. The exact masculine equivalent is Me'ir.

Meirav A variant spelling of Merav. *See* Merav.

Meirit (מְאִירִת) A feminine form of Meir. *See* Meir (*masculine section*). The exact Hebrew equivalent is Me'irit.

Meirona A variant spelling of Merona. *See* Merona.

Meital (מֵיטָל) From the Hebrew, meaning "dew drops." The exact Hebrew equivalent is Meital (Maytal). MASCULINE HEBREW EQUIVALENTS: Tal, Tali, Tal-Or.

Melanie From the Greek, meaning "black, dark." HEBREW EQUIVALENTS: Adara, Chachila, Tzila. MASCULINE HEBREW EQUIVALENTS: Adar, Kedar, Pinchas.

Melba A variant form of Melva. *See* Melva.

Melina From the Greek, meaning "song." HEBREW EQUIVALENTS: Mangena, Mangina, Shira. MASCULINE HEBREW EQUIVALENTS: Amiran, Zemer, Zimri.

Melinda From the Greek and Old English, meaning "gentle." HEBREW EQUIVALENTS: Adiva, Nediva, Na'ama. MASCULINE HEBREW EQUIVALENTS: Adiv, Na'aman, Nadiv.

Melissa, Melisse From the Greek, meaning "bee, honey." HEBREW EQUIVALENTS: Metuka, Mirit, Na'ama, Na'omi. MASCULINE HEBREW EQUIVALENTS: Avino'am, Matok, Meged.

Melita From the Greek, meaning "honey." HEBREW EQUIVALENTS: Devasha, Devora, Duvsha. MASCULINE HEBREW EQUIVALENTS: Devash, Yidbash.

Melitza, Melitzah (מְלִיצָה) From the Hebrew, meaning "parable." The exact Hebrew equivalent is Melitza. Achichud is a masculine equivalent.

Melody From the Greek, meaning "melody, song." HEBREW EQUIVALENTS: Mangena, Mangina, Ranita. MASCULINE HEBREW EQUIVALENTS: Amiran, Zemer, Zimri.

Melva A feminine form of Melvin. *See* Melvin (*masculine section*).

Melveen, Melvene Feminine forms of Melvin. *See* Melvin (*masculine section*).

Melvina A feminine form of Melvin. *See* Melvin (*masculine section*).

Menora, Menorah (מְנוֹרָה) From the Hebrew, meaning "candelabrum." The exact Hebrew equivalent is Menora. MASCULINE HEBREW EQUIVALENTS: Me'ir, Nahor, Nahur.

Menucha, Menuchah (מְנוּחָה) From the Hebrew, meaning "rest, peace." The exact Hebrew equivalent is Menucha. The exact masculine equivalent is Mano'ach.

Merav (מֵרָב/מֵירָב) From the Hebrew, meaning "the maximum, ultimate" or "abundance." The exact Hebrew equivalent is Merav. MASCULINE HEBREW EQUIVALENTS: Yitran, Yitro. In I Samuel 14:49, the name of King Saul's eldest daughter.

Mercedes From the Latin, meaning "mercy, pity." HEBREW EQUIVALENTS: Nechama, Ruchama. MASCULINE HEBREW EQUIVALENTS: Chanin, Rachaman, Rachmi'el.

Meredith From the Old Celtic, meaning "protector of the sea." HEBREW EQUIVALENTS: Chosa, Magena, Migdala. MASCULINE HEBREW EQUIVALENTS: Magen, Mivtach, Mivtachyahu.

Merelyn A hybrid name formed from Merril and Lyn. *See* Merril *and* Lyn.

Meret A pet form of Margaret. *See* Margaret.

Meri (מְרִי) From the Hebrew, meaning "rebellious, bitterness." The exact Hebrew equivalent is Meri. MASCULINE HEBREW EQUIVALENTS: Mardut, Mordechai, Nimrod.

Merida, Meridah From the Hebrew, meaning "revolt, feud." The exact Hebrew equivalent is Merida. The exact masculine equivalent is Mered.

Merideth A variant spelling of Meredith. *See* Meredith.

Merie A variant spelling of Meri. *See* Meri.

Meriva, Merivah (מְרִיבָה) From the Hebrew, meaning "feud, argument, revolt." The exact Hebrew equivalent is Meriva. The exact masculine equivalent is Meri.

Merla A variant form of Merle. *See* Merle.

Merle From the Latin and the French, meaning "bird," specifically a blackbird. HEBREW EQUIVALENTS: Da'ya, Gozala, Tzipora. MASCULINE HEBREW EQUIVALENTS: Gozal, Orev, Tzipor.

Merlin From the Old High German, meaning "falcon." Akin to Merle. *See* Merle.

Meroma (מְרוֹמָה) From the Hebrew, meaning "elevated, high, noble."

The exact Hebrew equivalent is Meroma. The exact masculine equivalent is Marom.

Merona (מֶרוֹנָה) From the Aramaic, meaning "sheep," or from the Hebrew, meaning "troops, soldiers." The exact Hebrew equivalent is Meirona. The exact masculine equivalent is Meiron.

Merrie From the Anglo-Saxon, meaning "joyous, pleasant." HEBREW EQUIVALENTS: Gilana, Marnina, Renana. MASCULINE HEBREW EQUIVALENTS: Marnin, Masos, Simcha.

Merrielle A pet form of Merrie. *See* Merrie.

Merril, Merrill Variant forms of Merle and Muriel. *See* Merle *and* Muriel.

Merry A variant spelling of Merrie. *See* Merrie.

Merryl A variant spelling of Meryl. *See* Meryl.

Merta A variant form of Marta (Martha). *See* Martha.

Meryl, Meryle Variant spellings of Merril. *See* Merril.

Mesilla, Mesillah (מְסִלָּה) From the Hebrew, meaning "path, road." The exact Hebrew equivalent is Mesilla. MASCULINE HEBREW EQUIVALENTS: Nativ, Shoval, Solel.

Mesora, Mesorah (מְסוֹרָה) From the Hebrew, meaning "transmission, tradition." The exact Hebrew equivalent is Mesora. The exact masculine equivalent is Masur.

Metuka (מְתוּקָה) From the Hebrew, meaning "sweet." The exact Hebrew equivalent is Metuka. The exact masculine equivalent is Matok.

Metzuda, Metzudah (מְצוּדָה) From the Hebrew, meaning "fortress." The exact Hebrew equivalent is Metzuda. MASCULINE HEBREW EQUIVALENTS: Bira, Cheilon, Ma'on.

Meyrav A variant spelling of Meirav. *See* Meirav.

Mia (מִיָה) A short form of Michaela. *See* Michaela. The exact Hebrew equivalent is Miya.

Mica A short form of Michal. *See* Michal.

Micha (מִיכָה) A short form of Michal. *See* Michal.

Michael Used occasionally as a feminine name. The exact Hebrew equivalent is Micha'el. *See* Michael (*masculine section*).

Michaela (מִיכָאֵלָה) The feminine form of Michael. The exact Hebrew equivalent is Micha'ela. The exact masculine equivalent is Micha'el. *See* Michael (*masculine section*).

Michaelann A hybrid name formed from Michael and Ann. *See* Michael *and* Ann.

Michaele A feminine form of Michael. *See* Michael (*masculine section*).

Michal (מִיכַל) A contracted form of Michael, meaning "Who is like God?" The exact Hebrew equivalent is Michal. MASCULINE HEBREW EQUIVALENTS: Micha, Micha'el. In I Samuel 14:49, the name of King Saul's younger daughter.

Michalina A pet form of Michal. *See* Michal.

Michel, Michele, Michelle Variant French forms of Michal. *See* Michal.

Micke, Mickey, Micki, Mickie Pet forms of Michal. *See* Michal.

Midge A variant form of Madge. *See* Madge.

Migda (מִגְדָּה) From the Hebrew, meaning "choice thing, gift" or "excellent." The exact Hebrew equivalent is Migda. MASCULINE HEBREW EQUIVALENTS: Matan, Matanya, Matityahu.

Migdala (מִגְדָּלָה) From the Hebrew, meaning "fortress, tower." The exact Hebrew equivalent is Migdala. The exact masculine equivalent is Migdal.

Migdana (מִגְדָּנָה) From the Hebrew, meaning "gift." The exact Hebrew equivalent is Migdana. MASCULINE HEBREW EQUIVALENTS: Magdi'el, Meged, Natan.

Mignon From the French, meaning "delicate, graceful, petite." HEBREW EQUIVALENTS: Adina, Adiva, Chana. MASCULINE HEBREW EQUIVALENTS: Amichen, Chanan, Chanina.

Mika A pet form of Michal. *See* Michal.

Mikhal A variant spelling of Michal. *See* Michal.

Mildred From the Anglo-Saxon, meaning "gentle of speech" or "gentle counselor." HEBREW EQUIVALENTS: Amira, Milka, Niva. MASCULINE HEBREW EQUIVALENTS: Dovev, Omer, Utz.

Mili (מִילִי) From the Hebrew, meaning "Who is for me?" or a Hebraized form of Millie. *See* Millie. The exact Hebrew equivalent is Mili.

Milka, Milkah (מִלְכָּה) From the Hebrew, meaning "divine" or "queen." Akin to Malka. The exact Hebrew equivalent is Milka. The masculine equivalent is Melech. In Numbers 26:33, one of Tzelophchad's five daughters.

Millicent From the Latin, meaning "sweet singer," or from the Old French and Old High German, meaning "work" or "strength." HEBREW EQUIVALENTS: Amal, Amalya, Amela. MASCULINE HEBREW EQUIVALENTS: Amatzya, Avram, Binyamin.

Millie, Milly Pet forms of Mildred and Millicent. *See* Mildred *and* Millicent.

Mim A pet form of Miryam. *See* Miryam.

Mimi A pet form of Miryam. *See* Miryam.

Mina A variant spelling of Minna. *See* Minna.

Minda (מִינְדָּא) A Yiddish form of Minna. *See* Minna.

Mindel (מִינְדְעל) A Yiddish pet form of Minda. *See* Minda.

Mindi A variant spelling of Mindy. *See* Mindy.

Mindy A pet form of Melinda or Mildred. *See* Melinda *and* Mildred.

Minerva The Roman goddess of wisdom. HEBREW EQUIVALENTS: Bina, Buna, Milka. MASCULINE HEBREW EQUIVALENTS: Ga'on, Navon.

Minette A French pet form of Mary. *See* Mary.

Minna A pet form of Wilhelmina. *See* Willhelmina.

Minnie, Minny Pet forms of Minna, Miriam, and Wilhelmina. *See* Minna, Miriam, *and* Wilhelmina.

Minta From the Greek, meaning "mint [an aromatic leaf]." HEBREW EQUIVALENTS: Ketzi'a, Tzeruya. MASCULINE HEBREW EQUIVALENTS: Mivsam, Yivsam.

Mira (מִירָה) A pet form of Miryam. *See* Miryam.

Miranda From the Latin, meaning "wonderful" or "adored one." HEBREW EQUIVALENTS: Hadarit, Sara. MASCULINE HEBREW EQUIVALENTS: Adi'el, Me'udan, Yehoyadan.

Mirel, Mirele (מִירֶעלֶע/מִירֶעל) Yiddish pet forms of Miryam. *See* Miryam.

Miri A short form of Mirit and Miryam. *See* Mirit *and* Miryam.

Miriam The Anglicized spelling of Miryam. *See* Miryam.

Miril (מִירִיל) A Yiddish pet form of Miryam. *See* Miryam.

Mirit (מִירִית) From the Hebrew, meaning "sweet wine." The exact Hebrew equivalent is Mirit. MASCULINE HEBREW EQUIVALENTS: Gafni, Gefanya, Gefen. Also, a variant form of Mira. *See* Mira.

Mirjam A Spanish form of Miriam. *See* Miriam.

Mirra A variant spelling of Mira. *See* Mira.

Miryam (מִרְיָם) From the Hebrew, meaning "sea of bitterness, sorrow," or from the Chaldaic, meaning "mistress of the sea." The exact Hebrew equivalent is Miryam. MASCULINE HEBREW EQUIVALENTS: Moshe, Peleg, Silon. In Exodus 15:20, the sister of Aaron and Moses.

Miryom A variant spelling of Miryam. *See* Miryam.

Mishaela (מִישָׁאֵלָה) A feminine form of Mishael. The exact Hebrew equivalent is Misha'ela. *See* Mishael (*masculine section*).

Missie, Missy A modern American name meaning "young girl." Also, a pet form of Melissa. *See* Melissa. HEBREW EQUIVALENTS: Bat, Bat-Sheva, Batya. MASCULINE HEBREW EQUIVALENTS: Ben, Ben-Tziyon, Na'arya.

Misty From the Old English, meaning "mist, darkness." HEBREW EQUIVALENTS: Laila, Lilit. MASCULINE HEBREW EQUIVALENTS: Adda, Anan, Anani.

Mitriya, Mitriyah (מִטְרִיָה) From the Hebrew, meaning "umbrella, screen, shade." The exact Hebrew equivalent is Mitriya. MASCULINE HEBREW EQUIVALENTS: Geshem, Malkosh, Matri.

Mitzi A pet form of Mary. *See* Mary.

Mitzpa, Mitzpah (מִצְפָּה) From the Hebrew, meaning "tower." The exact Hebrew equivalent is Mitzpa. MASCULINE HEBREW EQUIVALENTS: Armon, Armoni, Migdal.

Mizpa, Mizpah Variant spellings of Mitzpa. *See* Mitzpa.

Moira A Gaelic form of Mary. *See* Mary.

Mollie, Molly, Mollye Pet forms of Mary, Millicent, and Miriam. *See* Mary, Millicent, *and* Miriam.

Mona From the Irish, meaning "noble, pure." HEBREW EQUIVALENTS: Adina, Malka, Milka. MASCULINE HEBREW EQUIVALENTS: Adin, Adon, Zakai.

Monica A variant form of Mona. *See* Mona.

Monique A French form of Mona. *See* Mona.

Moraga (מוֹרָגָה) The feminine form of Moreg. *See* Moreg (*masculine section*). The exact Hebrew equivalent is Moraga.

Moran (מוֹרָן) A unisex name. From the Aramaic, meaning "our teacher." The exact Hebrew equivalent is Moran.

Morasha (מוֹרָשָׁה) From the Hebrew, meaning "legacy." The exact Hebrew equivalent is Morasha. The exact masculine equivalent is Morash.

Morena A variant form of Maura. *See* Maura.

Morgan From the Welsh, meaning "sea dweller." HEBREW EQUIVALENTS: Bat-Galim, Bat-Yam, Miryam. MASCULINE HEBREW EQUIVALENTS: Aviyam, Moshe, Peleg.

Moria, Moriah Variant spellings of Moriya. *See* Moriya.

Moriel (מוֹרִיאֵל) A unisex name. From the Hebrew, meaning "God is my teacher." The exact Hebrew equivalent is Mori'el.

Morine A variant form of Maureen. *See* Maureen.

Morit (מוֹרִית) From the Hebrew, meaning "teacher." The exact Hebrew equivalent is Morit. MASCULINE HEBREW EQUIVALENTS: Moran, Mori'el, Yora.

Moriya (מוֹרִיָה) From the Hebrew, meaning "God is my teacher." The exact Hebrew equivalent is Moriya. MASCULINE HEBREW EQUIVALENTS: Mori'el, Rabi, Yora.

Morna From the Middle English and German, meaning "morning," or from the Celtic, meaning "gentle, beloved." HEBREW EQUIVALENTS: Davida, Shachar, Yakira. MASCULINE HEBREW EQUIVALENTS: Ahuv, Ben-Shachar, Chavivel, David, Nadiv.

Morrisa, Morrissa The feminine form of Morris. *See* Morris (*masculine section*).

Moselle A name created to correspond to the masculine Moses. *See* Moses (*masculine section*).

Muriel From the Irish, meaning "bright sea," or from the Middle English, meaning "merry." HEBREW EQUIVALENTS: Marnina, Mazal, Renana. MASCULINE HEBREW EQUIVALENTS: Marnin, Mazal-Tov, Sason.

Mychal, Mykhal Variant spellings of Michal. *See* Michal.

Myra From the Greek and Arabic, meaning "myrrh," connoting bitterness. Also, from the Celtic, meaning "gentle, beloved." HEBREW EQUIVALENTS: Mor, Talmor. MASCULINE HEBREW EQUIVALENTS: Mara, Marata.

Myrel A variant spelling of Mirel. *See* Mirel.

Myriam A variant spelling of Miryam. *See* Miryam.

Myrna A variant form of Myra. *See* Myra.

Myrtle A unisex name. From the Persian, meaning "myrtle tree," a symbol of victory. The feminine Hebrew equivalent is Hadasa. The masculine equivalent is Hadas.

~ N ~

Naama, Naamah (נַעֲמָה) From the Hebrew, meaning "pleasant, beautiful." The exact Hebrew equivalent is Na'ama. The exact masculine equivalent is Na'aman.

Naamana (נַעֲמָנָה) From the Hebrew, meaning "pleasant." The exact Hebrew equivalent is Na'amana. The exact masculine equivalent is Na'aman.

Naami (נַעֲמִי) A variant form of Naomi. *See* Naomi. The exact Hebrew equivalent is Na'ami.

Naamia, Naamiah Variant spellings of Naamiya. *See* Naamiya.

Naamit (נַעֲמִית) From the Hebrew, meaning "an ostrichlike bird." The exact Hebrew equivalent is Na'amit. MASCULINE HEBREW EQUIVALENTS: Gozal, Tzipor.

Naamiya (נַעֲמִיָה) From the Hebrew, meaning "pleasant, sweet." A variant form of Na'ama. *See* Na'ama. The exact Hebrew equivalent is Na'amiya.

Naara, Naarah (נַעֲרָה) From the Hebrew, meaning "young girl." The exact Hebrew equivalent is Na'ara. The exact masculine equivalent is Na'ar. In I Chronicles 4:5, one of the two wives of Ashur of the tribe of Judah.

Nacha A variant pet form of Nechama. *See* Nechama.

Nada From the Slavic, meaning "hope." HEBREW EQUIVALENTS: Emuna, Tikva, Tzipiya. MASCULINE HEBREW EQUIVALENTS: Amon, Mivtach, Mivtachya.

Nadette A pet form of Bernadette. *See* Bernadette.

Nadia A variant form of Nada. *See* Nada.

Nadine A French form of Nada. *See* Nada.

Nadira From the Arabic, meaning "precious, scarce." HEBREW EQUIVALENTS: Adi'ela, Hadar, Hadarit. MASCULINE HEBREW EQUIVALENTS: Ada'ya, Adi, Adi'el.

Nadya (נָדְיָה) A Hebrew form of Nada, used in Israel. *See* Nada. The exact Hebrew equivalent is Nadya.

Nafshiya (נַפְשִׁיָה) From the Hebrew, meaning "soul" or "friendship." The exact Hebrew equivalent is Nafshiya. MASCULINE HEBREW EQUIVALENTS: Nafish, Nefesh.

Naftala (נִפְתָּלָה) From the Hebrew, meaning "to wrestle." The exact Hebrew equivalent is Naftala. The exact masculine equivalent is Naftali.

Nagida (נְגִידָה) From the Hebrew, meaning "noble, prosperous person." The exact Hebrew equivalent is Nagida. The exact masculine equivalent is Nagid.

Nahara (נָהָרָה) From the Hebrew and Aramaic, meaning "light." The exact Hebrew equivalent is Nahara. MASCULINE HEBREW EQUIVALENTS: Nahor, Nehorai, Nerli.

Nahari (נַהֲרִי) From the Aramaic, meaning "my light." The exact Hebrew equivalent is Nahari. MASCULINE HEBREW EQUIVALENTS: Nahor, Nehorai, Nerli.

Nahariya (נַהֲרִיָה) A variant form of Nahara. *See* Nahara.

Nan, Nana Pet forms of Nancy. *See* Nancy.

Nanci, Nancy Pet forms of Hannah. *See* Hannah.

Nanette A pet form of Anna and Hannah. *See* Anna *and* Hannah.

Nanine A variant pet form of Nanette. *See* Nanette.

Nanna A pet form of Hannah. *See* Hannah.

Naoma A variant form of Naomi. *See* Naomi.

Naomi (נָעֳמִי) From the Hebrew, meaning "beautiful, pleasant, delightful." The exact Hebrew equivalent is Na'omi. MASCULINE HEBREW EQUIVALENTS: Na'aman, Na'im, No'am. In Ruth 1:19, the mother-in-law of Ruth.

Narda From the Latin, meaning "scented ointment." HEBREW EQUIVALENTS: Bosma, Ketura, Livnat. MASCULINE HEBREW EQUIVALENTS: Bosem, Mivsam, Yivsam.

Nastasia A short form of Anastasia. *See* Anastasia.

Narelle From the Latin, meaning "narrative, short story." HEBREW EQUIVALENTS: Amira, Doveva, Dovevet. MASCULINE HEBREW EQUIVALENTS: Amarya, Dover, Imri.

Natalie A French and German form of the Latin, meaning "to be born, to be alive." HEBREW EQUIVALENTS: Chava, Cha'ya, Techiya. MASCULINE HEBREW EQUIVALENTS: Chiya, Nafshiya, Yechi'el.

Natania, Nataniah Variant spellings of Natanya. *See* Natanya.

Nataniela, Nataniella, Natanielle Variant feminine forms of Netaniela. *See* Netaniela.

Natanya (נְתַנְיָה) The feminine form of Natan (Nathan). Also, a variant form of Netanya. *See* Netanya. The exact Hebrew equivalent is Natanya.

Natasha A Russian pet form of Natalie. *See* Natalie.

Natasia A pet form of Anastasia. *See* Anastasia.

Nathalie A variant spelling of Natalie. *See* Natalie.

Nava, Navah (נָוָה/נָאוָה) From the Hebrew, meaning "beautiful, pleasant." The exact Hebrew equivalent is Nava. The exact masculine equivalent is Naveh.

Navit (נָוִית) A variant form of Nava. *See* Nava. The exact Hebrew equivalent is Navit.

Neala A feminine form of Neal. *See* Neal (*masculine section*).

Nealla A hybrid name formed from Neal and Ella. *See* Neal (*masculine section*) *and* Ella.

Nechama, Nechamah (נֶחָמָה) From the Hebrew, meaning "comfort." The exact Hebrew equivalent is Nechama. The exact masculine equivalent is Nachum.

Nechi A pet form of Nechama. *See* Nechama.

Nechusha, Nechushah (נְחוּשָׁה) From the Hebrew, meaning "copper, brass." The exact Hebrew equivalent is Nechusha. MASCULINE HEBREW EQUIVALENTS: Ard, Ardi, Arodi.

Nedara (נֶאְדָּרָה) From the Hebrew, meaning "adored, exalted." The exact Hebrew equivalent is Nedara. The exact masculine equivalent is Nedar.

Nedavia, Nedaviah, Nedavya (נְדַבְיָה) A unisex name. From the Hebrew, meaning "generosity of the Lord." The exact Hebrew equivalent is Nedavya.

Nediva (נְדִיבָה) From the Hebrew, meaning "noble, generous." The exact Hebrew equivalent is Nediva. The exact masculine equivalent is Nadiv.

Neena A variant spelling of Nina. *See* Nina.

Neesia A variant form of Nesya. *See* Nesya.

Negida (נְגִידָה) A variant form of Nagida. *See* Nagida. The exact Hebrew equivalent is Negida.

Negina, Neginah (נְגִינָה) From the Hebrew, meaning "song, melody." The exact Hebrew equivalent is Negina. MASCULINE HEBREW EQUIVALENTS: Shiron, Zemarya, Zemer.

Nehama A variant spelling of Nechama. *See* Nechama.

Nehara (נְהָרָה) A variant form of Nahara. *See* Nahara. The exact Hebrew equivalent is Nehara.

Nehira, Nehirah (נְהִירָה) A variant form of Nehora. *See* Nehora. The exact Hebrew equivalent is Nehira.

Nehora (נְהוֹרָה/נְהוֹרָא) From the Aramaic, meaning "light." The exact Hebrew equivalent is Nehora. The exact masculine equivalent is Nahor.

Nehura, Nehurah (נְהוּרָה) A variant form of Nehora. *See* Nehora. The exact Hebrew equivalent is Nehura.

Neila, Neilah From the Hebrew, meaning "conclusion, sealing." The exact Hebrew equivalent is Ne'ila. Chotam is a masculine equivalent.

Neima, Neimah (נְעִימָה) From the Hebrew, meaning "pleasant one." The exact Hebrew equivalent is Ne'ima. The exact masculine equivalent is Na'im.

Neirit A variant spelling of Nerit. *See* Nerit.

Nelda An Old English form of Eleanor, meaning "light." *See* Eleanor.

Nell, Nella Pet forms of Eleanor and Helen. *See* Eleanor *and* Helen.

Nellie, Nelly Pet forms of Eleanor. *See* Eleanor.

Nema A variant spelling of Nima. *See* Nima.

Neoma From the Greek, meaning "new moon." HEBREW EQUIVALENTS: Chadasha, Levana, Sahara. MASCULINE HEBREW EQUIVALENTS: Levanon, Yarchi, Yerach.

Neora, Neorah (נְאוֹרָה) From the Aramaic and Hebrew, meaning "light" or "shine." The exact Hebrew equivalent is Ne'ora. The exact masculine equivalent is Na'or.

Nerd From the Sanskrit, meaning "an aromatic plant." HEBREW EQUIVALENTS: Bosemet, Kida, Nirdi. MASCULINE HEBREW EQUIVALENTS: Mor, Tzeri.

Nerit (נֵרִית) From the Hebrew, meaning "candlelight." The exact Hebrew equivalent is Nerit. MASCULINE HEBREW EQUIVALENTS: Ner, Neri, Neriya.

Nerya, Neryah (נֵרִיָה) From the Hebrew, meaning "light of the Lord." The exact Hebrew equivalent is Nerya. MASCULINE HEBREW EQUIVALENTS: Ner, Neri, Neriya, Nerli.

Neshama, Neshamah From the Hebrew, meaning "soul, spirit, life." The exact Hebrew equivalent is Neshama. MASCULINE HEBREW EQUIVALENTS: Cha'yim, Yechi'el, Yocha'i.

Neshika, Neshikah (נְשִׁיקָה) From the Hebrew, meaning "kiss." The exact Hebrew equivalent is Neshika.

Neshima, Neshimah (נְשִׁימָה) From the Hebrew, meaning "breath." The exact Hebrew equivalent is Neshima. MASCULINE HEBREW EQUIVALENTS: Hevel (Abel), Nafish.

Nessa From the Old Norse, meaning "promontory, headland." Also, a short form of Vanessa. *See* Vanessa. HEBREW EQUIVALENTS: Artzit, Eretz. MASCULINE HEBREW EQUIVALENTS: Adam, Artza, Artzi.

Nessie A Welsh pet form of Agnes. *See* Agnes.

Nesya (נֶסְיָה) From the Hebrew, meaning "miracle of God." The exact Hebrew equivalent is Nesya. MASCULINE HEBREW EQUIVALENTS: Nes, Nisan, Nisi, Nisim.

Neta (נֶטַע) From the Hebrew, meaning "plant, shrub." The exact feminine and masculine Hebrew equivalent is Neta.

Netana (נְתַנָה) From the Hebrew, meaning "gift." The exact Hebrew equivalent is Netana. The exact masculine equivalent is Natan.

Netania, Netaniah Variant spellings of Netanya. *See* Netanya.

Netaniela, Netaniella (נְתַנִיאֵלָה) Variant forms of Netanya. *See* Netanya. The exact Hebrew equivalent is Netani'ela.

Netanya (נְתַנְיָה) A unisex name. From the Hebrew, meaning "gift of God." The exact Hebrew equivalent is Netanya.

Netina, Netinah (נְתִינָה) From the Hebrew, meaning "gift" or "resident, citizen." The exact Hebrew equivalent is Netina. The exact masculine equivalent is Natin.

Netiva (נְתִיבָה) From the Hebrew, meaning "path." The exact Hebrew equivalent is Netiva. The exact masculine equivalent is Nativ.

Netta A variant spelling of Neta. *See* Neta.

Netti A variant spelling of Nettie. *See* Nettie.

Nettie, Netty Pet forms of Annette and Antoinette. *See* Annette *and* Antoinette.

Neumi A variant form of Naomi. *See* Naomi.

Neva From the Spanish, meaning "snow," or from the Old English, meaning "new." HEBREW EQUIVALENTS: Chadasha, Neva, Shalgit. The masculine equivalent is Chadash. Also, a pet form of Geneva. *See* Geneva.

Nevia, Neviah (נְבִיאָה) From the Hebrew, meaning "prophet." The exact Hebrew equivalent is Nevi'a. The exact masculine equivalent is Navi.

Nia A pet form of the masculine name Niall, originally spelled Neil. *See* Neil (*masculine section*).

Nicci An Italian form of the Latin, meaning "victory." HEBREW EQUIVALENTS: Nitzcha, Nitzchiya, Nitzchona. MASCULINE HEBREW EQUIVALENTS: Netzach, Netzi'ach, Nitzchi.

Nichelle A variant form of Nicci. *See* Nicci.

Nicki, Niki, Nikki Pet forms of Nicole. *See* Nicole.

Nicola, Nicole Italian and French forms of the masculine name Nicholas. *See* Nicholas (*masculine section*).

Nicolette A pet form of Nicola. *See* Nicola.

Nicolle A variant spelling of Nicole. *See* Nicole.

Nigella A feminine form of the masculine name Nigel. *See* Nigel (*masculine section*).

Nikia, Nikki Pet forms of Nicole. *See* Nicole.

Nili (נִילִי) A unisex name. An acronym of the Hebrew words "the glory [or eternity] of Israel will not lie" (I Samuel 15:29). The exact Hebrew equivalent is Nili.

Nilit (נִילִית) A variant form of Nili. *See* Nili. The exact Hebrew equivalent is Nilit.

Nima (נִימָה) From the Hebrew, meaning "picture, portrait," or from the Greek, meaning "hair, thread." The exact Hebrew equivalent is Nima. The masculine equivalent is Nevat.

Nina A French and Russian pet form of Nanine, a form of Anne. *See* Anne.

Ninette A variant form of Nanette. *See* Nanette.

Nira, Nirah (נִירָה) The feminine form of Nir. *See* Nir (*masculine section*).

Nirel, Nir-El (נִיר-אֶל/נִירְאֵל) A unisex name. From the Hebrew, meaning "cultivated field of the Lord" or "light of God." The exact Hebrew equivalent is Nirel.

Nirit (נִירִית) An annual plant with yellow flowers, found in Israel. The exact Hebrew equivalent is Nirit. Also, akin to Nirel. *See* Nirel.

Nirtza (נִרְצָה) From the Hebrew, meaning "desirable." The exact Hebrew equivalent is Nirtza. MASCULINE HEBREW EQUIVALENTS: Chamadel, Chemdan, Nachman.

Nisa, Nissa (נִסָּה) From the Hebrew, meaning "to test." The exact Hebrew equivalent is Nisa. MASCULINE HEBREW EQUIVALENTS: Nes, Nisi, Nisim.

Nita (נְטָעָה) From the Hebrew, meaning "to plant." The exact Hebrew equivalent is Nita. MASCULINE HEBREW EQUIVALENTS: Neta, Neti'a, Nitai.

Nitza, Nitzah (נִיצָה) A unisex name. From the Hebrew, meaning "flower bud, blossom." The exact Hebrew equivalent is Nitza.

Nitzana (נִיצָנָה) A variant form of Nitza. *See* Nitza. The exact Hebrew equivalent is Nitzana.

Nitzanit (נִיצָנִית) A variant form of Nitza. *See* Nitza. The exact Hebrew equivalent is Nitzanit.

Nitzra (נִצְרָה) From the Hebrew, meaning "guard." The exact Hebrew equivalent is Nitzra. The exact masculine equivalent is Notzer.

Niva (נִיבָה) From the Hebrew, meaning "speech." The exact Hebrew equivalent is Niva. The exact masculine equivalent is Niv.

Noa, Noah (נֹעָה) From the Hebrew, meaning "wandering, wanderer." The exact Hebrew equivalent is No'a. MASCULINE HEBREW EQUIVALENTS:

Aminad, Golyat, Yagli. In Numbers 26:33, one of Tzelophchad's five daughters.

Noadya (נוֹעַדְיָה) From the Hebrew, meaning "appointed by God." The exact Hebrew equivalent is No'adya. In Nehemiah 6:14, a prophetess who was hired to discourage Nehemiah from completing the rebuilding of the walls of Jerusalem.

Noaha A feminine form of Noah. *See* Noah (*masculine section*).

Noelle A feminine form of Noel. *See* Noel (*masculine section*).

Noemi A variant form of Naomi. *See* Naomi.

Nofia, Nofiah, Nofiya (נוֹפִיָה) From the Hebrew, meaning "beautiful landscape." The exact Hebrew equivalent is Nofiya. The exact masculine equivalent is Nof.

Noga, Nogah (נוֹגַה) A unisex name. From the Hebrew, meaning "morning light, brightness." The exact Hebrew equivalent is Noga.

Noia A variant spelling of Noya. *See* Noya.

Nola From the Celtic, meaning "famous." HEBREW EQUIVALENTS: Degula, Hillela, Odeh'le'ya. MASCULINE HEBREW EQUIVALENTS: Hillel, Noda, Yehuda.

Nomi A variant form of Naomi. *See* Naomi.

Nophia A variant spelling of Nofia. *See* Nofia.

Nora, Norah From the Latin, meaning "honor, respect." HEBREW EQUIVALENTS: Hadura, Nediva, Nichbada. MASCULINE HEBREW EQUIVALENTS: Avinadav, Hadar, Nadav.

Noreen A variant Irish form of Nora. *See* Nora.

Noreena A variant form of Noreen. *See* Noreen.

Norene A variant spelling of Noreen. *See* Noreen.

Nori A pet form of Noreen. *See* Noreen.

Norma From the Latin, meaning "exact to the pattern, normal, peaceful." HEBREW EQUIVALENTS: Margaya, Menucha, Meshulemet. MASCULINE HEBREW EQUIVALENTS: Marg'oa, Sha'anan, Shalom.

Norrie A pet form of Nora. *See* Nora.

Notza, Notzah (נוֹצָה) A unisex name. From the Hebrew, meaning "feather." The exact Hebrew equivalent is Notza.

Notzi (נוֹצִי) A variant form of Notza. *See* Notza.

Nova From the Latin, meaning "new," referring to a star. HEBREW EQUIVALENTS: Chadasha, Kochava, Mazal. MASCULINE HEBREW EQUIVALENTS: Bar-Kochva, Kochav, Mazal-Tov.

Novela, Novella From the Latin, meaning "new, unusual." HEBREW EQUIVALENTS: Chadasha, Rishona. MASCULINE HEBREW EQUIVALENTS: Chadash, Rishon.

Noya (נוֹיָה) From the Hebrew, meaning "beautiful, ornamented." The exact Hebrew equivalent is Noya. The exact masculine equivalent is Noi.

Nura (נוּרָה/נוּרָא) From the Hebrew and Aramaic, meaning "light, bright." The exact Hebrew equivalent is Nura. The exact masculine equivalent is Nur.

Nuriah A variant spelling of Nuriya. *See* Nuriya.

Nurit (נוּרִית) A plant with bright red and yellow flowers, common in Israel. A variant form of Nura. *See* Nura. The exact Hebrew equivalent is Nurit.

Nurita (נוּרִיתָה) A variant form of Nurit. *See* Nurit. The exact Hebrew equivalent is Nurita.

Nuriya (נוּרִיָה) From the Hebrew, meaning "light of the Lord." The exact Hebrew equivalent is Nuriya. MASCULINE HEBREW EQUIVALENTS: Neriya, Neriyahu, Uriya.

❧ O ❧

Oda, Odah From the Greek, meaning "song, ode." HEBREW EQUIVA-LENTS: Negina, Ne'ima, Shira. MASCULINE HEBREW EQUIVALENTS: Zamir, Zemarya, Zemer.

Odeda (עוֹדְדָה) From the Hebrew, meaning "to encourage." The exact Hebrew equivalent is Odeda. The exact masculine equivalent is Oded.

Odedia A variant form of Odeda. *See* Odeda.

Odeh (אוֹדֶה) From the Hebrew, meaning "I will praise." The exact Hebrew equivalent is Odeh. MASCULINE HEBREW EQUIVALENTS: Hillel, Yehalel, Yehuda.

Odele From the Greek, meaning "ode, melody." HEBREW EQUIVALENTS: Negina, Shira, Zemira. MASCULINE HEBREW EQUIVALENTS: Zamir, Zemer, Zimri.

Odeleya (אוֹדְלְיָה) From the Hebrew, meaning "I will praise God." The exact Hebrew equivalent is Ode'le'ya. MASCULINE HEBREW EQUIVALENTS: Hillel, Yehalel, Yehuda.

Odelia, Odeliah Variant spellings of Odeleya. *See* Odeleya.

Odell A variant spelling of Odele. *See* Odele.

Odera (עוֹדְרָה) From the Hebrew, meaning "plow." The exact Hebrew equivalent is Odera. MASCULINE HEBREW EQUIVALENTS: Nirel, Nirya, Niv.

Odetta A pet form of Odele. *See* Odele.

Odette A variant form of Odetta. *See* Odetta.

Odiya (אוֹדִיָה) From the Hebrew, meaning "song of praise to God." The exact Hebrew equivalent is Odiya. MASCULINE HEBREW EQUIVALENTS: Hillel, Yehuda.

Oferet (עוֹפֶרֶת) From the Hebrew, meaning "lead, leaden." The exact Hebrew equivalent is Oferet.

Ofira (אוֹפִירָה) From the Hebrew, meaning "gold." The exact Hebrew equivalent is Ofira. The exact masculine equivalent is Ofir.

Ofna (אָפְנָה) From the Aramaic, meaning "appearance." The exact Hebrew equivalent is Ofna. MASCULINE HEBREW EQUIVALENTS: Nevat, Peni'el, Penu'el.

Ofnat (אָפְנַת) From the Hebrew, meaning "wheel." The exact Hebrew equivalent is Ofnat. MASCULINE HEBREW EQUIVALENTS: Galal, Galil.

Ofniya (אָפְנִיָה) A variant form of Ofna. *See* Ofna. The exact Hebrew equivalent is Ofniya.

Ofra (עָפְרָה) A unisex name. From the Hebrew, meaning "young mountain goat" or "young deer." The exact Hebrew equivalent is Ofra.

Ofrat (עָפְרַת) A variant form of Ofra. *See* Ofra. The exact Hebrew equivalent is Ofrat.

Ofrit (עָפְרִית) A variant form of Ofra. *See* Ofra. The exact Hebrew equivalent is Ofrit.

Ola, Olah (עוֹלָה) From the Hebrew, meaning "immigrant." Also, from the Old Norse, meaning "ancestor." The exact Hebrew equivalent is Ola. The exact masculine equivalent is Oleh.

Olga From the Russian and Old Norse, meaning "holy" or "peace." HEBREW EQUIVALENTS: Chagit, Chagiya, Kedosha. MASCULINE HEBREW EQUIVALENTS: Chaga, Kadosh, Zakai.

Oliva A variant form of Olive. *See* Olive.

Olive From the Latin, meaning "olive," a symbol of peace. HEBREW EQUIVALENTS: Za'yit, Zayta, Zaytana. MASCULINE HEBREW EQUIVALENTS: Za'yit, Zaytan.

Olivia A variant form of Olive. *See* Olive.

Olympia A name derived from the Greek mountain Olympus, on which the gods resided. HEBREW EQUIVALENTS: Bat-El, Betu'el, Ode'le'ya. MASCULINE HEBREW EQUIVALENTS: Avi'el, Betu'el, Iti'el.

Omenet (אוֹמֶנֶת) From the Hebrew, meaning "nurse, governess, rearer." The exact Hebrew equivalent is Omenet. The exact masculine equivalent is Omein.

Ona, Onah (עוֹנָה) From the Hebrew, meaning "season, period of time." The exact Hebrew equivalent is Ona. MASCULINE HEBREW EQUIVALENTS: Atari, Idan, Ido.

Oona A variant form of the Latin name Una, meaning "the one." The Hebrew equivalent is Rishona. The masculine equivalent is Rosh.

Opal From the Sanskrit, meaning "precious stone." HEBREW EQUIVALENTS: Hadara, Hadarit, Hadura. MASCULINE HEBREW EQUIVALENTS: Adi, Adin, Eter.

Ophelia From the Greek, meaning "serpent" or "to help." HEBREW EQUIVALENTS: Eli'ezra, Ezra'ela, Ozera. MASCULINE HEBREW EQUIVALENTS: Ezra, Ezri, Nachash.

Ophira A variant spelling of Ofira. *See* Ofira.

Ophnat A variant spelling of Ofnat. *See* Ofnat.

Ophra A variant spelling of Ofra. *See* Ofra.

Ophrat A variant spelling of Ofrat. *See* Ofrat.

Opra, Oprah Variant forms of Ofra. *See* Ofra.

Ora, Orah (אוֹרָה) From the Hebrew, meaning "light." Also, from the Latin, meaning "gold." The exact Hebrew equivalent is Ora. The exact masculine equivalent is Or.

Oralee, Ora-Li (אוֹרָה-לִי/אוֹרְלִי) From the Hebrew, meaning "my light." The exact Hebrew equivalent is Orali. The exact masculine equivalent is Orli.

Oranit A variant form of Ornit. *See* Ornit.

Oreiv A variant spelling of Orev. *See* Orev.

Orelle (אוֹר-אֶל) A variant form of Oriel. *See* Oriel.

Orev (עוֹרֵב) A unisex name. From the Hebrew, meaning "raven." In Judges 7:25, a Midianite leader when Gideon was judge. The exact Hebrew equivalent is Oreiv.

Ori (אוֹרִי) A unisex name. From the Hebrew, meaning "my light." The exact Hebrew equivalent is Ori.

Oria, Oriah (אוֹרִיָה) From the Hebrew, meaning "light of God." The exact Hebrew equivalent is Oria. MASCULINE HEBREW EQUIVALENTS: Me'ir, Or, Ori.

Oriana, Orianna (אוֹרִיעָנָה) Possibly derived from the Hebrew name Ori, meaning "my light [God]," plus *ana*, meaning "answered." The exact Hebrew equivalent is Oriana. MASCULINE HEBREW EQUIVALENTS: Me'ir, Ori, Orli.

Oriel, Ori-El (אוֹרִי-אֶל/אוֹרִיאֵל) From the Hebrew, meaning "God is my light." The exact Hebrew equivalent is Ori'el. MASCULINE HEBREW EQUIVALENTS: Avner, Ori, Orli.

Orit (אוֹרִית) A variant form of Ora. *See* Ora. The exact Hebrew equivalent is Orit.

Oriya, Oriyah (אוֹרִיָה) Variant spellings of Oria. *See* Oria.

Orla, Or-La (אוֹר-לָה/אוֹרְלָה) From the Hebrew, meaning "light is hers." The exact Hebrew equivalent is Orla. MASCULINE HEBREW EQUIVALENTS: Or, Orli.

Orlanda A feminine form of the masculine name Orlando. *See* Orlando (*masculine section*).

Orley A variant spelling of Orli. *See* Orli.

Orli, Or-Li (אוֹר-לִי/אוֹרְלִי) A unisex name. From the Hebrew, meaning "light is mine." The exact Hebrew equivalent is Orli.

Orlit (אוֹרְלִית) A variant form of Orli. *See* Orli. The exact Hebrew equivalent is Orlit.

Orly A variant spelling of Orli. *See* Orli.

Orna (אוֹר-נָא/אוֹרְנָה) From the Hebrew, meaning "let there be light" or "pine tree." The exact Hebrew equivalent is Orna. MASCULINE HEBREW EQUIVALENTS: Or, Oren, Oron.

Ornan A variant form of Orna. *See* Orna.

Orni (אוֹרְנִי) From the Hebrew, meaning "pine tree." The exact Hebrew equivalent is Orni. The exact masculine equivalent is Oren.

Ornina (אוֹרְנִינָה) A variant form of Orni. *See* Orni. The exact Hebrew equivalent is Ornina.

Ornit (אוֹרְנִית) A variant form of Orni. *See* Orni. The exact Hebrew equivalent is Ornit.

Orpa, Orpah (עָרְפָּה) From the Hebrew, meaning "neck," connoting stubbornness. The exact Hebrew equivalent is Orpa. MASCULINE HEBREW EQUIVALENTS: Akashya, Ikesh. In Ruth 1:4, a daughter-in-law of Naomi.

Oshra A feminine form of Osher. *See* Osher (*masculine section*).

Oshrat (אָשְׁרַת) From the Hebrew, meaning "my good fortune." The exact Hebrew equivalent is Oshri. The exact masculine equivalent is Oshri.

Osnat (אָתְנַת) An Egyptian name of uncertain meaning. Asenath is the Anglicized form. In Genesis 41:45, the wife of Joseph.

∼ P–Q ∼

Page, Paige From the French, meaning "attendant, server." HEBREW EQUIVALENTS: Ama'a, Shimshona. MASCULINE HEBREW EQUIVALENTS: Avdel, Ovadya, Potifar.

Palma From the Latin, meaning "palm tree." HEBREW EQUIVALENTS: Dikla, Tamar, Tomer. MASCULINE HEBREW EQUIVALENTS: Dekel, Itamar, Miklot.

Paloma A Spanish name derived from the Latin, meaning "dove." The exact feminine and masculine Hebrew equivalent is Yona.

Pam A diminutive form of Pamela. *See* Pamela.

Pamela From the Greek and the Anglo-Saxon, meaning "loved one, sweet one." HEBREW EQUIVALENTS: Ahuva, Chiba, Metuka. MASCULINE HEBREW EQUIVALENTS: David, Magdi'el, Matok.

Pandora From the Greek, meaning "very gifted." In Greek mythology, Pandora was the first woman who, out of curiosity, opened a sealed box and permited human ills to escape into the world. HEBREW EQUIVALENTS: Matana, Netanela, Netina. MASCULINE HEBREW EQUIVALENTS: Doron, Matanya, Navon.

Pania A pet form of Stephania. *See* Stephania.

Pansy An English flower-name. Also, from the French, meaning "to think." HEBREW EQUIVALENTS: Perach, Pericha, Pircha. MASCULINE HEBREW EQUIVALENTS: Parchi, Perach, Perachya.

Pat A pet form of Patricia. *See* Patricia.

Patience From the Latin, meaning "to suffer, persevere, endure." HEBREW EQUIVALENTS: Nitzcha, Nitzchiya, Nitzchona. MASCULINE HEBREW EQUIVALENTS: Avi'ad, Elad, Nitzchi.

Patrice A variant form of Patricia. *See* Patricia.

Patricia The feminine form of Patrick. *See* Patrick (*masculine section*).

Patsy A pet form of Patricia. *See* Patricia.

Patti, Pattie, Patty Pet forms of Patricia. *See* Patricia.

Paula From the Greek, meaning "small." HEBREW EQUIVALENTS: Delila, Ketana. MASCULINE HEBREW EQUIVALENTS: Katan, Tzu'ar, Vofsi.

Paulette A French pet form of Paula. *See* Paula.

Paulina The Spanish form of the French name Pauline. *See* Pauline.

Pauline The feminine French form of the masculine name Paul. *See* Paul (*masculine section*).

Paz (פָּז) A unisex name. From the Hebrew, meaning "gold, golden, sparkling." The exact Hebrew equivalent is Paz.

Paza (פָּזָה) A variant form of Paz. *See* Paz. The exact Hebrew equivalent is Paza.

Pazia, Paziah Variant spellings of Pazya. *See* Pazya.

Pazit (פָּזִית) A variant form of Paz. *See* Paz. The exact Hebrew equivalent is Pazit.

Paziya (פָּזִיָה) A variant form of Pazya. *See* Pazya. The exact Hebrew equivalent is Paziya.

Pazya (פָּזְיָה) From the Hebrew, meaning "God's gold." The exact Hebrew equivalent is Pazya. MASCULINE HEBREW EQUIVALENTS: Paz, Pazi, Upaz.

Pearl From the Latin and Middle English, meaning "pearl." HEBREW EQUIVALENTS: Penina, Segula, Tzefira. MASCULINE HEBREW EQUIVALENTS: Penini, Shoham, Shovai.

Pearla A variant form of Pearl. *See* Pearl.

Peg, Peggie, Peggy Pet forms of Margaret and Pearl. *See* Margaret *and* Pearl.

Pelia, Peliah (פְּלִיאָה) From the Hebrew, meaning "wonder, miracle." The exact Hebrew equivalent is Peli'a. MASCULINE HEBREW EQUIVALENTS: Pela'ya, Peleh, Peli.

Penelope From the Greek, meaning "worker in cloth" or "silent worker." HEBREW EQUIVALENTS: Amal, Amalya, Zeriza. MASCULINE HEBREW EQUIVALENTS: Amel, Ovadya, Oved.

Penina, Peninah (פְּנִינָה) From the Hebrew, meaning "coral" or "pearl." The exact Hebrew equivalent is Penina. The exact masculine equivalent is Penini. In I Samuel 1:2, the wife of Elkanah.

Penini (פְּנִינִי) A unisex name. From the Hebrew, meaning "pearl" or "precious stone." The exact Hebrew equivalent is Penini.

Peninia, Peniniah Variant spellings of Peniniya. *See* Peniniya.

Peninit (פְּנִינִית) From the Hebrew, meaning "pearly." The exact Hebrew equivalent is Peninit. The exact masculine equivalent is Penini.

Peniniya (פְּנִינִיָה) From the Hebrew, meaning "hen, fowl." The exact Hebrew equivalent is Peniniya. MASCULINE HEBREW EQUIVALENTS: Gozal, Tzipor.

Penney, Pennie, Penny Pet forms of Penelope. *See* Penelope.

Pepita A Spanish pet form of Josephine. *See* Josephine.

Pepper (פִּלְפֶּלֶת) From the Sanskrit word for peppercorn, a pungent spice. The Hebrew equivalent is Pilpelet.

Perach (פֶּרַח) A unisex name. From the Hebrew, meaning "flower, blossom." The exact Hebrew equivalent is Perach.

Peri (פְּרִי) From the Hebrew, meaning "fruit." The exact Hebrew equivalent is Peri (P'ri). MASCULINE HEBREW EQUIVALENTS: Peri'el, Porat, Pori'el.

Perl A Yiddish form of Pearl. *See* Pearl.

Perla A Spanish form of Pearl. *See* Pearl.

Peshe (פֶּעשֶׁע) A Yiddish form of Bashe. *See* Bashe.

Pessel (פֶּעסֶעל/פֶּעסֶל) A Yiddish form of Bashe. *See* Bashe.

Petra A feminine form of Peter. *See* Peter (*masculine section*).

Phebe A variant spelling of Phoebe. *See* Phoebe.

Philippa From the Greek, meaning "lover of horses." The feminine form of Philip. *See* Philip (*masculine section*).

Phoebe From the Greek, meaning "bright, shining one." HEBREW EQUIV-ALENTS: Behira, Me'ira, Ora. MASCULINE HEBREW EQUIVALENTS: Avner, Barak, Me'ir.

Phylicia A variant spelling of Felicia. *See* Felicia.

Phylis A variant spelling of Phyllis. *See* Phyllis.

Phyllis From the Greek, meaning "little leaf, green bough." HEBREW EQUIVALENTS: Nitza, Shoshana, Varda. MASCULINE HEBREW EQUIVALENTS: Efra'yim, Pekach, Pura.

Pia From the Latin, meaning "pious." The exact Hebrew equivalent is Chasida. The exact masculine equivalent is Chasid.

Pier A feminine form of Pierre, the French form of Peter. *See* Peter (*masculine section*).

Piper From the Old English, meaning "pipe player."

Pippa A pet form of Philippa. *See* Philippa.

Pircha, Pirchah (פִּרְחָה) From the Hebrew, meaning "flower, blossom." The exact Hebrew equivalent is Pircha. MASCULINE HEBREW EQUIVALENTS: Perach, Perachya, Tzemach.

Pita (פִּיתָה) From the Aramaic, meaning "piece of bread." The exact Hebrew equivalent is Pita. MASCULINE HEBREW EQUIVALENTS: Lachma, Lachmi, Lechem.

Piuta A variant spelling of Piyuta. *See* Piyuta.

Piyuta (פִּיוּטָה) A Hebrew form of the Greek, meaning "poet, poetry." The exact Hebrew equivalent is Piyuta. The exact masculine equivalent is Piyut.

Placidia From the Latin, meaning "tranquil, calm." HEBREW EQUIVALENTS: Menucha, Shalviya, Shlomit. MASCULINE HEBREW EQUIVALENTS: Avishalom, Meshulam, Shlomo.

Pnina, Pninah Variant spellings of Penina. *See* Penina.

Poda (פּוֹדָה) From the Hebrew, meaning "redeemed." The exact Hebrew equivalent is Poda. MASCULINE HEBREW EQUIVALENTS: Peda'el, Pedat, Pedatzur.

Pola The Italian form of Pula (a Croatian port city), meaning "rain." HEBREW EQUIVALENTS: Lital, Malkosha, Ravital. MASCULINE HEBREW EQUIVALENTS: Geshem, Malkosh, Matri.

Polly A variant form of Molly, which was at one time a popular form of Mary. *See* Mary.

Pollyanna A hybrid name formed from Polly and Anna. *See* Polly *and* Anna. Author Eleanor H. Porter (1868-1920) created the name for a fictional character who was eternally optimistic. Tikva is a Hebrew equivalent.

Pora (פּוֹרָה) From the Hebrew, meaning "fruitful." The exact Hebrew equivalent is Pora. MASCULINE HEBREW EQUIVALENTS: Pori'el, Pura.

Porat (פּוֹרָת) A variant form of Pora. *See* Pora. The exact Hebrew equivalent is Porat.

Poria, Poriah Variant spellings of Poriya. *See* Poriya.

Poriya (פּוֹרִיָה) A variant form of Pora. *See* Pora. The exact Hebrew equivalent is Poriya.

Portia From the Latin, meaning "hog." There are no Hebrew equivalents.

Presley A unisex name. From the Old English, meaning "priest's meadow." HEBREW EQUIVALENTS: Adama, Ya'ara, Ya'arit. MASCULINE HEBREW EQUIVALENTS: Hevel, Kahana, Kohen, Ya'ar.

Priscilla From the Latin, meaning "ancient, old." HEBREW EQUIVALENTS: Bilha, Keshisha, Yeshisha. MASCULINE HEBREW EQUIVALENTS: Kadmi'el, Yashish, Zaken.

Prudence From the Latin, meaning "prudent, wise." HEBREW EQUIVA-LENTS: Bina, Buna, Tushiya. MASCULINE HEBREW EQUIVALENTS: Haskel, Navon.

Prue A pet form of Prudence. *See* Prudence.

Pua, Puah (פּוּעָה) From the Hebrew, meaning "to groan, cry out." The exact Hebrew equivalent is Pu'a. In Exodus 1:15, one of the two midwives who delivered Hebrew babies.

Queena, Queene Variant forms of Queenie. *See* Queenie.

Queenie A nickname for Regina, from the Latin, meaning "queen." The Hebrew equivalent is Malka. The masculine equivalent is Melech.

R

Raanana (רַעֲנָנָה) From the Hebrew, meaning "fresh, luscious, beautiful." The exact Hebrew equivalent is Ra'anana. The exact masculine equivalent is Ra'anan.

Rachael, Rachaele, Rachayl Variant spellings of Rachel. *See* Rachel.

Rachel, Rachell (רָחֵל) From the Hebrew, meaning "ewe," a symbol of purity and gentility. The exact Hebrew equivalent is Rachel. MASCULINE HEBREW EQUIVALENTS: Adin, Adiv, Ra'anan. In Genesis 29:6, Jacob's wife, the daughter of Laban.

Rachela (רָחֵלָה) A variant form of Rachel. *See* Rachel. The exact Hebrew equivalent is Rachela.

Racheli A pet form of Rachel. *See* Rachel.

Rachelle A variant spelling of Rachel. *See* Rachel.

Rae A pet form of Rachel. *See* Rachel. HEBREW EQUIVALENTS: Bat-Shu'a, Mara, Marata. MASCULINE HEBREW EQUIVALENTS: Amos, Ben-Oni, Onan.

Rafa From the Arabic, meaning "well-being, good health." HEBREW EQUIVALENTS: Refa'ela, Refu'a, Terufa. MASCULINE HEBREW EQUIVALENTS: Asa, Rafi, Refa'el.

Rafaela, Rafaele Variant spellings of Refaela. *See* Refaela.

Rafi A unisex name derived from Refael and Refaela. *See* Refael (*masculine section*) *and* Refaela (*feminine section*).

Rafia A variant spelling of Rafya. *See* Rafya.

Rafya (רְפָיָה) From the Hebrew, meaning "the healing of the Lord." The exact Hebrew equivalent is Rafya. The exact masculine equivalent is Refa'el.

Rahel A variant spelling of Rachel. *See* Rachel.

Rahela, Raheli Variant forms of Rahel. *See* Rahel.

Raina, Raine (רֵיינֶע/רֵיינָא) From the Latin, meaning "to rule." Akin to Regina. *See* Regina. Also, from the Yiddish, meaning "clean, pure." *See* Rayna.

Raisa (רֵייסָא) From the Yiddish, meaning "rose." The exact Hebrew equivalent is Shoshana. The exact masculine equivalent is Shoshan.

Raise (רֵייסֶע) A variant form of Raisa. *See* Raisa.

Raisel (רֵייסל) A pet form of Raise. *See* Raise.

Raissa, Raisse Variant spellings of Raisa. *See* Raisa.

Raize (רֵייזֶע) A variant form of Raise. *See* Raise.

Raizel (רֵייזל) A pet form of Raize. *See* Raize.

Raizi A pet form of Raize. *See* Raize.

Rama (רָמָה) A unisex name. From the Hebrew, meaning "lofty, exalted." The exact Hebrew equivalent is Rama.

Rami, Ramie (רָמִי) Variant forms of Rama. *See* Rama. The exact Hebrew equivalent is Rami.

Ramit (רָמִית) A variant form of Rama. *See* Rama. The exact Hebrew equivalent is Ramit.

Ramona A feminine form of the masculine Raymond, meaning "peace" or "protection." Raymonda is a variant form. HEBREW EQUIVALENTS: Shlomit, Shulamit, Tira. MASCULINE HEBREW EQUIVALENTS: Shalom, Shelomo, Shemaryahu.

Ramot (רָמוֹת) A variant form of Rama. *See* Rama. The exact Hebrew equivalent is Ramot.

Rana A variant spelling of Raina. *See* Raina.

Ranae A variant form of René. *See* René.

Ranana A variant spelling of Raanana. *See* Raanana.

Randelle A feminine form of Randall. *See* Randall (*masculine section*).

Randi, Randy Feminine pet forms of Randolph. *See* Randolph (*masculine section*).

Rani (רָנִי) From the Hebrew, meaning "my song." The exact Hebrew equivalent is Rani. MASCULINE HEBREW EQUIVALENTS: Ron, Ronen, Roni.

Rania, Raniah Variant spellings of Ranya. *See* Ranya.

Ranit (רָנִית) From the Hebrew, meaning "joy" or "song." The exact Hebrew equivalent is Ranit. MASCULINE HEBREW EQUIVALENTS: Ron, Roni, Ronli.

Ranita (רָנִיתָה) A variant form of Ranit. *See* Ranit. The exact Hebrew equivalent is Ranita.

Ranny A pet form of Frances. *See* Frances.

Ranya (רַמְה) From the Hebrew, meaning "song of the Lord." The exact Hebrew equivalent is Ranya. The exact masculine equivalent is Zemarya.

Raphaela A variant spelling of Refaela. *See* Refaela.

Raphaelle A feminine form of the masculine name Raphael. *See* Raphael (*masculine section*).

Raquel A variant Spanish form of Rachel. *See* Rachel.

Raven From the Old French, meaning "to devour greedily." Also, a large black bird of the crow family. HEBREW EQUIVALENTS: A'ya, Efrona, Salit, Tzipora. MASCULINE HEBREW EQUIVALENTS: Efron, Paru'ach, Tzipor, Yarkon.

Ravid (רָבִיד) A unisex name. From the Hebrew, meaning "necklace." The exact Hebrew equivalent is Ravid.

Ravital (רְבִיטַל) From the Hebrew, meaning "abundance of dew." The exact Hebrew equivalent is Ravital. MASCULINE HEBREW EQUIVALENTS: Raviv, Tal, Tali.

Raviva (רְבִיבָה) A variant form of Reviva. *See* Reviva. The exact Hebrew equivalent is Raviva.

Ray, Raye Pet forms of Rachel. *See* Rachel. Also, from the Celtic, meaning "grace, gracious." *See* Grace.

Raya (רַע) A unisex name. From the Hebrew, meaning "friend." The exact Hebrew equivalent is Raya.

Rayna (רֵיינָא) A Yiddish form of Catherine, meaning "pure, clean." HEBREW EQUIVALENTS: Berura, Me'ira, Penuya. MASCULINE HEBREW EQUIVALENTS: Amizakai, Barur, Me'ir.

Rayne (רֵיינָע) A variant form of Rayna. *See* Rayna.

Rayzel (רֵייזֶעל/רֵייזְל) A pet form of Raize. *See* Raize.

Raz (רָז) A unisex name. From the Hebrew, meaning "secret." The exact Hebrew equivalent is Raz.

Razi (רָזִי) A unisex name. From the Hebrew, meaning "my secret." The exact Hebrew equivalent is Razi.

Razia, Raziah Variant spellings of Raziya. *See* Raziya.

Raziela, Raziella (רָזִיאֵלָה) From the Hebrew, meaning "God is my secret." The exact Hebrew equivalent is Razi'ela. The exact masculine equivalent is Razi'el.

Razil A variant spelling of Raisel. *See* Raisel.

Razilee A variant spelling of Razili. *See* Razili.

Razili (רָזִילִי) From the Hebrew, meaning "my secret." The exact Hebrew equivalent is Razili. MASCULINE HEBREW EQUIVALENTS: Raz, Razi, Razi'el.

Razina (רָזִינָה) A Hebrew form of Rosina. *See* Rosina. The exact Hebrew equivalent is Razina.

Raziya (רַזִיָה) From the Hebrew, meaning "secret of the Lord." The exact Hebrew equivalent is Raziya. The masculine equivalent is Razi'el.

Reatha A variant form of Rita. *See* Rita.

Reba (רִיבָּה) A pet form of Rebecca. *See also* Riva. The exact Hebrew equivalent is Reba.

Rebecca (רִבְקָה) From the Hebrew, meaning "to tie, bind." Animals were fattened before being tied and slaughtered, hence the secondary meaning of "voluptuous, beautiful, desirable." The exact Hebrew equivalent is Rivka. MASCULINE HEBREW EQUIVALENTS: Chemdan, Na'aman, Ra'anan. In Genesis 22:23, the daughter of Betuel; wife of Isaac.

Reda A variant form of Rita. *See* Rita.

Reena A variant spelling of Rina. *See* Rina.

Reeta A variant spelling of Rita. *See* Rita.

Refaela (רְפָאֵלָה) From the Hebrew, meaning "God has healed." The exact Hebrew equivalent is Refa'ela. The exact masculine equivalent is Refa'el.

Regan A variant form of Regina. *See* Regina.

Regina From the Latin, meaning "to rule," or from the Anglo-Saxon, meaning "pure." HEBREW EQUIVALENTS: Atara, Berura, Malka. MASCULINE HEBREW EQUIVALENTS: Avraham, Katri'el, Yisra'el.

Reina, Reine Variant spellings of Rayna. *See* Rayna.

Reishit A variant spelling of Reshit. *See* Reshit.

Reita A variant spelling of Rita. *See* Rita.

Reitha A variant spelling of Reatha. *See* Reatha.

Reizel, Reizl Variant spellings of Raisel. *See* Raisel.

Remiza (רְמִיזָה) From the Hebrew, meaning "sign, signal." The exact Hebrew equivalent is Remiza. The exact masculine equivalent is Remez.

Rena A short form of Regina or Serena. *See* Regina *and* Serena. Also, variant spellings of Rina. *See* Rina.

Renae A variant spelling of René. *See* René.

Renah A variant spelling of Rina. *See* Rina.

Renai A variant spelling of René. *See* René.

Renana (רְנָנָה) From the Hebrew, meaning "joy" or "song." The exact Hebrew equivalent is Renana. MASCULINE HEBREW EQUIVALENTS: Ranen, Ranon, Ronli.

Renanit (רְנָנִית) A variant form of Renana. *See* Renana. The exact Hebrew equivalent is Renanit.

Renata From the Latin, meaning "to be born again." HEBREW EQUIVALENTS: Chava, Cha'ya, Techiya. MASCULINE HEBREW EQUIVALENTS: Cha'yim, Chiya, Yechi'el.

René, Renée French forms of Renata. *See* Renata.

Renette A French pet form of René. *See* René.

Renina (רְנִינָה) A variant form of Renana. *See* Renana. The exact Hebrew equivalent is Renina.

Renita A Spanish pet form of René. *See* René.

Renni, Rennie Pet forms of Renata. *See* Renata.

Rephaela A variant spelling of Refaela. *See* Refaela.

Resa A pet form of Theresa. *See* Theresa.

Reshit (רֵאשִׁית) From the Hebrew, meaning "first, beginning." The exact Hebrew equivalent is Reshit. MASCULINE HEBREW EQUIVALENTS: Bechor, Rishon, Yiftach.

Reubena A variant spelling of Reuvena. *See* Reuvena.

Reut (רְעוּת) From the Hebrew, meaning "friend, friendship." The exact Hebrew equivalent is Re'ut. MASCULINE HEBREW EQUIVALENTS: Raya, Re'uel, Yedidya.

Reuvat (רְאוּבַת) A feminine form of Reuven, meaning "behold, a daughter!" The exact Hebrew equivalent is Re'uvat. The masculine equivalent is Re'uven.

Reuvena (רְאוּבֵנָה) A feminine form of Reuven, meaning "behold, a son!" The exact Hebrew equivalent is Re'uvena. The exact masculine equivalent is Re'uven.

Reva, Reeva (רִיבָה) Pet forms of Rebecca. *See* Rebecca. The exact Hebrew equivalent is Riva.

Reviva (רְבִיבָה) From the Hebrew, meaning "dew" or "rain." The exact Hebrew equivalent is Reviva. The exact masculine equivalent is Raviv.

Rexana The feminine form of Rex, meaning "king." HEBREW EQUIVALENTS: Atara, Malka, Tzefira. MASCULINE HEBREW EQUIVALENTS: Katri'el, Melech.

Reyna A variant spelling of Rayna. See Rayna.

Rhea From the Greek, meaning "protector of cities." HEBREW EQUIVALENTS: Avigdora, Magena, Shimrit. MASCULINE HEBREW EQUIVALENTS: Avigdor, Chetzron, Shemaryahu.

Rheba A variant spelling of Reba. See Reba.

Rheta A variant spelling of Rita. See Rita. Also, from the Greek, meaning "one who speaks well." HEBREW EQUIVALENTS: Amira, Devora, Niva. MASCULINE HEBREW EQUIVALENTS: Amaryahu, Imri, Niv.

Rhoda From the Greek, meaning "rose." The exact feminine and masculine Hebrew equivalent is Vered.

Rhode A variant form of Rhoda. See Rhoda.

Rhona A hybrid name formed from Rose and Anna. See Rose *and* Anna.

Rhonda From the Celtic, meaning "powerful river," or from the Welsh, meaning "good spear." HEBREW EQUIVALENTS: Arnona, Bat-Yam, Chanit. MASCULINE HEBREW EQUIVALENTS: Arnon, Aviyam, Siryon.

Ria A pet form of Victoria. See Victoria.

Rica A pet form of Ricarda. See Ricarda.

Ricarda A feminine Italian form of Ricardo. See Ricardo (*masculine section*).

Richarda A feminine form of Richard. See Richard (*masculine section*).

Richelle A feminine pet form of Richard. See Richard (*masculine section*).

Ricka, Ricki, Rickie Pet forms of Patricia, Rebecca, Ricarda, and Roberta. See Patricia, Rebecca, Ricarda, *and* Roberta.

Rickma (רִקְמָה) From the Hebrew, meaning "woven product." The exact Hebrew equivalent is Rikma. The exact masculine equivalent is Rekem.

Ricky A variant spelling of Ricki. *See* Ricki.

Rifka (רִיפְקָא) A Yiddish form of Rivka. *See* Rivka.

Rifke (רִיפְקֶע) A Yiddish form of Rivka. *See* Rivka.

Rifki A pet form of Rivka. *See* Rivka.

Riki, Rikki Pet forms of Erica. *See* Erica.

Rikma A variant spelling of Rickma. *See* Rickma.

Rimona (רִמוֹנָה) The feminine form of Rimon. *See* Rimon. The exact Hebrew equivalent is Rimona.

Rina (רִנָה) From the Hebrew, meaning "joy." The exact Hebrew equivalent is Rina. MASCULINE HEBREW EQUIVALENTS: Ranen, Rani, Ron.

Rinat (רִינַת) A variant form of Rina. *See* Rina.

Risa, **Rissa** A pet form of Theresa. *See* Theresa.

Rishona (רִאשׁוֹנָה) From the Hebrew, meaning "first." The exact Hebrew equivalent is Rishona. The exact masculine equivalent is Rishon.

Rita From the Sanskrit, meaning "brave" or "honest." HEBREW EQUIVALENTS: Abira, Amtza, Azri'ela. MASCULINE HEBREW EQUIVALENTS: Abir, Adir, Aviram. Also, a short form of Margarita. *See* Margarita.

Ritasue A hybrid name formed from Rita and Sue. *See* Rita *and* Sue.

Riva From the Old French, meaning "coastline, shore." Also, a pet form of Rivka. *See* Rivka.

Rivi (רִיבִי) A pet form of Rivka. *See* Rivka. The exact Hebrew equivalent is Rivi.

Rivka, Rivkah (רִבְקָה) From the Hebrew, meaning "to bind." Rebecca is the Anglicized form. *See* Rebecca.

Rivke (רִבְקֶע) A Yiddish form of Rivka. *See* Rivka.

Rivki, Rivkie, Rivky Pet forms of Rivka. *See* Rivka.

Roanna A hybrid name formed from Rose and Anna. *See* Rose *and* Anna.

Robbi, Robbie Pet forms of Roberta. *See* Roberta.

Roberta The feminine form of Robert. *See* Robert (*masculine section*).

Robertina A pet form of Roberta. *See* Roberta.

Robin, Robyn Pet forms of Roberta. *See* Roberta.

Rochel (רָאחֶעל/רָאכְל) A Yiddish form of Rachel. *See* Rachel.

Rochelle From the Old French, meaning "small rock." Also, a variant form of Rachel. HEBREW EQUIVALENTS: Avni'ela, Ritzpa, Tzuriya. MASCULINE HEBREW EQUIVALENTS: Achitzur, Tzur, Tzuri.

Rolanda A feminine form of Roland. *See* Roland (*masculine section*).

Roma (רוֹמָה) From the Hebrew, meaning "heights, lofty, exalted." The exact Hebrew equivalent is Roma. The exact masculine equivalent is Rom.

Romema (רוֹמֵמָה) From the Hebrew, meaning "heights, lofty, exalted." The exact Hebrew equivalent is Romema. The exact masculine equivalent is Romem.

Romi A variant pet form of Romema. *See* Romema.

Romia, Romiah Variant spellings of Romiya. *See* Romiya.

Romie A variant spelling of Romi. *See* Romi.

Romit (רוֹמִית) A variant form of Roma. *See* Roma. The exact Hebrew equivalent is Romit.

Romiya (רוֹמִיָה) A variant form of Romema. *See* Romema. The exact Hebrew equivalent is Romiya.

Ron (רוֹן) A unisex name. From the Hebrew, meaning "joy" or "song." The exact Hebrew equivalent is Ron.

Rona From the Gaelic, meaning "seal," or from the Hebrew, meaning "joy" or "song." The exact Hebrew equivalent is Rona. The exact masculine equivalent is Ron.

Ronalda A feminine form of Ronald. *See* Ronald (*masculine section*).

Ronda A variant spelling of Rhonda. *See* Rhonda.

Ronela, Ronella (רוֹנְאֵלָה) Variant forms of Ron. *See* Ron. The exact Hebrew equivalent is Ronela.

Roni (רוֹנִי) A unisex name. A variant form of Ron. *See* Ron. The exact Hebrew equivalent is Roni.

Ronia, Roniah Variant spellings of Roniya. *See* Roniya.

Ronili (רוֹנִי-לִי/רוֹנִילִי) From the Hebrew, meaning "joy is mine." The exact Hebrew equivalent is Ronili. MASCULINE HEBREW EQUIVALENTS: Roni, Ronli.

Ronit (רוֹנִית) From the Hebrew, meaning "joy" or "singer, song-ster." The exact Hebrew equivalent is Ronit. MASCULINE HEBREW EQUIV-ALENTS: Marnin, Ron, Roni.

Roniya (רוֹנִיָה) A variant form of Ron, meaning "joy of the Lord." The exact Hebrew equivalent is Roniya. MASCULINE HEBREW EQUIVALENTS: Ron, Roni.

Ronli, Ron-Li (רוֹן-לִי/רוֹנְלִי) A unisex name. From the Hebrew, meaning "song is mine." The exact Hebrew equivalent is Ronli.

Ronne A feminine pet form of Ronald. *See* Ronald (*masculine section*).

Ronnell A variant form of Ronela. *See* Ronella.

Ronni, Ronnie Feminine pet forms of Ronald. *See* Ronald (*masculine section*).

Ronnit A variant spelling of Ronit. *See* Ronit.

Ronny A variant spelling of Ronnie. *See* Ronnie.

Ronya (רוֹנְיָה) From the Hebrew, meaning "song of God." A variant form of Roniya. *See* Roniya. The exact Hebrew equivalent is Ronya.

Rori, Rory Irish feminine forms of Robert and Roderick. *See* Robert *and* Roderick (*masculine section*).

Rosa A popular Italian form of Rose. *See* Rose.

Rosabel From the Latin and French, meaning "beautiful rose." *See* Rose.

Rosalie A variant French pet form of Rose. *See* Rose.

Rosalind A pet form of Rose. *See* Rose.

Rosalinda A Spanish form of Rosalind. *See* Rosalind.

Rosaline A variant form of Rosalind. *See* Rosalind.

Rosalyn A variant form of Rosalind. *See* Rosalind.

Rosanna A hybrid name formed from Rosa and Anna. *See* Rosa *and* Anna.

Rosanne A hybrid name formed from Rose and Anne. *See* Rose *and* Anne.

Rose The English form of the Latin name Rosa, meaning "rose." The feminine and masculine Hebrew equivalent is Vered.

Roselotte A hybrid name formed from Rose and Lotte. *See* Rose *and* Lotte.

Roselyn A variant form of Rosalind. *See* Rosalind.

Rosemary A hybrid name formed from Rose and Mary. *See* Rose *and* Mary.

Rosetta An Italian pet form of Rose. *See* Rose.

Rosette A French pet form of Rose. *See* Rose.

Rosi, Rosie Pet forms of Rose. *See* Rose.

Rosina, Rosine Pet forms of Rose. *See* Rose.

Rosita A pet form of Rose. *See* Rose.

Roslyn A variant spelling of Rosalyn. *See* Rosalyn.

Rotem (רֹתֶם) A unisex name. From the Hebrew, meaning "to bind." Also, a plant found in southern Israel. The exact Hebrew equivalent is Rotem.

Rowena From the Old English, meaning "rugged land," and from the Celtic, meaning "flowery white hair." HEBREW EQUIVALENTS: Artzit, Dala, Delila. MASCULINE HEBREW EQUIVALENTS: Artza, Artzi, Lavan.

Roxane, Roxanna, Roxanne From the Persian, meaning "dawn, brilliant light." HEBREW EQUIVALENTS: Barakit, Bat-Shachar, Shacharit. MASCULINE HEBREW EQUIVALENTS: Avi-Shachar, Ben-Shachar, Tzafrir.

Roxie A variant spelling of Roxy.

Roxine A variant form of Roxanne. *See* Roxanne.

Roxy A pet form of Roxanne. *See* Roxanne.

Roz A pet form of Rosalyn. *See* Rosalyn.

Rozelin A variant spelling of Rosaline. *See* Rosaline.

Rozella A hybrid name formed from Rose and Ella. *See* Rose *and* Ella.

Rozina A variant spelling of Rosina. *See* Rosina.

Rubena A variant form of Reuvena. *See* Reuvena.

Ruby From the Latin and French, meaning "precious reddish stone." HEBREW EQUIVALENTS: Bareket, Margalit, Penina. MASCULINE HEBREW EQUIVALENTS: Avikar, Sapir, Shoham.

Ruchama (רוּחָמָה) From the Hebrew, meaning "compassion, consolation." The exact Hebrew equivalent is Ruchama. MASCULINE HEBREW EQUIVALENTS: Nachman, Nachum, Yerucham.

Rudelle From the Old High German, meaning "famous one." HEBREW EQUIVALENTS: Ya'el, Yehudit, Zimra. MASCULINE HEBREW EQUIVALENTS: Hillel, Shevach, Shimi.

Rue From the Old High German, meaning "fame." A variant form of Rudelle. *See* Rudelle.

Rula From the Middle English and the Latin, meaning "ruler." HEBREW EQUIVALENTS: Alufa, Malka, Sara. MASCULINE HEBREW EQUIVALENTS: Aluf, Elrad, Yisra'el.

Ruschel, Ruschele, Ruschell, Ruschelle Variant spellings of Rochelle. *See* Rochelle.

Rut The Hebrew form of Ruth. *See* Ruth.

Ruth (רוּת) From the Syriac and Hebrew, meaning "friendship." The exact Hebrew equivalent is Rut. MASCULINE HEBREW EQUIVALENTS: Amit, Amitai, David. In Ruth 1:4, the daughter-in-law of Naomi.

Ruthanna A hybrid name formed from Ruth and Anna. *See* Ruth *and* Anna.

Ruthi, Ruthie, Ruthy Pet forms of Ruth. *See* Ruth.

Ruti (רוּתִי) A pet form of Rut. *See* Rut. The exact Hebrew equivalent is Ruti.

Ryna A variant spelling of Rina. *See* Rina.

~ S ~

Saada (סַעֲדָה) A unisex name. A variant form of the masculine name Saad, meaning "support." Sa'ada is the exact Hebrew equivalent.

Saba (סָבָה/סָבָא) A unisex name. From the Aramaic and Hebrew, meaning "old, aged" or "grandfather." The exact Hebrew equivalent is Saba.

Sabaria A variant spelling of Tzabaria. *See* Tzabaria

Sabina, Sabine Feminine forms of the Latin Sabin, meaning "of the Sabines." The Sabines were an ancient Italian people who conquered the Romans in 290 B.C.E. Savina is a variant form.

Sabra (סַבְרָא/סַבְרָה) A unisex name. From the Arabic, meaning "cactus, prickly pear." The exact Hebrew equivalent is Sabra. Akin to Tzabara. *See* Tzabara.

Sabrina A pet form of Sabra. *See* Sabra.

Sacha *Also spelled* Sasha. A Russian pet form of Alexandra. *See* Alexandra.

Sadi A variant spelling of Sadie. *See* Sadie.

Sadie A pet form of Sarah. *See* Sarah.

Sadira (סָדִירָה) From the Arabic and Hebrew, meaning "organized, regulated." The exact Hebrew equivalent is Sadira. The exact masculine equivalent is Sadir.

461

Sady, **Sadye** Variant spellings of Sadie. *See* Sadie.

Safia An Arabic form of Sophia. *See* Sophia.

Sage A unisex name. From the Latin, meaning "wise." HEBREW EQUIVA-LENTS: Chochma, Ge'ona, Ge'onit. MASCULINE HEBREW EQUIVALENTS: Ish-Sechel, Navon, Zavin.

Sahara (סַהֲרָה) From the Hebrew, meaning "moon." The exact Hebrew equivalent is Sahara. MASCULINE HEBREW EQUIVALENTS: Chodesh, Yerach.

Saidye A modern spelling of Sadie. *See* Sadie.

Salida From the Old German, meaning "happiness, joy." HEBREW EQUIVALENTS: Sasona, Semecha, Simcha. MASCULINE HEBREW EQUIVALENTS: Sason, Simchon, Simchoni.

Salima A feminine form of Salim, meaning "tranquility." *See* Salim (*masculine section*).

Salit (סַלְעִית) From the Hebrew, meaning "rock, rocky." The exact Hebrew equivalent is Salit. MASCULINE HEBREW EQUIVALENTS: Even, Regem, Sapir.

Salli, **Sallie**, **Sally** Variant forms of Sarah. *See* Sarah.

Salome (שְׁלוֹמִית) From the Hebrew, meaning "peaceful." The exact Hebrew equivalent is Shlomit (Shelomit). The exact masculine equivalent is Shelomo (Shlomo).

Samantha From the Aramaic, meaning "listener." Akin to Samuela. *See* Samuela.

Samara (שׁוֹמְרוֹנָה) From the Latin, meaning "seed of the elm," and from the Hebrew, meaning "guardian." The feminine Hebrew equivalent is Shomrona. The masculine equivalent is Shomron.

Samie, **Sammie**, **Sammy**, **Sammye** Pet forms of Samantha and Samuela. *See* Samantha *and* Samuela.

Samuela (שְׁמוּאֵלָה) The feminine form of Samuel. *See* Samuel (*masculine section*). The exact Hebrew form is Shemu'ela (Shmu'ela).

Sandi A pet form of Sandra. *See* Sandra.

Sandra A pet form of Alexandra. *See* Alexandra.

Sandy A pet form of Sandra. *See* Sandra.

Sapir (סַפִּיר) A unisex name. From the Greek, meaning "precious stone." The exact Hebrew equivalent is Sapir.

Sapira (סַפִּירָה) A variant form of Sapir. *See* Sapir. The exact Hebrew equivalent is Sapira.

Sapirit (סַפִּירִית) A variant form of Sapir. *See* Sapir. The exact Hebrew equivalent is Sapirit.

Sara, Sarah (שָׂרָה) From the Hebrew, meaning "noble" or "princess." The exact Hebrew equivalent is Sara. MASCULINE HEBREW EQUIVALENTS: Adon, Aluf, Avihud. In Genesis 12:5, the wife of Abraham.

Sarai (שָׂרַי) The original biblical form of Sara. *See* Sara.

Sarali (שָׂרָלִי) A pet form of Sara. *See* Sara. The exact Hebrew equivalent is Sarali.

Saran, Sarann, Saranne Hybrid names formed from Sarah and Ann. *See* Sarah *and* Ann.

Sarel A pet form of Sarah. *See* Sarah.

Sareli A variant spelling of Sarali. *See* Sarali. Also, a feminine variant form of Yisrael (Israel). *See* Yisrael (*masculine section*).

Sarene A variant form of Sara. *See* Sara.

Saretta, Sarette Pet forms of Sara. *See* Sara.

Sari A variant spelling of Sarai. *See* Sarai.

Sarida (שָׂרִידָה) From the Hebrew, meaning "refugee, leftover." The exact Hebrew equivalent is Sarida. The exact masculine equivalent is Sarid.

Sarina, Sarine Variant forms of Sara. *See* Sara.

Sarit (שָׂרִית) A variant form of Sara. *See* Sara. The exact Hebrew equivalent is Sarit.

Sarita (שָׂרִיתָה) A variant form of Sara. *See* Sara. The exact Hebrew equivalent is Sarita.

Saryl (שָׂרִיל) A variant Yiddish form of Sara. *See* Sara.

Sasha *Also spelled* Sacha. A Russian pet form of Alexandra. *See* Alexandra.

Saula A feminine form of Saul. *See* Saul (*masculine section*).

Saundra A variant spelling of Sandra. *See* Sandra.

Savrina (סַבְרִינָה) A variant form of Sabra. *See* Sabra. The exact Hebrew equivalent is Savrina.

Savta (סַבְתָּא) From the Aramaic and Hebrew, meaning "grandmother." The exact Hebrew equivalent is Savta. The exact masculine equivalent is Saba.

Scarlet, Scarlett From the Middle English, meaning "red, ruby-colored." HEBREW EQUIVALENTS: Admon, Almoga, Odem. MASCULINE HEBREW EQUIVALENTS: Admon, Almog, Edom.

Schifra A variant spelling of Shifra. *See* Shifra.

Se'ara, Se'arah (סְעָרָה) From the Hebrew, meaning "storm, upheaval." The exact Hebrew equivalent is Se'ara. The exact masculine equivalent is Sa'ar.

Sechora, Sechorah (שְׂכוֹרָה) From the Hebrew, meaning "merchandise." The exact Hebrew equivalent is Sechora. MASCULINE HEBREW EQUIVALENTS: Avitagar, Machir.

Seema From the Greek, meaning "sprout." Akin to Cyma. HEBREW EQUIVALENTS: Nitza, Pircha, Shoshana. MASCULINE HEBREW EQUIVALENTS: Savyon, Shoshan, Tzemach.

Segula (סְגוּלָה) From the Hebrew, meaning "treasure" or "precious." The exact Hebrew equivalent is Segula. The exact masculine equivalent is Segel.

Sela (סֶלַע) A unisex name. From the Hebrew, meaning "stone, rock." The exact Hebrew equivalent is Sela.

Selda, Selde From the Anglo-Saxon, meaning "precious, rare." Also, from the Middle English, meaning "booth, hut." HEBREW EQUIVALENTS: Sapira, Segula, Yekara. MASCULINE HEBREW EQUIVALENTS: Sapir, Yahalom, Yakir.

Selena, Selene From the Greek, meaning "moon." HEBREW EQUIVALENTS: Chodesh, Levana, Sahara. MASCULINE HEBREW EQUIVALENTS: Levanon, Yarchi, Yerach.

Selila, Selilah (סְלִילָה) From the Hebrew, meaning "path." The exact Hebrew equivalent is Selila. The exact masculine equivalent is Salil.

Selima, Selimah Arabic feminine forms of Solomon, meaning "peace." *See* Solomon (*masculine section*).

Selina A variant spelling of Selena. *See* Selena.

Sellie A pet form of Selma. *See* Selma.

Selma From the Celtic, meaning "fair." HEBREW EQUIVALENTS: Levana, Na'ama, Na'omi. MASCULINE HEBREW EQUIVALENTS: Lavan, Livni, Ra'anan.

Sema A variant spelling of Seema. *See* Seema.

Serach (שֶׂרַח) From the Hebrew, meaning "spread out." The exact Hebrew equivalent is Serach. MASCULINE HEBREW EQUIVALENTS: Yazor, Yezi'el. In Genesis 46:17, the daughter of Asher, granddaughter of Jacob.

Serelle A pet form of Sarah. *See* Sarah.

Serena, Serina From the Latin, meaning "peaceful" or "cheerful." HEBREW EQUIVALENTS: Sha'anana, Shalviya, Shulamit. MASCULINE HEBREW EQUIVALENTS: Shalom, Shelomo, Yechi-Shalom.

Serenity A variant form of Serena. *See* Serena.

Serita A variant spelling of Sarita. *See* Sarita.

Severina From the Latin, meaning "friendly, friendship." HEBREW EQUIVALENTS: Achva, Amit, Amita. MASCULINE HEBREW EQUIVALENTS: David, Dodi, Yedidya.

Sevira (סְבִירָה) From the Hebrew, meaning "learned, reasonable, rational." The exact Hebrew equivalent is Sevira. The exact masculine equivalent is Savir.

Seviva, Sevivah (סְבִיבָה) From the Hebrew, meaning "environment, encirclement, surroundings, locality." The exact Hebrew equivalent is Seviva. The exact masculine equivalent is Saviv.

Shabetit, Shabtit (שַׁבְּתִּית) Feminine forms of the masculine name Shabbetai. *See* Shabbetai (*masculine section*).

Shachar (שַׁחַר) A unisex name. From the Hebrew, meaning "morning." The exact Hebrew equivalent is Shachar.

Shaina (שֵׁיינָא) A variant spelling of Sheina. *See* Sheina.

Shaindee A variant spelling of Sheindi. *See* Sheindi.

Shaindel, Shaindl (שֵׁיינְדֶעל/שֵׁיינְדְל) A variant spelling of Sheindel. *See* Sheindel.

Shaindi, Shaindie, Shaindy Variant spellings of Sheindi. *See* Sheindi.

Shaine (שֵׁיינֶע) A variant spelling of Sheine. *See* Sheine.

Shaked (שָׁקֵד) A unisex name. From the Hebrew, meaning "almond." The exact Hebrew equivalent is Shaked.

Shalhevet (שַׁלְהֶבֶת) From the Hebrew, meaning "flame." The exact Hebrew equivalent is Shalhevet. MASCULINE HEBREW EQUIVALENTS: Nur, Ud, Udi'el.

Shalva, Shalvah (שַׁלְוָה) From the Hebrew, meaning "tranquility, peace." The exact Hebrew equivalent is Shalva. MASCULINE HEBREW EQUIVALENTS: Shalev, Shalom, Shlomo.

Shamira (שָׁמִירָה) From the Hebrew, meaning "guard, protector." The exact Hebrew equivalent is Shamira. The exact masculine equivalent is Shamir.

Shan A pet form of Shannon. *See* Shannon.

Shana, Shanna Variant spellings of Shaina. *See* Shaina. Also, a pet form of Shoshana. *See* Shoshana.

Shandra A variant spelling of Chandra. *See* Chandra.

Shane A variant spelling of Shaine. *See* Shaine.

Shani, Shanie (שָׁנִי) A unisex name. From the Hebrew, meaning "scarlet [thread]." The exact Hebrew equivalent is Shani.

Shannen A variant spelling of Shannon. *See* Shannon.

Shannon A feminine form of Sean. *See* Sean (*masculine section*).

Shareen A variant form of Sharon. *See* Sharon.

Sharelle A variant form of Sharon. *See* Sharon.

Sharene A variant form of Sharon. *See* Sharon.

Shari A pet form of Sharon. *See* Sharon.

Sharilyn A hybrid name formed from Shari and Lyn. *See* Shari *and* Lyn.

Sharin A variant spelling of Sharon. *See* Sharon.

Sharleen, Sharlene Variant spellings of Charlene. *See* Charlene.

Sharon (שָׁרוֹן) A unisex name. From the Hebrew, meaning "a plain." The Sharon is an area of ancient Palestine extending from Mount Carmel south to Jaffa where roses grew in abundance. The exact Hebrew equivalent is Sharon.

Sharona (שָׁרוֹנָה) A variant form of Sharon. *See* Sharon. The exact Hebrew equivalent is Sharona.

Sharoni (שָׁרוֹנִי) A variant form of Sharon. *See* Sharon. The exact Hebrew equivalent is Sharoni.

Sharonit (שָׁרוֹנִית) A variant form of Sharon. *See* Sharon. The exact Hebrew equivalent is Sharonit.

Sharyn A variant spelling of Sharon. *See* Sharon.

Shaula (שָׁאוּלָה) A feminine form of Shaul (Saul). *See* Shaul (*masculine section*). The exact Hebrew equivalent is Sha'ula.

Shaulit (שָׁאוּלִית) A variant form of Shaula. *See* Shaula.

Shauna The feminine form of Shaun. *See* Shaun (*masculine section*).

Shava (שַׁוְעָה) From the Hebrew, meaning "scream, cry for help." Based on an expression in Exodus 2:23. The exact Hebrew equivalent is Shav'a. MASCULINE HEBREW EQUIVALENTS: Azri'el, Ezra.

Shavit (שָׁבִיט) From the Hebrew, meaning "comet, star." The exact Hebrew equivalent is Shavit. MASCULINE HEBREW EQUIVALENTS: Bar-Kochva, Kochav, Mazal.

Shawn A unisex name. A variant spelling of the masculine name Sean, a variant form of John. *See* John (*masculine section*).

Shawna A variant form of Shawn. *See* Shawn.

Shayna A variant spelling of Sheina. *See* Sheina.

Shayndel, Shayndl Variant spellings of Sheindel. *See* Sheindel.

Shayne A variant spelling of Sheina. *See* Sheina.

Shaynee, Shayni Pet forms of Sheina. *See* Sheina.

Sheba The Anglicized form of Sheva. *See* Sheva.

Sheena A Gaelic form of Jane. *See* Jane.

Sheera, Sheerah Variant spellings of Shira. *See* Shira.

Sheila, Sheilah Variant forms of Cecelia and Celia. *See* Cecelia *and* Celia.

Sheina (שֵׁיינָא) From the Yiddish, meaning "beautiful." HEBREW EQUIVALENTS: Na'a, Na'ama, Nava. MASCULINE HEBREW EQUIVALENTS: Adin, Shapir, Yafeh.

Sheindel, Sheindl (שֵׁיינְדֶעל/שֵׁיינדל) Pet forms of Sheina. *See* Sheina.

Sheindi, Sheindie, Sheindy Pet forms of Sheina. *See* Sheina.

Sheine A variant spelling of Sheina. *See* Sheina.

Shelby A unisex name. From the Anglo-Saxon, meaning "sheltered town." HEBREW EQUIVALENTS: Setura, Shamira, Shimriya. MASCULINE HEBREW EQUIVALENTS: Chasun, Eltzafun, Gonen.

Sheli (שֶׁלִי) A variant spelling of Shelley. *See* Shelley. Also, from the Hebrew, meaning "mine." The exact Hebrew equivalent is Sheli.

Shelia, Sheliah Variant spellings of Sheliya. *See* Sheliya.

Sheliya, Sheli-Ya (שֶׁלִי-יָה/שֶׁלְיָה) From the Hebrew, meaning "mine is God's." The exact Hebrew equivalent is Sheliya. MASCULINE HEBREW EQUIVALENTS: Eliya, Eliyahu, Ya'el.

Shella, Shellah Variant pet forms of Michelle. *See* Michelle.

Shellee, Shelley, Shelly Irish pet forms of Cecelia. *See* Cecelia.

Shelomit (שְׁלֹמִית) *Also spelled* Shlomit. From the Hebrew, meaning "peace." The exact Hebrew equivalent is Shlomit. The exact masculine equivalent is Shlomo. In Leviticus 24:11, the daughter of Divri of the tribe of Dan.

Shemuela A variant spelling of Shmuela. *See* Shmuela.

Sheree A variant form of Cheryl. *See* Cheryl.

Shereen An Arabic form of Sharon. *See* Sharon.

Sherelle, Sherrelle A variant spelling of Cheryl. *See* Cheryl.

Sherelyn A hybrid name formed from Sherry and Ellyn. *See* Sherry *and* Ellyn.

Sheri A variant spelling of Sherry. *See* Sherry.

Sheril, Sherill Variant spellings of Sheryl. *See* Sheryl.

Sherre, Sherri Variant spellings of Sherry. *See* Sherry.

Sherril, Sherrill Variant spellings of Sheryl. *See* Sheryl.

Sherrine A pet form of Sherry. *See* Sherry.

Sherron A variant form of Sharon. *See* Sharon.

Sherry A variant form of Caesarina, the feminine form of the Latin name Caesar, meaning "king." By extension, Sherry means "queen." The feminine Hebrew equivalent is Malka. The masculine equivalent is Melech.

Sheryl, Sheryll Variant spellings of Cheryl. *See* Cheryl.

Sheva (שְׁבַע) A unisex name. From the Hebrew, meaning "oath." Akin to Bat-Sheva. The exact Hebrew equivalent is Sheva.

Shevi A pet form of Bat-Sheva. *See* Bat-Sheva.

Shifra, Shifrah (שִׁפְרָה) From the Hebrew, meaning "good, handsome, beautiful," or from the Aramaic, meaning "trumpet." The exact Hebrew equivalent is Shifra. The exact masculine equivalent is Shefer.

Shimra (שִׁמְרָה) From the Hebrew, meaning "guarded, protected." The exact Hebrew equivalent is Shimra. MASCULINE HEBREW EQUIVALENTS: Shemarya, Shemer, Shimri.

Shimrat (שִׁמְרַת) From the Hebrew, meaning "guarded, protected." The exact Hebrew equivalent is Shimrat. MASCULINE HEBREW EQUIVALENTS: Shemaryahu, Shemer, Shimri.

Shimrit (שִׁמְרִית) From the Hebrew, meaning "guarded, protected." The exact Hebrew equivalent is Shimrit. MASCULINE HEBREW EQUIVALENTS: Shemaryahu, Shemer, Shimri.

Shimriya (שִׁמְרִיָה) From the Hebrew, meaning "God is my protector." The exact Hebrew equivalent is Shimriya. MASCULINE HEBREW EQUIVALENTS: Shemarya, Shemaryahu, Shimri.

Shimshona (שִׁמְשׁוֹנָה) The feminine form of Shimshon (Samson). *See* Samson (*masculine section*). The exact Hebrew equivalent is Shimshona.

Shiphra A variant spelling of Shifra. *See* Shifra.

Shir (שִׁיר) A unisex name. From the Hebrew, meaning "song." The exact Hebrew equivalent is Shir.

Shira, Shirah (שִׁירָה) A variant form of Shir. *See* Shir. The exact Hebrew equivalent is Shira. MASCULINE HEBREW EQUIVALENTS: Shir, Shiron, Yashir.

Shirel (שִׁירָאֵל) From the Hebrew, meaning "God's song." The exact Hebrew equivalent is Shirel. MASCULINE HEBREW EQUIVALENTS: Shir, Shiron, Yashir.

Shiri (שִׁירִי) A unisex name. From the Hebrew, meaning "my song." The exact Hebrew equivalent is Shiri.

Shirl A pet form of Shirley. *See* Shirley.

Shirlee, Shir-Lee Variant spellings of Shirli. *See* Shirli. Also, variant spellings of Shirley. *See* Shirley.

Shirley A unisex name. From the Old English, meaning "from the white meadow." HEBREW EQUIVALENTS: Ginat, Sharona, Yardeniya. MASCULINE HEBREW EQUIVALENTS: Gani, Sharon, Yarden.

Shirli, Shir-Li (שִׁיר-לִי/שִׁירלִי) From the Hebrew, meaning "song is mine." The exact Hebrew equivalent is Shirli. MASCULINE HEBREW EQUIVALENTS: Shir, Shiron, Yashir.

Shirra A variant spelling of Shira. *See* Shira.

Shlomit (שְׁלֹמִית) A variant spelling of Shelomit. *See* Shelomit.

Shmuela (שְׁמוּאֵלָה) The feminine form of Shmuel (Samuel). *See* Shmuel (*masculine section*). The exact Hebrew equivalent is Shmu'ela.

Shon A pet form of Shoshana. *See* Shoshana.

Shona (שׁוֹנָא) A variant form of Sheina. *See* Sheina.

Shoni, Shonie (שׁוֹנִי) Variant forms of Sheina. *See* Sheina.

Shoshan (שׁוֹשָׁן) A unisex name. From the Hebrew, meaning "lily," or from the Egyptian and Coptic, meaning "lotus." The exact Hebrew equivalent is Shoshan.

Shoshana, Shoshanah (שׁוֹשָׁנָה) Variant forms of Shoshan. *See* Shoshan. The exact Hebrew equivalent is Shoshana.

Shprintza, Shprintze (שְׁפְּרִינצָא/שְׁפְּרִנצֶע) Yiddish forms from the Esperanto, meaning "hope." *See* Hope.

Shu'a (שׁוּעַ) From the Hebrew, meaning "a cry, scream." The exact Hebrew equivalent is Shu'a. MASCULINE HEBREW EQUIVALENTS: Tzahal, Yovav. In Genesis 38:2, the wife of Judah.

Shuala (שׁוּעָלָה) From the Hebrew, meaning "fox." The exact Hebrew equivalent is Shu'ala. The exact masculine equivalent is Shu'al.

Shula (שׁוּלָה) A pet form of Shulamit. *See* Shulamit. The exact Hebrew equivalent is Shula.

Shulamit (שׁוּלַמִּית) From the Hebrew, meaning "peace, peaceful." The exact Hebrew equivalent is Shulamit. The exact masculine equivalent is Shlomo.

Shuli, Shuly (שׁוּלִי) Pet forms of Shulamit. *See* Shulamit. The exact Hebrew equivalent is Shuli.

Sibyl From the Greek, meaning "counsel of God." Also, from the Old

Italian, meaning "wise old woman." HEBREW EQUIVALENTS: Bina, Buna, Milka. MASCULINE HEBREW EQUIVALENTS: Achban, Utz.

Sidra (סִדְרָה) A unisex name. From the Latin, meaning "starlike." Also, from the Hebrew, meaning "order, sequence." The exact Hebrew equivalent is Sidra.

Sierra From the Latin, meaning "saw-toothed," a description of the formation of the tree branches in the mountain range of eastern California. HEBREW EQUIVALENTS: Aharona, Harda, Horiya. MASCULINE HEBREW EQUIVALENTS: Aharon, Harel, Shur.

Sigal (סִגָל) From the Hebrew, meaning "treasure." The exact Hebrew equivalent is Sigal. The exact masculine equivalent is Segel.

Sigalia A variant spelling of Sigaliya. *See* Sigaliya.

Sigalit (סִגָלִית) A variant form of Sigal. *See* Sigal. The exact Hebrew equivalent is Sigalit.

Sigaliya (סִגָלְיָה) A variant form of Sigal. *See* Sigal. The exact Hebrew equivalent is Sigaliya.

Siglia A variant spelling of Sigaliya. *See* Sigaliya.

Siglit (סִגְלִית) A variant form of Sigal. *See* Sigal. The exact Hebrew equivalent is Siglit.

Signora From the Latin, meaning "woman, lady." HEBREW EQUIVALENTS: Alufa, Gevira. MASCULINE HEBREW EQUIVALENTS: Adon, Adoniya, Aluf.

Silona (סִילוֹנָה) From the Greek and Hebrew, meaning "water conduit, stream." The exact Hebrew equivalent is Silona. The exact masculine equivalent is Silon.

Silonit (סִילוֹנִית) A variant form of Silona. *See* Silona. The exact Hebrew equivalent is Silonit.

Silva A variant form of Sylvia. *See* Sylvia.

Silvia A variant spelling of Sylvia. *See* Sylvia.

Sima (סִימָה) From the Aramaic, meaning "treasure." The exact Hebrew equivalent is Sima.

Simajean A hybrid name formed from Sima and Jean. *See* Sima *and* Jean.

Simcha (שִׂמְחָה) A unisex name. From the Hebrew, meaning "joy." The exact Hebrew equivalent is Simcha.

Simchit (שִׂמְחִית) A variant form of Simcha. *See* Simcha. The exact Hebrew equivalent is Simchit.

Simchona (שִׂמְחוֹנָה) A variant form of Simcha. *See* Simcha.

Simeona A variant form of Simona. *See* Simona.

Simla, Simlah (שִׂמְלָה) From the Hebrew, meaning "dress, garment." The exact Hebrew equivalent is Simla. MASCULINE HEBREW EQUIVALENTS: Salma, Salmon.

Simona (שִׁמְעוֹנָה) A feminine form of Simon. *See* Simon (*masculine section*). The exact Hebrew equivalent is Shimona.

Simone A French feminine form of Simon. *See* Simon (*masculine section*).

Sinai (סִינַי) A unisex name sometimes given to a person steeped in Torah learning. In Exodus 19:20, the name of the mountain on which the Torah was given. The exact Hebrew equivalent is Sinai.

Sindy A fanciful spelling of Cindy. *See* Cindy.

Siona A variant spelling of Tziyona. *See* Tziyona.

Sirel (סִירְל) A Yiddish form of Sara. *See* Sara.

Sirena A variant spelling of Serena. *See* Serena.

Sirke (שִׁירְקֶע/סִירְקֶע) A Yiddish pet form of Sara. *See* Sara.

Sisel (סִיסְל) From the Yiddish, meaning "sweet." HEBREW EQUIVALENTS: Metuka, Mirit. MASCULINE HEBREW EQUIVALENTS: Matok, Na'im, Yivsam.

Sisi A pet form of Cecilia. *See* Cecilia.

Sisley A variant spelling of Cicely. *See* Cicely.

Sissie, Sissy Variant spellings of Sisi. *See* Sisi.

Sivana (סִיוָנָה) The feminine form of Sivan. *See* Sivan (*masculine section*). The exact Hebrew equivalent is Sivana.

Sivia, Siviah, Sivya (צִבְיָה) Variant forms of Tzivya. *See* Tzivya.

Smadar (סְמָדַר) A unisex name. From the Hebrew, meaning "blossom." The exact Hebrew equivalent is Smadar.

Soferet (סוֹפֶרֶת) From the Hebrew, meaning "scribe." The exact Hebrew equivalent is Soferet. The exact masculine equivalent is Sofer.

Soleil From the French, meaning "sun." HEBREW EQUIVALENTS: Chamaniya, Shimshona. MASCULINE HEBREW EQUIVALENTS: Charsom, Koresh, Shimshon.

Solet (סֹלֶת) From the Hebrew, meaning "fine flour." The exact Hebrew equivalent is Solet. Kimchi is a masculine equivalent.

Sondra A variant spelling of Sandra. *See* Sandra.

Sonia A variant form of Sophia. *See* Sophia.

Sonja, Sonya Slavic forms of Sonia. *See* Sonia.

Sophia From the Greek, meaning "wisdom, wise one." HEBREW EQUIVALENTS: Bina, Milka, Tushiya. MASCULINE HEBREW EQUIVALENTS: Haskel, Utz, Yosha.

Sophie A French form of Sophia. *See* Sophia.

Sorale (שָׂרַאלֶע) A Yiddish pet form of Sarah. *See* Sarah.

Sorali, Soralie (שָׂרַאלִי) Yiddish pet forms of Sarah. *See* Sarah.

Soraya A Persian name of unknown origin.

Soreka (שׂוֹרֵקָה) From the Hebrew, meaning "vine." The exact Hebrew equivalent is Soreka. MASCULINE HEBREW EQUIVALENTS: Gafni, Gefen, Karmi'el.

Sorel, Sorol Pet forms of Sarah. *See* Sarah.

Sorka, Sorke (שָׂרְקֶע/שָׂרְקָא) A Yiddish pet form of Sara. *See* Sara.

Soroli A variant spelling of Sorali. *See* Sorali.

Spring A season of the year. From the Old English, meaning "to shoot up, to grow." The exact Hebrew equivalent is Aviva. The exact masculine equivalent is Aviv.

Stace A variant spelling of Stacey. *See* Stacey.

Stacey An Irish form of the Greek name Anastasia, meaning "resurrection, revival." HEBREW EQUIVALENTS: Chava, Cha'ya, Yechi'ela. MASCULINE HEBREW EQUIVALENTS: Amichai, Chai, Cha'yim.

Stacia, Stacie Variant pet forms of Stacey. *See* Stacey.

Stacy A variant spelling of Stacey. *See* Stacey.

Star From the Old English, meaning "star." The exact Hebrew equivalent is Ester. MASCULINE HEBREW EQUIVALENTS: Bar-Kochva, Kochav.

Staria A variant form of Star. *See* Star.

Starletta A pet form of Star. *See* Star.

Starr A variant spelling of Star. *See* Star.

Stefana, Stefania Feminine forms of Stephen. *See* Stephen (*masculine section*).

Stefanie, Stefenie Feminine forms of Stephen. *See* Stephen (*masculine section*).

Steffi A pet form of Stefanie. *See* Stefanie.

Stella From the Latin, meaning "star." The exact Hebrew equivalent is Ester. MASCULINE HEBREW EQUIVALENTS: Bar-Kochva, Kochav.

Stephane A variant spelling of Stephanie. *See* Stephanie.

Stephania, Stephanie, Stephenie Feminine forms of Stephen. *See* Stephen (*masculine section*).

Stevana, Stevena Feminine forms of Steven. *See* Steven (*masculine section*).

Su, Sue Pet forms of Susan. *See* Susan.

Suellen A hybrid name formed from Sue (Susan) and Ellen. *See* Susan *and* Ellen.

Sufa, Sufah (סוּפָה) From the Hebrew, meaning "storm." The exact Hebrew equivalent is Sufa. Sa'ar is a masculine equivalent.

Sulamit A variant spelling of Shulamit. *See* Shulamit.

Sultana From the Arabic, meaning "ruler" or "victorious." HEBREW EQUIVALENTS: Malka, Nitzchiya, Nitzchona. MASCULINE HEBREW EQUIVALENTS: Melech, Netzach, Nitzchi.

Summer From the Middle English and Old French, meaning "supporting beam." Also, a season of the year marked by growth and development. HEBREW EQUIVALENTS: Atalya, Sa'ada, Tzemicha. MASCULINE HEBREW EQUIVALENTS: Sa'adya, Tzemach, Yifrach.

Surel, Surell, Surelle Variant pet forms of Sarah. *See* Sarah.

Suri (שׂוּרִי) A variant form of Sara. *See* Sara.

Surilee (שׂוּרִילִי) A hybrid name formed from Suri and Lee. *See* Suri *and* Lee.

Susa (סוּסָה) From the Hebrew, meaning "horse." The exact Hebrew equivalent is Susa. The exact masculine equivalent is Sus.

Susan (שׁוֹשַׁנָה/שׁוֹשָׁן) From the Hebrew, meaning "lily." HEBREW EQUIVALENTS: Shoshan, Shoshana. The masculine equivalent is Shoshan.

Susanna, Susannah Variant forms of Susan. *See* Susan.

Susanne A variant form of Susan. *See* Susan.

Susette A pet form of Susan. *See* Susan.

Susi, Susie, Susy Pet forms of Susan. *See* Susan.

Suzanne A variant form of Susan. *See* Susan.

Suzette A French form of Susan. *See* Susan.

Suzy A pet form of Susan. *See* Susan.

Suzyn A variant spelling of Susan. *See* Susan.

Svetlana From the Russian, meaning "star." HEBREW EQUIVALENTS: Ester, Kochava, Mazala. MASCULINE HEBREW EQUIVALENTS: Kochav, Mazal.

Sybil, Sybille, Sybyl, Sybyle Variant spellings of Sibyl. *See* Sibyl.

Syd, Sydel, Sydelle Variant pet forms of Sydney. *See* Sydney.

Sydney A feminine form of the masculine Sidney. *See* Sidney (*masculine section*).

Sylvia From the Latin, meaning "forest" or "one who dwells in the woods." HEBREW EQUIVALENTS: Gana, Karmela, Ya'arit. MASCULINE HEBREW EQUIVALENTS: Karmel, Ya'ar, Ya'ari.

Sylvie A Norwegian form of Sylvia. *See* Sylvia.

Syma A variant spelling of Cyma, Seema, or Sima. *See* Cyma, Seema, *and* Sima.

✑ T ✑

Tabita, Tabitha From the Akkadian, meaning "goat." A variant form of Tevet, the tenth month in the Hebrew calendar. Its zodiacal sign is a goat. HEBREW EQUIVALENTS: Gadya, Ya'alit, Ya'el. MASCULINE HEBREW EQUIVALENTS: Ofra, Ofri, Terach.

Taffy The Welsh form of the name Vida, a variant form of David. *See* David (*masculine section*).

Taga (תֵּגָה) From the Aramaic and Arabic, meaning "crown." The exact Hebrew equivalent is Taga. MASCULINE HEBREW EQUIVALENTS: Katri'el, Keter, Kitron.

Tal (טַל) A unisex name. From the Hebrew, meaning "dew." The exact Hebrew equivalent is Tal.

Tali (טַלִי) A unisex name. From the Hebrew, meaning "my dew." The exact Hebrew equivalent is Tali.

Talia, Taliah Variant spellings of Talya. *See* Talya.

Talie A variant spelling of Tali. *See* Tali.

Talma (תַּלְמָה) From the Hebrew, meaning "mound, hill." The exact Hebrew equivalent is Talma. MASCULINE HEBREW EQUIVALENTS: Harel, Talmai, Telem.

Talmi (תַּלְמִי) A unisex name. From the Hebrew, meaning "spring of water." The exact Hebrew equivalent is Talmi.

478

Talmit (תַּלְמִית) A variant form of Talma. *See* Talma. The exact Hebrew equivalent is Talmit.

Talmon (תַּלְמוֹן) A unisex name. From the Aramaic, meaning "furrow." The exact Hebrew equivalent is Talmon.

Talmor (תַּלְמוֹר) From the Hebrew, meaning "heaped" or "sprinkled with myrrh, perfumed." The exact Hebrew equivalent is Talmor. MASCULINE HEBREW EQUIVALENTS: Mivsam, Mor, Yivsam.

Talor, Tal-Or (טַל-אוֹר/טַלְאוֹר) A unisex name. From the Hebrew, meaning "dew of the light [morning]." The exact Hebrew equivalent is Tal-Or.

Talora, Tal-Ora (טַל-אוֹרָה/טַלְאוֹרָה) Variant forms of Talor and Tal-Or. *See* Talor. The exact Hebrew equivalent is Tal-Ora.

Talya (טַלְיָה) A unisex name. From the Hebrew, meaning "God's dew." Also, from the Aramaic, meaning "young lamb." The exact Hebrew equivalent is Talya.

Tama, Tamah (תַּמָה) From the Hebrew, meaning "wonder, surprise" or "whole, complete." The exact Hebrew equivalent is Tama. The exact masculine equivalent is Tam.

Tamar (תָּמָר) A unisex name. From the Hebrew, meaning "palm tree" or "upright, righteous, graceful." The exact Hebrew equivalent is Tamar. In Genesis 38:6, the wife of Er, son of Judah.

Tamara, Tamarah (תָּמָרָה) From the East Indian, meaning "spice." HEBREW EQUIVALENTS: Nirdit, Tamar, Tamara. MASCULINE HEBREW EQUIVALENTS: Mivsam, Mor, Nardimon. Also, a variant form of Tamar. *See* Tamar.

Tami, Tammy Feminine forms of Thomas. *See* Thomas (*masculine section*). Also, pet forms of Tamara. *See* Tamara.

Tamra A shortened form of Tamara. *See* Tamara.

Tania, Tanja, Tanya From the Russian, meaning "fairy queen." HEBREW EQUIVALENTS: Malka, Malki'ela, Malkit. MASCULINE HEBREW EQUIVALENTS: Avimelech, Melech.

Tara (טָרָה) From the French and Aramaic, referring to a unit of measurement. Also, from the Aramaic, meaning "throw" or "carry." The

Hebrew equivalent is Tara. MASCULINE HEBREW EQUIVALENTS: Aryoch, Nasi, Yora.

Taralynn A hybrid name formed from Tara and Lynn. *See* Tara *and* Lynn.

Tari (טָרִי) From the Hebrew, meaning "fresh, ripe, new." The exact Hebrew equivalent is Tari.

Taryn A variant form of Tara. *See* Tara.

Tasha A pet form of Latasha or Natasha. *See* Latasha *and* Natasha.

Tate From the Anglo-Saxon, meaning "to be cheerful." HEBREW EQUIVALENTS: Rona, Roniya, Tzahala. MASCULINE HEBREW EQUIVALENTS: Tzahal, Yachdi'el, Yitzchak.

Tatum From the Middle English, meaning "lighthearted, happy." HEBREW EQUIVALENTS: Ditza, Gila, Roni. MASCULINE HEBREW EQUIVALENTS: Elez, Eliran, Marnin.

Tauba, Taube Yiddish forms of the German, meaning "dove." HEBREW EQUIVALENTS: Yona, Yonina, Yonita. MASCULINE HEBREW EQUIVALENTS: Tor, Yona.

Tavi A variant form of the masculine name David. *See* David (*masculine section*).

Tavita A pet form of Tavi. *See* Tavi.

Taylor Used most often as a masculine name. *See* Taylor (*masculine section*).

Tea A pet form of Althea. *See* Althea.

Techina, Techinah (תְּחִינָה) From the Hebrew, meaning "prayer, petition." The exact Hebrew equivalent is Techina. The exact masculine equivalent is Tachan.

Techiya (תְּחִיָה) From the Hebrew, meaning "life, revival." The exact Hebrew equivalent is Techiya. MASCULINE HEBREW EQUIVALENTS: Chai, Cha'yim, Yechi'el.

Teddi, Teddy Pet forms of Teresa and Theodora. *See* Teresa *and* Theodora.

Tehila, Tehilla (תְּהִילָה) From the Hebrew, meaning "praise, song of praise." The exact Hebrew equivalent is Tehila (T'hila). MASCULINE HEBREW EQUIVALENTS: Hila, Hillel, Mehulal.

Tehiya A variant spelling of Techiya. *See* Techiya.

Tehora (טְהוֹרָה) From the Hebrew, meaning "pure, clean." The exact Hebrew equivalent is Tehora. MASCULINE HEBREW EQUIVALENTS: Zach, Zakai.

Tekuma, Tekumah (תְּקוּמָה) From the Hebrew, meaning "revival, resuscitation, reestablishment." The exact Hebrew equivalent is Tekuma. MASCULINE HEBREW EQUIVALENTS: Amikam, Amishav.

Tema (טֶעמַא) A Yiddish form of Tamar. *See* Tamar.

Temara (תְּמָרָה) A variant form of Tamar. *See* Tamar. The exact Hebrew equivalent is Temara.

Temima (תְּמִימָה) From the Hebrew, meaning "whole, honest." The exact Hebrew equivalent is Temima. The exact masculine equivalent is Tam.

Temira (תְּמִירָה) From the Hebrew, meaning "tall, stately." The exact Hebrew equivalent is Temira. The exact masculine equivalent is Tamir.

Temma A variant spelling of Tema. *See* Tema.

Temple From the Latin, meaning "sanctuary, holy place." HEBREW EQUIVALENTS: Chagit, Devira, Kedushah. MASCULINE HEBREW EQUIVALENTS: Devir, Kadosh, Yom-Tov.

Temuna, Temunah (תְּמוּנָה) From the Hebrew, meaning "picture." The exact Hebrew equivalent is Temuna. MASCULINE HEBREW EQUIVALENTS: Dama, Micha'el.

Tenuva, Tenuvah (תְּנוּבָה) From the Hebrew, meaning "produce." The exact Hebrew equivalent is Tenuva. MASCULINE HEBREW EQUIVALENTS: Yanuv, Yifrach, Yitzmach.

Teresa The Spanish and Italian form of Theresa. *See* Theresa.

Teresita A Spanish pet form of Theresa. *See* Theresa.

Teri, Terie A pet form of Theresa. *See* Theresa.

Teriya (טְרִיָה) A variant form of Tari. *See* Tari. The exact Hebrew equivalent is Teriya.

Terrie, Terry Pet forms of Theresa. *See* Theresa.

Teruma, Terumah (תְּרוּמָה) A unisex name. From the Hebrew meaning "offering, gift." The exact Hebrew equivalent is Teruma.

Teshua, Teshuah (תְּשׁוּעָה) From the Hebrew, meaning "salvation." The exact Hebrew equivalent is Teshu'a. The exact masculine equivalent is Yehoshu'a.

Teshuka, Teshukah (תְּשׁוּקָה) From the Hebrew, meaning "desire." The exact Hebrew equivalent is Teshuka. MASCULINE HEBREW EQUIVALENTS: Chamadel, Chamadya, Chemed.

Teshura, Teshurah (תְּשׁוּרָה) A unisex name. From the Hebrew, meaning "gift." The exact Hebrew equivalent is Teshura.

Tessa A pet form of Theresa. *See* Theresa.

Tetty A pet form of Elizabeth. *See* Elizabeth.

Tevita A Fijian form of Davida. *See* Davida.

Thalia From the Greek, meaning "luxurious, flourishing." HEBREW EQUIVALENTS: Pirchit, Tara, Teriya. MASCULINE HEBREW EQUIVALENTS: Perach, Pura, Tara.

Thea A short form of Althea. *See* Althea.

Thelma From the Greek, meaning "nursing, infant," connoting youthfulness. HEBREW EQUIVALENTS: Alma, Aviva, Yenika. MASCULINE HEBREW EQUIVALENTS: Aviv, Bichri, Elam, Katan.

Theo A pet form of Theodora. *See* Theodora.

Theodora The feminine form of Theodore. *See* Theodore (*masculine section*).

Theora A short form of Theodora. *See* Theodora.

Theresa, Therese From the Greek, meaning "harvester, farmer." HEBREW EQUIVALENTS: Gana, Yardena, Yizr'ela. MASCULINE HEBREW EQUIVALENTS: Adam, Karmel, Yizr'el.

Thomasina A feminine form of Thomas. *See* Thomas (*masculine section*).

Tifara (תִּפְאָרָה) From the Hebrew, meaning "beauty" or "glory." The exact Hebrew equivalent is Tifara. MASCULINE HEBREW EQUIVALENTS: Hadar, Hod, Hodiya.

Tiferet (תִּפְאֶרֶת) A variant form of Tifara. *See* Tifara. The exact Hebrew equivalent is Tiferet.

Tiffani, Tiffanie, Tiffany From the Latin, meaning "three, the trinity." Also, from the Greek, meaning "manifestation of God." The exact Hebrew equivalent is Shelosha.

Tiki A pet form of Tikva. *See* Tikva.

Tikva (תִּקְוָה) A unisex name. From the Hebrew, meaning "hope." The exact Hebrew equivalent is Tikva.

Tilda A pet form of Mathilda. *See* Mathilda.

Tilla A variant form of Tillie. *See* Tillie.

Tillamae A hybrid name formed from Tilla and Mae. *See* Tilla *and* Mae.

Tillie, Tilly Pet forms of Mathilda. *See* Mathilda. Also, from the Latin, meaning "graceful linden tree." HEBREW EQUIVALENTS: Hadasa, Ilana, Tirza. MASCULINE HEBREW EQUIVALENTS: Ela, Miklot, Oren.

Timi A pet form of Timora. *See* Timora.

Timora (תִּימוֹרָה) From the Hebrew, meaning "tall," like the palm tree. The exact Hebrew equivalent is Timora. MASCULINE HEBREW EQUIVALENTS: Itamar, Tamir.

Timura (תִּימוּרָה) A variant form of Timora. *See* Timora. The exact Hebrew equivalent is Timura.

Tina A pet form of names such as Bettina and Christina. *See* Bettina *and* Christina.

Tira (טִירָא) From the Syriac, meaning "sheepfold," or from the Hebrew, meaning "enclosure, encampment." The exact Hebrew equivalent is Tira. MASCULINE EQUIVALENTS: Akiva, Tachan, Ya'akov.

Tiri (טִירִי) A variant form of Tira. *See* Tira. The exact Hebrew equivalent is Tiri.

Tirtza, Tirtzah (תִּרְצָה) From the Hebrew, meaning "agreeable, willing." The exact Hebrew equivalent is Tirtza. MASCULINE HEBREW EQUIVALENTS: Yishva, Yishvi. In Numbers 26:33, one of Tzelophchad's five daughters.

Tirza, Tirzah (תִּרְזָה) From the Hebrew, meaning "cypress tree." The exact Hebrew equivalent is Tirza. The masculine equivalent is Bros.

Tisa, Tissa (טִיסָה) From the Hebrew, meaning "flight, fleeing." The exact Hebrew equivalent is Tisa. Paru'ach is a masculine equivalent.

Tisha A pet form of Patricia. *See* Patricia.

Tita A variant form of Titania. *See* Titania.

Titania From the Greek, meaning "great one." HEBREW EQUIVALENTS: Atalya, Gedola, Gedula. MASCULINE HEBREW EQUIVALENTS: Gadol, Gedalya, Gidel.

Tiva (טִיבָה) From the Hebrew, meaning "good." The exact Hebrew equivalent is Tiva. MASCULINE HEBREW EQUIVALENTS: Tov, Toviya, Tuviya.

Tivona (טִבְעוֹנָה) From the Hebrew, meaning "lover of nature." The exact Hebrew equivalent is Tivona. The exact masculine equivalent is Tivon.

Tivoni (טִבְעוֹנִי) From the Hebrew, meaning "naturalist." The exact Hebrew equivalent is Tivoni. A masculine Hebrew equivalent is Teva.

Tizzie, Tizzy Pet forms of Elizabeth. *See* Elizabeth.

Toba A variant spelling of Tova. *See* Tova. Akin to the masculine Tobias.

Tobelle A pet form of Toba. *See* Toba.

Tobey A variant form of Toba. *See* Toba.

Tobi A variant spelling of Toby. *See* Toby.

Tobina A pet form of Toby. *See* Toby.

Tobit A variant spelling of Tovit. *See* Tovit.

Toby A pet form of Toba. *See* Toba.

Toda, Todah (תּוֹדָה) A unisex name. From the Hebrew, meaning "thanks, thank you." The exact Hebrew equivalent is Toda.

Toiba, Toibe (טוֹיבֶּע/טוֹיבָּא) From the Yiddish, meaning "dove." The exact feminine and masculine Hebrew equivalent is Yona.

Tomasina A feminine form of Thomas. *See* Thomas (*masculine section*).

Tomer (תּמֶר) A unisex name. A variant form of Tamar. *See* Tamar. The exact Hebrew equivalent is Tomer.

Toni A pet form of Antoinette. *See* Antoinette.

Tonia A variant form of Toni. *See* Toni.

Tonise A variant form of Toni. *See* Toni.

Tony A variant spelling of Toni. *See* Toni.

Topaza From the Greek, referring to a yellow variety of sapphire. The exact Hebrew equivalent is Sapira. The exact masculine equivalent is Sapir.

Tora, Torah (תּוֹרָה) From the Hebrew, meaning "teaching" or "law." The exact Hebrew equivalent is Tora. MASCULINE HEBREW EQUIVALENTS: Datan, Dati'el, Moran.

Tori (תּוֹרִי) From the Hebrew, meaning "my turtledove." The exact Hebrew equivalent is Tori. The masculine equivalent is Yona. Also, a variant form of Tora and a pet form of Victoria. *See* Tora *and* Victoria.

Torie, Torey, Tory Alternate spellings of Tori. *See* Tori.

Totie A variant form of Dottie, a pet form of Dorothy. *See* Dorothy.

Tova, Tovah (טוֹבָה) From the Hebrew, meaning "good." The exact Hebrew equivalent is Tova. The exact masculine equivalent is Tov.

Tovat (טוֹבַת) A variant form of Tova. *See* Tova. The exact Hebrew equivalent is Tovat.

Tovit (טוֹבִית) From the Hebrew, meaning "good." The exact Hebrew equivalent is Tovit. MASCULINE HEBREW EQUIVALENTS: Tov, Tovi, Tuviya.

Tracee, Tracey, Traci Variant spellings of Tracy. *See* Tracy.

Tracy From the Anglo-Saxon, meaning "brave." Also, a pet form of Theresa. *See* Theresa. HEBREW EQUIVALENTS: Abira, Abiri, Gavri'ela. MASCULINE HEBREW EQUIVALENTS: Gavri'el, Gevaryahu, Gever.

Trella A short form of Estella, the Spanish form of Esther. *See* Esther.

Tricia A pet form of Patricia. *See* Patricia.

Trina A short form of Katrina. *See* Katrina.

Trish, Trisha Pet forms of Patricia. *See* Patricia.

Tristana The feminine form of Tristan. *See* Tristan (*masculine section*).

Trix, Trixie, Trixy Pet forms of Beatrice and Beatrix. *See* Beatrice *and* Beatrix.

Truda, Trude Pet forms of Gertrude. *See* Gertrude.

Tsipora, Tsiporah Variant spellings of Tzipora. *See* Tzipora.

Tumi (תֻּמִי) From the Hebrew, meaning "whole, complete." The exact Hebrew equivalent is Tumi. The exact masculine equivalent is Tam.

Tuvit (טוּבִית) A variant form of Tova. *See* Tova. The exact Hebrew equivalent is Tuvit.

Tyna, Tyne From the British, meaning "river." HEBREW EQUIVALENTS: Bat-Yam, Dalya, Miryam. MASCULINE HEBREW EQUIVALENTS: Arnon, Ye'or, Ye'ori.

Tzabara (צַבָּרָה) From the Aramaic, meaning "to gather, assemble." Also, from the Arabic, meaning "cactus, prickly pear." The exact Hebrew equivalent is Tzabara. The exact masculine equivalent is Tzabar.

Tzabaria, Tzabariah Variant spellings of Tzabariya. *See* Tzabariya.

Tzabariya (צַבָּרְיָה) A variant form of Tzabara. *See* Tzabara. The exact Hebrew equivalent is Tzabariya.

Tzerua, Tzeruah (צְרוּעָה) From the Hebrew, meaning "blemished; insignificant one." The exact Hebrew equivalent is Tzeru'a. The exact masculine equivalent is Tzaru'a. In I Kings 11:26, the mother of Jeroboam ben Nevat.

Tzeruia, Tzeruiah, Tzeruya (צְרוּיָה) From the Hebrew, meaning "protected by God." The exact Hebrew equivalent is Tzeruya. MASCULINE HEBREW EQUIVALENTS: Eltzatan, Shemarya, Shimri. In II Samuel 2:18, a sister of King David.

Tzeviya, Tzeviyah (צְבִיָה) From the Hebrew, meaning "deer." The exact Hebrew equivalent is Tzeviya. The exact masculine equivalent is Tzevi.

Tzila, Tzilah (צִילָה) From the Hebrew, meaning "shadow." The exact Hebrew equivalent is Tzila. MASCULINE HEBREW EQUIVALENTS: Betzalel, Tzel, Tziltai.

Tziona A variant spelling of Tziyona. *See* Tziyona.

Tzipi (צִפִּי) A pet form of Tzipora. *See* Tzipora. The exact Hebrew equivalent is Tzipi.

Tzipia, Tzipiah, Tzipiya (צִפִּיָה) From the Hebrew, meaning "hope, anticipation." The exact Hebrew equivalent is Tzipiya. The masculine equivalent is Tikva.

Tzipora, Tziporah (צִפּוֹרָה) From the Hebrew, meaning "bird." The exact Hebrew equivalent is Tzipora. The exact masculine equivalent is Tzipor. In Exodus 2:21, the wife of Moses.

Tzipori (צִפּוֹרִי) From the Hebrew, meaning "my bird." The exact Hebrew equivalent is Tzipori. The masculine equivalent is Tzipor.

Tziporit (צִפּוֹרִית) A variant form of Tzipora. *See* Tzipora. The exact Hebrew equivalent is Tziporit. The masculine equivalent is Tzipor.

Tziril A Yiddish form of Sara. *See* Sara.

Tziyona (צִיוֹנָה) From the Hebrew, meaning "excellent." The exact Hebrew equivalent is Tziyona. The exact masculine equivalent is Tziyon.

Tziyonit (צִיוֹנִית) A variant form of Tziyona. *See* Tziyona. The exact Hebrew equivalent is Tziyonit.

Tzofia, Tzofiah, Tzofiya (צוֹפִיָה) From the Hebrew, meaning "watcher, guardian, scout." The exact Hebrew equivalent is Tzofiya. The exact masculine equivalent is Tzofi.

Tzurit (צוּרִית) From the Hebrew meaning, "rock." The exact Hebrew equivalent is Tzurit. The exact masculine equivalent is Tzur.

Tzuriya (צוּרִיָה) From the Hebrew meaning, "God is my rock." The exact Hebrew equivalent is Tzuriya. A masculine equivalent is Tzur.

ᕦ U ᕤ

Udi (עוּדִי) From the Hebrew, meaning "my torch." The exact Hebrew equivalent is Udi. FEMININE HEBREW EQUIVALENTS: Avuka, Masu'a.

Uga, Ugah (עוּגָה) From the Hebrew, meaning "cake." The exact Hebrew equivalent is Uga.

Ugit A variant form of Uga. *See* Uga.

Ugiya (עוּגִיָּה) From the Hebrew, meaning "cookie." Akin to Uga. The exact Hebrew equivalent is Ugiya.

Unita From the Latin, meaning "one, united." The exact Hebrew equivalent is Achava (Achva).

Uranit (אוּרָנִית) From the Hebrew, meaning "light." The exact Hebrew equivalent is Uranit. The exact masculine equivalent is Ur.

Uriela, Uriella (אוּרִיאֵלָה) From the Hebrew, meaning "light [flame] of the Lord." The exact Hebrew equivalent is Uri'ela. The exact masculine equivalent is Uri'el.

Urit (אוּרִית) From the Hebrew, meaning "light" or "fire." The exact Hebrew equivalent is Urit. The exact masculine equivalent is Ur.

Ursala A variant spelling of Ursula. *See* Ursula.

Ursula From the Latin, meaning "a she-bear." The exact Hebrew equivalent is Duba. MASCULINE HEBREW EQUIVALENTS: Dov, Dubi.

Uza (עֻזָה) A unisex name. From the Hebrew, meaning "strength." The exact Hebrew equivalent is Uza.

Uziela, Uziella (עֻזִיאֵלָה) From the Hebrew, meaning "my strength is the Lord." The exact Hebrew equivalent is Uzi'ela. The exact masculine equivalent is Uzi'el.

Uzit (עֻזִית) From the Hebrew, meaning "strength." The exact Hebrew equivalent is Uzit. The exact masculine equivalent is Uzi.

Uzza A variant spelling of Uza. *See* Uza.

～ V ～

Val A pet form of Valerie. *See* Valerie.

Valentina The feminine form of Valentine. *See* Valentine (*masculine section*).

Valeria A variant form of Valerie. *See* Valerie.

Valerie A unisex name. An English form of the French (derived from the Latin name Valeria), meaning "healthy, strong, courageous." HEBREW EQUIVALENTS: Abira, Eitana, Gavri'ela. MASCULINE HEBREW EQUIVALENTS: Gavri'el, Oz, Uzi'el.

Valery, Valorie Variant spellings of Valerie. *See* Valerie.

Vana A pet form of Vanessa. *See* Vanessa.

Vanda A variant form of Wanda. *See* Wanda.

Vanessa From the Middle English, meaning "to fan, agitate with a fan," an old method of winnowing grain. HEBREW EQUIVALENTS: Chita, Deganya, Garnit. MASCULINE HEBREW EQUIVALENTS: Dagan, Goren, Kimchi.

Vanna A pet form of Vanessa. *See* Vanessa.

Varda (וַרְדָה) From the Hebrew, meaning "rose." The exact Hebrew equivalent is Varda. The exact masculine equivalent is Vered.

Vardia, Vardiah Variant spellings of Vardiya. *See* Vardiya.

Vardina (וַרְדִּינָה) A variant form of Varda. *See* Varda. The exact Hebrew equivalent is Vardina.

Vardit (וַרְדִּית) A variant form of Varda. *See* Varda. The exact Hebrew equivalent is Vardit.

Vardiya (וַרְדִּיָה) A variant form of Varda. *See* Varda. The exact Hebrew equivalent is Vardiya.

Vasilia From the Greek and Russian, meaning "royalty." HEBREW EQUIVALENTS: Alufa, Malka, Sara. MASCULINE HEBREW EQUIVALENTS: Aluf, Melech, Yisra'el.

Vawn A feminine form of the masculine name Vaughan. *See* Vaughan (*masculine section*).

Veda From the Sanskrit, meaning "sacred understanding." HEBREW EQUIVALENTS: Bina, Buna, Tushiya. MASCULINE HEBREW EQUIVALENTS: Haskel, Yavin, Yosha.

Velma A pet form of Wilhelmina. *See* Wilhelmina.

Ventura From the Spanish, meaning "good fortune." HEBREW EQUIVALENTS: Ashera, Gadit, Mazal. MASCULINE HEBREW EQUIVALENTS: Asher, Maimon, Mazal.

Venus From the Latin, meaning "to love." In Greek mythology, the goddess of love and beauty. HEBREW EQUIVALENTS: Ahuva, Chaviva, Davida. MASCULINE HEBREW EQUIVALENTS: Ahuv, Ehud, Yedida.

Vera From the Latin, meaning "truth." Also, from the Russian, meaning "faith." HEBREW EQUIVALENTS: Amita, Amnona, Emet. MASCULINE HEBREW EQUIVALENTS: Amit, Amitai, Amnon.

Vered (וֶרֶד) A unisex name. From the Hebrew, meaning "rose." The exact Hebrew equivalent is Vered.

Verena, Verina From the Latin, meaning "one who venerates God" or "sacred wisdom." HEBREW EQUIVALENTS: Devora, Tehila, Yehudit. MASCULINE HEBREW EQUIVALENTS: Haskel, Hodiya, Yehuda.

Verita From the Latin, meaning "truth." HEBREW EQUIVALENTS: Amita, Amnona, Emet. MASCULINE HEBREW EQUIVALENTS: Amit, Amitai, Amnon.

Verity A variant form of Verita. *See* Verita.

Verna, Verne From the Latin, meaning "springlike" or "to grow green." Yarkona is a feminine Hebrew equivalent. Yarkon is a masculine equivalent.

Veronica A variant form of Berenice, meaning "bringer of victory." Also, from the Latin, meaning "truthful, faithful." HEBREW EQUIVALENTS: Emet, Emuna, Tikva. MASCULINE HEBREW EQUIVALENTS: Gover, Matzli'ach, Netzi'ach.

Vesta, Vestal In Roman mythology, the goddess of fire and purification. HEBREW EQUIVALENTS: Avuka, Shalhevet, Uri'ah, Uri'el. MASCULINE HEBREW EQUIVALENTS: Lahav, Lapid, Uri'ela.

Vi A pet form of Victoria and Violet. *See* Victoria *and* Violet.

Vici, Vicki, Vicky Variant pet forms of Victoria. *See* Victoria.

Victoria From the Latin, meaning "victorious." HEBREW EQUIVALENTS: Dafna, Hadasa, Nitzcha. MASCULINE HEBREW EQUIVALENTS: Gover, Matzli'ach, Netzi'ach.

Victorina, Victorine Pet forms of Victoria. *See* Victoria.

Vida A pet form of Davida. *See* Davida. Also, a variant form of Vita. *See* Vita.

Vikki, Vikkie, Vikky Pet forms of Victoria. *See* Victoria.

Vila A pet form of Vilhelmina. *See* Vilhelmina.

Vilhelmina A variant form of Wilhelmina. *See* Wilhelmina.

Vilma A variant form of Velma. *See* Velma.

Vina A pet form of Davina. *See* Davina.

Vinette A feminine form of Vincent. *See* Vincent (*masculine section*).

Viola A Middle English flower-name, from the Latin, meaning "violet." HEBREW EQUIVALENTS: Nitza, Shoshana, Varda. MASCULINE HEBREW EQUIVALENTS: Efra'yim, Pekach, Perachya.

Violet A variant form of Viola. *See* Viola.

Violetta A pet form of Violet. *See* Violet.

Virginia From the Latin, meaning "virgin, pure" or "maiden." HEBREW EQUIVALENTS: Rachel, Tamar, Zaka. MASCULINE HEBREW EQUIVALENTS: Itamar, Yesher, Yeshurun.

Vita From the Latin, meaning "life, animated." HEBREW EQUIVALENTS: Chava, Cha'ya, Techiya. MASCULINE HEBREW EQUIVALENTS: Cha'yim, Chiya, Yechi'el.

Vittoria A feminine form of Victor. *See* Victor (*masculine section*).

Viva From the Latin, meaning "live, alive." HEBREW EQUIVALENTS: Chava, Chaya, Techiya. MASCULINE HEBREW EQUIVALENTS: Chai, Cha'yim, Yocha'i.

Viveca From the Latin, meaning "alive." Akin to Viva. *See* Viva.

Vivi From the Latin, meaning "alive." HEBREW EQUIVALENTS: Chava, Cha'ya, Techiya. MASCULINE HEBREW EQUIVALENTS: Amichai, Cha'yim, Yechi'el.

Vivian, Viviana, Vivianna Variant forms of Vivi. *See* Vivi.

Vivica An alternate spelling of Viveca. *See* Viveca.

Vivien, Vivienne French forms of Vivian. *See* Vivian.

Vyvyan A variant spelling of Vivian. *See* Vivian.

～ W ～

Walda From the Old High German, meaning "to rule." HEBREW EQUIVALENTS: Atara, Malka, Sara. MASCULINE HEBREW EQUIVALENTS: Elrad, Malki'el, Yisra'el.

Wanda From the Old Norse, meaning "young tree," or from the Anglo-Saxon, meaning "wanderer." HEBREW EQUIVALENTS: Avishag, Hagar. MASCULINE HEBREW EQUIVALENTS: Gershom, Gershon, Golyat.

Weld A unisex name. *See* Weld (*masculine section*).

Wende, Wendey, Wendi, Wendy Pet forms of Genevieve, Gwendaline, and Winifred. *See* Genevieve, Gwendaline, *and* Winifred.

Wesley A unisex name. *See* Wesley (*masculine section*).

Whitney A unisex name. From the Old English, meaning "land near the water" or "white palace." HEBREW EQUIVALENTS: Armon, Armoni, Bitan. FEMININE HEBREW EQUIVALENTS: Armona, Bat-Yam, Levana.

Wilhelmina The English and Dutch form of Wilhelm (the German form of William), meaning "warrior" or "ruler." *See* William (*masculine section*).

Willa A pet form of Wilhelmina. *See* Wilhelmina.

Willene A pet form of Wilhelmina. *See* Wilhelmina.

Willow From the Middle English, meaning "to turn, twist, bend." The name of a genus of trees and shrubs having narrow leaves and flexible branches that blow easily in the wind. The exact Hebrew equivalent is Arava. MASCULINE HEBREW EQUIVALENTS: Alon, Etzion, Luz.

Wilma A pet form of Wilhelmina. *See* Wilhelmina.

Winifred From the Anglo-Saxon, meaning "friend of peace." HEBREW EQUIVALENTS: Menucha, Meshulemet, Shlomit. MASCULINE HEBREW EQUIVALENTS: Avshalom, Shalom, Shalum.

Winnie A pet form of Winifred. *See* Winifred.

Winnifred An alternate spelling of Winifred. *See* Winifred.

Winona A variant spelling of Wynona. *See* Wynona.

Wynette A diminutive form of Wynn or Wynna. *See* Wynn *and* Wynna.

Wynn, Wynne From the Welsh, meaning "white, fair, blessed." HEBREW EQUIVALENTS: Behira, Berucha, Levana. MASCULINE HEBREW EQUIVALENTS: Bahir, Baruch, Lavan.

Wynna A pet form of Gwendaline. *See* Gwendaline. Also, a pet form of Winifred. *See* Winifred.

Wynona A Sioux Indian name meaning "firstborn daughter." HEBREW EQUIVALENTS: Bakura, Bechira, Bechora. MASCULINE HEBREW EQUIVALENTS: Bachur, Bechor, Bichri.

❧ X–Y ❧

Xana, Xanna Pet forms of Susanna. *See* Susanna.

Xena From the Greek, meaning "great" or "stranger." HEBREW EQUIVA-LENTS: Atalya, Avishag, Gedola. MASCULINE HEBREW EQUIVALENTS: Gadol, Gedalya, Gidel.

Xenia From the Greek, meaning "welcoming, friendly." HEBREW EQUIV-ALENTS: Achava, Amit, Rut. MASCULINE HEBREW EQUIVALENTS: Chovav, David, Raya.

Xeriqua A variant spelling of Erica. *See* Erica.

Yaakova (יַעֲקֹבָה) From the Hebrew, meaning "to supplant." Akin to Yaakov. The exact Hebrew equivalent is Ya'akova.

Yaala (יַעֲלָה) A variant form of Yael. *See* Yael. The exact Hebrew equivalent is Ya'ala.

Yaalat (יַעֲלַת) A variant form of Yael. *See* Yael. The exact Hebrew equivalent is Ya'alat.

Yaalit (יַעֲלִית) A variant form of Yael. *See* Yael. The exact Hebrew equivalent is Ya'alit.

Yaanit (יַעֲנִית) A variant form of Yaen. *See* Yaen. The exact Hebrew equivalent is Ya'anit.

Yaara (יַעֲרָה) From the Hebrew, meaning "forest." The exact Hebrew equivalent is Ya'ara. The exact masculine equivalent is Ya'ar.

Yaarit (יַעֲרִית) From the Hebrew, meaning "pertaining to the forest." The exact Hebrew equivalent is Ya'arit. The masculine equivalent is Ya'ar.

Yael (יָעֵל) A unisex name. From the Hebrew, meaning "mountain goat" or "to ascend." The exact Hebrew equivalent is Ya'el.

Yaela, Yaella (יָעֲלָה) Variant forms of Yael. *See* Yael. The exact Hebrew equivalent is Ya'ela.

Yaen (יָעֵן) From the Hebrew, meaning "ostrich." The exact Hebrew equivalent is Ya'en. MASCULINE HEBREW EQUIVALENTS: Gozal, Tzipor.

Yafa, Yaffa (יָפָה) From the Assyrian and the Hebrew, meaning "beautiful." The exact Hebrew equivalent is Yafa. The exact masculine equivalent is Yafeh.

Yafit (יָפִית) A variant form of Yafa. *See* Yafa. The exact Hebrew equivalent is Yafit.

Yaira, Yairah (יָאִירָה) From the Hebrew, meaning "enlightened." The exact Hebrew equivalent is Ya'ira. The exact masculine equivalent is Ya'ir.

Yakira (יְקִירָה) From the Hebrew, meaning "valuable, precious." The exact Hebrew equivalent is Yakira. The exact masculine equivalent is Yakir.

Yalena, Yalina Russian forms of Helen. *See* Helen.

Yama (יָמָה) From the Hebrew, meaning "toward the sea" or "westward." The exact Hebrew equivalent is Yama. MASCULINE HEBREW EQUIVALENTS: Avigal, Aviyam, Ma'arav.

Yamina From the Arabic, meaning "proper." Akin to the Hebrew masculine name Yamin, meaning "right side." *See* Yamin (*masculine section*).

Yamit (יָמִית) From the Hebrew, meaning "pertaining to the sea." The exact Hebrew equivalent is Yamit. MASCULINE HEBREW EQUIVALENTS: Avigal, Aviyam.

Yara A variant spelling of Yaara. *See* Yaara.

Yardena (יַרְדֵּנָה) The feminine form of Yarden (Jordan). *See* Yarden (*masculine section*).

Yardenia, Yardeniah, Yardeniya (יַרְדֵּנְיָה) From the Hebrew, meaning "garden of the Lord." The exact Hebrew equivalent is Yardeniya. The exact masculine equivalent is Yarden.

Yarkona (יַרְקוֹנָה) The feminine form of Yarkon, meaning "green." The exact Hebrew equivalent is Yarkona. The exact masculine equivalent is Yarkon.

Yarona (יָרוֹנָה) From the Hebrew, meaning "sing." The exact Hebrew equivalent is Yarona. The exact masculine equivalent is Yaron.

Yasmin The Arabic name for any of various plants of the olive family (genus *Jasminum*) with fragrant flowers. HEBREW EQUIVALENTS: Bosma, Ketzi'a, Tamara. MASCULINE HEBREW EQUIVALENTS: Mivsam, Mor.

Yatva (יָטְבָה) From the Hebrew, meaning "good." The exact Hebrew equivalent is Yatva. MASCULINE HEBREW EQUIVALENTS: Tov, Tovi.

Yechiela (יְחִיאֵלָה) From the Hebrew, meaning "may God live." The exact Hebrew equivalent is Yechi'ela. The exact masculine equivalent is Yechi'el.

Yedida, Yedidah (יְדִידָה) From the Hebrew, meaning "friend" or "beloved." The exact Hebrew equivalent is Yedida. The masculine equivalent is Yadid.

Yedidela (יְדִידְאֵלָה) From the Hebrew, meaning "friend of God" or "beloved of God." The exact Hebrew equivalent is Yedidela. The masculine equivalent is Yedidya.

Yedidia, Yedidiah, Yedidya (יְדִידְיָה) A unisex name. From the Hebrew, meaning "friend of God" or "beloved of God." The exact Hebrew equivalent is Yedidya.

Yehiela A variant spelling of Yechiela. *See* Yechiela.

Yehudit (יְהוּדִית) From the Hebrew, meaning "praise." The exact Hebrew equivalent is Yehudit. Judith is an Anglicized form. The exact masculine equivalent is Yehuda (Judah).

Yeira, Yeirah (יְאִירָה) From the Hebrew, meaning "light." The exact Hebrew equivalent is Ye'ira. The exact masculine equivalent is Ya'ir.

Yekara, Yekarah (יְקָרָה) Variant forms of Yakira. *See* Yakira. The exact Hebrew equivalent is Yekara.

Yemima (יְמִימָה) Possibly from the Arabic, meaning "dove." The exact Hebrew equivalent is Yemima. The exact masculine equivalent is Yona.

Yemina (יְמִינָה) From the Hebrew, meaning "right hand," signifying strength. The exact Hebrew equivalent is Yemina. The exact masculine equivalent is Yamin.

Yenta A variant form of Yentil. *See* Yentil.

Yentil, Yentl (יֶענְטִיל) Yiddish forms of the Latin *gentilis*, meaning "foreigner, stranger." FEMININE HEBREW EQUIVALENTS: Gershona, Gi'oret. MASCULINE HEBREW EQUIVALENTS: Gershon, Gi'ora.

Yerusha, Yerushah (יְרוּשָׁה) A unisex name. From the Hebrew, meaning "inheritance." The exact Hebrew equivalent is Yerusha. The masculine equivalent is Morash.

Yeshisha (יְשִׁישָׁה) From the Hebrew, meaning "old." The exact Hebrew equivalent is Yeshisha. The exact masculine equivalent is Yashish.

Yetta, Yette, Yetti Pet forms of Henrietta. *See* Henrietta.

Yetzira, Yetzirah (יְצִירָה) From the Hebrew, meaning "creation, artifact." The exact Hebrew equivalent is Yetzira. MASCULINE HEBREW EQUIVALENTS: Asa'el, Asi'el, Elasa.

Yifat (יִפְעַת) From the Ugaritic and Akkadian, meaning "beauty." The exact Hebrew equivalent is Yifat. The exact masculine equivalent is Yafeh.

Yigala (יִגְאָלָה) From the Hebrew, meaning "to redeem." The exact Hebrew equivalent is Yigala. The exact masculine equivalent is Yigal.

Yimna (יִמְנָה) A unisex name. From the Hebrew and Arabic, meaning "right side," signifying good fortune. The exact Hebrew equivalent is Yimna.

Yiscah (יִסְכָּה) From the Hebrew, meaning "one who anoints." The exact Hebrew equivalent is Yiscah. MASCULINE HEBREW EQUIVALENTS: Chaza'el, Re'uven, Ro'i. In Genesis 11:29, the daughter of Haran, Abraham's brother.

Yisraela (יִשְׂרָאֵלָה) The feminine form of Yisrael. The exact Hebrew equivalent is Yisra'ela. *See* Yisrael (*masculine section*).

Yisrela (יִשְׂרָאֵלָה) A variant form of Yisraela. *See* Yisraela.

Yitra (יִתְרָה) From the Hebrew, meaning "wealth, riches." The exact Hebrew equivalent is Yitra. The exact masculine equivalent is Yitro.

Yitta (יִיטָא) A variant form of Yetta. *See* Yetta.

Yitti (יִיטִי) A Yiddish form of Yetta. *See* Yetta.

Yoanna (יוֹעֶנָה) From the Hebrew, meaning "God has answered." The exact Hebrew equivalent is Yo'ana. MASCULINE HEBREW EQUIVALENTS: Yehoshu'a, Yesha'ya, Yo'ezer.

Yochana, Yochanah (יוֹחָנָה) From the Hebrew, meaning "God is gracious." The exact Hebrew equivalent is Yochana. The exact masculine equivalent is Yochanan.

Yochebed A variant spelling of Yocheved. *See* Yocheved.

Yocheved (יוֹכֶבֶד) From the Hebrew, meaning "God's glory." The exact Hebrew equivalent is Yocheved. MASCULINE HEBREW EQUIVALENTS: Hod, Hodiya, Nehedar.

Yoela (יוֹאֵלָה) From the Hebrew, meaning "God is willing." The exact feminine Hebrew equivalent is Yo'ela.

Yoelit (יוֹאֵלִית) A variant form of Yoela. *See* Yoela. The exact Hebrew equivalent is Yo'elit.

Yoko From the Japanese, meaning "good, righteous." HEBREW EQUIVALENTS: Chasida, Tamar. MASCULINE HEBREW EQUIVALENTS: Chasid, Tzadik, Tzadok.

Yolanda, Yolande Possibly a form of the Old French name Violante, a derivative of Viola. *See* Viola. Also, from the Latin, meaning "modest, shy." HEBREW EQUIVALENTS: Anava, Anuva. MASCULINE HEBREW EQUIVALENTS: Anav, Anuv.

Yona, Yonah (יוֹנָה)   A unisex name. From the Hebrew, meaning "dove." The exact Hebrew equivalent is Yona.

Yonat (יוֹנַת) A variant form of Yona. *See* Yona. The exact Hebrew equivalent is Yonat.

Yonata (יוֹנָתָה) A variant form of Yona. *See* Yona. The exact Hebrew equivalent is Yonata.

Yonati (יוֹנָתִי) From the Hebrew, meaning "my dove." The exact Hebrew equivalent is Yonati. The exact masculine equivalent is Yona.

Yonina (יוֹנִינָה) A variant form of Yona. *See* Yona. The exact Hebrew equivalent is Yonina.

Yonit (יוֹנִית) A variant form of Yona. *See* Yona. The exact Hebrew equivalent is Yonit.

Yonita (יוֹנִיתָה) A variant form of Yona. *See* Yona. The exact Hebrew equivalent is Yonita.

Yora, Yorah (יוֹרָה) A unisex name. From the Hebrew, meaning "teach" or "shoot" or "kettle, pot." The exact Hebrew equivalent is Yora.

Yosefa, Yosepha (יוֹסֶפָה)   A variant form of Yosifa. *See* Yosifa. The exact Hebrew equivalent is Yosefa.

Yosifa (יוֹסִיפָה) A feminine form of Yosef (Joseph). *See* Yosef (*masculine section*). The exact Hebrew equivalent is Yosifa.

Yovel (יוֹבֵל) A unisex name. From the Hebrew, meaning "ram." The exact Hebrew equivalent is Yovel. The name is mentioned in Joshua 6:5.

Yudi (יוּדִי) A pet form of Yehudit. *See* Yehudit. The exact Hebrew equivalent is Yudi.

Yudis The Ashkenazic pronunciation of Yudit. *See* Yudit.

Yudit (יוּדִית) A short form of Yehudit. *See* Yehudit. The exact Hebrew equivalent is Yudit.

Yuli A variant form of Yulia. *See* Yulia.

Yulia, Yuliya Variant spellings of Julia. *See* Julia.

Yuta, Yutah (יוּטָה) From the Hebrew, meaning "braided hair." The exact Hebrew equivalent is Yuta. Esavis is a masculine equivalent.

Yvette A feminine form of Yves. *See* Yves (*masculine section*). Also, a Welsh form of Evan. *See* Evan (*masculine section*).

Yvonne A feminine French form of Yves. *See* Yves (*masculine section*).

✧ Z ✧

Zahara (זֳהֲרָה) From the Hebrew, meaning "to shine." The exact Hebrew equivalent is Zahara. The exact masculine equivalent is Zohar.

Zahari (זֳהֲרִי) A variant form of Zahara. *See* Zahara. The exact Hebrew equivalent is Zahari.

Zaharit (זֳהֲרִית) A variant form of Zahara. *See* Zahara. The exact Hebrew equivalent is Zaharit.

Zahava (זֳהָבָה) A variant spelling of Zehava. *See* Zehava. The exact Hebrew equivalent is Zahava.

Zahavi (זֳהָבִי) A variant form of Zahava. *See* Zahava. The exact Hebrew equivalent is Zahavi.

Zahira (זֳהִירָה) From the Hebrew and Arabic, meaning "shining bright." The exact Hebrew equivalent is Zahira. MASCULINE HEBREW EQUIVALENTS: Bahir, Ziv, Zohar.

Zaka, Zakah (זַכָּה) From the Hebrew, meaning "pure, clear, innocent." The exact Hebrew equivalent is Zaka. The exact masculine equivalent is Zakai.

Zakit (זַכִּית) A variant form of Zaka. *See* Zaka. The exact Hebrew equivalent is Zakit.

Zandra A variant form of Alexandra or Sandra. *See* Alexandra *and* Sandra.

Zara, Zarah (זָרָה) Variant forms of Sarah. *See* Sarah.

Zarina From the Persian, meaning "golden." HEBREW EQUIVALENTS: Ofira, Zehuva, Zehuvit. MASCULINE HEBREW EQUIVALENTS: Elifaz, Pazi, Zehavi.

Zariza, Zarizah (זְרִיזָה) Variant forms of Zeriza. *See* Zeriza. The exact Hebrew equivalent is Zariza.

Zavit (זָוִית) From the Hebrew, meaning "corner, angle." The exact Hebrew equivalent is Zavit.

Zayit (זַיִת) A unisex name. From the Hebrew, meaning "olive." The exact Hebrew equivalent is Za'yit.

Zeesi, Zeesie Pet forms of Zisa. *See* Zisa.

Zeeva (זְאֵבָה) From the Hebrew, meaning "wolf." The exact Hebrew equivalent is Ze'eva (Ze'eiva). The exact masculine equivalent is Ze'ev.

Zehara (זְהָרָה) From the Hebrew, meaning "light, brightness." The exact Hebrew equivalent is Zehara. The exact masculine equivalent is Zohar.

Zehari (זְהָרִי) A variant form of Zehara. *See* Zehara. The exact Hebrew equivalent is Zehari.

Zehava (זְהָבָה) From the Hebrew, meaning "gold, golden." The exact Hebrew equivalent is Zehava. The exact masculine equivalent is Zehavi.

Zehavi (זְהָבִי) A unisex name. A variant form of Zehava. *See* Zehava. The exact Hebrew equivalent is Zehavi.

Zehavit (זְהָבִית) A variant form of Zehava. *See* Zehava. The exact Hebrew equivalent is Zehavit.

Zehira (זְהִירָה) From the Hebrew, meaning "guarded, careful, cautious." The exact Hebrew equivalent is Zehira. The exact masculine equivalent is Zahir.

Zehorit (זְהוֹרִית) A variant form of Zehara. *See* Zehara. The exact Hebrew equivalent is Zehorit.

Zehuva (זְהוּבָה) From the Hebrew, meaning "gilded." The exact Hebrew equivalent is Zehuva. The exact masculine equivalent is Zehavi.

Zehuvit (זְהוּבִית) A variant form of Zehava. *See* Zehava. The exact Hebrew equivalent is Zehuvit.

Zeira (זְעִירָה) A unisex name. From the Aramaic, meaning "small, junior." The exact Hebrew equivalent is Ze'ira.

Zeita (זֵיתָה) An Aramaic variant form of Zayit. *See* Zayit. The exact Hebrew equivalent is Zayta.

Zeitana (זֵיתָנָה) A variant form of Zeita. *See* Zeita. The exact Hebrew equivalent is Zeitana (Zaytana).

Zekena (זְקֵנָה) From the Hebrew, meaning "old." The exact Hebrew is Zekena. The exact masculine equivalent is Zaken.

Zelda A variant spelling of Selda. *See* Selda.

Zemira (זְמִירָה) A unisex name. From the Hebrew, meaning "song, melody." The exact Hebrew equivalent is Zemira.

Zemora, Zemorah (זְמוֹרָה) From the Hebrew, meaning "branch, twig." The exact Hebrew equivalent is Zemora. The exact masculine equivalent is Zamir.

Zena A variant spelling of Xena. *See* Xena.

Zeriza (זְרִיזָה) From the Hebrew, meaning "energetic, industrious." The exact Hebrew equivalent is Zeriza. The exact masculine equivalent is Zariz.

Zeta A variant form of Zeita. *See* Zeita.

Zetana A variant spelling of Zeitana. *See* Zeitana.

Zetta A variant spelling of Zeta. *See* Zeta.

Zeva A variant spelling of Ze'eva. *See* Ze'eva.

Zevida (זְבִידָה) A unisex name. From the Hebrew, meaning "gift." The exact Hebrew equivalent is Zevida.

Zevuda (זְבוּדָה) A variant form of Zevida. *See* Zevida. The exact Hebrew equivalent is Zevuda.

Zevula (זְבוּלָה) From the Hebrew, meaning "dwelling place" or "palace." The exact Hebrew equivalent is Zevula. The exact masculine equivalent is Zevul.

Zila, Zilah, Zilla Variant spellings of Tzila. *See* Tzila.

Zilpa, Zilpah (זִלְפָּה) From the Hebrew, meaning "to sprinkle [water]." The exact Hebrew equivalent is Zilpah. MASCULINE HEBREW EQUIVALENTS: Yeziya, Zerika. In Genesis 29:24, the maid of Leah.

Zimra (זִמְרָה) A unisex name. From the Hebrew and Aramaic, meaning "song, tune" and "choice fruit." The exact Hebrew equivalent is Zimra.

Zimrat (זִמְרָת) A variant form of Zimra. *See* Zimra. The exact Hebrew equivalent is Zimrat.

Zimria, Zimriah, Zimriya (זִמְרִיָה) From the Hebrew, meaning "songfest" or "the Lord is my song." The exact Hebrew equivalent is Zimriya. The exact masculine equivalent is Zemer.

Zina A Russian pet form of the Greek name Zinaida, derived from Zeus, king of the gods. Also, a variant spelling of Xena. *See* Xena.

Ziona (צִיוֹנָה) A variant spelling of Tziyona. *See* Tziyona. The exact Hebrew equivalent is Tziyona.

Ziony (צִיוֹנִי) A pet form of Ziona. *See* Ziona.

Zipi A spelling of Tzipi. *See* Tzipi.

Zipora, Zippora (צִפּוֹרָה) Variant spellings of Tzipora. *See* Tzipora.

Zipori (צִפּוֹרִי) A variant spelling of Tzipori. *See* Tzipori.

Zira (זִירָה) From the Hebrew, meaning "arena." The exact Hebrew equivalent is Zira. MASCULINE HEBREW EQUIVALENTS: Mo'adya, No'ad, No'adya.

Ziril An Anglicized form of Tziril. *See* Tziril.

Zisa, Zissa (זִיסָה) From the Yiddish, meaning "sweet." HEBREW EQUIVALENTS: Metuka, Mirit. MASCULINE HEBREW EQUIVALENTS: Avino'am, Na'aman, No'am.

Zita A pet form of Theresa. *See* Theresa.

Ziva (זִיוָה) From the Hebrew, meaning "brightness, brilliance, splendor." The exact Hebrew equivalent is Ziva. The exact masculine equivalent is Ziv.

Zivit (זִיוִית) A variant form of Ziva. *See* Ziva. The exact Hebrew equivalent is Zivit.

Zizi A Hungarian pet form of Elizabeth. *See* Elizabeth.

Zlata (זְלַאטָא) A Polish-Yiddish form of Golda. *See* Golda.

Zlate (זְלַאטֶע) A variant form of Zlata. *See* Zlata.

Zoe From the Greek, meaning "life." HEBREW EQUIVALENTS: Chava, Cha'ya, Yechi'ela. MASCULINE HEBREW EQUIVALENTS: Chai, Cha'yim, Yechi'el.

Zofia A variant spelling of Tzofia. *See* Tzofia.

Zohar (זוֹהַר) A unisex name. From the Hebrew, meaning "light, brilliance." The exact Hebrew equivalent is Zohar.

Zohara, Zoharah (זוֹהֲרָה) A variant feminine form of Zohar. *See* Zohar. The exact Hebrew equivalent is Zohara.

Zoheret (זוֹהֶרֶת) A variant feminine form of Zohar. *See* Zohar. The exact Hebrew equivalent is Zoheret.

Zonya A variant spelling of Sonya. *See* Sonya.

Zophia A variant spelling of Sophia. *See* Sophia.

Zora (זָרָה) A variant form of Zara. *See* Zara.

Zsa Zsa A pet form of the Hungarian name Erzsbet, which is a variant form of Elizabeth. *See* Elizabeth.

Zvia A variant spelling of Tzeviya. *See* Tzeviya.

Zypora, Zyporah A variant spelling of Tzipora. *See* Tzipora.

INDEX OF NAMES
IN HEBREW SCRIPT

FEMININE NAMES

INDEX OF NAMES
BY MEANING

Almond
MASCULINE: Mandel, Shaked
FEMININE: Shaked

Almond tree
MASCULINE: Luz

Alone
FEMININE: Almana

Amber
FEMININE: Amber, Amberlee

Ambitious
FEMININE: Emilie, Emily, Emmy, Emmylou

Ancestor
MASCULINE: Olaf
FEMININE: Ola

Ancestry
MASCULINE: Alard, Allard

Anchor
MASCULINE: Agnon, Ogen

Ancient *See also* Old
FEMININE: Atika, Priscilla

Angel *See also* Messenger
MASCULINE: Angel, Angelo, Engelbert
FEMININE: Angela, Angelica, Angelina, Angeline, Angelique, Angelita, Angie, Angilee, Arela, Erela

Anger
MASCULINE: Evron, Yaziz
FEMININE: Evrona

Angle
FEMININE: Zavit

Animal fodder
FEMININE: Irit

Animals *See* Zoo; *specific animals by name*

Animated
FEMININE: Vita

Anklet
FEMININE: Achsa

Anointed
MASCULINE: Mashiach
FEMININE: Iscah, Levani, Yiscah

Anonymous *See also* Hidden
MASCULINE: Almoni
FEMININE: Almonit

Another
MASCULINE: Acher

Answer
MASCULINE: Anatot
FEMININE: Anina, Oriana

Ant
MASCULINE: Emmet, Nemuel

Antelope *See* Gazelle

Anticipation
FEMININE: Tzipia

Antiquated *See* Old

Anxious
MASCULINE: Doeg

Appearance
MASCULINE: Seth, Shet
FEMININE: Marit, Ofna, Ofniya

Appointed
MASCULINE: Seth, Shet
FEMININE: Noadya

April
FEMININE: Avril

Arena
FEMININE: Zira

Argument *See also* Conflict
FEMININE: Meriva

Army *See* Battle; General; Soldiers; Warrior

Artifact
FEMININE: Yetzira

Artist
MASCULINE: Aman

Ascend
MASCULINE: Eli, Jael, Yael
FEMININE: Aaliya, Aliya, Alla, Jael, Yaala, Yaalat, Yaalit, Yael, Yaela

Ash tree
FEMININE: Ashby, Ashleigh

Asked
MASCULINE: Saul, Shaul
FEMININE: Saula, Shaula, Shaulit

Assemble *See also* Gather
FEMININE: Sabaria, Tzabara, Tzabaria, Tzabariya

Assembly
MASCULINE: Daley
FEMININE: Atzira

Association *See also* Bind; Establishment
MASCULINE: Egged, Iggud
FEMININE: Aguda

Atmosphere
FEMININE: Aura, Avirit

Attendant *See* Servant

Aunt
FEMININE: Doda, Dodo

Authority symbol
MASCULINE: Gus, Gustaf, Gustav, Gustavus

Autumn
FEMININE: Autumn

Avenger
MASCULINE: Alastair, Alis, Alistair, Allistair, Allister, Altie

Awake
MASCULINE: Eiran, Er, Eran

Baby *See* Infant

Badger
MASCULINE: Brock
FEMININE: Girit

Bailiff
MASCULINE: Bailey

Baker
MASCULINE: Ofeh

Balcony
MASCULINE: Ziz, Zizi

Bald
MASCULINE: Calvin, Korach, Korah

Ban
MASCULINE: Isur

Bank (shore)
MASCULINE: Cliff, Clive

Banner *See also* Flag
MASCULINE: Nisan, Nison

Bard
MASCULINE: Devin, Devon

Bark (of plants)
FEMININE: Ketzia, Kezi, Kezia, Kezzi

Barrel maker
MASCULINE: Cooper

Barren
FEMININE: Ariri

Basin (sink)
MASCULINE: Agan

Basket
MASCULINE: Sali, Salu, Tene

Battle *See also* Conflict; Warfare
MASCULINE: Chad, Erve, Etgar, Harvey, Harvi, Herve, Lew, Lewes, Lewis, Louis, Ludwig
FEMININE: Blair

Battle spear
MASCULINE: Jarvis

Battlemaid *See* Warrior

Bay leaves
FEMININE: Bay

Bay tree *See also* Victor
FEMININE: Dafna, Dafne, Dafnit, Daphna, Daphnit, Dapna

Beacon *See* Light

Beam (rafter)
MASCULINE: Marish

Bean
MASCULINE: Fabian, Fabius, Pol
FEMININE: Fabiana

Bean farmer
MASCULINE: Fabian, Fabius
FEMININE: Fabia, Fabiana

Bear
MASCULINE: Art, Arthur, Artie, Arturo, Arty, Bear, Ber, Berel, Beril, Berish, Bern, Beryl, Byron, Dov, Dubi, Duv, Orson
FEMININE: Duba, Ursala

bold as
MASCULINE: Banet, Barnard, Barnet, Barney, Barr, Bernard, Bernardo, Bernarr, Bernd, Bernhard, Berni
FEMININE: Bernadette, Bernadina, Bernadine, Bernette, Bernine, Nadette

Bearer of glad tidings *See also* Messenger
FEMININE: Evangeline

Beauty and beautiful *See also* Fair; Grace; Handsome; Ornamented; Pretty
MASCULINE: Aden, Adin, Bell, Erv, Ervin, Erving, Erwin, Hada, Hadar, Irv, Irvin, Irvine, Irving, Japhet, Kailil, Kalil, Ken, Kene, Kenneth, Kennie, Kent, Naaman, Naom, Naveh, Noi, Noy, Raanan, Ranan, Shapir, Shefer, Yafet, Yefet
FEMININE: Abela, Ada, Adara, Adda, Adra, Amabel, Annabel, Arabel, Arabela, Arabelle, Beca, Beccie, Beckie, Beka, Bela, Belva, Berta, Bertha, Calla, Clarabella, Erwina, Gwen, Gwenn, Gwyn, Gwynn, Hadar, Hadara, Hadarit, Hadura, Indira, Jaffa, Jafit, Kiley, Mabel, Mabella, Mable, Naama, Naami, Naoma, Naomi, Navit, Neumi, Noemi, Noia, Nomi, Noya, Raanana, Ranana, Reba, Rebecca, Reva, Rheba, Ricka, Ricky, Riva, Schifra, Shaina, Shaindee, Shaindel, Shaindi, Shaine, Shana, Shane, Shayna, Shayndel, Shayne, Shaynee, Sheina, Sheindel, Sheindi, Sheine, Shifra, Shiphra, Shona, Shoni, Tifara, Tiferet, Yafa, Yafit, Yifat

Beaver meadow
MASCULINE: Beverley
FEMININE: Beverlee, Beverly, Bevya

Bee farm
MASCULINE: Beebe

Bees
FEMININE: Deb, Debora, Deborah, Debra, Deva, Devera, Devora, Devorit, Devra, Dobe, Dobra, Dovrat, Dvora, Dvorit, Lissa, Melissa, Missie

Beet
MASCULINE: Selek

Beginner
MASCULINE: Prentice, Prentiss

Beginning
MASCULINE: Janus, Orde
FEMININE: Reishit, Reshit

Behold
MASCULINE: Horace, Horatio

Bell clapper
MASCULINE: Inbal
FEMININE: Inbal

Belonging to me *See also* Possess
MASCULINE: Sheli

Belonging to one *See also* Possess
MASCULINE: Ain

Beloved *See also* Dear; Friend; Love and loving; Precious
MASCULINE: Ahuv, Alvan, Alvin, Azizi, Chaviv, Chavivi, Dab, Dabbey, Dabney, Dahvid, Daud, Dave, Davey, Davi, David, Davie, Daviel, Davis, Davy, Davyd, Dawson, Dewey, Didi, Dodic, Dovid, Dudi, Dudu, Ehud, Habib, Habibi, Haviv, Leeber, Leif, Liba, Lieb, Lieber, Lief, Loel, Lovell, Lowell, Miles, Tab, Tewel, Yadid, Yakar, Yakir, Yedid
FEMININE: Adora, Ahuva, Ahuvia, Ahuviya, Alvina, Amadea, Chaviva, Cher, Cheri, Cherilynn, Cherri, Cheryl, Darla, Darleen, Daryl, Davene, Davida, Davina, Davita, Doda, Dodi, Dodo, Dody, Haviva, Jedida, Kalila, Leeba, Liba, Libe, Libi, Libke, Lieba, Liebe, Lipke, Luba, Morna, Myra, Myrna, Pam, Pamela, Sheree, Sherelle, Taffy, Tavi, Tavita, Tevita, Vida, Vina, Yedida

Bend *See also* Flexible
FEMININE: Willow

Bequeath
MASCULINE: Grant

Best *See also* Choicest
FEMININE: Arista

Bestow *See* Gift

Biblical coin
MASCULINE: Beka

Big
FEMININE: Em, Emma, Emmie, Emmy, Emmylou, Lark

Bind *See also* Association; Chain; Imprison; Joined to
MASCULINE: Anuv, Asir, Rotem
FEMININE: Anuva, Atifa, Beca, Beccie,

Blooming
MASCULINE: Floren, Givol
FEMININE: Blossom, Chloe, Chloris, Cloe, Floreen, Florella, Floren, Florence, Florentina, Floria, Floriane, Florrie, Floryn, Flossie

Blossom
MASCULINE: Perach, Semadar, Smadar
FEMININE: Blossom, Nitza, Nitzana, Nitzanit, Perach, Pircha, Smadar

Boar
MASCULINE: Everett

Boat
MASCULINE: Kelley, Kelsey, Kelson, Kelsy, Tzi
FEMININE: Aniya, Chelsea, Kelci, Kelsey

Bold
MASCULINE: Arch, Archibald, Arky, Bailey, Cal, Cale, Caleb, Calev, Ferd, Ferdie, Ferdinand, Ferdy, Kalev, Kane, Keenan, Keene, Leopold, Noaz
FEMININE: Bernadette, Bernadina, Bernadine, Bernarda, Bernette, Bernine, Dara, Nadette

Bold as a bear
MASCULINE: Banet, Barnard, Barnet, Barney, Barr, Bernard, Bernardo, Bernarr, Bernd, Bernhard, Berni

Book copier
MASCULINE: Booker

Booty
MASCULINE: Baz

Border *See also* Boundary
FEMININE: Imra

Born
MASCULINE: Ethelbert, Noel
FEMININE: Latasha, Natalie, Natasha, Nathalie, Noelle, Tasha
born free *See also* Freedom
MASCULINE: Freed, Freeman
firstborn *See also* Eldest
MASCULINE: Primo
FEMININE: Reshit, Wynona
high born *See also* Noble birth
MASCULINE: Ethelbert
reborn (born again)
FEMININE: Ranae, Rena, Renae, René, Renette, Renita, Renni

Borrowed
MASCULINE: Mishael, Saul, Shael, Shaul
FEMININE: Mishaela, Saula, Shaula, Shaulit

Bottle
MASCULINE: Buki

Boulder *See also* Mountain; Rock
FEMININE: Chantal, Chantel

Bound *See also* Bind
FEMININE: Anuva

Boundary
MASCULINE: Berlin, Claibe, Claiborn, Gader
FEMININE: Gedera, Imra

Bountiful
MASCULINE: Cedric, Evyatar

Bow *See also* Knot; Tie
FEMININE: Aline, Gwendaline, Keshet, Wende, Wynette, Wynna

Bow maker
MASCULINE: Archer

Bowl
FEMININE: Gigit

Box
MASCULINE: Case

Boy *See also* Child; Son; Young; Youth
MASCULINE: Bubba, Lad, Naar, Sonny
FEMININE: Bambi

Braid
FEMININE: Yuta

Branch
MASCULINE: Agaf
FEMININE: Dahlia, Dalia, Dalit, Daliya, Dalya, Phylis, Phyllis, Zemora

Brass
FEMININE: Nechusha

Brave *See also* Bold
MASCULINE: Theo, Theobald
FEMININE: Erica, Erika, Fern, Marcella, Marcelle, Marcelyn, Marcia, Marcie, Marcilen, Marcy, Marsha, Reatha, Reda, Reeta, Reita, Reitha, Rheta, Riki, Rita, Ritasue, Tracee, Tracy, Xeriqua

Brave king
MASCULINE: Eric, Erik, Eryk

Bread
MASCULINE: Zemel
FEMININE: Pita

Breath
MASCULINE: Abel, Able, Hevel
FEMININE: Andra, Neshima

Bridge
MASCULINE: Bridge, Manford

Bright day
MASCULINE: Dagobert, Delbert

Bright promise *See* Optimism

Brightens
MASCULINE: Mayer, Meir, Meiri, Meyer, Myer

Brightness *See also* Brightens; Brilliance; Illustrious; Light; Shining; Sun; White; Wisdom
MASCULINE: Alva, Argus, Bahir, Bert, Berthold, Bertol, Berton, Burrut, Cy, Cyrus, Gimpel, Noga, Norbert, Xavier, Zahir
FEMININE: Bela, Berta, Bertha, Bertina, Bobbe, Bunny, Claire, Clara, Clarabella, Clare, Clarette, Clarice, Clarissa, Dana, Danette, Danna, Deanna, Deon, Di, Diana, Didi, Dion, Dyan, Dyana, Electra, Klara, Noga, Nura, Nurit, Nurita, Phebe, Phoebe, Ricka, Ricky, Robbi, Roberta, Robertina, Robin, Rori, Zehara, Zehari, Zehorit, Ziva, Zivit

Brilliance *See also* Bright; Light
MASCULINE: Ziv
FEMININE: Behira, Gladyce, Gladys, Ziva, Zivit, Zohar, Zohara, Zoheret

Brittany native
MASCULINE: Bret
FEMININE: Brittany

Broad (wide)
MASCULINE: Brad, Braden

Bronze
MASCULINE: Arad, Ard, Ardon, Arod
FEMININE: Arda

Brook *See also* Lake; River; Stream
MASCULINE: Beck, Hamilton, Hamlin, Jubal, Lynn, Peleg, Yuval

Brother
MASCULINE: Achban, Achi, Achiezer, Achihud, Achinadav
FEMININE: Achinoam

Brown
MASCULINE: Bronson, Bruno, Dunn, Floyd, Lloyd
FEMININE: Breindel, Brina, Bruna, Brune, Bryna

Brunette
FEMININE: Breindel, Brina, Bruna, Brune, Bryna

Brushwood
MASCULINE: Bromley

Buck *See* Deer

Bud *See also* Flower
FEMININE: Gemma, Nitza, Nitzana, Nitzanit

Budding *See* Blooming

Build
MASCULINE: Bani, Buni

Builder
FEMININE: Bona

Bull
MASCULINE: Buell

Bundle
FEMININE: Aguda

Burdened and burdensome
MASCULINE: Amasa, Ammos, Amos

Burn *See also* Fire; Flame
MASCULINE: Arden

Burst (explode)
MASCULINE: Peretz, Perez

Buyer
MASCULINE: Kaufman

Cabbage farmer
MASCULINE: Cole

Cactus
MASCULINE: Sabra, Tzabar
FEMININE: Sabaria, Sabra, Sabrina, Savrina, Tzabara, Tzabaria, Tzabariya

Cake *See also* Cookie
FEMININE: Uga, Ugit

Calm
MASCULINE: Placid, Salim
FEMININE: Placidia, Salima, Shalva

Camel
MASCULINE: Becher, Gamal, Gemali

Camp (protected area) See also Fortress
MASCULINE: Chester, Chet, Les, Lester, Linc, Lincoln
FEMININE: Tira, Tiri

Canal
MASCULINE: Biv

Candelabrum
FEMININE: Menora

Candle handler
FEMININE: Chandler

Candlelight
FEMININE: Neirit, Nerit

Candles, maker or seller of
MASCULINE: Chandler

Cape (cloak)
FEMININE: Aderet

Capital (geographic)
FEMININE: Bira, Biranit

Captain
MASCULINE: Seren

Careful
FEMININE: Zehira

Caress
FEMININE: Letifa

Caretaker See Servant

Caring
FEMININE: Caressa

Carrot
MASCULINE: Gezer

Carry
FEMININE: Tara, Taralynn, Taryn

Castle See also Fortified; Palace
MASCULINE: Armon, Berk, Borg, Briand, Burk
FEMININE: Armona, Armonit

Cathedral See also Church
MASCULINE: Goran, Gore

Cattle, grazing hill of
MASCULINE: Kile, Kyle

Cause, noble
MASCULINE: Ila, Ili

Cautious
FEMININE: Zehira

Cave
MASCULINE: Chor, Chori, Hori
FEMININE: Me'ara

Cedar
MASCULINE: Arzi, Arzon

Cedar panels
FEMININE: Ariza, Arza, Arzit

Cedar tree
FEMININE: Erez

Celebration
FEMININE: Chagit, Cleo, Clio, Hagit, Hillula

Celebrity See Famous

Celtic people
FEMININE: Brittany

Center
MASCULINE: Tabur, Taburi

Chain See also Bind
MASCULINE: Agnon, Asur, Ogen

Chalky
FEMININE: Giri

Challenge See also Battle
MASCULINE: Etgar

Champion See also Courage; Hero
MASCULINE: Neal, Neil, Neilson, Nelson, Niall, Nigel, Niles, Nils, Nyle
FEMININE: Neala, Nealla, Nia, Nigella

Channel (of water)
MASCULINE: Kile, Kyle

Chaplain
MASCULINE: Capp, Chapin, Chaplin

Character (nobility) See also Noble
MASCULINE: Sterling

Charcoal maker
MASCULINE: Cole, Coleman

Charming See also Grace
MASCULINE: Maksim
FEMININE: Chemda, Chen, Dulcia, Hemda, Hen, Maksima

Chase
MASCULINE: Chase, Chevy

Chastity
FEMININE: Agnes, Annice, Annis, Nessie

Cheer and cheerful *See also* Happiness; Joy
MASCULINE: Hi, Hilary, Hillary, Tate
FEMININE: Allegra, Cerena, Hilaire, Hilary, Hillary, Laris, Rena, Serena, Serenity, Sirena, Tate

Chest (box)
MASCULINE: Aran, Case

Chief *See also* Leader
MASCULINE: Cedric, Cole, Coleman, Conan, Malvin, Mel, Mell, Melvin, Melvyn, Meredith
FEMININE: Malvina, Melba, Melva, Melveen, Melvina

Child *See also* Boy; Daughter; Girl; Infant; Son; Young; Youth
MASCULINE: Chur, Churi, Clancy, Fairchild, Hur, Moise, Moishe, Moshe
FEMININE: Daisy, Greta, Gretchen, Gretel, Helenmae, Ketina, Madge, Mady, Mae, Mag, Maggie, Margaret, Margarete, Margaretta, Margarita, Marge, Margene, Margerie, Margery, Marget, Margi, Margit, Margo, Margy, Marji, Marjorie, May, Meg, Megan, Meret, Midge, Peg, Tillamae

Choice fruit
FEMININE: Zimra, Zimrat

Choicest
MASCULINE: Meitav
FEMININE: Eedit, Idit, Migda

Choir member *See also* Singer
MASCULINE: Gorman

Choose
FEMININE: Bara

Chosen one
MASCULINE: Corey, Cory, Nivchar
FEMININE: Bechira

Christ-bearer
MASCULINE: Chris, Christopher, Christy, Cristofer, Kris, Kristofer
FEMININE: Chrissy, Christina, Chryssa, Kicki, Kristin, Kristina, Kristine, Tina

Chump
MASCULINE: Shelumiel

Church *See also* Cathedral
MASCULINE: Kerby, Kermit, Kirby, Kirk
FEMININE: Kirsten

Cinnamon
MASCULINE: Kunama

Cipher
MASCULINE: Zero

Circle *See also* Cylinder
MASCULINE: Dur, Igul, Maagal
FEMININE: Akifa, Seviva

Citizen *See also* Nation
MASCULINE: Natin
FEMININE: Netina

City
MASCULINE: Granville, Ir, Orval, Orville
FEMININE: Bira, Biranit, Keret

Clapper, bell
MASCULINE: Inbal

Claw
MASCULINE: Clever

Clean *See also* Pure
MASCULINE: Zakai
FEMININE: Berura, Berurit, Beruriya, Berurya, Tehora

Clear (bright)
MASCULINE: Bahir, Zahir

Clear (pure) *See also* Pure
FEMININE: Behira, Beryl, Claire, Clara, Clarabella, Clare, Clarette, Clarice, Clarissa, Klara, Krystal, Zaka, Zakit

Clear glass
FEMININE: Chrystal, Crystal

Clearing
MASCULINE: Rodney

Clergy *See also* Chaplain; Minister; Preacher; Priest
MASCULINE: Abbe, Clark

Clerk
MASCULINE: Lavlar

Clever *See also*; Wisdom
MASCULINE: Herbert, Hubert, Huey, Hugh, Hugo, Sharp
FEMININE: Cassidy

Cliff
MASCULINE: Cliff, Erskine
FEMININE: Kaf

Clipping
MASCULINE: Gezer
FEMININE: Gezira

Cloak
FEMININE: Aderet, Gelima

Closed
MASCULINE: Ater, Setur
FEMININE: Akifa, Seviva

Cloth
FEMININE: Matlit

Clouds
MASCULINE: Anan, Anani, Idi, Ido
FEMININE: Iola

Clover
MASCULINE: Claibe, Claiborn, Clovis

Club (tool) *See also* Hammer
MASCULINE: Mace, Macey, Macy

Coal miner
MASCULINE: Colvin

Coal town
MASCULINE: Colby, Cole

Coastline
FEMININE: Riva

Coat of arms
MASCULINE: Shelet

Coin, biblical
MASCULINE: Beka

Coin, Israeli
FEMININE: Agora

Color *See also specific color by name*
MASCULINE: Guni

Comet
FEMININE: Shavit

Comfort and consolation
MASCULINE: Chami, Chemi, Chemia, Nachum, Nahum, Nechemia, Nechemya, Nehemia, Tanchum, Tanhum
FEMININE: Nacha, Nechama, Nechi, Nehama, Ruchama
one who offers
MASCULINE: Menachem, Menahem, Nachman, Nachmani

Comforter (blanket) *See also* Quilt
MASCULINE: Cody

Commission
FEMININE: Amala

Communal official
MASCULINE: Gabai

Companion *See* Friend

Comparison (likeness)
MASCULINE: Naf, Naftali, Naphtali

Compassionate *See also* God, compassion of
MASCULINE: Chanina, Itai, Ittai, Rachamim
FEMININE: Ruchama

Complete *See also* All
MASCULINE: Shalman, Tam, Tami
FEMININE: Tama, Tumi

Concealed
MASCULINE: Alemet, Amon, Nachbi, Setur
FEMININE: Geniza

Conceited *See* Egocentric

Conception *See also* Life
FEMININE: Concetta

Conclusion
FEMININE: Neila

Confederate states
FEMININE: Dixie

Conflict *See also* Contend; Tumult; Warfare
MASCULINE: Jeroboam, Madon, Yeravam
FEMININE: Hedda, Hedy

Confuse
MASCULINE: Bela

Conqueror *See also* Victor
MASCULINE: Jarvis, Vic, Victor, Vince, Vincent

Consecrated *See also* Holy; Sanctification
MASCULINE: Chermon, Chermoni, Hermon, Hermoni
FEMININE: Hermona

Consolation *See* Comfort and consolation

Constant
FEMININE: Connie, Constance

Constructed *See* Build

Container maker
MASCULINE: Cooper

Contend *See also* Conflict
MASCULINE: Yariv, Yisrael, Yisroel
FEMININE: Israela, Sareli, Shawna, Yisraela, Yisrela

Convulsion
FEMININE: Avit

Cook (preparer of food)
MASCULINE: Cook, Ofeh

Cookie
FEMININE: Ugiya

Copper
FEMININE: Nechusha

Coral
MASCULINE: Almog
FEMININE: Penina, Pnina

Cord (rope)
MASCULINE: Cord, Cordell
FEMININE: Cordelia

Corn sheaf
MASCULINE: Amir

Cornell tree
FEMININE: Corna, Cornelia

Corner
FEMININE: Zavit

Correspondence
MASCULINE: Agron

Cottage
MASCULINE: Byron, Kerby, Kibby, Kirby

Counsel *See also* Wisdom
MASCULINE: Al, Aldred, Alf, Alfred, Alfredo, Alson, Dob, Goddard, Hob, Hobs, Hopkins, Ralph, Randi, Randolph, Randy, Raoul, Raul, Rob, Robard, Robert, Roberto, Robin, Robson, Robyn, Rolf, Rowle, Rudolph, Rupert, Sandy, Sanford
FEMININE: Bobbe, Bunny, Randi, Ricka, Ricky, Robbi, Roberta, Robertina, Robin, Rori

Counselor *See also* Advisor
FEMININE: Alfreda, Mildred, Millie, Mindi, Mindy

Countryman
MASCULINE: Paine, Payne

Courage *See also* Bold; Champion; Hero
MASCULINE: Amitz, Anders, Andi, Andor, André, Andrew, Andy, Devlin, Drew, Dru, Helmut, Ometz, Riley, Valerie, Valery
FEMININE: Amtza, Andrea, Andye, Drew, Dru, Val, Valeria, Valerie, Valery

Courageous advice
MASCULINE: Ralph, Raoul, Raul, Rowle, Rudolph

Courteous
MASCULINE: Curt, Curtis, Kurt

Covenant
MASCULINE: Bris, Brit

Covered
MASCULINE: Atif, Hedley

Covering
MASCULINE: Chupah, Geled, Hedley
FEMININE: Atifa, Heaven, Magena, Magina

Crafty
MASCULINE: Atif, Naf, Naftali, Naphtali, Toolie

Crag
MASCULINE: Craig

Create
MASCULINE: Asa, Assa
FEMININE: Asaela

Creation
FEMININE: Asia, Asiya, Yetzira

Crooked
MASCULINE: Akom
FEMININE: Akuma

Cross over
MASCULINE: Ivri, Travis
FEMININE: Avira, Ivria, Ivriya

Crossbow
MASCULINE: Arbie

Crow
MASCULINE: Cornelius, Cornell, Crawford, Jay, Jayson, Kornell

Crown *See also* Royal
MASCULINE: Atir, Esteban, Kailil, Kalil, Keter, Kitron, Larry, Lars, Laurence, Laurie, Lawrence, Lorence, Lorn, Lorry, Stefan, Stefano, Stephan, Stephen, Stevan, Steven, Zer

FEMININE: Atara, Atura, Estefania, Kaile, Kalia, Kayla, Kelila, Kelula, Kitra, Kitrit, Kitron, Krayna, Kreindel, Kreine, Kryna, Kyla, Livya, Pania, Stefana, Stefanie, Steffi, Stephane, Stephania, Stevana, Taga

Cry *See also* Sing; Weep
MASCULINE: Jaron, Yaron
FEMININE: Pua, Shava, Shu'a

Crystal clear *See also* Clear (pure)
FEMININE: Krystal

Cub *See also* Lion
MASCULINE: Colin, Gur-Arye, Gur-Ari, Kefir

Cultivate *See also* Field (area of land)
MASCULINE: Nir

Cunning *See* Crafty

Curved
FEMININE: Akuma

Cushion
MASCULINE: Cody

Cut off
MASCULINE: Gideon, Gidi, Gidon, Gidone, Gidoni, Natik
FEMININE: Gidona

Cutting
MASCULINE: Geza
FEMININE: Gezira

Cylinder
MASCULINE: Galil

Cypress tree
FEMININE: Tirza

Dale *See* Valley

Dare
FEMININE: Dara

Daring *See also* Bold
MASCULINE: Noaz

Dark and darkness *See also* Black
MASCULINE: Darcy, Duane, Dwayne, Ofir, Ophir
FEMININE: Alata, Darcie, Laila, Leila, Maura, Maureen, Melanie, Misty, Morena, Morine

Dark in appearance *See also* Moorish; Negro
MASCULINE: Bruno, Delano, Duff, Floyd, Lloyd, Neal, Neil, Neilson, Nelson, Niall, Niles, Nils, Nyle
FEMININE: Neala, Nealla, Nia

Darkened
MASCULINE: Adar

Darling *See also* Dear
FEMININE: Cara

Date tree
FEMININE: Dikla, Diklit

Daughter *See also* Child
FEMININE: Bas-Sheva, Basha, Bashe, Basya, Bat-Yam, Bat-Tziyon, Bat-Sheva, Bat-Zion, Bat-El, Bat-Ami, Bat-Shua, Bathsheba, Batli, Batya, Beth-Ami, Peshe, Pessel, Shevi, Wynona

Dawn *See also* Morning
FEMININE: Aurora, Dawn, Roxane, Roxie, Roxine, Roxy

Day *See also specific days of the week*
MASCULINE: Dag, Dagobert, Damon, Delbert, Yemuel
FEMININE: Dana, Danette, Danna, Deanna, Deon, Di, Diana, Didi, Dion, Dyan, Dyana

Daybreak *See also* Dawn; Morning
FEMININE: Lacey, Lucette, Luci, Lucia, Lucie, Lucile, Lucinda, Lucy

Dear *See also* Beloved
MASCULINE: Darold, Darrell, Darrol, Leif, Lief, Yakar, Yakir
FEMININE: Careena, Carina, Carita, Cher, Cheri, Cherilynn, Cherri, Cheryl, Darla, Darleen, Daryl, Leeba, Liba, Libe, Libi, Libke, Lieba, Liebe, Lipke, Sheree, Sherelle

Death
MASCULINE: Than, Thane

Decrease
MASCULINE: Machi

Dedicated
MASCULINE: Chanoch, Enoch, Hanoch, Henech
FEMININE: Chanukah

Deed
FEMININE: Alila, Aliliya, Asia, Asiya

Deep (profound)
MASCULINE: Amok

Deer
MASCULINE: Afri, Ayal, Ayali, Ayalon, Buck, Bucky, Cerf, Dur, Elan, Hart, Hersch, Herschel, Hersh, Hershel, Hertz, Hertzel, Hertzl, Herz, Herzl, Heschel, Hesh, Heshel, Heshi, Hirsch, Hirsh, Ofar, Ofer, Ofra, Ofri, Opher, Tsvi, Tzevi, Tzvee, Tzvi, Tzvika, Zevi, Zvi
FEMININE: Ayala, Ayelet, Civia, Darbey, Doe, Fauna, Fawn, Fawna, Fawne, Fawnia, Gazella, Hertzela, Hertzliya, Herzlia, Hilma, Hindel, Hindi, Leola, Ofra, Ofrat, Ofrit, Ophra, Ophrat, Opra, Sivia, Tzeviya, Zvia

Deer keeper
MASCULINE: Harman

Deer meadow
MASCULINE: Darbey, Hartley, Raleigh

Defender *See also* Guard; Protect
MASCULINE: Leopold, Meredith, Seward

Delicate *See also* Tender
MASCULINE: Adina
FEMININE: Adeena, Adena, Adina, Aidel, Delicia, Edel, Eidel, Mignon

Delight
MASCULINE: Abinoam, Abiram, Adni, Avinoam, Eden
FEMININE: Delicia, Eden, Edna, Naami, Naoma, Naomi, Neumi, Noemi, Nomi

Deliverance
MASCULINE: Palti

Deliverer
MASCULINE: Xavier, Yishi

Demons *See also* Spirits
MASCULINE: Tzafreer
FEMININE: Lilit

Departure
FEMININE: Aziva

Descend
MASCULINE: Jared, Jarrod, Jered, Jordan, Jordy, Jori, Yarden, Yardeni, Yared, Yered
FEMININE: Jardena, Jordana, Jordi, Yardena

Descendant
MASCULINE: Jared, Jarrod, Yared

Descent, noble *See* Patrician

Desert (abandon)
MASCULINE: Arak, Arik
FEMININE: Arika

Desert oasis
MASCULINE: Neve

Desire and desirable
MASCULINE: Chemdat, Desi, Desiderio
FEMININE: Ava, Beca, Beccie, Beckie, Beka, Chamuda, Cheftzi-Ba, Chemda, Chemdat, Edna, Hefziba, Hemda, Hemdat, Hephziba, Hepzi, Hepziba, Lois, Nirtza, Reba, Rebecca, Reva, Rheba, Ricka, Ricky, Riva, Teshuka

Desolate *See also* Forsaken
FEMININE: Azuva

Despair of the Lord
MASCULINE: Josiah, Yoshiya, Yoshiyahu

Destiny *See* Fate

Destruction
MASCULINE: Avdima, Avdimi

Detachable
MASCULINE: Natik

Dew
MASCULINE: Avital, Avitul, Avtalyon, Raviv, Tal, Tal-Shachar, Tali, Talor, Taly
FEMININE: Lital, Maital, Maytal, Meital, Ravital, Raviva, Reviva, Tal, Tali, Talie, Talor, Talora

Diamonds
MASCULINE: Kimberley, Shamir
FEMININE: Kim, Kimberley

Digging
MASCULINE: Adir
FEMININE: Adira

Dignity
MASCULINE: Honor

Dim-sighted
MASCULINE: Cecil
FEMININE: Cecelia, Ceci, Cecil, Cecile, Cecilia, Cecily, Ceil, Cele, Celia, Cicely, Cis, Sheila, Sheli, Shellee, Shelley, Sheryl, Sisi, Sisley, Sissie

Dionysius (Greek god)
MASCULINE: Sidney, Sydney
FEMININE: Denice, Denise, Denyce, Syd, Sydney, Sid

Diseased
MASCULINE: Tzaru'a

Distinguished *See also* Honored
FEMININE: Efrat, Efrata

District
MASCULINE: Galil

Divine *See also* God
MASCULINE: Ambrose
FEMININE: Divina, Milka

Divine brightness
MASCULINE: Norbert

Divine gift
MASCULINE: Ted, Theo, Theodor, Todros, Tudor
FEMININE: Theo, Theodora, Theora

Divine helmet
MASCULINE: Ansel

Divine source of life
MASCULINE: Axel

Divine spear
MASCULINE: Oscar, Ossie

Divine strength
MASCULINE: Oscar, Ossie

Doctor *See also* Heal; Healer
MASCULINE: Assi
FEMININE: Assia

Doe *See also* Deer
MASCULINE: Daw

Dog
MASCULINE: Cal, Cale, Caleb, Calev, Kalev

Doll
FEMININE: Bambi, Buba, Bubati

Door
FEMININE: Delta

Dove
MASCULINE: Cole, Coleman, Jona, Jonas, Mal, Malcolm, Yon, Yona
FEMININE: Jemima, Jonina, Jonit, Paloma, Tauba, Toiba, Yemima, Yona, Yonat, Yonata, Yonati, Yonina, Yonit, Yonita

Dowry
MASCULINE: Zavad, Zavdi

Drawn out (of the water)
MASCULINE: Misha, Moise, Moishe, Mose, Moses, Moshe, Moss, Moy
FEMININE: Moselle

Dress
FEMININE: Simla

Duck
FEMININE: Idria, Idrit, Idriya

Dust
MASCULINE: Avak
FEMININE: Afra, Aphra, Avka

Dwelling *See also* Home; House
MASCULINE: Avgar, Bitan, Dir, Graham, Havelock, Maon, Norris
FEMININE: Dira, Doreet, Dorit, Leena, Lena, Zevula

Eagle
MASCULINE: Adler, Aquila, Arndt, Arne, Arnel, Arni, Arno, Arnold, Nesher
FEMININE: Arabel, Arabela, Arabelle, Arnett, Arnolde, Arnoldine, Ayit

Ear
MASCULINE: Ozni

Earnest
MASCULINE: Ernest, Ernesto, Ernie, Erno, Ernst

Earring
FEMININE: Agil

Earth *See also* Man; World
MASCULINE: Adam, Addison
FEMININE: Adama, Adamina, Eartha, Eretz
lover of
MASCULINE: Demetrius, Dimitry

East and eastern
MASCULINE: Anatole, Anatoly, Antal, Kedem, Kedma, Tolya
FEMININE: Kedma

Echo
MASCULINE: Adad, Hadad, Hed

Educated *See also* Enlighten; Knowledge-able; Learner; Wisdom
MASCULINE: Chanoch, Curt, Curtis, Enoch, Hanoch, Henech, Kurt, Maskil
FEMININE: Chanukah

Egocentric
MASCULINE: Gay

Egyptian name
FEMININE: Asenath, Asnat, Osnat

Elder *See also* Old
MASCULINE: Sava, Senior, Shneur
FEMININE: Keshisha

Eldest
MASCULINE: Bichri

Elected
MASCULINE: Corey, Cory, Gabai, Nivchar

Elevated *See also* Rise up
MASCULINE: Omar
FEMININE: Alta, Meroma

Elf ruler
MASCULINE: Aubrey, Avery

Elm
FEMININE: Samara

Eloquent
MASCULINE: Brian, Brion, Bry, Bryan, Ryan, Ryne

Embarrassment
MASCULINE: Buz, Buzi
FEMININE: Malbina

Ember
MASCULINE: Gomer
FEMININE: Gomer

Emblem *See* Banner; Flag

Emigration
FEMININE: Hagar

Eminent
FEMININE: Chandra, Shandra

Encampment *See* Camp; Enclosure

Enchanting
FEMININE: Alisia

Enchantment
FEMININE: Kesima

Encircle
FEMININE: Akifa, Seviva

Enclosure *See also* Closed; Garden; Park
MASCULINE: Ham, Hamilton, Hamlet, Link
FEMININE: Akifa, Corey, Cori, Correy, Corri, Corry, Courteny, Kori, Tira, Tiri

Encourage
MASCULINE: Oded
FEMININE: Odeda, Odedia

Endearing
FEMININE: Alisia

Enduring (lasting)
FEMININE: Durene

Enduring (suffering) *See also* Eternal
MASCULINE: Dante, Durand, Durant, Duryea
FEMININE: Patience

Enemy
MASCULINE: Iyov, Job

Energetic
MASCULINE: Eddy, Meretz
FEMININE: Mahira, Mehira, Zariza, Zeriza

Enlightenment *See also* Educated
MASCULINE: Jair, Maskil, Naor, Yair
FEMININE: Yaira

Envelop (protect)
MASCULINE: Lot, Lotan

Environment
FEMININE: Seviva

Envision
MASCULINE: Chazo

Era
MASCULINE: Idan

Escape
MASCULINE: Arak, Ira, Iran, Iri, Palti

Establish
MASCULINE: Yachin

Established
MASCULINE: Stacey
FEMININE: Komema

Establishment
MASCULINE: Mosad

Esteem *See* Dignity; High esteem; Honored; Respect

Eternal *See also* Enduring (lasting); Permanent
MASCULINE: Dante, Duryea, Elad

Eulogy
FEMININE: Eulalia

Evil
MASCULINE: Sig⋅⋅

Ewe *See also* Lamb; Sheep
FEMININE: Rachael, Rachel, Rachela, Racheli, Rachelle, Rae, Rahel, Rahela, Raquel, Ray, Rochel

Exact
FEMININE: Norma

Exalted *See also* Glory; High; Revered
MASCULINE: Adar, Aggie, Ali, August, Augustus, Austen, Chiram, Chirom, Hi, Hiram, Ila, Ili, Kareem, Karim, Marom, Nedar, Ram, Rama, Sami, Segev, Seguv, Yigdal, Zeb, Zebulon, Zevulun, Zvulun
FEMININE: Alta, Atalia, Athalia, Atlit, Nedara, Rama, Rami, Ramit, Roma, Romema, Romi, Romia, Romie, Romit, Romiya

Excellence
MASCULINE: Adif, Ben-Tziyon, Ben Zion, Benson, Bentzi, Burrut, Meged, Sion, Tziyon, Zion, Ziony
FEMININE: Siona

Excellent
FEMININE: Alita, Arista, Migda, Tziona, Tziyona, Tziyonit, Ziona, Ziony

Exceptional
MASCULINE: Angus

Excerpt
MASCULINE: Keta

Exiled
MASCULINE: Goliath, Yagli

Expert
MASCULINE: Aman, Maher

Expression (speech)
MASCULINE: Niv

Eyed, black
MASCULINE: Sullivan

Fabric pleater
MASCULINE: Trygve

Faced, black
MASCULINE: Duff

Fair *See also* Beauty; Handsome; White
MASCULINE: Al, Alain, Alan, Allan, Allen, Allyn, Alson, Alyn, Dwight, Erv, Ervin, Erving, Erwin, Fairchild, Finian, Gaylord, Gwynn, Irv, Irvin, Irvine, Irving, Wyn
FEMININE: Alaina, Alena, Allena, Alleyne, Allyn, Alva, Bianca, Blanca, Blanch, Elma, Enid, Gwen, Gwenn, Gwyn, Gwynn, Sellie, Selma, Wynette, Wynn

Fairy
FEMININE: Tania

Faith and fidelity
MASCULINE: Amin, Amitai, Amitan, Amnon, Fidel, Griffin, Griffith, Heman, Liel, Loy, Loyal, Truman
FEMININE: Amana, Amina, Connie, Constance, Emuna, Faith, Fay, Fayette, Fidelia, Fidella, Hope, Iris, Lela, Lelia, Veronica

Faith in God *See* God, faith in

Falcon
MASCULINE: Baz
FEMININE: Merlin

Falsehood
FEMININE: Kozbi

Falsifier
FEMININE: Cozbi

Fame of the land
MASCULINE: Arlando, Orland, Orlando, Roland, Rolando, Rolland, Rollen, Rollo, Rowe, Rowland
FEMININE: Orlanda, Rolanda

Family, noble
MASCULINE: Alfonse, Alphonso, Alsie, Alson, Lon

Famous
MASCULINE: Derek, Derrek, Dietrich, Dirk, Durk, Elmer, Elmo, Elmor, Filmore, Hili, Hillel, Maks, Malvin, Max, Maximilian, Maxwell, Mel,

Mell, Melvin, Melvyn, Merrill, Noble, Noda, Nolan, Noland, Osbert, Palu, Rodger, Rodgers, Roger, Yadua
FEMININE: Berta, Bertha, Degula, Maxa, Maxima, Maxime, Maxine, Nola, Rudelle, Rue

Farm
MASCULINE: Merton, Morton, Myrton, Newt, Newton, Wilton
FEMININE: Leena, Lena

Farm steward
MASCULINE: Granger

Farmer
MASCULINE: Calvert, Cole, Coleman, Fabian, Fabius, George, Jiri
FEMININE: Fabia, Georgeanne, Georgette, Georgia, Georgiana, Georgina, Gigi, Resa, Risa, Teddi, Teresa, Teresita, Teri, Terrie, Tessa, Theresa, Zita

Fate
MASCULINE: Goral
FEMININE: Fortuna

Father *See also* God; Grandfather
MASCULINE: Abba, Abbayei, Abbie, Abbot, Abin, Abina, Av, Avdan, Aviad, Aviasaf, Aviaz, Avichai, Avichayil, Avichen, Avida, Avidan, Avideror, Avidor, Avidror, Avigdor, Avihu, Avin, Avina, Evyatar, Lincoln
FEMININE: Abbe, Abbey, Abbie, Abby, Abigail, Avigal, Avigayil, Gail, Gale, Gayle
of individuals
MASCULINE: Abihu, Abimelech, Abinadab, Abinoam, Abiram, Avgar, Avida, Avidan, Avihud, Avikam, Avikar, Avimelech, Avinadav, Avinoam, Aviram, Avituv, Avizemer, Avron
FEMININE: Avichayil
of a mighty nation
MASCULINE: Abe, Aberlin, Abi, Abie, Abraham, Abram, Abrasha, Aviam, Aviasaf, Avraham, Avram, Avrom, Avrum, Avrumi, Brahm, Bremel, Ebril, Evril, From, Ibrahim
FEMININE: Abra, Avrasha

of spiritual movement
MASCULINE: Absalom, Avigal, Avishalom, Avital, Avitul, Avshalom, Avtalyon

Favorable
MASCULINE: Prosper

Favored
MASCULINE: Yefuneh

Fearless
MASCULINE: Almagor, Ralph, Raoul, Raul, Rowle, Rudolph

Feast and festivity
MASCULINE: Aga, Bondi, Chag, Chagai, Chagi, Hag, Haga, Hagai, Hagi, Yom Tov
FEMININE: Chagit, Chagiya, Hagia, Hagit, Holiday

Feather
MASCULINE: Notza
FEMININE: Notza, Notzi

Featherbed
FEMININE: Keset

Fee
FEMININE: Amala

Fence
MASCULINE: Gader
FEMININE: Gedera

Fern
FEMININE: Fern

Fertility
FEMININE: Ingrid

Feud
MASCULINE: Mered
FEMININE: Merida, Meriva

Fidelity *See* Faith and fidelity

Field (area of land) *See also* Garden; Meadow; Orchard; Valley
MASCULINE: Ainsley, Ashleigh, Bromley, Burleigh, Burley, Burr, Garth, Garvey, Harley, Hartley, Hayden, Heywood, Manley, Nir, Oakleigh, Oakley, Raleigh, Stan, Stanley, Stansfield
FEMININE: Amberlee, Blair, Idalee, Jennilee, Lauralee, Lee, Maisie, Maralee, Marilee, Marily, Surilee

Field (stadium)
MASCULINE: Champ, Champion

Field of the Lord
MASCULINE: Nirel, Niria, Niriel, Niriya, Nirya

Fifth
MASCULINE: Quentin, Quenton, Quincy, Quinn
FEMININE: Hamisi

Fig
FEMININE: Faga, Faiga, Faigel, Faygie, Feiga, Feigel, Feigi

Fig tree
FEMININE: Idra

Fight
MASCULINE: Yisrael, Yisroel
FEMININE: Israela, Sareli, Shawna, Yisraela, Yisrela

Fighting warrior *See* Warrior

Figs, house of
FEMININE: Bethany

Fire and fiery *See also* Candlelight; Ember; Flame; Passion; Spark; Torch
MASCULINE: Ashi, Edan, Eish, Esh, Lahav, Nur, Nuri, Ud, Udi, Uri
FEMININE: Enia, Enya, Lahav, Lehava, Medura, Urit, Vesta

Fire of the Lord
MASCULINE: Nuria, Nuriel, Nuriya, Nurya

Firebrand *See* Sword

Firm
MASCULINE: Eitan, Etan, Ethan, Eytan
FEMININE: Connie, Constance

First
MASCULINE: Rishon
FEMININE: Reishit, Rishona

First child of second husband
FEMININE: Adika

Firstborn
MASCULINE: Primo
FEMININE: Reshit, Wynona

Fish
MASCULINE: Dag, Fish, Fishel, Fishke, Fishkin, Fishlin, Fisk, Nun
FEMININE: Binit

Fish bone
FEMININE: Idra

Fish gill
MASCULINE: Zim

Flag *See also* Banner
MASCULINE: Degel
FEMININE: Digla, Diglat

Flag carrier
MASCULINE: Daglan
FEMININE: Dagal

Flag emblem
MASCULINE: Dagul

Flame *See also* Fire; Passion
MASCULINE: Edan, Lahat, Lahav, Lapid, Lapidos, Lapidot, Ud, Udi, Uri
FEMININE: Avuka, Lahav, Lehava, Medura, Shalhevet

Flash of light
MASCULINE: Barak, Bazak

Flatterer
FEMININE: Emilie

Flax
MASCULINE: Harlan, Harlin

Flaxen
FEMININE: Linnet

Fleeing *See also* Flee
MASCULINE: Arak, Palti
FEMININE: Tisa

Flexible *See also* Bend
MASCULINE: Linc, Lincoln

Flight (escape) *See also* Flee
FEMININE: Tisa

Flint
MASCULINE: Shamir

Flock
MASCULINE: Edri
FEMININE: Eder, Marona

Flock of sheep
MASCULINE: Eder, Maron

Flour
FEMININE: Solet

Flourishing *See also* Blooming; Grow; Prosperous
MASCULINE: Anthony, Anton, Erve, Harvey,

Harvi, Herve, Toni, Vern, Vernon, Virgil
FEMININE: Antonella, Cyma, Floreen, Florella, Floren, Florence, Florentina, Floria, Floriane, Florrie, Floryn, Flossie, Syma, Thalia

Flow *See* Descend

Flowers *See also* Blooming; Blossom; Bud; Garden
MASCULINE: Nitza, Nitzan, Perach, Pirchoni, Savyon
FEMININE: Aruga, Blima, Blossom, Blu, Bluma, Blume, Chavatzelet, Fifi, Fiorella, Fleur, Fleurette, Flora, Floreen, Florella, Floren, Florence, Florentina, Floria, Floriane, Florrie, Floryn, Flossie, Jasmina, Jasmine, Leilani, Lelani, Lila, Nirit, Nitza, Nitzana, Nitzanit, Nurit, Nurita, Pansy, Perach, Pircha

Folksy
MASCULINE: Amami

Food near the oak tree
MASCULINE: Adair

Food preparer
MASCULINE: Cook, Ofeh

Foot soldier *See also* Soldiers
MASCULINE: Troy

Ford
MASCULINE: Bradford, Clifford, Crawford, Stanford

Foreigner *See also* Stranger
FEMININE: Bab, Babette, Babs, Barbara, Barbi, Bobbe, Bunny, Yenta, Yentil

Foresee
MASCULINE: Chazo

Forester
MASCULINE: Forester, Foster

Forever *See* Eternal

Forget, causing to
MASCULINE: Manashi, Manasseh, Menas, Menashe, Menashi
FEMININE: Lotus

Forgetfulness *See* Lotus plant

Forlorn
FEMININE: Lorna

Formidable *See also* Strength
MASCULINE: Egan, Egon

Forsaken *See also* Desolate; Lonely
MASCULINE: Alman, Almon, Azuv
FEMININE: Azuva, Hagar, Lorna

Fortified
MASCULINE: Arlo, Walbert, Wilber, Wilbur
FEMININE: Bira, Biranit

Fortress *See also* Camp
MASCULINE: Chester, Chet, Maoz
FEMININE: Armona, Armonit, Avis, Metzuda, Migdala

Fortunate *See also* Blessed; Good fortune; Prosperous; Rich
MASCULINE: Anchel, Anschel, Anshel, Ascher, Aser, Asher, Asser, Edmond, Edmund, Feliks, Felix, Ned, Neddy, Prosper
FEMININE: Anchelle, Ashera, Audris, Falice, Felecia, Felecie, Feliciana, Felicite, Felisa, Oshrat, Phylicia

Fortune
FEMININE: Fortuna

Foundation (of support)
MASCULINE: Masad
FEMININE: Masada

Fountain
MASCULINE: Bruno, Gal, Mayan
FEMININE: Fontana, Gal, Gala, Galit

Four
MASCULINE: Arba

Fowl (animals)
FEMININE: Peninia, Peniniya

Fox
MASCULINE: Fox, Tod, Todd
FEMININE: Shuala

Fragment
MASCULINE: Gaziz
FEMININE: Geziza

Fragrance
MASCULINE: Bosem

Fragrant
MASCULINE: Myron

Fragrant spices, one who burns
MASCULINE: Gomer

Frankincense
MASCULINE: Livni
FEMININE: Levona

Freedom
MASCULINE: Amidror, Avideror, Avidror, Deror, Derori, Dror, Drori, Franchot, Francis, Frank, Frankie, Franklin, Franklyn, Franz, Freed, Freeman, Leopold
FEMININE: Deror, Fani, Fania, Fannie, Fanya, Fran, Francene, Frances, Francesca, Franci, Francine, Frani, Frankie, Liberty, Ranny

holiday of
MASCULINE: Pesach

mountain
MASCULINE: Fremont

Frequent
MASCULINE: Tadir

Fresh *See also* Clean
FEMININE: Raanana, Ranana, Tari, Teriya

Friday, born on
FEMININE: Fifi

Friendly
MASCULINE: Itai, Ittai
FEMININE: Xenia

Friends and friendship *See also* God, friendship of
MASCULINE: Aldwin, Alvan, Alvin, Alwin, Amitan, Arvid, Bailey, Bellamy, Berwin, Bub, Chavivi, Chovav, Chovev, Corwin, Dodi, Dodo, Elvin, Elwin, Khalil, Malvin, Mel, Mell, Melvin, Melvyn, Nadim, Noam, Norvin, Raya, Regem, Selwyn, Sherwin, Win, Winston, Yadid, Yedid
FEMININE: Aimee, Amity, Amy, Davene, Doda, Dodi, Dodo, Dody, Edina, Edna, Edwina, Fauna, Fawn, Fawna, Fawne, Fawnia, Jedida, Malvina, Melba, Melva, Melveen, Melvina, Nafshiya, Raya, Reut, Rut, Ruth, Ruthanna, Ruthi, Ruti, Severina, Yedida

Fringe
FEMININE: Kanaf

Fruit *See also specific fruits by name*
MASCULINE: Zimra
FEMININE: Asisya, Peri, Zimrat

Fruitful
MASCULINE: Edlow, Effi, Efraim, Efrat, Efrayim, Efrem, Efry, Ephraim, Fraime, Froim
FEMININE: Efrat, Efrata, Efrem, Pora, Porat, Poria, Poriya

Full-grown *See also* Man
MASCULINE: Carl, Carlos, Carlton, Carol, Carrol, Charle, Charles, Charley, Charlton, Chip, Chuck, Corliss, Karel, Karl, Karol
FEMININE: Carla, Carlotta

Furrow
MASCULINE: Talmon, Tel, Telem
FEMININE: Talmon

Fury
MASCULINE: Evron
FEMININE: Evrona

Future
MASCULINE: Atid
FEMININE: Atida

Gallant *See also* Hero
MASCULINE: Abiri
FEMININE: Abiri

Garden *See also* Flowers
MASCULINE: Bustan, Carmel, Carmen, Carmine, Gan, Gani, Garden, Garth, Garvey, Gina, Ginson, Ginton, Horton, Jardine, Karmel, Karmeli
FEMININE: Carma, Carmel, Carmela, Carmelit, Carmen, Gana, Ganit, Gena, Gina, Karma, Karmel, Karmela, Karmeli, Karmelit, Karmit, Karmiya, Yardenia

Garden of Eden *See also* Delight
MASCULINE: Eden
FEMININE: Eden

Garden keeper *See* Gardener

Garden plant
MASCULINE: Chavakuk, Habakuk

Gardener
MASCULINE: Ganan, Gardener
FEMININE: Hortense

Garment *See also* Vest
MASCULINE: Salman, Salmon, Seth, Shet
FEMININE: Simla

Garment cutter
MASCULINE: Taylor

Garnet
MASCULINE: Garnet

Gate
MASCULINE: Baba, Bava, Janus

Gather and gathering
MASCULINE: Asaf, Asaph, Asif, Daley, Tzabar
FEMININE: Asefa, Asifa, Atzira, Sabaria, Tzabara, Tzabaria, Tzabariya

Gay *See also* Happiness; Merry
FEMININE: Gay, Gaye

Gazelle
MASCULINE: Zeviel, Ziv
FEMININE: Ayala, Ayelet, Eilat, Gazella

General (of an army)
MASCULINE: Wal, Wallie, Wally, Walt, Walter, Wilt

Generation
MASCULINE: Amidor, Dor, Dori, Gildor
FEMININE: Doreet, Dorit, Dorota
father of
MASCULINE: Avidor

Generous
MASCULINE: Nadiv
FEMININE: Nediva

Gentle
MASCULINE: Aden, Adin, Adiv
FEMININE: Aidel, Edel, Eidel, Latifa, Linda, Lynda, Malinda, Melinda, Mildred, Millie, Mindi, Mindy, Morna, Myra, Myrna, Rachael, Rachel, Rachela, Racheli, Rachelle, Rae, Rahel, Rahela, Raquel, Ray, Rochel

Germany region
MASCULINE: Saxe, Saxony

Giant
MASCULINE: Og

Gift *See also* Divine gift; God, gift of
MASCULINE: Almadore, Doran, Dore, Doron, Geoff, Geoffrey, Gifford, Jef, Jeffers, Jefferson, Jeffery, Jess, Jesse, Matan, Matat, Nason, Natan, Nate, Nathan, Nati, Natin, Nitai, Noson, Shai, Teruma, Todros, Yishai, Zavad, Zavdi, Zeved
FEMININE: Aldora, Darona, Dodo, Dolley, Dolly, Dora, Doraleen, Dore, Doreen, Dorene, Doretha, Doretta, Dorina, Dorona, Doronit, Dorothea, Dorothy, Dorri, Dot, Eudora, Gisa, Glendora, Mana, Matana, Matat, Matea, Migda, Migdana, Natania, Natanya, Netana, Netina, Teruma, Teshura, Totie, Zevida, Zevuda

Gift of Isis
MASCULINE: Isador, Isidor, Isidoro, Iz, Izzie
FEMININE: Isadora

Gifted
FEMININE: Pandora

Gilded *See also* Gold
FEMININE: Eldora, Zehuva

Gill
MASCULINE: Zim

Girl *See also* Child; Maid; Young; Youth
FEMININE: Arleen, Arlene, Arlett, Arline, Arlyne, Colleen, Collette, Deidra, Deidre, Deirdre, Did, Gill, Gilla, Jill, Missie, Naara

Give *See* Bequeath; Gift

Gladiator *See also* Warrior
MASCULINE: Champ, Champion

Glass, clear
FEMININE: Chrystal, Crystal

Glen *See also* Valley
MASCULINE: Glen
FEMININE: Glenda, Glendora, Glenna, Glynda, Glynis

Glorify
FEMININE: Cleo, Clio

Glory *See also* Majestic
MASCULINE: Hercules, Hod, Pe'er, Segev
FEMININE: Glora, Gloria, Gloriana, Glory, Gloryette, Honor, Honora, Honorine, Nili, Nilit, Tifara, Tiferet

Go up *See* Ascend

Goat
MASCULINE: Afri, Gedi, Jael, Ofer, Ofra, Ofri, Opher, Yael, Zimran, Zimri
FEMININE: Jael, Ofra, Ofrat, Ofrit, Ophra, Ophrat, Opra, Tabita, Yaala, Yaalat, Yaalit, Yael, Yaela

Goatskin
MASCULINE: Giles, Gyles

God *See also* Divine; Faith; Holy
MASCULINE: Dom, Dominic
adorned by
MASCULINE: Adael, Adiel
FEMININE: Adiel, Edia
appointed by
FEMININE: Noadya
beloved of
MASCULINE: Didi, Eldad, Jed, Jedediah, Yedidia
FEMININE: Ahuvia, Ahuviya, Amadea, Yedidela, Yedidia
blessed of
FEMININE: Beruchiya
comforted by
MASCULINE: Chami, Chemi, Chemia, Nechemia, Nechemya, Nehemia
compassion of
MASCULINE: Chanania, Rachaman, Rachman, Yehochanan
counsel of
FEMININE: Sibyl, Sybil
creation by
MASCULINE: Asael, Asahel, Asiel
FEMININE: Asaela, Asiya
crown of
MASCULINE: Karniel, Kasriel, Kati, Katriel
day of
MASCULINE: Yemuel
dedicated by
MASCULINE: Sam, Samm, Sammy, Samuel, Samy, Uel

despair of
MASCULINE: Josiah, Yoshiya, Yoshiyahu
dew of *See also* God, sustainer
MASCULINE: Avital, Talia, Talya
FEMININE: Abital, Talia, Talya
face of
MASCULINE: Penuel
faith in
MASCULINE: Liel, Yachlel
FEMININE: Datya
fatherhood of
MASCULINE: Abbahu, Abi, Abida, Abinadab, Avi, Avia, Aviel, Aviela, Avihai, Avikar, Avimael, Avinadav, Aviram, Avivia, Aviviya, Aviya, Avuya, Eliav, Joab, Yoav
FEMININE: Avia, Aviela, Avivia, Aviviya, Aviya, Basha, Bashe, Basya, Bat-El, Batya, Peshe, Pessel
fear and honor of
MASCULINE: Tim, Timo, Timothy
festival of
FEMININE: Chagiya, Hagia
field of
MASCULINE: Niria, Niriya, Nirya
FEMININE: Nirel
fire of
MASCULINE: Nuria, Nuriya, Nurya
of fertility and peace
FEMININE: Ingrid
flame of *See also* God, light of
MASCULINE: Uria, Uriel, Uriya, Yuri
FEMININE: Uriela
of the forest
MASCULINE: Ossie, Oswald, Ozzi
friendship with
MASCULINE: Almodad, Elidad, Godwin, Reuel, Ruel
fruit of
FEMININE: Asia, Asisya
garden of
FEMININE: Gania, Ganya, Yardenia
gazelle of
MASCULINE: Zeviel
generosity of
FEMININE: Nedavia
gift of
MASCULINE: Avinatan, Avishai, Elnatan, Jon-Jon, Jonathan, Jonji, Jonni, Mat, Matania, Matanya, Matanyahu,

Mateo, Mati, Matia, Matis, Matitya, Matt, Mattathias, Matthew, Matti, Mattie, Matya, Nathanel, Netanel, Netaniel, Netanya, Netanyahu, Nethanel, Nethaniel, Tad, Thaddeus, Yehonatan, Yon, Yonat, Yonatan, Yoni, Yotan, Zavdiel, Zevadia
FEMININE: Deuela, Dodo, Dolley, Dolly, Dora, Doraleen, Dore, Doreen, Dorene, Doretha, Doretta, Dorina, Dorothea, Dorothy, Dorri, Dot, Glendora, Matea, Nataniela, Natanya, Netania, Netaniela, Netanya, Theo, Theodora, Theora, Totie

glory of
FEMININE: Yochebed, Yocheved

gold of
FEMININE: Pazia, Paziya, Pazya

good fortune from
MASCULINE: Gadiel
FEMININE: Gadiela

goodness of
MASCULINE: Tobe, Tobiah, Tobias, Toby, Toviel, Toviya, Tuvia, Tuviya, Tuviyahu

graciousness of
MASCULINE: Chanania, Chaniel, Ewen, Gian, Hanania, Hanina, Hans, Hansel, Hansen, Hanson, Ian, Ivan, Jack, Jackie, Jan, Jean, Johan, Johannes, John, Johnnie, Jon, Juan, Sean, Shane, Shanon, Shaun, Shawn, Yancy
FEMININE: Gianina, Ivana, Jan, Jane, Janel, Janet, Janetta, Janette, Jani, Janice, Janie, Janiece, Janina, Janis, Janita, Janlori, Janna, Jean, Jeanetta, Jeanette, Jeanice, Jeanie, Jeanine, Jeanne, Jeannette, Jeannine, Jehane, Jen, Jenat, Jenerette, Jenessa, Jenine, Jenna, Jennie, Jessica, Jessie, Jo-Anne, Jo, Joan, Joann, Joanna, Joanne, Johan, Johanna, Johanne, Johnetta, Johnna, Shan, Shannen, Shannon, Shauna, Shawn, Shawna, Sheena, Simajean, Yoanna, Yochana

greatness of
MASCULINE: Gedalia, Gedalya, Gedalyahu

habitation of
MASCULINE: Eldar

help and salvation
MASCULINE: Abiezer, Aviezer, Aviezri, Avishua, Azarel, Azaria, Azaryahu, Azriel, Azzi, Elazar, Eleazar, Eliezer, Eliseo, Elish, Elisha, Ellis, Elsen, Iezer, Ilie, Iliya, Is, Isa, Isaiah, Issa, Jere, Jeremiah, Josh, Joshua, Layser, Layzer, Lazar, Lazarus, Leeser, Leiser, Leser, Lesser, Lezer, Liezer, Moshael, Paltiel, Shai, Shay, Shaya, Shea, Yarom, Yehoshua, Yermi, Yeshaya, Yeshayahu, Yirmeya, Yirmeyahu, Yirmi
FEMININE: Alysha, Eliezra, Ezraela, Ezriela

hill of
MASCULINE: Galia, Galya
FEMININE: Galia, Galiya, Galya

horn of
FEMININE: Carnia, Carniela, Carniya

house of
MASCULINE: Betual, Betuel
FEMININE: Bethel

individual relationship with *See also* God, fatherhood of
MASCULINE: Duriel, Emmanuel, Gamliel, Ittai, Liel, Mani, Manni, Manny, Manu, Manuel, Moriel, Raziel
FEMININE: Gamliela, Shelia, Sheliya, Verena

joy of
MASCULINE: Ronel
FEMININE: Ronia, Roniya, Ronya

judgment of
MASCULINE: Dani, Daniel, Danil, Dannie, Donniel, Yadin, Yadon
FEMININE: Dania, Daniela, Daniele, Danit, Danita, Danya

kingship of
MASCULINE: Adriel, Elrad, Malcam, Malkam, Malkiel
FEMININE: Malkia, Malkiya

knowledge of
MASCULINE: Dael, Deuel, Yediel

light of *See also* God, flame of
MASCULINE: Aviur, Elior, Nirel, Niriel, Uriel

FEMININE: Eliora, Nerya, Nirel, Nuriah, Nuriya, Orelle, Oria, Oriana, Oriel, Oriya, Uriela

of light and sun
MASCULINE: Phoebus

Lord
MASCULINE: Adoniya, Eli, Eliah, Eliahu, Elias, Elie, Elihu, Elijah, Elio, Eliot, Elison, Eliya, Eliyahu, Elliot, Ellison, Elly, Elsen, Ely, Ilie, Ilija, Iliya, Ilya, Yoel
FEMININE: Adoniya, Eliya

loyal to
MASCULINE: Amania
FEMININE: Amania

manifestation of
FEMININE: Tiffani

mercy of
MASCULINE: Elchanan, Elhanan, Jochanan, Johanan, Yochanan, Yohanan

miracle of
FEMININE: Neesia, Nesya

name of
MASCULINE: Sam, Samm, Sammy, Samy, Shemuel, Shmuel, Shmuli, Uel, Zanvil
FEMININE: Shemuela, Shmuela

nation of
MASCULINE: Amiel, Amishaddai, Ammiel, Chanoch, Chiya, Eldad, Eliam, Eliata, Erel, Harel, Imanuel, Itai, Itiel, Kadmiel, Kemuel, Lemuel, Peniel, Penuel, Samuel

oath of
FEMININE: Anabeth, Anina, Annalisa, Bab, Bela, Belita, Bella, Belle, Beruchya, Bess, Bessie, Bet, Beta, Beth, Bethe, Betsy, Bette, Bettina, Betty, Donabella, Elisa, Elisabeta, Elisabeth, Elise, Elisheva, Elissa, Eliza, Elizabeta, Elizabeth, Elize, Ellis, Elsa, Elsie, Elyce, Elysa, Elza, Hazelbelle, Ilisa, Ilsa, Ilyse, Isa, Isabel, Isobel, Leesa, Leta, Lettie, Libbie, Lilibet, Lilybeth, Lisa, Lisi, Lissie, Livvie, Liza, Lizbeth, Lize, Lizette, Lizzie, Lys, Tetty, Tiie, Zizi, Zsa Zsa

ornament of
FEMININE: Adiel, Adiya

peace brought by
MASCULINE: Geoff, Geoffrey, Getzel, Godfrey, Gottfried, Jef, Jeffers, Jefferson, Jeffery, Shelumiel

perfection of
MASCULINE: Jotham, Yotam

praise for
MASCULINE: Hodiya
FEMININE: Hodia, Hodiya, Odeleya, Odelia, Odiya

prince of
MASCULINE: Asriel, Iser, Israel, Isser, Issi, Sruli, Yisrael, Yisroel
FEMININE: Israela, Sareli, Yisraela, Yisrela

protected by See also God, shadow of
MASCULINE: Elitzafan, Emanuel, Emmanuel, Mani, Manni, Manny, Manu, Manuel, Oshri, Shemaria, Shemarya, Shemaryahu
FEMININE: Chasia, Chasya, Emanuela, Hasya, Manuela, Shimriya, Tzeruia

refuge given by
MASCULINE: Adlai, Guriel, Maazya

remembrance of
MASCULINE: Benzecry, Zac, Zacharia, Zachary, Zackary, Zak, Zecharia, Zechariahu, Zeke, Zerachya

righteousness of
MASCULINE: Tzidkiah, Tzidkiyahu, Zedekiah

secret of
MASCULINE: Raziel
FEMININE: Eliraz, Razia, Raziela, Raziya

servant of
MASCULINE: Avdel, Avdiel, Obadiah, Obe, Osman, Osmand, Osmond, Ovadya, Ovadyahu
FEMININE: Gilda

shadow of
MASCULINE: Betzalel, Bezalel

sight of
MASCULINE: Peniel

song of
MASCULINE: Ronel
FEMININE: Rania, Ranya, Shirel, Zimria

splendor of
MASCULINE: Hadriel, Hodia, Hodiya
FEMININE: Hodia, Hodiya
strength from
MASCULINE: Atzalyahu, Avniel, Aziel, Cheskie, Chizkiya, Chizkiyahu, Ezekiel, Gab, Gabby, Gabe, Gabel, Gabi, Gabriel, Gavirol, Gavriel, Guriel, Haskel, Heske, Heskel, Hesketh, Heskiah, Hezekia, Jibril, Kaski, Kiel, Otniel, Saadia, Saadya, Tzuriel, Uziel, Uziya, Uzziah, Yechezkel, Zuriel
FEMININE: Aziela, Uziela
strength of
MASCULINE: Amatzia, Arel, Areli, Ariel, Aryel, Azazia, Eliaz, Eliram, Otniel
FEMININE: Amitzia, Ari, Ariel, Ariela, Arielle
of the sun
MASCULINE: Thom, Thomas, Tip, Tom, Tommi
FEMININE: Tami, Thomasina, Tomasina
teaching of
FEMININE: Horia, Horiya, Moria, Moriel, Moriya
thunder of
MASCULINE: Raamya
treasure of
MASCULINE: Tzefania, Tzefaniahu, Zefania, Zeph, Zephania
FEMININE: Adiya
with us
MASCULINE: Emanuel
FEMININE: Emanuela, Itia, Itiya, Manuela
vessel of
MASCULINE: Kliel
vineyard of
MASCULINE: Carmiel, Gefania, Gefanya
FEMININE: Carmia, Carmiela, Carmit, Carmiya
vision of
MASCULINE: Chaziel
voice of
FEMININE: Hedi, Hedya
wave of
MASCULINE: Galia, Galya
FEMININE: Galia, Galiya, Galya

who is like?
MASCULINE: Mica, Micha, Michael, Michal, Michel, Mickey, Miguel, Mika, Mike, Mikel, Mikhail, Miki, Misha, Mitch, Mitchel, Mychal
FEMININE: Mia, Mica, Micha, Michael, Michaela, Michaelann, Michaele, Michal, Michalina, Michel, Micke, Mika, Mikhal, Mychal, Shella
witnesses
MASCULINE: Adael, Adiel, Adlai
word of
MASCULINE: Amaria
work of
MASCULINE: Maaseiyahu
FEMININE: Amalia, Amalya
wrestled with
MASCULINE: Iser, Israel, Isser, Issi, Stacey, Yisrael
FEMININE: Israela, Sareli
yearning for
MASCULINE: Yachlel
youthfulness from
FEMININE: Elinoar

God acquires
MASCULINE: Elkan, Elkana, Elkin

God adds and increases
MASCULINE: Joce, Jody, Joe, Jojo, Jose, José, Joseph, Josephus, Sefi, Yos, Yosef, Yosei, Yosel, Yosi
FEMININE: Jodi, Joei, Joette, Joey, Josefa, Josephine, Josetta, Pepita, Yosefa, Yosifa

God answers
MASCULINE: Anaya, Elian
FEMININE: Edya, Eliana, Lian, Liana, Oriana

God builds and establishes
MASCULINE: Akim, Eliakim, Elika, Elyakim, Elyakum, Jehoiakim, Yakim, Yavneel, Yavniel, Yehoyakim

God is eternal
MASCULINE: Eliad

God is exalted
MASCULINE: Adoram, Atalia, Athalia, Yehoram, Yoram
FEMININE: Atalia, Athalia, Atlit

God hears/heard *See also* God, listens
MASCULINE: Ishmael, Shemaia, Shemarya, Shemaryahu, Shemaya, Yishmael

God heals
MASCULINE: Rafael, Rafe, Raphael, Refael, Refi, Rephael, Rephi, Rofi, Rophi
FEMININE: Rafaela, Rafi, Rafia, Rafya, Raphaela, Raphaelle, Refaela, Rephaela

God is joy
MASCULINE: Eliraz

God knows
MASCULINE: Eliada, Elyada

God listens *See also* God hears/heard
MASCULINE: Azania

God lives
MASCULINE: Chia, Chiel, Hiel, Jehiel, Yechiel, Yechieli, Yehiel, Yehieli, Yochai
FEMININE: Yechiela, Yehiela

God nourishes
MASCULINE: Jekuthiel, Kus, Yekusiel, Yekutiel

God redeems
MASCULINE: Geuel, Jeremais, Jeremiah, Jeremy, Jerrem, Jerry

God sustains *See also* God, dew of
MASCULINE: Avital
FEMININE: Abital, Avital

God willing
MASCULINE: Joel, Joelle, Yoav, Yoel
FEMININE: Eliava, Joal, Joela, Joelle, Joelynn, Yoela, Yoelit

Goddess
of earth and growth
FEMININE: Maia, Maya
of fire and purification
FEMININE: Vesta
of love
FEMININE: Aphrodite
of love and beauty
FEMININE: Venus
of the moon
FEMININE: Cindy, Cyndi, Cynthia, Sindy

of the rainbow
FEMININE: Iris
of wisdom
FEMININE: Minerva

God-like
MASCULINE: Ancel, Elvin, Elwin

Gods, Egyptian *See* Isis, love of

Gods, Greek *See also* Dionysius
FEMININE: Aphrodite, Caasi, Cassandra, Cassi, Cindy, Cyndi, Cynthia, Denice, Denise, Denyce, Hera, Hermine, Hermione, Pandora, Sindy, Venus, Zina

Gods, mountain of
FEMININE: Olympia

Gold and golden *See also* Gilded
MASCULINE: Aurel, Dor, Dori, Paz, Pazi, Zehavi
FEMININE: Aurea, Aurelia, Auriel, Aury, Gilda, Golda, Goldie, Iora, Ofira, Ophira, Ora, Orit, Paz, Paza, Pazia, Pazit, Paziya, Pazya, Zahava, Zahavi, Zarina, Zehava, Zehavi, Zehavit, Zehuvit, Zlata, Zlate

Golden, brownish-yellow
FEMININE: Amber, Amberlee

Golden-haired
FEMININE: Linnet

Good and goodness
MASCULINE: Avituv, Bonesh, Boni, Boniface, Boone, Litov, Naaman, Naom, Tabai, Tavi, Terence, Terri, Tiv, Tov, Tovi, Toviel
FEMININE: Agatha, Bonita, Bonnie, Dobra, Ghity, Gitel, Gittel, Gittie, Litov, Lois, Schifra, Shifra, Shiphra, Tiva, Toba, Tobelle, Tobey, Tobi, Tobina, Tobit, Toby, Tova, Tovat, Tovit, Tuvit, Yatva, Yoko

Good fortune *See also* Fortunate
MASCULINE: Adna, Eugen, Eugene, Gad, Gadi, Gene, Gluke, Lucky, Maimon, Maimun, Mazal, Oshri, Yimna
FEMININE: Glikel, Gluke, Oshrat, Ventura, Yimna

Goose
MASCULINE: Avaz

Governess
FEMININE: Omenet

Grace *See also* Charming
MASCULINE: Anson, Avichen, Chanan, Chanani, Chanina, Chen, Choni, Clem, Clement, Clemmon, Clemmons, Clemon, Esmond, Esmund, Evan, Evander, Evans, Ewen, Hanan, Hen, Honi, Ivan, Kal, Kalman, Kalonymos, Ray, Terence, Terri
FEMININE: Adiva, Alanna, Ana, Anabella, Anabeth, Anett, Aniela, Anina, Anita, Ann, Anna, Annabel, Annalisa, Anne, Annetta, Annette, Annie, Annika, Anya, Briana, Chana, Chani, Chaniette, Chanit, Charissa, Chen, Floriane, Georgeanne, Georgiana, Grace, Gracia, Graciela, Hana, Hani, Hanit, Hanna, Hen, Henda, Hendel, Hene, Heneleh, Henna, Ileana, Jerriann, Jo-Anne, Julianne, Kiley, Leann, Luan, Maryan, Maryanne, Michaelann, Mignon, Nan, Nancy, Nanette, Nanine, Nanna, Neena, Netti, Nettie, Nina, Ninette, Ray, Roanna, Rosanna, Rosanne, Ruthanna, Saran, Shan, Shannen, Shannon, Shauna, Tamar, Yvette

Grain *See also* Wheat
MASCULINE: Dagan, Garnet
FEMININE: Chita, Dagan, Daganit, Daganya, Dagen, Degania, Deganit, Deganya, Farrah, Nessa, Vana, Vanessa, Vanna

Grain dealer
MASCULINE: Brock

Grain thresher
MASCULINE: Moreg
FEMININE: Moraga

Granary
MASCULINE: Garner, Garon, Goren, Idra
FEMININE: Garnit

Grandfather
MASCULINE: Abimi, Aviav, Aviem, Avimi, Saba, Sava, Zayde, Zaydel, Zeide, Zeidel
FEMININE: Saba

Grandmother
FEMININE: Em, Emma, Emmie, Emmy, Emmylou, Savta

Grant
MASCULINE: Grant

Grape presser
MASCULINE: Gitai, Giti

Grapes
MASCULINE: Anav, Anavi, Eshkol
FEMININE: Anava

Grass
MASCULINE: Bentley, Landan, Landis

Gray *See also* Grey
MASCULINE: Doug, Douglas

Gray dwelling
MASCULINE: Graham

Great
MASCULINE: Magnus, Major, Maks, Manus, Max, Maximilian, Maxwell, Meredith, Nora, Rav, Rava
FEMININE: Magna, Maxa, Maxima, Maxime, Maxine, Tita, Titania, Xena, Zena, Zina

Greedy
FEMININE: Raven

Greek gods *See also* Dionysius
FEMININE: Aphrodite, Caasi, Cassandra, Cassi, Cindy, Cyndi, Cynthia, Denice, Denise, Denyce, Hera, Hermine, Hermione, Pandora, Sindy, Venus, Zina

Greek place-name
FEMININE: Lyda, Lydia

Green *See also* Sea-green precious stone
MASCULINE: Yarkon
FEMININE: Verna, Yarkona

Grey *See also* Gray
MASCULINE: Floyd, Lloyd

Groan
FEMININE: Pua

Ground *See also* Earth; Land
FEMININE: Eartha

Groundhog
FEMININE: Girit

Group
FEMININE: Aguda

Growth *See also* Flourish; Springtime; Sprout
MASCULINE: Ellery, Tzemach, Yaniv, Yigdal, Zemach
FEMININE: Cyma, Mae, May, Spring, Summer, Syma, Verna

Guard and guardian *See also* Defender; Protect; Protected; Watchman
MASCULINE: Bailey, Ed, Edd, Eddie, Eddy, Edison, Edson, Eduard, Edward, Edy, Er, Eri, Garret, Garreth, Garrett, Hi, Hilary, Hillary, Jarrett, Meltzar, Ned, Neddy, Roi, Shemer, Shimri, Shomer, Spencer, Stewart, Stu, Stuart, Tzofi, Ward, Zofi
FEMININE: Garret, Greer, Nitzra, Shamira, Shimra, Tzofia, Zehira, Zofia

Guard house
MASCULINE: Shimron

Guest
MASCULINE: Gaston

Guide
MASCULINE: Cicero, Guy

Hair *See also* Blond; Brunette
MASCULINE: Burl, Fairchild, Kerry
FEMININE: Delila, Dila, Flavia, Kerry, Linnet, Nema, Nima, Rowena, Yuta
red-haired
MASCULINE: Bayard, Clancy, Rufus, Rusty

Hammer *See also* Club
MASCULINE: Helem, Macabee, Makabi
FEMININE: Marcella, Marcelle, Marcelyn, Marcia, Marcie, Marcilen, Marcy, Marsha

Hand *See also* Claw; Right hand
MASCULINE: Jeb, Maynard
right hand
MASCULINE: Yamin, Yemin
FEMININE: Jemina, Yemina

Handsome
MASCULINE: Al, Alain, Alan, Allan, Allen, Allyn, Alson, Alyn, Beau, Erv, Ervin, Erving, Erwin, Hasan, Hussein, Irv, Irvin, Irvine, Irving, Jamal, Ken,
Kene, Kenneth, Kennie, Kent, Kevin
FEMININE: Linda, Lynda, Schifra, Shifra, Shiphra

Happiness *See also* Cheer; Joy; Merry
MASCULINE: Anchel, Anschel, Anshel, Ascher, Aser, Asher, Asser, Ayo, Edwin, Feliks, Felix, Gad, Gadi, Jay, Jayson, Said
FEMININE: Alitza, Aliza, Anchelle, Bea, Beate, Beatrice, Beatrix, Blythe, Chedva, Falice, Felecia, Felecie, Feliciana, Felicite, Felisa, Gada, Gadit, Gwyneth, Happy, Hedva, Leatrice, Meara, Phylicia, Salida, Tatum, Trix

Harbor
MASCULINE: Haven, Marin
FEMININE: Chelsea, Haven

Hare keeper
MASCULINE: Harman

Harmony (peace) *See also* Peace
MASCULINE: Al, Alan, Allan, Allen, Allyn, Alson, Alyn, Cosmo, Harmon
FEMININE: Alaina, Alena, Allena, Alleyne, Allyn, Harmony

Harp
MASCULINE: Kinori
FEMININE: Kinneret

Hart
MASCULINE: Cerf

Harvest
MASCULINE: Asif

Harvester
FEMININE: Resa, Risa, Teddi, Teresa, Teresita, Teri, Terrie, Tessa, Theresa, Zita

Hated one *See* Enemy

Haven *See* Sanctuary

Hawk
MASCULINE: Baz, Gavan, Gavin

Hayfield
MASCULINE: Hayden, Heywood

Hazel tree
FEMININE: Hazel, Hazelbelle

Hazelnut
FEMININE: Aveline, Avella

Head (leader)
MASCULINE: Dean, Dee, Deno, Rosh
FEMININE: Dean

Head of religious institution
MASCULINE: Abbe, Abbie, Pryor

Headland
FEMININE: Nessa

Heal
FEMININE: Althea, Tea, Thea

Healed
FEMININE: Rafaela, Rafi, Rafia, Rafya, Raphaela, Refaela, Rephaela

Healer
MASCULINE: Assi, Jason
FEMININE: Althea, Assia, Tea, Thea

Healing
MASCULINE: Asa, Assa, Rafa, Rafu, Raphu

Healthy
MASCULINE: Delano, Hal, Hale, Haley, Halley, Hollis, Valerie, Valery
FEMININE: Rafa, Val, Valeria, Valerie, Valery

Heap
MASCULINE: Dur
FEMININE: Doreet, Dorit, Talmor

Hearing
MASCULINE: Ozni

Hearing (listening) *See also* Listen
MASCULINE: Cimon, Clyde, Clydell, Otis, Shibi, Shimi, Shimke, Shimmel, Shimon, Si, Simeon, Simi, Simmie, Simon, Simpson, Symon
FEMININE: Simeona, Simona, Simone

Heart
MASCULINE: Cal, Cale, Caleb, Calev, Kalev, Lev
FEMININE: Cordis, Leeba, Liba, Libe, Luba

Heath
FEMININE: Heather

Heaven
FEMININE: Celeste, Lani

Heavenly *See* Divine

Heavenly star
MASCULINE: Joash, Yoash

Hebrew language
FEMININE: Ivrit, Ivrita

Hebrew person
MASCULINE: Ivri
FEMININE: Ivria, Ivriya

Hedge
MASCULINE: Woodie, Woodrow, Woody

Heel, held by
MASCULINE: Akavel, Akavya, Akevy, Aki, Akiba, Akiva, Akki, Cobe, Diego, Hamish, Jack, Jackie, Jackson, Jacob, Jacobo, Jacque, Jaimie, Jake, Jakob, James, Jamie, Jan, Jascha, Jim, Jimbo, Jimm, Jimmie, Kaufman, Kiva, Kobe, Koppel, Kovi, Kubi, Seamus, Yaacov, Yaakov, Yaki, Yankel, Yuki
FEMININE: Jackee, Jacklyn, Jacky, Jaclyn, Jacoba, Jacque, Jacqueline, Jacquelyn, Jacqui, Jaime, Jaymee, Jocelin, Jocelyn, Jodette, Joscelin, Joscelind, Josetta, Joslyn

Heights *See also* Hill; Mountain
MASCULINE: Aram, Giva, Givon, Hill, Hillard, Hilliard, Hobart, Hobert, Merom, Rom, Romem, Romi
FEMININE: Roma, Romema, Romi, Romia, Romie, Romit, Romiya

Helmet
MASCULINE: Corey, Cory

Help
MASCULINE: Ezer, Ezra, Ezri
FEMININE: Aida, Ezra, Ophelia

Helper
MASCULINE: Adolf, Adolph, Adolphe, Dolph, Ozer, Ozri
FEMININE: Adolpha, Camilla, Camillia, Kamilla

Hem
FEMININE: Imra

Hemp
MASCULINE: Harlan, Harlin

Hen
FEMININE: Peninia, Peniniya

Herd
MASCULINE: Eder, Maron
FEMININE: Eder

Herdsman
MASCULINE: Calvert

Hero or heroine *See also* Bold; Brave; Champion
MASCULINE: Abir, Abiri, Gavra, Gavri, Gever, Gordon, Gore, Guthrie, Igor, Lothar, Lother
FEMININE: Abiri, Bree, Gabi, Gabriela, Gabriele, Gavi, Gavriela, Gavrila, Gibora, Haley, Halie, Halle, Hallie, Haylee, Holis, Hollace, Hollis

Hewn stone
FEMININE: Gazit

Hidden
MASCULINE: Alemet, Almoni, Amon, Nachbi, Setur
FEMININE: Almonit, Geniza

Hiding place
FEMININE: Me'ara

High *See also* Exalted; Heights
MASCULINE: Alta, Alto, Altus, Aram, Erskine, High
FEMININE: Alita, Ardra, Bama, Meroma

High esteem *See also* Dignity; Respect
FEMININE: Antia, Antoina, Antoinette, Netti, Nettie, Toni, Tonia, Tonise, Tony

High place
MASCULINE: Hi, Hy, Hyland, Hyman
FEMININE: Giva, Givona

High-born
MASCULINE: Ethelbert

Hill *See also* Mountain
MASCULINE: Arlo, Art, Arthur, Artie, Arturo, Arty, Balfour, Bart, Barth, Bartholomew, Bartlet, Bergen, Berger, Brent, Darren, Darry, Darryl, Dary, Daryl, Edlow, Gal, Gali, Galia, Galya, Geva, Giva, Givon, High, Hill, Hillard, Hilliard, Hobart, Hobert, Howe, Kile, Kip, Kipling, Kyle, Loel, Lovell, Lowell, Lyn, Lyndon, Talmai, Tel, Telem
FEMININE: Artia, Brin, Bryn, Gal, Gala, Gali, Galit, Gilada, Giva, Givona, Talma, Talmit

Hind
FEMININE: Hilma, Hindel, Hindi

Hoeing
FEMININE: Adira

Hog
FEMININE: Portia

Hole *See also* Hollow; Pit
MASCULINE: Chor, Chori, Hori

Holiday *See also* Feast
MASCULINE: Bondi, Chag, Hag, Yom Tov
FEMININE: Holiday

Hollow *See also* Hole
FEMININE: Dimples

Holy *See also* Blessed; Consecrated; Pious; Sanctification
MASCULINE: Gerome, Gerre, Gerry, Hal, Hale, Haley, Halley, Hollis, Jere, Jerome, Jeromy, Jerrem, Jerry, Kadosh, Oleg, Olin, Selig, Selwyn, Zelig
FEMININE: Helga, Holli, Holly, Kadisha, Kedusha, Olga

Holy place
FEMININE: Temple

Home *See also* Dwelling; House
MASCULINE: Ham, Hamilton, Hamlet, Humphrey
ruler of *See* Lord

Homestead
MASCULINE: Trevor

Honest *See also* True; Trusted
MASCULINE: Amit, Amiti, Justice, Justin, Justus, Tam, Tami, Yashar, Yesher, Yeshurun
FEMININE: Amit, Amita, Reatha, Reda, Reeta, Reita, Reitha, Rheta, Rita, Ritasue, Temima

Honey
FEMININE: Honey, Lissa, Melissa, Melita, Missie

Honor *See also* Respect
FEMININE: Haron, Honor, Honora, Honorine

Honorable *See also* Noble
MASCULINE: Chori, Hori, Rodger, Rodgers, Roger, Yakar, Yakir
FEMININE: Atzila

Honored *See also* Ornamented
MASCULINE: Efrat, Hada, Hadar
FEMININE: Degula, Efrat, Efrata, Hadar, Hadara, Hadarit, Nora, Noreen, Noreena, Norene, Nori, Norrie

Hope *See also* Faith; Optimism
MASCULINE: Tikva, Wilfred
FEMININE: Erga, Faith, Gisela, Giselle, Gizela, Hope, Iris, Nada, Nadia, Nadine, Nadya, Pollyanna, Shprintza, Tiki, Tikva, Tzipia

Horizon
MASCULINE: Afek, Afik, Ofek
FEMININE: Afeka

Horn
MASCULINE: Karin, Karna, Karni, Keren
FEMININE: Carna, Carni, Karna, Karni, Karnit, Keren, Keryn

Horn of God *See also* God, horn of
FEMININE: Carnia, Carniela, Carniya, Karnia, Karniela

Horn of the sun *See also* King; Long life
FEMININE: Corna

Horse *See also* Rider
MASCULINE: Holden, Russ, Russel, Rusty, Sus, Susi
FEMININE: Susa
  groomer
  MASCULINE: Marchall, Marshal, Marshe
  herder
  MASCULINE: Stodard
  lover of
  MASCULINE: Felipe, Phelps, Phil, Philip, Phill, Phillip, Phillipe, Phillipp, Pip
  FEMININE: Philippa, Pippa

Hostage *See also* Imprison
MASCULINE: Homer

Hostess
FEMININE: Da'yelet

Hot
MASCULINE: Cham, Ham

Hotel *See* Inn

House *See also* Dwelling; Home
MASCULINE: Zeb, Zebulon, Zevulun, Zvulun

House of God
MASCULINE: Betual, Betuel
FEMININE: Bethel

House of Jacob
MASCULINE: Bilu

House steward
MASCULINE: Ossie, Oswald, Ozzi

Hummingbird
FEMININE: Corinna

Hunt
MASCULINE: Chase, Chevy
FEMININE: Chase

Hurt *See* Injure

Hyacinth
FEMININE: Hyacinth

Idol
FEMININE: Ashera

Ignorant
FEMININE: Loretta

Illustrious
MASCULINE: Adelbert, Bert, Bertin, Bertram, Bertran, Bertrand, Bertrem, Clarence
FEMININE: Bertina, Chandra, Shandra

Image
FEMININE: Imogen

Immigrant *See also* Stranger
FEMININE: Ola

Immortal
MASCULINE: Ambrose

Imperial *See also* Royal
MASCULINE: Caspar, Casper

Imprison *See also* Hostage
MASCULINE: Agnon, Asir, Asur, Ogen

Incandescent
FEMININE: Candace, Candance, Candice, Candida, Candy, Candyce

Incense
FEMININE: Ketura

Independence *See also* Freedom
FEMININE: Komema

Industrious
MASCULINE: Amery, Amory, Eiran, Emerson, Emery, Emil, Émile, Emory, Eran, Maher, Nemuel
FEMININE: Amalie, Amelia, Amilie, Emilia, Emilie, Emily, Emmy, Emmylou, Ida, Idalee, Idel, Idena, Idette, Ieda, Zariza, Zeriza

Infant
FEMININE: Thelma

Inheritance
MASCULINE: Yerusha
FEMININE: Yerusha

Inherited
MASCULINE: Masoor, Masur

Injure
MASCULINE: Tel, Telem

Inn
MASCULINE: Malon

Innocent *See also* Pure
MASCULINE: Zakai
FEMININE: Zaka, Zakit

Insignificant
FEMININE: Tzerua

Institution *See* Association; Establishment

Intelligence *See also* Wisdom
MASCULINE: Achban, Bina, Buna, Earl
FEMININE: Bina, Buna, Buni, Earla, Earlene

Investigate
MASCULINE: Buki, Tor

Iron
MASCULINE: Ferrin, Ferris

Irregular
MASCULINE: Akom
FEMININE: Akuma

Isis, gift of
MASCULINE: Isador, Isidor, Isidoro, Iz, Izzie

Island
MASCULINE: Brady, Carey, Cary, Holm, Holmes, Ismar, Itamar, Ittamar, Lyall, Lyle, Shelley, Shelly

Israel, glory of
MASCULINE: Nili
FEMININE: Nili, Nilit

Jacob, House of
MASCULINE: Bilu

Jade
FEMININE: Jade

Jail *See* Imprison

January
MASCULINE: Janus

Jewel
FEMININE: Emeralda, Esmeralda

Jewelry *See* Adorn; Anklet; Earring; Ornament

Joined to
MASCULINE: Lavey, Levi, Levitas, Lewi
FEMININE: Anuva

Journey
MASCULINE: Walker

Joy *See also* Happiness; Rejoicing
MASCULINE: Alitz, Aliz, Avigal, Bilga, Bilgai, Bilguy, Eliraz, Gil, Gili, Gill, Liran, Marnin, Masos, Ran, Ranen, Rani, Ranon, Ron, Ronel, Ronen, Roni, Sason, Seled, Simcha, Simha, Simkha, Sisi, Sos
FEMININE: Aleeza, Alitza, Aliz, Aliza, Alyza, Chedva, Ditza, Diza, Elza, Fradel, Frayda, Freida, Geela, Ghila, Gila, Gilada, Gilana, Gilat, Gili, Gilit, Happy, Hedva, Hen, Hillula, Jewel, Joice, Jovita, Joy, Joya, Joyce, Laetitia, Leta, Leticia, Letitia, Meara, Merrie, Merrielle, Merry, Ranit, Ranita, Reena, Renah, Renana, Renanit, Renina, Rina, Rinat, Ron, Rona, Ronela, Roni, Ronili, Ronit, Ronnell, Ronnit, Ryna, Salida, Simcha, Simchit, Simchona

Judges and judgment *See also* Judge; Law
MASCULINE: Avdan, Avidan, Dahn, Dan, Dana, Dani, Datan, Dathan, Dayan, Shafat, Shiftan, Yudan
FEMININE: Danette, Dani, Dania, Danie, Daniela, Daniele, Danit, Danita, Danya, Dayana, Deanna, Deena, Deenie, Dena, Deon, Dina, Dion, Idena

Judicious
MASCULINE: Ranier, Reg, Reginald, Reinhold, Rennie, Reynold, Ronald, Rondell, Ronnie
FEMININE: Ronalda, Ronne, Ronni, Ronny

Jug
MASCULINE: Kad, Kadi
FEMININE: Kadit

Juice
MASCULINE: Asis, Asisi
FEMININE: Asisya

Juicy
FEMININE: Asisa

Junior
MASCULINE: Zeira
FEMININE: Zeira

Juniper berry
FEMININE: Geneva

Just *See also* Honest
MASCULINE: Adlai, Justice, Justin, Justus, Tzadok, Zadok
FEMININE: Justina

Juvenile *See* Boy; Child; Girl; Young; Youth

Kernel
MASCULINE: Garin

Kettle
MASCULINE: Yora
FEMININE: Yora

Kimberlite
FEMININE: Kim, Kimberley

Kind *See also* Courteous; Pleasant
FEMININE: Elma

King and kingship *See also* God, Kingship of; Regal; Royal; Ruler
MASCULINE: Abimelech, Avimelech, Basil, Conan, Cornelius, Cornell, Daren, Darian, Darin, Dario, Darius, Elroy, Eric, Erik, Eryk, Kin, Kingsley, Kornell, LeRoy, Malki, Melchior, Melech, Reagan, Rex, Roy, Royal, Royce, Roye, Ryan, Ryne, Vasily
FEMININE: Darrene, Erica, Erika, Rexana, Riki, Xeriqua

King, father of
MASCULINE: Abimelech, Avimelech

Kiss
FEMININE: Neshika

Knife
MASCULINE: Dorian, Dorris
FEMININE: Dorea, Doria, Doris, Dorris

Knitted
MASCULINE: Sarug

Knot
MASCULINE: Kesher
FEMININE: Keshira

Knowledge *See also* Wisdom
MASCULINE: Avida, Kenen, Lamed, Yadua
FEMININE: Kendra, Kenna

Knowledgeable *See also* Educated
MASCULINE: Agur, Conan, Conrad, Konrad, Kurt

Labor *See* Toil
Lady
FEMININE: Dama, Dame, Damita, Dolores, Dona, Donabella, Donita, Donna, Donya, Gevira, Kyra, Signora

Lake
MASCULINE: Havelock, Lynn, Maris
FEMININE: Cherilynn, Geralyn, Jerrilyn, Lauralynn, Linn, Lyn, Lynette, Lynn, Maralyn, Marilyn, Marlyn, Merelyn, Sharilyn, Taralynn

Lamb *See also* Ewe; Sheep
MASCULINE: Talia, Talya
FEMININE: Agnes, Annice, Annis, Nessie, Talia, Talya

Lame *See also* Limp
MASCULINE: Claud, Claudell, Claudio
FEMININE: Claudette, Claudia, Claudine, Gladyce, Gladys

Land *See also* Earth; Fame of the land; Plain
MASCULINE: Artza, Artzi, Arza, Broderick, Cleve, Cleveland, Galil, Lambert, Rodney, Whitney
FEMININE: Eartha, Eretz, Rowena, Whitney

Landscape
MASCULINE: Nof
FEMININE: Nofia, Nophia

Large *See also* Big
FEMININE: Lark

Lark
FEMININE: Efroni, Lark

Lasting *See* Enduring (lasting)

Laughter
FEMININE: Isaaca
"he will laugh"
MASCULINE: Iaacov, Ike, Isa, Isaac, Isak, Isea, Issa, Itzhak, Itzig, Tzachi, Tzahi, Yitz, Yitzchak, Yitzchok, Yitzhak, Zac, Zak, Zik

Laurel (crown) *See also* Royal
MASCULINE: Larry, Lars, Laurence, Laurie, Lawrence, Lorence, Lorn, Lorry

Laurel tree
FEMININE: Magnolia

Laurels *See also* Victor
FEMININE: Dafna, Dafne, Dafnit, Daphna, Daphnit, Dapna, Kaile, Kalia, Kayla, Kelila, Kelula, Kyla, Lara, Laura, Lauraine, Lauralee, Lauralynn, Laure, Laurel, Lauren, Laurene, Lauretta, Lauri, Laurice, Loran, Loree, Loren, Lorri, Loryn, Loura, Luan

Law *See also* Judge
MASCULINE: Datan, Dathan, Din, Dotan, Dothan
FEMININE: Dotan, Tora

Lawmaker *See also* Ruler
MASCULINE: Solon

Lawn *See also* Grass
MASCULINE: Landan, Landis

Lawyer
MASCULINE: Dayan

Lead (metal)
FEMININE: Oferet

Leader *See also* Captain; Chief; General; Guide; King
MASCULINE: Alef, Aluf, Duke, Guy, Hal, Harlow, Harold, Heraldo, Katzin, Malvin, Mel, Mell, Melvin, Melvyn, Nasi, Sargeant

FEMININE: Alufa, Dean, Malvina, Melba, Melva, Melveen, Melvina

Leaf
FEMININE: Phylis, Phyllis

Learned *See also* Educated; Knowledgeable; Scholar
MASCULINE: Kane, Keenan, Keene, Savir
FEMININE: Sevira

Learner (one who learns) *See also* Beginner
MASCULINE: Lamed
FEMININE: Kendra, Sinai

Learner of Torah
MASCULINE: Sinai

Leathery covering
MASCULINE: Geled

Leftover
FEMININE: Sarida

Legacy
FEMININE: Morasha

Lemon
MASCULINE: Limon

Lens
FEMININE: Adasha

Lentil
FEMININE: Adasha

Leopard
MASCULINE: Namer, Namir

Libel
FEMININE: Alila

Liberal
MASCULINE: Erve, Harvey, Harvi, Herve
FEMININE: Fani, Fania, Fannie, Fanya, Fran, Francene, Frances, Francesca, Franci, Francine, Frani, Frankie, Ranny

Liberty *See* Freedom

Librarian
MASCULINE: Safran

Lie (falsehood)
FEMININE: Kozbi

Life *See also* Alive; Conception; Immortal; Live; Revival
MASCULINE: Axel, Chai, Chaim, Chayim, Cornelius, Cornell, Evelyn, Hai,

Haim, Haym, Hiam, Jaime, Kornell, Omri, Vida, Vitas, Vitya, Yechiya, Zoltan
FEMININE: Chava, Chavi, Elvita, Enid, Eva, Eve, Eveline, Evelyn, Evelyne, Evita, Evonne, Evy, Gilana, Gilat, Gilit, Hava, Havi, Haviva, Lavita, Neshama, Techiya, Tehiya, Vita, Zoe

Light *See also* Bright
MASCULINE: Amior, Anwar, Barak, Bazak, Benor, Gib, Gil, Gilbert, Gili, Gill, Gilli, Jair, Leor, Lior, Lucas, Lucian, Lucius, Luke, Lyor, Maor, Nahir, Nahor, Naor, Ner, Neri, Nerli, Noga, Nur, Nuri, Or, Ori, Orli, Oron, Sheraga, Shraga, Yair, Zahar, Zohar
FEMININE: Aileen, Ailene, Alcinda, Alina, Alyna, Behira, Daisy, Eileen, Elain, Elayne, Ele, Eleanor, Eleanora, Eleanore, Elen, Elena, Elenne, Elenor, Eleora, Elie, Elin, Elinoor, Elinora, Elinore, Ella, Ellen, Ellie, Ellin, Elly, Ellyn, Elyn, Galina, Gayora, Gilberta, Greta, Gretchen, Gretel, Heidi, Helaine, Helena, Helene, Heleni, Helenmae, Heline, Hella, Helmi, Helyne, Ileana, Ilene, Ilona, Lacey, Leanor, Leena, Lena, Lennie, Lenora, Leonora, Leora, Leorit, Lior, Liora, Liorit, Louella, Lucette, Luci, Lucia, Lucie, Lucile, Lucinda, Lucy, Luella, Lyor, Madge, Mady, Mae, Mag, Maggie, Maisie, Maor, Margaret, Margarete, Margaretta, Margarita, Marge, Margene, Margerie, Margery, Marget, Margi, Margit, Margo, Margy, Marji, Marjorie, May, Meg, Megan, Meira, Meirit, Meret, Midge, Nahara, Nahari, Nahariya, Nealla, Nehara, Nehira, Nehora, Nehura, Nelda, Nell, Nellie, Neora, Nerya, Noga, Nura, Nuriah, Nurit, Nurita, Nuriya, Ora, Oralee, Orelle, Ori, Oria, Oriana, Oriel, Orit, Oriya, Orla, Orley, Orli, Orlit, Orly, Orna, Ornan, Peg, Roxane, Roxie, Roxine, Roxy, Rozella, Sherelyn, Suellen, Uranit, Uriela, Urit, Yalena, Yeira, Zehara, Zehari, Zehorit, Zohar, Zohara, Zoheret

Light of God
MASCULINE: Nirel, Niriel, Zerachya

Lighthearted *See* Happiness

Liked
MASCULINE: Ahud

Likeness (similarity)
MASCULINE: Naf, Naftali, Naphtali, Toolie
FEMININE: Imogen

Lily
MASCULINE: Shoshan, Shushan
FEMININE: Hyacinth, Lili, Lilian, Lilita, Lilli, Lillian, Lilly, Lily, Lilyan, Lilybeth, Ritasue, Shon, Shoshan, Shoshana, Su, Suellen, Susan, Susanna, Susanne, Susette, Susi, Suzanne, Suzette, Suzy, Suzyn, Xana

Limp *See also* Lame
MASCULINE: Pesach

Linden trees
MASCULINE: Linc, Lincoln, Lindsay, Lindsy, Lyn, Lyndon
FEMININE: Lindsay

Lion or lioness *See also* Cub
MASCULINE: Ari, Arie, Arieh, Ario, Ary, Arye, Ben-Gurion, Gur-Ari, Gur, Gur-Arye, Guri, Guria, Gurya, Guryon, Junius, Kefir, Label, Lavey, Lavi, Leander, Lebush, Lee, Leib, Leibel, Leibush, Leigh, Leo, Leon, Lev, Lion, Lionel, Llewellyn, Loeb, Lowe, Lyon, Lyonell
FEMININE: Ari, Ariel, Ariela, Arielle, Gurit, Kefira, Leona, Leonia, Leonie, Leontine, Levia

Lion of God
MASCULINE: Arel, Areli, Ariel, Aryel

Listen *See also* Hear
FEMININE: Samantha, Samie, Samuela

Listened to
MASCULINE: Shamu'a

Lithe
MASCULINE: Linc, Lincoln

Little *See also* Small
MASCULINE: Lyall, Lyle
FEMININE: Careena, Carina, Carita

Lively
FEMININE: Alvita

Living *See also* Alive; Life; Reside
FEMININE: Chaya, Chayie, Viva

Locality
FEMININE: Seviva

Lodging
MASCULINE: Malon
FEMININE: Leena, Lena

Lofty *See also* Exalted
MASCULINE: Biddie, Birgit
FEMININE: Bridget, Bridgit, Brigida, Brigit, Brit, Rama, Rami, Ramit, Roma, Romema, Romi, Romia, Romie, Romit, Romiya

Logger of birch trees
MASCULINE: Barker, Birk

Lonely *See also* Forsaken
MASCULINE: Aluv, Azuv, Galmud
FEMININE: Almana, Aluva, Ariri, Azuva

Long (length)
MASCULINE: Lang

Long life *See also* Immortal
MASCULINE: Cornelius, Cornell, Kornell, Omri

Longing *See also* Hope
FEMININE: Erga

Lord *See* God

Lord and lordly *See also* Master; Noble
MASCULINE: Adir, Adon, Bari, Barrie, Barry, Cid, Cyril, Darry, Gevir, Hank, Harris, Harrison, Harry, Heinrich, Heinz, Henri, Henrique, Henry, Mar, Ty, Tyron, Tyson
FEMININE: Bari, Barrie, Etka, Etta, Harriet, Henia, Henrietta, Henya, Hetta, Ita, Itka, Itta, Maryetta, Yetta, Yitta, Yitti

Loss *See* Death; Destruction; Lost

Lost
FEMININE: Lorna

Lot (chance)
MASCULINE: Goral
FEMININE: Gorala

Lotus plant
MASCULINE: Arnan, Nalim, Shoshan
FEMININE: Lotus, Shon, Shoshan, Shoshana

Lovable
FEMININE: Annabel, Chemdat, Hemdat

Love and loving
MASCULINE: Ahava, Amand, Chemdat, Esmé, Philo
FEMININE: Ahava, Ahavat, Aimee, Amabel, Amada, Amanda, Amandalina, Amity, Amy, Caressa, Charity, Libida, Manda, Mandy, Venus

Loved *See* Beloved

Lover
MASCULINE: Chovav, Chovev, Ohev

Lover of horses
MASCULINE: Felipe, Phelps, Phil, Philip, Phill, Phillip, Phillipe, Phillipp, Pip

Lover of ships
MASCULINE: Kelvin

Lover of the earth
MASCULINE: Demetrius, Dimitry

Lover of the sea
MASCULINE: Darwin

Loyal *See also* Faith
FEMININE: Amania, Lela, Lelia

Loyal to the Lord
MASCULINE: Amania

Luck *See also* Good fortune
FEMININE: Glikel, Gluke, Mazal, Mazala, Mazalit

Lucky star
MASCULINE: Mazal-Tov

Luscious
FEMININE: Raanana, Ranana

Luxuriant
MASCULINE: Raanan, Ranan

Luxurious
FEMININE: Thalia

Lyre
MASCULINE: Kinori

Lyric
FEMININE: Lyric

Lyrical
FEMININE: Lirit

Maggot
MASCULINE: Tola

Magic
MASCULINE: Kesem
FEMININE: Kesima

Magician
MASCULINE: Ashaf

Maid or maiden
FEMININE: Alma, Aluma, Betula, Cora, Coreen, Coretta, Corette, Corinna, Corita, Erma, Ginger, Ginnie, Irma, Linda, Lynda, Maida, Virginia

Maimed *See* Cut off

Majestic *See also* Glory
MASCULINE: Adir, Avihud, Segev

Man (mankind) *See also* Earth; World; Young
MASCULINE: Adam, Addison, Anders, Andi, Andor, André, Andrew, Andy, Arsen, Arvid, Barzilai, Carl, Carlos, Carlton, Carol, Carrol, Charle, Charles, Charley, Charlton, Chip, Chuck, Corliss, Delano, Desmond, Drew, Dru, Eitan, Enos, Enosh, Fergus, Gavra, Gavri, Gever, Humphrey, Ish-Tov, Ish-Shalom, Karel, Karl, Karol, Lad, Lipman, Mandy, Manfred, Mani, Manin, Manis, Manish, Mann, Mannes, Manni, Manny, Newman, Norman, North, Oliver, Olivier, Ollie, Paine, Rodger, Rodgers, Rodman, Roger, Sava, Zusman
FEMININE: Adamina, Karla, Karleen, Karlene, Karlyn

Manly
FEMININE: Andye, Carla, Carlotta, Drew, Dru

Mantle
MASCULINE: Efrat
FEMININE: Efrat, Efrata, Gelima

Marble
MASCULINE: Dar

Married
FEMININE: Beula

Marsh
MASCULINE: Monroe

Marshy land
MASCULINE: Carr, Kerr, Seymore, Seymour, Si, Sy

Martial
FEMININE: Marcella, Marcelle, Marcelyn, Marcia, Marcie, Marcilen, Marcy, Marsha

Mason
MASCULINE: Mason

Master *See also* Lord; Teacher
MASCULINE: Adon, Adoram, Aluf, Gevir, Mar, Maran

Maximum
FEMININE: Mayrav, Meirav, Merav, Meyrav

May
FEMININE: Mae, Maia, May

Me *See also* Mine
MASCULINE: Li
FEMININE: Li, Mili

Meadow *See also* Field (area of land); Garden
MASCULINE: Abel, Able, Bentley, Berkeley, Beverley, Brad, Bradlee, Bromley, Darbey, Dudley, Dwayne, Farleigh, Greeley, Hanley, Ingmar, Kin, Kingsley, Lee, Leigh, Les, Lesley, Leslie, Presley, Raleigh, Roscoe, Ross, Shepley, Shipley, Shirley, Wayne, Wesley
FEMININE: Amberlee, Beverlee, Beverly, Bevya, Darbey, Idalee, Inga, Inger, Jennilee, Lauralee, Lee, Leland, Lesley, Maralee, Marilee, Marily, Meadow, Presley, Shirl, Shirlee, Shirley, Surilee, Wesley

Measurement
MASCULINE: Medad
FEMININE: Tara, Taralynn, Taryn

Melody *See also* Song; Tune
MASCULINE: Zemira
FEMININE: Carol, Carroll, Caryl, Karol, Karyl, Lorac, Lorelei, Mangena, Mangina, Melody, Negina, Odele, Odell, Odetta, Odette, Zemira

Memorial
MASCULINE: Zichri

Memory
MASCULINE: Benzecry, Zac, Zacharia, Zachary, Zackary, Zak, Zecharia, Zechariahu, Zeke, Zerachya

Merchandise
MASCULINE: Mercer
FEMININE: Sechora

Merchant
MASCULINE: Mercer

Mercury
FEMININE: Kaspit

Mercy and merciful See also Compassionate
MASCULINE: Clem, Clement, Clemmon, Clemmons, Clemon, Kal, Kalman, Kalonymos, Rachamim
FEMININE: Clementine, Mercedes

Merry See also Happiness; Joy; Revelry
FEMININE: Aliz, Gay, Gaye, Joice, Jovita, Joy, Joya, Joyce, Mabel, Mabella, Mable, Merelyn, Merril, Merryl, Meryl, Muriel

Messenger
MASCULINE: Aaron, Aharon, Angel, Angelo, Arke, Aron, Bedell, Bud, Buddy, Cal, Cale, Caleb, Calev, Camillus, Kalev, Malachai, Malachi, Malachy
FEMININE: Aarona, Aharona, Aharonit, Angel, Angela, Angelica, Angelina, Angeline, Angelique, Angelita, Angie, Angilee, Arela, Arni, Arnina, Arninit, Arnit, Arona, Aryn, Erela, Evangeline

Messenger summoner
MASCULINE: Sumner

Messiah
MASCULINE: Mashiach

Metal See Precious metals

Mighty See also Strength
MASCULINE: Amir, Ram, Rami, Sagi, Sagiv, Sagy

Military officer See also Captain; Officer; Soldiers
MASCULINE: Marchall, Marshal, Marshe

Mill
MASCULINE: Milford

Mill town
MASCULINE: Melton, Milton

Mindful
MASCULINE: Zakur

Mine See also Me
MASCULINE: Sheli
FEMININE: Liat

Minister
MASCULINE: Malachai, Malachi, Malachy

Minstrel
MASCULINE: Bard

Mint (plant)
FEMININE: Marva, Minta

Mir, associated with
MASCULINE: Miri

Miracles
MASCULINE: Nes, Ness, Nisan, Nisim, Nison, Nissi, Pele, Peli
FEMININE: Neesia, Nesya, Pelia

Mirage
FEMININE: Bavua

Mist
FEMININE: Misty

Mistress
FEMININE: Kyra, Mardi, Marita, Marta, Martha, Marthe, Merta

Mistress of the house See Lord

Modest
FEMININE: Jolanda, Yolanda

Monarchy See Royal

Month See also specific names of the months
MASCULINE: Levanon

Moon See also Goddess of the moon
MASCULINE: Levanon
FEMININE: Levana, Levani, Livana, Luna, Lunetta, Neoma, Sahara, Selena, Selina

Moorish (dark-skinned)
MASCULINE: Maurey, Maurice, Mauricio, Maurie, Maury, Morey, Mori, Moritz, Morrey, Morris, Morrison, Morry, Morse

Morning *See also* Dawn; Daybreak
MASCULINE: Shachar
FEMININE: Morna, Noga, Shachar, Talor, Talora

Morning dew *See also* Dew
MASCULINE: Tal-Shachar, Talor

Morning hours and demons
MASCULINE: Tzafreer

Morning light
MASCULINE: Noga

Moth
MASCULINE: Ash

Mother
FEMININE: Ena, Imma, Ina

Motto
FEMININE: Imra

Mound (of earth)
MASCULINE: Bart, Barth, Bartholomew, Bartlet, Gal, Talmai, Tel, Telem
FEMININE: Gal, Gala, Galit, Talma, Talmit

Mountain *See also* Boulder
MASCULINE: Aaron, Aharon, Alpin, Arke, Aron, Beaumont, Belmont, Benroy, Berg, Berger, Borg, Brent, Charan, Erskine, Fremont, Gomer, Haran, Harari, Harel, Marvin, Marwin, Mervin, Mervyn, Merwin, Montague, Monte, Montgomery, Monty
FEMININE: Aarona, Aharona, Aharonit, Arni, Arnina, Arninit, Arnit, Arona, Aryn, Harela, Olympia, Sinai

Mountain animals *See* Goat; Sheep

Mountain on which the Torah was given
MASCULINE: Sinai

Move ahead
MASCULINE: Lane, Yaziz
FEMININE: Lane, Layne

Musical
FEMININE: Lirit

Myrrh
MASCULINE: Mor
FEMININE: Myra, Myrna, Talmor

Myrtle tree
MASCULINE: Hadas, Myrtle
FEMININE: Dasa, Dasi, Dassa, Dassi, Hada, Hadas, Hadasa, Hode, Hodel, Hodi, Hude, Hudel, Myrtle

Myself *See* Me; Mine

Mythological names *See specific gods and goddesses by name*

Name *See also* Sacred name
MASCULINE: Kal, Kalman, Kalonymos, Shamai, Shamma, Shammai, Shem

Narrative
FEMININE: Narelle

Nation and nationhood *See also* Citizen; Countryman; Father of a mighty nation
MASCULINE: Amami, Ami, Amiaz, Amichai, Amidan, Amidar, Amidror, Amihud, Aminadav, Amior, Amiram, Amiran, Amiron, Amishaddai, Ammi, Amram, Arvid, Baram, Ben-Ami, Chanoch, Jeroboam, Lemuel, Leumi, Liam, Theo, Theobald, Tully, Yechiam, Yeravam
FEMININE: Ami, Amior, Bat-Ami, Beth-Ami, Leuma, Leumi

Natural
MASCULINE: Tibon, Tivi, Tivon

Naturalist
FEMININE: Tivona, Tivoni

Nature
MASCULINE: Teva

Navel (center)
MASCULINE: Tabur, Taburi

Navy
MASCULINE: Tzi

Neck
FEMININE: Orpa

Necklace
MASCULINE: Ravid
FEMININE: Ravid

Ne'er-do-well
MASCULINE: Shelumiel

Negro (dark in appearance)
MASCULINE: Phineas, Pinchas, Pinchos, Pincus, Pinhas, Pini, Pinkas, Pinkie, Pinkus, Pinky, Pinnie

Neighbor
MASCULINE: Shachna

New
FEMININE: Neva, Nova, Novela, Tari, Teriya

Night
MASCULINE: Delano, Layil
FEMININE: Laila, Laili, Layil, Laylie, Leila, Leili, Leyla

Noble and nobility *See also* Exalted; Patrician; Well-born
MASCULINE: Abelard, Adar, Adelbert, Adir, Al, Alard, Albert, Albie, Albrecht, Alfonse, Allard, Alphonso, Alsie, Alson, Atzil, Baron, Bert, Brian, Brion, Bry, Bryan, Chori, Earl, Edel, Elbert, Elbie, Elgin, Elmer, Elmo, Elmor, Ethelbert, Eugen, Eugene, Gene, Hori, Kareem, Karim, Lon, Nolan, Noland, Romi, Ryan, Ryne, Sagiv, Sterling
FEMININE: Alberta, Albertina, Atzila, Atzili, Audra, Audrey, Audrina, Bertina, Dona, Donabella, Donita, Donna, Donya, Earla, Earlene, Elberta, Ethel, Meroma, Mona, Monica, Monique, Nagida, Nediva, Negida, Sadi, Sadie, Sady, Saidye, Salli, Sara, Sarai, Sarali, Saran, Sarel, Sareli, Sarene, Saretta, Sari, Sarina, Sarit, Sarita, Saryl, Serelle, Serita, Sirel, Sirke, Sorale, Sorali, Sorel, Sorka, Soroli, Surel, Suri, Surilee, Tziril, Zara, Ziril, Zora

Noble birth
MASCULINE: Allison, Ethelbert
FEMININE: Ada, Adaline, Adda, Addie, Adela, Adelaide, Adele, Adelia, Adelina, Adeline, Adella, Adelle, Adelyn, Alanna, Alcina, Ali, Alice, Alicen, Alicia, Alisa, Alisia, Alison, Alissa, Alissyn, Allison, Ally, Allysin, Alyce, Alysa, Alyson, Alyssa, Delia, Dell, Elka, Elki, Leena, Lina

Noble cause
MASCULINE: Ila, Ili

Nocturnal *See* Night

Noise
MASCULINE: Raam

Nonsensical
MASCULINE: Kislon

Normal
FEMININE: Norma

North, person from
MASCULINE: Norland

Nose
MASCULINE: Cameron, Nachor
FEMININE: Cameron

Noted
MASCULINE: Shamu'a

Nourish
MASCULINE: Zan, Zane

Numbers *See specific numbers by name*

Nurse (medical)
FEMININE: Omenet, Thelma

Nut
MASCULINE: Egoz

Oak trees
MASCULINE: Dar, Darold, Derel, Derry, Eilon, Elon, Oakley
FEMININE: Alona, Alyonna, Ayla, Eila, Elona

Oath *See also* Pledge; Promise
MASCULINE: Arlan, Arlen, Arlin, Arlyn, Neder, Nidri, Sheva
FEMININE: Anabeth, Arleen, Arlene, Arlett, Arline, Arlyne, Bab, Bas-Sheva, Basha, Bashe, Bat-Shua, Bat-Sheva, Bathsheba, Bela, Belita, Bella, Belle, Bess, Bessie, Bet, Beta, Beth, Bethe, Betsy, Bette, Bettina, Betty, Donabella, Elisa, Elisabeta, Elisabeth, Elise, Elisheva, Elissa, Eliza, Elizabeta, Elizabeth, Elize, Ellis, Elsa, Elsie, Elyce, Elysa, Elza, Hazelbelle, Ilisa, Ilsa, Ilyse, Isa, Isabel, Isobel, Leesa, Leta, Lettie, Libbie, Lilibet, Lilybeth, Lisa, Lisi, Lissie, Livvie, Liza, Lizbeth, Lize, Lizette, Lizzie, Lys, Peshe, Pessel, Sheba, Sheva, Shevi, Tetty, Tiie, Tina, Zizi, Zsa Zsa

Observant (religious)
FEMININE: Dati, Datit

Occupational names *See specific occupations by name*

Ode
FEMININE: Oda, Odele, Odell, Odetta, Odette

Offering *See also* Gift
MASCULINE: Teruma
FEMININE: Teruma

Officer *See also* Captain
MASCULINE: Katzin, Marchall, Marshal, Marshe, Sargeant

Official *See also* Elected
MASCULINE: Gabai

Ointment
FEMININE: Narda

Old and older *See also* Ancient; Elder
MASCULINE: Al, Aldan, Alden, Alder, Aldo, Aldon, Aldous, Aldred, Aldren, Aldus, Alf, Alfred, Alfredo, Alson, Alter, Altie, Atik, Elden, Elder, Saba, Yashish, Zaken
FEMININE: Alda, Atika, Baila, Bayla, Bayle, Bilha, Keshisha, Lark, Priscilla, Saba, Sibyl, Sybil, Yeshisha, Zekena

Olive
MASCULINE: Zayit
FEMININE: Livia, Oliva, Olive, Olivia, Zayit, Zeita, Zeitana, Zeta, Zetana, Zetta

Olive plants
FEMININE: Yasmin

Olive tree
MASCULINE: Zetan

Omen *See also* Sign
MASCULINE: Siman-Tov

Omniscient
MASCULINE: Cato

One
MASCULINE: Adda, Alef
FEMININE: Oona

One (united)
FEMININE: Unita

Opal
FEMININE: Opal

Open
MASCULINE: Averel, Averil, Jephtah, Peretz, Perez, Yiftach
FEMININE: April

Opening (beginning)
MASCULINE: Janus

Opening (hole)
MASCULINE: Pekach

Oppress
MASCULINE: Tel, Telem

Optimism *See also* Faith; Hope
MASCULINE: Gib, Gil, Gilbert, Gili, Gill, Gilli
FEMININE: Pollyanna

Orator *See also* Speaker; Speech
MASCULINE: Cicero, Divri

Orchard *See also* Garden
MASCULINE: Ginson, Ginton
FEMININE: Carmela, Carmelit, Karmela, Karmit

Order (peace)
MASCULINE: Cosmo
FEMININE: Cosima

Order (sequence)
MASCULINE: Orde, Sadir, Seder, Sidra

Organization
FEMININE: Cosima

Organized
FEMININE: Sadira

Oriental
FEMININE: Laila, Leila

Ornament
MASCULINE: Atir
FEMININE: Achsa, Adi, Adie, Adiel, Adiela, Adiya, Maskit

Ornamented *See also* Adorn
MASCULINE: Hada, Hadar, Noi, Noy
FEMININE: Atura, Hadar, Hadara, Hadarit, Hadura, Noia, Noya

Ostentatious
MASCULINE: Cash, Cassius

Ostrich
FEMININE: Jaen, Yaanit, Yaen

Other
MASCULINE: Acher

Outstanding
MASCULINE: Angus

Owl
FEMININE: Lilit

Ownership *See also* Freedom
MASCULINE: Frank, Franklin, Franklyn

Ox
MASCULINE: Byk, Shor

Package (wrap up)
FEMININE: Ariza

Paid
MASCULINE: Shilem

Pal *See also* Friend
MASCULINE: Bub

Palace *See also* Castle
MASCULINE: Armon, Whitney
FEMININE: Whitney, Zevula

Palm carrier
MASCULINE: Palmer

Palm tree
MASCULINE: Tamir, Tamur, Tomer
FEMININE: Dikla, Diklit, Palma, Tamar, Tema, Temara, Temma, Timi, Timora, Timura, Tomer
island of palm trees
MASCULINE: Ismar, Itamar, Ittamar

Pancake
MASCULINE: Leviva
FEMININE: Leviva

Parable
FEMININE: Melitza

Paradise
MASCULINE: Eden
FEMININE: Eden

Park
MASCULINE: Warner, Warren, Werner

Park caretaker *See also* Gardener
MASCULINE: Parker

Partridge
FEMININE: Chogla, Hogla

Pass over
MASCULINE: Pesach

Passageway *See also* Gate
MASCULINE: Janus

Passion
MASCULINE: Ashi, Rees

Passover holiday
MASCULINE: Pesach

Pastureland *See also* Field (area of land)
MASCULINE: Hayden, Heywood

Patch (of cloth)
FEMININE: Matlit

Path
MASCULINE: Lane, Nativ, Salil, Shoval, Trace, Tracee, Tracey
FEMININE: Lane, Layne, Mesilla, Netiva, Selila

Patrician
MASCULINE: Paddy, Pat, Patrick, Payton
FEMININE: Pat, Patrice, Patricia, Patsy, Patti, Ricka, Ricky, Tisha, Tricia, Trish

Payer
MASCULINE: Yale

Peace *See also* Harmony; Rest
MASCULINE: Absalom, Al, Alan, Allan, Allen, Allyn, Alson, Alyn, Avishalom, Avshalom, Cosmo, Erin, Getzel, Godfrey, Gottfried, Harmon, Humphrey, Ish-Shalom, Mandy, Manfred, Mani, Manni, Manny, Manoach, Noach, Noah, Nomar, Oliver, Olivier, Ollie, Placid, Placido, Ramon, Raymond, Raymund, Salem, Salim, Salo, Saloman, Shaanan, Shalev, Shalom, Shalum, Shalvi, Shanan, Shelomi, Shelomo, Shilem, Shlomi, Shlomo, Shlomy, Sholom, Siegfried, Solomon, Wilfred, Zal, Zalki, Zalkin, Zalman
FEMININE: Aerin, Alfreda, Cerena, Chesna, Erin, Erna, Freda, Fredda, Frida, Frieda, Friedel, Fritzi, Ginnie, Harmony, Ingrid, Irena, Irene, Irenee, Irina, Jen, Jennie, Jennifer, Jennilee, Jenny, Livia, Menucha, Norma, Olga, Oliva, Olive, Olivia, Ramona, Ramot, Rena, Salome, Selima, Serena, Serenity, Shalva, Shelomit, Shlomit, Shula, Shulamit, Shuli, Sirena, Sulamit, Wende, Winifred, Winnie, Winnifred

Peacock
MASCULINE: Tavas

Pear
MASCULINE: Agas

Pearl
MASCULINE: Dar, Penini
FEMININE: Daisy, Greta, Gretchen, Gretel, Madge, Mady, Mae, Mag, Maggie, Margalit, Margalita, Margaret, Margarete, Margaretta, Margarita, Marge, Margene, Margerie, Margery, Marget, Margi, Margit, Margo, Margy, Marji, Marjorie, May, Meg, Megan, Meret, Midge, Pearl, Pearla, Peg, Penina, Penini, Peninit, Perl, Perla, Pnina

Pebble *See also* Stone
FEMININE: Coral, Coralee

People *See* Citizen

Peppercorn
FEMININE: Pepper

Perceptive *See also* Clever
MASCULINE: Sharp

Perfumed *See also* Myrrh
FEMININE: Talmor

Period of time
MASCULINE: Idan
FEMININE: Ona

Permanent *See also* Enduring (lasting); Eternal
MASCULINE: Eitan, Etan, Ethan, Eytan

Persevere
FEMININE: Patience

Petite
FEMININE: Mignon

Petition *See also* Praying and prayer
MASCULINE: Shela, Tachan
FEMININE: Techina

Picking (e.g., flowers)
FEMININE: Ketifa

Picture
FEMININE: Maskit, Nema, Nima, Temuna

Pile
MASCULINE: Dur
FEMININE: Doreet, Dorit

Pilgrim
MASCULINE: Palmer, Wal, Wally, Walt, Walter, Wilt

Pillar
FEMININE: Herma

Pillow
MASCULINE: Cody

Pine tree
FEMININE: Oranit, Orna, Ornan, Orni, Ornina, Ornit

Pious *See also* Zealous
MASCULINE: Aduk
FEMININE: Adika, Aduka, Frimcha, Fromet, Fruma, Frume, Frumet, Pia

Pipe player
FEMININE: Piper

Pit
MASCULINE: Cheifer

Pitcher
MASCULINE: Kad, Kadi
FEMININE: Kada, Kadia, Kadit, Kadiya, Kadya

Pity
FEMININE: Mercedes

Placid *See also* Peace
MASCULINE: Placid, Placido

Plains
MASCULINE: Sharon
FEMININE: Shareen, Sharelle, Sharene, Shari, Sharilyn, Sharin, Sharon, Sharona, Sharoni, Sharonit, Sharyn, Shereen, Sherron

Plant and planting
MASCULINE: Tzemach, Zemach
FEMININE: Nita

Plants *See also specific plants by name*
MASCULINE: Barkan, Harley, Nufar, Nuphar, Rotem, Shatil, Shatul
FEMININE: Fern, Heather, Kalanit, Lotus, Marganit, Marva, Nerd, Neta, Netta, Nirit, Rotem

Plaster
MASCULINE: Sid

Platform
FEMININE: Bama, Bima

Pleasant *See also* Kind
MASCULINE: Aden, Adin, Adiv, Eden, Ehud, Myron, Naam, Naaman, Naim, Naom, Shefer
FEMININE: Adiva, Elma, Jolene, Joletta, Jolie, Joliet, Latifa, Merrie, Merrielle, Merry, Naama, Naamana, Naami, Naamia, Naamiya, Naoma, Naomi, Navit, Neima, Neumi, Noemi, Nomi

Pleasure
FEMININE: Eden, Libida

Pledge *See also* Oath
MASCULINE: Arlan, Arlen, Arlin, Arlyn
FEMININE: Arleen, Arlene, Arlett, Arline, Arlyne

Plenty
MASCULINE: Cedric, Evyatar

Plough
MASCULINE: Nir
FEMININE: Nira, Odera

Plywood
MASCULINE: Lavid

Podium
FEMININE: Bima

Poems
FEMININE: Divan, Lyric

Poetry
MASCULINE: Bard, Devin, Devon, Singer
FEMININE: Devon, Eda, Lirit, Piuta, Piyuta

Polite *See* Courteous

Pomegranate
MASCULINE: Rimon
FEMININE: Rimon, Rimona

Pool
MASCULINE: Merrill

Poor
MASCULINE: Aluv
FEMININE: Aluva, Delila, Dila

Popular
MASCULINE: Amami

Port
FEMININE: Chelsea

Porter
MASCULINE: Porter, Sabal

Portion
MASCULINE: Keta
FEMININE: Mana

Portrait
FEMININE: Nema, Nima

Possession *See also* Belonging to me; Belonging to one
FEMININE: Beula

Pot
MASCULINE: Kad, Kadi, Yora
FEMININE: Yora

Pot-shaped area
MASCULINE: Bing

Powder
MASCULINE: Avak
FEMININE: Avka

Powerful *See also* Strength
MASCULINE: Aric, Berwin, Dick, Dix, Dixie, Dixon, Dyck, Dyke, Maynard, Ranier, Reg, Reginald, Reinhard, Reinhold, Rennie, Reynard, Reynold, Ric, Ricardo, Ricci, Ricco, Rich, Richard, Richardo, Richie, Rici, Rick, Rocco, Ronald, Rondell, Ronnie, Ryan, Ryne
FEMININE: Amitza, Amiza, Arnoldine, Aza, Chasina, Chasna, Erica, Erika, Hasina, Hasna, Riki, Xeriqua

Praise and praised
MASCULINE: Anthony, Anton, Cleo, Cleon, Clio, Hallel, Hila, Hili, Hillel, Jud, Juda, Judah, Judas, Judd, Jude, Judea, Judel, Judson, Seled, Shevach, Toni, Yehuda, Yehudi, Yuda
FEMININE: Antonella, Disa, Eeta, Eta, Etka, Eudice, Eudit, Hallela, Halleli, Hila, Hilana, Hili, Hillela, Ita, Itka, Itta, Jodeth, Jodi, Judi, Judith, Judy, Judythe, Odeh, Odeleya, Odelia, Odiya, Tehila, Yehudit, Yudi, Yudis, Yudit

Praise the Lord *See* God, praise for

Praying and prayer *See also* Blessing
MASCULINE: Atar, Bede, Shela, Tachan
FEMININE: Anina, Atira, Techina

Preacher
MASCULINE: Matif

Precious *See also* Beloved
MASCULINE: Azizi, Nadir, Selden, Yakar, Yakir
FEMININE: Kevuda, Nadira, Segula, Selda, Yakira, Yekara, Zelda

Precious metals *See* Brass; Bronze; Copper; Gold; Silver

Precious stones *See also* Diamonds; Garnet; Pearl; Ruby
MASCULINE: Beril, Beryl, Diamond, Jaspar, Leshem, Penini, Sapir
FEMININE: Bareket, Beryl, Bo, Gemma, Jade, Opal, Penini, Ruby, Sapir, Sapira, Sapirit, Topaza

Prepare (to do something) *See also* Ready
MASCULINE: Atid, Yachin

Present *See* Gift

Preserve
MASCULINE: Shemer, Warner, Warren, Werner

Pretty *See also* Beauty
MASCULINE: Beau
FEMININE: Bonita, Bonnie, Linda, Lynda

Prevaricator
FEMININE: Cozbi

Price
MASCULINE: Price

Prickly pear (cactus)
MASCULINE: Sabra, Tzabar
FEMININE: Sabaria, Sabra, Sabrina, Savrina, Tzabara, Tzabaria, Tzabariya

Priest *See also* Clergy
MASCULINE: Cal, Cale, Caleb, Calev, Kalev

Priest's meadow
MASCULINE: Presley
FEMININE: Presley

Priest's town
MASCULINE: Preston

Primer
MASCULINE: Alfon

Prince and princely
MASCULINE: Aluf, Arch, Archibald, Arky, Katzin, Nadiv, Nagid, Nasi, Prince, Princeton, Sar, Sari

Prince of God
MASCULINE: Asriel, Iser, Israel, Isser, Issi, Sruli, Yisrael, Yisroel
FEMININE: Israela, Sareli, Yisraela, Yisrela

Princess
FEMININE: Alufa, Sadi, Sadie, Sady, Saidye, Salli, Sara, Sarai, Sarali, Saran, Sarel, Sareli, Sarene, Saretta, Sari, Sarina, Sarit, Sarita, Saryl, Serelle, Serita, Sirel, Sirke, Sorale, Sorali, Sorel, Sorka, Soroli, Surel, Suri, Surilee, Tziril, Zara, Ziril, Zora

Produce
FEMININE: Tenuva

Profound
MASCULINE: Amok

Progenitor
FEMININE: Avi

Progressive
MASCULINE: Erve, Harvey, Harvi, Herve

Prohibition
MASCULINE: Isur

Promise *See also* Oath
MASCULINE: Neder

Promontory
MASCULINE: Garfield
FEMININE: Nessa

Proper
FEMININE: Yamina

Prophet *See also* Soothsayer
MASCULINE: Nachshon, Navi
FEMININE: Nevia

Prophetic powers
FEMININE: Caasi, Cassandra, Cassi

Prosperous *See also* Flourish; Rich; Wealth
MASCULINE: Edsel, Otto, Prosper
FEMININE: Ede, Edie, Edita, Edith, Edyth, Nagida, Negida

Protect (protector) *See also* Guard; Watchman
MASCULINE: Al, Alec, Alejandro, Aleksandr, Alessandro, Alex, Alexander, Alexandre, Alexandri, Alexis, Alix, Allix, Alson, Avigdor, Bil, Billi, Elex,

Esmond, Esmund, Hector, Helmut, Hi, Hilary, Hillary, Howard, Howie, Humphrey, Liam, Lot, Lotan, Magen, Nomar, Ramon, Raymond, Raymund, Sacha, Sander, Sanders, Sandor, Sandy, Sasha, Saunders, Sender, Tzofi, Warner, Warren, Werner, Wiley, Wilhelm, Will, Willi, William, Willie, Willis, Willy, Xander, Zander, Zofi

FEMININE: Aleksandra, Alexa, Alexandra, Alexandrina, Alexia, Alexis, Alix, Elka, Elki, Hera, Magena, Magina, Rhea, Sacha, Sandi, Sandra, Sandy, Sasha, Saundra, Sondra, Zandra

Protected
MASCULINE: Akevy, Aki, Akki, Cobe, Diego, Hamish, Jack, Jackie, Jackson, Jacob, Jacobo, Jacque, Jaimie, Jake, Jakob, James, Jamie, Jan, Jascha, Jim, Jimbo, Jimm, Jimmie, Kaufman, Kiva, Kobe, Koppel, Kovi, Kubi, Osman, Seamus

FEMININE: Chasia, Chasya, Gerda, Hasia, Hasya, Jackee, Jacklyn, Jacky, Jaclyn, Jacoba, Jacque, Jacqueline, Jacquelyn, Jacqui, Jaime, Jaymee, Jocelin, Jocelyn, Jodette, Joscelin, Joscelind, Josetta, Joslyn, Shimrat, Shimrit, Tzeruia

Protection *See also* Shelter
MASCULINE: Ansel, Randal, Randell, Randi, Randy, Shemaria, Shemarya, Shemaryahu, Siegmond, Sig, Siggi, Tzelophchad, Zelophehad

FEMININE: Anchelle, Hamutal, Ramona, Ramot

Protective shield
MASCULINE: Giles, Gyles

Proud
FEMININE: Gaya

Prudent
FEMININE: Prudence, Prue

Pure and purity *See also* Clear (pure)
MASCULINE: Zakai, Zaki
FEMININE: Agnes, Annice, Annis, Berura, Berurit, Beruriya, Berurya, Blanca, Blanch, Caasi, Caitlin, Caren,

Caron, Carren, Cathay, Catherin, Catherine, Cathi, Cathleen, Cathryn, Cathy, Dana, Danette, Danna, Deanna, Deon, Di, Diana, Didi, Dion, Dyan, Dyana, Ginger, Ginnie, Inez, Kaethe, Kai, Kara, Karan, Karen, Karin, Karina, Karon, Karyn, Kate, Katharine, Kathe, Katherine, Kathie, Kathleen, Kathryn, Kathy, Kati, Katrin, Katy, Kay, Kit, Kitty, Mona, Monica, Monique, Nessie, Rachael, Rachel, Rachela, Racheli, Rachelle, Rae, Rahel, Rahela, Raquel, Ray, Rayna, Rayne, Regan, Regina, Reina, Rena, Reyna, Rochel, Tehora, Trina, Virginia, Zaka, Zakit

Putty
MASCULINE: Merek

Quarrel
MASCULINE: Yariv

Queen and queenly *See also* Royal
FEMININE: Gevira, Hera, Malca, Malka, Malke, Malki, Malkit, Milka, Queena, Queenie, Sherelyn, Sheri, Sheril, Sherre, Sherril, Sherrine, Sherry, Tania

Quick
MASCULINE: Maher

Quicksilver
FEMININE: Kaspit

Quiet *See also* Peace; Silence
MASCULINE: Noach, Noah, Nomar, Ramon, Raymond, Raymund

Quilt *See also* Comforter (blanket)
FEMININE: Keset

Rafter
MASCULINE: Marish

Rain
MASCULINE: Geshem, Malkosh, Matri, Raviv
FEMININE: Lital, Pola, Raviva, Reviva

Rainbow
MASCULINE: Kashti
FEMININE: Iris, Keshet

Raise (bring up)
MASCULINE: Omen
FEMININE: Omenet

Ram
MASCULINE: Ayal, Ayali, Ayalon, Ramsay, Ramsey, Yovel
FEMININE: Yovel

Rare (uncommon)
MASCULINE: Nadir, Selden
FEMININE: Nadira, Selda, Zelda

Rational
MASCULINE: Savir
FEMININE: Sevira

Raven
MASCULINE: Bran, Brand, Brandan, Brandt, Corbet, Corbin, Corwin, Oreb, Oreiv, Orev, Raven
FEMININE: Oreiv, Orev, Raven

Ravine *See also* Valley
MASCULINE: Gai, Gaia, Guy
FEMININE: Corey, Cori, Correy, Corri, Corry, Courteny, Kori

Rays
FEMININE: Korenet

Ready *See also* Prepare
MASCULINE: Atid, Attai
FEMININE: Attai

Reasonable
MASCULINE: Savir
FEMININE: Sevira

Rebellion
MASCULINE: Meri

Rebellious *See also* Revolt
MASCULINE: Nimrod
FEMININE: Meri, Merie

Reborn
MASCULINE: Renay, René

Reckon time
MASCULINE: Idi, Ido

Record keeper
MASCULINE: Chancellor

Red *See also* Scarlet
MASCULINE: Admon, Adom, Bayard, Garnet, Odem, Royal, Rufus, Rusty
FEMININE: Aduma, Scarlet

Reddish stone
FEMININE: Ruby

Reddish-black
MASCULINE: Guni

Reddish-brown
MASCULINE: Armoni, Sorrell

Redeem
FEMININE: Yigala

Redeemed
FEMININE: Poda

Redeemer
MASCULINE: Goel

Redemption
MASCULINE: Igael, Igal, Iggy, Yigael, Yigal
FEMININE: Ge'ula

Reed
MASCULINE: Agmon, Kani, Kaniel, Read, Redd, Reed, Reid

Reestablishment
FEMININE: Tekuma

Refuge
MASCULINE: Adlai, Golan, Lew, Lewes, Lewis, Louis, Ludwig

Refugee
FEMININE: Avis, Sarida

Regal *See also* King
MASCULINE: Regis

Regional
MASCULINE: Azori

Regulated
FEMININE: Sadira

Rejoicing *See also* Joy
MASCULINE: Agel, Agil, Kay, Yagel, Yagil
FEMININE: Kai, Kay, Marnina

Religious
FEMININE: Dati, Datit
  head of religious institution
  MASCULINE: Abbe, Abbie, Pryor

Remembrance and remembering
MASCULINE: Benzecry, Yizkor, Zac, Zacharia, Zachary, Zackary, Zak, Zakur, Zecharia, Zechariahu, Zeke, Zichri

Remnant
MASCULINE: Sarid

Removable
MASCULINE: Natik

Renew
MASCULINE: Renay, René

Repair
MASCULINE: Mendel, Mendi, Mendl

Reputation
MASCULINE: Cimon, Shem, Shibi, Shimi, Shimke, Shimmel, Shimon, Si, Simeon, Simi, Simmie, Simon, Simpson, Symon
FEMININE: Simeona, Simona, Simone

Resemblance
MASCULINE: Dama
FEMININE: Halie

Reserved (shy)
FEMININE: Erna

Reside
MASCULINE: Blair, Dar
FEMININE: Dara

Resident
FEMININE: Netina

Resolute
MASCULINE: Ernest, Ernesto, Ernie, Erno, Ernst
FEMININE: Ernesta

Respect *See also* High esteem
MASCULINE: Rodman
FEMININE: Haron, Honor, Honora, Honorine, Kevuda, Nora, Noreen, Noreena, Norene, Nori, Norrie

Rest (relax) *See also* Peace
MASCULINE: Manoach, Noach, Noah, Shabbetai, Shabbtai, Shabtiel
FEMININE: Menucha, Shabetit

Resting place
MASCULINE: Neve

Resurrection *See also* Born again
MASCULINE: Anastasia
FEMININE: Anastasia, Nastasia, Natasia, Stace, Stacey, Stacia, Stacy

Resuscitation
FEMININE: Tekuma

Retiring
FEMININE: Erna

Return
MASCULINE: Yashuv

Revelry *See also* Merry
MASCULINE: Denis, Dennis, Denys, Ennis

Revered *See also* Exalted
MASCULINE: Aggie, August, Augustus, Austen
FEMININE: Antia, Antoina, Antoinette, Augusta, Augustina, Augustine, Gussie, Gustine, Netti, Nettie, Toni, Tonia, Tonise, Tony

Revival *See also* Born again
FEMININE: Anastasia, Nastasia, Natasia, Stace, Stacey, Stacia, Stacy, Techiya, Tehiya, Tekuma

Revolt
MASCULINE: Mered, Meri
FEMININE: Merida, Meriva

Reward
MASCULINE: Issachar, Sachar, Shalum

Rewarded
MASCULINE: Shalman

Rice
MASCULINE: Orez

Rich *See also* Prosperous; Wealth
MASCULINE: Adrian, Adrien, Aric, Daren, Darian, Darin, Dario, Darius, Dick, Dix, Dixie, Dixon, Dyck, Dyke, Edmond, Edmund, Edric, Edsel, Hadrian, Ned, Neddy, Odo, Reinhard, Reynard, Ric, Ricardo, Ricci, Ricco, Rich, Richard, Richardo, Richie, Rici, Rick, Rocco, Ryan, Ryne
FEMININE: Adria, Adriana, Adriane, Adrien, Alda, Bari, Barrie, Darrene, Ede, Edie, Edina, Edita, Edith, Edna, Edwina, Edyth

Riches
MASCULINE: Evyatar
FEMININE: Ashirut, Yitra

Rider
MASCULINE: Aric, Dick, Dix, Dixie, Dixon, Dyck, Dyke, Reinhard, Reynard, Ric, Ricardo, Ricci, Ricco, Rich, Richard, Richardo, Richie, Rici, Rick, Rocco, Ryan, Ryne

FEMININE: Rica, Ricarda, Richarda, Richelle, Ricka, Ricky

Ridicule
MASCULINE: Buz

Right (opposite of left) *See also* Good fortune; South
MASCULINE: Dexter, Yamin, Yemin
FEMININE: Jemina, Yamina, Yimna

Right hand
MASCULINE: Yamin, Yemin
FEMININE: Jemina, Yemina

Righteous
MASCULINE: Tzadok, Zadok
FEMININE: Chasida, Hasida, Tamar, Yoko

Ripe
FEMININE: Asisa, Tari, Teriya

Ripple
FEMININE: Adva

Rise up
MASCULINE: Idi, Ido, Timur, Yaziz

River
MASCULINE: Blane, Calder, Merrill, Rio, Romney
FEMININE: Dee, Rhonda, Ronda, Tyna

River bank
MASCULINE: Rip

River crossing
MASCULINE: Elford, Sandy, Sanford

River ford
MASCULINE: Wade

Road
MASCULINE: Nativ, Trace, Tracee, Tracey
FEMININE: Mesilla

Rock *See also* Boulder; Stone
MASCULINE: Art, Arthur, Artie, Arturo, Arty, Craig, Flint, Parnell, Pedro, Per, Perry, Pete, Peter, Pierce, Pierre, Piers, Rocco, Rock, Rockne, Rocky, Sela, Sili, Stone, Tzur, Tzuri, Zur, Zuri
FEMININE: Amberlee, Artia, Avna, Bo, Chantal, Chantel, Hindi, Kim, Kimberley, Petra, Pier, Rochelle, Ruschel, Salit, Sela, Tzur

Rock formation
MASCULINE: Kimberley

Rock of salvation
MASCULINE: Ebin, Evenezer

Rock quarry
MASCULINE: Dunstan, Dustin, Dusty

Roll
MASCULINE: Galil
FEMININE: Galila, Gelila

Roll up
MASCULINE: Walker

Rope *See also* Cord
FEMININE: Cordelia, Dalgia, Dalgiya

Rose
MASCULINE: Rohn, Vered
FEMININE: Raisa, Raise, Raisel, Raissa, Raize, Raizel, Raizi, Rayzel, Razil, Razina, Reizel, Rhoda, Rhode, Roanna, Rosa, Rosabel, Rosalie, Rosalind, Rosalinda, Rosaline, Rosalyn, Rosanna, Rosanne, Rose, Roselotte, Roselyn, Rosemary, Rosetta, Rosette, Rosi, Rosina, Rosita, Roslyn, Roz, Rozelin, Rozella, Rozina, Varda, Vardia, Vardina, Vardit, Vardiya, Vered

Round
MASCULINE: Saviv

Royalty *See also* Crown; King; Prince; Princess; Queen
MASCULINE: Alroy, Basil, Elroy, Kendrick, Kinsey, LeRoy, Regis
FEMININE: Corna, Kendra, Vasilia

Ruby
MASCULINE: Adom, Odem
FEMININE: Ruby

Ruby-colored
FEMININE: Scarlet

Ruddy
MASCULINE: Rory

Rugged land
MASCULINE: Rowe, Rowland

Ruler *See also* King; Lawmaker; Queen; Regal; Royal
MASCULINE: Alroy, Aric, Arndt, Arne, Arnel, Arni, Arno, Arnold, Dick, Dix, Dixie, Dixon, Don, Donald, Donnie, Dyck, Dyke, Edric, Eric, Erik, Eryk, Fred, Frederic, Frederick, Frits, Fritz,

Herbert, Hubert, Huey, Hugh, Hugo, Kendal, King, Macdonald, Mackenzie, Nagid, Ranier, Reg, Reginald, Reinhard, Reinhold, Rennie, Reynard, Reynold, Ric, Ricardo, Ricci, Ricco, Rich, Richard, Richardo, Richie, Rici, Rick, Rocco, Rockwell, Rocky, Rod, Roddy, Roderic, Ronald, Rondell, Ronnie, Rory, Ryan, Ryne, Ty, Tyron, Tyson, Vladimir
FEMININE: Arnolde, Bari, Barrie, Billie, Eeta, Eta, Etka, Etta, Ferida, Fredda, Frederica, Fritzi, Harriet, Henia, Henrietta, Henya, Hetta, Hilma, Ita, Itka, Itta, Mackenzi, Mackenzie, Maryetta, Mina, Minda, Mindel, Minna, Minnie, Raina, Rana, Regan, Regina, Rena, Rica, Ricarda, Richarda, Richelle, Ricka, Ricky, Ronalda, Ronne, Ronni, Ronny, Rori, Rula, Sultana, Velma, Vila, Vilhelmina, Vilma, Walda, Wilhelmina, Willa, Willene, Wilma, Yetta, Yitta, Yitti

elf ruler
MASCULINE: Aubrey

Rusty-haired
MASCULINE: Russ, Russel, Rusty

Sabbath *See also* Rest
MASCULINE: Shabbetai, Shabbtai, Shabtiel
FEMININE: Shabetit

Sabines, of the
FEMININE: Sabina

Sacred *See also* Consecrated; Holy
FEMININE: Augusta, Augustina, Augustine, Gussie, Gustine, Helga

Sacred name
MASCULINE: Gerome, Gerre, Gerry, Jere, Jerome, Jeromy, Jerrem, Jerry

Sacrificial knife
MASCULINE: Dorian, Dorris
FEMININE: Dorea, Doria, Doris, Dorris

Sailor
MASCULINE: Malach, Sapan

Saintly *See also* Angel

MASCULINE: Angel, Angelo

Salt
MASCULINE: Sal

Salvation *See also* God, help and salvation
MASCULINE: Ebin, Eliseo, Elish, Elisha, Ellis, Evenezer, Hosea, Hoshea, Ilie, Iliya, Josh, Joshua, Mosha, Yehoshua
FEMININE: Alysha, Teshua

Sanctification *See also* Blessed; Consecrated; Holy
MASCULINE: Kaddish, Kadish, Sinclair

Sanctuary
MASCULINE: Devir, Dvir, Haven
FEMININE: Devir, Devira, Dvir, Haven, Temple

Sapphire
FEMININE: Topaza

Sarcasm
FEMININE: Akitza

Sarcophagus
MASCULINE: Aran, Case

Saved
MASCULINE: Sal, Salvador

Savior
MASCULINE: Xavier, Yishi

Saxony resident
MASCULINE: Saxby

Scarce
MASCULINE: Nadir
FEMININE: Nadira

Scare
MASCULINE: Selden

Scarlet
MASCULINE: Shani

Scarlet (thread)
FEMININE: Shani

Scholar *See also* Wisdom
MASCULINE: Clark, Gaon
FEMININE: Geona

Scholarship
FEMININE: Idra

Scout (investigate)
MASCULINE: Tor, Tzofi, Zofi
FEMININE: Tzofia, Zofia

Scream *See also* Cry
FEMININE: Shava, Shu'a

Screen
FEMININE: Mitriya

Scribe *See also* Book copier; Writer
MASCULINE: Roman
FEMININE: Soferet

Sea
MASCULINE: Darwin, Delmor, Dylan, Lamar, Marino, Maris, Marlin, Marlo, Marlow, Marne, Marvin, Marwin, Meredith, Merrill, Mervin, Mervyn, Merwin, Morgan, Mortimer, Murray, Yam
FEMININE: Bat-Yam, Maren, Marina, Maris, Marisa, Marissa, Marna, Marni, Meredith, Merelyn, Merideth, Merril, Merryl, Meryl, Morgan, Muriel, Yama, Yamit

Sea-green precious stone
MASCULINE: Beril, Beryl

Seal *See also* Close
FEMININE: Rona

Sealing
FEMININE: Neila

Seaman
MASCULINE: Murray

Seasonal *See also specific seasons by name*
MASCULINE: Attai
FEMININE: Attai, Ona

Secret
MASCULINE: Jaspar, Raz, Razi, Raziel, Sodi
FEMININE: Aluma, Raz, Razi, Razia, Raziela, Razilee, Razili, Raziya

Secretary
MASCULINE: Chancellor, Chauncey

Section (portion)
MASCULINE: Keta

Secure *See* Fortified

See (behold)
MASCULINE: Horace, Horatio

Seed
MASCULINE: Garin, Zera

Seer *See also* Prophet
MASCULINE: Nachshon

Self-centered
MASCULINE: Gay

Selflessness
FEMININE: Lilo

Senior *See* Elder

Sequence
MASCULINE: Sidra

Sergeant
MASCULINE: Samal

Serpent
FEMININE: Belinda, Ophelia

Servant
MASCULINE: Avda, Avdi, Camillus, Lance, Lancelot, Malachai, Malachi, Malachy, Norris, Oved, Page, Porter, Sabal
FEMININE: Camilla, Camillia, Kamilla, Page

Servant of God
MASCULINE: Avdel, Avdiel, Obadiah, Obe, Osman, Osmand, Osmond, Ovadya, Ovadyahu

Servant of St. Columba
MASCULINE: Malcolm

Serve
MASCULINE: Serge, Sergei, Sergio

Server
FEMININE: Da'yelet, Page

Servile
MASCULINE: Avdon

Settlement
FEMININE: Keret

Shade
FEMININE: Mitriya

Shadow
FEMININE: Tzila, Zila

Shame
MASCULINE: Buz, Buzi
FEMININE: Buza

Share
FEMININE: Mana

Sharp
MASCULINE: Chadad

Sheaf
MASCULINE: Amir, Omer, Omri

Shearing
MASCULINE: Gaziz
FEMININE: Geziza

Shed (dwelling)
MASCULINE: Dir

Sheep *See also* Ewe; Lamb
MASCULINE: Eder, Maron, Meron, Shebsel, Shepsel, Zimran, Zimri
FEMININE: Marona, Meirona, Merona, Tira, Tiri

Sheep meadow
MASCULINE: Shepley, Shipley

Sheep shearer
MASCULINE: Sherman, Sherry, Sherwin, Sherwood

Shells, island of
MASCULINE: Shelley, Shelly

Shelter *See also* Protection
FEMININE: Amberlee, Idalee, Jennilee, Lauralee, Lee, Maralee, Marilee, Marily, Shelby, Surilee

Shepherd
MASCULINE: Holden, Roi, Shepard, Shepherd, Sheppard

Shepherd's hut
MASCULINE: Sheldon

Shield
MASCULINE: Giles, Shelet

Shining *See also* Bright
MASCULINE: Aaron, Aharon, Arke, Aron, Gray, Greg, Mayer, Meir, Meiri, Meyer, Myer, Sinclair, Zahir, Zerach, Zerah, Ziv
FEMININE: Aarona, Aharona, Aharonit, Arni, Arnina, Arninit, Arnit, Arona, Aryn, Electra, Korenet, Levina, Luna, Lunetta, Mazhira, Neora, Phebe, Phoebe, Zahara, Zahari, Zaharit, Zahira

Ships *See also* Boat
MASCULINE: Tzi
FEMININE: Chelsea
lover of
MASCULINE: Kelvin
FEMININE: Aniya

Shire district resident or servant
MASCULINE: Sherman, Sherry

Shoot
MASCULINE: Yora
FEMININE: Yora

Shoot up *See* Grow

Shopkeeper
MASCULINE: Berger, Burgess

Shore
FEMININE: Riva

Shrew
FEMININE: Belinda

Shrub
FEMININE: Heather, Neta, Netta

Shy
FEMININE: Erna, Jolanda, Yolanda

Sickness
FEMININE: Machla

Sieve
MASCULINE: Arbel

Sight
FEMININE: Marit

Sign (symbol) *See also* Miracles
MASCULINE: Ben-Tziyon, Ben Zion, Benson, Bentzi, Remez, Samal, Semel, Shelet, Siman-Tov, Siman, Sion, Tziyon, Xeno, Zeno, Zion, Ziony
FEMININE: Remiza

Signpost
FEMININE: Herma

Silence *See also* Quiet
MASCULINE: Duma

Silk
MASCULINE: Meshi

Silver
FEMININE: Arian, Ariana

Sincere
MASCULINE: Ernest, Ernesto, Ernie, Erno, Ernst

Singer *See also* Minstrel
MASCULINE: Gorman, Marnin, Singer
FEMININE: Millicent, Millie, Mollie, Ronit, Ronnit

Singing *See also* Song
MASCULINE: Aaron, Aharon, Anat, Arke, Aron, Jaron, Ranen, Ranon, Yaron, Yoran, Zamir
FEMININE: Aarona, Aharona, Aharonit, Anat, Arni, Arnina, Arninit, Arnit, Arona, Aryn, Lorelei, Yarona

Sivan
MASCULINE: Sivan
FEMININE: Sivana

Sixth
FEMININE: Fifi

Skin *See also* Dark in appearance; Fair; Moorish; Negro
MASCULINE: Geled, Or

Sky
FEMININE: Lani

Small *See also* Little
MASCULINE: Havel, Hussein, Ketina, Pablo, Paul, Pauley, Pavel, Poul, Powell, Vaughan, Zeira, Zuta
FEMININE: Katania, Ketana, Ketaniya, Paula, Paulette, Paulina, Pauline, Vaughn, Zeira

Smart *See* Clever; Wisdom

Smell, sweet
FEMININE: Basmat, Bosmat

Snake
MASCULINE: Nachshon, Phineas, Pinchas, Pinchos, Pincus, Pinhas, Pini, Pinkas, Pinkie, Pinkus, Pinky, Pinnie

Snow
FEMININE: Neva

Soil *See also* Earth
FEMININE: Adama

Sojourn
MASCULINE: Dar
FEMININE: Dara

Sold
MASCULINE: Machir

Soldiers *See also* Warrior
MASCULINE: Harman, Herman, Hermann, Kern, Miles, Myles, Troy, Ty, Tyron, Tyson
FEMININE: Armina, Meirona, Merona

Somerset
MASCULINE: Somers

Son *See also* Child
MASCULINE: Bani, Ben, Ben-Ami, Bengi, Benjamin, Benli, Benson, Benton, Bentzi, Bibi, Bin, Binjamin, Binyamin, Binyomin, Hevel, Jamin, Moise, Moishe, Moshe, Reuben, Reuvain, Reuven, Rube, Ruben, Rubens, Rubin, Ruby, Rueben, Ruvane, Ruvik, Shibi, Sonny, Yummy, Zindel, Zundel
FEMININE: Benette, Benjamina, Binyamina, Reubena, Reuvat, Reuvena, Rubena

Son of
MASCULINE: Mac, Mack, Mackey

Song *See also* Sing
MASCULINE: Avizemer, Avron, Leron, Liron, Lyron, Ran, Rani, Renen, Ron, Ronel, Ronen, Roni, Ronli, Shir, Shiri, Shiron, Zamir, Zemer, Zemira, Zimra
FEMININE: Arian, Ariana, Carol, Carroll, Caryl, Karol, Karyl, Leron, Liron, Lirona, Lirone, Lorac, Mangena, Mangina, Melina, Melody, Negina, Oda, Odiya, Rani, Rania, Ranit, Ranita, Ranya, Renana, Renanit, Renina, Ron, Rona, Ronela, Roni, Ronia, Roniya, Ronli, Ronnell, Ronya, Sheera, Shir, Shira, Shirel, Shiri, Shirli, Shirra, Tehila, Zemira, Zimra

Songbird
FEMININE: Bat-Shir, Gidron, Lark, Mavis

Songfest
MASCULINE: Shiron
FEMININE: Zimria

Songwriter
FEMININE: Eda

Soothsayer *See also* Prophet
MASCULINE: Anan, Anani
FEMININE: Cybil

Sophistication
FEMININE: Lavina, Lavinia

Sorrow *See also* Bitter
FEMININE: Dolores, Janlori, Lora, Loraine, Lori, Lorraine, Lorrin, Mardi, Marita, Marta, Martha, Marthe, Merta

Soul
FEMININE: Enid, Nafshiya, Neshama

Sound *See* Noise

South
MASCULINE: Darom, Nagiv, Negev, Teman, Temani
FEMININE: Daroma

Space *See* Heaven; Paradise; Sky

Spacious
MASCULINE: Yafet, Yefet

Spark
MASCULINE: Zik

Sparkling
MASCULINE: Paz
FEMININE: Paz, Paza, Pazit

Sparrow
MASCULINE: Galvin

Spasm
FEMININE: Avit

Speak *See also* Utterance
MASCULINE: Dovev

Speak kind words
FEMININE: Deb, Debora, Deborah, Debra, Deva, Devera, Devora, Devorit, Devra, Dobe, Dobra, Dovrat, Dvora, Dvorit

Speaker (spokesman) *See also* Orator
MASCULINE: Dover

Spear *See also* Sword
MASCULINE: Daro, Darrow, Gary, Gerald, Gerard, Gerardo, Gerhard, Ghary, Girard, Jerald, Jere, Jerold, Jerrald, Jerry, Kani, Kaniel, Oscar, Ossie
FEMININE: Rhonda, Ronda

Spearbearer
MASCULINE: Garvey, Gary, Gerald, Gerard, Gerardo, Gerhard, Ghary, Girard, Jerald, Jere, Jerold, Jerrald, Jerry, Lance, Lancelot
FEMININE: Geraldene, Geralyn, Geri

Speech (communication)
MASCULINE: Niv
FEMININE: Niva

Speech (oratory)
MASCULINE: Barnaby, Barney
FEMININE: Amira

Spices *See also* Cinnamon
MASCULINE: Mor
FEMININE: Basmat, Bosmat, Ketura, Pepper, Tamara, Tamra
one who burns
MASCULINE: Gomer
FEMININE: Gomer

Spirits
MASCULINE: Avira, Aviri, Damon
FEMININE: Avirit, Neshama

Splendor *See also* Glory
FEMININE: Gladyce, Gladys, Ziva, Zivit

Spokesman
MASCULINE: Dover

Spoon
FEMININE: Kaf

Spread
FEMININE: Serach

Spring (of water)
MASCULINE: Gal, Mayan, Talmi
FEMININE: Fontana, Gal, Gala, Galit, Talmi

Springtime *See also* Flourish
MASCULINE: Aviv, Avivi, Vern, Vernon
FEMININE: Abibi, Abibit, April, Aviv, Aviva, Avivi, Avivit, Avivith, Laverne, Mae, May, Spring, Verna

Sprinkle
FEMININE: Zilpa

Sprout
MASCULINE: Netzer, Nevat
FEMININE: Cyma, Seema, Sema, Syma

St. Columba, servant of
MASCULINE: Mal

Stadium
MASCULINE: Champ, Champion

Staff
MASCULINE: Degel

Stag *See* Deer

Star
MASCULINE: Cochav, Joash, Kochav, Kochavi, Mazal-Tov, Mazal, Mazel Tov, Yoash
FEMININE: Asta, Astera, Astra, Cochava, Eiit, Essa, Esta, Estella, Estelle, Ester, Esti, Eti, Hedy, Heidi, Hester, Hesther,

Kochava, Kochavit, Kokhava, Mazal, Mazala, Mazalit, Nova, Shavit, Sidra, Star, Staria, Starletta, Starr, Stella, Svetlana, Trella

Starlike
MASCULINE: Sidra

Starling
MASCULINE: Sterling

Stately *See also* Noble
MASCULINE: Tamir, Tamur, Timur
FEMININE: Temira

Statement
FEMININE: Imra

Steadfast *See* Enduring (lasting)

Steep
MASCULINE: Cliff, Clive

Steward
MASCULINE: Spencer

Stewardess
FEMININE: Da'yelet

Stick (together)
MASCULINE: Clay

Sticker *See* Thorn

Stinging
FEMININE: Akitza

Stone *See also* Rock
MASCULINE: Alson, Eban, Ebenm, Even, Sela, Shamir, Stan, Stanley, Stansfield, Stone
FEMININE: Avna, Chantal, Coral, Coralee, Gazit, Giza, Jade, Kirsten, Sela

Stone worker
MASCULINE: Mason

Stoning
MASCULINE: Regem

Storage
FEMININE: Geniza

Stork
FEMININE: Chasida, Hasida

Storm (upheaval)
MASCULINE: Sa'ar, Se'ara

Storm (weather)
FEMININE: Sufa

Story
FEMININE: Narelle

Stove
FEMININE: Kira

Stranger *See also* East; Pilgrim; Wander
MASCULINE: Avgar, Chetzron, Don, Donald, Donnie, Gaston, Gershom, Gershon, Gerson, Goliath, Hezron, Macdonald, Wal, Wallace, Wally, Wendel, Wilt
FEMININE: Bab, Babette, Babs, Barbara, Barbi, Bobbe, Bunny, Gershoma, Gershona, Hagar, Xena, Yenta, Yentil, Zena, Zina

Stream *See also* Ford
MASCULINE: Arnan, Arnon, Brook, Brooks, Doug, Douglas, Flint, Jubal, Linc, Lincolm, Noni, Peleg, Ray, Reece, Reo, Rhett, Yuval, Zerem
FEMININE: Arnona, Arnonit, Brook, Deror, Derora, Drora, Silona, Silonit

Strength *See also* Courage; Fortress; Iron; Mighty; Supernatural strength; Warrior
MASCULINE: Abir, Abner, Amatzia, Amir, Amotz, Amoz, Amtzi, Anders, Andi, Andor, André, Andrew, Andy, Arsen, Atzmon, Aviaz, Avichayil, Aviner, Avner, Avniel, Az, Azai, Azan, Azaz, Azazia, Azi, Aziz, Aziza, Barzilai, Bengi, Benjamin, Benson, Bentzi, Beril, Beryl, Bibi, Biddie, Bin, Binjamin, Binyamin, Binyomin, Birgit, Boaz, Brian, Brion, Bry, Bryan, Carl, Carlos, Carlton, Carol, Carrol, Charle, Charles, Charley, Charlton, Chip, Chuck, Corliss, Drew, Dru, Egan, Egon, Eitan, Etan, Ethan, Eyal, Eytan, Gibor, Giora, Guryon, Karel, Karl, Karol, Kidd, Lee, Leigh, Len, Lenn, Lennard, Lennie, Leonard, Leonardo, Li-On, Maoz, Maynard, Ometz, Oscar, Ossie, Otniel, Oz, Ozer, Ryan, Ryne, Sagi, Sagiv, Sagy, Sherira, Shibi, Uza, Uzi, Uzza, Uzzi, Val, Valentine, Valerie, Valery, Velvel, Volf, Wolf, Yummy
FEMININE: Abira, Amitza, Amitzia, Amiza, Amtza, Andrea, Andye, Arnett, Atzma, Audra, Audrey, Audrina, Aza,

Aziza, Briana, Bridget, Bridgit, Brigi-
da, Brigit, Brit, Carla, Carlena, Carley,
Carlina, Carlita, Carlotta, Carly, Car-
oline, Carolyn, Carrie, Carry, Char-
layne, Charleen, Charlene, Charlet,
Charlot, Charlotta, Charlotte, Cha-
sina, Chasna, Cherlene, Drew, Dru,
Effi, Elfreda, Etana, Fern, Gevura,
Gibora, Giora, Hasina, Hasna, Kari,
Karolina, Karolyn, Leena, Leona,
Leonia, Leonie, Lina, Lola, Lolli,
Lotta, Lyna, Millicent, Millie, Mollie,
Roselotte, Sharleen, Uza, Uzit, Uzza,
Val, Valentina, Valeria, Valerie, Valery,
Yemina

Strife *See also* Conflict
MASCULINE: Madon, Shutelach
FEMININE: Hedda, Hedy

Strongman *See* Hero

Stubbornness
FEMININE: Orpa

Student *See also* Beginner
MASCULINE: Lamed

Suffer
FEMININE: Patience

Sufficient
MASCULINE: Sagi, Sagy

Summer
FEMININE: Summer

Summer settlement
MASCULINE: Somers

Summoner
MASCULINE: Sumner

Sun *See also* God of the sun
MASCULINE: Cy, Cyrus, Heller, Sampson,
Samson, Shimshon, Sol
FEMININE: Shimshona, Soleil
god of
MASCULINE: Thom, Thomas, Tip, Tom,
Tommi
FEMININE: Phoebus, Tami, Thomasina,
Tomasina
horn of the *See* King; Long life
sunrise
MASCULINE: Anatole, Anatoly, Antal,
Tolya

Superior
MASCULINE: Ilai, Randal, Randell, Randi,
Randy
FEMININE: Eedit, Idit, Randelle

Superlative
FEMININE: Ila, Ilit, Ilita

Supernatural strength
FEMININE: Effi, Elfreda

Supplanted
MASCULINE: Akevy, Aki, Akki, Cobe,
Diego, Hamish, Jack, Jackie, Jackson,
Jacob, Jacobo, Jacque, Jaimie, Jake,
Jakob, James, Jamie, Jan, Jascha, Jim,
Jimbo, Jimm, Jimmie, Kaufman, Kiva,
Kobe, Koppel, Kovi, Kubi, Seamus,
Yaacov, Yaakov, Yaki, Yankel, Yuki
FEMININE: Jackee, Jacklyn, Jacky, Jaclyn,
Jacoba, Jacque, Jacqueline, Jacque-
lyn, Jacqui, Jaime, Jaymee, Jocelin,
Jocelyn, Jodette, Joscelin, Joscelind,
Josetta, Joslyn, Kobi, Yaakova

Support
MASCULINE: Masad, Saad, Saada, Saadi,
Saadli
FEMININE: Masada, Saada, Summer

Surprise
FEMININE: Tama

Surroundings
FEMININE: Seviva

Surveyor of land
MASCULINE: Rodney, Seker

Sustain
MASCULINE: Zan, Zane

Swallow (bird)
MASCULINE: Deror, Dror
FEMININE: Deror, Derora, Drora

Swallow (with one's throat)
MASCULINE: Bela

Sweetness
MASCULINE: Matok, Meged, Mesek, My-
ron, Naam, Naaman, Naom, Noam,
Syshe, Zusman
FEMININE: Basmat, Bosmat, Condi, Con-
doleeza, Dulcia, Metuka, Naamia,
Naamiya, Pam, Pamela, Sisel, Zeesi,
Zisa

Swiftness *See also* Deer
MASCULINE: Boaz
FEMININE: Mahira, Mehira

Sword *See also* Spear
MASCULINE: Brant, Gib, Gil, Gilbert, Gili, Gill, Gilli, Lahat
FEMININE: Gisela, Giselle, Gizela

Tail
MASCULINE: Zanav
FEMININE: Alya

Tailor
MASCULINE: Sarag, Webster
FEMININE: Taylor

Talk (eulogy)
FEMININE: Eulalia

Tall *See also* High
MASCULINE: Alta, Alto, Altus, Lang, Sagiv, Tamir, Tamur, Timur
FEMININE: Temira, Timi, Timora, Timura

Tattooed one
MASCULINE: Scott, Scottie

Teach and teaching
MASCULINE: Aaron, Aharon, Arke, Aron
FEMININE: Aarona, Aharona, Aharonit, Arni, Arnina, Arninit, Arnit, Arona, Aryn, Tora, Yora

Teacher *See also* Master
MASCULINE: Maran, Matif, Moran, Morenu, Mori, Rabi, Rav, Rava, Ravi, Yora
FEMININE: Moran, Morit

Temporary dwelling
MASCULINE: Bitan

Tender *See also* Delicate; Young
MASCULINE: Avrech, Terence, Terri

Tenth
MASCULINE: Tate
FEMININE: Dixie

Terebinth tree
FEMININE: Eila

Test
MASCULINE: Buki
FEMININE: Nisa

Testimony
MASCULINE: Gilad, Giladi

Thanks
MASCULINE: Toda
FEMININE: Toda

Thicket
MASCULINE: Bruce, Tod, Todd

Think
FEMININE: Pansy

Thirsty
FEMININE: Eeta, Eta, Etka, Ita, Itka, Itta

Thistle
FEMININE: Koranit

Thorn
MASCULINE: Dardar, Kotz

Thread
FEMININE: Nema, Nima

Three
FEMININE: Tiffani

Threshing floor
MASCULINE: Goren

Throw
FEMININE: Tara, Taralynn, Taryn

Thunder
MASCULINE: Raam

Thursday, born on
FEMININE: Hamisi

Tie (tied)
MASCULINE: Anuv, Kesher, Rotem
FEMININE: Anuva, Beca, Beccie, Beckie, Beka, Keshira, Keshura, Rebecca, Reva, Rheba, Ricka, Ricky, Riva

Tiger
MASCULINE: Tiger

Tile maker
MASCULINE: Tyler

Time
MASCULINE: Idi, Ido

Time period
MASCULINE: Idan

Timely
MASCULINE: Atid

Tithing
MASCULINE: Tate

Together
MASCULINE: Clay, Weld, Weldon
FEMININE: Iti, Itti, Weld

Toil *See also* Work
MASCULINE: Amal, Amali, Amel
FEMININE: Amal, Amela, Amila

Toiler
MASCULINE: Askan, Malvin, Mel, Mell, Melvin, Melvyn
FEMININE: Malvina, Melba, Melva, Melveen, Melvina

Topaz
FEMININE: Topaza

Torah learner
FEMININE: Sinai

Torch *See also* Fire; Flame
MASCULINE: Lapid, Lapidos, Lapidot
FEMININE: Avuka, Udi

Tower
FEMININE: Leena, Lena, Madalyne, Madelaine, Madeleine, Madelon, Madelyn, Mady, Madylin, Mag, Magda, Magdalen, Magdalene, Magdaline, Marla, Marlee, Marleen, Marlena, Marlene, Marley, Marli, Marlo, Migdala, Mitzpa, Mizpa

Town
MASCULINE: Alton, Ashton, Bart, Barth, Barton, Belton, Burrut, Burton, Carlton, Chilton, Clayton, Clifton, Clint, Clinton, Colby, Cole, Granville, Ir, Kin, Kingsley, Morton, Nevil, Newbold, Newt, Newton, Norton, Paxton, Preston, Princeton, Selby, Seton, Shelby, Shelton, Trygve
FEMININE: Shelby

Trader
MASCULINE: Chapman

Tradition
FEMININE: Masoret, Mesora

Tranquil *See also* Peace
MASCULINE: Placid, Salim
FEMININE: Placidia, Salima, Shalva

Transmission
FEMININE: Mesora

Transmitted
MASCULINE: Masoor, Masur

Traverse *See also* Cross over
MASCULINE: Travis

Treasure
MASCULINE: Matmon, Otzar, Ozar, Segel
FEMININE: Adiya, Segula, Sigal, Sigalia, Sigalit, Sigaliya, Siglia, Siglit, Sima, Simajean, Syma

Tree grower
MASCULINE: Grover

Trees *See also* Forest; Woods; *specific trees by name*
MASCULINE: Agaf, Branch, Elan, Geza, Ilan, Vern
FEMININE: Eilat, Elana, Ilana, Ilanit, Sierra, Vanda, Wanda

Trinity
FEMININE: Tiffani

Troops *See also* Soldiers
FEMININE: Meirona, Merona

Troubled
MASCULINE: Ammos, Amos
FEMININE: Baila, Bayla, Bayle, Bilha

True *See also* Faith; Honest
MASCULINE: Amitai, Amitan, Emmet, Truman
FEMININE: Elvera, Vera, Verita, Verity, Veronica

Trumpet
FEMININE: Schifra, Shifra, Shiphra

Trust *See also* Faith
FEMININE: Faith, Hope

Trusted (reliable) *See also* Faith
MASCULINE: Amin
FEMININE: Amina

Tuesday
FEMININE: Mardi

Tumult
MASCULINE: Tristan
FEMININE: Tristana

Tune *See also* Melody; Song
FEMININE: Zimra, Zimrat

Turban
MASCULINE: Efrat
FEMININE: Efrat, Efrata

Turn
FEMININE: Willow

Turtledove
FEMININE: Tori, Torie

Twig
FEMININE: Zemora

Twins
MASCULINE: Sivan, Teom, Thom, Thomas, Tip, Tom, Tommi
FEMININE: Sivana, Tami, Thomasina, Tomasina

Twist *See also* Flexible
FEMININE: Willow

Ultimate
FEMININE: Mayrav, Meirav, Merav, Meyrav

Umbrella
FEMININE: Mitriya

Uncle
MASCULINE: Achav, Ahab, Aisik, Dodi, Dodo

Unclean
FEMININE: Chel'a

Understanding (agreement)
FEMININE: Veda

Understanding (insight)
MASCULINE: Bina, Buna, Yavin
FEMININE: Bina, Buna, Buni

Unite
MASCULINE: Weld, Weldon

Unity
FEMININE: Cosima, Harmony, Unita, Weld

Universe
MASCULINE: Cosmo

Unlucky
FEMININE: Mallory

Unsullied *See* Pure

Unusual
FEMININE: Novela

Upheaval
MASCULINE: Sa'ar, Se'ara

Uplift
MASCULINE: Eli

Uppermost
FEMININE: Ila, Ilit, Ilita

Upright *See also* Honest
MASCULINE: Amit, Amiti, Tomer, Yashar, Yesher, Yeshurun
FEMININE: Amit, Amita, Komema, Tamar

Uproar
MASCULINE: Tristan
FEMININE: Tristana

Utterance *See also* Speak
MASCULINE: Imri
FEMININE: Amira

Vain
MASCULINE: Cash, Cassius

Valiant and valorous
MASCULINE: Ben-Chayil, Casey, Farrel, Val, Valentine
FEMININE: Andrea, Casey, Charlayne, Charleen, Charlene, Cherlene, Sharleen, Valentina

Valley
MASCULINE: Dale, Dalin, Dall, Dallas, Dallin, Gai, Gaia, Gilmore, Glen, Guy, Kendal, Ogden, Tilden, Vail, Val, Vale, Walden, Waldo, Wendel
FEMININE: Bika, Dale, Dayle, Deena, Denna, Gayora, Glenda, Glendora, Glenna, Glynda, Glynis

Valuable
FEMININE: Yakira, Yekara

Value (cost)
MASCULINE: Price

Value (rare)
MASCULINE: Selden

Vapor
MASCULINE: Hevel

Verdant
FEMININE: Chloe, Chloris, Cloe, Laverne

Vessel of God
MASCULINE: Kliel

Vest
MASCULINE: Efod, Eiphod

Viaduct
MASCULINE: Biv

Victory *See also* Conqueror
MASCULINE: Anat, Colin, Jarvis, Mansur, Nicholas, Nicolas, Niel, Nike, Sayer, Siegmond, Sig, Siggi, Vic, Victor, Vince, Vincent, Win, Winston, Winthrop
FEMININE: Anat, Berenice, Bernice, Bernine, Bernita, Colette, Dafna, Dafne, Dafnit, Daphna, Daphnit, Dapna, Dasa, Dasi, Dassa, Dassi, Eunice, Hada, Hadas, Hadasa, Hode, Hodel, Hodi, Hude, Hudel, Lara, Laura, Lauraine, Lauralee, Lauralynn, Laure, Laurel, Lauren, Laurene, Lauretta, Lauri, Laurice, Loran, Loree, Loren, Lorri, Loryn, Loura, Luan, Magnolia, Myrtle, Nicci, Nichelle, Nicki, Nicola, Nicolette, Nicolle, Nikia, Ria, Sultana, Veronica, Vi, Vici, Victoria, Victorina, Vikki, Vinette, Vittoria

View
FEMININE: Belva

Vigor (vigorous) *See also* Energetic
MASCULINE: Hod, Meretz

Village
MASCULINE: Melville, Winthrop

Vine
MASCULINE: Gefen
FEMININE: Gafna, Gafnit, Gefen, Ivy, Lata, Soreka

Vineyard
MASCULINE: Carmel, Carmeli, Carmen, Carmi, Carmiel, Carmine, Gafni, Gefania, Gefanya, Karmel, Karmeli, Kerem
FEMININE: Carma, Carmel, Carmeli, Carmen, Carmia, Carmiela, Carmit, Carmiya, Karma, Karmel, Karmeli, Karmelit, Karmiya, Kerem

Violet
FEMININE: Jolanda, Vi, Viola, Violet, Violette, Yolanda

Virgin
FEMININE: Adara, Adra, Camilla, Camillia, Ginger, Ginnie, Kamilla, Virginia

Virile
MASCULINE: Gavri
FEMININE: Carla, Carlena, Carley, Carlina, Carlita, Carlotta, Carly, Caroline, Carolyn, Carrie, Carry, Kari, Karolina, Karolyn, Leena, Lina, Lola, Lolli, Lyna

Virtuous
MASCULINE: Zaki

Vision of God
MASCULINE: Chaziel

Vocabulary
MASCULINE: Agron

Volunteer
MASCULINE: Askan

Voluptuous
FEMININE: Beca, Beccie, Beckie, Beka, Edna, Reba, Rebecca, Reva, Rheba, Ricka, Ricky, Riva

Vulture
MASCULINE: Aya, Ayya, Nesher
FEMININE: Aya, Ayya

Wagon
FEMININE: Agala

Wagon maker
MASCULINE: Dwayne, Wayne

Waiter
MASCULINE: Meltzar

Wales
MASCULINE: Bris, Brit, Briton

Walking
MASCULINE: Ambler

Wandering *See also* Stranger
MASCULINE: Errol, Eryle, Nanod, Wendel, Yagli
FEMININE: Noa, Noaha, Vanda, Wanda

Warden
MASCULINE: Kay

Wares
MASCULINE: Mercer

Warfare *See also* Battle; Conflict
MASCULINE: Gunther
FEMININE: Hedda, Hedy

Warm
MASCULINE: Cham, Ham

Warmth
FEMININE: Chamutal

Warrior (warlike) *See also* Conqueror; Gladiator; Spearbearer; Victor
MASCULINE: Alger, Armand, Armando, Armen, Armond, Boris, Boyd, Carney, Chad, Duncan, Edgar, Edmond, Edmund, Evan, Evander, Evans, Everett, Ewen, Gad, Gadi, Garvey, Gary, Gerald, Gerard, Gerardo, Gerhard, Ghary, Gideon, Gidi, Gidon, Gidone, Gidoni, Girard, Gunther, Hal, Harlan, Harold, Heraldo, Jerald, Jere, Jerold, Jerrald, Jerry, Kelley, Lothar, Lother, Marc, Marcel, Marcelo, March, Marco, Marcus, Marcy, Marek, Mari, Mario, Marius, Mark, Marko, Marshe, Martin, Matel, Miles, Mo, Modi, Moe, Mordecai, Mordechai, Mordicai, Mordke, Mordy, Morris, Morrison, Motel, Moti, Muki, Myles, Ned, Neddy, Orven, Orvin, Oscar, Ossie, Owen, Rodger, Rodgers, Roger, Sloan
FEMININE: Avril, Billie, Ede, Edie, Edita, Edith, Edyth, Eloise, Elouise, Emmylou, Gada, Gadit, Geraldene, Geralyn, Geri, Gertrude, Gidona, Heloise, Heralda, Hilda, Hildegard, Hildi, Hili, Hilla, Hilma, Ida, Idalee, Idel, Idena, Idette, Ieda, Janlori, Jeralee, Jeralyn, Jeri, Jerriann, Jerrilyn, Kalee, Kelley, Kelli, Lora, Loraine, Lori, Lorraine, Lorrin, Lou, Louella, Louisa, Louise, Luella, Luisa, Luise, Lula, Lulu, Martelle, Marti, Martina, Mathilda, Matilda, Matti, Matty, Matya, Maud, Mina, Minda, Mindel, Minna, Minnie, Morrisa, Tilda, Tilla, Tillamae, Tillie, Truda, Velma, Vila, Vilhelmina, Vilma, Wilhelmina, Willa, Willene, Yvette

Watch *See* Guard

Watchman *See also* Guard
MASCULINE: Gregory, Howard, Howie, Shomer
FEMININE: Tzofia, Zofia

Water *See also* Brook; Canal; Ripple; River; Sea; Stream; Wave; Well; Whirlpool
MASCULINE: Moise, Moishe, Mose, Moses, Moshe, Moss, Moy, Trent
FEMININE: Dahlia, Dalia, Dalit, Daliya, Dalya, Mayim, Silona, Silonit, Talmi, Zilpa

Water channel
MASCULINE: Afek, Afik

Waterfall
MASCULINE: Eshed
FEMININE: Cherilynn, Geralyn, Jerrilyn, Lauralynn, Linn, Lyn, Lynette, Lynn, Maralyn, Marilyn, Marlyn, Merelyn, Sharilyn, Taralynn

Wave (of water)
MASCULINE: Gal, Gali, Galia, Galya
FEMININE: Adva, Gal, Gala, Gali, Galit, Gayil, Gene, Geneva, Genevieve, Wende

Weak
FEMININE: Baila, Bayla, Bayle, Bilha

Wealth *See also* Prosperous; Rich
MASCULINE: Ashir, Gevir, Hon, Jess, Jesse, Jethro, Osher, Otto
FEMININE: Ashira, Ashirut, Audris, Dari, Jessica, Jessie, Jethra, Oshra, Yitra

Weary
FEMININE: Laya, Lea, Leah, Leann, Leatrice, Leiah, Leya, Lia, Liya

Weasel
FEMININE: Chulda, Hulda

Weaver
MASCULINE: Oreg, Webster

Week *See specific days of the week*

Weeps *See also* Cry
FEMININE: Lora, Loraine, Lori, Lorraine, Lorrin

Welcoming
FEMININE: Xenia

Weld
MASCULINE: Weld, Weldon
FEMININE: Weld

Well (of water)
MASCULINE: Be'eri, Howel, Rockwell, Rocky, Sewell
FEMININE: Einat

Well-being
FEMININE: Rafa

Well-born *See also* Noble
MASCULINE: Ethelbert, Eugen, Eugene, Gene, Owen
FEMININE: Ena, Eugenia, Eugenie

Well-bred *See also* Noble
MASCULINE: Earl
FEMININE: Earla, Earlene

Well-known *See* Famous

Westward
FEMININE: Yama

Wheat *See also* Grain
FEMININE: Chita

Wheel
MASCULINE: Ofan
FEMININE: Ofnat, Ophnat

Whelp (cub)
MASCULINE: Colin

Whirl
MASCULINE: Storm

Whirlpool
MASCULINE: Eddy

Whisper
MASCULINE: Dovev

White *See also* Bright; Fair
MASCULINE: Alban, Albin, Albion, Alva, Dwight, Finian, Galvin, Gwynn, Laban, Lavan, Levanon, Livni, Whitney, Wyn
FEMININE: Alba, Albina, Bianca, Blanca, Blanch, Candace, Candance, Candice, Candida, Candy, Candyce, Fiona, Gwen, Gwenn, Gwyn, Gwynn, Levana, Levani, Livana, Livna, Livnat, Wynette, Wynn

Whiten
MASCULINE: Blake, Blanchard, Malachai, Malachi, Malachy
FEMININE: Malbina

Whole
MASCULINE: Hal, Hale, Haley, Halley, Hollis, Shalem, Shalum, Tam, Tami
FEMININE: Tama, Temima, Tumi

Widow
FEMININE: Almana

Widower
MASCULINE: Alman, Almon

Wild ass
MASCULINE: Arodi

Willing
FEMININE: Tirtza

Willow trees
MASCULINE: Sal, Willard, Willmer, Willoughby
FEMININE: Arava, Willow, Wilma

Wine
MASCULINE: Denis, Dennis, Denys, Dion, Ennis
FEMININE: Meerit, Miri, Mirit

Wine press
MASCULINE: Yekev
FEMININE: Gat, Gita, Gitit

Wing
MASCULINE: Agaf
FEMININE: Kanaf

Winged
FEMININE: Aletta

Wisdom *See also* Clever; Counsel; Educated; Lawmaker; Learned; Scholar; Understanding (insight)
MASCULINE: Alvis, Bina, Cassidy, Clark, Elvis, Feibush, Feivel, Feiwel, Haskel, Heske, Heskel, Kane, Keenan, Keene, Navon, Phoebus, Ranier, Reg, Reginald, Reinhold, Rennie, Reynold, Ronald, Rondell, Ronnie, Sage
FEMININE: Athena, Bina, Cassidy, Prudence, Prue, Ronalda, Ronne, Ronni, Ronny, Safia, Sage, Sibyl, Sonia, Sonja, Sophia, Sophie, Sybil, Zonya, Zophia

Witchcraft
MASCULINE: Kesem
FEMININE: Kesima

With me
FEMININE: Iti, Itti

Witness
MASCULINE: Adi

Wizard
MASCULINE: Ashaf

Wolf
MASCULINE: Adolf, Adolph, Adolphe, Dolph, Lupo, Lupus, Seff, Velvel, Volf, Wolf, Wolfgang, Ze'ev, Zev
FEMININE: Adolpha, Lupita, Zeeva, Zeva

Woman *See also* Lady
FEMININE: Sibyl, Signora, Sybil

Wonder
MASCULINE: Palu, Tema
FEMININE: Marvel, Pelia, Tama

Wonderful
FEMININE: Marenda, Miranda

Wood
FEMININE: Evonne, Ivette, Yvette, Yvonne

Wooden causeway
MASCULINE: Bridge

Woods (forest) *See also* Forester
MASCULINE: Bruce, Forest, Forrest, Heywood, Holt, Keith, Kelley, Norwood, Roscoe, Ross, Shaw, Silas, Silvan, Silvester, Sy, Sylvan, Sylvester, Wal, Walden, Waldo, Wallie, Wally, Walt, Walter, Wilt, Wood, Woodie, Woodrow, Woody, Yaar
FEMININE: Kalee, Kelley, Kelli, Silva, Silvia, Sylvia, Sylvie, Yaara, Yaarit, Yara

Wooly
FEMININE: Lana

Word *See* Speak; Utterance

Words for singing
FEMININE: Lyric

Work *See also* Toil
MASCULINE: Amal, Amali, Amel
FEMININE: Amal, Amalia, Amalie, Amalya, Amelia, Amilie, Emilia, Millicent, Millie, Mollie

Worker *See also* Toiler
FEMININE: Penelope, Penney

World *See also* Earth; Man
MASCULINE: Desmond

Woven
FEMININE: Rickma, Rikma

Wreath *See also* Crown
MASCULINE: Atir, Kailil, Kalil, Zer
FEMININE: Atara, Bay

Wrestling
MASCULINE: Iser, Israel, Isser, Issi, Naf, Naftali, Naphtali, Stacey, Toolie
FEMININE: Naftala

Wretched *See also* Forsaken; Poor
FEMININE: Aluva

Write
MASCULINE: Roman

Writer *See also* Scribe
MASCULINE: Lavlar

Yearning
FEMININE: Erga

Yellow
MASCULINE: Boyd

Yellow-haired
FEMININE: Flavia

Yew wood
MASCULINE: Yves

Yields
MASCULINE: Yale

Young and youngster *See also* Boy; Child; Daughter; Girl; Maid; Son; Tender; Youth
MASCULINE: Avrech, Elem, Junior, Lad, Naar
FEMININE: Deidra, Deidre, Deirdre, Didi, Missie, Naara

Youth and youthful *See also* Baby; Cedar tree; Child; Infant; Springtime; Young
MASCULINE: Bichri, Erez, Jule, Julian, Julius, Virgil
FEMININE: Abibi, Abibit, Aviva, Avivit, Avivith, Erez, Gillian, Jewelia, Jillian, Joliet, Jule, Julee, Juleen, Jules, Julia, Julian, Julianne, Julie, Julienne, Juliet, Julieta, Juliette, June, Mae, May, Yuli, Yulia

Zealous

MASCULINE: Aduk, Kanai, Rhys, Rice

FEMININE: Aduka

Zeus

FEMININE: Zina

Zimrat

FEMININE: Zimrat

Zion, child of

MASCULINE: Ben-Tziyon, Ben Zion, Ben-son, Bentzi

FEMININE: Bat-Tziyon, Bat-Zion

Zoo

MASCULINE: Bivar

Zealous
MASCULINE: Aduk, Kanai, Rhys, Rice
FEMININE: Aduka

Zeus
FEMININE: Zina

Zimrat
FEMININE: Zimrat

Zion, child of
MASCULINE: Ben-Tziyon, Ben Zion, Ben-son, Bentzi
FEMININE: Bat-Tziyon, Bat-Zion

Zoo
MASCULINE: Bivar